D0113909

INTIMATE
WORLDS

INTIMATE WORLDS

WORLDS

Life Inside the Family

MAGGIE SCARF

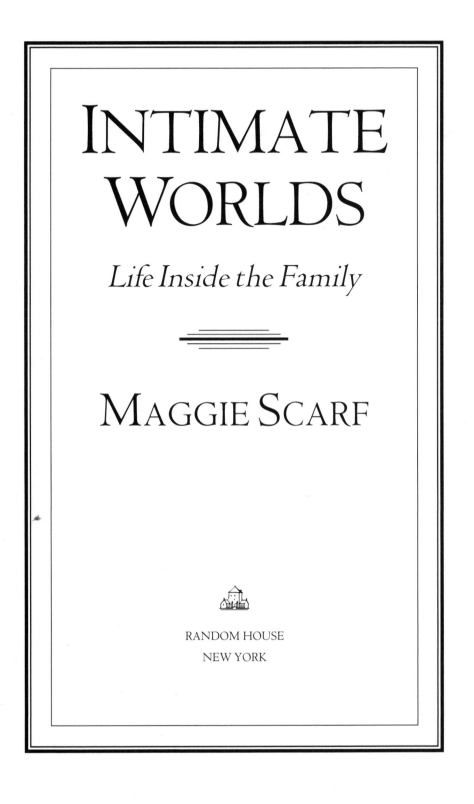

RANDOM HOUSE

NEW YORK

Library of Congress Cataloging-in-Publication Data
Scarf, Maggie
Intimate Worlds / by Maggie Scarf
p.   cm.
ISBN 0-394-56543-6
1. Family psychotherapy. 2. Family—Mental health.
3. Family—Psychological aspects. I. Title.
RC488.5.S28 1995
616.89′156—dc20   95-827

Manufactured in the United States of America on acid-free paper
2 4 6 8 9 7 5 3
First Edition

It is to my husband, Herb,
the beloved pal of a lifetime,
and to the family that we created together,
that this work is lovingly dedicated.

Author's Note

The families whose interviews have been used in these pages have agreed to let their stories be told, with minor changes as far as identifying details (names, geographical locations in some cases, wife's or husband's profession, etc.) are concerned. The family stories described here are, therefore, factual, aside from the omission or change of such unnecessarily specific and revealing information.

Acknowledgments

How, on looking closely at a wide range of different kinds of families, can one go about teasing out those factors associated with family health and happiness, as distinct from those factors involved when the members of the family are feeling miserable and the system itself is functioning poorly? This is clearly one of the most basic questions to be asked about the family—and yet, until my path happened to cross that of Dallas psychiatrist Leonora Stephens, I hadn't been able to focus upon it with clarity and precision, nor had I realized that one could actually address and answer it in a straightforward, systematic way.

It was Leonora Stephens, then training director of the Southwest Family Institute of Dallas (she is now in private practice and is also associate professor of psychiatry at the University of Texas Southwestern Medical School), who first introduced me to the Beavers Systems Model; and it is she who has, over the subsequent seven-plus years, helped me to truly comprehend this empirically tested scale of family competence and well-being in ever greater depth and detail. And, in the course of what has become a very long, important, and warm association, Leonora Stephens has truly been *there* for me—a kind, patient guide, and the smartest, most perceptive of mentors. To be candid, I find it hard even to imagine what this long process of interviewing, researching, and writing about families would have been like without Leonora Stephens's remarkably astute, discerning, and supportive presence throughout. I am deeply, deeply grateful to her.

I am also profoundly obliged to another crucially important friend and mentor, psychoanalyst John Zinner, M.D. Dr. Zinner, who is on the faculty of the Washington School of Psychiatry and maintains a private practice in Bethesda, Maryland, is one of the founders of the object-relations approach to family treatment. It was under Dr. Zinner's brilliant tutelage that I began to fully grasp the ways in which *outer presences*—actual relationships we've had with significant people in our lives—are internalized as *inner presences*, which are often remarkably influential in shaping our present-day existence. It was he, too, who taught me to recognize that the family group can, like the individual person, become gripped by unconscious fantasies—basic, unquestioned assumptions that result in the repetitious playing out of old agendas deriving from the parents' own pasts in their families of origin. My hope is that what I learned from John Zinner, in what was a school for one, is faithfully reflected in the pages that follow.

I would also like to offer a collective acknowledgment of my gratitude to the entire faculty of the Washington School of Psychiatry. The Washington school is the intellectual hub of object-relations family theory and therapy in this country, and this remarkable group of clinicians, teachers, and researchers (some are all three simultaneously) welcomed me into their midst and made me feel like one of the family. The important connections that I forged at the Washington School of Psychiatry have proven crucial to my thinking not only about families in general, but about the family I myself grew up in, and the family world that my husband and I created together.

Although everyone associated with the Washington School was extremely generous in offering me assistance, there is one particular person who merits especially enthusiastic words of appreciation. This is Hannah Fox, M.S.W., C.S.W., who is now the director of the Metropolitan Center for Object Relations Theory and Practice and a clinician in private practice in New York City and Teaneck, New Jersey.

During the final years of my work on this book, Hannah Fox and I met on a regular basis to talk about the families I was then interviewing. These discussions proved not only fascinating to me personally, but also integral to my understanding of the hidden forces at play in the life of the family. In truth, I never left Hannah Fox's presence without carrying away with me some truly novel, unexpected, and thoroughly intriguing ways of thinking about families.

From the very outset of this engrossing project, I was also meeting regularly with a highly experienced, thoroughly knowledgeable family therapist named Katherine E. B. Davis. Katherine Davis, M.S.W., C.S.W., is now in private practice in New Haven, Connecticut, but she was for many years the clinical director of the Hamden Mental Health Center. With her, as with so many of the other experts I came to know throughout the course of this work, I shared that wonderful mixture of common interests, mentoring, and friendship. She kept me steadfastly on track in terms of thinking systemically—staying well aware, for example, of the subtle manner in which one family member's apparently senseless, self-destructive behavior often served a protective, equilibrium-maintaining function for the system as an emotionally bonded and interconnected entity.

Another much appreciated facilitator, also present from the very beginning of this endeavor, was New Haven psychologist Robert A. Horwitz, Ph.D. With the permission of the families he was treating, Dr. Horwitz, then president-elect of the Connecticut Psychological Association, invited me into the sanctum of his consulting office to meet with them along with him. The passionate intensity of such clinical encounters with all or most family members present is, I hope, accurately depicted in Part Two, where one of the families he and I saw together over the course of a year, the Maguires, is discussed at length. (See "Level 4: The Polarized Family— the Tyrant and His Subjects.")

I would also like to express my heartfelt thanks to the administrative and staff members of Elmcrest Psychiatric Hospital in Portland, Connecticut—and most especially to Lane Ameen, M.D., its medical director, and to Bernard Langenauer, M.D., vice-president of psychiatric services—who offered me the opportunity to do research on a unit for adolescents in crisis, and then assisted me in every way possible. Often, in my experience, it is very hard for an outsider to make a comfortable place for herself within a medical/psychiatric hierarchy. This is because everyone on the staff—every nurse, every psychiatrist, every family clinician, every recreational worker—has his or her own well-defined turf and particular duties to accomplish. But at Elmcrest Hospital's Chapman Unit, the staff members (especially clinicians Linda Bowen and Irene Haskew) not only helped and advised me, they also made me feel supported and appreciated.

I had, from the very beginning of this enterprise, been reading voluminously—reading not only on my own, but under the guidance of Jesse D. Geller, Ph.D., associate clinical professor of psychology in psychiatry and (at the time) director of the Psychological Services Clinic at Yale University. Professor Geller led me, in an orderly and yet delightfully wide-ranging manner, through the most important papers in the object-relations literature, starting with Freud's exquisite "Mourning and Melancholia" and moving on through the work of Melanie Klein, R.W.D. Fairbairn, D. W. Winnicott, and Wilfred R. Bion—the great thinkers in the field. I was also accorded a somewhat similar, much shorter but also quite marvelous course in object-relations theory by one of the foremost modern scholars in the area, the widely renowned writer and psychoanalyst Stephen A. Mitchell, M.D.

I have focused, thus far, upon those valued colleagues whom I came to know in the course of this study of families; now I would like to offer my grateful accolades to those theorists and clinicians who have been my close associates, mentors, friends throughout much of my career. These include my longtime buddies Carol Nadelson, M.D., professor of psychiatry at Harvard University and editor in chief of the American Psychiatric Press; Anne Peretz, M.S.W., founder and president of the Family Center in Somerville, Massachusetts; and Stuart Johnson, M.S.W., whose deliciously clever "family homework assignments" will be encountered later on in this book (see Chapter 21, "Family Tasks"). I also want to thank psychologist Betsy S. Stone of Stamford, Connecticut, who contributed some wonderful therapeutic-homework tasks of her own, and with whom I had several important gear-unblocking conversations along the way. Betsy Stone is not only a valued colleague, but a cherished daughter.

Other people richly deserving of my appreciative thanks include Dr. W. Robert Beavers, originator of the Beavers model, and his long-term collaborator and co-author (*Successful Families*) Robert H. Hampson, both of whom have been extraordinarily generous and helpful in sharing their time and expertise.

So are my warm thanks due to Judith Grunebaum, M.S.S.S., of the department of psychiatry at Harvard Medical School's Cambridge Hospital. In the course of talking to me about one family, Judy Grunebaum taught me much about all families; from her, I learned to fully appreciate the concept of the parentified child, who is fated to experience a sense of failure and existential guilt (or, in some cases, unquenchable rage) because he or she is being called upon to support the parent and fill the parent's needs in a way that no small child can ever really succeed in doing.

Grateful thanks are also due to the many other experts and specialists of different kinds with whom I have consulted along the way. To these individuals, who work in such varied fields as infant-mother attachment, eating disorders, alcoholism, resilient children, family ethnicity, and many other family-related areas, I would like to express my great appreciation— and also an apology for not having the space to be able to list you separately here; you are too many.

For the resources needed to travel far and wide to see so many diverse theorists, researchers, experts of all stripes and hues, I do want to extend my heartfelt thanks to the Smith Richardson Foundation, Inc., which generously supported this work over an extended period of time. I also want to add a special word of thanks to Smith Richardson board member Dr. Edward F. Zigler, Sterling Professor of Psychology and director of the Bush Center in Child Development and Social Policy at Yale, who has shown me the most unfailing kindness and encouragement throughout the years that this study of families has required.

When it comes to expressing my gratitude and thanks to the many, many families who volunteered to be interviewed for this project, however, let me confess that I find myself almost tongue-tied. All that I can say is that talking with you, often admiring you, on occasion even jealous of you, frequently worrying about you, thinking endlessly about you, comparing my own families (of the past and of the present) to your family, has been one of the most extraordinary experiences of my lifetime.

Finally, a fond word of appreciation to someone who has been a friend and staple of my professional life, my assistant Felicia Naumann Dickinson. Felicia Dickinson has been part of my writing life and office support system for so long that I am not sure I could go on breathing without her. The indefatigable Jean Emmons provided me with the speedy library help that is so much a part of what I need in order to maintain my forward motion; Jean not only managed to keep up with my requests, but brought me dusty tomes from the Yale library stacks that she thought might prove useful (and which often did).

And now, at last, like a child who has saved a favorite piece of chocolate for last, I come to Kate—Kate Medina, my thoroughly astute, dazzlingly intelligent editor, who manages to be tactful and benevolent at the same time as she is remarkably keen, objective, and clear-sighted.

Somehow it has happened, as Kate and I noticed recently, that a good deal of time has passed since our initial meeting in the early 1970s; here we are, more in harmony than ever, and we seem to have spent a good deal of our professional lives together. I must admit that, even though the two of us have shared a close collaboration throughout these many years, I am still at times taken by surprise by the recognition that Kate Medina is nothing short of a genius at what she does. Her tremendous focus as an editor, her way of stepping back from the work and looking at it as a whole—of thinking, seeing, reshaping—is indelibly imprinted upon every page of this book, as it is imprinted on so much of this writer's understanding of her craft. All that I can say is that my gratitude to her, as a colleague and dear friend, is immeasurable.

MAGGIE SCARF
Jonathan Edwards College, Yale University
February 1995

Contents

Acknowledgments   xi

Introduction   xxi

PART ONE

Level 5: The Family in Pain—Ghost-Ridden, Leaderless, Confused

1. Acting Out the Pain: The Child as Symptom Bearer and Delegate   3

2. The Beavers Scale of Family Health and Competence: Levels 1–5   23

3. Family Legacies: The Ways in Which the Past Invades the Present   37

4. Styles of Relating: Emotionally Enmeshed and Emotionally Disengaged Families   50

5. The Genogram: The Family's Existential Blueprint for Being   62

6. Closely Connected People: The Family Script, Projective Identification, and Paradoxical Tasks   76

PART TWO

Level 4: The Polarized Family—The Tyrant and His Subjects

7. Establishing Order and Predictability: The Emergence of a Tyrant   97

8. A Core Family Dynamic: The Oppressor and the Oppressed   107

9. Struggling for Control: The Bulimic Strategy   123

10. Re-creating the Pain of the Past: An Attempt at Resolution   138

PART THREE

The First Loves of Our Lives—Patterns of Intimacy and Attachment

11. Early Development: Of Love and Survival   163

12. Intimacy: Patterns in Human Attachment   175

13. What Would the First Sentence of Your Own Autobiography Be?   192

PART FOUR

Level 3: The Rule-Bound Family—A Stable, Nontyrannical Form of Governance Emerges; the Problem of Intimacy Is Unresolved

14. A Rule-Bound Emotional World: Control of the Self and of the System Is Established; Intimacy Remains Elusive   209

15. Her Side of the Genogram—an Enmeshed Family System and a Quasi-Incestuous "Family Affair": Toni Gifford   219

16. His Side of the Genogram—a Chilly, Distanced Family: Henry Gifford   242

17. Opposites Attract—or Are They Opposites? The Merging of Two Family Styles   254

18. Alcohol and the Family   273

19. Intimacy, Self-knowledge, and Self-esteem   287

PART FIVE

Family Boundaries and Therapeutic Tasks

20. Self Boundaries and Family Boundaries   309

21. Family Tasks   319

PART SIX

Levels 1 and 2: Adequate and Optimal Families—
Where Boundaries Are Clear, Conflicts Are Resolvable; as One
Ascends Toward the Top of the Family Competence Continuum,
a Trust That Good Things Will Happen in Human Encounters
Grows and Prevails

22. An Important Part of Loving: Acknowledging Human
    Separateness   341
23. Why Some Children Thrive Despite Early Family Trauma   370
24. Love: Unconditional, or Conditional/Earned   384
25. Resolving Conflict, Managing Power   398
26. Journeying Home   412

Appendixes

APPENDIX I

Directions for Mapping One's Own Family on the Beavers
Systems Model 427

APPENDIX II

Interview Outline: A Sampling of the Topics Raised, Questions
Asked, Self-Reflective Exercises Frequently Used in the Course of
Interviewing Families 433

Selected Bibliography   439
Index   453

Introduction

When I began work on this book about families, I was surely well accustomed to dealing with difficult, emotionally charged subjects. In my previous books, I had dealt with some highly flammable topics—women and depression in the case of *Unfinished Business: Pressure Points in the Lives of Women*, and marital relationships in *Intimate Partners: Patterns in Love and Marriage*. But nothing had quite prepared me for what happened when I began exploring the subject of the family: Here was every charged topic and every emotional dilemma that I could possibly have thought of—and some I couldn't possibly have imagined.

In the beginning, I was somewhat bowled over, not only by what I was seeing and hearing in the family groups I interviewed, but also by the complex responses these intense and powerful interviews aroused in me, especially those that evoked memories of my own difficult family of origin. And yet I was enthralled by the family stories being told to me, many of which sounded like the plots of novels, replete with many secrets and unsolved mysteries.

It was inevitable that, in the course of being interviewed for this book, people found that old family trunks locked away in the attic of everyone's awareness would be suddenly opened up, and that unnoticed or ignored intergenerational truths would abruptly and unceremoniously come to light. At times, these feeling-laden family matters were hastily thrust back out of everyone's sight; on other occasions, the members of the family were eager to confront their issues squarely and get to work on resolving them.

As I slowly gained my bearing, and grew in understanding, I began to view the family unit as a great emotional foundry, the passion-filled forge in which our deepest realities—our sense of who we are as persons, and of the world around us—first begins to form and take shape. It is within the enclave of the early family that we learn those patterns of being, both of a healthy and a pathological nature, which will gradually be assimilated into, and become a fundamental part of, our own inner experience.

It is within the family, too, that we start forming assumptions and expectations about what things are likely to happen in close relationships. It is here that each of us develops an emotional template of sorts, an internal blueprint for later adult existence. And so ingrained are the family's ways of being that, at an unconscious level, their truths seem unassailable. The way it was in our early families appears to be *the way of the world and the way things are*, rather than one particular family's way of relating and seeing things.

Overall, it has taken eight years for me to explore and digest the extraordinary material that I gathered as I journeyed into the private world of the family, and to write *Intimate Worlds.* Along the way, however, I came to recognize that while each family's narrative is unique, rich, complex, and compelling, *all* families are struggling with a limited set of core issues: power, and how to manage it; intimacy, and how to achieve it; conflict, and how to resolve it. Every member of every family I talked to was also dealing with the issue of individuality, of being "me, myself"—that is, trying to develop one's own authentic personhood while retaining a sense of belonging.

I soon became familiar with the maladaptive strategies families repeatedly make use of in the struggle to cope with (or avoid facing up to) core family concerns. These strategies, which come into play automatically, include emotional triangling, and the tactic of scapegoating—sacrificing one member of the family group to save the emotional system at large. I was also made continually aware of the poignant, tremendously powerful influence of the past—each parent's past, in his or her own family of origin—in setting the tone and establishing the emotional patterns of the current family's daily existence. This strong urge to re-create the unfinished business of the past in the family's present-day life often manifests itself in ways that are nothing short of eerie; the shadow cast by the family tree is truly an astonishingly long one.

Starting Out—by Going Home

During the late 1980s, when I was beginning research for this book, I went to a large conference in Dallas, Texas, at which some impressive figures in the field of family theory and therapy were offering a diverse smorgasbord of lectures and workshops.

In the course of a jam-packed few days I heard about many of the latest developments in the field—theoretical models of family life, new techniques for family improvement. These huge conferences often have the air of a meeting at the United Nations. There are envoys from the major schools of family theory and treatment—Structural, Strategic, Bowenian, Contextual, Behavioral, and Object-Relations Family Therapy, for example—and also representatives of less-established schools. All are vying for attention and adherents.

In the midst of the plethora of differing approaches, I felt the need for a time-out. So, scanning the catalogue of offerings, I decided to go to a workshop that sounded somewhat frivolous. It had the oddball title "Taming Your Gremlin, or, Your Ego May Not Be Your Amigo," and it was being led by someone whose name I'd never heard before: Richard D. Carson, M.S.W.

I came a bit late, assuming that I would be one of a small handful of people there. But I was mistaken; when I arrived, I found myself in a large room so crowded with people that not enough seats were available. Chairs had been shifted to the side walls, and those of us who had come in at the last minute were asked to sit on the floor, using the wall in back of us for support.

The workshop leader began the session by putting us into a light trance, using deep-breathing exercises and a few progressive-relaxation techniques. Soon I found myself floating, although hyperaware of Mr. Carson's quiet voice.

He was instructing us to bring to mind a house we'd once lived in during our childhood. We were to summon up a visual image of ourselves at roughly the age we'd been when living in that house (I pictured myself at age six or seven). We were to see ourselves as standing across the street from the house, focusing upon it carefully, and recalling the details of its appearance.

I envisioned myself standing directly in front of the bakery opposite our house, where I'd buy myself an after-school chocolate éclair whenever I could. I was staring at the storefront of the house I'd grown up in, but a trolley car (the number 34) passed in front of me, obscuring my view momentarily. Then I saw our house again—the front part of the ground floor was my father's paint-and-wallpaper store—and I felt a sense of apprehension wash over me.

As a young child, I'd struggled hard to understand what was so fundamentally different—wrong, amiss—about our family, and I had worked out two possible explanations. One line of theorizing had it that we were lesser mortals because we lived behind a store in a mainly residential neighborhood. The other major conjecture was that we weren't as good as other families, because in our family there were four children, while in the other neighborhood families, there were only two. . . .

As if from afar, I heard the soft, soothing voice of Richard Carson instructing me to cross the street, slowly, slowly, and then approach the door of the house.

It was strange, this sense of duality. In one part of my mind I knew I was still me, and yet in another part of my mind I was experiencing myself as a child, looking carefully in both directions and wary of the occasionally heavy traffic.

Then I had crossed the street, and stood gazing at the black and white tiles beneath the large storefront windows (I wasn't able to bring to mind anything that might have been on display there). The disembodied voice of Mr. Carson came to me: "Now, knock on the door."

I felt fearful. If I came in via this front entrance, I might offend or anger my always unpredictable father, who could be dealing with a customer (he got into bitter quarrels with his customers all the time). I usually entered the house through the backyard after school, and my mother, working in the kitchen, humming her favorite song ("The Bluebird of Happiness"), greeted me with pleasure.

But here I was, in the prescribed imagery of this moment, and I dutifully knocked on the front door. To my surprise, the workshop leader then told me that I myself—the adult I am now—was opening the door to myself, as a child. The grown-up "me" was welcoming the much younger "me," and leading her slowly into the house's interior. I was to look around and recall, as well as I could, just what each of those rooms had looked like.

Fortunately, my father didn't seem to be in the store; but when I'd passed through the dining room and living room, the six- or seven-year-old "me" looked up trustingly into the face of the grown woman who was holding my hand. I realized then that that person wasn't, strictly speaking, me; she was some amalgam of myself and my beloved mother. I felt a rush of intense, little-girl emotion, for I'd worshiped my mother, and wanted so urgently for her to be happy.

This thought brought with it an acutely painful upsurge of sorrow; but at that moment I heard Richard Carson's voice recalling me to the main business of the imagery exercise. The adult "self," we were being instructed, was to look deeply into the eyes of the child "self," and to think of one thing we'd really like to tell him or her. If there was just one thing that we, as grown-ups, wished that child could have known, what might that thing be?

My own response popped into my mind immediately. I had a vivid picture of the older woman's hands dropping onto the little girl's shoulders as she looked down at the child with sympathy and affection. "You are really going to be all right," my adult self said to my child self, "and things are going to get much better than you can possibly imagine." Oh, how I wish I could have had that comforting bit of foreknowledge way back then, for the family world that I grew up in was tremendously scary, difficult, and depriving.

But what *had* been wrong, and what had made it so? Granted that my own early hypotheses—the problem was that we lived behind a store; the problem was that there were four children in the family instead of two—had surely not been correct, how could those questions be responded to now? I knew as little as ever. But what that somewhat shocking experience of finding myself, in my imagination, at home, told me was that even though I was now an adult woman, with a husband and with three grown daughters who were raising young families of their own, the family I'd grown up in was not lost somewhere, in the haze of the past and of fading memories. It was, in the most immediate sense, vividly alive inside me.

And it was, I think, from this moment onward that I was no longer a researcher and writer, engaged in a somewhat abstract study of the family; I was a person who was studying, not without some ambivalence and pain, but also with remembered moments of great love, the family I myself had come from, and the issues, resolved and unresolved, with which that experience of growing up had left me.

Inside the Private World of the Family

I began this study of the family in the same way I'd embarked upon all previous research endeavors, which is to say by talking to people about their lives in semistructured, but flexible, intensive interviews. I was trying to understand, from as far inside the emotional system as possible, how each family's own small universe had been constructed.

Interviewing whole families was, at the outset, a strange and perplexing experience. For now, instead of talking to one individual (woman) alone, or to two people involved in an intimate attachment, I was frequently talking with an entire roomful of people, including some very young children. It could at times be dismaying, but it was also amazing and rewarding. I was finding each family's tales of the past, as well as the dilemmas they were struggling with currently, intensely dramatic and compelling. And how could they not be, considering that the dramas of families—which have to do with loving, losing, power, intimacy, conflict, and the pressure of the past to reassert itself in the present—*are* the major dramas of our lives?

What I found, as I became more skilled in conducting these interviews, was that the members of the families I was talking to became easier too, more comfortable, readier to open up about their experiences. And in the course of these conversations, extraordinary family recollections and stories were continually emerging—stories that were, I must say, usually told to me with great poignancy and eloquence.

In many of these recountings, there were recurring, quite serious family issues—problems with alcoholism, eating disorders, or the violation of important sexual boundaries—that seemed, like a bridge across time, to link one generation to the next. There were also many situations in which a particular member of the family saw in an intimate other (a child, a spouse) aspects of his or her own inner being that were being stoutly repudiated (see Chapter 6, "Closely Connected People: The Family Script, Projective Identification, and Paradoxical Tasks"). But everywhere, in the many different worlds of the families to which I was being admitted, I was finding those patterns of caring and longing, intimacy and solitude, power and self-esteem, freedom and confinement to which we are all introduced in the original family—which is to say, the first human environment with which we become acquainted.

A Rising Tide of Family Information

My taped interviews with families were, I soon found, piling up faster than I could sort and file them, and I was feeling uncertain about how I was ever going to put it all together. I had thought I would look at families in terms of how they were structured—traditional, single-parent, blended, and so forth—but the issues being raised in my interviews crisscrossed through all family forms and modes of organization.

And so the great question was, How was I to bring order and clarity to this rising tide of family information, how to place this huge amount of material into a really useful, organizing framework? How, for that matter, was I to address certain fundamental questions that still seemed too vague and slippery to answer—such as, What is a good family? What makes one family capable of creating a happy environment for its members, while another family seems continually fraught with covert or overt tensions, and is producing symptomatic offspring?

Family Competence and Well-being: The Beavers Systems Model

As my interviews with families proceeded, I began tracking those core family concerns—power, intimacy, conflict—that kept manifesting themselves continually, in one guise or another. How was the family handling the issue of power? In other words who, in the intimate group, had power, and how was that power being managed?

I found myself becoming ever more sensitized to the power struggles and power coalitions that pervade some families' lives, and increasingly aware of the harm that could ensue when the appropriate family hierarchy became unbalanced—when, for instance, a member of the parental generation and a member of the child generation had formed a coalition to undermine the legitimate authority of the other parent/spouse.

I was equally intrigued by the dilemmas relating to intimacy—to the overarching, often perplexing question of how the members of a family group could remain connected and yet at liberty to develop their own individual, separate personhood. And I was just as interested and on the alert to the important issue of how the members of the family customarily dealt with conflict.

All families, as I well knew, experience some degree of overt or covert conflict (as do all social groups of other sorts). But what seemed to be of vital significance was not that such differences and conflicts existed; what mattered, and mattered greatly, was how these differences and conflicts were customarily responded to. Did the members of the family withdraw from overt disagreement, so that they eventually found themselves feeling inauthentic, isolated, and alienated? Or did people argue often and openly, without ever being able to get clear about what their basic differences actually were? Finally, could the members of the family get their emotional laundry washed and put away—that is, focus upon and clarify their real issues, negotiate their differences, and then proceed to resolve them?

Somewhere around this time, by sheer good luck, I happened to attend a conference on marriage and the family in New Orleans, and to go to a lecture being given by the psychiatrist Leonora Stephens. Dr. Stephens was speaking on the subject of "borderline families"—which in this context, as she carefully explained, meant families classified as on the border between "severely dysfunctional" and "midrange" on a family evaluation scale called the Beavers Systems Model. I found the lecture riveting, for I recognized in Stephens's description of the "borderline family" several of the families I was interviewing extensively at the time. (And also, to be frank, I found an uncomfortable resemblance to the family that I myself had grown up in.)

I was fascinated, above all, by Stephens's lively, animated description of the Beavers Systems Model, a family assessment device that is used for clinical and research purposes, and that until then I'd been only vaguely acquainted with. For here, I realized, was a group of researchers thinking in systematic ways about not only intimacy, power, and conflict, but also a range of other important family concerns (such as the family's mythology, in terms of how congruent its beliefs about itself are with observable reality). As I listened to Leonora Stephens lecture about the Beavers Scale of family competence and functioning, many of the data that I had been gathering in the course of my interviews with families suddenly began to come together, make sense, fit into a coherent framework.

For what the Beavers schema offered was a way of understanding family competence and functioning as viewed along points on a scale or continuum. This clinical device contained structural blueprints of five major patterns of family life, with the most troubled families at one end of the continuum and the most competent, successful families at the other. Using meticulous descriptions of these five very different kinds of family systems, Beavers and his colleagues were able to relate a family's current level of health and competence to certain specific, recognizable factors, and also to describe how families at different levels of the continuum typically operate.

The five major family systems are as follows: In families at the low end of the Beavers continuum ("severely disturbed" families), chaos and incoherence reign. Then, moving upward, one encounters the more orderly but tyrannical "borderline" system; then the "midrange" family, with its "internal referee"; and, at the top of the scale, families belonging to the "adequate" and "optimal" groups.

The Beavers researchers were, I realized, not only looking at family patterns in a systematic, illuminating manner; they were also attempting to address the important issue of how such patterns, if they happened to be proving painful and destructive, might possibly be altered. For instance, what specific changes are necessary in order for a midrange family to move upward to an adequate—or even optimal—level of health and functioning on the Beavers Scale?

The Beavers Systems Model had, as I soon learned, been first devised by psychiatrist W. Robert Beavers in the early 1970s; since that time, the model (originally known as the Beavers-Timberlawn Family Evaluation Scales) has been subjected to over twenty-five years of empirical testing, refinement, subsequent study, further elaboration, and revision. (The original version of this assessment device was, interestingly enough, constructed in the course of a study of healthy, successful families. Such studies have been relatively rare; it is symptomatic families who usually garner scientific attention.)

Over the past two and a half decades, the Beavers model has also been scrutinized carefully with respect to its usefulness in assessing varying kinds of families, including single-parent families, inner-city families with a developmentally disadvantaged child, families in therapy at the Southwest Family Institute in Dallas (a research and training center founded by Dr. Beavers), and a large sample of nonclinical volunteer families, recruited through churches, temples, and schools.

Since the particulars of the model are described at length in Chapter 2, "The Beavers Scale of Family Health and Competence: Levels 1–5," I will not discuss them in further detail here. I do want to emphasize, however, that this is a *developmental schema*, which lays out the core issues and maturational tasks that families at different levels of the scale are struggling to deal with; as shall be seen, the major, preoccupying concerns of a family system located at the bottom of the scale will look very different from those of a family somewhere in the middle of the continuum. It is also important to remember that the families described in these pages are those families *as seen at a certain point in time*. No family's position on the Beavers health and competence ladder is fixed for all time; predictably, over the course of the family life cycle, some families will move upward on the scale, while others will regress and take a downward course.

A word must be said, at this juncture, about my reasons for beginning this book with a discussion of a family in severe distress, one that is located at the most troubled end of the Beavers continuum. Starting at the bottom of the family health and functioning ladder will, I believe, make it much easier for the reader to appreciate the nature of the successive developmental tasks being mastered as the ladder of family competence and well-being is ascended.

The Power of the Family

Throughout my work on this project, I was not only interviewing families, but attending courses on the family, workshops and conferences on the family, and also reading, reading, reading. It was at the Columbia School of Social Work that I came across an intriguing article written by a family clinician and researcher named Connie Hansen. In the mid-1960s, Hansen had lived with three different "normal, healthy" families sequentially, spending a full week in each household; her goal was to study patterns of interaction in families that were viewed as well functioning and successful.

But in one of the three families, Hansen found herself becoming distressed by the father's constant attacks on his wife and children. She was also troubled by the mother's persistent efforts to get closer to the children—for when her youngsters did draw nearer to her, the mother immediately backed off, leaving them feeling confused and rejected. Although Hansen did manage to preserve her carefully neutral researcher's stance, she found herself developing physical symptoms: daily headaches that lasted from waking to sleep (despite as many as six aspirins a day); nightmares of an intensity she'd never previously experienced; and backaches, which she'd never had at all before.

The real marvel was, however, that within twenty-four hours of Hansen's move out of this household and in with the next family, every single one of these symptoms had disappeared! This researcher's account, though written in a thoroughly balanced, unsensational manner, did provide a powerful demonstration of the strong reactions that families can generate in their members (even temporary ones like Hansen, who was, after all, only a member of the family for a week).

I was much taken by this brief report because, in the course of my own interviews with families, I had often had comparable experiences. The pulling, magnetic forces at play within a family can be so powerful that on occasion one finds oneself responding to the group's vibes and "catching" (for better or for worse) its general mood state. Sometimes, at the end of a long, intense interview, I would find myself departing the household in a state of tension, feeling inadequate, upset, even despondent. On other occasions, including times when I'd arrived feeling somewhat hard-pressed, cranky, and harassed, I left the interview feeling validated, confirmed, on top of the world. Such was the family group's capacity (*even when it was someone else's family*) to engender, mirror, and reflect "good-and-valued" or "bad-and-unwelcome" aspects of the individual self.

The Mates Are the Architects of the Family: My Parents' Marriage

An early photograph of my mother and father (both now deceased) stands on a bedroom bureau, in a place where my gaze encounters it often. It must have been taken around the time of their wedding; she looks so limpid, so wide-eyed, so tentative. He was more than twice her age when they married, and his jaw juts out sternly, as if he were her irritated parent.

I pause before this photograph, puzzled, lost in reverie. "The marital relationship is the axis around which all other family relationships are formed. The mates are the 'architects' of the family," wrote family therapist Virginia Satir many years ago. The family that my parents constructed seems, in retrospect, somewhat less like a single edifice than like a compound—one that contained two central administrative buildings, from which mutually contradictory sets of decrees and rules regularly emerged. Those dictates emerging from Administrative Building Number 1, my father's base of operations, were often harsh, sometimes quite erratic, at times not even comprehensible. But Administrative Building Number 2, in which my mother functioned, was dedicated to the work of moderating and softening the effects of these initial, dictatorial commands; at times, we children were even advised on ways to go about ignoring my father's orders completely. Still, in her old-country way, my mother always did insist that "he is your father, and you must respect him."

Looking up, I catch sight of myself in the mirror over the dresser. There is a faintly ironic smile on my face, linked, no doubt, to what seems the almost laughably obvious truth that when I began this exploration of families in general, I had certain subliminal objectives of my own. I wanted, of course, to try to understand my own family—not only the family that I grew up in, but also the family that my husband and I created together.

I pick up my parents' photograph, stare at their images. My father's is distinct and clear, my mother's much hazier, as though each stood in a separate light. She is all softness, soft dark hair and a dark V-necked blouse. Lining the V is a long strand of pearls; even they are not well defined, but glimmering vaguely. She tried to leave my father, she told me, when my oldest sister was still an infant.

"What could I do, though? Where could I go?" She always sighed when she got to that point in the story. She couldn't have survived, with a tiny baby, in a country whose language she didn't yet know. My father had brought her to this country as a bride (his third wife) from Warsaw, and eventually she'd had to bend to the yoke of that marriage.

Sometimes, in the evenings, I would sit with my mother, watching her shovel coal into our basement furnace, her face flushed and beautiful in the flickers of light. She told me stories about her girlhood—about her well-loved merchant father who had died young, leaving the family destitute, and about her widowed mother who, like the old woman in the shoe, had had to tell her daughter she could no longer keep her, and that my father's offer of marriage must be accepted.

My mother told me, too, about the handsome captain of the boat that had brought her to America. He had really *admired* her—but she was already promised, on her way to be married. I was so filled with regret about that lost possibility, that romance that had never come into being. If only I could have changed her history, willed an elopement with that unknown captain! "You'll be happy someday, Mommy, you'll see," I, her little confidante, assured her. I willed it to be so, and, when I was a child, believed it would be so, absolutely—but things didn't happen according to my plan.

My parents divorced when I was fifteen years old, and although my mother did remarry, a decade later, she seemed to have lost whatever talent she once might have had for living in a comfortable, mutually respectful relationship with a man; she feared the male's superior power, which she believed in, without question, and she distrusted all men profoundly.

So it was I, her youngest daughter, who had taken on what is usually the spouse's role, that of comrade and intimate. The intensely strong and close relationship that I shared with my mother throughout my early years was, as I now fully recognize, a classic instance of what is known as "parentification" (see Chapter 8, "A Core Family Dynamic: The Oppressor and the Oppressed," and also Chapter 19, "Intimacy, Self-knowledge, and

Self-esteem"). This is the topsy-turvy situation that ensues when the parent, instead of nurturing the immature child, requires the child's nurturance instead. Instead of focusing upon my needs, my mother had transformed me into her caring parent—her loving, overly responsible confidante, who wanted nothing more on earth than to save her, to see the Bluebird of Happiness alight at last in her life.

Clearly, a phrase like "the parentified child" implies that one could register legitimate complaints about my mother's behavior—and yet, search my heart as I may, I find it impossible to blame her. What springs into my mind instead is the awful picture of her as an eighteen-year-old girl in a strange land, without language or resources, and in the power of a remote and tyrannical man who was old enough to be her father, but was mine instead.

Memories of Early Love

In the late 1970s (my mother was still living at the time, though unable to speak or write intelligibly as the result of a stroke) I had an experience that transported me back into the heart of my original family with a sense of immediacy that I found nothing less than startling. It happened, quite by chance, when I was gathering material for an article on a clinic for insomniacs, which I was writing for *The New York Times Magazine*.

In order to demonstrate to me the beneficial effects of biofeedback, the sleep researchers I was interviewing suggested that I allow myself to be hooked up to a biofeedback device and simply experience body-muscle relaxation for myself. What this device "fed back" to the sleep patient, they explained, was ongoing information about the state of his or her own muscular tension—most particularly, what kinds of things caused the muscles to loosen up and what things tended to make them tighten and grow rigid.

Accordingly, I rested on a comfortable sofa in a soundproof room, with electrodes on the mobile, reactive muscles of my forehead, and a set of earphones over my ears. I soon became aware that each time I thought about something that made me feel taut and anxious, I could literally "hear" my own facial musculature clenching. The biofeedback mechanism translated the electrical charge of the muscles into sounds: What I heard, then, was a rapid barrage of click-click-clicks.

It didn't take me very long to discover that certain kinds of thoughts produced an avalanche of noise. When I thought about writing the sleep article, for example—about how hard it would be to summarize the latest research findings on the disorders of sleep, and the newer ways of treating them—the uproar in my ears was overwhelming. Other thoughts, however, tended to slow the clicks down. When I set myself to thinking those thoughts, I was rewarded by hearing a widely spaced click . . . click . . . click.

And nothing, I found, could slow the sounds down so effectively as imagining myself as a small infant lying on a table, kicking my legs, "talking" and laughing with my mother. When I brought this picture—complete with the vision of my smiling mother leaning over me—to the center of my mind, there were actually extended periods when I heard no clicks at all.

It was as though my feelings about the mother of my infancy were still there, inside my muscles and my thought processes, fully intact. They lay there, coiled within my brain cells; and those feelings had the power, at the deepest level of my being, to relax me and make me happy.

Beneath all later experiences, it seemed, there still existed that central and fundamental image: myself as the young baby of my mommy. When it came to self-inducing a state of calmness and contentment, no other imagined scene had the same capacity to cut off those clicks completely. That baby-with-her-mommy was as present-tense and vividly alive inside me as ever.

The "Good-Enough Mother"

At the furthest reach of my memory—a small, lit isle surrounded on all sides by obscurity—is a riot of tickling, myself and my sisters lined up on a big wide bed. I think I must have been about two years old. My mother was taking turns with us, tickling and kissing our bellies, and oh, it was delicious! I have a memory of laughing and laughing, to the point of pain; of wanting another turn, but at the same time being afraid of having one. . . .

It is true that over the course of time, inevitably, the scales of infantile idealization fell from my eyes; I came to see my mother as the fallible, and in some ways quite unbending, even obstinate human being that she was. As she aged, she seemed to grow more opinionated and eccentric, ever more identified with my father's (now her ex-husband's) view that a woman's proper role was to be a secondary figure, submissive, without personal aspirations. I believe she saw my evolving writing career as a kind of aberration, as if I were a female masquerading in a male's clothing. A good woman's rightful sphere should be limited to home, children, religion.

And yet . . . In those early years, when it most counted, my mother was always there for me, a loving, dependable, wryly humorous, generous-spirited (I would say gallant) human being. I did, as I said earlier, spend my childhood in an oppressive, discordant family atmosphere—ridden with marital tensions and desperate sibling rivalries. But somehow, along the way, my mother was able to give me what I needed to grow on, and somehow I was able to take in and absorb the nurturance that she offered.

My mother was the "good-enough mother" of whom the famed British psychiatrist D. W. Winnicott has written—that intuitive, empathetic maternal caregiver who fosters her young baby's "capacity for going on being" and spontaneously developing her or his own authentic personhood (or "true self," as Winnicott put it). Despite all later differences between us, the mother of my earliest years made me feel satisfyingly well loved, and accorded me a certain permission and degree of space in which to do my growing. And it was within the setting of this first, trustworthy relationship, which *felt* so reliable (whatever its later shortcomings), that, so I believe, I became the particular human being I am.

This is, I must hasten to say, not merely one person's—my own—singular story. For a very widely accepted theoretical view is that within this special emotional context—the powerful love bond that grows up between the helpless, dependent infant and the nurturing caregiver—the very foundation stone of the personality is laid down (see Part Three: "The First Loves of Our Lives: Patterns of Intimacy and Attachment"). Indeed, there is now good scientific evidence supporting the view that it is within this crucial first relationship that the brain itself is being structured—that our cognitive capacities, our ways of responding emotionally, and our patterns of perceiving the world are being slowly developed. Thus, what is woven into the very tapestry of the self is the all-important other.

The First Organization

The family is the first social organization with which the fledgling human being comes into contact. As such, observes the British psychiatrist A. C. Robin Skynner, "the family stands in a peculiarly central, crucial position. It faces inward to the individual, outward toward society, preparing each member to take his place in the wider social group by helping him to internalize its values and traditions as part of himself." It is within the family that we imbibe and incorporate the skills and knowledge that will one day enable us to live outside it.

What we learn in this intensely emotional social system (all families are emotional little groups, even those that display no emotionality whatsoever) is a particular set of rules, regulations, and expectations about our own and other people's behavior that eventually become taken for granted as the way of the world, *obvious matters that everybody knows about.* We learn, among other things, what an adult woman is like and what an adult man is like, and how the two sexes relate. This learning occurs, as a matter of course, from our observations of our parents' behavior, for we are witnesses to what goes on between them even as our consciousness awakens.

We take this first environment of our lives inside us as a rough-hewn interior blueprint for later emotional relating. The nurturing, enculturating family is the place in which we learn about what kinds of feelings are acceptable, appropriate, and tolerable—and what feelings are not allowable at all. As Dr. Theodor Lidz points out in *The Person,* "It is in the family that patterns of emotional reactivity develop and interpersonal relationships are established that pattern and color all subsequent relationships."

It is within this first human organization, too, that each of us is first exposed to a broad array of teachings on almost every conceivable subject—ranging from fidelity and trustworthiness to religion and politics to personal risk-taking as opposed to playing things safe. These lessons, internalized during what is essentially a long period of basic training for later life, become the substrate from which significant aspects of our thinking, our motives, our directives, our ways of being, and our very personalities are formed. What we learn within the family are the most unforgettable lessons that our lives will ever teach us.

How, though, could it be otherwise? It is within the context of the original family that our own personhood, our game plan for being in close relationships, and our ways of being in the world outside the family (which can vary from "The milieu around us is safe and welcoming" to "You can't trust anyone outside the family") have first taken shape. The family is the earliest, most basic environment in which we learn about what things we are—or are not—entitled to, and about whether people are reliable and trustworthy.

As psychologist William R. Looft has written, "Everyone carries around within him a model of man—a personalized conception of the nature of human nature, a common-sense notion about 'the way people are.' He may not be able to verbalize precisely just what his personal theory about human nature is, but he clearly has one, for it is implicit in what he does to, for, and about other people."

Our development of a unique, personal theory about the nature of human nature gets under way very early in life, in our original families, where we begin immediately to internalize the information we must have in order to devise our own individual blueprints for later, independent being.

Family Volunteers

Who in the world would ever volunteer to participate in an intensive, self-revealing family interview? This is a question I am frequently asked, and the best, most honest answer I can offer is "Just about anyone with whom you might be acquainted." In the past eight years, I have interviewed some fifty families, a substantial subset of them at quite considerable length; but had my own time permitted, I could have talked with many more. There were a large number of families on my list of volunteers whom I was simply unable to see; but the list was quite long and each set of family interviews was in and of itself engrossing, absorbing, highly demanding of time and energy.

Where did these volunteer families come from? Again, the answer is "Everywhere." Some responded when, in the course of a speaking engagement, I asked for interested members of the audience to write down their name, family composition, telephone number, and address, and hand them to me at the end of the lecture. Many people did. Other families came to me through contacts in the public school system, some through local religious organizations. A corporate-executive pair whom I met at a dinner party asked me if I was including remarried families in my study, and then eagerly volunteered to be interviewed. Some of the families were in clinical treatment, and agreed to let me sit in on the therapy as a participant-observer. Other families were those I encountered during a tour of research duty at Elmcrest Hospital in Portland, Connecticut, on a ward devoted to the care of adolescents in crisis.

From the point of view of economic and social status, the families I saw ranged from quite wealthy to comfortably middle-class; there were also many families that were uncomfortably middle-class and struggling hard to meet their commitments, as well as families living in poverty-ridden areas, including inner-city ghettos. I also interviewed (as I'd originally set out to do) family groupings of widely varying forms, designs, structures. But by the time it came to actually sitting down and writing, my framework for thinking and talking about families had changed in certain fundamental ways.

Object-Relations Family Therapy

When I first embarked on this trek into the heartland of the family, I brought only two tentative goals in my mental backpack. The first of these goals was that of using these abundant family data to illustrate and explain basic aspects of systemic family theory and treatment as they exist today.

This initial aim proved readily achievable, and in the pages that follow many facets of family theory and therapy are touched upon. There is, however, a particular emphasis upon one way of thinking about families, which is known as the object-relations approach.

Object-relations family therapy has its early roots in psychoanalysis; it is, therefore, oriented toward understanding not only the outer life of the family but its inner, unconscious world as well. Broadly speaking, this rich and wonderfully subtle theory is based upon two fundamental assumptions: first, that we humans come into the world ready to love, to link, and to connect; and second, that we also enter life with an innate longing for growth and differentiation, a need to develop our own authentic personhood.

The technical word "object" can, by the way, be translated as "love object"; the term "object relations" means "relations between persons involved in ardent emotional attachments." These attachments can exist in the outer world of reality or as residues of the past—that is, inner presences, often unconscious, that remain vigorous and very much alive within us.

New Forms of Family Structure

The second goal that I'd set out with was that of taking a close, considered look at the newer family structures—such as single-parent families, remarried, "reconstituted" families, etc.—that had been emerging in recent years and were becoming ever more commonplace. How were the members of these new kinds of family groups actually faring? My original working plan was to focus upon—and eventually write about—the special problems and concerns confronting people living in the representative "dual-career" family, the "single-parent" family, the "remarried" family, and so forth. But as far as meeting this second goal was concerned, I soon found myself running into insuperable problems.

For in actuality, two families with identical kinds of structures could and often did evidence more points of difference than they did similarities. When I looked at the various single-parent families I was talking with, not one of them could be construed as representative of single-parent families in general. This was also true of the remarried families I was interviewing. While, broadly speaking, these "reconstituted" families had the same organizational form, what could be said about any one of them was not necessarily relevant to any of the others.

It Is Family Functioning, Not Family Structure, That Matters Most

Furthermore, it had become clear to me along the way that a family's mode of functioning—the members' customary patterns of being together and interacting with one another—rather than its structural composition was of primary importance. *It was family functioning, not form, that mattered most.* If I kept the spotlight of my attention fixed steadily upon family health and competence I could, I realized, transmit a lot of valuable information—information that people would find useful in their everyday lives.

But this, inevitably (and I must say, regrettably), made it imperative for me to keep the variable of family structure constant. For, if I were to describe a remarried, reconstituted family as existing at the bottom of the Beavers ladder, that would suggest that all stepfamilies are inevitably going to be severely distressed and dysfunctional. And similarly, if I were to present a single-parent family as "optimal," the top of the scale (while all the families below them were two-parent families), it would imply that single-parent families are the only, best, and healthiest kind of family structures to live in.

Thus, in order to avoid such implications vis-à-vis family form (and with the consoling knowledge that one can't usefully compare apples and oranges, anyhow), I have focused the discussion that follows upon families that are, structurally speaking, similar: These are not remarriage families, and both parents are present in the household. It should, nevertheless, be well understood that *any* family, whatever its structure, can locate itself upon the Beavers family functioning scale (see Appendix I). This assessment instrument is focused upon family competence and well-being, not upon family composition, and what follows in these pages is applicable to all families everywhere.

PART ONE

LEVEL 5:
THE FAMILY IN PAIN—

Ghost-Ridden, Leaderless, Confused

Acting Out the Pain: The Child as Symptom Bearer and Delegate

It was a mild, slightly drizzly afternoon in late February, and we were in a therapeutic meeting with the Anderson family. Present were the parents, Susan and Ralph; the patient, fifteen-year-old Dave; clinician Linda Bowen; and myself. Dave Anderson's younger sister, Cheryl, had been expected to attend, but once again her parents had arrived at the hospital without her.

I was disappointed, for Dave had now been on the Chapman Unit for seventeen days. He was moving ever closer to the date of his discharge from Elmcrest, which is a psychiatric hospital in Portland, Connecticut, but his twelve-year-old sister had not yet appeared; she had merely sent along one excuse after another. I wanted very much to meet Cheryl, particularly to hear her own version of a disturbing incident that Dave had recounted to a staff member shortly after his admission.

It appeared that several weeks before Dave's hospitalization, on a Sunday afternoon when the senior Andersons were out of the house, the adolescent had threatened his sister with the family gun. According to Dave's telling of the tale, Cheryl had been grounded at the time, which meant that she wasn't permitted to leave the house or use the telephone.

As soon as their parents were gone, however, Cheryl had taken off and disappeared for several hours. Then, on her return, she had called a friend and refused to end the conversation until her infuriated older brother had put the gun to the side of her head and threatened to pull the trigger if she didn't hang up immediately.

That was Dave's version, but there was some question about whether or not Cheryl had indeed been grounded on that Sunday in the first place. Susan Anderson, on learning of the incident, had insisted that Cheryl hadn't been grounded on that day; her punishment had ended the Friday before. The children's father, Ralph Anderson, had no recollection of anything to do with that particular Sunday; he'd simply seemed mystified, and been unable to add anything definitive to the discussion.

I wondered what Cheryl herself would have to say, if and when we ever met her. Had she taken her tall, strapping older brother's threat seriously, and actually been in fear of her life? Was it her belief that the weapon had been loaded at the time? Thus far, we'd been unable to get a clear answer as to whether the family gun was usually kept loaded. It was as if the Andersons, as a group, couldn't get together on certain basic facts of their mutual life, couldn't settle on some jointly accepted, shared family reality—a typical feature of severely disturbed, Level 5 families (see Chapter 2, "The Beavers Scale of Family Health and Competence: Levels 1–5") in which mystification and disjointed thinking are the norm.

The Family's Symptom Bearer

It is a well-known axiom of family therapy that the so-called "symptom bearer" in an emotional system is often not the most disturbed or distressed person living there. The symptomatic individual, often a young child or adolescent, is merely the one who sounds the bugle and alerts outsiders to the fact that help is needed within the domestic stockade.

It is the symptoms or difficulties (depression, truancy, drug use, eating disorder, promiscuity, and so on) of the "identified patient" that require clinical intervention. Treatment then becomes available to the others in the emotional system, for the family as an entity is usually drawn into the process of therapeutic healing.

Long before the family ever does enter treatment, however, it can be assumed that the symptom bearer has been playing a key role in the emotional system's ongoing functioning. As the Chapman Unit's director, Peter Smith, M.D., once put it, "The symptoms that eventually bring an adolescent into the hospital have been serving some purpose to someone long before the patient ever arrives here. There is *always* some reason for those symptoms being there in the first place."

The family's intense focus upon a youngster's disturbing behavior has in fact been helping to keep the emotional system operational and functioning—at least to some extent, and for a period of time. For, as long as everyone can remain preoccupied by the delinquency or depression or suicidal ideation of the disturbed teenager, other, potentially more dangerous matters (for example, the parental couple's painfully remote, ungratifying, or even rapidly disintegrating relationship) can be brushed to one side and ignored.

According to psychiatrist Smith, the impressive display of diversionary fireworks created by the family's symptom bearer is serving to maintain an area of silence around some *other* source of terrible anxiety. There is some feared happening—perhaps the sudden emergence of an open discussion about painful underlying concerns that are being camouflaged by evasion, mystification, double-talk, and a variety of other communicational ploys.

For if there were ever frank talk about Father's affairs, or Mother's drinking, or about the sexual deadness of the marital partners, who could predict what catastrophes might happen? The emotional system, as an entity, is invested in *not knowing* something that everyone is doing his or her best to suppress and avoid.

Although the family members may not realize it at the time of a youngster's psychiatric hospitalization, it is by then not only the patient but the *system as a whole* that is in dire need of the institution's parenting—its strict rule-making, which provides organization, and its psychological support, which offers a safe, empathetic environment in which the family's frightening dilemmas and its conflicts can be explored.

For the emotional system's unaddressed issues are, predictably, linked to the patient's symptoms, whatever those symptoms may be. This is why the Chapman Unit's fundamental rule of thumb is that *psychological things matter*. The family's underlying concerns must be confronted while the adolescent is still in the hospital and a caring staff is there to support the people in the emotional system through what will inevitably be a punishing ordeal for all of them, not for the young patient alone.

Typically, however, the family's agenda is a very different one. They want to have their adolescent "repaired," preferably without ever approaching, much less exposing, those underlying emotionally charged issues and conflicts that no one in the system wants to even think about, much less try to deal with. In truth, the people in the system *will* need to confront their issues—to focus on and deal with the real sources of their distress—but the growing realization that this *must* happen doesn't make drawing closer to the painful places any easier. Drawing closer to the pain can feel like that awful moment on the Ferris wheel when one has reached the terrifying summit and halted: One is about to descend precipitously.

Diagnosis: Oppositional Defiant Disorder

Until the time of their son's hospitalization, the Andersons had been able to use the strategy of the ostrich, to assume that problems one didn't acknowledge openly were problems that one didn't have to deal with. The members of the family had simply stuck their collective heads into the ground until the group's anxieties could no longer be contained. (Clearly, the most obvious signal that a family's tensions are no longer containable is the fact that one of them requires inpatient psychiatric care.)

Dave Anderson, a tall teenager with straight brown hair and attractive aquiline features, had been admitted to Elmcrest with the major diagnosis of oppositional defiant disorder, ODD. ODD is listed among the disorders of infancy, childhood, and adolescence in the current (1994) *Diagnostic and Statistical Manual of Mental Disorders,* and is characterized by the following symptoms.

The child: 1) often loses temper; 2) often argues with adults; 3) often actively defies or refuses adults' requests or rules; 4) often deliberately annoys people; 5) often blames others for his or her mistakes or misbehavior; 6) is often touchy or easily annoyed by others; 7) is often angry and resentful; 8) is often spiteful or vindictive;

According to the psychiatric manual, if a pattern of negativistic, hostile behavior lasts at least six months, during which four (or more) of the above symptoms have been present, a diagnosis of oppositional defiant disorder is applicable. This clinical description has always struck me as a somewhat comical one: It sounds very like "This is a *bad kid,*" translated into official language.

But in Dave Anderson's case it wasn't funny. By the time he arrived at Elmcrest, Dave was showing signs of serious impairment and emotional disturbance, both at home and in school. At school, this muscular, good-looking ninth-grader had been getting mostly F's in his courses, and was also behaving disruptively in the classroom—he'd been scaring both his classmates and his teachers with his unpredictable outbursts of irritability and rage.

Eventually, the school authorities at Dave's suburban junior high school had concluded that something was very deeply amiss—and his parents, when called in to confer with school officials, had certainly agreed. For at home, Dave was throwing loud tantrums on an almost daily basis. He'd also begun taking off in the family car without permission or a driver's license; he had run away from home on one occasion, and was in general behaving in a variety of threatening, potentially violent ways. As the senior Andersons saw it, their adolescent son was either completely out of control, or a hairsbreadth away from being so.

The upshot of an escalating series of disturbing incidents involving Dave Anderson—and the series of school-and-family conferences following upon them—was that the school district's consulting psychiatrist had been contacted and asked to make a thorough psychological evaluation of the boy. That physician had recommended inpatient hospitalization, without deferral or delay—which was why Dave Anderson was here at Elmcrest now.

Dave had arrived on the unit in a state of total fury—a fury that, in this particular instance, I considered completely understandable: His mother and father, having told their children that they were all going out for a Sunday drive, had instead brought their teenage son to Elmcrest and signed him in, involuntarily, without any prior notice or warning.

Although the Andersons had done this on advisement, lest Dave put up some resistance or run away, I thought that they'd received somewhat questionable guidance. For from the adolescent's point of view, being driven to a mental institution with no idea that he was about to be committed must have been experienced as the most horrifying kind of family ambush and betrayal.

A Secondary Diagnosis: Dysthymia (Chronic Low-Grade Depression)

My first glimpse of Dave Anderson was on the Monday morning after that surprise Sunday hospitalization. A meeting of the entire unit was in progress, and he was sitting slumped far down on a long red leather banquette, looking as if he were anywhere but present in this room.

A red nylon baseball cap had been pulled down over Dave's eyes, and his head hung over his chest, so that he made eye contact with nothing other than his own large, unlaced high-top sneakers. Even though there were young people seated on either side of him, and everyone was sitting so close together that their shoulders touched, the newcomer's posture and mien seemed to declare both his isolation from the group and the pure rage he was feeling. He had been put into this bizarre situation by his parents, but the nonverbal message he was transmitting very clearly was that nothing in the world could force him to *be* here, in the sense of participating or becoming involved.

Since then, however, seventeen days had passed, and in that time the changes wrought in this young person were nothing short of dramatic. Part of Dave's striking improvement could have been due to the effects of treatment with antidepressants, for it had been learned, at the time of his admission, that recently he'd been losing weight and having difficulty falling asleep. He was also having trouble concentrating, lacked energy, and had been entertaining transient thoughts of suicide—all signs and symptoms of an underlying depression.

Dave had therefore been given a secondary diagnosis, dysthymia (from the Greek, "bad or ill spirits"). And in the past week or so, either in response to the medication (although it usually takes about three weeks before a patient fully experiences an antidepressant's effects) or to other things that were happening on the ward, his mood and mien had been slowly but most definitively brightening.

"I Hate My Parents' Guts and They Hate *Me* Too"

The basic problem, as Dave had stated grimly during his first session with clinician Linda Bowen and myself, was that "I hate my parents' guts and they hate *me* too." He didn't need to be here, he'd said furiously, and he didn't know why he *was* here, because he certainly wasn't crazy in any way. "My parents *lied* to me to get me here," he'd then added, his face a stony mask of rage.

Over the past two and a half weeks, however, we and everyone else on the unit had seen that rigid mask start to crumble, revealing a vulnerable, needful adolescent underneath.

Both Linda, Dave's primary therapist, and I, who'd been involved with the family from the very outset,* felt a particularly tender spot in our hearts for this boy. For, while Dave was actively playing out the role of the family delinquent and "bad boy," there was a way in which he seemed to be covertly offering himself up as the family lightning rod—bringing down upon himself the cascade of crackling, sizzling, undischarged tensions that were coursing throughout the entire Anderson household.

Today, Ralph and Susan Anderson, looking somber and thin-lipped, had shrugged out of their coats, apologizing to Linda and me for Cheryl's nonappearance. Dave, however, didn't look unhappy; he was, perhaps, relieved at his kid sister's absence, because he had a frightening agenda for today's meeting.

Instead of getting into the habitual fighting mode with his parents, he was planning to open up and talk honestly with them about his real problems and issues. He was going to be direct with them and tell them about how he'd been feeling; he would be making himself vulnerable to them in ways he'd never done before.

In a family system such as the Andersons'—one in which the members' customary style of interacting is emotionally distant and hostile—this was surely a monumentally courageous undertaking. For in disengaged, severely troubled systems such as theirs, opening up and making oneself vulnerable is far likelier to be punished than it is to be rewarded.

I suppose that, since I know this, Dave's behavior at the outset of the session shouldn't have surprised me as much as it did. But I was in fact dismayed, and in no way prepared for the profound change that had come over him in the brief two hours since I'd seen him. Then, during daily

---

*I was doing research on families at Elmcrest during this time.

group therapy with his adolescent peers, he'd been remarkably forthcoming, even voluble, about himself, his issues, his emotions.

Dave had even gone so far as to acknowledge to the other patients in the group that he knew he was being helped here—not failing to add, however, that he was still enraged about having been dumped into a psychiatric hospital with such devious lack of forewarning. After *that*, he'd asked the group rhetorically, how could he ever trust his parents again?

Still, he'd conceded, he knew that being on the Chapman Unit, and being forced to open up about his problems—to recognize how much hurting there was beneath all of the rageful talk and bad behavior—had enabled him to look more closely at his own attitudes and at the self-destructive situations into which those attitudes were leading him.

"And now, what's the piece of work that you yourself have to do next?" Linda Bowen, in whose office this peer-group therapy session was taking place, had asked her young patient directly.

"Take responsibility for my part of the problem," Dave had responded without hesitating, "and then get my parents to take the part of it that's theirs." Then, after a brief silence, he'd added thoughtfully that he was coming to realize that maybe he wasn't the monster of the universe, after all, and that maybe some of the family conflicts were being misdirected, sent to the wrong address . . . but for some reason, all of his mother's rage seemed to have his name on it, and his name alone.

"My mom won't let her anger out on anyone but me," he'd complained, looking perplexed. "No matter what I do, it's always the *wrong* thing to do. And you know, it's *impossible* to beat someone at a game when they're making up the rules as they go along." The other patients in the clinical group had not only responded sympathetically, but had offered Dave thoughtful and discerning feedback.

They'd urged him to approach his folks directly, without anger, in a way that would enable him to let them know how much he was actually suffering, and how very ready he was to put an end to his own share in the ongoing family hostilities. This, Dave had agreed to do without hesitation, and yet now that he was face-to-face with them, he seemed to have been struck completely dumb.

I stared at him as he sat there, slouched down in his seat, legs spread wide, looking infuriated and avoiding all eye contact with those present. The baseball cap he wore had been pulled low down over his forehead. Where was the straightforward person who'd decided to be forthcoming, to take responsibility, and to try to meet his parents on some middle ground?

Linda Bowen's gaze met mine briefly, but neither she nor I said anything. We waited; the rancor in the room was palpable, even though not a word (aside from the explanation of Cheryl's absence) had been uttered. I looked at Susan Anderson, an intelligent, peppy woman who worked full-time as an insurance analyst. Mrs. Anderson, as one couldn't fail to remark, sat through every one of these sessions with her arms folded tightly across her bosom.

It was as if she were trying to contain herself, to keep her evident exasperation from erupting uncontrollably. Or perhaps, alternatively, she was trying to protect herself from harm.

The mother met my eye, half-smiled, and shook her head, as if to say that nothing could possibly be done with this sullen, unruly son of hers. Ralph Anderson's face betrayed nothing; he sat there fiddling with the fountain pen clipped to the pocket of his blue pinstriped shirt. Dave's father was the chief supervisor of maintenance in a large Hartford hospital, but he looked like a chairman of the board. He had the air of a man who could wait this silence out.

It was the clinician who said, at last, "Do you want to tell your parents how you've been doing, Dave?"

But the adolescent, without raising his head, merely murmured something unintelligible into his shirt. I leaned forward. "What was that, Dave? I couldn't quite hear you."

"I said 'I'm doing *great*,' " he responded sardonically. "It's just like school, except that instead of doing detention time I do table time. Ten *hours*. Same thing; it's just that they call it by a different name here."

Dave had leaped spontaneously into the role of the bad, troublemaking outcast.

Linda Bowen smiled wryly, raised an eyebrow, said, "Overall, though, you haven't been in a lot of trouble on the unit—isn't that right? You've actually been doing what you needed to do, the exception being your behavior when you first got here."

But Dave's father, stiffening, cut in to ask in a forbidding tone of voice, "Ten hours—for what?"

Dave shrugged. "To do my journal . . . answer questions . . . write some essays." He was describing a ten-hour stint on "Focus," not ten hours in "Time Out," but the mere suggestion of misbehavior had certainly aroused his father's interest and attention.

The Patient Status Ladder: Taking Self-responsibility Instead of Acting Out One's Problems

"Focus" is an intermediate level on the Chapman Unit's status ladder; a patient's status has to do with his or her current capacity for taking self-responsibility. The unit's status levels vary upward from "Entry," to "Escort," to "Needs Constant Observation" (for potentially suicidal teenagers or those who may "elope," that is, run away), to "Fifteen-Minute

Checks," to "Focus," the midpoint status on the ladder to which Dave had been referring.

The person on Focus goes through a series of reflective exercises, which include essay and personal journal writing, designed to help him to stop acting out his distress and fix his attention upon the real, underlying concerns. *These have to do, predictably, with things that are happening in the family.* The real work of the Chapman Unit involves helping the patient get into conscious contact with the painful family issues that he or she has been so assiduously avoiding.

Above Focus on the status ladder are Levels 2, 3, and 4 (which is the highest ranking), all of which denote the patient's increasing capacity for insight and growing ability to monitor and control his or her own behavior. At these higher levels, for example, a young female victim of sexual abuse would *not* try to communicate her distress by overdosing with pills, wrist cutting, or some other form of self-harm. She would be more capable of talking with others about what had happened to her and about the intense rage and self-loathing that such experiences had left in their wake.

Can Anyone Listen Without Going Crazy?

A brief, uneasy silence had settled upon us. Linda Bowen ended it by telling the Andersons that Dave was actually being quite cooperative on the ward, able to deal with his issues, giving good feedback to others, keeping up with his schoolwork, and making a very respectable showing academically. "The most difficult time Dave seems to have is in these family sessions—he acts the way he's acting now. But this is not typical of the way he acts on the unit."

The therapist gave Dave's parents a long, quizzical look; her forehead was raked with thoughtful furrows. Then she turned to the patient. "That's right, isn't it?"

"Yeah, because if I do well on the unit there's a *payoff*, something in it for me," Dave muttered in a low, embittered tone of voice.

I tried, without success, to meet his eye; but he was feeling too offended to look at anyone directly. "The way you're acting here is *not* what I see on the unit; this isn't what other people see either," I observed, adding that he didn't have this attitude ordinarily; he tended to be cooperative and do what he was supposed to do.

I was addressing his averted head, but Dave turned to me unexpectedly, met my gaze, and half-smiled. Then he said, with a mixture of candor and cynicism, that if he was rude and obnoxious in this office it was because he knew he could get away with it. "On the unit, they would have stuck me in

Time Out by now," he acknowledged with a shrug and one of his rare, thoroughly engaging grins.

"That tells me that there are other ways that you are finding to cope with, or vent, your frustration and anger," his father cut in reprovingly.

"Yeah. Ways that I've never known before," the boy mumbled.

"Well, then, I think that's something that should probably be explored a bit more. That there is another, more productive way to vent your frustration and your anger," Ralph Anderson declared.

"Oh, *yes*, Dad"—Dave stared at his parent aggressively—"there are lots of ways! But the main way, in our family, would be talking. Talking, if there were somebody to talk to, somebody who could listen without going *crazy*—"

Mr. Anderson blinked several times, but made no reply.

When I looked back at Dave, his head was hanging down over his chest again; he had the air of a criminal or penitent. Was it easier for him to behave on the unit, I asked him quietly, because people were, in fact, listening to what he had to say?

"I just don't have any *trust* in the people I have at home," the teenager blurted out, "and they have no trust in me, either. That's why I don't talk to them. Because if I—"

"—I don't think that's true," his father cut in to say imperiously.

Dave's mother caught my eye, shook her head. The expression on her face was ironic, but I had no idea what message she was trying to convey. Although Susan Anderson hadn't said a word thus far, I had been experiencing her presence very powerfully throughout. I had the curious, perhaps thoroughly groundless, notion that she was somehow stage-managing much of what was being enacted in this office now.

"Okay, Dad, you tell *me* what I think is true!" David was gripping the sides of his chair, as if trying to keep himself seated. "Whatever *you* think is true is true!"

"*You* may perceive that, but I don't perceive that." The father maintained his own position coolly and deliberately; we had arrived at an impasse. The Andersons seemed to have no means of relating to one another except through their mutual anger, disapproval, and disappointment. It was as if anger itself were the primary glue that linked the members of the group and held the system together.

In families such as theirs, however, one may take it as a given that beneath the overt anger there is always covert longing—an intense yearning that things might be otherwise. But that longing is perceived to be so dangerous—one could be hurt or seriously damaged if one dared to make oneself vulnerable—that it has been exiled from everyone's conscious awareness, and an air of utter hopelessness pervades the atmosphere.

A Son's Yearning for His Father's Love and Attention

Linda Bowen inhaled deeply, exhaled, then looked around at each of the family members in turn. "We're at a pretty important juncture, and we need to be clear." She smiled at Dave's parents warmly, as if to help them relax and to soften the impact of the remarks that were to follow.

"Dave has a lot of trouble talking about certain things—especially with you two—so I guess I'll have to act as more of a translator than I really like to be." She hesitated momentarily, and the Andersons, although looking wary, nodded eagerly as if urging her to continue.

"The truth is that what we've been hearing pretty consistently, throughout his stay, is that Dave is feeling that people here are listening to him, and responding to him—that they really *care* about him, too. And what I seem to hear him saying now is that he doesn't feel the people at home can connect with him emotionally, or that they care about where he's at, not at all. What I hear him saying is that, at some level, the reason he acts up is to get the attention in a negative way—because getting it in a positive way doesn't work out."

Ralph Anderson countered immediately, his voice composed but chiding, "I think the opportunity to talk is there, and we have certainly *had* a lot of discussions about different things. But those discussions always get to an endpoint, which is his saying 'I want to do such-and-such,' and if you don't agree with him, the discussion ends there."

"We're not talking about what I want to *do*!" Dave burst out suddenly. "We're talking about how I *feel*! We're talking about *why* I have problems, and *who* I can come to when I do!" The teenager's voice was becoming choked up, and there were sudden tears rolling in his eyes. "I don't feel that I trust you guys enough—or that we have enough of a relationship so I can *talk* to you—" Dave spoke in brief snatches, as if he were constantly being interrupted by wind-gusts of emotionality. "And that's what I'm really saying—and that's why I blow up and get angry with you—that's why I have a very, very bad temper—" He was crying unabashedly now.

I looked over at his parents expectantly, awaiting some response, but none at all was forthcoming. Susan Anderson merely unfolded her arms and refolded them, putting the other arm on top. Dave, still sobbing, was looking at them too, his expression far more wistful and childlike than antagonistic and attacking.

He said, in a low, humbled tone of voice, that he supposed that the opportunity for him to talk *was* always there, and that sometimes his parents did go through the motions of listening. "But still, it never seems to register somehow," he added, heaving up a jagged breath. "I don't feel I have a mother-son or a father-son relationship with either one of you."

Though he was talking about both relationships, Dave's eyes were fixed solely upon his dad. He then went on to cite what he termed a "prime-time example" of the ways in which he felt his father tuned him out.

Last fall, the two of them had unearthed an old, very elaborate set of trains (complete with boxes and cars and switching stations) that had been gathering dust in the family attic. Dave had proposed that he and his dad set up the trains together, and his dad had agreed to this plan very readily. "Remember what you said when I asked you if you wanted to do it?" the son now demanded painfully. "You said 'Yes, that sounds like a great thing we can do together'—your exact words. 'Yes, that sounds like a great thing we can do together, as a father-son thing.' "

Dave was weeping as he spoke, in great heaving gusts, and his father sat there as if paralyzed, a stunned expression on his face.

Those trains were running now, the teenager went on, and the lights were on; the entire system had been wired. "*I* wired it. And I don't know—maybe it's just me—maybe I am really going crazy and I do belong in this place, but it didn't *look* like it was a father-son thing that was going on," Dave protested accusingly, through his tears. "Maybe it's just in my head, but I didn't *see* a father and a son working on it. I saw a son down there doing it and thinking, 'Yeah, Dad will come down tomorrow and help.' Or 'Yeah, he'll come down this weekend and help—' "

The self-abandoned sobs of this large, strapping adolescent, in his Tropicana sweatshirt and faded dungarees, were so painful that I felt tears springing to my own eyes. I looked at Dave's parents, who sat bolt upright in their chairs, eyes widened and faces stiff with tension, like people gazing at a natural catastrophe. Why couldn't either one of them reach out to their son, try to comfort him at this moment?

Ralph Anderson folded his own arms over his chest, crossed one trouser leg over the other, then cleared his throat and said reasonably, "You know, I come home at suppertime and you're down in the basement working on it, and I do go and see what you're doing, advise you a bit on how things should be set up." He sounded patient, logical, astonishingly remote. "You've asked me questions about how I wanted something done. But basically I left a lot of it to you, because I considered that an adventure for you—"

That was a clear and obvious cop-out—and, to be sure, Dave recognized it as such. "Oh, it was *great*," he told his father ironically, "but I didn't expect to be doing it on my own." The moment of maximum vulnerability was passing, and I heard the animosity returning to his voice.

For a moment the father was silent, thoughtful; then he shrugged briefly, said, "I agree that maybe we should have found more time to work on it. But see, with a lot of things going on—and three or four other people in the house to think about—I'm surprised or I guess even disappointed that you couldn't say, 'Hey, I need more of your time.' " This parent was finding it hard to meet his son halfway and to acknowledge what might be his own part in the ongoing difficulties between them.

"I didn't *need* your time—I just expected it, because you said you and I would do this thing together!" Dave's voice was choking up again, and he launched into a confused, angry tirade which halted suddenly on a piteous, longing note. "Since you'd *said*, 'Yeah, that sounds like a great thing we can do together,' I kept hoping that maybe you were going to come back down and work on it—and do things with me—and then you didn't."

Dave's father was clearly at a loss. Ralph Anderson was confident when it came to dealing with his son's anger, but he had no idea what to do when it came to responding to this kind of naked emotional appeal. He made a few oratorical statements to the effect that he did want to have a better relationship with Dave, but the real import of his message was vague, and his voice sounded curiously detached.

"Can I ask you a question, Mr. Anderson?" I leaned toward him. He turned his head in my direction and I found myself staring into his wide gray eyes; he nodded. "How are you feeling right now?" I inquired quietly.

"I feel kind of down," he replied.

Tiptoeing Closer to the Chasm: What Everyone
in the Family Knows, and Nobody in the Family Ever
Talks About

Clinician Linda Bowen was leaning toward Ralph Anderson too. "Doesn't it kind of grab your heart a little bit, seeing Dave this way?" she asked him disingenuously; a somewhat sheepish nod was the father's only reply.

"Did you ever realize how much he craved spending some time with you?" she persisted; the parent shook his head. Dave was now slumped over in his seat again, his shoulders heaving and his face buried in his hands.

At that moment, I met the mother's eye and asked her if she gave some credence to the things that Dave had been saying—that nobody in the family seemed to have much time for him, and he was feeling ignored and discounted. Susan Anderson jumped slightly, but then shrugged her shoulders carelessly as if to say she didn't consider the question a particularly pertinent one. "Some . . . maybe. But the *other* part is his expectation that everything will happen on his time and according to his own plans.

"And I think that's really what Ralph is saying," she added, sounding dejected herself. "That the particular time David chooses to want you to *be* with him, and to *do* things with him, may not necessarily be a time that is appropriate for the rest of the family." But even as she spoke, as if by means of some inner sorcery, her air of hopelessness and discouragement was being transformed into one of angry annoyance.

"Actually, in *most* of the situations I can think of it is *David* who decides when to do things and whether or not we're going to do them at all. David *makes* the decisions," she declared, in a clipped and antagonistic tone of voice, adding that it wasn't David who was being ignored and discounted; it was he and he alone who controlled everything that happened in the entire household. "He controls how it runs, when it runs, and whether or not it runs," declared the mother, her voice and posture suffused with exasperation and outrage. I realized that she was staring at me belligerently, looking like a defendant who knows she is innocent and yet expects the judge to come back with a thoroughly misguided and erroneous verdict.

There was a silence, which I ended by asking her how she thought their daughter, Cheryl, fit into the family picture—most especially, in terms of permitting herself to be controlled. "She *doesn't* fit in. She leaves. She departs," Susan Anderson answered tersely. "She spends an awful lot of time in her room. Because David *controls* the television—"

"Cheryl doesn't like the conflict," her husband explained very reasonably.

"—and she doesn't want to be around when everybody is yelling and screaming. So she feels pretty left out," Dave's mother chimed in, in an easier, more morally secure–sounding tone of voice. I stole a glance at Dave, the family desperado, who was sitting hunched over in his seat, elbows on the knees of his faded dungarees, face hidden in the large, open palms of his hands. Why, I wondered, had neither of his parents responded to him when he'd been trying so hard to open up to them?

Then I turned to Linda Bowen, whose bemused expression seemed to reflect my own preoccupation. She rolled her chair around in such a way that she was positioned to look at her adolescent patient's parents head-on and very directly. "Is there someone else in here who needs to look at what *she* is doing, or at what *he* is doing?" she inquired pointedly. Neither of the Andersons replied.

The clinician turned to Susan Anderson, fixed her gaze upon the mother exclusively, and then held it steadily as she continued. "Because what I'm seeing and hearing right now is that Dave's *not* being oppositional; he's *not* being defiant; he's talking very appropriately about his feelings. And yet, your anger comes through whenever we're talking about him. . . . Do you see how you're sitting there with your arms all folded tight together, like that?"

Dave's mother looked down at her arms for a brief moment, but didn't concede the point by unfolding them.

"It's real rage that you have for Dave," continued Linda evenly, "just real *rage*, you know. And I'm wondering if it is indeed directed at him— because I'm not quite certain that it is."

"I don't feel that it's directed at him," answered Dave's mother, and I looked at her in amazement. "*I* think it's directed at the situations that have come up, and that I've had to deal with," she added mysteriously, stealing a sidelong, heavily ironic glance at her husband, who looked away from her.

The Andersons were tiptoeing closer to the chasm, the family secret that (at least according to Mrs. Anderson) everyone in the family really did know about, but that nobody ever talked about openly.

A Strategy for Averting Catastrophe: Emotional Triangles

As a geometrical form, one conceives of the triangle as something static existing in space—a simple figure with three sides and three points of intersection (the vertices) at which the sides intersect. In family-systems terms, however, "triangle" has taken on a highly specialized meaning. In this theoretical context, triangles are viewed not as static shapes but as *three-way relational processes*, happening in time.

Certain types of triangles are, it should be said, of particular concern to systematically oriented thinkers; these are the fixed emotional triangles (therapist Salvador Minuchin calls them "rigid triads") that have become entrenched within the family system. Such triangles are, simply, extremely predictable, patterned, endlessly repeating sequences of interaction in which three mesmerized family players are involved.

Fixed emotional triangles come into being, by and large, as a short-term solution to a looming and seemingly unresolvable problem—usually, escalating tensions in a two-party relationship. When the couple system is being rocked by anxieties and conflict—anxieties that may indeed pose a threat to the system's ongoing existence—a semiautomatic, quite commonplace response is to introduce a third party (or a loaded topic, such as money or drinking) onto the scene. Then, the pair can focus their attention and energies on the third leg of the triangle (our child, your lover, my interfering mother, our budget, your alcoholism) and avoid facing up to the really terrifying issues that are actually dividing them (Do you care for me anymore? Do I want to stay in this relationship?) and that feel far too scary to attempt confronting.

Introducing the third party or charged subject (about which the couple can then wrangle endlessly) into a two-person relationship can best be understood as an attempt to stabilize an emotional system that feels endangered, perhaps even fatally so. The underlying advantage of the triangle is that when tensions in the twosome have escalated upward into the danger zone, the pair's possible responses are somewhat limited in nature. They can either face up to and deal with their relational dilemmas, or be forced, as the strain and pressure rise beyond endurance, to end the relationship completely. Bringing a third party into the interaction allows for a variety of responses other than these two polar extremes (that is, settle their issues or break up).

Coalitions

A three-person group allows for a number of different coalitions. Any two of the individuals can join together, covertly or overtly, against the third. For example, the couple's distress, when handled in this roundabout manner, can be expressed in ongoing fights that one of the parents is having with a child. *The real key to understanding triangles is to think of them as serving to decrease the level of tension, create stability, and help the partners to avoid painful change* (change for the better, alas, included).

Triangling a third party into a two-person relationship is, however, only a "peace in our time," not a long-range solution. For while the original sources of the tensions (the partners' unresolved conflicts or feelings of emotional emptiness) do become lost to view, eventually the "solution" itself becomes the source of serious new difficulties, and frequently of serious family pathology.

The Andersons were certainly a good case in point, for Dave's "oppositional defiant disorder" was seen by everyone in his world as the primary source of the family's difficulties—it was the reason for his hospitalization and for the treatment he was receiving. But his mother's cryptic comment to the effect that the anger she'd been directing toward her son was really anger about something entirely different—the mysterious "situation" which her husband seemed eager to avoid discussing—certainly did suggest the strong probability that wife, husband, and son were highly interconnected in what is known as a "detouring-attacking" triangle.

Family triangles do, as noted, come in a variety of forms and configurations, and the detouring-attacking triangle is, in my own view, a particularly toxic one. In this kind of three-way interaction, unresolved tensions that really have to do with the marital relationship are routinely deflected and detoured by the couple, who become allies in their ongoing attacks upon their intractable, incorrigible child. And in this respect, the triangulated offspring's *acting out is really serving to stabilize, protect, and maintain the emotional system*, to keep it from breaking apart.

For as long as the necessary family triangle exists, it serves the purpose of preventing things from getting worse (or being resolved and improving, to be sure). Thus, to the degree that the Andersons' attention remained riveted upon their son's oppositional, defiant behavior—and to the degree that he cooperated by causing continual upsets and commotions in the family—the ultimate catastrophe in their *own* relationship could be avoided.

A Loving Child

How do the members of a family know its truths without ever having been explicitly told them? Young Dave Anderson, when his mother alluded to anger about a mysterious "situation," seemed to sense that something unfathomable and threatening was taking place. He even appeared to have some crude, inchoate comprehension of what it might be, even though he had certainly never indicated any factual knowledge of the family secret; if he knew something, it was not at the level of conscious awareness.

Dave simply sat there staring at his mother, scorn etched upon his attractive, regular features. "You can't direct rage at situations, you can direct it at *people*," he said to her loudly. "You can be mad at somebody for *doing something*, but you can't just be mad at—at something—at, I don't know what—because somebody has to *do* something." His voice was rising to a shout.

"Maybe it's not rage," Ralph Anderson offered incoherently, his tone bland.

"Situations just don't pop out of *here*." Dave, pointing at the side of his own head, stared angrily at his mother and disregarded his father's comment entirely.

"Maybe it's more frustration than rage," the father persisted. He seemed to be running interference, lest this discussion veer too close to any particular "situation" that might indeed provoke rage by its very nature. I realized at that moment how frightened both the parents looked; they seemed almost stupefied by alarm and embarrassment.

The facts of the matter were (as everyone in this room *except* Dave well knew) that fourteen years earlier Ralph Anderson had had an affair—an affair resulting in an illegitimate child. Neither his fifteen-year-old son nor his twelve-year-old daughter had been told anything about the existence of this half-sibling, a boy who, at almost thirteen, was several months older than Cheryl and two years younger than Dave.

Still, Susan Anderson was sure that both children really *did* know the outlines of the situation. For, as she had told Linda and me privately, there had been occasions when they'd overheard certain conversations, had seen money orders and other documents and had even asked questions about them. Dave and Cheryl were, in their mother's view, well aware of the family secret but were blocking what they knew from their own conscious understanding.

What I was finding somewhat eerie, though, was the way Dave's complaints had focused on the train project that had never quite materialized—that is to say, on his father's seeming lack of investment in the relationship they shared. For in fact Ralph Anderson was (to some still-unknown degree) invested elsewhere, in this other son and family, who existed in another town in another state, and of whom Dave himself seemed to be completely unaware.

Mr. Anderson was, as I knew, sending support money to the other family, but I didn't know what they meant to him—and neither, it appeared, did his wife. All that Susan Anderson had told us was that the family's move from upstate New York to Connecticut, four years earlier, had been motivated by the wish to extricate this family from an uncomfortable proximity to that "situation."

"Look, guys, somebody's got to *cause* frustration." Dave slapped both hands down on the tops of his thighs, hard, as if for emphasis. "You guys have to *own up* to some of these things. You guys have got to talk—to tell who you're mad at, who you're frustrated with! This is what *I'm* trying to do now; this is basically how *I* feel." Tears had started to his eyes again, and he said, his voice choked, "Every time, it's—it's—'Meet me halfway, Dave.' —Well, I met you guys halfway. I stayed in this hospital without trying anything. I've done everything they asked me to do. I've been good, and I haven't been in Time Out. I feel that *I've* gone at least half of the way." He was starting to weep again, and it was painful to see him struggling to hold the sobs back.

"So what is it you're asking of your parents now?" I questioned the teenager softly, dropping my eyes and fixing them on his unlaced high-top sneakers. "I see them not owning up to anything," he answered immediately. "Not talking about a thing! 'Oh, I'm frustrated at a situation.' " He mimicked his mother's remark sarcastically. "You can't be angry at a *thing*, Ma. I can't be mad at that plant." I looked up in time to see him pointing at a tired-looking ivy that sat on Linda Bowen's windowsill.

"I may not *want* it, and feel real *annoyed* about it, but it's not anger at the plant—it's anger at the *person* who put it there." His tears had given way to acrimony again, but before his mother could hurl her return volley of blame, the therapist rolled her office chair nearer to Dave's seat and then sat looking directly into his face. She waited until their gaze was mutual and connected.

Then she asked quietly, "So what do you think your parents are angry about?"

"Me." He looked away from her, looked out the window with tears standing in his eyes. He was, it seemed to me, serving as the container of all the family harm and badness. Not only was he diverting his mother's rage from his father, but he was helping both of them to manage their secret and all the anxiety and pain that doing so entailed. "Dave," I said suddenly, "I think you are a very loving child."

The Andersons looked at me in stupefaction, but Linda Bowen met my gaze and almost imperceptibly, she nodded.

The Adolescent Delegate

It seemed self-evident that as long as Dave's anger, delinquency, school failure, and acting out were serving a significant function, in terms of holding the precarious family system together, it would be difficult for his folks to give up their dogged focus upon his "irresponsible and uncontrollable" behavior. But there were also, it seemed to me, subtler and less apparent reasons why these middle-aged parents might actually "require" that their adolescent child become an impulsive, antisocial, and uncontrollable person.

For, as theorist Helm Stierlin, M.D., has observed, people in their middle years often send their maturing offspring out into the world as "delegates"—envoys entrusted with the mission of embodying and acting out the parents' own suppressed, denied, and highly conflicted inclinations.

As Stierlin writes in his classic work, *Separating Parents and Adolescents,* the "delegating mode comes into play when a parent enlists an adolescent son to resolve his own conflicts over delinquent tendencies. This parent covertly encourages his son to become a delinquent and then attacks him for doing so." The bad child, in other words, does his dutiful but emotionally restricted sire's unconscious bidding by acting out *in the real world* those forbidden impulses that the upright parent has refused to recognize as aspects of his own inner experience.

A promiscuous young female may, for example, be acting out her highly repressed, virtuous mother's stifled wantonness and denied sexuality. Or (as one might speculate was happening in the Anderson household) a younger male may be acting out his principled, moral, law-abiding father's own asocial, aggressive, "bad boy" tendencies. In such instances, the impossible and uncontrollable adolescent is in some deep sense the family's thrill provider. He or she has been entrusted with the mission of bringing excitement into the parents' impeccably "good" yet routine and colorless existence.

The very word "delegate," it should be mentioned, means "one designated to act for or represent another or others." The adolescent delegate is, in this respect, the child who has taken on the burden of doing for the parent or parents what cannot even be thought about, much less enacted in the world of reality. The sexually faithful but erotically starved middle-aged mother cannot, for example, possibly conceive of herself as someone so depraved that she would take pleasure in the arms of a series of different lovers. In this sense, her promiscuous child is this parent's proxy—a part of the parent's extended, but vehemently suppressed and repudiated inner reality.

The daughter is, in brief, acting out the parent's own hidden, disavowed agenda. And it is for this reason, writes Stierlin, that "the adolescent will be covertly encouraged to commit and seek punishment for those delinquent acts about which the parent himself harbors (chiefly unconscious) guilt." The middle-aged parent can then mete out to the bad, impulsive, out-of-control adolescent those punishments she or he secretly believes (or, in Ralph Anderson's case, actually *knows*) himself to deserve.

The delegated offspring's primary task is thus, according to Stierlin, "to be mischief maker, troubled, crazy, etc., in order for the parent to be reassured that *he himself* [my emphasis] is not bad, crazy, etc., after all." Seen from this point of view, the maturing young person can be understood to be helping the parent handle (in a vicarious fashion) the guilty pangs emanating from a harsh and often unbearably punitive conscience.

CHAPTER 2

The Beavers Scale of Family Health and Competence: Levels 1–5

It is by now well recognized that the famous opening line of Leo Tolstoy's *Anna Karenina*—"All happy families resemble one another; every unhappy family is unhappy in its own way"—is a beautiful statement but a fallacious one. It is *unhappy* families who are more likely to resemble one another, for they tend to rigidify into certain recognizable, limited stances. The hallmark of the happy family is its variability, its ability to be flexible and to cherish its members' individuality, whereas unhappy families tend to become trapped in fixed patterns of responding and in nonnegotiable positions—to get stuck, in other words.

It is of course obvious that radically different emotional climates, rules, roles, and patterns of being exist within different families; but in what *specific* ways do these families actually differ? In recent years, researchers have been attempting to codify and to examine rigorously what transpires within a relatively competent, harmonious, well-functioning family group, as contrasted with one whose members are distressed and disturbed.

Among the many family assessment instruments now available is the well-known Beavers Systems Model. This is a clinical scale that researchers use to classify families according to level of health and competence. All families are viewed as existing on a continuum that ranges from the most perturbed family system at one end to the least troubled system at the other.

The Beavers Systems Model (formerly the Beavers-Timberlawn Family Assessment Scale) is named after its principal originator, the psychiatrist

W. Robert Beavers, who was for many years director of the Southwest Family Institute in Dallas. In over thirty years of work with this assessment/diagnostic instrument, Beavers and his colleagues have been subjecting their hypotheses about how families function to ongoing scientific testing; they use both individual family members' self-reports, and observational ratings of the family as a whole. Thus, their evolving theories have been buttressed by valid empirical findings—a rarity in the teeming family theory and therapy marketplace, where an astonishing variety of competing points of view, sects, gurus, charismatic leaders, and schools of serious thought abound.

In its simplest terms, the central, compelling theme that has emerged from the Beavers research is that *different family systems operate at differing, but very clearly recognizable, levels of health and competence;* and any given family's current level of functioning can usually be described with a surprising degree of precision. Beavers has, moreover, taken a maverick approach within the field of family assessment, inasmuch as he and his co-workers have made healthy, competent families as important a focus of their attention as families that are distressed and perturbed.

The Beavers Systems Model is thus not primarily pathology-oriented (as many such family diagnostic instruments are). Rather than limit themselves to the study of what can go wrong—of processes that are destructive to the members of the system and to the system itself—these scientists have also looked carefully at healthy, competent families over an extended (five-year) period. A considerable part of this effort has, in other words, been geared toward understanding, in the most exact terms possible, what can go *right* within the family setting, and what specific sorts of family interactions tend to make it do so.

The Beavers Systems Model:
Five Family Developmental Levels

Briefly, the five major family developmental levels on the Beavers health and functioning graph are as follows. Families at Level 1, "optimal" families, are the most competent on the scale. Next to this topmost group are the Level 2 "adequate" families. Level 3 is called "midrange." This is the most densely populated cluster; in most studies, about 60 percent of families seem to fit into this "midrange" category. After the midrange is Level 4, the "borderline" family; and finally, at Level 5, the least well functioning end of the spectrum are families that are "severely disturbed."

Family systems operating at these five different planes of emotional development are, as will become quite evident, not only struggling with profoundly different kinds of dilemmas, but struggling to deal with these dilemmas in profoundly different kinds of ways.

Levels 1–5: An Overview

A brief overview of the different kinds of family worlds described in the Beavers Systems Model follows; each level will also be elaborated upon in subsequent chapters.

I will begin with the chaotic systems at the bottom rung of the competence ladder, for the movement upward on the scale, from worse to better, clearly illuminates the basic nature of the developmental tasks that must be mastered along the way to a family's healing and improvement.

Level 5: The Family in Pain (Severely Disturbed)

The *family in pain* is an emotional system in a state of confusion and turmoil. This kind of family world is comparable to a nation in a state of civil disorder; nobody seems to have authority; no one is able to enforce rules or effect needed changes; real leadership is totally lacking.

In this disjointed family realm, there are no durable, straightforward predictabilities, no clear-cut ways of behaving that one can be certain will lead to good outcomes. The operational rules of the system, to the extent that such rules exist, are in perpetual flux, always mystifying, always changing. And if one member of the group (say, the mother) attempts to articulate an idea, someone else inside the emotional system (father, grandparent, teenage child) will negate or dispute it in an almost automatic, reflexive fashion. To add to the general air of confusion, the mother may then acquiesce to the opposing idea, without acknowledging that it is at total variance with her own suggestion. Or, if never contradicted, she may simply backtrack and contradict herself.

This is an amorphous world, a world without any reliable or even discernible hierarchy or governance. *No* member of the system is capable of achieving clarity, of taking a personal stand and maintaining it long enough to ensure that new and better things can happen. A sense of murky uncertainty pervades the entire system, creating feelings of terrible apprehension and danger—a sense of danger that is by no means limited to the present or to fears of what may happen in the future. For severely disturbed families are ghost-ridden, haunted by the unmourned, unmetabolized, unresolved sorrows and miseries of the past. Indeed, if the severely disturbed family had a motto emblazoned upon the gate to its domain, it would be "Loss (and therefore change of any sort) is intolerable."

In these severely compromised systems, even the expectable losses and partings associated with the passage of time (children growing up and leaving the nest; the decline of aging parents) are frequently denied and disavowed, for there is an underlying sense that change and loss will prove intolerably painful, far too painful to be managed. For this reason, what emerges is a sticky, pervasive sense of stasis and stagnation; it is as if biological time itself isn't even ticking along (or as if its ticking can be disregarded and ignored).

While life itself, with its expectable transitions as well as its unforeseen disruptions and setbacks, will bring a train of demands for adaptive change, these chaotic and yet fundamentally rigid systems can come up with nothing other than the most stilted and stereotypic modes of responding. The family in pain tends to do what it has always done before, without ever seeming to notice that what it does has not been working.

What one tends to see, at this developmental level, are the same dreary, no-win sequences recurring over and over again. It is as if the members of the system are in an unspoken collusion to keep their collective attention away from the real sources of their suffering—for the underlying issues are too freighted with pain to bear consciously knowing about, much less reflecting upon, experiencing, feeling.

Depending upon the nature of the family's relational style ("family style" is itself an important topic, which I shall discuss), the dilemmas and conflicts within the system may be covert and smoldering or they may be overt and explosive; but they are, in any case, perennially unresolvable. For the members of the Level 5 family can neither focus on their issues and concerns with any reasonable degree of clarity nor can they even think about them in a coherent fashion.

To an outsider, it sometimes seems as if the people in this kind of family cosmos are oddly dedicated to promoting a state of mutual obfuscation. Their discussions are riddled with sudden, evasive shifts of topic—the question asked is not the question that is answered—and there is a frequent failure to recall certain facts that are of monumental emotional importance to the hearer ("I thought I'd told you about the abortion; maybe I didn't"). Certain remarks, moreover, are simply met with silence, as if the statement itself had been dropped into a well—which has the effect of disqualifying both the speaker and whatever words he or she has spoken.

The net result of these, and a host of other confusing and disorienting conversational techniques, is that in severely disturbed systems, meaning is routinely fragmented and *life itself makes no sense*. What families at this level of development lack, in the most fundamental way, is *coherence*. A sense of coherence and clarity is, in fact, what everyone in this terrifyingly chaotic kind of system is struggling desperately to achieve.

Level 4: The Polarized Family (Borderline)

In the *polarized family*, matters have improved somewhat, but only to a limited degree. For as part of a desperate effort to master the disorder seen in the severely disturbed systems below them, borderline families have gone to the opposite extreme. Instead of having no rules, they have nothing but *inflexible, black-and-white rules*—rules designed not only to control the actions, but the thoughts and feelings of everyone within the intimate system.

Borderline families live in the polarized world of either/or: You're either in control or you're out of control; you're either all bad or you're all good; you're either all right or you're in the wrong entirely. You are the parent of a perfect family or the parent of a family full of monstrous ingrates. In this kind of emotional universe, there is not much gray area, nor is there space for negotiation of individual differences. For at this developmental level, the terrifying disorganization of the severely disturbed Level 5 system has been replaced by a dictatorship. Utter disorder has been supplanted by strict overcontrol, and anarchy overcome by the advent of a tyrant.

And disagreeable as life in this kind of emotional system might appear to be, it does represent a developmental advance over the terrifying chaos that exists below it on the scale. For the authoritarian family world that has been created *is* preferable to the confusion and formlessness that lurk at Level 5.

An analogy might be made to the welcoming of a strong dictatorship in a country whose cultural institutions are breaking down, whose criminal justice system has ceased to function, and whose economy is out of control. In the face of total disorganization, the loss of personal freedom seems a small sacrifice; *any* government, however repressive, is felt to be preferable to no government at all.

Seen from this point of view, the emergence of the tyrant feels—and *is* in truth—adaptive for everyone concerned. Life is not so incoherent and unstructured that what happens is likely to be unpredictable and unintelligible. The family despot has imposed his own ironclad expectations, rules, and regulations upon the group, and thus replaced potential disarray and confusion with a state of martial law.

The problem is that while his behavior may, in the short run, have brought order out of disarray, in the long run it becomes untenable to everyone. For the tyrant, in his struggle to maintain control, has imposed *rigid ways not only of behaving but of thinking and feeling* upon the members of the intimate group. His stern jurisdiction extends into the internal life of every person in the household; it is he who hands down the decrees about which ideas, wishes, emotions, and behaviors fall within the range of the acceptable. The overlord then defends these edicts with a force buttressed by his own underlying panic—for in this world of polar opposites, he experiences himself as being either in total control or as having no control whatsoever. And if he is out of control, chaos threatens.

In these polarized families, the organizational rules have come into existence not only in order to stave off family-wide chaos but to impose a sense of order in the internal world of everyone within the household. The intractable problem that pervades these intimate systems is, however, that maintaining total dominion over other people's thoughts and feelings—their wishes, longings, strivings (such as a growing adolescent's striving for autonomy)—may be effective in the short run but is doomed in the long one. For, like murder, human complexity will out—and inevitably, as in other totalitarian systems, a rebellious fifth column develops.

For even if the individuals in the family have no conscious wish to defy or resist the prevailing order, they cannot remain in their highly oversimplified roles and positions forever. Being human, they will find themselves experiencing a great variety of diverse thoughts, ideas, and emotions, even if such thoughts and feelings are forbidden in their family world. They may feel angry, sad, inadequate, or just plain ambivalent—even though mutually inconsistent or just plain unwelcome thoughts and feelings are unforgivable violations of the system's operational code.

In borderline, Level 4 families, an air of constraint settles on everyone; the rules of the emotional system cannot be challenged. This is not due solely to fear of the dictator's power; it is also due to a prevalent dread that once control is lost, the system itself will go completely haywire; the family itself may splinter and fall apart.

It is for these reasons that the members of the intimate group live under mutual surveillance, struggling to think and feel the permissible thoughts and emotions. But they live, always, with the lurking fear of the family bogeyman—the ever-present threat that someone's essential individuality, differentness, actual thoughts, wishes, and ideas will suddenly burst out and come into view. And when this happens (as it will, because human nature cannot be suppressed indefinitely), it will be seen, within this emotional framework, as vile badness or utter insanity—but in any case, as treachery of the most inexcusable sort. For it flies in the face of one of the polarized system's most basic precepts, which is that nobody in this family world is supposed to state an individual, differentiated position—"I disagree with what you said"; "I'd prefer staying home this afternoon"; "I feel upset by what you did"; and the like—or, worse yet, to maintain that position in the face of the tyrant's disapproval.

The tyrant runs the system, not by means of conflict resolution and compromise, but by means of intimidation and control. Control is, in fact, the paramount issue that families at this level of emotional development are grappling with, and the intermittent power struggles they experience can be truly ferocious.

Thus, while Level 4, borderline families have actually solved the problem of coherence that pervades the formless Level 5 system below them, they have done so at great psychic cost—by establishing a despotic, totalitarian mode of existence. It is nevertheless true that the Level 4 family system *has* developed structure—rules which make life predictable—and the people in this system are truly better off.

Level 3: The Rule-Bound Family (Midrange)

The *rule-bound, Level 3 family* represents yet another advance upward on the family developmental continuum. In this midrange emotional system, the issues of both coherence *and* control have been dealt with and resolved. Midrange families are not formless and confused; neither do they need to exist under a state of martial law. They certainly do *not* (as do Level 4, borderline families) require a tyrant whose decrees are handed down in terms of strict absolutes.

This is because the midrange, Level 3 family has figured out how to maintain order and control in a less primitive, cartoonlike fashion. In these families, control is no longer external—something imposed upon its members by an oppressive dictator—but rather comes from within each individual member of the group. Midrange families use the tremendous power and influence inherent in close relationships in order to keep the people within the emotional system in line. And indeed, if the members of this system were to devise a motto for their own family coat of arms, it would be *If you loved me, you would always do all the particular things that you well know will meet with my approval.*

In the midrange family, feeling worthy, loved and lovable, good about oneself is contingent on obeying the dictates of the emotional system.

If, for example, a wife takes it as a given and obvious rule of living that "A good man spends all his free time with his family," then being a "good man" clearly involves behaving in this particular fashion.

Suppose, however, that the husband is invited to go off on a weekend expedition with his old college buddies—and suppose, furthermore, that he wants very much to go. Given that his relationships with his wife and children are important to him, and that he does want to be a good spouse and parent (as defined by the emotional system's rules), he is immediately confronted with one of two possible—and equally disagreeable—choices.

He can either abide by the family by-law (and feel disappointed and resentful) or he can defy the rule and go off for the weekend feeling like a rotten louse—that is, guilty. Whichever of these courses he chooses, the regulation itself remains inflexibly in place, because at this developmental level, the rules of the system are far more important than anyone within it.

THE INVISIBLE REFEREE

In the rule-bound family's world, the coercion to behave in certain acceptable ways does not come from external sources (which is why the tyrant can be dispensed with); the coercion comes from within each member of the group and from the manifold rules for being a good person that have been taken in by every one of them. Thus, rules such as "A good woman always keeps a spotless house" and "A loving wife always wants to have sex whenever her partner does" may be among the code of regulations for living that the people in the emotional system have internalized. And if rules like these are indeed on the family books, then the female partner (like the husband in the earlier example) can follow either the path of compliance or that of defiance and guilt.

If she takes the former path and abides by the rules of the emotional system, she may find herself—for reasons that are often quite unclear to her—tense, irate, and perhaps suffering from a good deal of unexplained depression (because the rules of the system impel her to harshly suppress her own authentic thoughts and feelings). If she takes the latter path—lets the house get untidy from time to time, or tells him that she's not in the mood for sex—she may be perceived as a bad, slovenly creature or as a "frigid," unfeminine, and unloving sexual partner *not only by her spouse but by herself.*

The rule-bound emotional system is one in which the regulations for honorable living are ubiquitous and dominate almost every aspect of existence. The omnipresent difficulty is, however, that when obedience to the rules takes precedence over any effort to figure out what one actually wants, it is almost impossible to make contact with one's own psychological insides—that is, with one's real thoughts, true wishes, and actual preferences.

If, for instance, the wife in the above example happens to be someone who doesn't want to put her energies into keeping her house impeccably clean, she may feel compelled to do so, because a spotless home is written into the marital and family by-laws. Or it may be that the wife actually prefers to have sex less often than her spouse does, or in a less routinized manner—and in their intimate world the policy is that it happens every other night. She may conform and feel resentful, or not conform and feel guilty; but what she *won't* have, in the midrange system, is the option to think about whether or not the rule itself makes much sense to her.

Doing something because one "ought" to do so is very different from doing it because it is an expression of one's own genuine preference. But in the rule-bound family what one does is, by and large, what one is supposed to do and what is expected of one—or one feels culpable, blameworthy.

In such an atmosphere, the members of the Level 3 family often behave as if they are being surveilled by a spectral watcher or what psychiatrist Robert Beavers has termed "the invisible referee"—a faceless judge or perhaps an entire imagined audience of "good people" who are scrutinizing every aspect of one's thoughts, feelings, and behavior. Under the sway of this invisible referee's authority and domination, the people in the system become genuinely confused about whether they are thinking certain thoughts or acting in certain ways because they want to or because it is wanted of them.

For example, the father who might like to go off on a camping weekend with his friends may not even be capable of knowing consciously that he does want to go. The system's rules take precedence over the capacity to experience certain wishes, thoughts, needs, feelings; and even though the pressure to be one's own real self continues to exert itself, the family's regulations for being a worthy person exert counterpressures of even greater strength and force. The rules and regulations feel vitally necessary, because *midrange systems are pervaded by the belief that human beings are basically uncaring and untrustworthy.*

There is no faith that a family member will behave in loving ways spontaneously. Thus, an adult daughter may faithfully obey the rule "You should call your parents once a week," but it feels vastly different to call home because it's expected rather than to call home because one is really eager to talk to the folks. The very need for such a rule betrays a lack of confidence that she would ever want to call home if left to her own devices.

In families at the midrange level, the rules are felt to be critically necessary because they keep the people in the system behaving in the ways that good, close, and loving family members *ought to.* The dilemma is, however, that even though the rules *do* serve to regulate everyone's behavior very effectively, they throw up an invisible yet very real barrier against spontaneous, authentic, close relating.

For one cannot say to the partner or to the family, "This is who I am," if doing so flies in the face of the system's operational regulations. And if one ever did so, the feedback would very likely be a reprimand: "A good, loving person would think (or feel or be) otherwise." It is as if, in the backdrop of the family theater, there is a kind of Greek chorus commenting on everyone's behavior. Their constant refrains are "They say—" and "Everyone knows—."

But who, actually, are "they" or "everyone"? Driven by the rules as they all are, the members of the midrange family would find this a difficult question to answer.

THE PROBLEM OF INTIMACY

The rules have, of course, been brought into play to provide security, stability, and predictability to the behavior of everyone in the system; the difficulty is that these selfsame rules interfere seriously with the development of genuine closeness. For true intimacy has to begin with people trying to come to grips with who they really are and what they actually do think and feel (as distinct from knowing what they "should" think and feel) and being willing to come to one another with this honest, if not always perfectly congenial and welcome, information.

Real relationship involves having a place to go with one's not-so-pretty thoughts. Real relationship involves being able to bring one's ambivalent feelings out into the open, and to do so with a sense of safety, which in turn must derive from the knowledge that one will be heeded and attended. But in the rule-bound emotional system, it is far more important to be who one "should be" than to be who one actually is at the moment.

Admittedly there is, in *all* family systems, a certain amount of tension between meeting the needs of the self and meeting the needs of the group as an emotional entity. But what tends to happen at the midrange level is that the richness of the individual's subjective experience becomes truncated as he or she struggles valiantly to be the person that "they" or "everyone" will find acceptable.

The problem intrinsic to the midrange system is that if a person cannot get in touch with his own real feelings—cannot become connected to his or her own inner world in a manner that is vivid, genuine, and alive—it is truly impossible ever to get to know another person intimately either. Being heard as who one is, and hearing the other as who he or she is, is the loving service that true intimates offer to one another routinely.

In truth, when it comes to getting intimate, no stand-in for the real self will do. For intimacy involves the capacity to expose one's genuine (if not always palatable) thoughts, feelings, and needs to the close person or people in one's life. It involves making oneself vulnerable by daring to say forthrightly, "This is who I am, warts and all." This could only be hazarded if one were fairly confident that the feedback would be supportive—that to be honestly oneself would be within the pale of what is humanly permissible.

In the midrange family, however, the internalized rules themselves preclude this from happening. *The rules rule, because the system is operating on the basic assumption that the guidelines to behavior must be in place because no one would ever do the right and loving thing of his or her own accord.* What has been sacrificed, in the service of the manifold "shoulds" and "oughts," is intimacy itself, and intimacy is indeed the major issue with which the people in this rule-bound world are struggling.

Level 2: The Adequate Family; and Level 1: The Optimal Family

Adequate and *optimal* families may be referred to in the same categorical breath, so to speak, because these relational systems are in many ways far more similar than they are different. Families at this healthier end of the clinical ladder share fundamental characteristics—most especially, their ability to be comfortable with both their loving feelings and with their feelings of annoyance and frustration. The members of the intimate group can, in other words, take personal responsibility for their mixed, ambivalent thoughts and emotions.

Adequate and optimal families are also much alike in their ability to display flexible responses to life events, and to focus on their issues and on the tasks at hand with a good degree of goal-direction and clarity. While these competent systems are, of course, not totally devoid of conflict—there is no group of individuals, indeed no individual human being, without mixed thoughts and feelings about a great variety of matters—there is, in such families, generally very little conflict that is found to be unresolvable.

For while the members of any family group do have to struggle with their share of strong differences, matters of disagreement, and occasional outright battles, these more capable, successful families are pervaded by a deep sense of trust in the dependability and reliability of their underlying connection. Because their fundamental relationships with one another *feel* so secure, there is always the sense that "We can work it out"; the vitally important relational web that links them will not be dangerously threatened.

Power, Control, Intimacy: Core Family Issues

Power is always a major focus of concern, overtly or covertly, in every human grouping. As one ascends the Beavers Scale from the least competent and functional families to the most competent and functional families, clear differences in the ways in which power, control, and intimacy issues are managed become strikingly apparent.

In families at the bottom of the clinical ladder (Level 5, severely disturbed), no member of the family is clearly in charge. These basically structureless, ungoverned families are without any real, discernible hierarchy; the only rule is that there is no reliably consistent rule; "Anything goes" is the household's basic credo. In this kind of emotional system, efforts to establish control are generally covert and indirect, and since *no one* in this family world has real power that can be used effectively, the system itself feels dangerously random and chaotic.

In families at the next level up (Level 4, borderline), the situation has of course improved, but only to a certain degree. While some sense of order has been established, these polarized systems are characterized by persistent (but never completely successful) efforts to establish patterns of dominance and submission. The all-pervasive difficulty here is that while dictatorial rule is certainly better than no coherent structure at all, this form of family government eventually does become completely untenable.

Fierce power struggles—which always involve some family member's desperate effort to establish his or her own separateness and individual humanity—inevitably erupt.

Such control battles may surface in the overt form of emotional explosions, or in the more covert form of emotional symptoms (for example, anorexia nervosa). In the polarized family, however, the power struggle can never really be resolved and settled. For in this kind of extravagantly oversimplified either/or system, all is understood in terms of diametric opposites (you are either omnipotent *or* you are totally helpless). Thus, the more subtle, intricate, complex gray areas of negotiation and compromise have no place or existence whatsoever. At this level of family functioning, the ongoing struggle for control has—and can have—no imaginable conclusion, so the unresolvable conflict rages on endlessly.

At the next higher rung of the Beavers ladder (Level 3, midrange), the people in the system have certainly recognized the tremendous power and influence inherent in close relationships; they also know very well how to use that power to keep the emotional system running smoothly. Families at this developmental plane have mastered the problem of control by establishing a more complex and differentiated set of organizational rules. The disconcerting difficulty pervading the system is, however, that the stable structure thus created is being maintained by means of manipulation, intimidation, and guilt. Even though the emotional system does operate effectively, everyone within it is feeling emotionally constricted, guilt-laden, and discomfited. The myriad rules about what a "good person" should think and feel make the members of these families feel controlled from within.

Furthermore, because certain thoughts and feelings are not acceptable within the system, the internal world of every member of the family starts feeling "bad" and dangerous. Indeed, it is often the case that people in a rule-bound world will confuse having had a "bad," unacceptable thought with actually having done something terrible.

Very commonly, in order to defend themselves from the sense of shame, guilt, and inner badness, the members of the midrange group will deny, repress, or project onto others thoughts and feelings that have been deemed impermissible and unthinkable. It is almost as if the family members have labored together to build a tall prison, whose walls are made entirely of rules, and then they've all leaped inside it and locked the door behind them.

Flexibility and Structure: Key Aspects of Family Health

As one moves upward on the health and competence continuum, it will be useful to bear in mind the fact that families at Level 2 (adequate) are located between the midrange and optimal families on the Beavers Scale. Adequate, Level 2 is, in fact, an in-between kind of category, for while families assessed as "adequate" have a great deal in common with the optimal families above them on the Beavers ladder, they also bear some resemblance to the less capable, rule-bound families one rung below them.

The adequate family is like the rule-bound family in its occasional tendency to use emotionally coercive tactics—to try to resolve conflicts by means of intimidation and guilt. There will also be times when the members of an adequate family are not supposed to think certain thoughts, or to have certain feelings, which are considered out of bounds within the emotional framework. *Such methods of control are by no means the norm* in adequate families (as they are in midrange families) but to the extent that they are present in the system they do impose limits on the closeness, trust, and good feeling that the members of the intimate group can confidently share.

Adequate families are more like optimal, Level 1 families in their performance rating; both groups do extremely well when it comes to meeting the developmental needs of their individual members. The parents in the adequate family have formed an effective coalition, and they work well as a team (though their marital relationships may not be quite as emotionally rewarding as are those of the optimal couples above them on the scale). At these higher levels of family development, the nature of the rules and the structure of the hierarchy are in dramatically sharper focus; the way in which the organization operates (who is in charge, and under which circumstances) are now well defined and clear to all concerned.

Most important of all, however, the rules of the family system are not viewed as edicts that have been engraved in stone; they are seen as human rules, made by fallible human beings—rules that can, under the appropriate circumstances, come into question and undergo change. And it is in this particularly crucial respect that adequate families and optimal families are most similar.

Healthy, competent emotional systems are flexible—although families assessed as adequate are somewhat less so. While both these emotional systems operate very effectively, in terms of doing the right thing, the adequate system's wheels don't always move around easily; some pain and individual loneliness are present. In adequate families, one simply doesn't see the same relatively constant sense of closeness and delight—that real pleasure in one another's company—so evident in the optimal families above them at the top of the scale.

Family Happiness and Power Sharing

The most competent family systems are egalitarian ones, in which *equal overt power is shared by the parents* in a manner that is mutually attentive to and respectful of each other's sometimes different viewpoints. In purely political terms, one would call the optimal family a democratically organized group, with strong, clear, joint leadership at the head of its government, and a citizenry (the younger generation) with a voice that will be heard and responded to reliably.

In these workable intimate systems, negative affects such as anger, frustration, sadness, discouragement—even despair—are viewed as part of the human package, rather than as unwelcome, dangerous, or potentially destructive forces. In this kind of emotional atmosphere, a full range of feeling can be expressed because *all feelings (not just those that are in line with the family's agenda and self-image) are taken to be the "facts" of someone's existence at that particular moment*—at that particular moment, it must be emphasized, and not until the end of time.

In these families, angry feelings and sad feelings are thus not merely "allowed" or "permitted"; they are expected to exist, welcomed, and even embraced as aspects of a loved family member's own unique humanity. It is, in truth, this readiness to acknowledge and experience the hard and distressing parts of life that makes it possible for the people in the system to own and take responsibility for their genuine feelings and to feel quite naturally entitled to do so.

In this familial environment, individual differences are not viewed as threatening; simply being oneself is never seen as badness or a betrayal of the group. Differences are not merely tolerated by the group; they are seen as enriching to everyone. Here, as well, space is allotted—a plot of personal autonomy in which each member of the family can grow as a separate being without sacrificing his or her sense of belonging within the larger relational system. And it is this very comfortable sense that one can get close without being swallowed up in other peoples' needs, or in their communal myth-making, that makes intimacy feel safe—or, indeed, possible at all.

CHAPTER 3

Family Legacies: The Ways in Which the Past Invades the Present

It was at our subsequent meeting that the Andersons' family secret emerged. On this occasion, Susan Anderson was sitting directly across from me, arms tightly folded across her chest, her cheeks flushed and her lips pursed. Dave's younger sister had finally appeared and now sat beside her mother, looking frightened. Cheryl Anderson was a chubby girl with long hair; her hazel eyes never rested upon anyone else in the office. It seemed to me that she found the idea of being inside a psychiatric institution unnerving.

Dave's father looked anxious, too, and as if he were getting more anxious by the moment; therapist Linda Bowen had begun this session by launching directly into the subject of his wife's simmering, ongoing fury. "What became very clear in our last session is, I think, that Dave does sense your anger," she said to the mother straightfowardly, "and that you *are* very angry. And really, it's okay to talk about that—it's an important part of what we need to talk about today." Mrs. Anderson, her naturally high color deepening, nodded her head in agreement.

"Another thing I think is that a part of you is very weary and exhausted," Linda went on, her voice sympathetic, and the mother nodded, her irate, exasperated facial expression crumpling into one of worry and sadness. "And I wonder if you'd be able to talk to Dave about that. I wonder if you could tell him that you *are* his mom and that you *do* love him—but that you're really mad and you're *tired*." She paused; Dave's mother, looking perplexed by the question, frowned and didn't reply.

Linda continued. "The last time we met, Dave was certainly able to tell you both some difficult—and I think, extremely *painful*—things. To tell you about how much he's been hurting, and his feeling that he's not got a real relationship going—not with either one of you. I think it was *hard* for him to come out and say those things—that it took a lot of courage—but what he was saying felt pretty real to me."

"I'm sick and tired of it all, that's for sure," Susan Anderson allowed bitterly.

"I've been sick and tired of it for *ten years*": Dave echoed her words immediately.

"So this has been going on for a long, long time." Linda picked up on the boy's remark without turning her gaze from his parent. "And correct me if I'm wrong, but it's my own sense that you've been the main person dealing with it. That your husband's been"—she hesitated briefly—"present in the household throughout all of these troubles, but that *you* are the main person dealing with Dave. And you're really pretty sick of it, aren't you?"

"Yes," the mother answered tersely.

"Is there some part of you that wishes your husband were a little bit more involved, and took some of the burden off your shoulders?" This question was the clinician's, but for some reason Susan turned to face me and nodded, as if asking "Do you *see*?" It was as if she wanted me to understand that she was not the unreasonably irate parent that she might appear to be—to understand that her partner had not been doing his share or supporting her at all, and that her rage was therefore warranted.

Then she turned back to Linda Bowen, who was asking her whether there was some part of her that was actually mad at her husband—mad about all the things that had been happening, that she was being forced to deal with on her own. "Sure," said the mother, without a moment's hesitation.

"I guess that in a way it's easier to duke it out with Dave, isn't it?" The therapist looked at Mrs. Anderson quizzically. "Because your son *fights back*, and somehow I have the idea that your husband doesn't." In the charged silence that ensued, I noticed that the teenager was no longer slouching in his seat but was sitting bolt upright and transfixed by what was being said.

"No, Ralph just *leaves*," Susan acknowledged indignantly, and I had an odd intuition at that moment. It was the idea that Ralph Anderson, perpetually fleeing a pitched battle with his wife, was somehow leaving his son behind as hostage. Linda Bowen must have had a similar notion, for she smiled a brief, ironical smile.

But her tone remained friendly, supportive. She looked at Mrs. Anderson and said, "It's *hard* to be angry—and it's *hard* to quarrel, too—

with someone who refuses to be angry back at you. Who won't even hang around long enough to fight it out." Then she turned to the father, said almost gaily, "Maybe you need to stick around and duke it out with your wife a little more, and *not* leave the fight . . . hmmm?" Ralph Anderson met her gaze, but stared at her blankly, as if what she'd said was incomprehensible.

A Mother's Rage

Since the time of our last family meeting, Dave had been preoccupied by the subject of his mother's rage. Why was she so angry? Was her anger directed at him or at a "situation"—and if the latter, what was the "situation" and how did it involve him? He was, he'd admitted, just beginning to understand how much there was that he really didn't know, and his agenda for today had been to find out more about what was actually going on. But now he sat there, his body posture limp, looking furious and saying nothing.

"We've been making a lot of good progress," Linda observed thoughtfully, as if contemplating the wider family landscape from a distance. "You, Dave, have shared a lot of honest feelings with your family, and your parents are being honest too. Mom has been able to say that a part of her is angry at you, but a part of her is angry at Dad as well." Then she paused, regarded the top of her patient's lowered head, frowned slightly. "Do you have any idea why your mom would be angry at your dad?" she asked him.

"Because of his— I don't know— I don't give a— I don't *care*, either," the teenager muttered, not raising his head and looking at her.

"Because of his . . . ?" Linda cocked her head to one side again, smiled an inquiring smile that he couldn't see, then sat back in her chair and waited. After a few moments Dave said something unintelligible into his chest, something in which I could discern only the phrase "I don't know" again.

"So there's no specific thing that you know of that would be making your mother really mad at your father?" I asked in a low voice. To my surprise, Dave looked up and met my gaze directly. He shook his head, looked lost and confused. I was puzzled, for his mother had been insisting, from the very outset, that she was quite certain that the children *were* aware of Ralph's illegitimate child and of the other family's existence.

It was my belief, and Linda's too, that having this matter put out on the table, in plain sight of everyone, had been high on Susan Anderson's agenda since the beginning of her son's hospitalization. Dave's mother believed the children needed to be told they had a half-sibling, but maintained that it was not up to *her* to do the telling—the problem was not one of her own creating. Her position was that speaking openly to Dave and

Cheryl (about what she believed they already did know, covertly) was her husband's responsibility, and his responsibility alone.

"Maybe we can help you, and fill you in," Linda Bowen said to Dave; but then she paused, turned to his younger sister, and asked if she had any idea what might be making her mother angry at her dad.

Cheryl jumped. "What's making her mad at him? —I don't know." She rolled her eyes, made a silly face at her brother and her parents, grinned in embarrassment.

"There's no reason you can think of?" The clinician repeated her question, in a searching tone of voice, but Dave's sister merely stared and shook her head.

Linda Bowen turned back to the mother, saying nothing, but letting her eyes linger upon Mrs. Anderson for the next several moments. Then she looked at Ralph Anderson in the same slow, scrutinizing fashion. "How about Mom and Dad? Can they perhaps give us a reason?" she asked in a level tone of voice.

I had known in advance that opening up the issue of the father's other family was something that needed to happen. It was a dilemma that the Andersons would have to confront before it tore them all apart—but still, I felt frightened by the course upon which Linda Bowen was now embarking.

Ralph Anderson, clearing his throat hastily, said, "I think that a lot of the school involvement, and Dave's problems—*she* has dealt with most of that." He nodded in his wife's direction. "A lot has to do with frustration level—she's the one who has been dealing with a lot of these things. And I guess that I tend to be more tolerant—a lot of things bother her—and I think that creates some friction as well."

The burden of Dave's father's message seemed to be that there would be far less conflict in the household if his wife were less emotionally reactive. Susan shot him an exasperated look, but made no verbal response, nor did either of the children.

Linda Bowen paused, gazed around the room, her glance touching briefly upon each member of the family in turn. "Is this the explanation for Mom's anger, or does someone here have something else to add?"

No one did.

Dave was sinking lower in his chair as if he were crumpling from within and every bone in his body were dissolving. He seemed at that moment to be the physical embodiment of the potential disaster that everyone in this system feared might be about to materialize and then emerge into the open.

No one spoke. We sat there, for the next few minutes, in a tension-filled silence that I began to find almost physically painful.

Revelations

It was Linda Bowen who ended the conversational stalemate. "I think there's one issue that everybody knows about—at least Mom *says* everybody knows about it—and that no one talks about at all. Is that true?" She looked at Susan Anderson, who pursed her lips and said, "Yes, but as I said, *I'm* not going to be the one to raise it."

"But does everybody actually know about it?" the therapist asked.

"It's *his* problem," the mother replied, with a baleful glance at her husband.

Linda attempted to clarify the situation again, "Yes, but *does* everybody know about it?" she asked. Mrs. Anderson nodded her head, looked at the children, and responded challengingly, "Ask them."

"Maybe if somebody would give me a *clue*," said Dave in a low, caustic tone. "Maybe if somebody would give me an idea of what we're *talking* about . . ." He continued to grumble angrily into his own chest, but it was impossible to hear what he was saying.

Ralph Anderson sat up straight in his seat; he cleared his throat. "Well, I think everybody's alluding to the fact that you have a half-brother," he said to his son. "It's something that hasn't been talked about a lot, but it's not really any deep, dark secret. Mom knows. It's something that we meant to—" He hesitated for a moment. "We were going to talk with you about this when we needed to."

Dave and Cheryl stared at their father in amazement.

"Did you know about this, Dave?" Linda asked her patient. Dave shook his head and said in an aggrieved voice, "No."

"I think that on some level he certainly did," his mother put in, her voice taut yet packed with an angry energy.

Ralph Anderson, adjusting the collar of his shirt, shot his wife a look of gratitude. "Yes, this is something that has been talked about, to some degree, before. To some extent," he repeated uncomfortably. "I know that the question has come up in reference to a money order; I don't remember which of you asked the question. Questioned that money order at a particular time . . . But it's just something that is *there*, even though we haven't really talked about it an awful lot."

I looked at Linda Bowen, who appeared dismayed by the fact that the revelation had clearly taken the children completely by surprise. I felt shaken too. "You had no idea?" the therapist was asking Cheryl, who merely shook her head, very slowly, from side to side. "What does he *mean* by a half-brother?" she demanded truculently.

"A son who lives in upstate New York," her father replied evenly, "which was the main reason for our moving here. To get away from that situation." He spoke as if nothing so far out of the ordinary were actually being communicated. "And I think it was *you* who asked about the money order—that was quite a while back. Maybe it didn't register," he said, as if her failure to listen had been part of the reason why this news was so startling to her now.

But the daughter, gaze fixed upon him, held up her hand as if to halt this onslaught of dry explanation. "No, no, wait a minute. *What* half-brother and *who* do you mean?"

"He means that we have a half-brother," Dave said sarcastically, each word he uttered clipped and definite. "Who lives in New York." Cheryl's head swiveled slowly on her neck as she turned to meet her brother's gaze. "We do?" she asked him disbelievingly.

"That's what he just said," Dave's voice was heavy with irony.

For a moment, no one spoke, and I glanced at Susan Anderson's face. The anger and strain seemed to have washed out of it; she looked, in fact, like the cat who has swallowed the canary: triumphant, full, and gratified. It was as if she had just won a major conquest in the ongoing household war. Hitherto, it was *she* who had appeared to be the unreasonably hostile, bitchy, bad guy in the group, but now the *real* identity of the family culprit had been revealed.

"You know," she said suddenly, meeting my eye, "I went to the marriage counselor last night—by myself, Ralph couldn't make it. And one of the things the counselor said to me was 'You've got to realize that this kid could show up on your doorstep at any moment. And how would *you* feel, if you were in Dave or Cheryl's place, and you suddenly discovered, from out of nowhere, that you had a half-brother you didn't even know about?' "

She smiled. "I had to laugh, because that actually did happen in my own life."

I stared at her. "It did?"

The Past Invades the Present

In ordinary family life, as psychiatrist Jill Savege Scharff has observed, the past does continue to exist and to be constantly replayed in the present-day relationships of everyone in the household. "Every family system, healthy or unhealthy," writes Scharff, "is imbued with or invaded by the past that is woven into its fabric."

This is especially true in families that qualify as severely disturbed on the Beavers Scale, for in these emotional systems the past has not only invaded the present but, very often, overwhelmed it. The Level 5 family is pervaded by the eerie sense that, while the hands of the clock have gone on moving forward in real time, time's passage hasn't actually registered. What once was, now *is*; the family's past is its present, and its present (or some ingenious variation upon key thematic concerns) is a great predictor of its future direction.

I gazed at Susan Anderson's fixed smile, which seemed ever more incongruous as she continued speaking. Her parents, she explained, had been divorced when she was ten years old, and she and her siblings hadn't seen a lot of their dad after the breakup. She hadn't even known that her father was planning to remarry, until one day when she and her mother happened to run into him on the steps of the local hospital.

"My mother asked him if he was visiting a friend or a relative, and my father said, 'Relative,' that's all," recounted Susan. "He looked at his watch"—Dave's mother imitated the gesture of a man hurriedly checking the time—"and he said, 'I've got to go,' and then walked off pretty fast." She laughed sardonically, as if at a strange but comical recollection.

Her mother's curiosity had been aroused, Susan said, and she herself had been dispatched to the front desk to find out exactly who it was that he'd been visiting. "I found out that there was a lady in the maternity ward who had just had a baby, and that she was my father's wife. So that's how I found out I had a half-brother." While that joyless smile never left Dave's mother's face, I saw the wounded expression in her eyes and heard the betrayed child's indignation in the sound of her voice.

Susan Anderson (then Clark) was thirteen years old at the time, and her divorced parents were both living in the same small town in Vermont in which they had grown up. I looked at her and observed quietly, "So it's in a slightly different form, but it's the same story the second time around." She nodded. "Yes, that's how I found out I had a half-brother." The woman her father had married, she added ("I guess you'd call her my step-mother"), was six months pregnant at the time of the ceremony, and also had a two-year-old illegitimate daughter of her own. Her father had adopted this child. "My dad *did* parent his kids from that marriage, though one of them wasn't even his own," she said gloomily.

But her father had never really parented Susan and her two brothers, the children of his first marriage, despite the fact that he'd lived quite near to them geographically. "When I think about it, I do resent some of the things he did to us," Susan admitted, a hair-thin crack of vulnerability sounding in her voice. "Such as, tell us he'd pick us up on Sunday afternoon, and never show up . . . and this was not a one-time occurrence."

Dave's mother was now talking openly about deep, poignant girlhood feelings of disappointment and resentment, but her present-day anger—that ongoing rage at her unruly, unmanageable child—seemed to have diminished dramatically. And, picturing this angry woman as a tender, half-formed, almost adolescent young female waiting in vain for her indifferent father to appear, I found myself feeling awfully sad on Susan Anderson's behalf.

Emotional Legacies: The "Shocking, Unwelcome Newborn" Reappears

Families often have recurrent, emotionally charged thematic concerns, whether these be "inappropriate anger," "parental abandonment," "depression," "alcoholism," "inability to mourn effectively," "overclose attachment between a parent and a child," "difficulties in dealing with life's expectable separations and losses," or any of a host of other problematic possibilities.

These family issues are like emotional legacies, passed along from generation to generation, picked up here and there and worked upon anew by different individuals in different locations on the family tree. They are particularly evident around expectable life-cycle transitions, one example of which is the passage from being a couple alone to being the parents of a new, first baby.

If, as therapists Elizabeth A. Carter and Monica McGoldrick observe in *The Family Life Cycle*, "one's parents were basically pleased to be parents and handled the job without too much anxiety, the birth of the first child will produce just the normal stress of a system expanding its boundaries from two to three members. If, on the other hand, parenting was a *cause célèbre* of some kind in the family of origin of one or both spouses, and has not been dealt with, the birth of a baby will produce heightened anxiety for the couple making the transition to parenthood."

The progressive way-stations along the course of the family life cycle—marriage, the birth and raising of children, the departure of children from the household, retirement, and death—are handled with more or less anxiety and distress, depending upon how well such difficult transitions have been dealt with in the emotional system earlier. It is from our vitally important and needed others that we have taken in the basic blueprint of our life's program; it is within the family that we have learned the cues about how matters should proceed, and about what things may be expected to happen. And, in sometimes subtle and sometimes glaringly obvious ways, we tend to live out our own updated version of *their* truths and the particular version of reality with which they have presented us.

Nowhere, it should be noted, does this creation of a "template" or "blueprint" become more evident than in families in which traumatic events or downright abuse or neglect has occurred. As authors Richard Kagan and Shirley Schlosberg note in *Families in Perpetual Crisis*, such families "typically act out themes which have never been resolved. The mother who was raped, brutalized, and betrayed by her family at age 13 finds her own daughter sexually abused at the same age in a seemingly unstoppable cycle of multigenerational trauma. The parent who was sent to an institution as an adolescent may find herself petitioning the court for placement of a delinquent son at the same age."

Where painful experiences have proven too hot to handle—to process psychologically, and eventually to resolve—rigid re-creations of the same experiences are often seen in the next and in subsequent generations. That was why I viewed the reappearance of the "shocking, unwelcome, and intruding newborn" in Susan Anderson's life as a riveting and by no means coincidental occurrence.

For while she herself seemed to view this duplication of an emotionally loaded set of circumstances as nothing other than a bizarre fluke of fate, the family drama currently being staged had all of the earmarks of a faithful reenactment. *What was being repeated in the outer world was the same terrible scene that lived inside her: the central experience of being utterly abandoned by an already neglectful, unconcerned, emotionally uninvolved male.*

"Individuals who have lived with inconsistent, immature, and erratic parents are not able to grieve their losses," as Kagan and Schlosberg write. "Instead, because of a lack of nurturing attachments that would have allowed them to deal with traumas, they are mired in their rage." Those harsh and distressing early experiences that we have been unable to deal with tend to be resurrected later on in our lives, often in ingenious disguises.

Freud's Repetition Compulsion

As Freud noted in his brilliant treatise on the repetition compulsion (see Chapter 5) this "need to repeat" traumatic events in our lives may have to do with an ongoing effort to gain a sense of mastery and control. For, when we go through a "Play it again, Sam" episode, we create a fresh opportunity to confront certain matters that, for a vulnerable child, were experienced as far too overpowering and overwhelming to cope with or to try to manage. Perhaps (we think) it will come out differently this time around. We will, in any case, be transported to a time and place with which we are deeply, if painfully, familiar.

In this blatant repetition of a past family scenario, Susan Anderson's husband—like her sexually wild and emotionally unavailable father—had suddenly presented her with a new boy child of his own who seemed to have come out of nowhere. And if this later treachery had been cut to an old and very familiar pattern, it also presented her with a fresh opportunity to struggle with an old dilemma.

In the unconscious world, Susan had reconnected with the first loved male in her life, and with what had happened between them. And if she herself was now frantic with rage, it was because she was struggling to cope with the same pain and shock that she'd had to accommodate as a young female adolescent.

But how, I wondered, had she managed to find the very partner who would collude with her to make this happen? Had she *known*, when she'd met him, that Ralph Anderson was the person who would agree to play the leading man's role in this particular restaging—that he would help her to confront the past in the present, and to deal with her father's indifference and rejection once again?

It is, of course, true, as most marital clinicians will testify, that a couple's life together is guided by the beacon of very powerful inner expectations. In sometimes imperceptible and sometimes glaringly apparent ways, intimate partners come together in unconscious unison to make their deepest, oldest prophecies become their present-day realities.

Still, in this particular instance, the precision of the internal radar system that had led *this* woman to *this* man seemed beyond any efforts at intellectual comprehension. What could readily be understood, however, was why this mother expected her adolescent son to develop into an irresponsible, untrustworthy, uncontrollable, and reckless human being. David Anderson was, at fifteen, moving from his boyhood into young (sexual) adulthood. And if, in the process, he was becoming everything that his mother expected a male to become, he was in some real sense meeting his mother's truest, most deeply held expectations.

Coming into the Family Inheritance

I noticed that the vertical frown line which had appeared between Linda Bowen's eyebrows in the course of this discussion was slowly and relentlessly deepening. Clearly nonplussed by the children's stunned reaction to their father's revelation, the therapist now addressed Ralph Anderson directly.

"I think that perhaps Dave and Cheryl need to have a bit more explained to them. Cheryl, in particular, must be wondering about what money orders have to do with half-brothers—do you know what I mean?" Mr. Anderson nodded, as if to say he was prepared to offer his full cooperation, but it was clear that if he'd been capable of pressing a magic nerve in his wrist and vanishing on the spot, he wouldn't have hesitated for a moment.

The father cleared his throat, turned to his daughter, and said, "The money orders are for child support—things like that." Cheryl shifted her position on her seat, as if to withdraw bodily, then stared at him as if she didn't know him. "So what was all that stuff about why we moved here?" she asked him, her tone surly and hostile.

"I think basically that was the reason for our moving to Connecticut," he repeated evenly. "Getting away from that situation—"

"So in other words my life has been built on lies!" Dave suddenly shouted, half rising from his chair. "I mean, you guys *know* that! You guys are always after me about *my* lying! 'Is your homework done? I don't believe you,' " he mimicked them, looking from Ralph to Susan and then back again. His internal needle had swung all the way from hopeless apathy to intense fury, and the possibility that he might become physically assaultive registered upon the faces of everyone present.

Still, his mother goaded him further by retorting, "Well, David, you have certainly told us a great many lies of that sort."

"I want you to know *I* was told that the reason we were moving to Connecticut was that Mom and Dad had *better job offers*," the boy announced fiercely. But at the same time he sank back into his chair, slumping as if overwhelmed from within. "*Mom* had a better job offer," Cheryl chimed in. "At least, that's what was told to us. . ." Her voice trailed off, and she looked lost and bewildered.

"Mom *did* get a better job offer," Ralph said, sounding as if his patience were being tried. And Susan said, "A much better job offer—and that is why we moved. Because we wouldn't have moved here if I hadn't." It was as if Ralph's prior explanation had been negated and disqualified on the spot.

I was feeling disoriented, as if I'd lost the sense of this discussion somehow. Which of the two explanations was the true—or at least the truer— one? Had the family's move to Connecticut been motivated primarily by economic factors, or had they all been in flight from Ralph's shadow family and that "situation" in upstate New York? Once again, as had been the case in the incident in which Dave had threatened Cheryl with the gun, it was difficult to achieve a sense of clarity about who had done what things and for which particular reasons.

Achieving clarity would, in this current instance, have involved the father's taking full emotional responsibility for his betrayal of the family. It would also have involved both parents' making themselves accountable for having lied to their kids (protective though their reasons for lying might have been). But instead, the conversation was either getting stalled in evasions or laboring along on apparently irrelevant sidetracks. I found myself slouching downward in my chair so that my own posture began to mirror Dave's.

How could either of the children in this family fully respond to this traumatic insult—their father was suddenly also someone else's father— when the very facts of the situation kept shifting and changing? The entire discussion had gotten derailed. What had started out to be an open interchange about some shocking new information—the existence of someone in the family system of whom the children had been completely unaware—had become a somewhat muddled argument about why the family had moved from New York to Connecticut, and whether or not (and how much) the parents had been lying.

In severely disturbed, Level 5 families, such confused and mystifying communications are the norm. As Dr. W. Robert Beavers notes in *Psychotherapy and Growth*, there are, in these families, "frequent incoherent topic shifts and an overall lack of clarity, though individual statements are usually comprehensible. There is great impermeability to each other's communicative efforts." In plainer language, everyone talks (or perhaps shouts), but no one seems to take in what anyone else has said, to understand it, or perhaps even to *hear* it in the first place.

"The disorganization, ineffective discipline and hostile, attacking behavior are so pervasive that negotiation is impossible; goals cannot be defined, much less attained," Beavers continues. "Discipline tends to be both harsh and sporadic, reflecting a 'what's-the use?' attitude."

I looked at Cheryl and Dave, who had fallen silent; they both seemed lost and uncertain. Nobody appeared to be telling these youngsters that there were rules, limits, and an order of things in this chaotic family territory, where the laws were not really codified, comprehensible, enforced. The clinician's gaze had settled upon the children also, and upon her patient most particularly. "Can you tell your mom and dad how you're feeling about what you've just found out?" Linda Bowen asked Dave quietly.

"I've been *lied to*," he answered furiously.

" 'Lied to.' " She echoed his phrase, her voice low. "And how does being lied to make you feel?" He shot her an irritated look. "I dunno" was the extent of his response.

"Does it make you feel angry? Sad? . . . You're looking a little sad at this moment." I myself thought that he looked far more angry and frightened than anything else, but in any case he neither nodded nor replied.

He was tuning her out, and a dismal sense of stasis and stuckness settled down upon the rest of us. Even though the storm had broken, and the father's secret been revealed, the family climate remained as tense and ominous as it had been before anything had happened.

"Dave," I said finally, "the last time we met you were talking about wanting your folks to take their part of the responsibility for what's been going on." His head was bent forward, his hair sloping downward, and he didn't look up when I spoke. "And that's what they're starting to do right now—you know that, don't you?—own up and take responsibility for things you and Cheryl didn't even know about. I guess, though, it's not easy when it happens . . . ?" Without raising his head, he nodded slowly as if to say "No, it really isn't."

Linda nodded too, and said to him, "It was a *hard* thing for them to do. Because they knew it would hurt you kids, and because it's a difficult thing for them to talk about. But," she added suddenly, "Mom seems completely relieved." Everyone in the office, even Dave, turned to look at Susan.

Perhaps, I thought, she was finding it a relief to have her own anger explained and justified, and to see her husband so clearly identified as the *real* family bad guy. But Susan merely smiled and said offhandedly that talking about this particular issue was really nothing new to her; she'd already discussed Ralph's illegitimate child with a number of the many marital counselors she'd seen.

"Everybody says I'm still angry about it, and that it should be forgiven and put behind us. . . . But when you tell me I have to forgive I can tell you that that's *never* going to happen." The smile remained fixed, but her eyes bulged and her low voice was suffused with wrath.

"Still," she added, "there's a big difference between what I feel about it now and the way I felt about it a few years ago." She paused, drew herself upright in her chair, and said in an imperious tone: "I think I've made peace with myself and, for the most part, with Ralph. We have a very *clear* understanding of how we go forward in the future as far as that kind of activity is concerned." I took this to mean that the deceiver and betrayer had promised not to lie to her or to deceive or betray her anymore. The children looked at her in bafflement, but neither of them said a word.

But what, I wondered, would constitute "betrayal" in her eyes? Did Susan Anderson have a clear idea about how much contact her husband had with his other son at this very moment? And if he ever did see his shadow family in upstate New York (whom he was supporting financially), would that be viewed as "treachery" by his wife? There was so much about this husband and parent that I myself found hard to fathom, so much that seemed completely mysterious and impenetrable.

"So what is this kid's name, and how old is he?" Cheryl demanded suddenly. Mr. Anderson cleared his throat, and told his daughter that the boy was now twelve, almost thirteen, years old, and that his name was Ralph—Ralph Junior.

Dave's listing head swung upward; he stared at his parent in disbelief. So did Cheryl, whose jaw fell open and who drew in a sharp breath of total amazement. She made a comic face, the pop-eyed, exaggerated caricature of a person looking wildly startled—but it was clear that she was seriously shaken.

This half-brother who had appeared so suddenly on the family horizon was the son that their father had either named, or allowed to be named, after himself. What's more, this new family member (*was* he a family member?) had obviously been conceived in the time period between her "real" older brother's birth and her own.

Before my eyes, Cheryl Anderson was coming into her family inheritance. She was taking in her mother's unmetabolized and undigested anger at an irresponsible, false, untrustworthy male.

CHAPTER 4

Styles of Relating: Emotionally Enmeshed and Emotionally Disengaged Families

There are families in which autonomy, the need for personal space, and a sense of independence are highly emphasized. The people in these emotional systems often feel more at ease with expressions of their individuality and differentness than they do with expressions of endearment and affection.

In other, antithetical, kinds of systems, the family's emphasis tends to be on closeness and a sense of ongoing emotional contact; in these families, the members tend to be less comfortable with differences of opinion and points of view (which could lead to conflict) and much more at ease with expressions of intimacy and warmth.

But what is important to note is that any family's style of intimate relating may be associated with—and yet is by no means synonymous with—that family's level of competence and well-being. *Whether the family's style of interacting happens to place great emphasis upon emotional closeness or to emphasize autonomy has nothing whatsoever to do with that family's developmental level.*

Relational style exists independently of the group's health and functioning as reflected on the Beavers Systems Model.

Centripetal families, on the Beavers continuum, are those that incline inward, emotionally—that tend to turn to the intimate group for the fulfillment of their emotional needs.

Centrifugal families tend to view the sources of emotional fulfillment and gratification as existing outside the family orbit, rather than inside it.

Family Style Is Only That—a Style

These different modes of family relating are, as renowned theorist Salvador Minuchin, M.D., has observed, simply styles of human interaction (which he terms "enmeshment" and "disengagement"), and not necessarily signs of well-being or of emotional disturbance.

It is only at the extremes of the engagement-disengagement continuum—where family members are intrusively overinvolved (enmeshed) or oddly indifferent and detached (disengaged)—that areas of possible pathology begin to emerge. For, fascinatingly enough, as a family's competence and sense of well-being decline, the group's tendency to adhere strictly to one style of being or the other seems to increase in tandem.

Families at the lower end of the clinical ladder live either in a state of suffocating emotional fusion *or* in an atmosphere almost completely devoid of warmth, caring, and positive feeling. It is as if the less-functional families have reached a fork in the roadway of their lives, and made a stark stylistic choice: either to be fused together in an "undifferentiated family ego mass" (to use theorist Murray Bowen's famous term)—or, alternatively, to be out of real affective touch with one another, isolated, distant, disconnected.

If the family has taken the "enmeshed" branch of the road, the people in the group have become so warm, loving, and emotionally overinvolved that individual differences are disallowed and frequently just plain obliterated.

If the family has moved off to the other, "disengaged," style of being, the right to personal space is surely being upheld, and differences are being emphasized, but signs of caring and affection are in short supply.

Within *enmeshed* emotional systems at the lower-functioning end of the Beavers Scale (severely disturbed, borderline, and some midrange), expressions of a family member's individual differentness simply cannot be tolerated. The members of the family suppress feelings of negativity, disagreements, and oppositional viewpoints, and often do so without ever being consciously aware that such feelings exist within them. Simply being who one is—authentically one's own self—is routinely disallowed in a highly overconnected and overreactive enmeshed/centripetal-style emotional world.

Within the *disengaged* family at the lower-functioning end of the Beavers Scale the antithetical situation prevails. In the disengaged system, expressions of anger are freely permitted, but neediness is seen as intolerable. The covert rules of the family club permit members to blow off their bitterness and fury at the slightest provocation, but disallow any expressions of their softness, hurting, or vulnerability. It is as if everyone in these emotional systems, whose customary relational mode is one of animosity and disconnection, has gone through a kind of combat training in which he or she has learned to stifle expressions of weakness and any flickering wish or hope of making a warm, intimate connection. In such detached, remote (aside from angry episodes), unempathic families, any effort to move closer to someone else in the group tends to be ignored, condemned, or even punished.

In brief, *the less healthy and well functioning the family organization as reflected on the Beavers Scale, the greater is its tendency to rigidify into one stylistic extreme (overinvolved and invasive) or the reverse one (remote and disengaged).*

And when this occurs, the members of the nuclear group are either never in any disagreement or they are in angry conflict almost nonstop.

Whichever of these two sharply divergent pathways the less competent family may have taken, human ambivalence—the normal capacity to feel loving and affectionate at some times, and withdrawn, annoyed, or angry at others—seems to have vanished from the relational system entirely.

Ethnic Considerations: A Side Note

Any family's style of being is, of course, deeply affected by its ethnic origins, and by the cultural values that a particular community holds to be most meaningful. For example, as authors Monica McGoldrick, John K. Pearce, and Joseph Giordano note in *Ethnicity and Family Therapy*, "WASP families are likely to feel they have failed if their children do not move away from the family and become independent . . . while Italian families are likely to feel they have failed if the children do move away."

Families of British-American origin, note these clinicians, both gain and suffer from their most important cultural trait, hyperindividualism. "They tend to be good at self-reliance, self-sufficiency and self-control and rather less good at maintaining mutually giving relationships, tolerating dependency, and integrating and expressing emotional experience." Jewish families, on the other hand (like Italian families), place great emphasis on the children "as extensions of their parents and on the importance of family togetherness," and, as McGoldrick, Pearce, and Giordano point out, "these values are so strong that Jewish children rarely leave home without a good deal of turmoil in their wake."

The Changing Face of Family Style over Time: As Children Grow and Develop, Their Area of Personal Space Must Enlarge

It is true that everyone who grows up within a family must continually struggle with the basic human dilemma of how to remain close to other members of the group and yet not sacrifice one's own individual uniqueness and differentness.

As we grow from infancy to adulthood, the slow evolution into maturity is supported by the care and understanding of those around us. It is our parents' love and concern that, over time, become integrated into our inner experience in ways that make it possible for us to understand, nurture, and care for ourselves.

But if this watering, tending, and feeding process is of vital importance, so is the loving caretaker's toleration of some degree of private, inviolable turf—a space in which personal growth can take place in a progressive, orderly fashion. In this territory of the self, secure from the invasion of insistent parental fantasies, the developing youngster can blossom into the unique person he or she needs to become—"me, myself," as the great theorist of adolescence Peter Blos, M.D., has put it.

What this requires is flexibility.

Changes in the Family's Basic Operational Style Need to Occur over Time

In a family with young children, the rules and regulations must lean in the direction of a more emotionally enmeshed mode of functioning. In these early years, the parents must try to "feel for" and with the offspring—to empathize into the little person's skin. A blurry interpersonal boundary between nurturer and child is *adaptive* when children are small, and so what works best at this phase of family living is a warm, home-focused, inward-looking, centripetal style—a sense that everyone's needs can and will be met within the magic demarcation of the family circle.

But with the passage of time, and the child's steady growth and development, the boundary between the self and the parent continues to emerge; individual differences make themselves increasingly known. A mother may expect her little daughter to be someone who is feminine and winsome, and instead find herself with a daughter who is an active, assertive tomboy. If the family system has made the appropriate shift from the normally more enmeshed mode of functioning characteristic of the early years, such subjectively based differences will be respected.

As the family's life cycle advances and the developing generation approaches puberty, the competent emotional system alters progressively in the direction of a more disengaged style of relating. During this phase of family living, the youngsters' biologically and socially driven urges to explore the world outside the nest, and to begin to make a life among their own peers, are in the ascendant. The well-functioning system experiences a natural shift into an increasingly outward-directed style of being.

Healthy, competent families seem to have the flexibility to achieve this

necessary transformation over time; they can be, at first, more centri-
petally home-focused, and then successively more and more centrifugally
oriented, as their maturing children's needs and circumstances require.

Less capable, less adept family systems experience such changes as difficult or downright impossible. These families seem to adhere to *one style*
(emotionally fused or emotionally disconnected) and then cling to it as if
no other way of existing as a group were imaginable.

In either case, the greater the family's distress, the greater is its tendency
to become mired in one way of relating or its opposite. Indeed, at Level 5,
these two major dimensions of family functioning—style and competence—seem to bleed into one another, to overlap and merge.

In severely disturbed systems, the family members exist either in a state
of suffocating overinvolvement (rigid enmeshment) or in an atmosphere
almost completely devoid of caring, concern, and affection (rigid disengagement).

Enmeshed (Inward-Focused) Level 5 Families: Groupthink

If the family is operating in an enmeshed, inward-focused style, its
members are so overconnected and entangled that expressions of a particular individual's differentness from the other people in the system cannot
be tolerated. The people in the emotional system tend to suppress feelings
of negativity, disagreements, and opposing viewpoints—often without any
awareness that they might be harboring such conflictual feelings.

This kind of system requires, as a condition of membership, that everyone banish his or her "bad" feelings (which certainly include the wish to
be a separate, different person), even if this involves losing touch with
one's own inner reality. Just being who one is—authentically oneself—is
routinely disallowed in the severely disturbed, centripetal emotional
system.

In such overconnected and enmeshed families, the members of the intimate group are constantly reading one another's facial expressions in
order to devise a completely congruent, agreed-upon family viewpoint. If,
for instance, Dad wears a slight frown after the departure of a houseguest,
someone is sure to make a remark about how long the guest stayed or how
dull her conversation was, about the annoying quality of her table manners
or the obnoxiousness of her giggle. Everyone else will have something to
add, and everyone will be in general agreement.

Very predictably, positive feeling and high-voltage empathy among the
members of the family will prevail. In this atmosphere of groupthink, no
one can think of breathing on his or her own, or of harboring a dissenting
or negative point of view. To disagree or get annoyed—or downright
angry—is completely unimaginable behavior.

The Adolescent Transition: Separating from the Emotionally Fused, Inward-Focused Family

In this world of unchanging sameness and harmony, the normal biological changes that accompany puberty tend to arrive as a dismaying blow; they send a thrill of horror throughout the overattached, emotionally fused group. Because, in these severely distressed systems, the passage of time is routinely being denied, the very process of growing up and growing apart—an expectable part of the human developmental program—is seen as a ruthless assertion of a family member's own individuality and uniqueness, and a terrible betrayal of the group as an entity.

For in enmeshed, Level 5 systems, the mere idea of someone's growing up and becoming adult brings with it the thought of that person's ultimate departure—and in these families, to think of a member's leaving is indistinguishable from the thought of that person's death.

Developing Symptoms (Anorexia Nervosa and Other Disorders): A Way of Being "Me, Myself"

Thus, moving into adolescence and maturing sexually are experienced as antifamily offenses. This is the reason why, during the adolescent transition, serious and even life-threatening problems can take root and develop. In severely impaired, emotionally entangled systems, clinical symptoms—particularly the syndrome of anorexia nervosa—are highly likely to develop.

One can understand why and how this would happen. For clearly, in this kind of demanding, cloying familial atmosphere, the dilemma of the developing young female would be "How can I dare to grow up and become 'me,' if becoming 'me' involves losing the love of those whom I love and upon whom I so depend?" The self-starvation of the anorectic youngster provides a solution of sorts, though admittedly a highly paradoxical one.

Refusing to eat is an assertion of one's control over one's own bodily self. Obviously, no one can make a person who's not hungry consume the food that others have set down before her. In this sense, the anorectic youngster's lack of hunger is a form of rebellion, a way of being "me, myself" without taking overt responsibility for doing so. She is, after all, not being blatantly negative; she is just without appetite, that's all.

Equally important in this context is the fact that self-starvation can offer a way out (a weird one, to be sure): It interrupts the seemingly relentless movement forward of the maturing young female's biological clock. Severe weight loss impedes or halts the development of secondary sexual characteristics, such as breast growth and menstruation. Thus, if a young woman becomes sufficiently skinny, she is likely to make the wonderful discovery that she can make her menstrual periods vanish. This triumph over her own body appears to support the adolescent's delusory notion that she need not necessarily go on growing up and developing into her own independent womanhood; she can halt the onward rush of time.

It is for these underlying reasons that anorexia nervosa may be experienced as the most ingenious of possible solutions. The symptoms may *feel* both protective and preservative—to the adolescent herself (she can remain a perpetual daughter) and to the family system as a whole (which seems unable to tolerate the notion of growth, separation, and departure). The illness may, in short, help to foster the developing girl's illusion that the awful risks attendant upon growing up and leaving home—first and foremost, the risk of being read out of the emotional system and abandoned—can be postponed or avoided.

According to Beavers et al., separating and individuating adolescents in severely distressed, centripetal systems are at enhanced risk not only for anorexia nervosa, but for such severe disturbances as agoraphobia, depression, and even schizophrenia. For, as the maturing younger members of the family become engaged in the ordinary—and ordinarily painful—work of trying their wings and attempting brief test flights into adulthood, the magnetic emotional forces around the family either impede their liftoff or act to ricochet them back into the family—with symptoms, dire financial need, or some other form of dependency.

Disengaged (Emotionally Disconnected) Level 5 Families

In severely disturbed, disengaged families the very opposite tendencies prevail. While the developing adolescent in an enmeshed, centripetal family appears to be caught in sticky flypaper, the adolescent in a disturbed, emotionally disconnected family often experiences a total lack of the affectional glue that might make anyone within the family system want to stay there.

In these rejecting, conflict-ridden households, there are few or no positive, warm emotional alliances between the members of the family. Each person in the system lives on another planet as far as the others are concerned, and most (or all) of them are fueled by intense feelings of rage and disappointment. Here, the primary lesson that is being taught is that one must always keep one's guard up; vulnerability and weakness are bad, unacceptable, and dangerous.

A Family World in Which Anger Feels More Comfortable
Than Neediness

The people in this kind of emotional system learn very early in their lives to be far more comfortable with their anger than they can be with their normal human neediness. The fundamental lesson being driven home is that exposing one's soft underbelly by reaching out to make a positive connection with someone else is hazardous, even stupid behavior. For in emotionally avoidant systems, it is held to be self-evident that everyone is always out to hurt you; expressions of one's negativity are, therefore, the only forms of expression that are safe.

In a world perceived as always unpredictable, baffling, and threatening, the natural desire to form close, warm, loving attachments must be rigorously suppressed and denied. An expression such as "I know you don't give a damn about me, and I don't give a damn about *you*, either" appears to be the safest and most judicious stance a person can take.

In the view of psychiatrist Leonora Stephens, an expert on the Beavers Systems Model, the parents in severely disturbed, disengaged families can be thought of as teaching their children the most important lesson they themselves have ever learned. This is, basically, that the human world is a harsh and merciless place in which one's needs cannot possibly be met, and in which *even experiencing one's neediness can expose one to terrible pain* and to serious emotional damage.

"In Level 5, centrifugal families, the parents or older siblings may beat up the 'crybaby' in order to teach him that weakness and vulnerability are bad," Stephens observed in the course of an extended discussion. In a perverse way, notes the therapist, by showing their anger these parental caretakers are showing their love and concern.

"Anger *is* their mode of caring, and in fact the visible evidence of their involvement," Dr. Stephens points out. "Because if that child didn't really *matter* to you, how could you be driven to distraction by his or her behavior?"

Leaving Home, Disengaged Style

Over time and most inevitably, the growing youngsters in this hostility-driven system internalize the family's rageful mode of relating. They begin to experience themselves as containing few if any tender, loving feelings (just as, in the mirror-image situation, the members of the enmeshed family system have learned to experience themselves as devoid of any angry feelings whatsoever).

Indeed, the children in these families learn to believe that they *need* their rage, not only as a protective shield against their own inner pain but as a means of walling themselves off emotionally from any verbal or physical mistreatment being inflicted upon them. And, unlike the separating and individuating youngsters in an enmeshed system, who are having trouble leaving home, the separating adolescents in a disengaged system often find themselves in the position of being *extruded* from the family—or feeling forced to flee it—much too early in their lives and in the course of their development.

But interestingly enough, despite the apparently stark differences between them, Level 5 enmeshed *and* disengaged families actually do have something very much in common. For *in neither of these troubled emotional systems is the apprentice generation being groomed for an eventual independent adulthood.*

The growing and maturing children are not being prepared for a future in which they will be distinct, separate individuals, connected to but different from the families in which they have been raised. Instead, they are caught in a way of being, neither comfortably able to stay in the family nor comfortably able to leave the family behind them.

The Focus of the Family's Anxieties

Dave Anderson, unready and unprepared as he was to embark upon a life of his own, often threatened to leave home once he reached the age of sixteen. There seemed to be no reason to stay in his eruptive, rage-filled family atmosphere one day longer than was legally required.

In truth, frustration and dissension were everywhere in the Anderson household, and the ubiquitous strain was affecting every one of them. Both the children were, under the circumstances, finding it impossible to meet their own growth and individuation needs in a progressive, orderly fashion. Neither Dave nor Cheryl was paying attention in class, turning in homework assignments, or giving any thought to his or her eventual graduation from high school; the possibility of going on to college or to some form of technical training was far from either youngster's mind. There was such a sense of futility in the air, so much a "What's the use?" kind of feeling that the idea of a better or different tomorrow seemed inconceivable.

And if, at present, Dave was the focus of the family anxieties (and of his deeply disappointed mother's deflected rage), I found it not farfetched to suppose that his younger sister might one day be in a similar position herself. It was, in truth, not hard to imagine that a shockingly unexpected newborn (an out-of-wedlock pregnancy) might lie somewhere in Cheryl's not very distant future.

The Boundary Between the Self and the Other

One might suppose that in such distant and disengaged emotional systems the tendency to cross the boundary between the inner self and the self of someone else in the family would not be very great. In these angry, remote, distant groups, confusing one's own thoughts and feelings with the thoughts and feelings of, say, a spouse or child would seem far less likely than it would in enmeshed, overinvolved emotional systems, where oneness, harmony, and similarity are being emphasized.

But while this is to some degree the case, there do seem to be interpersonal boundary violations in both centripetal and centrifugal families at the lower end of the family developmental ladder. In these Level 5 systems, as Robert Beavers has noted, "it is often difficult to tell who is parent, who is child, or to distinguish between one and another member of such a family as to beliefs, feelings, perceptions and wishes."

Young Dave Anderson certainly did appear, in his mother's eyes, in the guise of the terrifying, powerful male whose lack of control and impulsivity "ran the household" and everyone who lived there; in other words, less like a dependent son than a powerful parent. Dave was indeed the very embodiment of his mother's bad internal presence—the bad father, and then bad husband—who lived inside her and whom she had now gotten outside herself by projecting him onto her adolescent child.

She was fighting out with Dave an internal conflict—a conflict involving a wild, irresponsible, uncaring man—that had been going on within her for much of a lifetime. But which of this mother's beliefs, feelings, perceptions, and wishes about her son really had to do with him, and which of them were efforts to externalize—*and see in Dave*—old dilemmas that existed within her own being? In these chaotic, desperately charged circumstances, it was hard to know where the grown woman's skin truly ended, and where her adolescent son's skin began.

The Internal Tormentor: His True Identity

Susan Anderson's own confusion about the identity of the internal tormentor was further evidenced by the way in which she tended to talk about her son and her husband interchangeably. One sometimes lost the sense of which "bad, impossible male" she was referring to; she spoke of them as if they were one and the same untrustworthy, uncaring human being.

Toward the close of the family session just described, for example, Linda Bowen asked Dave's mother, "Do you think that perhaps just by virtue of *seeing* this pattern—your way of duking out with Dave some of the anger that really belongs in your relationship with your husband—you may in fact be able to alleviate some of those angry feelings?" In these clos-ing moments of the discussion, it should be said, Mrs. Anderson appeared much calmer, potentially more receptive to taking in what was being said to her.

Linda's voice and expression were diffident, and yet she clearly wanted to convey a sense of her own tentative hopefulness. But the mother only frowned, looked at her doubtfully, then looked at me, shook her head, and said dismissively, "I don't think that's where the anger is at all."

I wasn't sure what she meant. "Whose anger?" I asked her.

"Mine. I don't believe I'm angry at him for that. So I don't think that's going to change or to improve."

"Why, then, are you angry at him?" put in Linda. I wasn't sure who "him" referred to, and it seemed to me that the clinician was looking a bit perplexed herself. I felt even more disoriented when Susan Anderson answered coolly and cryptically, "I think a lot of it is just a difference in style."

"A difference between you and Dave?" I asked her, shaking my head slowly in puzzlement. "No, between *Ralph* and myself," she answered impatiently.

Glancing over at Linda, I could see that she seemed momentarily stymied, caught in the family's confusion. "A difference in the way you parent?" she asked after a while.

The mother shrugged. "The way we parent . . . the way we look at life . . . the way we do everything," she said, with a look of helpless yet angry resignation. Her truculent expression seemed to say that while she and her family needed help, and wanted help, the world (and the therapist) had nothing to offer them that could possibly be useful.

"Again," Linda Bowen said quietly, "it's anger that really needs to be between you and your husband, and that gets placed on Dave instead."

But Mrs. Anderson shot down this insight immediately. "A lot of it *is* dealing with Dave, and the things that he does," she said, in a determined tone of voice. She was sticking to the story as she knew it, which was that the major problem in the family was her acting-out, uncontrollable, delin-quent son. But she was sticking to *its reverse* as well, which was that the major problem was her husband, who had deceived his family and who looked at life, parenting, and "everything we do" in ways that were differ-ent, uncaring, and harmful.

Mrs. Anderson was, in other words, directing all of the blame and anger in the world toward her husband without acknowledging that she was at the same time attributing everything bad and destructive in the world to her adolescent child. Such confused, incoherent thinking and communicating reflected the internal chaos that she, and everyone else in this emotionally disengaged, deeply distressed Level 5 family, was experiencing.

The Naked Shift: Stating a Strong Position and Its Reverse Simultaneously

In thus *stating a strong position and simultaneously asserting its opposite*, Susan Anderson appeared to be engaging in a form of verbal sleight-of-hand that the Beavers researchers have termed "the naked shift." According to Beavers, a naked shift occurs when "the statement of one's personal subjective view is followed by the statement of an opposite position, without any of the necessary glue to acknowledge ambivalence."

In the above instance it was, of course, not exactly the two sides of an ambivalent stance that were in question (this would have sounded more like "My impossible son is the source of all my problems; he's the light of my life, and I've adored him from the moment he was born") but the object of the mother's anger that was fluctuating wildly.

Susan Anderson was saying, in almost one and the same breath, that the cause of all the family's pain and distress was her son Dave, and that the cause of all their pain and distress was her husband. But she did, in any event, seem unaware of the maddening inconsistency of her statements, and of the imperative need to reach a stable bottom-line conclusion and to plant her personal flag (however provisionally) at that place.

Individuals who live in severely disturbed emotional systems are often unable to do this. They seem incapable of formulating a clear, individually based stand and saying, "This is what *I* think, feel, believe, am going to do about a certain problem or issue." Or, alternatively, if they do succeed in stating a firm point of view, they often rapidly annul it by moving to another—but logically incompatible—position. And it is this rampant confusion about where anyone actually does stand that contributes to the familial atmosphere of murkiness, futility, and outrage. For, when the nature of reality is provisional and meaning itself is precarious, life feels extremely dangerous and at times even downright crazy.

CHAPTER 5

The Genogram: The Family's Existential Blueprint for Being

A few weeks after Dave Anderson's discharge from Elmcrest, I drove out to see the family at their small suburban house in Glastonbury, Connecticut. As I began unloading my interviewer's gear—tape recorder, colored pencils, sketch pad for working on the family genogram (an overview of the family's relational history)—Dave's mother, father, and sister sat down on the sofa in a row. It was clear that I was to sit in the over-sized chair just opposite them.

Dave himself didn't join us until his mother called him; at her request, he dragged in a rocker from his bedroom. He had a half-smile of welcome on his face, but didn't meet my eye or actually greet me. He simply set the rocking chair down nearest to Cheryl's end of the sofa and dropped into it—not directly next to his sister, but at the dead center of that end of the living room. The tableau thus created was that of a family group (mother, father, daughter) and an outsider.

Dave had situated himself strategically to occupy the center of the group's attention: to bring upon himself the lion's share of praise or blaming. I smiled, not only at him but at each member of the family, then spent a few moments looking around at a semicircle of, most surprisingly, amicable, anticipatory faces.

This was not at all what I'd expected; the Andersons' last session at the hospital had ended in a wild shouting match about the terms and conditions of the home contract (which is basically a negotiated agreement laying out the responsibilities the patient is to assume on his return, the major goals he will be striving for, and the consequences to be expected if he doesn't abide by the rules). In fact, the family mêlée that had erupted in the course of working out the home contract had almost led to Dave's being escorted from the room under guard.

Now, however, I had been ushered into a household that appeared to be under very little strain. "Correct me if I'm wrong, but it looks as if things have been going better since Dave's been home." The Andersons, as if surprised by this comment, looked at one another, then looked back at me and shrugged; nobody, however, said a word.

I turned to Dave, as if obeying the group's unspoken directive that he was the person upon whom I was to focus. "So I'm wondering, is this impression of mine a fairly accurate one?" I asked him.

"Yup," he replied, with a small smile and a backward rock of his chair.

"It's like the tension in the air is gone," put in Cheryl, in a tone of spooky amazement.

What's Changed?

What had brought about this marked shift in the family atmosphere? When I put this question to Dave directly, he merely lifted his shoulders lightly. "No idea," he replied airily, picking up the baseball hat he wore and then replacing it with the brim facing sideways.

I felt a momentary surge of irritation, but when I asked Dave if he believed that certain things in his life had actually changed as a result of his hospitalization at Elmcrest, the teenager answered in a serious tone of voice. "I think a *lot* changed. I don't know what, but things definitely changed . . . My attitude." I waited, but he said nothing further.

"So, you think the most important thing that happened had to do with your own attitude's having changed—is that right?" I said at last.

"I wouldn't say it changed completely"—he sounded as if he were cautioning me—"but it *did* change." Was it my imagination, or was his voice pitched lower, closer to the baritone range, since I'd last seen him? Was it now less a boy's voice than the voice of a grown male? My momentary annoyance had vanished, to be replaced by the natural liking I felt for Dave Anderson.

Glancing over at his parents, I realized that I'd never before seen them regarding their adolescent son with so little exasperation on their faces. I turned to Dave again, asked quietly, "Would you relate this change in your attitude to the fact that you got to express some of your real feelings to your folks—or maybe even to your just having gotten in touch with those feelings yourself?"

He shook his head back and forth slowly, as if to say he had no idea; but at the same time, he shoved his baseball cap around again in such a way that his full face was exposed. It was as if he were telling me that he was ready, now, to make contact.

"Probably," he said at last, in an emotionally present, if somewhat wary, tone of voice. I asked him then if he could help me orient this discussion by talking, as specifically as possible, about *which* feelings he'd been able to get in touch with during his time at Elmcrest.

"Oh, *everything*," he answered, "everything and *anything* that had to do with something I felt—except, basically, anger. The anger *always* came out, but anything else was . . ." He hesitated, then stopped, and I had a mental picture of his unfinished sentence flapping in the air like laundry on a half-empty clothesline.

Then he commenced afresh, saying that when he'd entered Elmcrest, he hadn't trusted anybody or anything. "I didn't trust *myself* to say the things I felt—unless it was being pissed off." Perhaps, he added, he'd had some vague notion that there were other kinds of feelings inside him, but he'd been pretty much out of contact with them, and unable to talk about his feelings with anyone. I was struck by the self-awareness of these remarks.

A real transformation had occurred (or, at least, been initiated), for the angry teenager I'd first glimpsed on the Chapman Unit had been sick with rage, affectively vacant and unreachable. *That* adolescent had been estranged from his inner world, while *this* adolescent seemed to be in real contact with his own psychological insides. Dave seemed, in short, far *less pressured to act out his inner pain and far more capable of thinking about it, feeling it, expressing it verbally.*

I was leaning toward him attentively, like a fisherman trying to reel in a large catch with as much delicacy and care as could be mustered. "Tell me, even more precisely, if you can," I said, "about what the issues actually were—I mean, what kinds of things you might have been feeling, but weren't able to talk to other people about." I smiled, "Aside, of course, from the anger, which you *were* able to communicate."

Dave didn't return my smile, nor did he respond for several moments. "Confusion," he said, at last. "I'm not sure *what* else. Probably, being scared." I stole a look at his mother, who was staring at this nondefiant, nonoppositional son as if she didn't really know him. She didn't look completely pleased.

"Scared of what?" I prompted him.

"Oh, scared of everything. Scared of life, scared of school. Scared of *everything*," he repeated. I asked Dave then if his newfound ability to verbalize his fears and discuss them with other people on the ward—his peers, the staff—had made those feelings seem a little less scary somehow. "I don't know if they got less scary, but I understood them more. To an extent," he added at once. "I understood, at least, some of the things that had really been messing me up."

"Which were?" I asked, believing that I knew quite well what he would say.

He would talk, I felt sure, about the eruption of the family secret, and about the ways in which he and his mother had become partners in rage when it was a "situation" involving his father that was at the real eye of her ongoing fury. He might go back, as well, to the painful subject of the Christmas trains, and of his inability to work out a connected relationship to his father. But Dave alluded to none of the above.

"Oh, my own attitude about who was in control," he answered, and I looked at him in surprise. Had he lost all sense of clarity (perhaps even *memory* itself) about the core family issues that had been discussed during his hospitalization at Elmcrest?

It was as if Dave Anderson had suddenly thrown himself upon the family sword, declaring self-sacrificially, "No matter what else happens, folks, *I* will always be the bad guy and the source of all the hurting and confusion here." The problems in this family (as he was defining them) seemed to have to do with his own bad attitude, and his bad attitude alone.

Lost in Confusion: The Level 5 Family in Pain

Turning back to Dave, I observed that he had indeed undergone real change during his stay on the Chapman Unit, and that the staff members had been well aware of the fact. "Everyone realized that you were getting in touch with your issues; but what I'm wondering now is how much you yourself link this change"—I waved a hand that included everyone in the family—"with the very specific matters that we all talked about together."

As if to indicate that he had no idea what I might be referring to, Dave shook his head; the expression on his face was blank. The major, still unresolved dilemmas, which had been taken out for public inspection during his hospitalization at Elmcrest, had apparently been shoved back under the family rug. And if that was in fact true, then after a post-hospital honeymoon period, the Andersons would eventually return to the status quo ante. Dave would step back into his role of special child, the hub of the family triangle and the cause of all his parents' worries and their anguish.

I waited in silence for the adolescent to meet my eye, but he was now looking down. "You know, we were all together as a group a number of times," I observed softly, "and we discussed a number of issues. We talked about your trying to connect with your dad around the setting up of the trains. We talked about the family secret that was exposed."

I hesitated, then decided not to mention the inflammatory matter of his mother's duking out with Dave what was really anger at his father and "a situation" for which Dave himself was in no way responsible. But I did ask the boy whether any of those discussions had been particularly helpful to him, either in terms of understanding the things that were going on in the family, or in terms of understanding more about the things that were going on inside himself. "Not really," he said, looking up at me with a flat, deadpan expression.

"I mean—yeah, a lot of stuff came out in the open," he amended after a moment, "and, like Cheryl said, a lot of the tension was gone when that happened. . ." His voice trailed off, leaving me feeling suddenly adrift, as if I'd found myself afloat on a raft in a wide, wide sea and unable to locate an orienting horizon.

"I mean, maybe—I don't know," he went on, sounding vague and doubtful. "It's some of *both* things, I suppose—some, that I got to talk; some, that I *heard* some stuff too. It's not just another photo in the photo album, like . . . you know. What I'm thinking about is the picture in my father's desk of my stepbrother—or half-brother, that's what he is, I guess."

Was he alluding to a real photo that might be in his father's desk drawer, or was this a photo of his own imagining? I was feeling lost, without a spar of solid understanding to cling to. And we were in darkly menacing, shoal-filled waters—somewhere between what was known and what was not known, what was talked about and what was not talked about, what was indubitably the most threatening and dangerous material that the family had yet to face clearly and attempt to deal with. But at Level 5, it is clarity itself that is most dreaded.

The Unnoticed Links Between the Past and the Present: Genograms

There is, in my opinion, no mode of approach to the family that is as gentle, noninvasive, and yet powerfully evocative as the technique known as the family genogram. The genogram, first devised by family theorist Murray Bowen, M.D., is in one sense just a simple, straightforward history-taking device, similar to the medical histories taken by physicians. Answers to direct questions are solicited. For example, the medical patient may be asked, "Have you ever had an operation? What for?" and the information thus provided gives the doctor a quick overview of the person's present state of health, and his or her current or potential difficulties.

The same is true of the family genogram; what the researcher or clinician does is ask a series of explicit, if somewhat mundane-sounding, questions. For example, "What is your father's name? Is he living? What kind of work does he do, or has he retired? Can you give me a few adjectives that would capture his particular qualities, such as 'tough,' 'gentle,' 'friendly,' 'reserved'?"

Such questions are direct and straightforward; and yet as the answers accumulate, they tend to produce a deluge of rich associations, half-remembered bits of information, available but never-before-focused-upon memories, and a wide variety of other unpredictable responses. And somehow, in the course of these interviews, the past looms up in ways that often astonish the family members, and I am led, as if by sonar guidance, to the heart of the family's existence.

Clearly, the genogram is, at a superficial level, merely an efficient method of gathering factual information about a particular small group's shared past. And in fact this mode of questioning does succeed in eliciting, rapidly and efficiently, a clear diagram containing a good deal of general information: the names of all the important players in the family, the dates of significant happenings (births, marriages, divorces, deaths, accidents, retirements, illnesses) and a broad-brushed, if admittedly somewhat crude, overview of the family's positive resources and the particularly conflicted areas in which trouble has, historically, tended to develop.

But because the family facts being gathered are laden with emotional associations, this guided interview serves to steer the conversation toward insistent family themes and patterns: divided loyalties; charged issues (alcoholism; marital instability; problems in dealing with separations and losses); and those emotionally laden scripts that tend to reemerge repeatedly within the system. And inevitably, in the course of what seems to be a dry process of data gathering, many seemingly disconnected family facts swim into focus. In many instances, *new* information also emerges—information which an important person in the system has somehow never even heard about earlier (indeed, this happened several times during my series of interviews with the Andersons).

Overall, what the family genogram tends to document and highlight are the myriad (and sometimes uncanny) ways in which people tend to remain deeply loyal and internally committed to the extended family's existential blueprint for being—even when they neither want nor mean to be, and, in some instances, even when they believe they are no longer connected to their families of origin in any way at all.

For, as the family members' relational history over time is gathered and concentrated upon in their presence, what stand out in high relief are the strong but hitherto often unrecognized links between the family's past history and the issues that individuals in the family are struggling with in the present.

A Roistering, Womanizing Man

Life on the Chapman Unit was so pressured and intense that I'd found few opportunities to spend time alone with the senior Andersons during Dave's brief sojourn there. Although I'd met with Ralph and Susan briefly (in the small office that had been put at my disposal during my tenure at the hospital), it was not until my series of home interviews with the family began that I was able to reconstruct the history of what each parent's own early life had been like.

Susan and Ralph Anderson were both small-town kids. Susan had been raised in rural Vermont, and Ralph in a similarly rural area of upstate New York. Both were the children of blue-collar families; Susan's father had, she told me, worked for the railroad. These days she never saw him, and spoke to him on the telephone only once every couple of years. She felt distant from her dad, and they had almost no relationship to speak of.

Her father's second marriage had eventually failed also—because, Susan believed, of his incessant, incorrigible playing around. He was now in his mid-sixties, and married for a third time; she had no idea whether this third marriage had worked out any better than the others, and a shrug of her shoulders let me know that she didn't much care.

Glancing down at the genogram I'd begun constructing, I noted that Susan herself was the eldest child of her father's first, ten-year-long marriage, and asked her if she had any ideas about why her parents' marriage had ended. She nodded and said bleakly, "Because of my father's extramarital affairs, and because he was never around."

Her father sounded like a roistering, womanizing man, I remarked wryly; and to my surprise, this brought an indulgent smile to the middle-aged woman's face. Her father had been married three times, she said, and two of his brides had been pregnant.

"Who was the other wife who was pregnant?" I asked, and when she hesitated, I looked down at the sketch pad on my lap quickly, confirming what I already knew. Susan said, in a flat tone of voice, that she had been born six months after her parents' marriage.

So she herself had been conceived out of wedlock—a perhaps unwelcome, or perhaps ambivalently welcomed, surprise. "Unplanned, unanticipated baby," I noted just above her name on the family genogram.

The Andersons had met one another in the small town in upstate New York where Ralph himself had grown up. Susan, as a single young woman of eighteen, had moved there with a new job as a computer programmer and had a new apartment of her own. When I asked the couple, as I do routinely, to describe the circumstances of that first meeting—and, most particularly, what qualities had first attracted them to each other—the father suddenly tuned into the conversation and came alive in a way I'd never seen him do before.

Mischief Night

Ralph Anderson exchanged a glance with his wife, and they both began laughing. They had met, he told me, on the night before Halloween, when Ralph had been out "raising hell, spraying foam, throwing eggs and stuff" with a crowd of neighborhood kids. Afterward, the whole gang had gone to Susan's. "We all piled into her place, took showers, and cleaned up and got the egg and stuff out of our hair. And that was the first time the two of us ever saw each other."

Ralph laughed again, looking more engaged and interested than I'd ever seen him. They had all come to her apartment, Susan explained with an amused, ironic smile, because she was the only young person anyone knew who happened to have a place of her own. I smiled too; to me, it sounded like such a beguilingly preadolescent story.

I asked Dave's father how old he'd been at the time; to my surprise, he said nineteen, adding, however, that "most of the other guys in the crowd were a good deal younger." I laughed, commented that nineteen seemed to me a wee bit old to be careering around town playing Mischief Night pranks. "Actually, he was twenty," Susan commented dryly; but she laughed, and was clearly enjoying herself.

Ralph leaned forward, explained breezily that he'd "just been out raising hell and doing the kinds of crazy things that young males do." I looked at him for a moment, feeling struck by the strangest, most peculiar notion. When his wife had first encountered the man who would one day become her life partner, it had been on Mischief Night, and he had been running wild—doing "the kinds of crazy things that young males do" and behaving like an overage delinquent. His behavior had, in other words, been reminiscent of that roistering, feckless man who'd been the first loved male in his daughter's life, and the first male who'd ever betrayed her.

Re-creating and Reenacting Charged Themes of Childhood: Marital Collusion

Compared to Susan's family of origin—Yankees who'd lived in the same area of New England for the past thirteen generations—Ralph Anderson's family were comparative newcomers to America. His grandparents had immigrated to this country from Canada; he came from a Scottish-Irish-English background.

I asked Ralph to tell me something about what his *own* father, now in his mid-sixties, was like. Dave's father answered that his own father had always been an extremely hardworking man, someone who'd put in long hours and who'd eventually become a respected jack-of-all-trades in the construction business. I wrote "hardworking" to one side of his father's name on the genogram.

Ralph himself was the oldest of three siblings, two boys (neither of them named after the father) and a youngest girl. His father had, he recounted, worked in a lime quarry for a period of time, and had often had to take a couple of trips during the night to check the pumps—"he'd make sure they were working right and pump the water out. Then, there was one period when he was traveling to a job in Massachusetts; he worked *all the time*, at a variety of stuff—did what he needed to provide."

Then the son appended: "Probably at the expense of a lot of other things."

"Such as?" I inquired, but he merely shrugged.

There was a short silence. "Family-type things," he resumed suddenly, as if out of nowhere. "Instead of working so many hours, he might have had more time to spend with people, and to do things." He fell silent again, but it had been a rare display of real feeling. Had he himself once missed his own father, and yearned for his companionship as much as Dave was yearning for a "real relationship" with him now?

Ralph Anderson's mother, now in her early sixties, had been a full-time housewife and mother until her children reached school age; then she'd worked on a packaging and production line in a factory for a period of time. When asked to give me a couple of adjectives that might best describe her, those that came to her forty-two-year-old son's mind immediately were "nervous" and "overprotective."

Then he said somewhat guiltily, "I had some others in mind a moment ago, but I can't think of them now."

"The first thing that comes to *my* mind," put in Susan with acerbity, "is that she's always worried about what everybody else is going to say and think. 'What will the neighbors think? What will the minister say?' " She made a face, mimicking her mother-in-law's frightened expression. "She only focuses on things *outside* herself. She would never have gotten divorced, because what would the neighbors say about *that* one?" Susan laughed sarcastically.

Was she implying that her mother-in-law would most certainly have opted out of her marriage if she'd only had the courage to do so?

I turned to Ralph. "And what kind of marriage would you say their marriage was—is *now*, for that matter?" He looked at me as if I'd asked him a question in an unknown language, his expression uncomprehending and blank. "Passive resistant," his wife answered for him.

I didn't turn to her, for at that moment I started getting the uncomfortable feeling that Ralph was receding from this conversation, going away somewhere inside. I fixed my gaze upon his deep-set light-gray eyes as intently as I could, experiencing as almost physical the struggle to keep his attention. "Passive resistant," I repeated her words aloud and slowly.

Why was he retreating, renouncing the authority to speak for himself so readily? "His father just *leaves* if he doesn't like what's going on," Susan added to her original comment.

Ralph Anderson sat there saying nothing, even though it was *his* life that was under discussion; he himself seemed to have nothing to add or to contribute. I kept my eyes fixed steadily upon his, but found him well able to meet my gaze in the absence of any real interpersonal engagement. I could feel my sense of discomfort growing.

"And it's your mother who *makes* what's going on happen?" I was struggling hard to maintain the semblance of an interaction with someone who didn't feel as if he were really present. "I don't know that I'd describe it exactly that way. I think a lot of it is what you might call 'tolerance,' " he answered blandly. "I think my father's very tolerant in terms of doing things *her* way, and doing them when *she* wants to do them."

His parents' marriage was, according to this thumbnail description, one that certainly bore some resemblance to his own. For his marriage to Susan, as Ralph had portrayed it, was a relationship between an overly "nervous" woman and a more "tolerant" male spouse. Next to his father's name on the family genogram, I added to "hardworking" the words "tolerant" and "passive resistant."

If Susan Anderson had imported significant aspects of her own past into this marriage, her husband had not neglected to bring in parts of his own childhood in his original family as well. But then such collusions to re-create and reenact certain charged themes of childhood, which involve a mutual exchange of projections, always do require the participation of *two* interested parties.

As many clinicians and theorists have noted, marital partners often come together to elaborate upon certain missing, deeply unconscious, parts of their earlier life narratives. And together, they recapitulate certain critical scenarios from the past—or some ingenious variation upon those charged scenarios—not only in the service of mastering the past, but often simply as part of an unconscious effort to *understand* what has happened. (See Chapter 10, "Re-creating the Pain of the Past: An Attempt at Resolution.")

Negative Maternal Attention and Intrusive Caring

I am glad I had the wit or presence of mind to ask Ralph Anderson which issues, in particular, his father had been more "tolerant" about. "Oh, it was just that, you might say my mother was a worrier," he said. "And something that might spark her and get her going was—I got the picture, or got the feeling, anyhow—not of major consequence to *him*."

He believed, he added in a philosophic aside, that fathers in general tend to be more lenient toward their sons than mothers ever are. His own mother had certainly responded in exaggerated ways to what had been no more than normal teenage antics on his own part. "I was just doing the kind of young male things that people have done *forever* when they're growing up," he declared, a spark of animation returning to his voice.

His father's stance had been that of the listener. "He always listened, always heard her out, but he probably didn't voice a lot of judgments." Ralph grew silent, a gloomy expression on his face. I wondered if he believed that his father's judgments, if ever voiced, would have come down on his own side.

The bottom line had been, in any case, that Ralph's dad had never taken any clear-cut stand for or against him at all. While his mother had been trying to ride herd on her adolescent son's behavior, Ralph's father had stood back and "held the coats" in what sounded like an ongoing quarrel between a nervous maternal parent and a maturing young male with a few wild oats to sow.

"What do you think your mother feared you might do?" I asked Ralph Anderson directly. He jumped slightly, as if startled by the forthrightness of the question. How well the flanks of his accessibility were guarded! How rarely anyone—and this included practiced members of the Elmcrest staff—tried to penetrate the invisible protective shield with which he surrounded himself. Ralph Anderson was certainly skilled, as the children of invasively overprotective parents often are, in the technique of being absent while present as a means of emotional survival.

"Oh, get into trouble, probably," he answered, after a brief pause. "Drink too much. Get into an accident or get hurt in some kind of fight." He laughed scornfully and, for that moment, looked as defiant and oppositional as his son.

Despite his mother's suspicious nagging and constant complaining, Ralph added, he had always been well behaved—"relative to being that age, of course." He had, in fact, been a quite responsible young person, he asserted. The edge of irritation was creeping back into his voice, I noticed—with relief, for it meant that he was staying involved.

"My mother was really *very* overprotective"—he leaned forward in his seat, elbows propped on his knees—"and she had a real hard problem with the leaving-the-nest syndrome." Even earlier, he added, she'd been much harder on him than on his siblings; he hadn't even been allowed to go out and play with the kids in the neighborhood. "If the kids wanted to come to our house, that was fine, and . . ." He shrugged, but left the sentence uncompleted.

The father's voice, alive momentarily with irritation, now began winding down on an even, flat, and explanatory note, as if an inner battery were running out of juice. As a child, Ralph Anderson seemed to have had a specially charged meaning for his mother—like Dave, who was the potentially out-of-control bad boy in this generation. The parent, like his son, had received a goodly share of negative maternal attention and intrusive caring.

I gazed at Ralph thoughtfully, trying to imagine just *why* his mother had seemed so sure this son needed constant watching and around-the-clock supervision. "Do you think your mother ever worried about you getting into any trouble that was specifically sexual in nature—getting some girl-friend pregnant, perhaps?" I asked him.

Ralph nodded; the ghost of a smile flickered across his face. He uncrossed his legs, then recrossed them with the bottom leg now on top. "Oh, yes. Yes, indeed. I remember, in fact, that when I told her that Susan and I were getting married, she asked me if we were doing it because we *had* to." He laughed, but Susan, sitting next to her husband on the sofa, jumped as if she'd been touched with a cattle prod. Clearly, she'd never heard any mention of this particular dialogue before.

She turned her entire torso, looked at her husband briefly, then swiveled back to face me. Her eyes, a tawny brown with yellow lights in them, were glinting angrily. Fixing her gaze upon mine, she leaned toward me and said bitingly, "Ralph's kid sister, Karen—*kid*, she's almost forty now!—has never gotten married, but she does have a child. It's an out-of-wedlock child, the kid of some guy that she hardly even knew—some Mexican—almost like a one-night stand. She's been in California now, for a few years, hiding out." She shot another tight-lipped look at her husband, who only nodded.

"Quite a few years," he agreed composedly.

"Does your mother know about your sister's baby?" I asked Dave's father. But before he could respond, Susan turned to him and demanded harshly, "How old is this kid—three? Two or three, certainly, before your mother found out that he even *existed*."

She turned back to me, added acidly, "His folks never talk about this baby, nor do they talk about the other one—*his* illegitimate child." She compressed her fingers into the familiar hitchhiker's position, thumb pointing in her spouse's direction. "They just *pretend* that none of this ever happened, and that those kids aren't even on this planet," she added.

"So," I said to Ralph quietly, "your parents do know about your out-of-wedlock son?" He nodded. "Then your folks have two grandchildren whom they have pretty much nothing to do with?" I asked him in the same quiet voice.

He answered calmly, "Yes, I guess you might say so."

Discardable Children, Partners, Parents, and Entire Families

So Ralph Anderson's parents had not only one, but two illegitimate grandchildren. And, for a woman like his mother, who'd been described as highly preoccupied with keeping up appearances and much concerned about respectability, this was a curiously high score indeed. Out-of-wedlock births were a pervasive issue in this family; so were half-disclosed secrets. It occurred to me then that Ralph himself, who "believed" he'd been born about a year after his parents' marriage, might have been an illegitimate child also. He had certainly held some special meaning for his mother, who'd treated him differently from his siblings.

I was staring down at the family genogram. "So many unexpected or unwanted or unacknowledged or abandoned babies in this system," I murmured. I didn't actually realize, until I heard the odd, strained sound of my voice, just how unnerved I was feeling. The issue of the "unwanted, unexpected baby" was like a bridge across time, affectively linking each generation to the next one.

It was as if these extracurricular babies—these human remnants of transitory or failed relationships—were being extruded from the family's consciousness like so much unwanted debris. The entire extended emotional system seemed to be permeated by the sense that expendable infants and discardable children, partners, parents, and entire families, for that matter, could be banished somehow, shipped off to some parallel universe that was paradoxically both within the family's orbit and outside its boundaries completely.

In this family, it was hard to say which people were actually in the emotional system and which were outside it—and this is, it should be said, a frequent characteristic of the severely disturbed and emotionally distanced, Level 5 system. Unlike the too-tight and confining boundary of the enmeshed family, which restrains its maturing members and won't allow them to leave, the boundary of the seriously disturbed, disengaged family often seems to be too loose, to lack any clear-cut boundary demarcating it from the world outside it.

In these disjointed, emotionally disconnected families, so many different people—ex-husbands and ex-wives, children of other marriages and liaisons, casual girlfriends and boyfriends, grandparents and other substitute parents—seem to drift onto the family stage for a time and then drift off into obscurity once again. The Andersons were, in comparison to many other disengaged families at this developmental level, relatively high functioning and intact; the adult cast was relatively unchanging.

Still, the question "Who are the members of this family?" would clearly not have been a simple one to answer. Was Ralph Anderson's illegitimate son—clearly related to Dave and Cheryl by ties of blood—to be thought of as in this family or out of it? How much of himself was the father putting into that relationship? For that matter, was that son a National Merit Scholar or a low-performing dropout? And what about the boy's mother? Was she in some sense related to this family, or was she not? Most important of all, how, practically speaking, did the "real" Anderson family mean to deal with the existence of the family in upstate New York?

These were matters that the Andersons, as a group, still seemed utterly unable to confront.

But over time, underneath the ricocheting anger and the confusingly incoherent, always unresolvable family quarrels, I sensed pain and a growing panic that seemed to become ever more insistent over the course of the succeeding months. During the post-Elmcrest honeymoon period, the issue of the shadow family had been stowed away; but, as I'd feared, there was no chance that it could stay there and fester without polluting the entire family atmosphere eventually.

And sure enough, by May Cheryl was telling me privately that she'd been trying desperately to learn more about her half-brother, but that her father refused to answer her questions. Dave reported that he and his mother were spending all their time in the family's weekly outpatient therapy sessions arguing and battling; he felt he was "back on the road to hell" and would be rehospitalized within the course of the coming year. Susan Anderson told me that she had no idea whether or not her husband was in contact with his other family at this time—he claimed that he never saw them, but she suspected that he did—and Ralph Anderson stonewalled in our private conversations and told me nothing whatsoever.

CHAPTER 6

Closely Connected People: The Family Script, Projective Identification, and Paradoxical Tasks

The Andersons were entangled in an old family script, a present-day reenactment of elements of the parents' conflicted early love attachments. Susan's script, generated in her original family, revolved around a relationship between an abandoned daughter and her uncaring, sexually out-of-control dad. Ralph Anderson's script, taken from his own early life, had to do with a "nervous, worrying, overinvolved mother" (the role in which his wife was now cast) and with a "more tolerant, emotionally distant father" (his own role). Fifteen-year-old Dave was a figure with whom both parents were deeply familiar, the "defiant young male"—the male who, in both their family scripts, is being reined in, but wants to sow his wild oats and run free.

This re-creation of distressing but deeply familiar scenarios, containing key elements from both parents' early histories, was being evoked by means of an extraordinary psychological mechanism—one that is ubiquitous in family life: "projective identification." The way in which this psychological process operates involves one individual's projecting into an intimately connected other (a marital partner, a particular child) certain stoutly denied, repudiated aspects of the projector's own inner being.

This displacement of what is inside the self into what is outside the self occurs at an unconscious level. The person who is doing the projecting then begins to interact with the other individual as if he or she were the very embodiment of the thoughts, feelings, and ideas that the projector is so steadfastly disavowing and disinheriting.

The Concept of Projective Identification: Seeing in the Other What Cannot Be Tolerated in the Self

When it comes to making sense of what happens between people involved in close relationships, there is no concept more powerful and explanatory than the concept of projective identification. An awareness of this psychological process can, in my own view, provide a view of the underlying scaffolding of long-term emotional attachments that could never be achievable otherwise.

As a term, "projective identification" has, admittedly, a somewhat intimidating sound. But it can be explained, and becoming informed about the concept is well worth the minimal learning effort involved. For, once a real appreciation of this phenomenon has been absorbed (at both the intellectual and emotional levels), a remarkably useful way of understanding what goes on in long-term love attachments will have been added to one's repertoire of interpersonal skills.

First of all, let it be said that no single, universally accepted definition of projective identification is currently available; instead, there is a large, still-mushrooming clinical literature about the meaning of the term and about how this psychological process operates. Projective identification has, moreover, been widely written about under a number of differing guises and aliases—such as "irrational role assignment," "trading of dissociations," "externalization," "defensive delineation," "evocation of a proxy," "the family projection process," and "scapegoating." Indeed, the process called "delegation," which was described a bit earlier—and which involves a parent seeing in an adolescent child denied and disowned aspects of his or her own inner reality—is indistinguishable from projective identification.

But basically, whatever name one may give to it, projective identification is a defensive process of the ego—in other words, a psychological maneuver that a person uses in order to defend himself or herself from experiencing inner pain and conflict. What this defense mechanism involves is the projection of a denied, unwanted, and unrecognized aspect of the self into an intimately connected other (a spouse, parent, sibling, child, even a close friend), in whom this missing piece of the self is then "rediscovered."

Projective identification is, in brief, a way of ridding oneself of unacceptable parts of one's inner world (such as anxiety, deep sadness, feelings of frailty and inadequacy, suppressed rage) and then perceiving in someone else's thoughts, feelings, expressions, and behavior what one simply cannot tolerate or take ownership of, as part of one's own inner being.

In certain instances, as theorists John Zinner and Roger Shapiro have pointed out, it is not the despised but the cherished aspects of themselves that family members have split off and projected into others within the group. A mother may, for example, see her daughter as happy and popular, and refuse to recognize aspects of the girl that are in fact sad, lonely, and despairing. It is as if the mother has projected the most positive parts of her inner world (her most treasured dreams and unmet longings) into her offspring for a kind of emotional safekeeping. She cannot then respond realistically to her daughter's real problems, shortcomings, and failures, for she cannot countenance the daughter's being different from the way in which she herself needs to see her.

Far more frequently, however, it is the negative, repudiated aspects of the projector's self—such as a profound sense of his or her own unacceptability—that are split off and "located" in the unconscious projection's receiver. And if that individual happens to be a dependent child, she or he will often oblige by being hopelessly shy and awkward, growing fat, becoming delinquent or school-phobic, or developing other social and interpersonal problems. The child's strong tendency will be to meet the internally conflicted parent's expectations and be the unacceptable, undesirable individual in his or her stead.

What motivates the child to collude with the parent in this way? As Zinner and Shapiro explain, "From the very formation of a new family, unconscious assumptions exert an important influence on behavior. Marital choice is motivated by a desire to find . . . [a love] . . . object who will complement and reinforce unconscious fantasies. Prior to their birth, children are introduced into their parents' fantasies, and from birth onward, a variety of parental coercions interact with the child's own . . . [temperament] to fix him as a collusive participant in the family's hidden agenda."

Given the family drama, they explain, with its fabric of conscious and unconscious themes, and an actively engaged but often unwitting cast, it is by means of projective identification that certain family roles are created and maintained. For the needful child's strong tendency is to *accept* the parent's projections, *identify* with the parent's expectations, and *become* what the parent expects or needs him to become. This is true throughout the dependent years of childhood, but especially true at the nodal point of adolescence, when the process of identity formation is rapidly accelerating.

A Wonderful Transformation of "What Is Part of Me" into "What Is Definitely *Not* Part of Me"

To take another example of this phenomenon in action, let us say that a father, in order to avoid confronting his own denied feelings of vulnerability, ineffectiveness, and unmanliness, sees in his scholarly adolescent son the very embodiment of the cowardly sissy—someone who is hope-lessly undefended, fainthearted, and passive. The parent, who perceives himself as strong, masculine, and in control, may then become preoccu-pied with worries about his son's deficiencies and weaknesses. Furthermore, not only will the father see in his son the frail and sissified individual he himself fears being; he will start interacting with the young-ster as though the boy were the living realization of his own deepest fears about male failure and inadequacy. In other words, the "strong and robust" parent sees in his "weakling" of a son those inner feelings of inept-ness, uncertainty, and unmasculine fragility that he himself is so stead-fastly denying and disavowing.

In such a situation, I must hasten to add, the father has by no means made a conscious decision to think the thoughts he is thinking and behave in the way that he is behaving. On the contrary, as noted earlier, this displacement of what is inside the self to what is outside the self (but located nearby, in a closely connected other) occurs at an unconscious level. What is involved here is one person's defending himself from a painful internal conflict—in this case, a conflict about male adequacy—by projecting outward certain anxiety-laden aspects of his own inner experi-ence and then perceiving them as existing only in his adolescent offspring.

In the above instance the father has, by means of projective identifica-tion, effected a wonderful transformation of "what is part of me" into "what is definitely *not* part of me"; he is, in fantasy, splitting off and subtracting a piece of his own subjective self and adding this unwanted part of his inner world to the projection's recipient, his son. Weakness, vulnerability, being "too soft" are now seen, by the hale and sturdy parent, as integral parts of his maturing child's own subjectivity. Then—and this is crucial to the process—*the youngster will be subtly cued, goaded, and pres-sured into feeling and behaving in ways that are congruent with his parent's fantasies about him.*

This insistent interpersonal coercion to feel, think, and act in ways that will verify the projector's fantasy is by no stretch of the imagination an imaginary one. "This is," as psychologist Thomas Ogden has observed in his classic article "On Projective Identification," "*real pressure* [my italics] exerted by means of a multitude of interactions between the projector and the recipient."

A Ventriloquist and His Dummy

It would be convenient to envision the process of projective identification in terms of Edgar Bergen and Charlie McCarthy—that is, in terms of a ventriloquist and his dummy. Let us suppose, for instance, that there is a wife who views herself as gentle, soft-spoken, mild-mannered, and never angry, but who is in fact struggling with deep feelings of unconscious rage. In order to deal with her own sternly submerged hostile feelings (which, like all repressed feelings, are insistently pressing for recognition, but about which she feels highly conflicted), the wife may think, feel, and behave in impeccably nonaggressive, reasonable, controlled, and rational ways, while recognizing anger only as it becomes manifest in the behavior of her overbearing, short-fused, and sometimes totally out-of-control mate.

If this marital pair is involved in a projective-identification relationship (if she is never angry and he is always quick to anger, the likelihood of this is very high), the wife can be understood to be making a circuitous, second-hand, Rube Goldberg–like connection with her own unconscious wrath and rage by way of the hostile expressions of her mate. It is primarily through his angry behavior—about which she assuredly feels extremely critical, but with which she unconsciously identifies—that she can make contact with those dissociated aspects of her own inner experience about which she feels so painfully conflicted.

It is, furthermore, primarily through the medium of his outbursts that she is able to achieve at least some partial release of her own thoroughly repudiated and disavowed rageful feelings. Suppose, however, that the designated recipient of this never-angry wife's projective fantasy (whom she relies upon to speak her anger for her) doesn't actually happen to be feeling the least bit irritable when she needs him to express angry emotions on her behalf. Rest easy: If the couple is involved in a projective-identification system, he is likely to be feeling quite furious about something very quickly. And, in the ensuing debacle, the wife (the ventriloquist) can truly be said to be operating her partner's strings, while her easily ignited spouse is both experiencing and expressing her anger for her.

The husband is also, it should be recognized, protecting her from the pain of confronting her own internal conflict—which may have to do with her having learned that the normal anger everyone feels from time to time is thoroughly unacceptable in a female—by assuming the starring role in any and all of their angry scenarios. It is as if, when there is rage in the atmosphere to be vented (his own or his partner's), the responsibility for feeling it and giving it expression is the husband's and the husband's alone. He serves as the Charlie McCarthy of the relationship—or at least he does so insofar as emoting angrily is concerned.

Where Does the Self End and the Other Begin?

If the male partner, in the above example, is doing something for his intimate partner (expressing her anger), she is always sure to be doing something for him as well. In marital projective-identification systems, there is never a unidirectional process afoot; there is always a subliminal barter in which two interested participants are involved. For, unlike the parent-offspring projective-identification system, in which the vulnerable, dependent child has been inducted and trained into a particular role, the spouses were initially attracted to each other by the realization that they could strike an unconscious deal.

It is therefore fair to say that if a husband is colluding with his wife to take over split-off parts of her inner world, she is sure to be carrying certain denied, disavowed feelings and attitudes of his (perhaps his feelings of sadness, vulnerability, and weakness) that cannot be tolerated at the level of conscious awareness.

Projective-identification systems involve unconscious trade-offs, and it is for this very fundamental reason that a profound confusion between self and other inevitably develops at the very heart of projector-receiver relationships. For if the quick-to-anger husband in the above example is required to experience and to enact his partner's rageful feelings for her, where can it be said that *his* inner world ends and *her* inner world begins?

And how can he, if she is carrying his denied feelings of helplessness, perhaps even of frank despair, ever begin to take inner ownership of the denied sorrow that is truly within his own being?

As long as she embodies and expresses all the grief and neediness in the relationship (she is the ventriloquist's dummy, here) he can never make conscious contact with his own feelings of sadness: never explore them, think about them, learn more about them—and, above all, *never ask to be comforted in his sorrow.*

In projective-identification systems, which always involve mutual distortions of both the self and the other, the very tangible interpersonal dilemma that emerges—and that creates endless marital and family woe—is that *the anxiety-laden internal conflict that one person is experiencing becomes transposed and transformed into the ongoing strife between two or more people.*

Where Speech Is an Instrument of Unhappy Interactions: Level 5 Families

As my series of interviews with the Andersons continued, it became ever clearer that Dave's role in the family script—that of the out-of-control delinquent male troublemaker—was one that he was always prepared to play at a moment's notice. In the natural setting of his home, he was growing ever more surly; I sometimes found it hard to remember that during most of his hospitalization, this teenager had been cooperative, empathic with his peers, able to keep up with his schoolwork, rarely angry, and never explosive.

But as the months of spring gave way to early summer, fermenting pressures in the household seemed to be insistently demanding that an angry, rebellious, self-loathing troublemaker reappear on the scene. Dave was behaving in a myriad of ways well calculated to provoke rejection and punishment; I myself was wondering what had become of the clearly troubled, frightened, but essentially likable adolescent who'd talked so candidly and thoughtfully about himself, and about his life, during his brief sojourn on the ward.

Perhaps, I speculated, this teenager's experiences in his primary family had taught him that being "the incorrigibly bad one" was his only ticket of admission into *any* kind of relationship with either of his parents; perhaps Dave's "badness" had brought him the only attention and sense of personal efficacy that were available. For it is true that from the dependent, needful child's point of view, *any* relationship—even a pathological relationship—will always be preferable to the horror of having *no* way of connecting to the parental caregiver at all. (See Part Three, "The First Loves of Our Lives.")

Over time, the subject of Ralph Anderson's second family seemed to have receded into the shadows; to my knowledge, it had hardly been discussed since Dave's hospitalization. So, shortly before our interviews were to conclude, I decided to raise the subject at a family meeting at which all members were present. "Have you talked to the kids any more about their half-brother?" I asked the father directly. "Or has the subject not come up again since that session at Elmcrest?"

Mr. Anderson met my gaze levelly and cleared his throat, then replied, "I don't think it's come up very much. I did talk with Cheryl that same night, perhaps, about one or two things—more curiosity things than anything else. But it hasn't really come up, otherwise." He sounded remote.

"Have you talked with Dave about it too?" I inquired calmly.

The father looked at a corner of the ceiling for a moment, then said, "I think maybe we did talk, one time in the car. Not in specifics, but in generalizations . . . He didn't really have any questions. But we have talked about it some, yes," he answered evasively.

I asked Ralph Anderson if he'd found it a relief to have the whole matter out in the open. Was he more comfortable now, knowing that he wasn't carrying this loaded piece of information around in a private satchel, and that everyone in the family was at least aware of it? Or, I inquired, would he have preferred that the information *never* come out?

The middle-aged parent, urbane and unfazed, crossed and recrossed his legs, then answered neutrally, "I think it's probably better that it's out. I don't really think of it as a *relief*, because I don't picture that as having been the problem. We—Susan and I—did talk about it, after leaving Elmcrest that evening, and we don't, either one of us, think of it as a real relevant issue." As he spoke, my gaze slid over to Dave's younger sister, whose eyes were rolling wildly as if she'd just heard the most improbable and patently absurd statement imaginable.

The sight of her silly pantomime made me smile. "Does someone else here think this *is* a relevant issue?" I asked her; she only giggled, didn't reply. "Cheryl, your eyes are rolling around in your head like marbles," I said, and the twelve-year-old giggled again. "What is it supposed to be relevant *to*?" she asked me, in a slyly innocent tone of voice.

Dave suddenly started laughing, slapping his thigh, for reasons that were not clear to me. I was, I realized, starting to feel a bit queasy, as if reality itself were rolling beneath me and I were experiencing a kind of existential seasickness. It was as if I'd suddenly become a member of this incoherent emotional system, and my own innate sense of the orderliness of things was somehow being negated and demolished. Language itself seemed to be being used in a somewhat perverse, disinformational style.

According to Dr. John Zinner, a pioneer of the psychoanalytically oriented family therapy movement, it is ordinarily in conversation with one another that family members "share their feelings and increase their understanding of one another's fears, longings, and perceptions." In highly troubled family systems, however, the view that talking is an invaluable resource is often completely nonexistent.

In these families, as psychotherapist Zinner has written, "talking has lost its positive communicative and expressive value. Instead, speech has become an instrument of unhappy interactions—a vehicle for expressing aggression, for engendering guilt, for acting out competitive urges, for lowering self-esteem." Instead of being seen as a means of clarifying issues and improving reciprocal understanding, saying what one actually thinks is viewed, says Zinner, "as a hazardous venture which is very likely to lead to a catastrophic outcome."

Certainly, in the Anderson family, talking often seemed to be a way of generating anxiety, confusion, and haziness—of inundating ordinary common sense and coherence in an overflow of ambiguous, self-contradictory verbiage. This is typical of severely disturbed, incoherent, Level 5 systems: Talking doesn't seem to serve the purpose of making things clearer and better; it seems, very frequently, to make the facts themselves unreliable and capricious, leaving one feeling helplessly confounded.

I turned, gazed at Mrs. Anderson, who seemed distracted and was being uncharacteristically quiet. "Susan, what are you thinking about? You seem so . . . absorbed," I said in a friendly tone of voice. It was an effort, on my part, to back away from the hot topic of her husband's other child and of the family in upstate New York, for it was around this subject that the incoherent, crazy-making talk and Dave's inappropriate laughter had in fact erupted.

A familiarly tight, irritated expression spread itself across the mother's features immediately. "I think it's more some people's *actions* that cause the problems here," she stated, looking at her son grimly and meaningfully. "As for the other stuff, I, too, don't think of that as having really been a relevant piece."

I drew in a sharp breath, trying not to look as startled as I felt. How could it not be relevant? Furious as Susan Anderson had declared herself to be about "a situation," she was now summarily dismissing the importance of her children's half-sibling and of the other family that *this* family was supporting financially. Even though she herself had lobbied to reveal the story openly—and had then declared her husband's betrayal to be in the realm of the "unforgivable"—she was maintaining that this issue was "irrelevant" to everything else that was happening in the family at this time.

"To be honest," she continued energetically, fixing a baleful look upon Dave, "I don't think that there's *ever* as much tension in the house when a certain person makes at least *some* effort at compliance with rules as there is when every single minute is devoted to defying *every rule that was ever made.*" The fault, in other words, lay with Dave.

Then, breaking the angry glare, Susan turned back to me once again. "David's *whole life* is dedicated to being negative and oppositional," she stated firmly, as if to eradicate once and for all any lingering doubts on this subject that I might be harboring. It was as if she were letting me know that a wild, angry, delinquent son was the only kind of son that could belong to her.

Obviously, whatever understanding of their truly pressing, vital issues the Andersons might have gleaned during Dave's hospitalization had simply vanished in the family quicksand. The family-wide fantasy that Dave and Dave alone was at the root of all their difficulties—and that if he straightened up, all of their problems would vanish—continued to hold sway. And to this end, a colossal shared emotional blindness was necessary.

The Family Myth as Emotional Thermostat

As psychiatrist Antonio J. Ferreira observed in his acclaimed paper "Family Myth and Homeostasis," a family system's overarching myth tends to be "called into play whenever certain tensions reach predetermined thresholds among family members and in some way, real or fantasied, threaten to disrupt ongoing relationships. Then, the family myth functions like the thermostat that is kicked into action by the 'temperature' in the family. Like any other homeostatic mechanism, the myth prevents the family system from damaging, perhaps destroying itself."

In other words, the family's inner image of itself—however illusory or misguided that inner image or myth may be—functions as a kind of safety valve. The family's myth is, suggests Ferreira, a "survival mechanism," a belief-based glue that serves to bind the emotional system together, no matter how tenuously a family's mythic image of itself may correlate with reality.

And in point of fact, the crucial significance of the family myth as safety valve had never been clearer to me than it was at that particular moment; the Andersons had never responded with so united a voice before. The father's response, when I'd asked him if he'd had more discussions with his children about their half-sibling, had been to meet my eye coolly and tell me that the topic wasn't "relevant"; Cheryl had begun making faces and clowning; Dave had started laughing crazily, at nothing in particular; and Susan Anderson had chimed in to agree that the subject was an irrelevant one.

This family's deeply held myth, which was that *Dave's behavior was the cause of all the pain and trouble in the household*, evidently had to be maintained no matter what the costs of maintaining this myth might be.

Man of Mystery

What felt odd to me was that the more time I spent with the father of this family, the less I felt I knew him. Generally speaking, Ralph Anderson was affable enough, but he often seemed to be a spectator of what was happening in the family rather than an affected participant. At times, he even seemed like an undercover agent—someone who was living his life as if he were on a highly secret mission and would be exposed to grave danger if his real identity, thoughts, feelings, wishes, and motives were ever to be sorted out and known.

It wasn't that this parent retreated into silence. Ralph did speak, and in fact from time to time would take the floor and launch into lengthy, moralizing orations. These usually occurred when I was talking with the entire family, and the extemporaneous lecture was always directed toward Dave (whose response was to tune his father out). I, too, felt myself tuning out emotionally, for it wasn't clear how much of what the father said was actually *meant*; the voice with which these dull, rote recitations were delivered simply didn't feel authentic.

Perhaps this parent's occasional harangues about such things as "responsibility" and "living up to expectations" were a form of atonement to his spouse for his own bad, irresponsible behavior. I wasn't sure, and to be frank, I never could quite resolve the question of whether Ralph Anderson meant a bit of what he said in these occasional rebukes, or whether he was, in fact, subliminally cheering his defiant, boldly masculine son onward. It was simply impossible to come anywhere near penetrating this secretive parent's "cover"; what I knew about Ralph Anderson, I knew at the most superficial level, and even this information was, to some degree, suspect.

Certainly, the nature of his relationship with that shadowy other family remained unclear to me; nor did Susan and the children appear to know much more than I did. They must, I thought, be feeling as excluded and shut out by him as I was, and I was certainly feeling increasingly frustrated and ignored.

As mid-June approached, my interviews with the Andersons were drawing toward their natural termination; I was, moreover, about to go away on a long working vacation. But as the time for my departure neared, I found myself feeling increasingly concerned about them. I was not only worried, but feeling guilty as well: Walking away from the family, at that point in time, felt disturbingly like walking away from the scene of an accident.

The Andersons were, as I knew, in a weekly outpatient therapy group, but their family therapy didn't appear to be helping. I was leaving, and they were seeming ever more hopelessly stuck. It was at this tense, distressing juncture that, providentially, I happened to get in touch with a colleague and highly valued mentor, psychiatrist Leonora Stephens, for it was Leonora who made the wonderful suggestion that I leave each member of the Anderson family with a "gift"—the gift of a personalized therapeutic homework assignment.

Bypassing the Family's Resistance to Change: Therapeutic Tasks

Severely disturbed families will predictably show an almost automatic resistance to change, for these systems are pervaded by the dread that truth-telling may lead to terrible consequences. Thus, while life within the family world may be painful, the people in the system are at least dealing with the devil they know. The feeling is that dealing with the devil they *don't* know—confronting their issues directly—carries the risk of totally intolerable outcomes.

For example, a once-deserted daughter like Susan Anderson might, if she were ever to confront her rage at the present-day betraying male in her life, unleash a boundless, limitless fury and find herself being utterly abandoned again. This is why she was so stuck in her own unresolved and unresolvable ambivalence—in her desire for change, and her profound opposition to real change ever taking place.

Level 5 emotional systems are locked in place by fear—by fear, and by the deep belief that if things stay just as they are, they surely won't get much better but at least they won't become completely intolerable. A woman who, like Susan Anderson, has been completely abandoned in her girlhood, fears nothing more than being abandoned once again—no matter how empty and unrewarding the relationship may be.

The basic issue that severely disturbed families are struggling with is the need to achieve clarity; but, at the same time, clarity is what everyone in the system is also struggling actively to avoid. For while the members of the system may be finding the ongoing chaos almost unbearable, there is an important sense in which they all experience the turmoil as vitally protective and necessary.

The reason is, very simply, that thinking clearly and confronting issues forthrightly may lead to unthinkable outcomes. Therefore, disturbing and repugnant though the endless conflict in the family may be, it still feels safer to deny, avoid, and obfuscate the fundamental issues rather than to take the chance of facing them—and it is here, around the problem of resistance, that therapeutic tasks can prove remarkably handy.

For these simple clinical "homework assignments" are essentially devices that can be used effectively to bypass the emotional system's inherent resistance to change of any kind (which of course includes the resistance to improvement). Therapeutic tasks are designed to give the members of the family a taste of the honey of what life could be like if everyone did things just a little bit differently.

Be warned: At first blush these tasks may sound peculiar; in practice however, they often prove to be amazingly powerful curveballs. In any case, the following set of therapeutic assignments, devised jointly by myself and Dr. Leonora Stephens for the members of the Anderson family, will serve as exemplars of what these homework tasks are like, how they are used to bypass the family's unconscious resistance to change, and why they exert their sometimes quite miraculous effects. (A more general discussion of clinical homework tasks, and many other examples, can be found in Chapter 21, "Family Tasks.")

A Set of Personalized Therapeutic Assignments

Task 1. For the "the man of mystery"—the remote, solitary, and emotionally detached father of the family, the following assignment was worked out. Mr. Anderson's task was to schedule a fifteen-minute press conference once a week, during which he would respond to his wife and children's many unanswered questions, including questions about their recently discovered half-sibling and about the family that lived in upstate New York.

The family members attending the press conference were, as I instructed them, to formulate their questions carefully, just as real reporters at a presidential press conference might do. They were, in brief, to respect the fifteen-minute limit for receiving the answers to questions that actually were on everyone's mind, even though at present no one was discussing them openly.

This weekly press conference would, as I explained it to the father, give all the members of the family—particularly the children—a structured space of time in which to ask him the many things they'd been too hesitant or too fearful to ask before. (One question of intense concern to Cheryl, as she had confided in a private interview, was whether—*and when*—she and Dave would ever get to meet their half-brother.)

Task 2. The therapeutic task designed for Susan Anderson, whose self-other boundaries were weak and blurry, was to stop focusing so exclusively upon all the irresponsible men in her life, whose behavior she couldn't control anyhow. Her "homework," a small but powerfully instructive step in this direction, was simply to do a single nice thing for herself on a daily basis.

This could be, as I instructed her, a very minor thing—perhaps buying herself a small gift, such as a blouse or a pair of gloves. It could be nothing other than taking time out to go to the library; it might be getting someone else in the family to prepare that particular evening's meal.

What, one may ask, is the rationale underlying this simple-sounding task? It is the following: By this daily act of concentrating upon what *she could do to take care of and nurture her own self,* this mother would begin refocusing her attention on her own needs and away from her obsessive concern with her son's defiant, wild, uncontrollable behavior. Then, instead of saying to herself, "My life would be fine if my awful son [or "my husband," or "my father"] were more responsible," Susan Anderson could begin moving toward a position in which she became able to say to herself, "*I* can be responsible for making myself have a good life, and I can start doing that right now."

The ultimate purpose of this clinical assignment (which is an autonomy-enhancing device) is to help a person take ownership of the legitimacy of her own needs, including the need to enjoy some of life's simple pleasures. Simply getting into the habit of meeting a small need of her own every day would mark a small beginning in the important work ahead for this wife and parent, which was to establish some separate and individual personal territory of her own.

Task 3. What of Dave's younger sister, Cheryl? It was clear that she would profit from a clinical assignment that would garner her the parental attention that she so desperately needed. For, as her older brother had reported during peer-group therapy, Cheryl was already beginning to follow Dave down the path that he called "the road to hell."

It was true that at the time of our interviews, this twelve-year-old had stopped doing her homework and was on academic probation, but the family's gaze was so riveted upon Dave (males being the designated bad guys in this family) that nobody seemed to actually care about the girl's increasingly self-destructive conduct. Cheryl's assignment was, therefore, in the nature of a quid pro quo.

In exchange for giving up certain misbehaviors, such as failing to turn in her homework, she was to become entitled to fifteen minutes of her parents' undivided attention on three designated evenings per week. This would, as I told the assembled family members, involve both parents sitting down opposite Cheryl and according her their undivided attention. Her mother and father would simply *listen to their daughter talk about herself and her own issues* without making any response. The quid pro quo was, in short, that the daughter would behave in ways that would improve her school performance and her parents would spend time *hearing her out* in return.

Task 4. The clinical assignment devised for Dave was, necessarily, of a very different sort. Given that he was at present devoted to being defiant and oppositional, the task set for him had to be highly indirect and paradoxical in nature.

There are a number of so-called "paradoxical strategies" now commonly in use; these can sound particularly bizarre. Paradoxical tasks can best be thought of as a kind of psychological aikido, that martial art in which the opponent is maneuvered into using his own strength (in this case, the strong resistance to change) against himself.

The therapeutic task devised for Dave Anderson was one commonly known as "prescribing the symptom." What this involves is *not* exhorting the symptomatic person to stop what he is doing (direct demands have, in any case, not been working), but instead telling him to go on doing exactly what he is doing *because it is so helpful to those around him.*

Thus, rather than suggesting that Dave work harder to control his defiant, oppositional behavior, I urged him to *continue making trouble,* because his doing so was clearly of vital importance to others in the family. His rebellious acting out was actually, as I remarked, in the nature of a loving gift that he was giving to his mother—a caring son's way of protecting his parent from her pain.

For, I observed thoughtfully, as long as his mother remained riveted upon all of the bad things *he* was doing, she could avoid ever having to deal with the losses and injuries she had suffered. His mom need never focus upon herself, or upon the tragic events of her girlhood, or upon the betrayals that had transpired later on in her lifetime.

What is so devilishly clever about paradoxical strategies is that they put the person receiving the instructions into a logical bind. In this case, if Dave continued to be bad (defiant and oppositional) he was actually being good, behaving in exactly the ways that others in the family (especially his mother) wanted him to. How to continue acting out in a new framework in which "badness" was being recast as "helpfulness" was thus rendered manifestly unclear.

Not surprisingly, Dave responded to this homework task angrily. Why, he demanded, should I suggest that he go on being bad—he was being bad already! Such a suggestion was, moreover, not only "stupid" but highly insulting to a teenager whose claim to fame was his incorrigible badness.

I nodded understandingly, but added blandly that he really did deserve everyone's congratulations for his loving behavior, and that it was important that he continue helping his mother out in these vital, indispensable ways (or that he do so until she seemed readier to handle all the grief and the pain that she was so clearly incapable of managing now).

Furthermore, if he should happen to notice his mother looking sad or upset—or if she seemed about to get into a battle with his dad—it was Dave's important responsibility to distract her from her pain by doing something totally outrageous. The only small proviso included in these instructions was that the teenager was to continue being defiant and oppositional without endangering his own future.

Thus, as I told him, if he noticed his mother looking sad and needing to be diverted, he should use a tactic such as talking offensively, cursing obscenely, or maybe just throwing dirty towels around the bathroom—anything that would enrage her without doing harm to himself.

These tactics were, as I noted, far preferable to failing to do his homework, flunking out of school, or sneaking off in the family car for a dangerous joyride. Dave's homework assignment was, in summary, to continue being the defiant, oppositional family trouble-generator, but to do so without escalating into behaviors so self-destructive that they might land him in a long-term residential facility—or, worse yet, in jail.

Why and how might a paradoxical task of this sort prove effective? The answer is that paradoxical strategies are both marvel-producing and enraging because there is simply no way around them—and this is so because *a good paradoxical intervention always rests upon a true statement.*

In the present instance, it was true that Dave Anderson was showing his love for his parent by protecting her from her inner pain and conflict in the only way he knew. By keeping his mother focused upon his own uncontrollable badness and irresponsibility, Dave was helping her to *keep her gaze concentrated on the present tense.* Susan Anderson need never (as long as her son's acting out continued to keep the household in a state of confusion and chaos) fear having to look backward and turn into a pillar of salt as the grief of a lifetime was reawakened.

Achieving Clarity (and a Small Miracle)

Whether or not therapeutic tasks of this kind are actually ever carried out, simply assigning them provides a wonderful means of exposing the real nature of the emotional system to everyone concerned. For, by merely outlining each individual member's homework task in the presence of the other people in the family, the ways in which the system is operating are suddenly brought into dramatic focus.

The Andersons' tasks would, for example, address the father's isolation and distancing from the family; the mother's loss-haunted, obsessional focus upon the "uncontrollable male"; the daughter's feelings of lostness and her need for parental attention; and the son's function as the system's symptom bearer and—paradoxically—its savior. The tasks had introduced a high measure of clarity into the emotional system, for they had, willy-nilly, exposed the things that were actually going on beneath the system's impervious surface of confusion, turmoil, and obfuscation.

But did I believe that the Andersons would actually follow through, and do their homework tasks as instructed? Not really.

Although Ralph did agree to hold a weekly press conference, he did so in his customary distant, unreadable manner. Susan Anderson seemed enthused about a task that would involve her doing more nice things for herself, while Dave, as noted above, told me belligerently that he was making lots of trouble already. "Fine," I reiterated, "then all you have to do is continue with what you're doing." Cheryl was intrigued, not only by her own assignment but by her father's. She liked the idea of the press conference, because, as she said, "I'm feeling kind of . . . maybe not completely, but *somewhat* . . . abandoned by Dad."

Nevertheless, to be honest, I did not place great hope in the prospect of the Andersons carrying through with their designated agendas. As things turned out, I was mistaken.

When I came back from vacation and contacted the family again, I found that in fact they had done so. Ralph Anderson had held his press conference a couple of times, and Cheryl had plied him with questions. Dave had said he really had no questions, and Susan had said she didn't either (although she had voiced a great many unanswered questions in private interviews with me).

After that, the family press conferences had ceased; but Susan was still doing something nice for herself daily. Cheryl, too, was continuing to trade special time with her parents for good behavior, although, as her mother conceded, this wasn't always being observed with sufficient regularity.

As for Dave, he had really been much easier throughout the summer. He was working as an auto mechanic's assistant at the moment, and the entire household had been far more peaceful. "Of course we still don't know whether or not David's going to be put back a year because of the time he lost at Elmcrest," Susan told me, "and that will make a big difference to *him*. So I'm feeling a lot of anxiety about that at the moment, but I'm trying hard to take responsibility for my own anxiety, and not, you know, start projecting it onto him."

I was taken aback—no, startled. This mother now seemed fully aware that she might be projecting her own feelings onto her son, when a few months earlier she'd been unaware that the two of them really did occupy different skins, and that Dave had a subjective reality fundamentally different from her own.

Everyone in the family was feeling pretty good, Mrs. Anderson continued, and things were going fairly well in general. "I'm really glad to hear that, Susan," I said to her quietly. I was actually feeling jubilant at the news.

Had it been the therapeutic tasks that made a difference? Had the family therapy sessions they were attending begun at last to have an impact? Who cared? Everyone loves a miracle, even a small miracle, and the emotional system had clearly shifted in a positive direction.

Moving Upward and Downward on the Family Health and Competence Continuum

It is important to reiterate that the varying levels of health and functioning on the Beavers family assessment scale are *not* fixed diagnostic categories, labels that, once applied to a particular family, will adhere forever, not subject to change or modification.

Families can move upward or downward on the clinical scale; thus, during one phase of its life cycle, the Level 5, severely disturbed family may show a sudden growth spurt and move up to Level 4, Level 3, or (rarely) even higher, just as a midrange, Level 3 family system may regress and move downward on the scale.

What sorts of things would have to happen in order for a family like the Andersons to make real strides upward on the developmental continuum? Could a family functioning at this severely disturbed level ever lift itself up by its own bootstraps—advance significantly upward on the Beavers ladder without therapeutic assistance?

The answer is that while it's possible, it is not very likely; the Level 5 system is basically organized in such a way as to *avoid* coming to grips with its own issues. It is as though these emotional systems are committed to kicking sand into their own communal eyes, and remaining muddled, obscure, and unfocused. The confusion is experienced as necessary, for the members of these families are terrified of ever getting into conscious touch with those painful, unmourned losses which, if truly experienced, might prove completely overwhelming.

For the Andersons, real contact with their "hot" and urgent issues—the parents' marital suffering, the existence of the father's second family— would mean facing up to *and feeling* the reality of the father's betrayal. It would mean truly experiencing the subliminal threats of abandonment that his betrayal unavoidably raised (after all, he'd abandoned that other family, hadn't he?).

Achieving clarity about their issues would mean, moreover, not only confronting the pain but having to *deal with* the pain—and, along the way, having to encounter a number of very down-to-earth, practical dilemmas. Would the half-siblings ever meet? In what specific ways would the existence of the other family be dealt with? These were among the pressing questions that the Andersons, as a family, needed to think about, and about which they would have to make some decisions.

Doing so would, however, arouse a host of conflictual, intensely ambivalent feelings within every single one of them. And herein lies another, extremely problematic feature of the Level 5 system: The people in these severely troubled families are unable to come to grips with even the normal human ambivalence that every one of us experiences as part of everyday life. Their way of dealing with ambivalence is to simply deny it, pretend that it doesn't exist.

Perennially Unresolved Ambivalent Dilemmas

Ambivalence, let it be said, is endemic to the human condition. Mixed feelings and inner conflict about a great range of daily concerns—for instance, "I want to put in heroic hours at the office, and get promoted to a partnership" versus "I feel I'm missing out on my kids' childhood, and I want to spend more time at home with them" would be an example of the kinds of powerful inner crosscurrents with which most of us must struggle.

By and large, a healthy, functional way of dealing with ambivalent feelings is to allow oneself to experience the pain of the inner conflict, suffer it through to its resolution, eventually come down more on one side of the matter or the other, and then tailor one's behavior accordingly. But the members of the Level 5 emotional system tend to deal with ambivalence by *not* dealing with it, by simply refusing to recognize that two warring and diametrically opposite tendencies are actually present within them.

Thus, Susan Anderson could maintain and readily express two mutually contradictory points of view simultaneously—"My husband's betrayal of me and of the family is unforgivable"; "My husband's other child and other family are not really relevant issues"—without seeming to perceive the impossible incongruity between them. And this was, it seemed to me, only one among a number of this mother's unresolved dilemmas. For, by telling me privately that she had a great many questions about her husband's present connection with his other family, and then raising *no* questions at the father's "press conference," Susan seemed to be saying both "I want to know more about Ralph's other family" and "I can't stand the idea of hearing anything about them," simultaneously.

Indeed, everyone within this severely troubled emotional system appeared to be crying out "We need to have some clarity and coherence in our lives," and yet adding, sotto voce, "We're terrified of what might happen if things ever *did* get straightened out, so let's hope that nothing ever changes." But instead of acknowledging the existence of a whole range of strong internal contradictions, and resolving their ambivalent feelings by making some choices about how they should be handled, the members of a Level 5 system will usually attempt to deal with ambivalence by ignoring it.

It is as though, in these rigid family systems, the strong need and wish for change exists crazily side by side with its opposite face, the strong wish for no change whatsoever. The upshot is that in the world of outer reality, nothing actually happens—the inner conflict persists without resolution or outcome. And this is among the fundamental reasons why a Level 5 family will usually need some therapeutic help in getting out of the existential corner into which it has painted itself.

The basic lesson that the members of these distressed emotional systems need to absorb is that, over the long run, the chaos and turmoil will not really shield them from their pain. They also need to learn (and can do so, in the right clinical circumstances) the difficult lesson that actually facing up to one's losses and one's grief is not only survivable, but often remarkably healing.

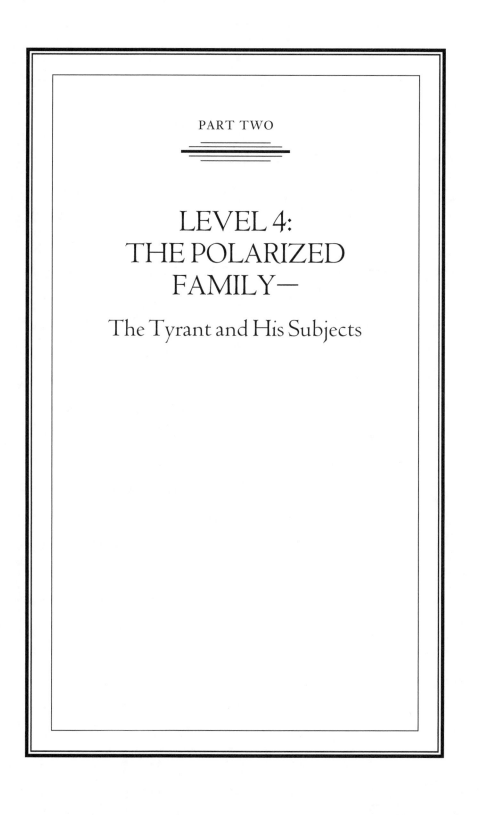

PART TWO

LEVEL 4:
THE POLARIZED
FAMILY—

The Tyrant and His Subjects

Establishing Order and Predictability: The Emergence of a Tyrant

The members of the Level 5 family try, as we have seen, to manage the problem of ambivalence in a fundamentally irrational fashion—by behaving as if it's possible to maintain two diametrically opposite internal stances at the same time ("I adore my daughter above all else"; "My daughter has given me so much trouble and hardship that sometimes I wish she'd never been born"). By the time one ascends the Beavers Scale to the level above, however, this is no longer the case. Families at Level 4 on the clinical continuum have come up with a novel technique for dealing with ambivalence, a technique strikingly different from that seen in the chaotic systems below them.

In these Level 4, "borderline" emotional systems, developing a cogent, clear-cut point of view *does* become possible—and this clearly represents a genuine developmental advance. Nevertheless, it must be said that families at this maturational level deal with ambivalence in a remarkably crude and primitive fashion. Instead of totally refusing to acknowledge the existence of ambivalent feelings and untenably discrepant points of view (which is what happens at Level 5) the borderline family tends to pick up a metaphoric meat cleaver and split the ambivalence cleanly down the middle.

The members of these polarized emotional systems live in the stark, oversimplified world of either/or, a world that contains no middle ground of ambiguity. In this kind of system, there can be no faltering, no uncertainty; the expectation is that each member of the family cast will embody and express *either* one side of an inner ambivalence *or* the other one. Thus, if you're not the top dog, you're the bottom dog; if you're not the saintly caretaker, you're the self-centered egoist; if you're not the competent one, you're the dope who never knows how to get anything accomplished.

In the borderline family, a person is his or her oversimplified character in the family production, and can be nothing other. Indeed, a distinguishing characteristic of these emotional systems is the pervasive fear that, given one false or even hesitant step on anyone's part, chaos and disorder will follow. Human complexity, being "of two minds" (at least, until one has resolved an inner ambivalence), is simply out of bounds.

The polarized Level 4 system's basic credo is that unless everyone remains in his or her designated family role, things may spin completely out of control—the system itself may fragment, dissolve into disarray and incoherence. It is, in fact, this *deeply feared loss of control*—a loss of control that could result in total formlessness and anarchy—that serves to lock everyone in the polarized family into his or her unidimensional, stereotyped position.

And it is this selfsame threat—the threat of imminent disorganization—that has typically produced a tyrant, someone who, at some point in time, has stepped forward and said, "Okay, I will create order and governance by taking over and becoming the dictator here." The Level 4 emotional system can best be understood as one that has been struggling with the threat of utter anarchy and confusion that exists at the developmental level below it and has, in the process, come up with its own set of better—and yet far from perfect—solutions.

In the Either/Or World of the Maguire Family: An Always-Angry Husband and a Never-Angry Wife

I sat in on the weekly treatment sessions of the Maguire family over a nine-month period. Clare Maguire, forty-four, was an ex–Pan Am stewardess who'd met her husband when he was a passenger on a transatlantic flight; Matt Maguire, forty-six, was a self-made man, someone from a desperately poor first-generation Irish immigrant background who'd developed a highly successful computer business and made himself a multimillionaire.

The couple had been married for eighteen years; they had twin sons, Carl and Bobby, age fourteen, and a daughter, Katie, age sixteen. It was Katie who was the designated patient, or symptom bearer, in this family, for she was what is termed a normal-weight bulimic—someone who goes on wild food binges and then resorts to self-induced purges in order to maintain her weight within the normal range.

Much that was transpiring within the Maguire household indicated that the family was functioning at a borderline level on the Beavers Scale.

Certainly, when it came to the Level 4 emotional system's tendency to split the ambivalence down the middle, the parental couple presented a living exemplar. For, in their effort to deal with the strong internal conflict that most of us experience about both *feeling* angry and *expressing* anger, Matt and Clare Maguire had polarized into two diametrically opposing positions. Each partner personified, embodied, and gave voice to one half of the ambivalence: Clare experienced herself as "without anger" and always eager to avoid any conflict, while Matt was perennially on the edge of an outburst.

Of course the human truth is that no one is uniquely without anger, just as no one is nothing but angry all the time; these highly exaggerated postures falsify the complexity of everyone involved. But in the Level 4, polarized family world, the maintenance of such adamantly held positions is experienced as vitally necessary to family discipline and order. The operational rules of the borderline system have indeed come into existence in order to stave off family-wide chaos and create a sense of governance and control—and the effort has proven, to a considerable degree, successful.

Families at this developmental level *are* far better regulated and more organized than the Level 5 families below them on the scale. The household tyrant's efforts have imposed some real coherence and regularity upon the emotional system, fending off the anarchy and disarray that everyone subliminally fears. But while, in the short run, the family despot has reformed the system and imposed a clear-cut set of rules and regulations, in the longer run his reign becomes totally untenable.

The tyrant rules by stern decree, and his area of control and command extends throughout the entire domestic terrain—including the internal world of everyone in the household. He sets the rules about which thoughts, feelings, ideas, wishes, behaviors, and ways of being are to be considered permissible. But the problem is that this flies in the face of human nature itself.

It is simply impossible to contain individual complexity in this harshly autocratic fashion indefinitely. Such an effort is, as family expert Leonora Stephens has observed, rather like an attempt to stuff five pounds of flour into a three-pound sack—it will leak out or burst out somehow. Someone's unique and essential differentness from his or her role in the family drama will suddenly make itself known. And when this does happen (as it must, in the course of time) it will produce frantic, system-wide reverberations.

The basic operational rule in the Level 4 emotional system is that the individuals in the family are *not* supposed to state a differentiated, personal position ("*I* am, wish, want, would prefer," and the like) and to maintain it. The tyrant rules the family, not by means of collaboration and conflict resolution, but by means of autocratic domination and control—a control that is not to be questioned.

A Family Edict: Everyone Must Eat the Same Breakfast

It had not been Katie Maguire's bulimia that served to bring her entire family into outpatient treatment. For, even though the sixteen-year-old had been bingeing and purging throughout much of the past summer, her parents had been completely unaware of any such problems when they sent her back to boarding school at the beginning of September.

Nevertheless, the Maguire family's coming into therapy did seem, in some curious way, to have been the result of a conscious effort on their adolescent daughter's part. It was almost as though Katie had decided she was going to shake up the system's unhappy equilibrium and set some needed changes into motion. She'd make *a move*, however reckless and irrational that move might appear to be—and she had certainly done so.

It had been in the immediate wake of the teenager's flamboyant "bust" in an uproarious drinking episode (she'd been discovered, partying and drunk, in the boys' dorm at her boarding school) and her subsequent expulsion that the school authorities had insisted Katie Maguire enter therapy as a condition of her reinstatement. And, since treating an adolescent often involves working with the patient's family as well, the rest of the Maguires had come into therapy also.

For the parents, this schedule involved a certain amount of traveling, for they lived in a wealthy enclave in Greenwich, Connecticut, some seventy miles away from Katie's boarding school. But every other Tuesday, either Matt or Clare, or both parents, came in for a therapeutic session with their daughter, psychologist Robert Horwitz, Ph.D., and me (on the alternate weeks, we met with Katie alone). When their crowded after-school sports schedules permitted, Katie's younger brothers, Carl and Bobby, attended these family meetings also.

But on the particular day when the topic of the Maguires' breakfast rule ("Everyone must eat the same breakfast") arose, the only members of the family present were sandy-haired Katie and her attractive, quite young-looking mother, Clare. The subject of the breakfast rule actually came up in conjunction with Katie's description of how, toward the end of a recent holiday weekend in Vermont, her father had abruptly driven off, leaving the rest of them openmouthed and shaken.

Katie's belief was that her dad had departed in that sudden, shocking manner because her kid brothers were being sloppy and lazy, tossing their clothes and ski gear around everywhere and creating a sense of total disorder. "We'd brought two cars up to our condo," Katie explained to Dr. Horwitz and me, "and my dad said, basically, 'Screw it,' and took off, because nothing was getting done. We weren't leaving on time . . . we weren't . . ." She paused, a puzzled expression appearing on her face.

"We weren't being—um, productive enough to get the house in order, as it should be, for us to all go home as a family. So my dad just said, 'I'm going,' and he left." The young girl was offering a rationale for her father's behavior, and yet she herself looked devastated.

"*I* don't think that's why he left," put in her mother at once.

Katie's head wheeled in her mother's direction. "*Why*, then?" she asked, her voice sounding plaintive.

"You went upstairs" was the older woman's brisk response; then, turning to face the psychologist and me, she added, "My husband has this *thing*, which is like a blanket rule in our family. And the rule is that what's good for one is good for everybody; that's that. So if I'm making lunch, and I'm fixing him a ham-and-cheese sandwich, and there's someone in the family who doesn't like ham-and-cheese sandwiches, that person is out of luck. It's absolutely a *sin* if I make anyone something different."

The mother scanned our faces briefly, as if hoping there were some explanation for this behavior that one of us might have read about in a textbook. When neither of us replied, she continued, "I don't *get* that—I mean, this is *not* something I consider important. Maybe because I was an only child, and whatever I wanted for lunch I got. I'm not used to this 'We're in a group and so we all do the same thing' approach."

Katie had, I noticed, picked up a long hank of hair from the crown of her head and was now twisting it around and around again. Clare Maguire turned to me, fixed her gaze fully upon mine. "The last morning we were up in Vermont, I was making some pancakes, and one of my sons—Carl—doesn't *like* pancakes. He doesn't *eat* them. So he came into the kitchen and said, 'Oh, great, you made pancakes; that's swell for all of you, but what am *I* going to have?' So I said, 'Well, the grill is hot; do you want a couple of fried eggs?' " She paused, shot a quick, guilty look at Bob Horwitz, then shrugged: "I'm sure my husband thinks I did this to just really drive him crazy."

Then she resumed telling the story. "Matt was at the sink, and he turned around and said, 'Are you making a different breakfast for somebody?' " She mimicked the deep bass, angry, threatening voice in which these words had been spoken. "I mean, he just lost it—he went berserk—and I said that yes, well, I *had*."

She did realize, she added immediately, that this was something that might upset her husband; but it simply hadn't been in her mind at that moment. "As soon as he reacted that way," continued Clare, "I remembered that this is really a big deal for him. And I guess it *is*—it's just one of those crazy, unresolved things that happen in our family all the time."

She turned to Katie. "So then Dad just left the kitchen, got dressed, and said, 'I'll see you at home,' and took off. But that's what sparked his leaving." She shrugged. Although the story she'd told was an upsetting one, Clare Maguire didn't seem awfully rattled; and I was struck by how much more equanimity and self-assurance this woman seemed to possess when her authoritarian spouse wasn't present.

"*I* call it communism," Clare added, almost gaily. "And I know I shouldn't make light of it, but I really don't *get* it. But I guess the fact that we've never sat down and really tried to hash this one out—and find out what's underneath it—makes it one of those crazy little issues that comes up every once in a while in our family."

"Or maybe a crazy big issue," observed the clinician quietly. I wasn't exactly sure what he meant; but I myself was busily attempting to construct some theory that might explain Matt Maguire's behavior. I gazed at these two handsome females, Matt's wife and his daughter, and asked them how they explained it to themselves.

Clare believed it had to do with her husband's feelings about luxury—about the children being spoiled and demanding things that were not being offered them. "My husband grew up in a family where there was just *what there was*—and that didn't include any luxury or pampering—and so I think he really sees it as *subversive* when somebody wants something special or different from what the rest of the family is getting."

But the daughter's own theory was a very different one. She said she thought that her father set such demanding rules "in order to satisfy his own simplistic values." When I shook my head as if to say I didn't quite understand, Katie explained that her father was a very, very *organized* man who liked to have everything very clear-cut, tidy, and systematic. "He's very *demanding*, and I think—to him—it represents just a little tad of disorganization or difference or conflict when somebody wants something different." Still, there was a somewhat nonplussed look on the adolescent girl's face, as there was on her mother's also.

Conscious and Unconscious Rules

It is now widely recognized that *the family is a rule-governed system*. That is, family members interact with each other in a highly repetitive, orchestrated fashion; what happens in families, on a daily basis, is by no means random. On the contrary, the behavior of every member of the group is patterned in ways that are curiously constant and predictable. Everyone within the group acts as if he or she is operating according to institutional by-laws—rules of the family game that are accepted as something immutable.

As family theorist Don D. Jackson pointed out in a famous essay published in the mid-1960s, "Both common sense and clinical observation argue for the organized nature of family interaction. If there were not some circumscription of the infinity of possible behaviors in which its members might conceivably engage, not only the daily chores but the very survival of the family unit would be in question."

People living in a family need to know, generally speaking, who will do what and when it will happen. If there were no understanding, for example, about who would be responsible for the grocery shopping, then there would either be no food on the family table or the food purchases would be duplicated in ways that were costly and wasteful. Rules develop very naturally as a way of increasing the family unit's efficiency.

It is easier for everyone to behave according to certain interdigitating understandings, such as "The women in this family are responsible for marketing and cooking" and "The men in this family are responsible for lawn mowing and automobile maintenance," than to have to work out these decisions on each and every occasion. So family rules come into being.

A family rule is, very simply, a group-wide norm by which (implicitly or explicitly) everyone has agreed to abide. And these rules of the family game are, as psychiatrist Jackson was the first to observe, basically *relationship agreements* pertaining to the rights, privileges, duties, and constraints upon everybody living in the household.

Some rules apply only to particular members of the group; an example might be "The children in this family may not take food out of the refrigerator without permission." Other rules apply to everyone in the family; for instance, "No one shall control anyone else" or "Father will overtly run the show, but Mother's covert authority must be respected." *But the crucial thing to be understood about family rules is that some exist at the level of everyone's shared awareness, while others are simply not part of the group members' conscious knowledge at all.*

Family rules that are implicit and unconscious are the rules of the game that everyone abides by but that nobody ever talks about openly. It is as if there is a group-wide injunction against discussing these unwritten family laws, or, for that matter, even being aware of their existence. Yet these implicitly understood and observed family regulations—such as, "We never discuss the affair that Mom is involved in" or "We don't allude to the religious differences of the two sides of the family" or "Dad's escalating obesity is a topic that is out of bounds, in terms not only of what can be talked about but of what can be *thought* about, too"—may be influencing everyone within the system in a covert and yet tremendously powerful fashion.

According to Stamford, Connecticut, psychologist Betsy Stone, a conscious and explicit family rule is one that can be clearly and openly articulated: "Mom always takes care of the finances"; "We don't allow junk food in the house." Explicit family rules can be talked about and questioned—perhaps fought about bitterly, on occasion—but they tend to cause fewer long-term difficulties than do the implicit and unconscious rules of the game. For these rules are simply beyond discussion; no one really "knows" of their existence, even though everyone obeys them in a quasi-hypnotic fashion.

Not doing so would be unimaginable. If one were to breach an implicit family rule, and know what is not supposed to be known, the results (so everyone supposes) would be catastrophic. It is out of loyalty to the group as an entity that certain feelings, thoughts, perceptions, and ideas are labeled taboo: *out of order.*

In Complete Control or Completely out of Control

What, I began to speculate, might be the Maguires' explicit and conscious *and* implicit and unconscious rules of family life—most particularly, the rules relating to food? It had certainly not escaped my notice that Katie's choice of symptoms was one that, in this particular situation, gave her an added measure of autonomy. A family tyrant could force her to eat what she was supposed to eat at the time when she was supposed to eat it, but her bulimic symptoms offered her a wonderful way of spitting it out right afterward.

In any event, though, what was strikingly clear was that Matt Maguire believed, in the most literal fashion, that everyone in his family should be a clone of sorts—that it was each member of the family's wifely or filial duty to have the same (*his*) wants, feelings, thoughts, and ideas. It was as if he were striving to banish "differentness"—that is, separate personhood—by dictatorial fiat.

This father was attempting to impose a state of martial law, not only upon the family as a whole unit but upon the inner world of everyone inside it. They were all to want what *he* wanted, *when* he wanted it—and in borderline, Level 4 families, it is the awful fear of loss of control that locks everyone into uncompromising, stereotyped positions such as this one. For in these families, it will be remembered, a state of either/or prevails: *You are either in total and complete control or you are out of control completely.*

Matt's reaction to the incident involving the substitution of eggs for pancakes was certainly a striking example of this phenomenon in action. For this father was not only enraged by his son's asking for a different breakfast, and his wife's beginning to cook it; he was just as deeply threatened by the boy's having an independent preference of his own. It was as if this demonstration of his offspring's separate, subjective reality—of an inner life distinct from that of the rest of the family—jeopardized the very integrity and soundness of the group as a whole.

The father's precipitate departure, in the wake of this insurrection, had been nothing other than the enactment of an abandonment scenario. What Matt Maguire seemed to be saying, not only to his son but to everyone else in the family, was "If you threaten me by breaking ranks—by displaying your separateness and differentness—then I will counterattack by deserting you first."

In families at this developmental level, issues having to do with separation and loss—including the expectable losses involved when children grow up and move in the direction of becoming autonomous, adult persons—are extraordinarily charged. Such families are, as theorist John Zinner has noted, often in the grip of a powerful, unconscious assumption: that to individuate into a separate, different person and then to leave the original family is an act of terrible betrayal (rather than being, as it is, a part of the normal, expectable human program).

To become one's own person (to prefer eggs to pancakes) is, in and of itself, a violation of the fixed, unbending rules of the family game. "Behaviors that herald separation and autonomy are experienced by parents, not as desirable goals for the adolescent," Zinner writes, "but rather as a narcissistic injury, to which the parents react with narcissistic rage." His teenage son's stepping out of line and wanting eggs instead of pancakes had been experienced by Matt Maguire as an infuriating blow to his own sense of mastery, control, self-esteem.

All three of the Maguire children were, at this phase of the family's life cycle, on the launching pad and preparing for takeoff. Katie was already away at boarding school, and Carl and Bobby would be leaving for boarding schools in the near future. In truth, everything was changing, and changes call for flexibility, for multiple options.

But the strict, uncompromising nature of this kind of family's black-and-white rule system could not be challenged by its members because of the dread (which was actually ubiquitous) that once control was lost it would be lost completely and irretrievably. This was, it seemed to me, the real reason for Matt's having reacted with such anger and terror. If his son wouldn't obey his clearly stated edict, and if his wife abetted that disobedience, family anarchy and disintegration threatened.

In polarized, Level 4 families, it may be that something as apparently trivial as wanting eggs rather than pancakes is a gross violation of the family's regulations—or it may be that feelings relating to anger, sadness, and sexuality, and even ambivalence of any sort, are forbidden. Transgressions of a rule will in any event be seen, within this family's framework, as mad or bad, but in any case completely traitorous.

There is never, in these systems, a sense that each person can be accorded the personal space to develop into an individual, unique self, and that that will be perfectly acceptable to everyone else in the group. There is, on the contrary, the underlying belief that everyone's behavior must be kept under tight control according to the iron laws of dominance and submission.

In Matt Maguire's case, a real, fatherly wish for perfect family harmony—which to him meant wall-to-wall agreement with his own inclinations and desires—obviously flew in the face of human reality, which is that people are diverse and complex in their needs, outlooks, and wishes. Because he could not have the total control he required, he'd reverted to a sense of feeling totally, frighteningly *out of control*—and he'd stormed out and driven home by himself. There could be a holiday weekend in Vermont that met his stringent guidelines, or there would be no holidaying; there was no possible position between these two extreme ones.

In this polarized family, you were always either one thing or the other—all bad or all good, totally in the right or entirely in the wrong. You were, as Matt Maguire saw it, either the father of the perfectly well behaved, compliant family or the father of a family full of self-centered ingrates. In this kind of emotional world, there is not much gray area, not much space for negotiation of differences, and so the Maguires' weekend in the country had ended in disarray, mutual perplexity, and fury.

CHAPTER 8

A Core Family Dynamic:
The Oppressor and the Oppressed

Matthew Maguire was, at age forty-six, a remarkably successful, wholly self-made man. His own father had been a poor day laborer, and his mother had worked in a soap factory; he himself had never gone to college, because his family had been unable to afford it. He had nevertheless managed to establish a self-owned business in the rapidly expanding field of computers; he ascribed his own phenomenal success to "luck, pure luck—just being in the right place at the right time."

Just plain luck could, however, be only part of a far more complex explanation. Today, at the outset of a meeting at which all family members were present, I asked the father admiringly just how he'd managed to accomplish so extraordinary an economic metamorphosis. What had enabled him to move from the poverty of his own family—poverty so severe that he remembered actually going hungry at times—to his current state of affluence, which included ownership of a comfortable house in Greenwich, Connecticut, a large boat, and a ski condo in Vermont?

Instead of looking flattered, Matt Maguire's expression became darkly resentful. He was, as he never failed to let his family know, a man in a state of simmering fury, a man who seemed to have one foot outside the door of an entire lifetime. He was just completing the process of signing off on the sale of his computer business, and he would be sailing off to the Caribbean in two weeks in order to put the Maguires' boat into winter storage. But when—and whether or not—he would be coming home again remained a very open question.

Now he stared at me, and in reply to my question said bitterly: "How did I do it? I *worked hard.*" Then he added, "That's all I've ever done, my entire life—work hard for other people." He looked around at his wife and children, scowling, as if their very existence burdened him.

I saw one of his twin sons, Carl, shoot a pleading, impatient look at his mother. The message of his glance seemed to be, as I translated it for myself, "Why in hell don't you *say* something, why don't you ever *confront* him?" But Clare Maguire simply sat there, silent, looking as helpless, scared, and disempowered as her adolescent children.

I felt my own discomfort level rising; not only was Matt's rage, and their fear of it, infectious, but I myself am the daughter of a tyrannical father. I had been here before, and knew well what they were feeling, even at the level of my own tense and constricted corpuscles.

I wondered if Bob Horwitz would break the deadlock of this awful moment, but he didn't. Instead he fixed a questioning gaze upon Clare, as if to say: "The ball's in your court; what comes next, in this family's sequence?"

Clare Maguire, looking like a distraught witness who'd been summoned to court against her will, buttoned, then unbuttoned, then buttoned again the collar of her ivory shirt. Clare had come into this afternoon's meeting exuding an air of energy, vitality, and youthfulness, looking more like Katie's older sister than her parent. But now, in the wake of her spouse's aggression, Clare's complexion turned pasty-white and her features became set and frozen. Her head began drifting gently forward, to hang down as if she were ashamed of the testimony that she had to give.

"Getting into confrontations," murmured the mother, in a low, embarrassed voice, "is not one of my favorite things. If my life were to be perfect, it would mean never having to lock horns with anybody over anything.

"That would be my *wish,*" she added quickly, as if acknowledging its impossibility. "Having come out of a family where there was a lot of discord, confusion, yelling, and verbal abuse—I would like to never, *ever* have to deal with stuff like that."

Just then, the frenzied blaring of an ambulance siren halted the conversation and we waited for the noise to subside. We were accustomed to these brief interruptions; Bob Horwitz's office is close to the Yale–New Haven hospital complex and not more than a block from the emergency-room entrance.

In the noise-imposed interval, I studied the fourteen-year-old Maguire twins. Bobby and Carl were perfect biological replicas—blond, with handsome features and tall, well-formed, muscular frames. Although they participated little in the general conversation, they sat side by side, and occasionally I saw one of them nudge the other and exchange a cryptic look or smile.

If, in this family universe, each individual seemed somewhat like an isolated planet—remote and distanced from the others—then the twins appeared to be the two entities with the most gravitational pull between them. Their gestures indicated that these two were in some kind of ongoing emotional contact. Still, one only had to look at them to realize that they were involved in a concerted, somewhat endearing effort to enable other people to differentiate between them fairly easily.

The Compliant Good Son and the Moody "Troubled" One

Bobby Maguire had a well-scrubbed face and an open, alert expression. His hair was clipped short, in a clean-cut, almost military fashion. His clothing was preppy but comfortable-looking—a denim work shirt, blue sweater, tan cords, and sneakers. Bobby's customary stance in the family was that of the cooperative, nonconfrontational good soldier, while his twin brother occupied the opposite role. Carl was the moody, alienated "troubled one," and he had decked himself out accordingly.

Not only was the adolescent dressed in black from head to toe, in clothing of uncertain vintage, but he had also set himself apart from his twin by means of a most distinctive hairstyle. On the left side of his head, Carl's hair was trimmed down almost to the scalp, while on the right side an exaggeratedly long swath of hair had been permitted to grow out. That hair hung down behind his ear like a piece of smooth golden fabric, and in the lobe of his right ear a small stud earring glinted.

Historically, as Dr. Horwitz and I had already learned, it was this "moody, alienated" child who had always been the major focus of the family's anxieties. Everyone (and this included Matt himself) spoke of Carl as being too much like his father—tense, uncommunicative about his feelings, and high-strung. Even now, in the wake of Katie's dramatic emergence as the "identified patient" in the family, I had the distinct impression that it was Carl (named after Clare's father, Carl, who'd lived with the Maguires until his death this past June) who unnerved his folks far more than did his bulimic, acting-out older sister.

True, until just recently, Katie had been a relatively docile and pliable youngster, helpful at home and a high-performing student at school. This was, perhaps, why her parents didn't appear to be taking their daughter's problems all that seriously. I myself had the distinct impression that, at some level, Matt and Clare were minimizing Katie's difficulties, not comprehending their full magnitude.

It was as if the fact that she'd been caught carousing drunkenly with a couple of male seniors were being seen as a form of adolescent high jinks. Nor had her parents been able to take in and absorb any real understanding of the ultimate dangerousness (to the young girl's health *and* to her looks) of the bulimic symptoms with which she was struggling.

Fear of Confrontation: A Maternal Pattern

Clare Maguire resumed speaking. "The truth is," she said, her tone apologetic, "I'm really not a screamer, or a—a wave-maker of any kind. I mean, if I were to describe my perception of my own mother and father, I would say that *she* was the peacemaker and that *he* did all the ranting and raving and screaming and insisting on being the powerful one, and all that sort of thing."

The mother halted, as if to contemplate the unbidden, perhaps taboo thought that her own marriage seemed to be cut from the selfsame pattern. Then she added slowly, "It's sort of eerie, in a way, because it's so very similar to . . ." Glancing guiltily at her husband, she let the sentence trail off, veering quickly away from the danger.

"I'm an only child"—Clare shifted course smoothly—"so I had a perfect view of what went on between my folks. And I don't know how much truth there is in this, but they say that whether you like it or not, there are a lot of things about having watched your mother—seen *who* she was, and *how* she behaved—that you take on for yourself, whether or not you mean to do it, or want to." She spoke rapidly, as if she couldn't change the subject from "marriage" to "mothers and daughters" quickly enough.

Katie, who, like her brother Carl, had arrived at this meeting dressed all in black—black sweater, black leggings, black boots—had been sitting silently in her seat until this moment. She looked, as always, as if she could have stepped out of a glossy magazine ad; she was the American dream girl, sandy-haired, strong-featured, leggy, and attractive. True, her face was slightly broken out this afternoon, and her hair was a little stringy, as if it needed washing; but she couldn't have prevented herself from looking winningly handsome if she'd wanted to.

She had been sulking, but now the subject of mothers and daughters (which was perhaps stirring fears about her own daughterly fate) seemed to bring her to angry life. Shifting position, she sat up very straight and declared to no one in particular: "Last summer, when things at home were really awful, I was talking with one of my brothers. And we were just talking about how it really sucked, just being there, and we agreed that we didn't understand why Mom and Dad shouldn't get a divorce. Because, I mean, that's the easy way out, isn't it?" Her eyes were fixed upon the far wall, past the circle of chairs in which we were convened.

"Were you thinking," asked Bob Horwitz, "that it would be better for the three of you kids, or better for them?" His voice sounded loud in the startled silence that had followed Katie's outburst.

"Better for everyone." Her voice was tart. "Not that I think divorce is *good*," she added, meeting his gaze, "but what's the point of subjecting children to a marriage that doesn't work, instead of just splitting up?"

A Family-Wide Unconscious Assumption:
Confronting Dad Will Lead to Disaster

According to Katie, she and her brothers were all sick of the ongoing tension and the never-ending arguments. "No"—the daughter amended that statement immediately, in an indignant tone—"you couldn't call what happens in our house 'arguments.' They're *not* arguments, because arguments involve two people—equally—who are yelling back and forth at each other. But when stuff goes on at our house, it's just *Dad* who's always doing it."

I met and held her gaze for a moment, then for some reason turned to look at the twins. Carl was staring gloomily down at his hands, which were folded, fingers entwined, upon his lap. Bobby, however, was looking at his older sister as if awed and amazed by her outspokenness. "You mean it's your dad who's always making loud remarks?" Dr. Horwitz asked her.

Katie turned back to him and nodded. "Yeah, and it seems as if everything *annoys* my dad; everything gets on his nerves. So he'll start yelling his head off, about something or other, and then just—*storm out*, leave the room!"

Her voice dropped, took on a forlorn note. "But nobody ever gets to say a word to him directly. You *can't* yell back at him—not at *my* dad—not unless you feel like getting kicked out of the house."

"Does that include your mother?" the therapist asked her, in a pleasant, equable tone, as if they were engaged in an ordinary conversation and her parents were not present and listening.

Katie nodded again. "No matter *what*," she went on, "my father has the upper hand in absolutely everything. And even if my parents aren't in an argument, my mom is still—it's as if she's way *below* him. It just seems to me that my mom is always trying to keep the lid on, but I still wouldn't even call what goes on at home 'arguments.' "

"Then what would you call them, Katie?" I asked her, leaning forward in her direction. She turned an agitated face toward me, "I don't know. I don't know a *word* for them. It's just like—upheavals. But I really don't know what to call them—'major disturbances,' maybe. The problem is, we never talk about any of these things—when they happen, or later—because we *can't argue back*.

"Or at least we *feel* we can't argue back," she amended, then said: "Gee, if I were as *rude* to my dad as he is to me, it would be like—like—" She stopped short, as if at the brink of the unimaginable. "I would be *dead* if I did that," she said at last.

Katie seemed, at that moment, to be articulating a fantasy that was affecting everyone in the Maguire household in a powerful fashion. This fantasy was, as well as I could phrase it to myself: "Dare to challenge or confront Dad directly, and death and devastation will follow." It is shared unconscious beliefs of this sort (known, in the technical literature, as "basic unconscious assumptions") that underlie and lead to the establishment of certain covert but unbreakable family rules—in this case, "You don't confront Dad."

But what I found myself wondering about, just then, was whether this group-wide belief had ever actually been tested in reality by any one of them. Was the father of this family as terrifyingly dangerous as they all believed him to be?

An Always-Imminent Battle

Clare Maguire's efforts to evade open conflict produced a perpetually breathless sense in the household—the sense of an always-imminent battle, a fight on the verge of breaking out. What was easy to lose sight of, in one's natural sympathy with her victim stance, was the role that she herself played in the repetitive sequence of events.

Clare's unwillingness to take a stand, to defend herself and her children, was feeding into her husband's ability to "rant and rave" at anyone in the family and to go unchallenged. As matters now stood, no differences of opinion between individual family members could ever be discussed, nor could real disagreements be resolved in a mutually satisfying fashion. This wife and mother simply ducked every confrontation she possibly could, without seeming to notice that in point of fact this was *not* preventing arguments from happening.

Matt and Clare Maguire were, in fact, continually arguing—and these arguments were highly disturbing to their children. Clare's own reading of events was, however, that the open fights that erupted were simply those she hadn't succeeded in avoiding.

Now Dr. Horwitz, gazing thoughtfully at the mother, said slowly and reflectively, "What I'm wondering about is whether your ability to simply let these episodes go by, without much challenge, is part of why Matt behaves in the way that he does. And I'm wondering, too," he added, "if this is something that results in Katie and the boys feeling abandoned—left to fend for themselves in a situation in which they feel there's no one able to protect them."

"Are you trying to say," she asked him, looking thoroughly frightened, "that you think I should confront Matt at the time these things—these—these—*outbursts*—are happening?" Then, almost reflexively, she turned to me, as if for female support. I, another woman, would surely understand that she was being asked (by a male) to contemplate the unthinkable; I would understand that an angry man could never be opposed openly. And I, although I *am* in fact capable of challenging an angry man, felt myself resonating to her fear as reflexively as a harp string; once upon a time, I had been a little girl who was scared to death of her own dad.

Still, I couldn't help but wonder about the degree to which Clare Maguire's evident apprehension might be based on things that were real and current in her present life. Did she feel physically vulnerable—as if this large, tense husband of hers might, at some point, lose control and attack her or one of the children? Or had he done so already? I returned the mother's gaze, and said to her with sympathetic frankness, "As things stand now, Matt's like someone who runs in an election unopposed—he's going to win, every time."

Almost as soon as these words were uttered, I realized I was allying with Clare-the-victim and defending her. I was being swept into this family's highly polarized portrayal of itself, in which one partner was cast in the role of the complete victim and the other played the total tyrant.

At that moment, as if instinctively, Bob Horwitz turned to Matt and said, "One thing about this conversation that worries me is that you're ending up being portrayed as the bad guy. And something that's true about families is that there *aren't* really any bad guys. What there are is bad patterns—which get going and seem to have a life of their own, so that no one knows how to stop them."

Everyone, including me, looked at him dubiously. From a theoretical point of view, I understood what he was saying: The tyrant and the victim are often in a collusive, unconscious deal, in which the tyrant carries all the rage and aggression, while the victim carries the helplessness and vulnerability for the pair of them. Nevertheless, the emotional force of this family's drama—especially for someone as familiar with the plot as I am—was hypnotic, and it would have been awfully easy to buy into their black-and-white, good guy–bad guy self-presentation.

An Eerie Similarity

Matt Maguire's facial expression in repose—a wry, somewhat sardonic half-smile—hadn't changed much throughout the earlier part of the session. Even seated, the father of this family looked tall, a large, broad-shouldered, masculine presence. There was something faintly cinematic about the atmosphere this man created around himself. Matt Maguire had the star's air, the expectation that he would naturally command center stage and be found captivating and compelling.

I found myself wondering, not for the first time, if there was an unseen presence in this room—another woman in the picture who would, perhaps, be accompanying this restless, dissatisfied man on his upcoming long sail to the Caribbean? Then I realized, with a start, that he was well aware of my careful inspection.

He was, in fact, nodding at me, urging me or even pleading with me to speak up and say something. What? I felt confused, as if I'd received, in that flash of nonverbal communication, an SOS of some kind—one whose meaning I couldn't decipher. But the nearest words that I could have put to it, if I had been asked to write it down, would have been "Please reach out to me, if you can receive this; I'm feeling frightened."

I had the sudden intuition, then, that the family dictator was feeling fragile and uncertain—an intuition that I found disconcerting. It was hard to keep in mind, in this system filled with polar stereotypes, the notion that the guy in the black shirt, the menacing tyrant, might be someone who was also, at some level, needy, uncertain, and dependent.

I turned back to his wife, who had suddenly brought up the same topic that she'd been so eager to avoid just a short while earlier. Clare Maguire was reflecting once again about the "eerie similarity" between what was happening in her present-day family and what life had been like in her family of origin.

An Internalized Diagram for Being: The Degraded, Peacemaking Female

"When you think about it, it's almost as if we're all passing this whole scenario along," Clare said. "And you know"—she was speaking in the somewhat halting voice of someone whose words are being uttered even as she's discovering what her thoughts are—"I've sometimes thought that maybe, when Matt gets into these big upsets, that this *monster*—this *ogre*—is really not that powerful at all. But I think—no, I'm *sure*—that the reason I don't jump right in and start yelling back at him when these situations come up is because I revert to being seven or eight years old. And whenever this happens, he's my father, and I just wouldn't *dare* . . ."

So the inviolable rule "You don't confront Dad" had not originated in this generation. As she spoke, the mother's gaze lit briefly upon every person in the office *other* than her husband, whom she studiously avoided looking at directly. Then she added, "It's not that I'm really an adult confronting another adult, in an adult situation. I get clicked back to what this reminds me of, which is 'Don't you *dare* open your mouth!' "

Undoubtedly, the basic, system-wide assumption here was that the male parent in the household was never to be challenged because, as Katie had said, one "would be dead" if one ever dared to try it. "That's one thing I never *did* do—open my mouth in front of my father. I never confronted him—it wouldn't have gotten me anywhere. And besides," Clare added childishly, "it would have been disrespectful."

We all fell silent in the wake of that statement. I felt a surge of sympathy, almost painful, for this aging, pretty woman's lifelong struggle to please and placate men who were simply not ever going to be appeased and mollified. Then I noticed that Katie, next in line and ready to inherit the role of the degraded, peacemaking female, was gazing at her mother open-mouthed.

I turned to look at the father, who was now leaning forward in his seat; he seemed to be absorbed in what was happening, and far less preoccupied with himself.

"But, you know, there's more to this than just my not fighting back," Clare resumed, after a pause. Her voice was rising in pitch, sounding clearer and more certain. "Because there are times when Matt'll say to me, 'Being married to you is just like having a fourth child'—that he wishes I'd participate more in some of the things that have to happen."

She turned to face her husband. "Like the paperwork, you know? And I'll say to you, 'The paperwork is certainly not one of my strengths, but I'm willing to try.'" She shrugged, turned away, and appealed to Bob Horwitz and then to me: "But then *he'll* say that that's too juvenile an atti- tude on my part, and he'll insist on doing it all himself."

She shrugged again and said to the entire assemblage, almost flippantly, "I guess we're a good, disturbed couple, because he's the responsible, older adult, which helps me to remain very irresponsible in certain areas." And, I thought, very helpless and powerless as well.

"But, you know"—Clare turned back in Matt's direction—"I'd *like* to let go of the off-balance part—I really would. I don't enjoy how off-balance our relationship is, but it's as if I don't know how to change or be differ- ent." He didn't respond, but merely lifted his shoulders as if to say "I don't know how to, either." So she turned to the assemblage at large, and said, "Well, that's the way it is; but still, the wheels turn, the family goes on and, for better or worse, life continues."

A Relational Model: The Tyrant, the Victim, and Their Young, Dependent Witnesses

The internalized model of a family that Clare Maguire had brought with her to adulthood was, in its essential structure, a system that involved the "peacemaking," placating woman; the "ranting and raving" man; and the defenseless children with a "perfect view" of the things that were happen- ing between their parents.

Her husband's own family background had, on the face of it, been radi- cally different from her own. For while Clare's family had been comfort- ably middle-class, and white Anglo-German Protestant, Matt's had been first-generation Irish Catholic and lived at poverty level, even dipping below it occasionally. These marital partners had, nevertheless, had strik- ingly similar experiences in their original families.

Both had been witnesses, in their early years, to a marriage between a tyrant and a victim. The only difference was that, in Matt's case, the powerless spouse had been his father, who'd been subject to paralyzing depressive episodes and sometimes unable to continue work. It was as if the marital system with which Clare had been so familiar had been flipped over or turned inside out. For in Matt's early years, it had been the female partner who'd usurped the domestic power and control, leaving the male partner helpless and impotized.

His mother had been, as this forty-six-year-old son described her, "vicious-tempered," while his father had been "totally spineless." Thus, although the person in the "tyrant" shoes and the person in the "victim" shoes had been of different genders, the all-powerful/utterly powerless relational system had been essentially the same. And if Clare's inner image of a relationship between a male and a female had to do with the woman's being deprecated and dominated, Matt's internalized view was one in which the man had been overwhelmed and defeated. This must have threatened his very sense of efficacy, his sense of maleness itself.

Matt himself had had to take over—to function, early in his life, as the man of the house. He could not, over the course of his childhood, slowly grow up and become a man *like* his father; instead, Matt had been forced to be his male parent's replacement.

He had had to step into enormous shoes very early, and to fill the responsible, patriarchal position that had been vacated. Now, having sold his thriving business at age forty-six, this middle-aged father had the stated ambition "to try and catch up" with all the enjoyment of life that he'd had to forgo throughout his boyhood.

"I started working very early. *Very* early," he complained, in the same aggrieved tone of voice. "Beginning with a job as a paperboy at the age of eight. I *always* worked. So I saw my friends get to go away to college—and come home in the summers and have a ball—and I just got out of high school and had to get a job immediately. I feel, now, that I deprived myself of a lot, doing that. And I don't want to go on depriving myself—I want to catch up."

"And 'catching up' means having fun, enjoying yourself?" I asked him.

" 'Catching up' means *doing nothing*," he said, with indignation in his voice. "And not having to do things for *other people* . . . *They* can do for me. Catch-up time is payback time," he added—more, I thought, for the benefit of his family than for myself.

There was a brief silence, during which his expression began slowly softening, and the father murmured as if to himself: "Catch-up time is somebody getting my slippers for me. . . . *That's* catching up. . . ." The look on his face was beatific.

"I don't see how that jibes with being all by yourself on a boat," Bob

Horwitz observed lightly. I looked at the psychologist swiftly; did he, too, have the thought that there might be someone else along on that trip to the Caribbean? But Matt simply stared at the psychologist as if he were being obtuse. "Well, *doing* for me," he said, with a brusque shrug.

He himself, the father added, had been "doing for others" ever since he could remember, helping out in a desperately poor household. "But I don't believe I was doing *for myself*, not ever," he stated angrily, turning to glare, briefly, at each of the children and then, wordlessly, at his wife.

It was almost as though some sort of existential debt had been declared in arrears, and Matt Maguire were now embarked on a mission to obtain his own well-merited but infuriatingly overdue payment. He had never, ever gotten back the degree of caretaking that he'd had to give out so early in his life, and so now his number one priority was to give that caretaking to himself.

The Parentified Child: Destructive Entitlement

It was an early innovator in the field of family therapy, the psychiatrist Ivan Boszormenyi-Nagy, who introduced into the clinical literature the concept of the "parentified child." This is the child who, according to Boszormenyi-Nagy's definition, has been destructively exploited by the adult generation.

As Boszormenyi-Nagy and his co-author, Barbara Krasner, have observed in *Between Give and Take*, "the relational misuse of small children to satisfy the possessive, dependent, destructive, or sexual needs of one or several adults" results in massive loss of trust on the part of the offspring. The parental caretakers, who are, in the natural sequence of events, expected to nurture and protect their child, are the very people who are overburdening and demanding impossible or inappropriate care and nurturance *from* him or her.

'Lasting damage takes place, write these therapists, when the young lose faith in the integrity of those around them and conclude that they are living in "an intrinsically exploitative and manipulative world." It is at this point that children develop a sense of what Boszormenyi-Nagy termed "destructive entitlement"; that is, they adopt the assumption that, because their most basic human needs were poorly attended to or totally unmet during the long, dependent years of childhood, an existential debt has accumulated. Destructive entitlement is the sense that one is *owed to*.

What Matt was referring to as "catch-up time" and "payback time" was his own sense that it was now or never when it came to making good on the pleasure-and-enjoyment debt that had been accruing throughout his entire lifetime. The unspent credit, in his inner ledger, had reached an intolerably high level; as Boszormenyi-Nagy and Krasner write, "Why should the 'child,' now grown, give someone better than he got? . . . The relational unfairness of the last generation has spilled over and become consequential for the present generation."

This parent's sense of grief about the loss of his own childhood was erupting now, in the middle of his life, in the context of his relationships with his own children, whom he viewed as recalcitrant and unappreciative and by whom he felt totally exploited.

The Family Bad Guy

At forty-six, Matt Maguire was simultaneously cognizant of his maturing children's movement into the kind of adolescence he himself had once yearned for—unburdened and carefree—and angrily aware of his own role as the family bad guy.

"You mentioned my being the family bad guy," he said to Bob Horwitz shortly before the session's end, "and I get a *lot* of that. I get a lot of that from the boys, and I feel it now from Katie—that I'm an unsettling faction in the family." He felt, the father complained, as if he were getting in everybody's way, and being forced to impose his own will upon them all in order to get anything accomplished.

It was a thankless, draining job, and he was thoroughly sick of it. "It's as if I'm this terrible *drag* that no one in the family wants to deal with. So"— the father drew himself up and sat tall in his seat—"rather than telling them something for the nine hundredth time, I'm getting out of it. See, understand?" His expression was surly; he was saying, in so many words, that if the members of this family didn't plan to shape up and reform into the kind of family he wanted, his own plan was to desert them.

Still, despite its irascible overlay, there was not only anger but anxiety in the father's voice. I leaned forward and asked him whether anyone in the family had been urging him *not* to go, or at least to return to them soon. At this, Matt bridled and told me that nobody had. "Not a *single person*," he reiterated in an affronted tone, adding that when he'd talked about possibly getting home in time for Thanksgiving, Katie had suggested that he might want to stay down there a little bit longer. He shot an angry look at his daughter.

Then he turned to stare at Carl and Bobby. They, too, he muttered, probably saw his coming absence as a way of lessening the level of tension in the household. "Not only will there be *less* tension, I'm sure there'll be *no* tension . . . because *I'm* the visible source of tension when I'm there." Neither of his sons responded, nor did they meet their parent's eye; they merely shifted in their chairs apprehensively.

As Matt himself saw it, the central issue was that for him, living in a clean, orderly house was important; and for the rest of the family, this didn't seem to matter. "I wish it did, but it doesn't, and I could go on and on—and maybe they could, too—but after a while, nobody wants to listen or to hear me. . . . So, okay, let me find out what *I* need—" He was threatening abandonment again.

"—and then if other people want to live another way, that's fine for them," he concluded, landing back in the loveless (if responsible and controlling) position in which he tended to find himself. "It's too *much*," he burst out suddenly, his expression darkening. There were never, ever family conversations about anything pleasant, he continued, his voice rising indignantly. "We can't get past *breathing* from day to day, let alone actually *enjoy* anything. So I really feel like I'm not just taking the boat down for warm-water storage; I'm escaping."

No one said a word. "A lot of it is—I just don't feel *appreciated* in any way," the father acknowledged, out of nowhere, "and it was so different for me, the way *I* grew up—you *had* to work. You had to; there was no other way. And now I feel that's all I've been doing—and I can't get an ounce of sentiment from my wife or children. I want it *badly*," he added, in a hurt, offended voice, "but it's just not happening." Matt seemed to be coming into contact, however briefly, with the feelings of grief and longing that lay deep within, buried underneath the wrath and resentment.

But he quickly reverted to his angry stance again, asserting that aside from his obvious economic function, the people in his family just didn't seem to care about him—not even now, when he was threatening to go out of their lives and possibly never come back. He was, it seemed to me, hoping and needing to hear them say that they wanted him to stay, or that they would be awaiting his return, but his life had not taught him that there were *other* ways to get his emotional needs met than by means of control, imprecations, and intimidation.

"I just don't feel loved at all! It's a drag," the father cried out suddenly, painfully, as if the words were being wrenched from him against his own will. "And these *self-serving* kids—oh my God. I know they're young, but still it's not *right*, I'm sure it's not right. The way *I* had to grow up—I don't know; maybe you can't expect other people to appreciate that. Still"—he looked at his sons, his face suffused with outrage—"if you had just an ounce of responsibility—just an *ounce*—" The twins didn't move, but sat there upright, as stiff-backed as marines during an inspection.

"It sounds, Matt," I said to their father, hearing the slight flutter in my own voice as I spoke, "as if it's hard to watch them have a real childhood when you were forced to go out and work so hard so early in your own life."

He made no response, so I continued: "You didn't quite have a chance to have a real childhood yourself, and here you are, providing it for all of them."

"Yes," he said, and the countenance he turned to me was calmer. "You're right, and I don't know if I'm begrudging them the childhood at all, or if all I want or need to hear is: 'I'm a kid, and having it good, and thanks for giving me the opportunity.' That's really it. I want them to be kids, but—" He stopped, turned back to Carl and Bobby, and shook a reproving finger at them. "But just don't shit on me—don't expect it all to fall in your lap—it's not automatic."

Matt Maguire's simmering anger, always ready to bubble up, had been rekindled by an inner source of combustion. His adolescent children were, after all, getting what he himself had never had—a carefree, financially untroubled youth—and they didn't seem to feel overly obligated to listen to him, follow orders, show their appreciation and their awareness that there might be things owing to *him* in return.

Parental Projective Identification: Projecting, Perceiving, and Attacking in One's Child or Children What Has Once Been Repudiated and Condemned Within the Self

It was as if, within this middle-aged father, two opposite internal images of an adolescent boy were struggling to gain primacy and expression. One was the inner imago of a good, hardworking teenager in relationship to a demanding, "vicious-tempered" mother who had forced him to become the breadwinning man of her household.

The other was the inner imago of the carefree (therefore "selfish") boy who wanted to go off and have fun with the other teenagers, to evade the responsibilities being prematurely thrust upon him by his oppressive parent. It was this bad, self-centered "inner boy" whose needs Matt now wanted to catch up with and gratify, and whom he had reinvoked and now perceived and roundly condemned in the behavior of his adolescent sons.

They were the youngsters who were playful ("irresponsible"), who enjoyed life (were "unappreciative"), and who were as happily self-involved ("selfish") as he himself had never been permitted to be. He was now projecting, perceiving, and attacking *in his sons* the adolescent self-absorption and lightheartedness that he'd once had to repress and condemn in himself.

Resurrecting the Past: An Old Inner Conflict Externalized and Struggled with in the Present

The fact that Matt Maguire's extraordinary success had made it possible for his kids to have what he'd never had might have been a source of psychic healing, pride, and gratification. But Matt was, as his rage about his past so clearly indicated, still entangled in the skeins of a highly conflicted early attachment.

He was reenacting, with the family he and Clare had created, certain charged aspects of his own early history—most strikingly, the relationship that had once existed between an overburdened boy and his harshly demanding mother. It was as part of an unconscious but very real effort to deal with the past that this father had induced his adolescent offspring onto the family stage, given them their designated roles, and drafted them into the restaging of his own internal dilemma.

It was in this fashion that *the unresolved conflict inside him had been externalized and transposed into an outer conflict that was very palpable and real.* It had now become an ongoing fight between himself and his "self-centered" adolescent children, one that was occurring in the world of outer reality.

What this parent now perceived in his children was the irresponsible, self-absorbed lightheartedness that must have been, during his own young years, a savagely repressed part of his own inner being. For throughout the dependent years of childhood and early adolescence—the years of paramount need for parental support—even having such feelings would have been a highly threatening experience. If he didn't meet his hard, strong-willed mother's demands, he might lose her nurturance completely.

His mother's love was, as the growing youngster perceived it, *conditional upon his performance, and had to be earned.* And the punishment for not going out to work for the family as she demanded might be the loss of her necessary love and her caring. So the inner boy who'd really wanted to go off with his friends and enjoy himself had been forced underground and out of conscious awareness—as had the attendant feelings of anger and resentment. Such feelings were lethal, too dangerous to contemplate. If he "had" such feelings—and if his superpowerful parent were to know he had those feelings—he might be abandoned completely.

Now, however, many years later, in his interactions with his "ungrateful and unappreciative" sons, Matt was recreating a relationship in which he himself had once participated and which lived on inside him, unprocessed and unresolved. He was reenacting, with his children, his own early experiences; but he himself was now cast in the role of the browbeating parent, while his sons occupied the role of the growing boy who really wants to have a carefree life of his own and is not being permitted to do so.

Matt Maguire had, in this present-day resurrection of that charged relationship with his mother, identified with her cruelly demanding values. Now *he* was the harsh disciplinarian who wanted his boys to give up their playful carefreeness and become as prematurely adult and responsible as he'd had to be. And his sons, *as he perceived them*, had become the latter-day personification of the resentful, self-absorbed bad "inner boy" who had once been so ruthlessly suppressed and banished from his own conscious awareness.

In this updated version of his family script, Matt had projected into his sons the repressed and silenced half of an old inner ambivalence—and in them he saw the outrageous backsliding, anger, and rebellion that he'd never dared connect with during that earlier period of his own life. Now, grieving and brooding over his lost childhood, this father saw his maturing children's wishes to enjoy themselves—and to begin developing inner and outer lives of their own, apart from the needs of the family—as the utter treason it would have been had he himself ever dared to try it.

Matt was reliving the past, but this time in the role of his "vicious-tempered" and exacting parent. He simply could not see his sons as individual and separate persons, because they represented one side of the internal conflict that had been raging inside him for a lifetime—a polarized conflict about *either* "enjoying life" *or* "being a responsible member of the family."

Curiously enough, this middle-aged parent could be fully articulate about his own desire for "catch-up time" and "payback time" in order to pursue his own boyhood dream of lighthearted fun and enjoyment. Matt was now about to cruise off on the family's boat for an undetermined period of time amid an ominous haze of threats about not returning and disconnecting from the family completely.

But the image of the lighthearted, irresponsible youth, as it lived on within him, surely did not exist independently of its polarized opposite: the inner image of a boy in relationship to a demanding, attacking maternal parent. Thus it was that even as he embarked on the voyage that would remove him from the burdens of caring for the family—as he sailed off to recapture his lost adolescence, ignoring the half-grown children who needed their father to be there for them during this complex, transitional period of their own lives—Matt Maguire had to be hearing within himself the critical voice of the woman who had first insisted that he assume his manly family burdens and forgo his own carefree childhood.

And even as he loudly proclaimed his independence from his ungrateful, rebellious, uncaring family, he must have been, in his subjective world, experiencing his "internal mother's" ceaseless rebukes and her outrage. It was this attack from within, unendurable and unanswerable, that was exploding in anger at his "self-indulgent, irresponsible" offspring. The unresolved emotional issues of the past, now being rekindled by his adolescent children's initial efforts at separation and individuation ("breaking ranks," in the father's view), were being reinvoked and reenacted as paramount issues of the Maguire family's very present-day reality.

CHAPTER 9

Struggling for Control:
The Bulimic Strategy

After Christmas, Katie Maguire returned from the vacation break with a peculiar story to tell. This was one of our alternate-week sessions, and Bob Horwitz and I were meeting with her alone. Even so, the teenager buried her face in her hands, giggled nervously, and said that while something strange had occurred when she was home from boarding school, she might not be ready to talk with us about it.

A moment later, though, she sat bolt upright, an arch grin on her face, her head tilted jauntily sideward, and launched into the tale. "It was on Christmas Eve, and I was wrapping presents in my room," she recounted, "and I heard my parents having sex. And I—ugh!—I just wanted to get out of there. I almost threw up. It was just like . . . oh, something *disgusting*. I ran downstairs and I was sweating and shaking and my brother Carl said to me, 'What's wrong?' And I said, 'Oh, they're having sex.' So we all tiptoed back up there and listened."

Katie flipped her head back suddenly, for her thick brown-blond hair was sliding down her forehead and over her eyes. I'd noticed that she liked to use her hair to play a kind of toddler's peekaboo: "Now I see you, and now you're here; but whenever I want to, I can let my hair slip forward and make *you* disappear completely."

"It was so *gross*," she went on excitedly. "It sounded like a porno. Their bed is really *antique*, and it was squeaking. I couldn't look at them for the next three days."

She subsided into her chair as if the thrill of the revelation had lasted no longer than it took her to make it. For a few moments not a further word was spoken. Then she added sullenly, "What's worse is how they don't even get along. I mean, if they got along and were lovey-dovey all the time, fine. But they *don't* get along; they *fight*. I was so grossed out by them doing that—I mean I couldn't believe it. And it ruined my whole vacation." Katie laughed contemptuously. "It was hard to think of them as Mom and Dad after that."

"Is that a first?" Dr. Horwitz asked, his voice neutral, and the teenager's wary gray-blue eyes fixed upon him reflectively. Katie Maguire was, I reflected, at once an extremely attractive young woman and a frightened sixteen-year-old child.

"No," she said at last, "I've heard them have sex before that, when I was younger. But I'd never really *thought* about it; sex didn't have much of an impact on me, I suppose." This time, she admitted, she'd been extraordinarily shocked and disturbed; in her own view, her younger brothers had actually responded far more "maturely" than she had. "Carl and Bobby just went back to watching TV, and *I* was the one who was grossed out. Like, I kept running down and saying to them: 'Don't you want to go up there and listen?' "

Dr. Horwitz, inclining toward her slightly, said calmly, "You sound as if you were pretty interested. . . . Otherwise, why would you have wanted to do that?" I almost laughed, for I could not imagine any teenage daughter *not* being intensely curious about the situation Katie was describing.

Katie began giggling nervously again. "It was just—I had to make sure that I wasn't making it up. I said to myself, 'Wait, this isn't happening,' so then I'd go up again. And then it was, 'Oh, God, they *are* having sex,' so I'd go running back downstairs."

"Was the door shut?" I asked, wondering whether her parents had simply been behaving obtusely or had been staging some odd kind of exhibitionistic event. Katie nodded; the door had been closed, and the lights were off, she told me. "It was early—before dinner—around seven-thirty, and both of them were completely crocked."

Dr. Horwitz raised a questioning eyebrow. "On Christmas Eve? Is that a family tradition, getting drunk on Christmas Eve?"

Katie frowned, shook her head. "No, but they drank a *lot* this past vacation, and I think, if some of my friends from school had been there, they'd have thought my parents were *lushes*. But my mom and dad only drink because . . . well, my dad just drinks to relax himself, after going out on a ski patrol, or out on the slopes . . . whatever. After a couple of martinis, he is *blitzed*, though." She laughed indulgently, as if her father were her naughty but amusing child.

Matt Maguire had, despite his bluster and threats, returned from the Bahamas in time for the Thanksgiving holiday, and he now seemed to be on an open-ended work furlough while the Maguires lived off the proceeds from the sale of his business. The family had just returned from a three-week Christmas vacation, which they'd spent at their ski house in Vermont.

Sex, Hunger, and Family Boundaries

"As for Mom, she drinks at night so she won't really care how much she eats," Katie now continued, in an earnest tone, "and then she'll really *pig out*. One night, my mom pigged out until she threw up—it was disgusting, so *sick*. But she'll eat so much that she can't even *move*. She doesn't eat all day, not until dinner, and she says that if she *doesn't* drink, then she doesn't gorge out.

"The alcohol increases her appetite," Katie explained, almost pedantically, as if instructing us upon the effects of the drug. But then she burst out laughing at the notion of her mother's lust for food going so dramatically out of control. I thought at once of Clare Maguire's remark to the effect that "there are a lot of things about having watched your mother— seen *who* she was, and *how* she behaved—that you take on for yourself, whether or not you mean to, or want to," and it occurred to me that another mother-daughter pattern was at play here.

Certainly, "pigging out" and "bingeing" were terms that could be used synonymously. And since Katie was still struggling with her bulimic symptoms—using periodic junk-food gorgings as a form of emotional solace, and purges as a means of controlling potential weight gain—this little tale of family life seemed to me a most significant one. As their adolescent daughter saw it, Clare Maguire drank in order to release all constraints about food and dieting, and Matt Maguire drank in order to be "blitzed" for the forthcoming evening.

"You said the noises you heard from your parents' room sounded like a porno," Dr. Horwitz now observed. "Have you seen some porno movies yourself?"

Katie nodded and, to my amazement, answered that her dad and her grandfather (Clare's father, who'd lived with the family until his recent death from kidney disease) had watched X-rated movies together on a regular basis. "And you— were you watching with them?" I asked, trying to sound unworried and to keep the sense of concern out of my voice.

What, I was wondering, were this family's rules (both explicit and conscious, *and* implicit and unconscious) insofar as sexual privacy was concerned? And even more specifically, what were the Maguires' rules in regard to the drawing of sexual boundaries between the older and the younger generations?

As family therapist Harry J. Aponte has observed, it is typically the case that when a parental couple wants to make love, they will be mindful and considerate of other members of the household. The husband and wife "will plan sexual activity at a time and place that will allow them privacy from the children." Because the boundary around their sexual activities as spouses must exclude the children, the partners "must plan their sexual life in such a way that it does not subvert their functions as parents."

Were Clare and Matt Maguire, as a general rule, accustomed to maintaining their sexual privacy—so that leaping into bed on Christmas Eve, with their adolescent daughter wrapping gifts in an adjoining bedroom, represented a "binge" of some kind on their part?

Covert Control and Overt Compliance: Hiding/Hurting the Self

Katie Maguire's bulimic symptoms could, it seemed to me, be understood as a form of compromise—a way of *not* confronting her parents about their escalating, frightening quarrels and of *not* challenging overtly her father's tyrannical, overcontrolling reign. She could appear to be the compliant, attractively pleasing young female she was supposed to be, while secretly having it her own way by bingeing on the sweet, fat-filled, high-calorie foods that were "forbidden" in the appearance-conscious world of her family.

In this covert fashion, Katie could both angrily rebel (take control, and eat what she chose to eat) while undoing the interpersonal consequences of her greedy, wickedly impulsive, willful behavior. And the vomiting of the food, as she'd noted later on in a private diary that she'd asked me to read, left a feeling of "cleanliness and purity" inside.

In some curious way, I thought, each of these gorging and purging episodes resembled a small, self-contained morality play. For, as I read through the journal Katie had given me, I quickly recognized that the dramatic action always began with the buildup of feelings of intense, inner neediness—a mounting, insatiable craving, and an accompanying angry tension about the ways in which her real and pressing emotional hunger was being ignored.

The junk-food binge seemed to be part of a frantic effort to nurture and soothe herself—to meet her own needs and give herself what nobody else was willing or able to give her—during which she "fell from grace" and capitulated into unbridled, gluttonous sinfulness. She reveled in her gobbling down of the sweet "nourishment" from which she sought comfort, calm, and satiation. In this frenzy of self-feeding she was, symbolically, serving in two roles: She was both herself as baby and her own sustenance-providing caretaker.

All too soon, however, the initial almost manic elation experienced at the outset of her solitary feast began to subside. Nevertheless, as Katie described it, she continued "chowing down" the bags of cheap cookies and chocolates with which she'd supplied herself. It was as though there were no limit to her needfulness and hunger, no bottom to the inner emptiness she was trying to fill.

She ate until she could, literally and physically, swallow nothing more. At this point, she always started to feel slightly queasy, nauseous, guilty, "fat," "disgusting"—so she put two fingers down her throat and was soon spewing everything forth. At last, in the immediate aftermath of the episode, Katie Maguire experienced the inner purification associated with atonement.

It was as if all the need, desperation, and angry poisons within her had been evacuated, along with the too-rich and too-copious food she had gobbled down. Her loss of impulse control and "fall" into wild and unstoppable eating had been expiated by means of the gut-wrenching, physically violent act of purgation. And while she might feel despondent and ashamed about what had just occurred, she *did* feel different, some-how. The entire incident was over—at least until the next time—and meanwhile Katie had, in some perverse fashion, taken charge of her own life and fed herself.

What Actually Causes Bulimia Nervosa?

It is undeniably the case that there are many young adolescent females who spring from family backgrounds as difficult and problematic as Katie Maguire's (or, for that matter, far more so). Why had she, in particular, developed bulimia nervosa; and what causative factors do, in general, lie at the root of this dangerous, and at times even fatal, psychiatric dysfunction?

The answer to the latter question is that no one is completely certain. Bulimia nervosa has existed, as an official mental disorder, for only a very short period of time. But what *is* clear is that bulimia is highly prevalent, particularly among females, and that it is growing ever more so. The binge-purge syndrome afflicts the population at a ratio of nine to ten women to every man, and recent estimates suggest that as many as 3 percent of college-age females suffer from bulimia (less than 1 percent of young females are anorexic.)

Experts cannot, however, point to any single, unitary antecedent of the binge-purge syndrome. There seem, instead, to be an array of risk factors associated with the disorder's emergence, and some of them are sociolog-ical rather than psychological in nature.

Our society's current rage for skinniness is, most certainly, important among them. So, moreover, is the fact that this culture's view of what is to be considered fat has been changing over the past several decades. By way of example, an arresting study of Miss America contestants indicated that there was a significant *decrease* in both the body measurements and the body weights of Miss America aspirants in the twenty-year period between 1959 and 1979. In other words, as this research work (published in 1980) demonstrated, the "ideal female body" has been losing weight from the 1960s onward.

Later studies have only underscored this finding by showing that the winners of the Miss America pageant have consistently been significantly lighter than the other contest contenders. The beauty ideal of the late twentieth century is, apparently, someone who is not only "the fairest" but "the thinnest" in the land.

This understanding of what is beautiful and admirable in a female body is surely not lost upon the developing adolescent girl. From pubescence onward, the fledgling female's body shape has been in the process of total transformation. She has rounded out, become more curvaceous, and developed a cushion of womanly fat in the breasts and the buttocks.

This is all part of normal sexual maturation—the prepubertal female's body contains 10 to 15 percent more fat than that of her male age peer, while after puberty girls have twice as much body fat as boys do. The female at risk for bulimia is, however, someone who is *unnerved* by the metamorphosis her body is undergoing.

Because of her own deep-seated uncertainty about her worth and value as a human being, she is hypersensitive to these physical changes and profoundly miserable about them. So linked in her mind are "fat" and "unacceptability" that this extra, unfamiliar body fat feels to her like a humiliating public exposure of her inner sense of inadequacy and failure.

The "extra" pounds are, in her own mind, the symbolic equivalent of a billboard that has been slung over her chest and that she is being forced to carry with her wherever she goes—a huge placard advertising to the world her real valuelessness, lack of self-control, and incompetence. She must get rid of this damning weight very rapidly, at any cost, for she feels unmasked, deeply shamed, and mortified.

So she goes on a severe, self-punishing diet—which is the typical way bulimia gets started. It is in precisely this innocuous-seeming fashion— just going on a sharply restrictive diet, or a series of such diets—that an array of physiological responses comes into play in order to defend against *what her body experiences as a state of famine.*

One such predictable response to a starvation diet will be an ardent preoccupation with food and with eating. The person who is fasting may not be consuming any food, but she finds it difficult to think about anything else. Another reaction to intense hunger will be her body's fierce and natural urge to compensate for the deprivation. She will experience an enormous urge to eat—to eat vast amounts of food—in order to counter-act the acute craving that prolonged self-starvation brings. And in time, the urge to binge becomes overwhelming; the dieter's sense of control and self-mastery begin to falter.

What tends to happen is that, in the course of trying to assert total control over her own biological nature, the bulimic person loses control completely. She starts to eat not only "forbidden food," such as sweets and junk food, but to eat as much and as rapidly as she can (Katie often binged, for want of anything better, on whole loaves of white bread and peanut butter). Moral abstemiousness has led to glorious license.

But the fantastic, gluttonous gorging that ensues must be erased from her existence as soon as it has occurred. So she purges, takes laxatives or diuretics, or becomes involved in frantic exercising (frequently, she does several of these things), and becomes obsessed with undoing the damages related to her fall from the diet wagon. And in time, if the full-blown syndrome of bulimia nervosa develops, she will become so absorbed in this ritualistic dieting-bingeing-and-purging cycle that her weight will become the essence of her self-identity.

What she weighs will be the only aspect of herself that she considers important, the sole basis upon which she forms her self-judgments. If her weight drops she will feel, fleetingly, like a worthy, even triumphant human being. But if she puts the pounds back on, or gains even more—as will occur, inevitably, in the course of her yo-yo relating to food—she will feel like a bloated, loathsome, and (to use one of Katie Maguire's favorite words) "disgusting" monstrosity.

The Bulimic Diagnosis

Although bulimic symptoms had certainly been described in the psychi-atric literature of the nineteenth century, bulimia nervosa was not formally defined as a discrete clinical entity until very recently, in 1980. Before then, bulimic behaviors tended to be viewed as a peculiar variant, or accompaniment, of anorexia nervosa.

This was because it had been recognized that a significant number of individuals who initially starve themselves eventually switch to bingeing and purging as an alternate method of controlling their weight. It was known, too, that some anorexics engage in both behaviors at once—that is, they fast strenuously and engage in bingeing and purging as well.

But there are also so-called normal-weight bulimics—Katie Maguire was among them—who may go on diets often, but never do become involved in the severe self-starvation of anorexia. To distinguish those whose bingeing is the *primary* disturbance from those who are anorexic and bulimic, the newly defined psychiatric illness called bulimia nervosa was added to the psychiatric canon in the third (1980) edition of the *Diagnostic and Statistical Manual of Mental Disorders.*

The distinguishing features of bulimia, as set forth in the most recent, revised (1994) version of the diagnostic manual (*DSM-IV*) are the following:

A. *Recurrent episodes of binge eating. An episode of binge eating is characterized by both of the following:*

  (1) *eating, in a discrete period of time (e.g., within any 2-hour period), an amount of food that is definitely larger than most people would eat during a similar period of time and under similar circumstances*
  (2) *a sense of lack of control over eating during the episode (e.g., a feeling that one cannot stop eating or control what or how much one is eating.)*

Katie Maguire, who kept a food-behavior diary throughout the course of therapy, was clearly diagnosable by means of this criterion.

B. *Recurrent inappropriate compensatory behavior in order to prevent weight gain, such as self-induced vomiting; misuse of laxatives, diuretics, enemas, or other medications; fasting; or excessive exercise.*

Some of these last-named symptoms of bulimia, such as fasting or excessive exercise, are of course not always easy to distinguish from what would be considered normative feminine behavior in a society that strongly idealizes the slender female frame. Engaging "in vigorous exercise in order to prevent weight gain" (as in the above) and being "overconcerned with body shape and weight" (as appears in item D, below) seem to me to be diagnostic criteria for which an overwhelming number of women could currently qualify. For in our culture, an attractive, appealing woman is a thin one.

C. *The binge eating and inappropriate compensatory behavior both occur, on average, at least twice a week for three months.*

Katie's food-behavior diary indicated that she was not clearly diagnosable by means of this standard. For she binged erratically, depending on the degree of stress, rejection, and disappointment that she happened to be experiencing—and how capably she was managing to handle things. Some weeks, she didn't engage in any binges at all, while others she did exceed this twice-weekly average.

D. *Self-evaluation is unduly influenced by body shape and weight.*

Katie was clearly triumphant when her weight was at an acceptably low level, but when it crept higher, she felt like "disgusting" scum. As far as this approach to food was concerned, however, she was clearly being affected by the behavior of a mother whose own self-appraisal was much influenced by her weight, and who was, in a sense, bulimic also. For Clare Maguire had a habit of fasting all day and drinking liquor in the evening as a prelude to "pigging out." Indeed, as Clare had acknowledged, she hadn't had a normal relationship to food since going on a strict diet in her early adolescence. She had gone on that diet against the express wishes of her mother—who was, by the way, seriously overweight.

E. The disturbance does not occur exclusively during episodes of Anorexia Nervosa.

This statement is meant to underscore the current psychiatric position that bulimia nervosa is to be viewed as a mental disturbance in its own right, one that is not necessarily linked to anorexia nervosa, as was once believed.

Onset

The classical life moment in which bulimia begins is the transitional era spanning middle to late adolescence and very early adulthood. This is a period during which the individual is typically engaged in the work of separating her own self from the family matrix and defining herself as a differentiated human being.

Some clinicians and researchers believe that bulimia nervosa is a disorder of maturation, a breakdown that occurs as the young female is in the final phases of the adolescent transformation from dependent child to self-sufficient young adult. Specialists Susan C. Wooley and Ann Kearney-Cooke of the Eating Disorders Clinic at the University of Cincinnati Medical School have, for instance, proposed that anorexia nervosa represents severe problems surrounding the entrance into adolescence, while bulimia nervosa represents severe difficulties in leaving adolescence behind.

In the early phases of the adolescent transition, the major tasks involve the development of one's sexual being and the accompanying transfer of interest and energy into the world that lies outside the family. The anorexic individual staves off the development of secondary sexual characteristics by means of self-starvation; she becomes emaciated, falls below the critical weight at which menstruation will occur, and collapses back into the family's embrace.

The bulimic person has, suggest these experts, usually managed to negotiate the tasks of early adolescence in a successful fashion. She has become differentiated as a sexual human female, become less invested within the family, and is much more involved in the world of her peers. But, write Wooley and Kearney-Cooke (in the *Handbook of Eating Disorders*), "she falters later in the establishment of intimacy and authenticity and in peer relationships and in the separation from her family. She seems to know the steps but cannot dance."

Emotional Illiteracy: Freud's Alexithymia ("No Word for Emotions")

A real and very important risk factor in the development of bulimia nervosa has to do with a person's customary style of dealing with her own thoughts and feelings. Often, bulimics are peculiarly out of touch with their inner signals, as lost as pilots flying through the world without any radar contact with the ground. They deal with their own feelings—particularly distressing feelings—in a muddled, undifferentiated fashion, as if they themselves are completely incapable of tuning in and deciphering them.

It was Freud who first noted and described this peculiar form of disability, which he called "alexithymia" (a word derived from Greek roots that means "no word for emotions)." Individuals afflicted by this disorder seem unable, as he observed, to identify and discriminate between their varying internal mood states; it is as if they lack the most basic vocabulary to describe to themselves the things that are happening inside them.

It is most certainly not only bulimics who suffer from this inability to tune into their own feelings and name them correctly. This condition, which can perhaps best be characterized as a form of emotional illiteracy, is in my own view a not at all uncommon one—especially among men, who receive much intensive early training in distancing themselves from certain proscribed feelings, such as those having to do with vulnerability, the need for closeness, and feelings of inadequacy and weakness.

According to Inge Ortmeyer, director of clinical services at the Wilkins Center for Eating Disorders in Greenwich, Connecticut, bulimics (and also individuals suffering from other forms of eating disorder) often do have great difficulty recognizing and classifying their own internal experiences. Instead of knowing, for example, whether she is feeling bored, sad, irritated—or, for that matter, whether she is hungry or has a headache—the alexithymic individual simply experiences a massive inner disquietude. She is, rather like a preverbal child, *conscious* of her bodily sensations, but finds it hard to identify and describe the ideas and feelings associated with them.

So weak is the wattage of the alexithymic's inner spotlight that she can even find it problematic to make the distinction between a physical complaint, such as a headache, and a state of emotion such as anxiety or even loneliness. She may be feeling globally unhappy, but be unable to sort out her feelings, label them correctly, and figure out the sources from which they may have sprung. She may even be unable to discriminate between such differing states of feeling as boredom, anger, and sadness. All she is aware of is generalized unpleasure, feeling *down*.

As Dr. Graeme T. Taylor has observed in the *Harvard Medical School Mental Health Letter*, people afflicted by alexithymia have so much difficulty distinguishing between their varying bodily complaints and differing emotional states that they cannot "read feelings as signals of inner conflict or responses to external situations [and they] tend to concentrate on the associated physical sensations."

It is, suggests Taylor, the alexithymic person's inability to regulate her or his own physiological responses to stress that drives her or him into some form of (often self-destructive) action. Many such individuals, as he asserts, feeling overwhelmed by unreadable impulses and mounting pressures from within, "try to reduce emotional tension through physical activity: binge eating, sex, alcohol and drug abuse, compulsive exercise."

Because the person is so out of contact with her inner world, however, she doesn't really know for sure whether she is feeling anxious, sad, lonely, or hungry; she is, therefore, incapable of figuring out what to do in order to restore herself to calmness. It is because she cannot meet her own needs and soothe herself that her agitated state must be relieved by some form of external activity. So, rather than attempting to focus upon feelings that could be frustrating, upsetting, or unbearably painful, the alexithymic and bulimic person focuses upon her fat cells.

It is her fat cells that have become the metaphor for those aspects of her inner text (such as anxiety and rage) that are affecting her profoundly but are nevertheless obscure and illegible. So she *takes action*. She turns to bingeing in order to evade and numb and avoid those unwanted, unruly feelings within herself, and—instead of endeavoring to decipher and to deal with them—she "eats herself into oblivion" instead.

The Body Is the Enemy

In thinking about bulimia nervosa, the complex influences of heredity must also be taken into serious account. For if a developing young female has been genetically programmed to have a very slender body build, she will never have to become involved in frantic efforts to force her weight downward in the first place.

It is by now very well established that different individuals who eat similar amounts of food and engage in similar amounts of exercise can have vastly dissimilar body weights; what is crucial is the way in which a given person's body stores food and the way in which her body burns up energy. An impressive amount of scientific data, much of it garnered within the last two decades, indicates that, diet though we may, our body weight tends to float to its own genetically ordained "set-point."

Although an individual's body weight is, obviously, susceptible to wide fluctuation, "the adult weights of most animals and humans are actually quite stable," as psychologist Richard E. Keesey states in the *Handbook of Eating Disorders.* A good deal of research evidence now supports the theory that we are each born with an internal pointer that insists on being at a certain natural number on our body's predetermined inner scale.

It is known, as Keesey points out, "that body weight, if displaced from the normally maintained level, is subsequently restored to the initial level." This is the dieter's dilemma: The individual who loses weight by means of sharply restricting her food intake frequently finds herself back once again in the weight range at which she started.

Worse yet, she often finds that she is even *heavier.* For self-starvation has a paradoxical effect upon the body, which responds defensively to what it experiences as a state of extreme deprivation. What happens, in response, is that as part of a self-preservative effort, the body initiates a system of rationing and conservation of its resources. As part of this effort, the body's capacity to store fat increases and its resting metabolic rate declines.

This makes it far easier for the individual to maintain "emergency" fat supplies and more difficult to burn them away—which would, obviously, be of vital importance if the individual really were starving. But the upshot of this situation is that the dieter finds that, over the course of time, she stores fat more readily and finds it increasingly difficult to lose it by fasting or by heroic efforts at exercising.

So, for a person who is genetically predisposed to have a heavier body build (and who may not be eating significantly greater quantities than her best friend, who is skinny), restrictive, severely controlled dieting doesn't actually provide the answer. Nevertheless, the notion that weight, like height, is to some large degree an inherited aspect of our being is one that we, as a society, find very difficult to accept and believe in.

We can certainly understand that some people are born tall and some are born short; that some people have blue eyes and some have brown eyes; but we find it almost impossible to contemplate the notion that some people are born to have heavier body builds and some are born to be lighter. Body weight appears to us to be associated with moral worth and stamina—something that *can* and *should* be under a person's control.

There is a world of blame for stocky, chubby people (especially females) and admiring accolades for those who are thin. The slender person is someone who, in our view, eats sparely, and the fat person is someone who overindulges. To be appropriately lean and attractively feminine, all she would have to do would be to eat less. "In fact," as Keesey notes, "variation in food intake often fails to produce the expected change in body weight."

The critical factors are actually *the way in which an individual metabolizes food, and the amount of fat that is stored in her fat cells.* These are inborn aspects of the person's physiology, and they have a high genetic and familial component. In the case of Katie Maguire, her grandmother was reported to have been "obese," and her own mother had developed a lifelong eating disorder in attempting to get her own weight down to an acceptably slim, sexually attractive level when she herself was in adolescence.

Now Katie was in the initial stages of what might well be a long war against her own body and biology. And, whether or not a familial inclination to develop a heavier build had been bequeathed to her, what *was* being modeled for her was Clare's own abnormal relation to food and to eating.

Katie's mother was giving her, by the powerful setting of a maternal example, the sense that one can take *control* of one's body and force it into a certain mold by maintaining a stern, adversarial stance against it. The result was that neither the older nor the younger woman experienced her body as a place in which she could live harmoniously. The body was the enemy, to be harshly overpowered and dominated—at any cost, and by any means necessary.

The Physical Consequences of Bulimia

Would her bulimic symptoms simply be a temporary "solution" to Katie Maguire's ongoing difficulties, or would her bingeing and purging prove to be an intractable, established way to deal with her life's problems? It was still too early to make any sound predictions, and a recent physical examination had indicated that nothing serious was amiss—at least, not thus far.

Over time, however, bulimia nervosa can produce a formidable array of medical consequences. These include fatigue, sore throat, ulcerations of the esophagus, and possible heart disturbances, due to the depletion of bodily electrolytes (mainly potassium) caused by constant vomiting.

Katie had certainly experienced some of these symptoms already. Her throat, as she'd noted in the diary she'd given me, was perennially sore; also, frequent exposure to the acids coming up in her stomach contents was making her esophagus feel raw, inflamed, and damaged. Given time, paradoxically, these powerful substances were likely to affect not only Katie's health but her appearance: The acids in human vomitus are so caustic that they can strip the porcelain enamel from a bathroom sink or toilet bowl.

Regurgitated stomach acids can also lift enamel from the teeth, which is why people who engage in chronic vomiting tend to experience loss of tooth enamel, and tooth discoloration too. This dental erosion is, it should be said, also caused by the oversweet nature of what is being consumed during the gorging phase of a typical bulimic episode. But in any event, the natural consequence of creating an oral environment suffused with food sugars and corrosive stomach acids is the wearing away of tooth enamel.

When this happens, the teeth become shortened, and spaces may develop between them; this is one side effect of bulimia that is *irreversible*. Thus, a psychological disorder engendered by the need to look beautiful—to be slim, "feminine," and attractive—can ultimately have extraordinarily damaging, deleterious effects upon the perfect exterior for which so much is being sacrificed.

Shortened, stubby, yellowed teeth are not desirable and captivating— nor are the enlarged salivary glands which often give the bulimic person's cheeks a swollen, raccoonlike appearance. Katie might, if her bulimia persisted, be trading in her face for her figure.

An Intergenerational Issue: Weight and Lovableness

As Clare Maguire had intimated, this was not the first generation of the family in which weight and being-loved-and-lovable had become confounded during the adolescent years. For Clare, the only child of a mother of Scottish and English ancestry and a father whose ethnic origins were Austrian, had always been extremely close to her mother until her own teenage years. They had in fact been more like girlfriends than mother and daughter, and certainly had been trusted companions in oppression when it came to handling the explosive, tyrannizing head of the household.

But with the onset of puberty, Clare, who'd always been a somewhat plump little girl, had decided that she wanted to lose weight. "I was getting interested in boys, and I refused to keep eating all the sweet stuff my mom loved to make," she recounted. Her mother, whose way of emotionally nourishing her child involved preparing rich dessert treats for her, had for some reason experienced this decision as a form of emotional rejection.

According to Clare, neither her relationship with her mother nor her relationship to food had been "normal" since that phase of her life. And even though the series of fasting diets that she'd initiated at the time *had* proved effective—she'd slimmed down quickly, and become quite popular and attractive—the negative aftereffects of this period had been enormous and unending. For her bond with her mother (now deceased) had never again been as close, warm, and trusting, nor had Clare and her body been on friendly, comfortable terms from that time to the present.

For from then onward, her mundane needs for food as sustenance had been viewed by her as *bad* impulses coming from within—impulses that had to be mastered and controlled. And now, many years later, as the mother of an adolescent daughter, she was finding herself unable to model a normal relationship to food. Just as the distinction between giving real emotional nourishment and offering sweet foods as a form of loving had been unclear in Clare's own mother's mind, so it was unclear in her own.

As far as *this* mother was concerned, refusing to bring home sweet chocolate cookies and cakes from the market (the very junk food Katie so loved to binge on) was confounded with a refusal to give her daughter her maternal love and caring—and this confusion remained the case long after she'd become aware of Katie's bulimic symptoms. For, like her own mother before her, Clare Maguire was having real difficulty in drawing a clear distinction between "feedings" that are physical and those that are emotional in nature.

CHAPTER 10

Re-creating the Pain of the Past: An Attempt at Resolution

One of the great arenas of human passion is, as clinician Jay Haley has observed, ordinary family life and the successive dilemmas that arise when men and women mate and rear children. The story of each and every family is the story of that family's development over time. "Symptoms appear," writes Haley in *Uncommon Therapy*, "when there is a dislocation or interruption in the unfolding life cycle of a family. . . . The symptom is a signal that a family has difficulty in getting past a stage in the life cycle."

Family distress or outright pathology can, obviously, develop at any phase of the family narrative; but in the view of theorists Elizabeth A. Carter and Monica McGoldrick, the successive changes to be managed are incremental until the blossoming of the adolescent offspring. The advent of adolescence, as these authors write in *The Changing Family Life Cycle*, "ushers in a new era because it marks a new definition of the children within the family and of the parents' roles in relation to their children." Even in the best of circumstances, this is a deeply unsettling stage of any family's existence, for everyone in the system is suddenly being called upon to adapt to a dizzying array of biological, psychological, and social changes.

Merely in physical terms, the maturing offspring's height is changing—the rapid growth spurt of early puberty is on the order of three to four inches a year—and his or her interior organs are also rapidly increasing in size. Far more strange and unnerving, however, are the changes in hormonal status, which promote the development of secondary sexual characteristics.

This sudden outpouring of chemicals, newly circulating within the youngster's body, brings about profound shifts in his or her thoughts and feelings, which now become more erotic and aggressive in nature. To the developing adolescent, such preoccupations often feel alien, dangerous, foreign—as if they ought to be in someone else's head, rather than his or her own. For the widespread biological changes ushered in by puberty are, it must be remembered, being unleashed upon what is still to some extent a child's being.

The fact that so much is happening so rapidly produces, not surprisingly, a sense of inner disorientation. This sense of disorientation is linked to and underlies the notoriously roller-coaster-like mood swings of the adolescent, who is now subject to sudden bursts of happiness and high energy that alternate with moods of unhappiness, sluggish apathy, and hopeless boredom. This is a phase of human living when long riffs of feeling miserable are normal.

For it is during this phase of life that the metamorphosing child/young adult is engaged in the exquisitely painful task of separating from home base—slowly detaching "who I am as a person" from "who I am as the child of my parents." This process involves loss and grief, for the adolescent is parting from the only world he or she has ever lived in, and the first love relationships he or she has ever known. These selfsame lost and mournful feelings are also, it should be said, being experienced by the now middle-aged parents, whose *own unresolved separation issues, sexual issues, and identity issues are being reactivated* during this stressful epoch of the family life cycle.

It was certainly true, in the case of the Anderson family, that Dave's adolescence had ignited unresolved issues of his mother's—issues having to do with male sexuality, with the sense of helplessness and rage she'd once felt in the face of her father's "incessant playing around" and his neglect of herself and her siblings. Now, her suddenly mature-looking son's "irresponsibility and wildness" were reawakening in her the deep memories associated with that first loved male in her life, and with her inability to get him to love—or even notice—her in return.

The adolescent epoch is a long and protracted phase of the family life cycle, one which stretches from the eldest child's early prepubescent stirrings to the departure of the youngest sibling as a fledgling adult. It is a stage of family living that sorely strains the adaptational resources of everyone concerned, and the pressures generated can and often do reverberate into seemingly unconnected areas of the lives of the older generation.

Thus it was, in my own view, not coincidental that at a time when Matt Maguire's adolescent children were in the process of leaving home, he himself was suddenly kicking up his heels, wanting to be freed of all responsibility and to catch up with the fun and enjoyment he felt he'd missed out on earlier. This father was experiencing his children's natural movement outward from the family as treason and betrayal on their part, and a frightening, totally intolerable loss of control on his own.

Individuation: Becoming "Me, Myself"

Bob Horwitz and I had been working diligently to support Katie Maguire's natural developmental push in the direction of individuation (becoming "me, myself"), and she was doing well. Katie was, during this period, engaged in the prolonged work of "hatching" and slowly disengaging her own separate, unique, and different self away from the family nesting place. For this was, of course, a time of her life when, as the adolescent theorist Peter Blos has written, the "shedding of family dependencies, the loosening of infantile ties to become a member of society at large, or simply of the adult world" is in order.

Katie needed to feel that, as an autonomous individual, she would be able to assert control over her world and take care of herself. She needed to "own" her body and her personhood openly, rather than express her control and her self-ownership only by means of her secret bulimic debauches. The effort, in our sessions, had been to point out the myriad small, daily incidents in which she could take charge, feel competent, and get her own needs met very adequately.

Something as simple as being able to say "Sorry, I can't hang out now," if she happened to be busy when a friend stopped by her room, was for her new and thoroughly daring. Before, she'd felt so unsure of herself and so socially needy (though she never gave an outward appearance of being needy) that she'd allowed herself to live at the mercy of everyone else's momentary impulses, programs, and agendas.

Now she was managing matters quite differently in a number of seemingly trivial but actually highly significant ways. Her mood had stabilized recognizably, and she'd seemed to be gaining some real awareness of the way in which she binged in order to ward off feelings of depression, hopelessness, and anger.

We were therefore taken aback, not to say dismayed, when, just after her school's four-day February vacation weekend Katie came in looking thoroughly miserable and lost. All she said, in a sullen, complaining tone of voice, was "I feel really, really *fat* this week. Like—*disgusting*," and then she flopped into her customary chair dejectedly. She looked sallow and tired, and her face was broken out.

Out of Control

Although she sat there morosely, saying nothing, everything about Katie's appearance—the expression in her eyes, the very way she held herself—was transmitting a multitude of nonverbal messages about how awful, helpless, and out of control she was feeling. Indeed, if this scene had been filmed for a silent movie, not a word of explanatory text would have been needed to convey this young person's intense suffering and real anguish.

I myself was experiencing a leaden sense of impotence, a virus of hopelessness and frustration, that was mixed with some anger as well. It was as if Bob Horwitz and I had been working on an elaborate sand castle, and an inevitable tide was moving in to obliterate it. For over this past weekend there had been a long, unchaperoned house party at the family's ski condo up in Vermont—a plan proposed by Katie, to which her parents had (for reasons I found myself totally unable to fathom) freely assented.

Katie Maguire, at age sixteen—*bulimic*, moreover—was awfully young to be expected to handle so complex an event as a weekend sleep-over party for an unspecified number of her prep school classmates. There was, furthermore, to be no adult on the premises (although Katie's parents were staying in a nearby ski cabin with friends of their own). Neither Bob Horwitz nor I had heard a word about this plan until it happened to come up, quite casually, during a meeting with the entire family—and by that time, Kate's guest list had grown to a total of sixteen boys and girls. Her dad was supplying the beer keg.

As parents, the Maguires didn't seem to be providing their daughter with well-calibrated, successively greater challenges in order to help her develop a sense of her own competence and self-sufficiency; instead, they were tossing her into a totally unregulated, sexually stimulating, unsupervised situation in a completely sink-or-swim fashion. From a systemic point of view, they were flipping over from a state of "total control" to its opposite, "no control"; once again, I wondered about the nature of their family's rules for dealing with sexuality and intergenerational boundaries. Were these parents, in an unconscious but very powerful fashion, making use of their daughter to provide them with a zing and excitement they felt their own lives to be lacking?

In any event, by the time Bob Horwitz and I had learned about it, the vacation house-party plans were already set; the best assistance that anyone could offer Katie was to help her foresee the kinds of problems that might arise over that weekend, and the ways in which she might be able to deal with them. But as things turned out, *nothing* could have prepared her for so grueling, unstructured, and uncontrolled an experience.

For, as she began describing it now, there had been heavy drinking, crashers from other parties, drug use, stuffed-up toilets, no hot water, and demands on the food supply that she, as hostess, had been totally unable to handle. And finally, in the hours just before dawn on Saturday morning (when the revelers were at last asleep in their sleeping bags), Katie had gone into the kitchen and started bingeing.

On that first occasion, for lack of anything better, she had taken a loaf and a half of sliced Wonder bread, concocted a huge stack of butter-and-orange-marmalade sandwiches, then gulped them down as fast as she could swallow them. After that, she'd slipped out behind the house, put her fingers down her throat, and vomited it all up. Then she'd buried the half-digested food in the snow.

That had been only the beginning, though; throughout the weekend, her bingeing and purging had increased and intensified. The biggest difficulty she'd encountered, as she narrated the story now, had been dealing with her friend and running companion, Ben. Ben had appointed himself her "conscience" and was trying to help her in her efforts to control her bingeing.

Her worst fear had been that Ben might be aware of what was happening. "I felt like he was *watching* me all the time, even when he wasn't in the house," she recounted, then laughed joylessly. "So all the time, I kept thinking, 'Shit, he's going to *see me* eating all this,' or 'Shit, he's going to *catch me* throwing up.'"

But if Ben had been aware of what was going on, he'd never said anything to Katie directly. He'd simply made her feel guilty, foul, and sneaky, and she'd been awfully low and depressed ever since the long holiday weekend. Before going up to Vermont, moreover, she'd gotten her weight down to 115 pounds; now she weighed an unthinkable, completely *disgusting* 120.

Still, she insisted, she was far from sorry about having given the party. In retrospect, she was actually glad to have had the opportunity to host such a "cool" occasion—even though, as she admitted, it hadn't been an experience that she would want to repeat very often in the future. If she was now feeling down, rotten, worthless, angry, and "used" by many of the school friends who had been guests—as well as offended by her own bulimic orgy of this past weekend—then the pathway to her personal redemption was a clear one.

She would abstain completely from the sweet junk food that she so adored (and binged on) and start eating "wholesome" food only. She would lose that extra weight, and at 115 pounds—or perhaps even 110—she would feel happy, healthy, and in control of her life and her fate once again.

St. Valentine's Day

It was toward the close of that particular session that Katie Maguire dropped a sudden therapeutic bombshell. "Wow, my mom sent me a *package* for Valentine's Day," she said excitedly, perking up. Then she shot a challenging look in my direction and started giggling. "There were three bags of chocolate chip cookies in it, and then two bags of yogurt-covered raisins. I'd *asked* for just the raisins. . . . No"—she shrugged briefly as if to say the issue was an unimportant one—"actually I asked for *both* of them."

She turned to the psychologist and gave him the faintly taunting look she'd given me. "There was a *letter*, too," she continued, "and my mom said that she had very *mixed* feelings about sending me the cookies, that she wasn't sure whether she should do so or not. But she *did* hope that by now I had learned that they're a treat and not a drug—"

Katie stopped, put both hands to her temples, and combed her fingers through her hair, lifting it high and outward, like a wide frame around her face. She grinned. "I was *so* psyched up to eat the cookies that I had a whole bag and a half right away," she said enthusiastically. "They were the Pepperidge Farm, really big ones. . . . 'Big Nantucket' is what they're called."

She released the hair and shook her head so hard that light-colored locks flew around her head momentarily. "I went running through the dorm, then, getting rid of the rest of them—opening doors and just throwing them on people's beds. Then, yesterday, I got another package—a neighbor from home who always sends me cookies. I ate a few and gave the rest away, because if I kept them I'd eat them all." She was speaking rapidly, an arch, complicit expression on her face. "Except that I still have all the yogurt-covered raisins. But I can *deal* with raisins," Katie assured us shrilly.

She was talking very fast, without conversational pauses, as though the last thing in the world she wanted was a response from Bob Horwitz or me. We were witnessing, it seemed to me, an outpouring of a good deal of barely digested, deeply conflictual emotional information. I glanced briefly at the psychologist, met his eyes for a fleeting moment, questioning him silently about what *he* might be making of a mother's sending such a gift to her bulimic child.

The association that had popped instantaneously into my own mind was to the story of Snow White, and to the poisoned apple brought to her as a gift by the jealous stepmother (an older woman). The apple is, of course, a universal symbol of sexuality and fertility; the still-beautiful but deeply envious stepmother's objective is to destroy a feared rival for the admiration of the king and to remain "the fairest in the land" herself.

It was undoubtedly true that Clare Maguire, like most mothers, wanted her maturing daughter to grow up into a lovely and attractive woman. As psychologist Hilary J. Beattie, Ph.D., has observed (in "Eating Disorders and the Mother-Daughter Relationship") a mother's "own narcissism is heavily invested in her daughter's appearance and social [and other] success, which leaves both in a difficult 'double bind.'" For the mother wants her child, whom she experiences as a proxy for herself, to be the "fairest in the land," and at the same time she often finds it difficult to cede her own position to her nubile, sexually challenging competitor.

What's more, as Beattie notes, the younger female's push toward independence frequently "triggers the mother's unresolved conflicts over separation and loss derived from *her* relationship with *her own* mother" (my italics). The mother "fears to lose the symbiotic, nurturing relationship with her daughter and is often unconsciously threatened by the girl's growing sexual attractiveness." Although it was very clear to me that Clare Maguire loved her daughter deeply, was she (in a manner outside her own awareness) sending Katie poisoned apples?

Food is, certainly, the most concrete possible symbol of maternal nurturance. Sweet, dangerous, forbidden junk food was the enigmatic "gift" that Clare had sent to her bulimic daughter. But when a mother sends her eating-disordered offspring the very foodstuffs that the girl is known to binge on, then what is the Valentine's Day message being delivered? And what message, or messages, was Katie hearing?

"Tell me, what did you make of your mother's gift?" Bob Horwitz asked her, at that moment.

Red Roses and the Holiday of Love

For a moment Katie looked at him uncomprehendingly, as if he'd asked the question in a foreign language and she were waiting for the translation to come to her via an earphone. "I don't like throwing up anymore," she said at last, in a somber tone. "My throat *hurts.* It's a hassle, too, because the bathroom I've been using is being repainted this week—I explained this to Ben in a letter I wrote him just after one of our big *confidential* talks. . . ." Her tone was derisive; she seemed to be mocking either Ben's fruitless role as her "conscience" or his trust in her own involvement and honesty.

But then she sighed, slumped down against the back of her leather chair, and said gloomily, "I can't even *think* about throwing up, because Ben and I are such good friends." So, despite her sarcasm, her friend's watchful caretaking was actually affecting her; it was he who was taking over her self-regulating functions, since she could not maintain control of them herself. For this she felt gratitude, but also anger and rebelliousness. "He asked me to go with him to the spring ball—it's black-tie—this weekend."

She had dealt with the subject of her mother's gift by not responding to the question at all.

I felt cheered by the news of Ben's invitation. I liked the sound of this young man, Katie's friend, jogging companion, and (at this moment, necessary) caretaker. Ben might now be emerging in the more romantic guise of a Prince Charming—the young lover who would protect her and come to her rescue. These thoughts must have been reflected on my features, for Katie, bright and sensitive as she was, seemed to make an unconscious connection with my fantasy immediately. "It's not *me* he likes, it's my roommate, Rachel," she said scornfully. "In fact, I was sure he was going to ask her."

"But he did ask you," I responded, somewhat too rapidly. I leaned back in my chair, took in a breath, then asked curiously, "Is Rachel going with somebody else?"

"I'm sure all the guys are too intimidated to ask her, because she is *so pretty*," Katie replied in a flat, depressed-sounding voice. Then the weather of her mood shifted suddenly once again. "Oh! Dad sent me three chocolate roses for Valentine's Day," she said brightly. "I was so happy! And the reason it was such a good present—I told Dad this on the phone— was that even though they *were* chocolate, they were far too beautiful to eat. I didn't want to mess them up, because they were so *pretty*. They were red."

"They were made out of red chocolate?" Dr. Horwitz asked, leaning forward in his seat, both hands clasped over one of his knees.

"Yes," said Katie excitedly, "each had a long, long stem like a lollipop stem, which was wrapped in green paper. And then at the top was a red chocolate rose, with little green leaves all around it."

Had she eaten them eventually? I asked her, and Katie grinned, hanging her head like a naughty schoolchild. "I had two on one day, I think," she said, "though not at the same time. And then one on another day. No, I gave the other one away, I think—to a guy named Jay.

"And then," she added vivaciously, "I received a carnation from a guy named Brian, the one I used to go with in my freshman year, who was so abusive and mean."

We were being hustled past any discussion of her father's gift as rapidly as we had been hurried past her mother's. "I didn't even know Brian knew I *existed* anymore," Katie said.

"But his flower wasn't the edible kind?" Dr. Horwitz asked her wryly. No, said Katie coolly, as if ignorant of the implications of the question.

Brian's carnation didn't have any romantic meanings, she hastened to explain, because he had another girlfriend now. "It was just nice to know that he was thinking of me," she said, looking gratified momentarily; then her expression darkened again, abruptly. "So why do I feel so *fat* now?" she demanded.

"I mean, it's not only that I *am* fat; I feel *different* too. My stomach feels like it's tied up in a knot." If she did go to the dance with Ben, she added wretchedly, she had nothing whatsoever to wear; those five extra pounds meant that none of her dresses would fit her without ugly bulges. "What can I *do?*—I can't really go. I have nothing, and I feel too totally *disgusting*," she protested, in a tone of frantic despair.

Katie was, as one could not fail to notice, resolutely dodging any encounter with her feelings about her parents' gifts, and focusing instead on her own self-loathing. It was easier, perhaps, to experience frustration and anger at herself than at them, because while she was in part adult she was still in large part also her parents' unfinished, still needy, and dependent child—and at some gut level, she didn't want the messages of their Valentine's Day gifts (which bore the scent of sabotage) unscrambled.

Katie's Dream

Still, just prior to this afternoon's meeting, the teenager had been drawn into the work of decipherment via a vivid dream that she'd had. As it happened, Katie had had three class periods free that afternoon, and she'd fallen asleep on her bed when she'd curled up in order to catch up on some homework. She'd had the following dream, which she described to us in the closing minutes of the session:

> I was having another party, only this one was in the summer, not the winter. I'm not sure where we were—home in Greenwich, I think— but I'd left a bunch of people at the house, and was going into town with my mother, *who was the same age as I was.* [My italics]. The two of us were just hanging out, because we were best friends. So we went into David's Cookies, and there was a pretty big line, and we went to stand in it, next to each other, holding hands. But then Ben was there, and he took his two big hands and grabbed us by the necks and slammed us both right up against the wall! And he stood there and looked at us, then let us down, stood back and laughed and walked away. I did what I usually do—my usual nervous laughter—and my mom did too. When we finally got up to the counter, my dad was there. I mean, he was *behind* the counter, and it was my birthday, and my mom and my dad gave me this big cookie—it was *huge*. And it said "Happy Birthday, Katie" and I was sitting up on the counter, eating it and sharing it with everyone in the store.

Katie seemed to be struggling, in this dream, to sort out the difference between those who were encouraging her to give in to the uncontrolled expression of her appetites (her parents) and the young male friend (Ben) who was attempting to take charge of her appetites for her. Benign though his intentions might be, Ben's behavior (as she experienced it) was that of someone taking tyrannical control of her—picking her up by the neck, slamming her against the wall, and *forcing* her not to eat what was forbidden.

She was the utterly passive victim in her dream, a figure devoid of power and self-responsibility. Her alternatives were to be strangled (by Ben) or to be dangerously and excitingly overfed by Matt and Clare. In this dream sequence, moreover, Katie's mother was not envisioned as caregiver and protector; she was seen as a best friend, confidante, and peer.

This was, of course, a reflection of the extended family's reality, for just as Clare had been her own mother's "pal" and confederate in the ongoing battle with a tyrannical male, Katie was taking over the role of feminine ally in the conflict between the male tyrant and the female scapegoat going on in the Maguire household.

At the same time, this mother's Valentine's Day gift seemed to speak of some deeply suppressed rivalry with the maiden-daughter who could quite conceivably become not only healthy, lovely, and happy, but capable of surpassing her mother in appearance *and* in life opportunities. Far more importantly, the gift seemed to me to be freighted with another message, which was "Don't get too well and leave me behind; don't abandon me." In families at this level of development, *the words* ("I want my daughter to be healthy and happy, and to go on to have a happy life of her own") *very frequently don't match the actions* (whose message here was "Stay sick and dependent; I need to have you go on needing me").

For Katie, beginning to eat normally (if and when that happened) would be a real declaration of her own autonomy—but deep in her heart, I believed, there existed the counterpart to her mother's fear. A daughter's irrational dread, in this kind of circumstance, is that if she *does* surpass her maternal parent—if she becomes more beautiful, successful, or both—her still-loved, still-needed mother may either be overwhelmed and die, or else desert her completely. Such a declaration of independence and wellness was one that Katie, at this point in her life, was still very far from being capable of making.

The Early Life History of the Bulimic

According to psychoanalyst Kent Ravenscroft, the bulimic's earliest experiences in life have often been extremely problematic. She is someone whose needs have either been ignored or attended to inconsistently, or whose own wishes and preferences have been systematically disregarded by an overbearing, overprotective parent or parents. There has been no personal growing space provided in which she feels at liberty to sort out who she is and what she wants and needs as the unique human individual she is in the process of becoming.

Most important, the individual at risk for bulimia is someone who has not quite negotiated the all-important transition from being soothed and regulated by the caretaking mother to being able to soothe and regulate herself.

Typically, very early in life, the nurturing parent's calming influence—"There, there, it will be all right"—comes to the developing child from outside the self; in the process of growth, it is internalized. Eventually, in the course of time, "mother" is experienced as a helpful, soothing, and advising voice *from inside.*

In the bulimic's case, however, it is food (the sweet, rich food of the binge) that serves as compensation for the emotional goodies and supplies that have not been forthcoming, and the purge becomes a means of projecting *outside* the self everything within it that is experienced as spoiled, ungratifying, and rotten. Writes Ravenscroft, "Normal weight bulimia, with its onset predominantly in midadolescent females, is an eating disorder caused by specific interrelated personality and family pathology. Characteristically, the mother is in a relatively hostile-dependent, masochistic relationship with her husband. . . . Typically, the father is somewhat counterdependent, counterphobic and sadistic with his wife, while overstimulating and rejecting with his daughter."

This is a good thumbnail description of the Maguires' relationship. Clare was submissive and oppressed; Matt was tough, macho with the women, and inappropriately seductive with his daughter. He had sent Katie, his bulimic child, an edible bouquet of red roses on St. Valentine's Day, which is a celebration of passion and love. As a symbolic gesture, this offering of red roses was, clearly, unduly exciting—an invitation not only to a loss of impulse control (that is, an invitation to binge on chocolate), but to cross the generational boundary that separated them. He was, in a sense, wooing her, remembering her even though his real affectional partner had received no Valentine's Day remembrance whatsoever (as Matt admitted when I asked him about it directly).

At one level, this father had simply sent a Valentine's Day gift to his adolescent daughter, who was away at boarding school. Yet at another, metaphorical and mythical, level, Matt was engaging in a kind of emotional incest—involving Katie in all that was destructive, forbidden (like her gorging and purging), and impassioned. He was also *doing something* to his wife. For by inviting Katie into a "romantic" relationship and ignoring Clare, he was obviously violating the marital boundary and setting up the two females as competitors for his affection. Katie was now the first and fairest in the family land, while empty-handed Clare, unremembered on St. Valentine's Day, was her daughter's older, disappointed rival.

Was he also sending Katie the message that everything she needed, in terms of love and sustenance, could just as well be found at home—and that she need never really leave them? As clinician Kent Ravenscroft observes, the bulimic and her family are particularly vulnerable to difficulties around the familial and personal tasks relating to differentiation and leave-taking.

This is the period during which the family drama tends to reach its emotional climax. "Facing the necessity of . . . 'launching' their adolescent female, the parents, themselves in their midlife crisis, must face the prospect of an empty nest and their marital impasse," he writes. It is in the midst of this period of heightened vulnerability that a family crisis of some kind tends to occur—one that exerts a regressive pull upon the daughter.

This is what I feared might happen to Katie. She might, in Ravenscroft's words, "collapse loyally back into the family" and either never leave home (due to her bulimic illness) or do no better than replicate the situation with an eating disorder of her own and (eventually) a tyrannizing, abusive mate. Meanwhile, her parents' gifts, sent to her on the holiday of love, had been freighted with a serious communication, which she certainly seemed to have heard.

This communication was "Don't get too independent, healthy, and self-sufficient, because we still need your manifold services here. Mom needs a female friend and confidante, Dad needs a sexy young lady to woo, and the emotional system as a whole needs a symptom bearer who will help to keep the focus off their painful marital impasse. So do get better, but of course not *so much better* that we become less central and are left feeling desolate and stranded."

This message, like an irresistible siren call, appeared to have diverted her and captured her attention. And now Katie, veering backward and off her own life's course, was moving into a perilous stretch of water, dotted with concealed shoals and subject to treacherous family riptides. For in the wake of St. Valentine's Day, her bingeing and purging escalated alarmingly.

Re-creating the Pain of the Past: Freud's Repetition Compulsion

Why is it that people tend to re-create, in their present-day lives, the very same situations that brought them so much suffering in the past? How does it happen that a woman who, like Clare Maguire, has grown up as the daughter of a tyrannical, overpowering man eventually gets herself into a long-term, intimate relationship with a man who bullies and frightens her? Or, if that woman has carefully selected a partner who is *not* initially abusive and becomes so later on, what subtle, unconscious aspects of his and her behavior seem to promote his becoming abusive eventually?

It was Freud who first drew attention to the curious frequency with which people behave as if they are under powerful internal pressure to stage reenactments of early relational dilemmas. He named this tendency (which he found difficult to integrate into his own evolving theory) the "repetition compulsion." It was, in his view, "a way of remembering" the emotionally crucial events of the past—a remembering that took place not in conscious memories and reflection, but in unconsciously motivated present-day action.

It was not only neurotics, as the psychoanalyst observed, but "some normal people" who seemed thus impelled to continually reexperience certain distressing early situations—a recurring dramatization, in the person's current life, of events that once brought him or her only misery and suffering. It was as though, in the plasticity of infancy and childhood, a *mode of existing in close relationships* had been impressed upon the individual, and, from this adaptive mold, a rough-hewn pattern had been created. Henceforth, it was with this unconscious pattern that he or she seemed to be working, in such a way that remarkably similar life sequences or scenarios inevitably developed.

This palpably real, *clinically observable* need to restage and reenact certain early, intensely charged situations is like a behavioral tic of some kind. For, as Freud noted, each repetition of the central theme or scenario, culminating in the same disappointment and grief, was nevertheless immediately followed by another very much like it.

"This 'perpetual recurrence of the same thing,'" he wrote, "causes us no astonishment when it relates to active behavior on the part of the person concerned and when we can discern in him an essential character trait which always remains the same and which is compelled to find expression in a repetition of the same experiences. We are much more impressed by cases where the subject appears to have a passive experience, over which he has no influence, but in which he meets with a repetition of the same fatality."

What was striking was the way an individual might blindly, repeatedly, and apparently "passively" suffer the same fate over and over again. A person might, for example, divorce his alcoholic wife and marry a woman who was *not* alcoholic, but who then developed a progressively more serious drinking problem over the subsequent decade. Or, to take another instance, a wife might be in a physically violent relationship with one marital partner, leave him, and then find that her new, quintessentially nice, gentle lover or husband is becoming increasingly abusive (perhaps slapping her face during quarrels). When a recurring destiny or central theme of this kind becomes manifest in a person's life, a powerful subliminal thrust in this direction must be posited.

Nevertheless, as Freud himself freely admitted, this peculiar tendency to restage and reenact early, and distressing, relational experiences was inexplicable in terms of his own evolving theoretic doctrine. For psychoanalytic theory, as it then stood, was rooted in the idea that a unitary biological force propels and guides all human activity. This was "libido," the life instinct, which Freud viewed as animated solely by powerful sexual energies and guided by the "pleasure principle"—that is, the universal tendency to behave in ways that will maximize pleasure and minimize physical and psychological pain.

What, in such a theoretical cosmos, could possibly explain an individual's seeking out and reenacting old, unhappy situations? What could impel that person to deliberately repeat—in a variety of perhaps overtly different but always covertly identical circumstances—the trauma and pain of a much earlier phase of his or her existence? Such patently self-destructive behavior seemed, as the founder of psychoanalysis reflected upon it, to point to the presence of some hitherto unrecognized internal forces. There must be some "demonic," primitive, aggressive instinctual energy, arising from within, that could prompt an individual to actively court misery-inducing, self-damaging experiences.

It was to some large degree his speculations about the repetition compulsion that eventually led Freud to believe in a biologically based "death instinct." For while it was easy to understand (on the basis of the pleasure principle) why highly pleasureful behavior would tend to be repeated, the clearly discernible need to reenact hurtful, self-wounding experiences was explainable only if understood in a wider biological context. "If it is true that—at some immeasurably remote time and in a manner we cannot conceive—life once proceeded out of inorganic matter, then, according to our presumption, an instinct must have arisen which sought to do away with life once more and re-establish the inorganic state," he wrote in the *New Introductory Lectures on Psychoanalysis*, published in 1932.

Alongside the life-enhancing, progressive, libidinal drives, he suggested, there were disintegrative drives tending in a backward-looking, self-harm-seeking direction. For, he argued, the need to re-create painful experiences spoke of an urge not only to hurt but to annihilate the self. Alongside the wish to be, which is the life instinct, there existed a deep desire to be no longer. To this Freud gave the name "thanatos," the death instinct, describing it as an innate "urge to return to an earlier state" and ultimately to the inorganic, unexcited, tensionless state that prevailed before life itself began.

Repetitive Reverberations

In his extensive discussions of the "need to repeat" early, familiarly painful experiences, Freud's attention was clearly focused upon the life trajectory of the individual human being. But as other, later theorists have noted, repetitive reverberations of a similar sort frequently occur on the family level as well. If, for instance, one steps back and views the extended system as *an emotionally connected whole*, one quickly comes to recognize the existence of core emotional sequences that seem to surface over and over again. This "recurrence of the same thing," to use Freud's phrase, is, in other words, apparent not only in the life course of the individual human being, but of the family system in its entirety.

Very clearly, in the Maguire family, the domestic drama of Clare's earliest years—which involved a powerful, furious male, a helpless, weak female, and the defenseless offspring who served as their audience—had been replicated in the present generation. So, less overtly and plainly, had been the family structure of Matt's earliest years, which involved a harsh, aggressive parent (mother), a deprecated, defeated parent (father), and the children who felt caught between them.

In Matt's case, the genders of the aggressor and the victim were switched, but the emotional system had been polarized in the selfsame manner as had his wife's. *Their original families' problematic way of handling power (so that one parent was all-powerful, the other totally powerless), which had brought such pain to both of them in the dependent years of their childhood, was structurally identical to the one the Maguires had re-created in the present generation.*

What could explain their having deliberately revived, in their own intimate relationship, a version of an infantile scenario that had once been experienced as highly distressing and upsetting? Freud's explanation of the repetition compulsion—that it is motivated by an innate death instinct, which drives the organism to seek self-harm and ultimate annihilation—is by no means the universally accepted one. Indeed, the whole concept of the death instinct has remained controversial, and many experts have questioned the existence of such a biologically based, self-destructive inner human force. (I myself find it intellectually unconvincing.) Many later theorists have, however, offered a variety of other possible explanations of the repetition compulsion. An extensive literature has in fact grown up around this single but utterly fascinating human conundrum.

Mastering the Past: An Alternative Explanation of the Compulsion to Repeat

One popular hypothesis about the repetition compulsion is that it represents an effort to master events that, during the vulnerable years of early childhood, were experienced as too overwhelming and anxiety-producing to perceive, let alone to deal with and assimilate. This view of "the urge to repeat painful experiences" has it that re-creating the past *as an adult* is a way of confronting anew what could not be confronted during the vulnerable, powerless childhood years, when one was so utterly needful and dependent.

As analyst Nathan P. Segel, M.D., has suggested (in an article entitled "Repetition Compulsion, Acting out, and Identification with the Doer"), restaging charged aspects of the past may be seen as an "attempt to master the stimuli by actively repeating aspects of the [unpleasantly]. . . stimulating experiences that were passively imposed, without warning or preparation."

For example, a woman who grew up in a household in which the father was a compulsive gambler or alcoholic may become involved in a present-day re-creation of that central scenario in which her spouse is now cast in the role of the addict. The husband in this case may indeed gamble, drink too much, eat too much, or smoke excessively; but whatever addictive behaviors he actually does manifest, he can also be understood to be embodying and enacting *for her* the man who lives on inside her head— that early object of her infantile devotion, who was so impulse-ridden, out of control, and unreliable.

This wife is, at the level of her own conscious awareness, predictably enraged by her partner's behavior; she berates him endlessly, while striving desperately to cure him or at least help him cure himself. But at an unconscious level, she is using him as the recipient of (and stand-in for) all the rage that she once felt and that, if unprocessed and unresolved, still lives on within her—her deep anger against the original betrayer, her beloved and totally undependable dad.

What is crucially different about this current rendition of the family drama, however, is that—unlike the one she was conscripted into as a child—this rendition of the dream has (albeit unconsciously) been set into motion by the woman herself. This time around, she is not really a passive actor; she has become actively engaged as the play's producer instead. Admittedly, she may not enjoy the ongoing dramatization at all—it may cause her very real pain—but as (unconscious) author of the script, she has attained some measure of mastery over the very same circumstances that once threatened to overwhelm her. What once happened *to her* are the same kinds of things that she herself, propelled by unconscious forces, is *causing to happen* in this subsequent revival.

In a way, her active re-creation of key aspects of the family script surely does to some degree reflect a simple effort to discharge enduring anxieties about certain deeply felt infantile experiences. But even more importantly, the restaging and replaying of the drama (the "recurrence of the same thing") can be seen as an effort to alter and rewrite the original playbook.

For if, in this case, the woman can only succeed in making her spouse stop drinking—or overeating, or betraying her sexually, or doing whatever he does that makes her feel as helpless, disregarded, and defenseless as she once did—then she may be able to put a new, happier ending to the old, unhappy script. Her fantasy (which exists outside of her own awareness) is of at last getting the love and stable caring of the good parent, if only she can bring the third act to another, profoundly different conclusion.

In this sense, her struggle to resurrect the past in her present-day relationships can be seen as a hopeful effort—an effort directed at trying again, creating fresh opportunities for mastering old, unresolved dilemmas. And if the sequence of the dramatic action does feel painfully familiar, it cannot be otherwise, for her life has told her that this is simply the only show in town.

Reconnecting, Emotionally, with the First Love Objects of Our Lives: Another Possible Explanation of the Repetition Compulsion

The adult man or woman who becomes engaged in repeating stressful experiences of the past may be attempting to master the past, but all too often he or she simply repeats the past without ever discovering a means of bringing the original script to a different, more gratifying conclusion. It is, suggests psychoanalyst John Zinner, as if there is a powerful and very *real* psychological force, deriving from within, which seems to push the individual along in the old and all-too-familiar directions, from beginning to end. That human tidal force, pressing for recapitulation of *what has been*, compels a person to do things in the same ways they were done earlier in his or her lifetime.

For example, a father whose dearest wish was to be different from his own father—more available and much less critical—may be startled to discover himself behaving in a very similar fashion with his own children (most especially, one or more of his sons). The negative scenarios that caused him such pain in his own youth are being repeated faithfully, without significant alterations or addenda. It is as if the passionate lessons of childhood, having been so well learned, are resistant, at a profoundly unintentional, unwilled level, to being *un*learned.

As rational, thinking human beings, observes Zinner, we may want and choose to do things differently, but as feeling, emotional beings, we often find it difficult to resist flowing into the experiential channels our earliest experiences have formed. Perhaps a reason why we tend to find ourselves in the same (often painful) situations, facing the very same dilemmas all over again, is that *repeating the past is a way of remaining psychologically connected to the past*—it is a way of *keeping the past active and alive in the present.*

A world in which there was an ongoing battle between a tyrannical male and a helpless female was, for example, one that Clare Maguire had lived in since time immemorial. And as hurtful as reliving this situation might have been for her, it did re-create the entire feeling of what being in that relationship, with that father, had been like. For, when the past is thus faithfully reenacted in the present, the net effect is that *the lost love object— the parent—isn't lost anymore.*

Seen in this light, Matt's heightened restlessness and anger throughout these past months could be understood as helping Clare to make living contact with her own deeply loved yet "ranting and raving" father—the grandparent who had lived with them until this past June, and whose loss the entire family had been grieving. Similarly, this mother's ambivalently competitive relationship with her maturing daughter, as evidenced by her subversive Valentine's Day gift—and Katie's own eating disturbance— were also echoes of a past that was being lived out in the present.

In truth, the current mother-daughter relationship could be seen as a fairly faithful restoration of the relationship that Clare had shared with her own mother—which is to say, one in which the younger woman had to pay a price for growing into her own femininity and beauty. Such recapitulations of early, charged experiences with a parent or parents can be seen as a way of getting the lost love objects back once again.

For in this here-and-now enactment of the original relationship with the object of one's intense feelings (the parent), one repeats a version of what once did happen, thereby reinvoking the old ghosts and bringing them to life in one's present-day, external reality. Thus, instead of making the internal separation from the earlier, problematic, unresolved attachments, one re-creates "more of the same thing" and plays out the same scene, again, again, and again.

Still Another Hypothesis: Remaining in a Familiar Relational World

Another possible explanation of the repetition compulsion, one I have written about elsewhere (*Intimate Partners: Patterns in Love and Marriage*), has to do with the simple observation that we all tend to get into patterns of relationships that are known to us. If the daughter of a harsh and tyrannical father marries a man who is or becomes harsh and tyrannical, her behavior can be understood in terms of her staying in a world with which she is thoroughly familiar.

She knows, from long experience, what life is like when you live with a man of this kind. What she doesn't know is what life would be like with a man who is peaceful and gentle; she may view him as unmanly in the first place. (Clare considered Ben, Katie's jogging companion and "conscience," a boring and uninteresting fellow.) What is painful and familiar is often preferable to what is unfamiliar and alien.

For even though what is known may be frankly unpleasant at a conscious level, the unknown is often so far off the charts of one's existence that it tends to be perceived either as dull or as absolutely terrifying. A calm relationship with an even-tempered male would, for Clare, have been like stepping off a pier into an unknown, indistinct void—an experience for which nothing in her life had prepared her.

The knowledge base from which we operate is, by and large, what was learned in our original families. We do things, for the most part, as we saw them done or as a reaction to the way we saw them done. As family therapist Patricia Meyer observed in *The Family Life Cycle*, practically everyone's life course is grounded in a likeness of—or opposition to—the life course of the parents. "In other words," she writes, "an individual follows the behavioral patterns that he or she has experienced, or establishes behavioral patterns *opposite* to those experienced in growing up."

The suggestion here is that we speak, in our lives, the emotional language we first learned—or that the outer limit of our creativity is usually no more than doing the reverse. Clare Maguire had imbibed the understanding, very early in her life, that a man and a woman related in a tyrant-and-martyr fashion. Matt Maguire had learned, early in his own life, that a woman would be a tyrant unless she was ground down completely. So he had, in effect, flipped the relational system over to become its own opposite—tyrannical husband–martyred wife—but not effected any change in the basic operational mode of the system, which was as polarized as it had always been.

Matt had learned, too, that a boy who wanted to have fun was a bad, irresponsible boy, just as Clare had learned that a girl who diets was a bad, presumptuous temptress who might well lose her mother's love in the process of becoming (too) attractive. It might be that these charged aspects of the past were being repeated because these parents hadn't the faintest notion that other ways of living (as spouses *or* as parents) were possible.

Perhaps, however, the very widespread—but usually thoroughly unnoticed and unrecognized—"need to repeat" charged aspects of the past stems from the simple truth that the past has provided us with our internal guideposts for living. Doing things differently, therefore—changing the family drama in significant ways—is an act of creativity, of first imagining and then implementing the construction of an alternate kind of reality. This is truly hard to do when the internalized blueprint for living, etched on our very beings in our original families, seems to allow for no other reality whatsoever. We stay in the familiar relational world because it is the only world that we know and that feels right.

Counting Blessings

By early June, as the school year drew to a close, the feeling of crisis in the Maguire household had diminished considerably. There was no longer the sense that every circuit on the family's central switchboard was lit up, flashing and frantically sending out a general alarm. Clare and Matt seemed to be quarreling much less, and the pressures on Katie, the family symptom bearer, had therefore lessened as well.

Katie had begun wearing a lovely old silver chain and a heavy silver bracelet that had been left to her by her grandfather, and was now never without them. We were then approaching the anniversary of Clare's father's death, and there was a sense that the family's period of mourning for this longtime member of their household was drawing to a close.

Matters had calmed down, but it could not be said that any transformational miracles had taken place. Matt was still overbearing and tyrannical, unable to take inner responsibility for the aspects of himself that he was projecting onto his "bad, self-seeking, selfish and fun-loving, irresponsible" adolescent children and onto the wife he saw as inattentive, immature, disorganized, and covertly rebellious.

Clare was still the passive, devalued victim, unable to entertain the notion of challenging an angrily critical, "ranting and raving" man directly. In a host of ways (albeit with certain elaborations, variations, and additions) the central themes of the past were still being played out in the family's present existence.

Thus, although everybody was clearly feeling better—perhaps because the therapy sessions provided a safe forum in which there was some opportunity to speak one's piece and be heard—the basic structure of this Level 4 polarized emotional system was unchanged. The Maguires had not moved upward on the family developmental scale, but neither had they descended into the chaotic, confused, disorganized Level 5 world that existed directly below them.

Of course, *this family had not come into therapy because they wanted to change.* The Maguires had come to treatment under duress, as a condition of Katie's being allowed to return to school after her expulsion—*and if people lack the inner motivation to change, then widespread changes are surely not likely to happen.*

No one can, for instance, stop smoking or drinking for somebody else. The decision to do so must be made and maintained by the person who will undergo the suffering associated with the withdrawal. Similarly, undergoing psychological change can be painful, and enduring the pain of making changes is not usually feasible (for an individual or for a family) if the terror of the unknown and unfamiliar is more acute than the pain of keeping things just the way they are.

Things could, after all, change for the worse and not for the better, for while transformation of the emotional system may herald the promise of something different and more gratifying, it can also bring with it the threat of unknown, unsustainable losses—not only losses in the external world (the family might split apart), but losses in the world within the individual members of the group. In some curious way, to the degree that Clare stopped repeating the past and resurrecting "the way it once was," she would lose her living contact with that deeply disappointing, frustrating, and at times frankly hateful—but deeply compelling, worshiped, and yearned for—relationship with that first love of her earliest life, her dad.

Letting go of this profound connection to an "internal parent" (and the reason we often falter when called upon to do so) is difficult, because however complex and anguished that connection may have been, we find it hard to surrender the precious illusion that someday, somehow, we will receive the perfect love and nurturance that we still unconsciously hope for and await.

This is prominent among the many powerful reasons why changing is often such a difficult, downright agonizing process, and why some couples and families (the Maguires were among them) simply cannot, or don't want to, truly commit themselves to the attempt. Another powerful reason is, of course, the sense of danger associated with moving into an emotional system that is unfamiliar and in which the rules of the game (and the endpoint or goal of any sequence) are thoroughly and frighteningly unclear. After all, the daughter of a tyrant knows how to interact with an oppressive, dictatorial male, but what she doesn't know are the expected moves—who she should be and what she should do—in the presence of an amiable, considerate partner who treats her as an equal.

The common human tendency is to cling to the world we know (however unpleasant that world may be) because the pain of changing and of attempting to live in a world we don't really understand feels extremely scary. Many clinicians have noted how often a couple in marital therapy, who have obviously been feeling better and interacting in a much healthier way, will suddenly drop out of treatment with the most garbled sorts of explanations. Alongside the wish to grow (up) and develop psychologically, there seems to exist an attendant reluctance—a fear, or even terror, of what is strange, even though what is strange does represent an obvious improvement.

Thus, in circumstances that involve treatment having been imposed rather than chosen, the clinician may certainly lead the proverbial horse to the well, but no one can really make it lean over and drink deeply of the waters of insight. Still, in the Maguire family's case, it could be said that if the horse hadn't ever drunk very deeply from the well, it had at least not leaped off a cliff on its way there; nor had it, on arrival, jumped into the water and drowned itself.

During these past months, Katie Maguire had not gotten into any difficulties as serious and potentially irreversible as those that had brought her into treatment in the first place. This was a blessing to be counted, because, as any psychotherapist who works with adolescents will surely attest, terrible outcomes are never further than a hairsbreadth away. And Katie had, at the beginning of the school year, appeared to be on a rapid spiral downward. She was not only a secret bulimic; she was also flouting the school's rules, drinking, and inviting serious disciplinary action to descend upon her.

So, when one added up the column of this year's achievements, it could be said that Katie had not, in the subsequent months, gotten expelled for alcohol or drug use, nor had she made a serious suicide attempt (although she had muttered vaguely suicidal threats when she was feeling depressed, "fat," and angry). She hadn't managed to suddenly find herself in risky, unsafe circumstances—situations in which she might have gotten raped or otherwise assaulted—nor had she gotten accidentally pregnant. At year's end, Katie had completed her course work adequately, if not as brilliantly as she was capable of doing, and been elected captain of next year's lacrosse team.

Given this daughter's agitation and the whole group's escalating anxieties when we'd first encountered them, the possibilities for calamity had actually been enormous—but no calamities had occurred. So, if there had been no family transformation in the course of therapy, neither had any of the numerous possible disasters transpired.

When summer vacation began, the Maguires took a furlough from therapy, and in the fall (not surprisingly) they did not reappear. But Bob Horwitz, in frequent contact with the school's counseling staff, did learn that Katie had returned from the vacation looking fit and in good spirits. Her younger brothers, Carl and Bobby, had now entered the same boarding school, and she was visibly pleased to have them there.

As for Katie's bulimic symptoms, the school authorities, though remaining watchful, reported that there seemed to be no sign of them whatsoever. The family was doing well, and if the emotional system's ghosts had not been fully exorcised, they had receded. Everything was under control, at least for the present.

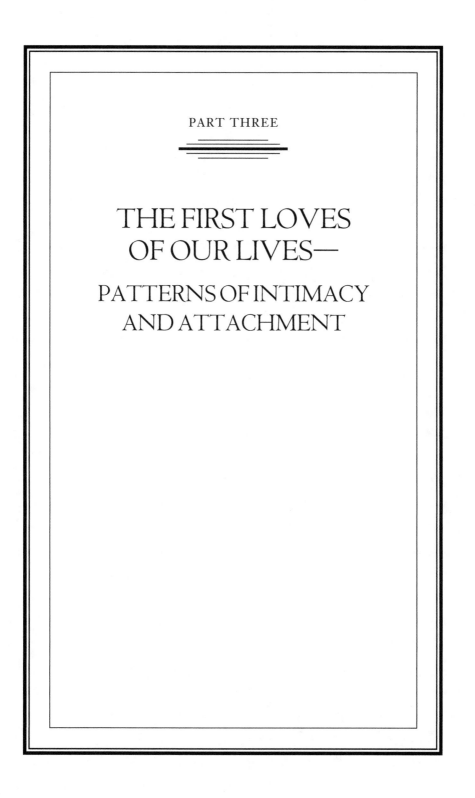

PART THREE

THE FIRST LOVES
OF OUR LIVES—
PATTERNS OF INTIMACY
AND ATTACHMENT

CHAPTER 11

Early Development:
Of Love and Survival

Earlier, I quoted psychologist William R. Looft to the effect that "everyone carries around within him a model of man—a personalized conception of the nature of human nature, a common-sense notion about 'the way people are.' He may not be able to verbalize precisely just what his personal theory about human nature is, but he clearly has one, for it is implicit in what he does to, for, and about other people." Our development of a unique, personal theory about the nature of human nature gets under way very early in life—*at birth, in our original families,* where we begin immediately to internalize the information we must have in order to devise our own individual blueprints for later, independent being.

Present at Birth: The Need for Human Contact

On what basis could one possibly assert that the newborn is beginning to theorize about the human world (even in the most primitive fashion) from the moment of birth onward? How could anyone know what a young infant actually can perceive, be aware of, think about, feel, or understand?

The answer to this question is that within the past decade and a half, a truly startling revolution in infant research has occurred, and the new data on early infancy are remarkably compelling. Broadly speaking, this experimental work has brought about a shift away from intensive study of the development of the young baby as a separate individual to a focus on the developing baby in the context of his important attachments. (Although I prefer to avoid it, I have used the generic "he" in this discussion so as to avoid awkward repetition of "he or she." The developmental data apply equally to female and male babies.)

Thus, while psychological studies of early physical and mental developmental landmarks (such as when the baby can sit, stand, comprehend that an object covered by a blanket still exists under the blanket, and so on) continue apace, an important focal interest of the most recent research has been *babies in relationship with their attachment figures.* For it now seems clear that the newborn person becomes assimilated into the human universe within the framework of these first, crucially significant love bonds.

What has also emerged from the "infant research revolution" is an extraordinary picture of the neonate—a picture quite different from the one that earlier, psychoanalytic theorists had sketched in. Instead of a passive, asocial creature, struggling for reduction of instinctual tensions and for quiescence, the newborn babe seems to be an active little organism who comes into the world eager for experiences and primed (in the sense of being hard-wired) for getting into passionate relationships.

The *need for human contact* constitutes the primary motivating force that drives the behavior of the developing human being. Closely watched and rigorously studied preverbal infants have, very recently, "told" us (see Chapter 12, "Intimacy: Patterns in Human Attachment") that it is in our human nature to become entangled in intensely charged love relationships with our adored and needed caretakers from the moment of our birth onward.

Critical Periods of Early Growth: When Patterns of Attachment Are Established (and May Go Awry)

It was the late, great theorist Dr. John Bowlby who, far in advance of the revolution in infant research (which was made possible by technological advances), first put forth the heretical suggestion that there was a crucial biological link between "human loving" and "survival." During the early 1950s Dr. Bowlby, a psychoanalyst, became interested in the burgeoning new science of ethology, the study of animal behavior in the wild. Ethology, he was coming to believe, might possibly provide psychoanalysis with a more rigorous way of looking at human behavior.

By means of extensive and meticulous observations, ethologists were then gaining a whole new understanding of how social behavior, especially family relationships, developed in the lower species. These biologists were working with concepts such as "instinct," "conflict," and "defense mechanisms"—terms that sounded familiar to a psychoanalytic theorist.

What intrigued Bowlby most was the clear demonstration that there were, in the lower animals, certain "sensitive" or "critical" periods of early growth during which development might go permanently awry. For example, the young chick, which usually shows an instinctive pecking response after one day, never does so at all if it is kept in darkness for the first fourteen days of its life. And the strong tendency of the mallard duckling to follow a moving object—which in nature, of course, is usually the mother—never becomes manifest if the duckling sees no moving object within its first forty hours. The newborns of these species appeared to arrive in the world *preprogrammed to flourish in the ordinary, expectable environment that would greet them.*

Evidently, total darkness was not what the chick's genetic endowment had prepared it for—and, having failed to learn to peck during the "critical" phase of its development, it faced starvation. In the case of the duckling, following the first moving object was a strategy that worked well—as long as the mother duck was there to be followed. Trailing in her wake promoted survival; but if the environment failed to produce the object, following behavior never developed.

Also, as Konrad Lorenz's famous work on "imprinting" in young geese had demonstrated, the wrong moving object might be followed on occasion. A young gosling, faithfully trailing after the first moving object it saw during the "critical" phase, soon became more and more focused upon and attached to it, even when it was something ridiculously inappropriate—such as a moving human being (Dr. Lorenz himself), or a large cardboard box that had been set into motion. The baby goose was genetically prepared to engage in following behavior, and readily became fixated upon whomever or whatever that moving object happened to be.

Obviously, nature's adaptive strategies were by no means flawless. In the lower species, natural capacities and smoothly operating behavioral patterns could be rendered pathological and self-destructive by unexpected forces operating within the environment. Fascinated by these ethological revelations, John Bowlby began to wonder if they were in fact relevant to human infancy. Were there similar "sensitive" or "critical" phases during which environmental pathogens might affect the baby's development in a particularly virulent way?

Human Attachment and Individual Survival

A common behavior pattern seen in human infants is, of course, the strong tendency to develop a powerful emotional attachment to the magical adults who care for him or her—to mother, first and most intensely. Bowlby had for many years been studying the passionate infant-caretaker bond, but, as he told me in the course of a series of conversations that we had in the 1970s, before encountering the work of the ethologists he had always been at a total loss to explain the basis upon which this love relationship actually forms.

A common psychoanalytic belief, to which Bowlby himself could not fully subscribe, was that the baby's first experience of loving arises within the context of nurturant services rendered. That is, the vulnerable infant awakens into consciousness in the arms of the one who tends to his physical needs, who holds, rocks, and, most important of all, feeds him. According to this point of view, love comes into being and flourishes in the atmosphere of pleasure and gratification that follows upon the relief of instinctual tensions, particularly the powerful tension of hunger. This model of how the baby's tie to the caretaker is formed has sometimes been called the "kitchen cupboard theory of loving."

But John Bowlby, who'd begun looking at human attachment through what he called his "new ethological spectacles," began to conceive of loving as a natural and biologically rooted behavioral sequence. Was it not possible that becoming emotionally bonded to the parent was, for the human infant, what following was for the gosling or duckling—a genetically prepackaged mode of interacting and behaving in the average, expectable milieu that the neonate would enter?

The instinctual tendency to form a close, loving bond with the primary caretaker could, on reflection, be understood as biologically advantageous. For a strong, innate tendency to become emotionally attached to the parental caretaker would surely have had a real survival value in the primitive environment in which *Homo sapiens* evolved.

Loving, after all, promotes certain kinds of behavior, prominent among which is the tendency to want to stay close to the object of one's affections. The baby who fell in love with his parent, and who elicited her loving feedback, procured not only her nurturance but the protection provided by her presence. The infant's instinctual behavior patterns, as Bowlby argued in his classic three-volume work *Attachment and Loss*, become sharply focused upon what appears to be a particular set goal—that of keeping the caregiving person nearby. In the normal, expectable course of events, the mother who adored her young adorer would not wander off and leave him unattended. In the natural habitat, where carnivorous animals roamed, the proximity of the watchful, agile parent enhanced her offspring's chances of survival.

It is certainly reasonable to suppose that the young of our species, in common with many of the lower animals, developed behavioral patterns that proved adaptive during our long prehistory in the wild. Those individuals who behaved in certain ways lived long enough to reproduce and to pass along roughly similar kinds of appropriate genetic instructions. Over time—by which is meant eons of evolutionary time—behavior was subtly shaped along certain lines that had proven effective.

Bowlby's fascinating thesis, set forth in *Attachment and Loss*, is that those babies who formed an intense emotional bond with their human caretakers were the ones who survived to produce descendants. It is the need for the parent's protection that mediates what he termed "attachment behavior," which he came to see as a biologically rooted behavioral pattern.

In this regard, it is necessary to remember that the primitive environment is the one in which we humans became human, and it is the milieu to which our species adapted. Civilization is relatively new under the sun: It accounts for roughly one percent of human history, and there is no evidence that we have, as a species, undergone biological changes in this brief illuminated moment of evolutionary time.

During our long prehistory in a wild habitat, where lions, saber-toothed tigers, and other carnivores roamed, life's every passing moment was precarious and dangerous. That tasty morsel, the immobile young human infant, required the loving parent's constant protection and unfailingly vigilant caretaking. That is why, theorized Bowlby, this very human behavior called loving became part of the genetic package.

If *keeping the mother nearby* enhances a baby's feelings of well-being it is, according to Bowlby, because the mothering person's hovering presence once had a very real life-and-death significance. The young infant's need for the parent's protection was once so paramount that her nearness came to be experienced as akin to security itself, and her absences as dangerous and alarming. Thus it is that simply having the mother be there feels like an end in itself, a satisfying outcome, conferring feelings of contentment and safety upon her lovestruck little offspring.

Social Releasers: "Signs" and "Signals" That Promote Social Interactions

Psychoanalysts had speculated at length about instinct and instinctive behaviors; but ethologists were then, as Bowlby told me, engaged in studying instinctive behavior in the lower species experimentally. They were also framing some interesting explanatory concepts about instinct, such as the difference between causation and function. For example: What causes a certain behavior (such as eating) to get under way, and what function, or adaptive purpose does that particular behavior serve?

In the case of eating, what generally causes an animal to start to consume food is an empty stomach or a drop in the level of blood sugar, which signals a state of hunger to the brain. But the function of eating is, of course, the nourishment and replenishment of the body. This may seem simple and obvious, but in the course of their studies of what made certain behaviors commence, ethologists had made an important discovery: Some instinctual behaviors are activated by "signs"—simple stimuli in the environment.

The young herring gull, for instance, responds to the sight of a red spot by opening its beak wide in order to receive food. That red spot is an environmental signal; it resembles the red spot on the beak of the food-bringing adult gull parent. Similarly, a male robin responds to the sight of red feathers in his territory by displaying attack behavior; red feathers are a visual signal that a competitor is present, for they look like the feathers on the breast of a rival male. In dozens of species, such simple "signs" in the environment—the color of a beak, the spread of a tail, a song or a call—bring about behavioral responses. Because they bring about social interactions of varying kinds—for example, initiating courtship, mating, or feeding of the young—these stimuli are called "social releasers."

This way of looking at behavior led Bowlby to begin speculating about the human infant's smile. There was and is no question that the baby's smiling response, which appears sometime between the first two and three months of life, evokes powerful feelings in the adults around him. As the infant gazes into the mothering person's eyes, coos at her, and smiles up endearingly, she feels that he "recognizes" her and knows her as his own, very special person. His behavior is, in a word, enchanting—and, in another word, adaptive, because it binds the parent lovingly to him.

What John Bowlby found particularly intriguing were the numerous studies of what evokes smiling in young infants. These indicated quite consistently that a two- or three-month-old baby was actually *not* responding to a particular person, but to a "sign," or gestalt pattern in his environment. An early (1946) study of the smiling response had in fact demonstrated that when infants were presented with different painted masks, they smiled much more at the ones that looked like frontward-facing people—with foreheads, paired eyes, a slitlike horizontal mouth, and the like.

What appeared to transfix and delight the babies most of all were two eyes in the appropriate places on a mask that was in motion, bobbing up and down about eight inches from the baby's face. The mask looked and "behaved" much as a friendly human adult might look and behave, and it elicited enormous smiles from the young infant subjects in the study.

The babies would not, however, respond with smiles to a mask—or a human face—seen in profile. Nor would any of the infants smile even at his or her own mother's face, when seen in profile. The human face in profile was not the environmental sign-stimulus to which the baby was innately "preset" to react. The human infant, it appears, responds with joyous smiles to a visual configuration resembling the frontal human face, in much the same spirit that the baby herring gull gapes for food automatically at the sight of a red spot like the one on its parent's beak.

Smiling in young infants is, in other words, an innate reaction to an environmental stimulus to which our species is selectively sensitive. The smiling response is a "social releaser" for our species. In the case of the baby herring gull, the social behavior that ensues involves feeding; in that of the human baby, it involves getting into a spirited social exchange with the all-important human caretakers.

And the infant's smiles do have extraordinarily powerful effects upon those around him, most especially upon that central figure of early life, the mother (or father, or another primary caregiver). The mothering person is the person preferred above all others. As the developing infant becomes more familiar with her, he "follows" her with her gaze, orients himself to her, and smiles at her more frequently and broadly than he smiles at anyone else. She, in turn, becomes enraptured by her baby's joyful, friendly overtures; they enslave her, binding her tightly and lovingly to her dependent little worshiper.

Prewired for Loving

Is it not wonderful that the infant, whose survival is so dependent upon parental involvement, instinctively behaves in ways that will promote the formation of a charged love attachment with the all-important, protective, nurturing caretakers? The baby likes and responds most to what is most human, and other human beings are what his fate most depends upon.

It is as if the infant comes into the world primed to set up an intense communication with the mothering figure who will be there to greet him. The empirical evidence in support of such a position, as Bowlby told me, was by no means as plentiful as it would become in the flood tide of the "infancy research revolution" that was to follow later on. But the handful of studies then available did support the idea that the newborn is preadapted to react differentially to certain humanlike stimuli. Infant research carried out in the early 1960s had, for instance, already demonstrated that babies prefer voices and voicelike responses to all other sounds presented to them.

The evidence suggested that human infants might be biologically "prewired" to respond in ways that would promote the crucially important human connection. "My main thesis," stated John Bowlby in a seminal paper entitled "The Nature of the Child's Tie to the Mother," is that the growth of the child's attachment to the caretaker is predictably "expressed through a number of instinctual responses, all of which are primary . . . and, in the first place, relatively independent of one another. Those which I am postulating are sucking, clinging, following, crying and smiling." (Cooing and babbling, he added in a footnote, might well represent a sixth.)

These spontaneously appearing infant behaviors were, in his view, the separate strands from which the rich and passionate infant-caregiver attachment would in the course of time be woven. Of these five adaptive responses, the earliest to be manifested were crying and sucking. And crying was (like the smiling response) a social releaser. "As regards crying," wrote Bowlby, "there is plentiful evidence from the animal world . . . that crying evokes instinctual responses in the mother. . . . Probably in all cases the mother responds promptly and unfailingly to her infant's bleat, call or cry."

It seemed clear, he added, that similar impulses were evoked in the human parent. And no one would dispute the fact that crying is a powerful signal of the infant's distress and a clarion call to parental activity. The baby's wails may be signaling hunger, alarm, cold, discomfort, or the need for contact of some kind (such as holding or rocking). But crying does, in almost all cases, bring the mother to her infant's side swiftly and engage her in an intensive interaction with her baby. As she tries to discern and satisfy his need, she is finding out a lot about her little offspring; she is getting to know what things will calm him down, and the difference between his various kinds of crying behaviors (from mildly fussy to urgently demanding).

It is, by the way, interesting to note that babies' cries have an intensely aversive, anxiety-arousing effect upon human adults; researchers have not yet been able to ascertain precisely why this is so. But people in general (one doesn't have to be the parent of the baby) find the sound of an infant's crying very hard to tolerate. A baby's cries are powerful stimuli, and the adults around him will usually be very active in trying to discover what he needs in order to be calmed and to bring his crying to an end.

From a social point of view, sucking is different. Pleasurable and gratifying as it may be, being fed requires only that the mother's breast (or a bottle) be there. During feeding, the newborn gazes up at the nurturer, whom he is capable of seeing—and mutual gazing is an important part of the emotional glue that will serve to bond the pair. It is, incidentally, well worth noting that until the young infant's accommodative vision has matured (which happens between three and four months) he or she can focus *only* on objects that are about eight to ten inches away—the distance between his own cradled position at the breast or bottle, and his mother's face.

Still, maternal behavior is less intensely interactive around the feeding experience than it is around such "social releasers" as crying and smiling. And as Bowlby saw it, theorists tended to place far too much emphasis on sucking and orality. Sucking is an innate neurological response of great and obvious importance, but, he maintained, it is *not* more primary than other spontaneously appearing behaviors—crying, smiling, and clinging to the caretaking parent.

In most species of our nearest relations, the primates, clinging appears before sucking. A newborn chimpanzee climbs up, or is placed by its mother, on her chest. Once there, the baby chimp clings for hours; only after some time does he find the nipple and begin to suck. The human infant, far less mature at birth than his primate cousin (probably because a human baby's head could not pass through the birth canal if it were fully developed), does retain vestiges of this same powerful gripping response. If a stick is placed in a newborn baby's grasp, he can hang on and support his own weight. But clinging to the mother, like following when able, is part of the human infant's repertoire that will appear later on in the developmental sequence.

The baby's quintet of instinctual responses—sucking, crying, smiling, clinging, following—will of course mature at different times during the first months of life. But they do have what Bowlby called a "predictable outcome," that of connecting the mother to her child emotionally and keeping her in his close vicinity. Crying and smiling, most especially, cause her to respond. The fact that what makes a baby smile most is the sight of a human face is, as the analyst observed wryly, not exactly due to happenstance.

In the course of the first year of life, the infant's disparate innate behaviors become integrated and focused on the all-important, vitally needed, utterly worshiped maternal caretaker. The developing baby then displays the full range of attachment behavior—behavior directed toward keeping the mother nearby with every bit of innate emotional armament that can be mustered. The baby starts crying and protesting when his favorite person goes away, follows after her whenever able, clings to her when frightened, and greets her ecstatically when she returns after an absence. He is punishing her departures by making it difficult for her to leave, and rewarding her returns in ways that will promote her getting back as soon as possible. What the baby does *automatically* is to let her know, by means of his behavior, how utterly necessary she is to his sense of safety, well-being, and security.

In this respect, the human infant's behavior strongly resembles that of our monkey and ape relations. Ethological observations of infant primates in the wild show that they, too, prefer staying close to their mothers and, like human toddlers, rush to her side at the least sign of alarm. This *intense need to keep the mother nearby* is, according to Bowlby and his followers, as strong as the need to be fed by her. Proximity to the mother is experienced as a satisfying thing, an end in itself, ensuring her protection, especially from strangers and potential predators.

The Function of Loving

Over a century earlier, in his masterwork *The Origin of Species*, Charles Darwin had observed that each species is endowed with its own particular repertoire of behavioral patterns in the same way that it is endowed with its own particularities of bodily form and structure. What an organism instinctively *does*—its mode of responding to its environment—is as crucial to its survival as are its anatomical structures.

In the natural world, and over eons of time, behaviors that were biologically advantageous for a species tended to be preserved and improved upon, through chance variations that proved beneficial. In the lower species, as Darwin observed, all of the "most complex and wonderful instincts" had emerged in just this fashion—and in his three-volume work on attachment theory, John Bowlby now argued that human love bonding was perhaps the most wonderful among them.

Human loving is, in all its awesome complexity, basically a way of being that promotes individual and species survival. While it is, asserted the psychoanalyst, to some degree variable and modifiable, love bonding is fundamentally an innate behavioral pattern—a pattern we share with other primates, who also form intense mother-infant attachments.

Each new human individual, proposed Bowlby, comes into this world as an active self, biologically prepared to become emotionally connected to the other who will be waiting there to greet him. It is within the context of this first, enchanted relationship that the young infant's behavior becomes organized and that he or she learns what may be expected from the environment. The first adults that any of us come to know *are* in fact "the environment," the mirror in which we first gaze upon ourselves in reflection and begin to discover who we are.

The Self and the Other: The Crucial First Relationship

The "sensitive" phase of human infancy is, thus, that period of early life when the first passionate emotional ties are coming into being. Because the parent's love has had, throughout evolutionary millennia, an underlying and very real survival value, the baby experiences his human partner's proximity as necessary for psychological survival. Such an attachment figure must be there if development is to proceed in a normal fashion.

The need to form a close attachment with a special someone appears to be crucial not only for the baby's emotional but for his physical well-being and development. As a renowned study of foundling-home infants carried out by Dr. René Spitz demonstrated, emotionally unattached babies may "fail to thrive" and simply waste away. The infants in the Spitz study, all of whom were well fed and well housed—but not being attended to by any special, involved individual—displayed unmistakable mental and physical deficits within the first year of life. Despite the fact that they were being cared for in a clean, hygienic environment, with one nurse assigned to every eight individuals, these babies (all of whom had been separated from their prison-inmate mothers at four months) were unable to sit or stand, cried often, never smiled, and had not begun to develop language. They were apathetic, listless, and caught infections easily; several simply died.

Does it seem too farfetched to wonder if the human infant, like the gosling, enters the world preprogrammed to become focused upon and emotionally attached to a special other individual? And to wonder if, should the environment fail to provide that unique someone who becomes wonderfully familiar and expectably *there*, the baby becomes disorganized and despairing, and experiences himself as horribly isolated, in an emotional vacuum? It is as if, in the absence of a warm and engaged other, the human self cannot flourish and develop.

Love Hunger Is on a Par with Food Hunger

The idea that ethology might provide a solid base for psychoanalytic theorizing was, as Bowlby told me in the 1970s, initially a simple act of faith. Although there were a variety of fascinating speculations about how the young infant experienced his world, few analytic thinkers (Anna Freud and Margaret Mahler were the striking exceptions) based their theorizing on the direct observation of infant behaviors. The scientific approach Bowlby was championing involved not only meticulous baby-watching, but baby-watching through ethologically focused eyeglasses.

Suppose one looked, as precisely and analytically as possible, at what caused a particular behavior—crying, for example. Was the baby hungry, or was the baby wet, cold, and uncomfortable? And what was the crying behavior's function on that particular occasion? Fully understanding the function of a behavior, in ethological terms, involves taking careful note of what brings about its ending or consummation. If, in a particular sequence, the crying infant becomes calm and peaceful when the mother begins to rock his cradle, rub his back rhythmically, and speak or sing to him, then it may be inferred that it is the comfort of her human presence that has served to bring his crying to an end.

While the baby's crying can and frequently does signal hunger or physical discomfort to the parent, there are certainly numerous instances in which its sole function seems to be that of bringing her close, engaging with her, procuring her reassuring, soothing presence and attentions. Love hunger is, theorized Bowlby, on a par with food hunger—a powerful, fundamental inborn need that must be satisfied within the neonate's intimate (family) environment. The human infant's social and interactive needs are *primary*, he insisted.

This view of the baby's essential nature ran counter, as noted earlier, to the prevailing theoretical winds of the time (which still continue to claim many adherents). For Freud's thinking about infancy was profoundly different. He viewed the human infant as a passive actor in the opening scenes of life's commencing drama; the baby was not even, psychologically speaking, a separate self—an "I." "An infant at the breast does not as yet distinguish his ego from the external world as the source of the sensations flowing in upon him," he wrote in *Civilization and Its Discontents.* For the neonate, there was no boundary between inside and outside, the self and the other person.

In the Freudian schema, the infant's major efforts were not directed toward engaging with the caregiver but toward minimizing and controlling those instinctual tensions (such as hunger) that perpetually threatened to overwhelm his vulnerable little being. The young baby did not seek out experiences so much as he tried to ensure that experiences did not flood him with intolerable, unmanageable stimulation.

But an impressive body of recent experimental findings has not really borne out this conception of infant nature; instead, a somewhat different picture of the human newborn has emerged. There is now a widely held and increasingly respected view that, as psychologist Sheldon Cashdan observes in *Object Relations Therapy,* "the mind and psychic structures that comprise [*sic*] it . . . evolve out of human interactions rather than out of biologically derived tensions. Instead of being motivated by tension reduction, human beings are motivated by the need to establish and maintain relationships." In brief, we enter life raring to become involved with those around us, and most especially with that special attachment figure, the mother—she whom we adore with all our being, and upon whom our being literally depends.

CHAPTER 12

Intimacy: Patterns
in Human Attachment

Like a high-powered microscope with wonderfully clear resolution, the recent rapid progress in the field of infant research has brought into much sharper focus the elaborate substructure of human attachment. And certainly, if this remarkable scientific work has taught us anything about our human nature, it is that loving precedes language.

For it is in the infant year, the year "without speech," that we learn a nonverbal mode of loving, one that will be retained throughout our lifetime. We learn, too, whether or not it's possible to meet our two most fundamental human requirements—the need for closeness (intimacy) and the need to be a separate self (autonomy)—simultaneously, or if one need must be sacrificed in order to gratify and realize the other.

Without Speech

Well in advance of the recent upsurge of experimental work with young babies, there were many highly speculative theories about how the infant experiences life in a mute world (the word "infant," deriving from the Latin, means "without speech"). Until very recently, however—given the newborn's obvious inability to answer questions—there has been a dearth of empirical data.

Did the neonate enter life charged with sexual and aggressive tensions, which were seeking release, as Freud had suggested? Or did the newborn come into existence dominated primarily by the need (to use E. M.

Forster's incomparable phrase) to "only connect" with those around him, as many later theorists believed? What, in its most pristine state and before the environment had stamped its powerful impress upon the nascent individual, did the human package come equipped with?

These were very basic questions—questions about the essential nature of human nature *before* the influence of culture had made itself felt—but of course the newborn infant could not possibly answer them. It seemed patently impossible for anyone to really ascertain what human neonates could see, hear, feel, think, "know," and experience. The inner life of the infant was, or at least seemed to be, forever out of the range of adult contact, much less open to systematic scientific investigation.

But fascinatingly enough, and just within the past couple of decades, a highly sophisticated new technology has produced an explosion of information. Researchers are, at present, able to pose astonishing "questions" to their tiny preverbal subjects, and they are receiving some extraordinary "answers."

It has now become clear that the newborn comes onto life's stage equipped with a great many hitherto unrecognized competencies, and that he or she goes about the all-important business of establishing emotional connectedness in an efficient, dedicated fashion. The infant's perceptual abilities, when it comes to innate skills that will facilitate bonding and relationship, verge on the mysterious or even magical. Take, for example, the matter of sound—that is, the baby's capacity to hear, attend, and respond to those around him.

The Recognition of the All-Important Other: Does It Begin in Utero?

According to researchers Anthony J. DeCasper and William P. Fifer, human responsiveness to sound begins in the third trimester in utero and becomes quite sophisticated by birth. Young infants are not only adept listeners, they are extremely discriminating listeners to speech sounds. In an experiment involving babies no more than a few days old, psychologists DeCasper and Fifer demonstrated that the newborn is acutely sensitive to the sound of his mother's voice, and can tell the difference between her voice and that of another female.

What these psychologists did was to place an electronically bugged nipple (pacifier) into the baby's mouth, a nipple which was hooked up to two audiocassette machines. On one machine was a recording of the mother reading Dr. Seuss's *And to Think That I Saw It on Mulberry Street*. On the other was a recording of another woman reading the same material. The infant, equipped with tiny earphones, soon discovered that by sucking on the nipple in a certain pattern of bursts and pauses, he or she was able to produce the sound of the mother's voice. The infants quickly learned the pattern of sucking that would activate the mother's voice; they produced it far more often than they did the voice of the other woman.

"We now report that a newborn infant younger than 3 days of age can not only discriminate its mother's voice but will also work to produce her voice in preference to the voice of another female," stated the researchers in a 1980 article in *Science* magazine. The neonate's clear preference for the maternal voice, they wrote, "suggests that the period shortly after birth may be important for initiating infant bonding to the mother." This is remarkable, and especially so when one realizes that as recently as 1960 it was believed that the newborn could neither hear nor see at birth.

The above experiment is a good model of the manner in which developmental researchers now get infants to give responses to their questions. Working to produce the mother's voice by emitting a particular pattern of sucks and pauses is the baby's way of saying "I not only recognize her voice, but prefer her voice, and by means of my behavior I will show it."

Many kinds of questions have been posed to babies in this fashion. For example, in another such experiment—this one involving three-day-old infants—psychologist Aidan MacFarlane put the babies on their backs and then put breast pads taken from their nursing mothers on one side of their heads. On the other side of each infant's head a breast pad saturated with another nursing mother's milk was placed.

Would the baby turn his head in one direction more than in the other? The question being asked here was, of course, whether or not the infant could discriminate between the smell of his own mother's milk and that of another woman. And in fact, the neonate was able to do so. For no matter which side the mother's breast pad was placed on, he would turn his head in that direction.

Prewired for Loving

It is now well documented that infants look longer and harder at those visual stimuli (patterning of features; curves; angles; and so on) that are most "facelike" in appearance. A clear-cut preference for such stimuli can be demonstrated even in very young infants, as Robert L. Fantz showed in a series of pioneering studies carried out in the early 1960s (that is, well in advance of the current revolution in the field).

Fantz's baby subjects, all under five days old, were presented with six possible visual images to look at. In varying orders of succession, these were three plainly colored surfaces (white, yellow, and red) and three different patterns (a bull's-eye, a human face, and newsprint). The infants, three of whom were under twenty-four hours old, fixated longest upon the visual "target" that most resembled the human face.

Their next favorite was the bull's-eye, after which came the newsprint; the plain white, yellow, and red surfaces received very little attention. Clearly, infants liked patterns more than solid-colored surfaces (even if the colors were bright ones), and they found the visual pattern of the human face most diverting and worthy of investigation.

"Whatever the mechanism underlying this interest," commented psychologist Fantz in a 1963 article in *Science*, "it should facilitate the development of social responsiveness, since what is responded to must first be attended to." The newborn seemed to be cunningly prestructured in ways that would promote recognizing and relating to other human beings.

In this early research, as in the later upsurge of experimental work with infants, it was by means of *what the baby did* (for example, fixated on a visual stimulus for a longer or shorter time) that the investigator's questions were "answered." In this way, the speechless world of the infant was being penetrated, and wherever one looked in the growing body of data, the neonate was found to be more perceptually competent a creature than anyone had ever imagined.

I Can Match My Behavior to Your Behavior: Loving Precedes Language

Newborns between the ages of twelve and twenty-one days could, as was demonstrated experimentally by researchers Andrew N. Meltzoff and M. Keith Moore, even imitate the facial gestures of adults. If, for example, an adult stuck out his tongue or pursed his lips, the infant was highly liable to respond by doing the same thing a little less than three seconds later. The babies' ability to perform this imitative task was thoroughly surprising, for it indicated an innate capacity to make a mental link between an action that was seen and an action that was then performed.

It was as if, were the baby able to speak, he would say, "I see you doing that action, which feels a certain way to me, and which I can repeat." It is a way of matching the social gesture of the other with a social gesture of one's own. As psychologist Meltzoff observed in a book entitled *Social Perception in Infants*, "Imitation . . . taps fundamental social processes. It involves the infant's recognition that he can do what another person does, that he is in some sense *like* the adult model" (my italics). In such an interaction, one cannot think of the newborn as "merged" with the adult caretaker but rather as a self (or proto-self) relating to another human being.

Infants are, we now know, capable not only of imitating facial gestures but of imitating adult expressions of emotion as well. As researcher Tiffany M. Field and her colleagues reported in a 1982 article in *Science*, thirty-six-hour-old babies can distinguish between the facial expressions of happiness, sadness, and surprise. They will, most readily, perceive and reproduce the smile, frown, or surprised look displayed on the face of an adult model.

These and a vast number of other experimental results have by no means failed to attract psychoanalytic attention. As Dr. Doris K. Silverman observed in a recent article in *Psychoanalytical Psychology*, "a new development among neonate observers is the awareness of newborns' highly developed state, of their awareness of the external world, of their active eliciting of responsiveness, and of the intricate, synchronistic mother-infant relationship that fosters bonding."

Love Play: Life's Gloriously Charged First Dialogues

By two months of age the infant's eyes are well able to coordinate at most distances; the larger environment is no longer blurred and is well into focus. Now he can not only look around but has the capacity to fixate his gaze upon the gaze of the primary attachment figure (and others in the family circle); he delights one and all by showing signs of recognition, of "knowing" them.

During this phase of life, when the baby is visually proficient but still unable to move about on his own, he is as intensely sociable a little creature as ever in his life he will become. Nothing exists but the here and the now, the smile or the frown of the moment.

He is especially keen on faces that are speaking, and he regards these with the utmost fascination. And, while he spends much more of his time interacting with the maternal caregiver than with anyone else, he is getting to know the other players on the family stage as well. As he smiles, coos, and babbles, he is making eye-to-eye contact with those around him, and they are usually quite responsive to his captivating overtures.

It is within the context of these early face-to-face interactions (most especially the joyful gazing and vocalizing interchanges with the primary caretaker) that the infant gets his first experience of being a self in a gloriously charged dialogue with another person. And it certainly does seem plausible to suppose, as some infant researchers have suggested, that during these early games of love (whose only "goal" is shared mutual delight) we get a very powerful foretaste of what *the self being with the other*—intimacy—is like.

"I"-to-"I" Contact

Imagine a mother leaning over the rail of her four-and-a-half-month-old baby's crib. The baby has been fussing slightly, having just wakened after a nap. "He*loooo*," she says brightly, in the higher-pitched voice to which she has automatically shifted (we humans seem to have innate knowledge of the higher voice ranges and contours of sound that infants prefer). The baby orients himself to her, focuses his gaze upon hers intently. Then he coos up at her for a moment.

"Oh, so you're *glad* to see me," she murmurs, leaning farther inward and giving the infant's belly a slow little jiggle that is in accord with the rhythm of her speech. Momentarily taken aback, the infant draws in a sudden breath and then looks up at her attentively. She waits. The pair seem transfixed, lost in each other's eyes. "Hel-*lo?*" she repeats, with a little smile. She leans down to plant a brief kiss upon the baby's belly, and this time he responds with a hearty chortle. Then he begins "talking" up at her earnestly, his arms and legs flailing excitedly.

He is not only responding joyously to his human partner's latest advance; he is tuning her own behavioral dials up a bit higher. For as his level of arousal heightens, so does hers. And, as her "turn" in their dialogue comes around again, she resumes at an even more enthusiastic level. *"Hello,"* she says, making an exaggerated mock-surprise face this time around. The infant stares up at this fantastic new input, looking amazed and enthralled. He gazes up at her, waiting.

The maternal caregiver, eager for more of her baby's smiles, laughter, and vocalizing, now leans over to give his belly a long nuzzle—one that sends him into a paroxysm of pleasure. He laughs and pumps his little limbs about, but then suddenly turns his head away and is silent. He has passed beyond what researcher Daniel Stern terms the "optimal level of stimulation," and their socializing has become too agonizingly delicious to bear.

By averting his head and breaking eye contact, the baby has called a halt; he needs a time-out in order to calm himself. Babies will do this with regularity during face-to-face play—call a halt to the turn-taking interchange with the partner—in order to soothe themselves and restore their own equilibrium. This is the infant's way of providing himself with a necessary rest-stop along the mounting scale of his and the loving other's mutual excitement.

Although aversion of the head is the usual way in which a baby will say "Whoa, this is becoming too much to tolerate," there are other ways in which a suspension of the dialogue can be created. The infant can lose eye contact by closing his lids, or his eyes may simply glaze over and become unfocused so that he is looking at nothing and nobody in particular. Or his gaze may become "avoidant" and sweep past the partner without ever actually alighting upon her. These are all baby ways of saying, "For the moment at least, I don't want this interaction to continue."

Eye Love: Creating and Breaking Contact

Some infant-caregiver couples may spend as long as a hundred seconds locked in mutual gazing, a phenomenon that researchers refer to as "eye love." Although no one can explain exactly why it should be so, mutual gazing is inherently highly stimulating and arousing. Looking deeply into someone's eyes while that person looks back into one's own eyes is a stirring, even electrifying experience. It can feel thrilling or enraging, depending on the social context in which it happens to be taking place. (In certain animals, apes and dogs, for example, direct gaze is a threat behavior; staring is a signal of aggression.) As adults, we will sustain eye-to-eye contact for only a few seconds at a time unless we are either falling in love, or about to make love, or getting into a serious fight.

In all other kinds of human social situations, mutual gazing—two grown-up individuals looking wordlessly into each other's eyes—will not be sustained for very long. Someone will glance away, for focal eye contact elicits such intense feelings on both extremes (loving, angry) of the emotional continuum. In the case of caregivers and their infants, however, prolonged visual regard is the norm. A mother and her baby will spend a lot of time looking deeply into one another's eyes, and enjoying it.

In any case, this intense way of being together fills them both with excitement, creating a highly charged affective climate between them. It is, however, so exciting that one partner or the other (in most cases, the infant) frequently needs to break the gaze and take a time-out. He is feeling overstimulated and actually *is* overstimulated, physiologically. For, as infancy researcher Tiffany Field has recently demonstrated, about five seconds before the baby averts his face and takes a breather his heart rate accelerates suddenly and dramatically. By breaking off the highly thrilling eye contact, he can slow his heart rate back down to its baseline within five seconds. And after a very brief interval, the infant is usually feeling ready to turn back to the caregiver for more exchange of gazes, smiles, and stimulating "conversational" vocalizing.

Regulating the Self and the Relationship

Thus, the baby is a full interactive partner in the regulation of the relationship, with veto power over the proceedings on a moment-to-moment basis. He can control his own level of engagement and regulate his inner state by means of looking at, or looking away from, the maternal caregiver. Far from being passive, the infant retains a good deal of control over the interaction, and the sensitive parent allows him to take this control most readily. She respects the baby's need to take a periodic breather, and permits him to pace his own level of arousal and stimulation by averting his gaze whenever necessary.

There are, however, mothers who cannot cede control in this fashion. They will not allow the infant to "take over" in the ordinary way, and to regulate the beginnings and endings of these exciting face-to-face episodes. Instead of permitting the baby to take some time out to cool down, as will happen periodically throughout this highly exciting social exchange, this kind of mother fails to respect the request being made when her baby turns his gaze away.

She experiences this, suggests researcher Daniel Stern, as a "micro-rejection," and instead of waiting for baby to return to the exchange voluntarily, she escalates the intensity of her own behavior—gets louder and more demanding, makes funnier, more exaggerated faces, etc. It is as though in order to maintain her command she must keep the baby involved, no matter what. And if all her efforts to recapture his attention prove ineffective, the unempathic partner may pursue him by moving around and putting herself in the very place to which his gaze has turned. She has invaded his privacy space, and simply won't let him alone.

It is in this kind of circumstance that eye-glazing and other infant methods of saying no must be resorted to by the baby. He may even have to call a halt to the dialogue by adopting a posture of refusal, such as arching his body away or going totally limp in the passive protestor's position with which we are all so familiar. And, if this is the way things ordinarily happen between the partners, then the maternal caregiver is depriving the baby of the important experience of being able to self-regulate—that is, to control his own level of excitement and stimulation effectively.

In this kind of situation, what the baby is learning, long before language, is that one can either be in a close relationship *or* take care of one's own needs, but one can't do both things simultaneously.

A Mother and Two Sons: A Secure Relationship and an Anxious-Avoidant Relationship

In a remarkable paper that appeared in 1971, psychiatrist Daniel Stern examined the ordinary face-to-face play of a mother and her fraternal twin babies. What was illuminating about this work was that Stern studied what happened between the mother and each of her infants in such fine detail that ordinarily hidden aspects of the relationships suddenly sprang into clear sight.

The "microanalytic" method of inquiry used in this research, then fairly new, is now in widespread use; Stern himself was among those who pioneered the use of new technologies in order to study mother-infant interactions in very precise and fine-grained detail. In the above study, the young (twenty-five-year-old) mother sat on the floor during a series of ordinary face-to-face play sessions with her three-and-a-half-month-old boys. While she interacted with her sons in the "natural habitat" (her own living room), the two boys, Mark and Fred, each sat in his own infant seat facing her.

The mother's firstborn son, Mark, was the one she considered to be more like herself; that is, "active." This was an opinion she had formed during her pregnancy, for that baby had done much more kicking in utero. She saw the second son, Fred, as more "passive," like his father. She did, as it happened, have some ambivalent feelings about her husband, and most especially about her husband's passivity.

In the course of a series of typical play sessions, a portable video camera recorded a portion of the proceedings—a twenty-minute segment of mother-twins interaction. Eventually, a selected portion of the videotape was converted into 16mm film and subjected to intensive frame-by-frame analysis using a hand-cranked movie viewer, so that the film could be moved backward and forward, stopped in place, and so forth. This made it possible for Stern to study each frame carefully—to examine what happened between the mother and each twin on, literally, a split-second ($\frac{1}{24}$ second) basis. And the social exchange between the mother and "active" Mark, when compared to the social exchange between the mother and "passive" Fred, was found to be surprisingly different.

When the mother and Mark were in the face-to-face position, Mark remained oriented to her and engaged in the customary facially animated exchanges until one or the other of them looked away. When one partner *did* look away, so did the other. Each could thus cue the other to orient and exchange loving gazes or to be comfortably separate and looking in another direction. Theirs was a wonderfully satisfying, mutually regulated dialogue; they could be together or apart, with equal, uncomplicated easiness. At the end of this typical segment of face-to-face play interaction, baby Mark was quite calm.

When the mother turned to Fred, however, things proceeded in a very different fashion. Each time she oriented herself to Fred and looked at him, he began orienting himself away; he would not sustain eye contact for much longer than about a second. Then the mother, instead of permitting Fred to avert his gaze (as she had permitted Mark to do), attempted to pursue him. As Fred turned away, she went after him, trying to engage with him ever more demandingly and invasively. But the baby resisted her—until she gave up and turned back to look at Mark.

As soon as she began orienting herself to Mark, Fred turned in his mother's direction. He oriented himself to her and looked at her as if to solicit her gaze and her loving attention. And so it went, in this interactive system which was *also* mutually regulated, but in a highly disagreeable fashion. The mother and Fred seemed to have developed an approach-avoidance relationship, for as one moved closer and initiated the exchange of loving gazes, the other could be depended upon to turn away.

Each partner appeared to be cuing the other *not* to make or sustain much gratifying "I-to-I" contact. Thus, while the mother and Mark prompted each other to *look at the same time* and then *turn away at the same time*, the mother-Fred pair could neither get it together nor experience any moments of separateness. As Stern pointed out in his discussion of this study, what happened between the mother and each infant was rather like an interactive dance—a waltz, in which both knew the steps and executed them together.

In a waltz, wrote Stern, "certain steps and turns will be cued by one partner—in between those cues both know the program well enough to move synchronously for short periods." The mother-Fred dance was one that both partners clearly knew very well, and that neither one of them was enjoying.

As the psychiatrist noted, "Fred can neither stay face to face with mother for long, nor remain faced away from her for long. . . . A vicious cycle, *cued by specific behaviors of mother and infant*, is repeatedly instituted. The cycle is also time-consuming so that mother and Fred generally spend more time interacting together. It is, however, mutually unsatisfying."

Although they monitored each other's behavior constantly and were continually preoccupied with one another, infant and caregiver could neither get together in a gratifying manner nor leave each other alone. At the end of a typical face-to-face play interaction, Fred was upset and his mother was unable to soothe him.

As this work demonstrated, each twin was in a highly structured but very different interactive system with the mother. As a result, Mark and Fred were learning profoundly different lessons about social living. Fred was learning that one could neither become truly engaged (intimate) with the other nor could one quite disconnect from her influence for a moment (and be a separate person). Mark was learning that one could be emotionally engaged *and* separate and autonomous with equal facility. Experiences of togetherness, and experiences of the self alone, occurred in a continuously pulsating balance.

Clearly each of the twins, at age three and a half months, was internalizing a very different (if still quite rudimentary) set of "rules" and expectations about how the interaction would go, and indeed about the basic nature of human relatedness. And, reported Stern, at age twelve to fifteen months, Fred was a far more fearful and dependent child, with transient phobias (he was terrified by the vacuum cleaner), who could neither wander far from his mother nor look at her directly. His reaction to strangers was an intense one. Mark, on the other hand, "greets people well, makes prolonged eye contact . . . wanders off more freely and gets deeply engrossed in play without any regard for mother's whereabouts," related Stern. One twin had a secure attachment to the mother; the other twin had what is known as an "anxious, avoidant" attachment, and these two very different mother-son relationships were deeply rooted in a world without words.

The Mother-Infant Bond: A Mutual-Regulation Model

What had gotten the highly aversive mother-Fred "dance" going in the first place? Could one say that this mother-infant misattunement was due to aspects of the baby's own inborn temperament? Or was the responsibility to be laid at the door of a powerful maternal fantasy about Fred's inherent failings—the "passivity" which she saw as being so much like his father's, and about which she seemed to have negatively charged feelings? The answer to this question is most probably "Neither."

In a mutual-regulation model of infant-caretaker behavior, the most that one can say is that *the system itself isn't working well;* both partners may feel rejected, disturbed, and unable to change things, but both are influencing the relationship in such a way that things remain the same. If there is one important lesson that the recent revolution in infancy research has taught us it is that the mother-infant bond is an interactive one. Both participants play a role in shaping the developing attachment and regulating what happens between them.

And infants, it must be remembered, do come into the world with certain temperamental inclinations and biases. A constitutionally high-strung newborn may, for example, respond to an anxious parent in a way that derails the dialogue between them and gets the relationship off to a detrimental beginning.

A more robust baby, on the other hand, will certainly experience the overwrought caregiver's lack of availability, and yet will work very hard to engage her. Infants bring a whole biologically based repertoire of responses to the caretaker. Some babies will be completely undone by a very minor amount of maternal depression, while others seem able to weather a fairly major emotional disturbance in the parent without undue emotional damage.

Who the baby is affects and "shapes" the mother's behavior in ways that are very powerful—just as powerful as the ways in which the mother "shapes" the baby's responses. And, from the earliest days onward, infant and caregiver monitor and influence each other's behavior.

"Watch, Wait, and Wonder": Therapy for Parent-Infant Couples

It was the great child analyst and pediatrician D. W. Winnicott who, long before the current upsurge in infant studies, made the famous observation "There is no such thing as a baby." What Winnicott meant by this remark is that there is no way to comprehend the human infant's behavior in isolation from the all-important relationship with the first caretaker.

To understand the baby, asserted Winnicott, one must understand the baby and mother together—and the body of scientific knowledge now available has surely borne the truth of this statement out. What makes for synchrony and shared pleasure, or for misattunement and mutual frustration, is the fit between baby and parent and the system they create together.

In the mother-Fred instance, for example, a reasonable hypothesis might be that this twin's inborn constitution—which another parent might have experienced as delightfully placid and even-tempered—had negative meaning for this particular mother. The caretaker's intense feelings about the baby's "passivity," in conjunction with certain givens of baby Fred's native temperament, had led to the emotional discordance between them.

That being said, is it possible that so distressing a pattern of infant-parent relating can be halted once the aversive "waltz" between the partners has gotten started? Happily, the answer is that it can, for an increasingly sophisticated understanding of maternal-infant interaction has led to the development of new kinds of "couples therapies" for poorly functioning or outright symptomatic mother-baby pairs.

Among the relatively new forms of treatment is one that, while not yet in widespread use, is certainly on the cutting edge of infant psychiatry. This mode of intervention, which is known as the "Watch, Wait, and Wonder" technique, may sound too simple to bear any relationship to "therapy," but its effects are powerful and can magically transform a mother-baby relationship, even in certain highly pathological situations (for example, when the baby is suffering from a global "failure to thrive").

Watch, Wait, and Wonder sessions are conducted in a small (some twelve feet by eighteen feet) childproof room, with a mat on the floor and colorful toys strewn around. During the first half of the time allotted (which will be roughly an hour, in toto), the mother is instructed to get down on the floor with her baby, but to *let the infant initiate play.* This is the Golden Rule to be followed: The parent is to let her infant take the lead throughout the play session, always being careful *not* to take over the activity and start directing it. (Enforcing the rule will, on occasion, require some gentle coaching on the part of the therapist.)

This elementary instruction—"Stay back, and let the baby do all the initiating"—subtly alters the parent's role in the interaction, so that she becomes the observer of her infant's efforts to engage rather than the person who is to take charge of and direct them. It also blocks the mother from playing out her own scenarios in such a way that the baby is being used as an emotional prop in her own internal drama. The infant is the sole initiator, and is therefore able to have an enormous say over what transpires between the pair.

The parent simply *watches* her baby, *waits* for him to take the lead, and *wonders* about who he really is—which is quite different from knowing everything about him in advance, because she has already incorporated him into her own subjectivity. (Even in utero, it will be recalled, the mother of the twins in the Stern experiment "knew" that baby Fred was the more passive one—an attribution which, for her, held unpleasant connotations.)

The first part of the Watch, Wait, and Wonder sequence—the play sequence—is followed by a discussion, during which mother and therapist talk over what just happened (while the baby continues playing on the floor). In the course of this reflective period, the mother will be asked what she observed about her child during a play session in which the baby did all the initiating and her own role was limited to that of the responder and follower.

What tends to surface rapidly in this discussion are those aspects of the infant-led play that served to trigger anxiety in the parent—so much anxiety that she found it impossible to follow the Golden Rule of noninterference and began intruding, prohibiting, taking over and directing the play, or simply tuning out and perhaps even falling asleep. As Elisabeth Muir, a pioneer of the Watch, Wait, and Wonder method, explains, "The mother may comment on something that puzzled her or that was difficult to tolerate. . . . This allows an opportunity for the therapist to explore with the mother what was difficult about it, what thoughts she had about it, and if there are connections to other experiences."

This can in turn, observes Muir in an article describing the Watch, Wait, and Wonder technique, lead directly "to an unfolding of the mother's own experiences with her own mother in the past, or with her spouse in the present and thence back into her past. Slow and careful exploration of anxious moments can reveal some core relational problems of the mother that are being re-enacted in her relationship with her baby, and can thus allow some insight into how she might be repeating patterns from her past in her new relationship with her baby."

In ongoing problematic situations, such as the mother-Fred relationship, a timely psychotherapeutic intervention can serve to create synchrony and mutual pleasure between a thoroughly mismatched and disaffected pair. For parent-infant therapies are geared toward helping the caregiving parent disentangle her own life experience and view of herself from her perceptions and attributions vis-à-vis her baby.

Thus, while in that particular instance it was clear that the baby's temperamental style (Fred was the more placid twin) was inborn and not subject to change, what *could* be changed was the mother's capacity to see her young baby in a more objective, less emotionally burdened fashion. Clearly, for the mother of the twins, "passivity" represented something historical that was negatively toned—which was why she tended to invade baby Fred's space whenever she feared that he wasn't being appropriately "active."

A Watch, Wait, and Wonder approach to the problem would, in this kind of circumstance, help the parent step back and get to know her baby for who he really is when he *isn't* being intruded upon and goaded into unwanted activity; and it would help the parent explore the bad feelings associated with "passivity" that existed in her own internal world.

Love's Underlying Rhythms

Long before language and symbolic thinking come into play, we transmit and receive a great variety of complex and powerful interpersonal messages through other channels, using the dialect of gaze, facial expressiveness, body movement, and rhythmic vocalization. From the first moment of life, suggests infancy researcher Beatrice Beebe, we are always seeking ways of being engaged with the caregiver, and ways of being separate from her also.

According to Dr. Beebe, who uses fine-grained microanalytic methods of study to examine infant-caretaker looking, motion, and vocalizing patterns, the very nature of human attachment is such that ways of moving "in" and moving "out" of the relationship are always being negotiated and renegotiated on an ongoing basis. As the partners create the mutual gaze and break the mutual gaze—as they move their bodies toward and away from each other, as they vocalize in unison or engage in turn-taking "dialogues"—the relationship is being regulated from moment to moment by both members of the pair. In the process, the "rules" of the interaction are being structured and codified.

"Basically, every infant-caregiver couple is always working on some kind of balance," Dr. Beebe told me. "They are always involved in developing answers to such questions as 'How do we get engaged? What happens when we're engaged? How long can we stay engaged? When do we move out; how long do we stay out; what prevents coming back and what facilitates coming back?' These things are being arbitrated from day one onward."

As microanalyses of film and audiotapes have consistently demonstrated, baby and mother are adjusting their behaviors to one another on a split-second basis. And, while neither partner is in complete control of the relationship, each is always monitoring and influencing the other to make subtle shifts in a particular direction so that both can get on the same behavioral wavelength. "When you study what's happening at this microscopic level, you see that what one individual does is always affecting the other," Beebe told me. "When [the] baby smiles, the mother's eyes brighten and she begins to smile, and this is a critical piece of experience—

seeing in the other person's expression some kind of immediate correspondence to one's own subjective feeling state."

When this happens, the infant is not only inviting the caregiver to join with him in his own internal state; he is also seeing in her face the gratifying effects of his own behavior. And, while mother and infant are responding to each other in a variety of modalities—looking, vocalizing, body movement—it is in the face most of all that the other's responsive pleasure and delight can be seen and fully realized. It is as if each partner's joy and elation were being sent out and returned with compound interest. Each partner's rising delight *can be seen* in the facial expression of the other.

The ongoing mutual regulation of the mother-infant relationship is so subtle and swiftly moving that many significant events happen in fractions of seconds, so rapidly that the unassisted eye could not possibly observe them. But microanalytic researches have indicated the remarkable degree to which both members of the pair are continuously monitoring and influencing each other to match their behaviors—to bring their facial expressions, vocal rhythms, and so on into concordance in order to remain emotionally attuned.

Space as Well as Closeness: Infant-Mother Attachment

A recent study of vocal rhythms, carried out by psychologist Beatrice Beebe and colleagues Joseph Jaffe, Stanley Feldstein, Cynthia Crown, and Michael Jasnow, examined the patterns of sounds and silences in typical infant-caretaker "dialogues." At the outset of this research, the babies were all four months old, and the investigators were looking for three possible measures of whether infant-caregiver partners were influencing each other's vocal patterns.

The first of the three measures was the duration of each partner's separate utterance. Were the mother and infant matching each other when it came to the length of their vocalizations? For example, if the mother said "Hiya hiya," and the baby said "Ennnh ehh ahhhh," would each distinct vocal emission (her first "hiya" and the baby's initial "ennnh," for example) tend to be similar in timing?

The second measure studied was the duration of the pauses *within* each string of utterances, while it remained the same speaker's turn. For instance how long, on average, did a mother pause between her first "hiya," her next one, and then the one after that? And how long did a baby pause between the "ennnh" and the "ehhh" and the "ahhhh" sounds within his own turn at the conversational microphone? These are called "intrapersonal" pauses.

The third measure being looked at was the length of the pauses *between* one person's turn and the other's. When the mother's turn had ended, how long did it take before the baby began to vocalize in response? When the baby's turn was over, how long did she take before she replied? These pauses are called "switching pauses," because they mark the transition from one speaker to the other.

Using a sophisticated statistical method called time-series analysis, the researchers posed the following questions: On average, did the duration of the partners' vocalizations, intrapersonal pauses, and switching pauses tend to correlate? Did mother and baby monitor each other's behavior and influence each other to change in the direction of "getting it together"— that is, to track and match the rhythms of sound and silence in their mutual communication?

The answer was yes on all three of the above measures—but most strikingly on the third. In terms of switching pauses—the time between when one speaker's turn ends, and the other's vocalizing turn begins—the yes results were clearest and most definitive. Even so, the outcome of this research proved surprising in a way that had been completely unexpected.

The investigators had assumed, at the outset of the study, that those mothers and infants whose vocal patterns were most closely coordinated would prove to be those with the best relatedness. In other words, where there was close following and matching of vocal rhythms, it was expected that the babies would be seen to show optimal development when reexamined at the age of one year. But what emerged very clearly was that this was not at all the case.

Infant-caretaker pairs who were very high trackers (who, on average, matched the durations of their switching pauses the most precisely) were not doing very well. They were, in fact, doing just as badly as those pairs who were undertrackers (where there was little correlation between switching pauses, which indicated that the pair had less than usual relatedness). The best outcomes were among infant-and-mother pairs who were tracking and matching the switching pauses *moderately* well.

These "midrange" babies, who were in the majority of the group, were found to be "securely attached to their caretakers" at age one year, to have "easier temperaments," and to have "high cognition." They not only felt safer and more confident, were happier and more equable, but they could *think* more clearly as well. This was a very nice statistical demonstration that the elegant relatedness that infant and mother share *requires space as well as closeness.*

One could speculate that, in the overtracking pairs, the infant and mother were both too vigilant, too wary, too concerned about what the other was doing. To have true togetherness, permission for separateness is required, and the high trackers seemed unable to give it to one another.

The infant-mother couples in the largest, moderately tracking group, appeared most flexible and fluid in their tracking and matching of vocal behaviors. It was as if each partner assumed that the other would be there even if the following and matching were not perfectly coordinated at every possible moment in time. They neither stayed rigidly in touch, nor did they fall out of contact as did the undertrackers, who were therefore not really relating well.

The Substructure of Human Attachment

What is wonderful about microanalytic studies of infant-caregiver interactions is, observes Beebe, the insight that they offer into the very substructure of human attachment itself. For it is within the context of this subtle yet powerful early connectedness that the infant's expectations about being with another person are becoming organized. It is with our eyes, faces, body movements, and patterns of sound and silence that we first learn to communicate our own states of feeling, receive other people's emotional messages, and share our internal world with another. We learn about loving nonverbally.

Of course, once language and symbolic functioning come into play the existence of this other mode of communicating may be obscured, but it is a mode we retain throughout our lives. The special language of loving, which is spoken with the eyes, with speech rhythms, with bodily postures and movements is, says Beebe, the "underbelly of every attachment and every love." *This is the way we love, the way we connect to anyone.* If, therefore, any among us were to write the true and complete story of his or her life, the first chapter would consist of nothing other than blank pages. We learn an extraordinary amount about loving long, long before we ever have the words to describe it.

CHAPTER 13

What Would the First Sentence of Your Own Autobiography Be?

"If you were going to tell or write the story of your life—which would, of course, begin when you were a small infant in your own family—what would the first sentence of your autobiography sound like?" This was one of the questions I usually posed, during the course of my interviews with families, to everyone in the group who was old enough and willing to try to answer it.

For every one of us has an autobiographical tale to tell, a narrative that commences at birth, in our family of origin, and is then elaborated upon over a lifetime. Much of what we learn very early in life is *not* language-based; thus, we develop sets of deeply rooted expectations, ingrained "rules" about what is supposed to happen in relationships, memories in the form of mental imagery, which cannot be spoken about because they have never been experienced verbally. These are, in a way, "unthought thoughts" (we do not yet have words, which are the necessary tools for thinking and reflection), and they derive from that watery, formless period of our prehistory when structured understandings—what infancy researcher Daniel Stern calls "islands of consistency"—were first emerging out of a jumbled stream of sensations, perceptions, and experiences.

This is the world of personal Genesis, the world that existed before language came into being. But the autobiographical account of a life (so far as the person himself or herself knows it) can only be thought about or communicated verbally. And since we must avail ourselves of language in order to even think about our experiences—which is to say, what has happened to us as we perceive it—we can go no further back in time than to the opening of the text, as we know it.

The gates of the earliest, first garden, in which we once dwelt "without speech," are forever closed to us. Even our earliest mental images of that primeval time will have become imagery to which words are now attached, in order to facilitate reflection and thinking. So we must start with a text, a story told (to the self or to others), a story with an opening sentence and an environmental backdrop, which in human terms is always the original family.

The Opening Chords of a Composition

Every human being, let me say, has a family history, whether it is remembered, fashioned in his or her fantasies, or a combination of both of the above. Even the parentless foundling, who is connected to no one in reality, creates a mental family—a family peopled with involved and caring figures of the imagination. The autobiographical story each of us carries around inside his or her head is a story of the family, for the family is where life normatively begins.

And the family, for its own part, organizes around its young and around generations of its own experiences of rearing them. That is why that simple-sounding question—"What would the first sentence of your own life story sound like?"—often elicited astonishing answers, answers that were as true to much of what then followed in that person's life as the opening chords of a musical composition are true to the rest of the work. Whether it was in a major key (which would convey happy, pleasant, trusting feelings), or in a minor key (conveying sorrow, disquiet, feelings of melancholy), the first line of the composition created a particular mood and stated the thematic content of the life history the individual had constructed and was continuing to work on—and that statement's tonal quality, as I heard it and reflected upon it, was a true one.

The World the Newborn Enters

Long before the infant is born in reality, he is born in the fears, fantasies, hopes, and expectations of the important people around him. As infancy specialist Bert Cramer, M.D., has observed, "A baby's first birth is in the parents' heads, in their past histories, and in their psychological makeup." The world the infant enters is by no means a social and emotional vacuum, nor is it populated only by himself and the beloved caregiver, to whom he becomes so passionately connected.

For even though it is the relationship between baby and mother that has been emphasized in the foregoing discussion, the infant forms ardent relationships with other members of the family cast—with the father, most certainly, and with siblings, if there are any; with grandparents, aunts, uncles, cousins, close friends of the family, and with mothering substitutes, such as day-care workers, baby-sitters, nursemaids.

The baby's lively connections are manifold, and the varying characters in his life offer him different kinds of experiences. When it comes to playing, for example, he may find Dad a rowdier and more thrilling companion than Mom—Dad likes to throw him up into the air and catch him, which scares him a bit but excites him enormously. He may enjoy being with the bubbly adolescent baby-sitter who is, herself, practicing the art of parenting and wants nothing more than to entertain, divert, and please him. He may find his long, quieter afternoons with enamored Grandma delightful.

But early in life—and for that matter, throughout our lives—we tend to develop that special relationship with a vitally important *other* whose very existence serves to confer feelings of safety and security. It is this unique human partner (the first attachment figure, early in life; later on, the intimate partner) who provides us with an emotional home base, a sheltering place we can run to when anxieties, dilemmas, and difficulties arise.

"Attachment behavior tends to be most obvious when the attached person is frightened, fatigued, or sick," writes Dr. Inge Bretherton in *Growing Points of Attachment Theory and Research*, "and [it] is assuaged when the attachment figure provides protection, help, and soothing." That is why merely knowing that one's important other is available and responsive provides a strong and pervasive sense of well-being. It is, similarly, why knowing or fearing the opposite—that the other is unavailable or indifferent—can generate such terrifying feelings of abandonment and danger.

It Is "Under the Eye of the Other" That the Self Comes into Being

Is it, then, true that at the outset of life there is *one* crucially important attachment figure, a single special partner upon whom the infant focuses intently and who becomes programmed into the neonate's very psyche? Or does the young baby form other, equally important loving attachments, and become just as emotionally involved with the father or with a substitute caregiver with whom he or she may be spending a good deal of time?

The most recent thinking among infant specialists is that there can certainly be more than a single passionate relationship in the very young child's life. According to attachment theorist Bretherton, there is actually "a small hierarchy of familiar figures" to whom the baby becomes preferentially devoted. But still, most experts in the field do maintain that there is predictably *a principal attachment figure* who is, like the pope, the first among equals.

As the eminent Edward E. Zigler and co-author Mary E. Lang observed in *Child Care Choices*, "Research has now shown that babies can form attachments to other significant people in their lives, such as fathers, grandparents and siblings, but the most central and important bond is almost always to the mother. The importance of secure attachment . . . [to the mother] is that it gives the child a sense of trust, a feeling that the world is a good place."

Life's earliest love duets, the beautifully rhythmic exchanges of the young baby and the adored, cherished caregiver, are those enacted while this attachment is coming into being. It is within the context of this primary, vitally important human bond that "mental models," or ways of thinking about the self-with-the-other, begin to coalesce and to assume form and shape. From the dawn of personal time, we seek relatedness, and at the same time we seek to make sense of the relatedness we experience.

Thus, as Inge Bretherton points out, "if an attachment figure frequently rejects or ridicules the child's bid for comfort in stressful situations, the child may come to develop not only an internal working model of the parent as rejecting but also one of himself or herself as not worthy of comfort. Conversely, if the attachment figure gives help and comfort when needed, the child will tend to develop a working model of the parent as loving and himself or herself as a person worthy of such support."

It is in the beloved and needed primary caregiver's eyes that one first sees oneself, and it is from that reflection that a sense of *who one is* to some large degree is derived. As Jean-Paul Sartre observed in *Being and Nothingness*, it is "under the eyes of the other" that the story of the self originates.

I Overwhelmed Her

We all do, of course, keep ongoing mental records (not always completely accurate ones) from which we devise the central story lines of our lives even in the process of their unfolding. We want—no, *need*—to make sense of what has happened to us, to impose coherence and meaning upon our experiences. As Daniel Stern has commented, "the intrinsic motivation to order one's universe is an imperative of mental life." As the nascent human being develops consciousness of self, he begins to tell himself an autobiographical story (to which he himself is giving structure, as he goes along), and the family is where this narrative commences.

"I was overwhelming to my mother, I think," said one man, an architect who was in his early fifties when my interviews with the family got under way. "And because I overwhelmed *her*, it seems to me that I *felt* overwhelmed, right from the very beginning."

This gentle, rather private individual was in a first marriage (he and his wife had been married for almost thirty-two years) and he was the father of a teenage son, who was soon to leave for college, and of two grown daughters, who were already out of the home. An important aspect of his own early history had been, he believed, simply being born at the wrong time in his parents' lives—in the midst of the Great Depression of the 1930s, just after his father's small manufacturing business had gone under.

"It was bad enough for them just *having* a child at that particular time, but having one who was premature and very underweight was, I think, a disaster," he recounted, looking somewhat guilty as he spoke, like a guest who had, through some scheduling error, arrived at a thoroughly inconvenient moment.

His mother had been "overwhelmed," he reiterated, by his arrival. "She always said that I *cried* all the time, and that she couldn't figure out what I wanted—or what *she* should do—first. She'd laugh about it too, saying that I was so tiny and funny-looking—I was only three and a half pounds, and spent a long time in the incubator—that she didn't want people to look in the carriage and *see* me. She was too embarrassed." He himself blushed slightly as he spoke.

This man in his middle years had, by dint of an unusual creative talent, built up a successful architectural business; he had clients throughout the United States and in Europe as well. At the same time he was, and always had been, extremely involved and active in local and statewide politics. On one occasion, he'd even been offered an opportunity he found quite captivating—to run for a high state office—and he'd thought very long and hard about doing it. He'd really wanted to run, as he acknowledged in a rueful tone of voice, and certainly would have done it had he not experienced the prospect as more "terrifying" than it was "challenging."

It had been one of the most difficult decisions of his lifetime, but eventually, after some prolonged and painful introspection, he'd felt it necessary to turn the offer down. He simply couldn't summon up what he referred to as "the necessary inner resources," because novel situations and new ventures were, for him, always potentially overwhelming.

His mother's pervasive anxieties had, he thought, invaded him very early and completely, and as a result he'd always lived with a certain subliminal dread—a "morbid doubtfulness" that his own performance might not prove satisfactory, and that any risks he took might expose him to humiliating failure and the utter loss of respect of those around him.

It was for this reason, as he explained, that he tended to limit what he attempted—and within these self-defined limits, he could enjoy long riffs of relative satisfaction and contentment. But situations that were adventurous, and involved unknown and unforeseeable factors—such as a bid for high political office—were outside those limits, for they were situations in which he might not be capable of reassuring himself (and everyone else) that he was in control and perfectly competent. The sleeping dogs of apprehension had taken up permanent residence within him and could be wakened by any hint of risk-taking or dangerousness.

"I can see the anxiety in my own eyes very early," he recounted, rising suddenly and going to a bookcase to take down an old family album. "Here is a photograph of me at age one and a half, and it's right *there*." He pointed: In the photo he was sitting in a high chair in a white sailor suit, and I could see most readily what he meant: His eyes were wide open, fearful, staring. "I remember what I *felt* like, even then," he said, quietly.

At the time of the financial crash of the late 1920s, his mother had had to return to her widowed father's home ignominiously, bringing with her a failed husband (who was eighteen years her senior) and a "homely" underweight baby whom she felt incompetent to care for. "I think I knew, almost before I knew anything else, that she couldn't handle me; I was too much for her.

"I knew, too, that I would have to take care of *her*—she couldn't manage things," he added, "and that I'd have to take care of *myself* somehow as well." The frightened look on his face at this moment was, I thought, the duplicate of the look on the face of the toddler in the photo album.

The Visual Cliff

Had this man's sense that he was "overwhelming" to his mother been communicated to him even in that wordless world of infancy before textually recorded time? How early in life could her own anxieties and fears have been communicated to her infant offspring?

A remarkable series of experiments begun at the University of Colorado Health Sciences Center in the late 1970s has provided strong evidence that babies pick up and interpret their mothers' emotional expressions with great accuracy by the latter months of the first year of life. Not only is the young infant very capable of discriminating between the mother's differing facial expressions—Does she look happy? Does she look fearful?—but the infant also makes active use of these emotional signals in situations that are to any degree ambiguous and uncertain.

The classic experiment in this area of infant research involves the use of a construction known as the "visual cliff." The "cliff" is no cliff, but is an optical illusion. In reality, it is a table covered with thick Plexiglas and divided into two halves. On the "shallow" side of the cliff is a brightly patterned surface; as the infant crawls along the table, this pattern can be seen directly underneath the acrylic sheet. On the "deep" side of the cliff, the patterned surface is about thirty inches under the Plexiglas; in this way, the appearance of a clifflike drop-off is created.

The baby is not ever, of course, in any real danger of falling over the visual cliff, which is solid Plexiglas, but when he comes to the cliff's "edge" he does experience it as mildly frightening. In an early study devised by Mary D. Klinnert for her doctoral dissertation, the psychologist positioned both an attractive Ferris wheel toy and the mother at the far, or "deep," end of the table.

The infant, predictably enough, was lured forward by both the toy and the sight of the parent standing at the other side. But on arriving at the apparent drop-off, the youngster found himself in a highly uncertain situation. Was it dangerous to go on moving forward, or wasn't it? On the one hand, he wanted to reach the toy and get to his mother; on the other hand, the consequences of continuing were unclear. In this position of ambiguity, as Mary Klinnert demonstrated, the infant pauses at the cliff's edge and *looks at the face of the parent.*

He is appraising the situation by seeking emotional information about whether to proceed or to retreat. It is as if the baby is asking, "Is it all right to come forward, or is it dangerous? What do you think?" The mother's facial expression, it was found, had dramatic effects upon her infant's subsequent behavior. If she (by prearrangement with the experimenters) assumed a smiling, joyous expression, the baby was highly likely to cross the deep side and crawl happily toward her. But if, as instructed, the mother put on a fearful facial expression, the infant would not continue.

Instead, the baby would vacillate for a while around the "edge" of the visual cliff, then retreat to the shallow side, looking and acting upset. He was, in other words, safe, but distressed and sorely disappointed. The desired toy, and Mother herself—life's prizes of the moment—were unreachable, for her emotional signaling had warned him that getting to them was far too dangerous.

The Star Her Infant Steers By

How the mother feels about a particular situation is reflected in her facial expression, and her facial expression communicates to the baby what he should feel and how he should respond. In situations of ambiguity and uncertainty, her emotional signals are the star her infant steers by.

As Daniel Stern remarks in *The Interpersonal World of the Infant,* "One could argue that the infant is not only looking at mother for an appraisal . . . but is also looking to see which of the infant's own conflicted states is being matched or attuned to." In other words, does her fearful expression tell him that she is feeling the same fear he feels? Or does her happy expression match his pleasure in the journey, and convey to him that it is safe to continue onward despite his apprehension about crossing the "cliff"? Out of his own mixed feelings, the infant will select the one that coincides with what his mother seems to be experiencing. He will, in short, match his own emotional state with hers.

The way young infants appraise a situation by "reading" the caretaker's facial expression is now viewed as an important aspect of the regulation of social behavior. It is called social referencing and is an efficient means of letting the baby know what he needs to know very rapidly—for example, "This makes me scared; *you* should be scared" or "This is great fun, going down the slide; you should try it."

The mother's emotional advice is sought in a great variety of circumstances—at the approach of a stranger, to take another example. The fear, anger, joy, or pleasure on her face will communicate information about the baby's basic question, "Is this person okay?" But in some instances, social referencing sets up a kind of emotional contagion—what John Bowlby called a "catching of fears," of sweeping feeling-states of anxiety and distress.

In *The Interpersonal World of the Infant*, Daniel Stern describes one mother who used what he called "depressive signals" to control her one-year-old son's ordinary exploratory behavior. Whenever the boy did something clumsy or careless, such as knock something over or disarrange his toys, the mother would let out what Stern called "a multi-modal depressive signal."

"This consisted of long expirations, falling intonations, slightly collapsing postures, furrowing the brows, tilting and drooping the head, and 'Oh, Johnnys' that could be interpreted as 'Look what you've done to your mother again,' if not 'What a tragedy that your clumsiness with that toy train has caused the death of another dozen people.'" While such behavior is expectable in a one-year-old, this mother was indicating that her son's conduct was willfully bad, upsetting to her, and far too depressing for her to handle.

Gradually, reports Stern, this little boy's exuberant one-year-old behavior became more circumspect. To be as noisy, exploratory, and active as he (a typical one-year-old) would have liked to be would have overwhelmed the very person he needed there to care for him.

Her emotional signaling had taught him that he shouldn't want to do certain things or even to have certain kinds of feelings. "Social referencing permits the mother to determine and to alter to some degree what the infant actually experiences," explains Stern. "And affect attunement [that is, the matching of emotional states] permits the infant to know if what he or she experiences is shared by the mother and thus falls into the realm of the shareable."

A Disturbing Metaphor

In the case of the architect who felt that his birth had "overwhelmed" his mother, the concept of the visual cliff had an immediate and important impact. It was, in fact, a metaphor that he found quite disturbing. I had mentioned the visual cliff during one of our early interviews, and he returned to the topic in every one of our subsequent conversations.

"For me it was as if, at the edge of the visual cliff, the anxiety on my mother's face always told me: 'Don't cross! It's too dangerous! Turn back!' " he recounted. All throughout his boyhood, he had been cautioned ad infinitum about every possible danger. " 'You'll hurt yourself; you'll scrape your knee; you'll break your arm; don't *try* it!' These were the things I heard, over and over again—that the world was dangerous, and anything I tried out there would surely harm me."

The notion of the visual cliff could, he said, explain the trajectory of his entire life. It explained why he had become a shy, worried little boy, afraid of his own aggressive feelings and fearful that his anxious mother would be undone by even the slightest hint of aggression on his own part. It explained why novel things in his life were never experienced as welcome challenges, but as frightening and potentially overwhelming ordeals.

The look on his mother's face had always haunted him: "*Her* feelings of dread came, I think, to invade me; they're in my very corpuscles," he told me. As a small child, he had searched her face for information about life, and the emotional information he read there had scared him in ways that he had only recently come to fathom and to appreciate. Although, in the outside environment, this man certainly appeared to be extremely competent, and was clearly talented and successful, in the inner world he was a man on a tightrope from which he could tumble at any moment. His mother's nameless fears and dreads—that things were too much for her, that she was on the verge of being completely overwhelmed—were inside him and pervaded his own sense of being and his reality.

Autobiographical Beginnings

"I was a wanted baby, born into a loving and happy marriage, but I know that my mother was unable to breast-feed me," an attractive young mother of two adopted children, ages six and eight, told me. This wife's only complaint about her life seemed to be a pervasive unease about whether or not her physician husband's affections were going to stray sometime in the future. "So you could say that things were right—the stars were in the heavens—except for that one cloud. I always felt that she was disappointed in me, preferred my younger brother somehow. Maybe I was more of a burden, because I suffered from asthma; I don't know. But I felt it was difficult for her to have me as a little girl—I wasn't exactly the daughter she'd wanted." (Was she not, perhaps, the wife her husband wanted either?)

"I was born during a hurricane, and my mother never let me forget it," I was told by a twenty-seven-year-old computer analyst, the mother of two small children, ages three and five, and the wife of a middle-management executive. I found myself looking speculatively at this young woman's head of flaming red hair. "My mother always said that for the first couple of years of my life, it matched my personality perfectly," she added, "and actually, there's *always* been a *lot* of anger between us."

"I began my life in pain," said a forty-four-year-old poet and novelist, who was in a second marriage and the father of two daughters and a step-daughter, all teenagers. "I suffered from very severe colic, and also had an undescended testicle for almost the first year of my life. So I was in a great deal of pain, on and off—pain that couldn't be soothed. And my earliest experiences were of this bodily suffering, that my mother couldn't relieve, and of her sense of impotence, of rage, of sadness about being unable to comfort her beautiful little baby boy."

He hesitated, then added in a low, almost inaudible voice, "I probably learned, very early, to manage experiences on my own. That promoted, very early, a sense of estrangement and aloneness."

"My mother was six months pregnant when my parents married, so I know I was a mistake." So spoke a forty-eight-year-old biologist, who was the mother of an adolescent son and a preteenage daughter, and who was married to a psychiatric researcher. "I was the child of refugees who'd fled to England from Austria, and I think my mother, especially, always felt that what she had lost she could lose again very easily. So she trained us, myself and my brother, to be ready to lose everything and everyone at any moment—to not get too attached, and to be ready to make it on your own. She was *harsh*, because she felt that you had to be tough in order to survive.

"In a way, what my mother wanted was totally paradoxical, which was for us to be completely under her control and yet to be totally independent people," she said, with an unmistakable animosity in her voice. "We were supposed to have a very small mental bag packed all the time, a bag that would make us self-sufficient and keep us *alive*. What this produced was two very enraged little children, who were totally repressed and almost unable to communicate with other people."

"If you had asked me that a decade ago, I would have started my life story by saying 'My mother loved me, and I loved her, a *lot*,'" said a thirty-four-year-old magazine editor, divorced and the mother of a four-year-old son. "I would have said my mother *saved* me, because everyone else in my family was so crazy. But lately, I've come to see what was going on between us a lot differently—to see that I was, in many ways, neglected. I was a waif. So I guess I'd start the story *now* by saying: "I was born, and no one paid much attention." She looked bereft.

Born with a Caul

"I was the result of a moment of passion, and for that reason I've always felt both a strange obligation and a great sense of specialness," said another woman, also in her early thirties, who was seven months pregnant with the couple's first child at the time we began our interviews.

The "strange obligation" she felt was to live up to that romantic standard in some way—to be endlessly, deliciously lovable. And she always had, she acknowledged, felt extraordinarily lucky, even charmed. "It was as if I were born with a caul—a gift and a mark simultaneously," she explained. The "mark" had to do with the fact that feeling special does not necessarily prepare one for the reality of a life in which one may not be viewed as so wonderfully special by everybody outside the family.

Her difficulties, she said, had always had to do with expecting everything to work out in a magical fashion. "I don't ever imagine that things might go badly for me," she admitted, "and when they do I'm totally unprepared, and very deeply shaken." Being born with a figurative caul, she said, had imbued her with a certain belief that if she were only infinitely pleasing, and always followed the advice of those who loved her, then those others would assume responsibility for her decisions.

She had gotten married, in her mid-twenties, in a reckless and unthinking fashion. That first marriage, undertaken despite the fact that there were already evident and serious difficulties in the relationship, had ended before the first year was completed. "I knew there were real problems, but I had this unrealistic belief that if only I were lovable enough anyone would want to take care of me." She smiled wryly and shook her head. "I've had to accept a great deal more responsibility for what happens to me than I was able to do in my earlier adulthood," she said, patting her belly as if to reassure the infant growing inside her that she would be able to parent it responsibly.

"I've had to develop my own strength—to learn how to take care of me. But still," she added, after a momentary pause, "the flip side of that coin is still there. Believing that you're special gives you an optimistic, believing, cheerful attitude toward life, and a lot of that trusting, happy-go-lucky feeling is still there."

Motifs in Life and Music

The first sentence of anyone's life story, like the thematic idea introduced at the beginning of a musical work, sets a tonal mood that will be revisited continually as the composition develops. For centrally important motifs, in music and in life, tend to reemerge even if in somewhat altered and in some cases even unrecognizable guises.

If, in his tenth opus, a composer introduces a certain musical theme, hints of that same theme can usually be discerned in the works that have preceded it. It is as if certain preoccupying concerns—and manifold variations upon those concerns—exert a mysterious force to which the theme's creator ineluctably returns.

As we grow, it need hardly be said, differing instruments can be heard, and the number of performers in the orchestra expands. A despairing theme, played in the minor key of suffering and grief—"I was born in pain, and my mother could not soothe me"—may be obscured, and counterthemes of great joy and sweetness may prevail for long periods.

This had indeed been true in the case of the novelist, who had had many alternative life experiences that were gratifying and rewarding. Yet the early realization that his mother could not help him or give comfort had taught him, he told me, to "manage experiences on my own and not depend on others for help. That promoted, I believe, a sense that I could rely on no one but myself."

This basic theme, restated in variations that had become increasingly ornamented, elaborated upon, and embellished, was an underlying motif that could reappear at any moment. It was a theme of dissonance, which, in life and in harmony, struggles toward and even demands resolution.

A very different opening statement—"I was born with a caul"—had been that of the young expectant mother who'd assumed that she would always be cared for by virtue of her innate specialness and lovability. While her life had offered her convincing experiences that this was not really so, the familiar thematic motif was still present.

"I have a tendency to be the fool who rushes in where angels fear to tread," she acknowledged, "because I still have trouble believing that things may in fact go badly." She felt peculiarly charmed, as if all she had to do was stand there until the good things that she anticipated occurred. Her major thematic idea had been declared, and played itself out in its infinite variations—some quite inconsistent with the original idea, for they were sad and disappointing in nature. And yet what remained was the initial joyous, fulfilled quality of the opening statement.

It is back to this central idea that the melodic threads of our experiences lead us, for the variations upon a theme are always intimately bound up with it. Even when it appears that an initial thematic idea has vanished from our lives, it will usually reemerge later on in the composition. These particularly charged notes are fixed in our memories, for they are the ones that were heard at our life's very beginning.

I Was Born and Nobody Noticed

It is, nevertheless, important to take note of the fact that different individuals will adopt to the same thematic substrate in strikingly different ways. The wife and mother of two young sons who told me wryly that the first sentence of her life story could well be "I was born and nobody noticed" might have developed a strong, underlying motif: "I guess I wasn't worth much, because I wasn't considered deserving of anyone's attention."

But this woman, a lawyer and actively engaged politician, had turned this early negative experience of herself into a positive asset. She had, in what was unquestionably a highly adaptive way of turning things around, said, "I'll make sure that I *command* attention by putting myself in a central, visible position." At the time of our interviews, she was running for a high elective office, and it looked as though she would win (she did).

But had she, on the other hand, simply accepted that early neglect as something merited, and internalized a sense of herself as unworthy of attention, she might have given up on herself in any one of a variety of ways, such as dating abusive men or taking drugs, while saying to herself, "Who gives a damn, and what does it matter, anyway?" Different people can, in other words, compose very different kinds of lives on an infrastructure of similar, even identical early experiences.

Born Adult

"I was born adult," said Toni Gifford, the mother of a seven-year-old daughter and also eight months pregnant at the time our interviews began in the winter of 1990. Toni, the wife of a lieutenant commander in the Navy, explained her answer further: "I think I came out adult, because right from the start, I had a lot of responsibility and had to take care of everyone in the family." I smiled, for Toni Gifford had chosen nursing as a profession, and then become a therapist later on in her career.

"Not only did I have to take care of the younger children—there were six of us, in a very devout Catholic family—but I had to take care of my parents, because there were problems there, oh, as far back as I can remember. And somehow it was *my* duty—*I* had to keep them together. So I was always very vigilant, always checking things out, always eternally *wary*."

She laughed, as if at herself, but looked troubled simultaneously. "The story of my life started out this way: 'I was born and then I took charge immediately.' " And indeed she was someone who, as I came to recognize during the course of the interviews, had never for a moment relaxed her need to keep the system going and take care of everyone in it.

Thus it is that in life's first relationships, in the families into which we are born, each of our personal narratives begin—and the first sentence of the story is a compelling one. For in her present-day family, which was functioning at a midrange level of health and competence (See Part Four: "Level 3: The Rule-Bound Family"), Toni Gifford was as watchfully in command and overburdened emotionally as she had been in her original household.

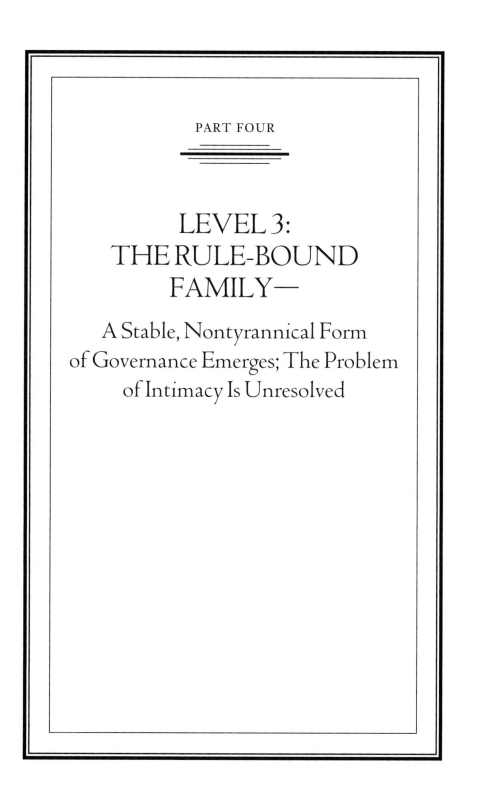

PART FOUR

LEVEL 3: THE RULE-BOUND FAMILY—

A Stable, Nontyrannical Form
of Governance Emerges; The Problem
of Intimacy Is Unresolved

A Rule-Bound Emotional World: Control of the Self and of the System Is Established; Intimacy Remains Elusive

The Beavers Scale of family health and functioning, it will be recalled, ranges upward from the least competent, "severely dysfunctional" family (Level 5), to Level 4, "borderline," to Level 3, "midrange" (more families fit into this category than into any of the others), and then to Level 2, "adequate"; at the most adaptive end of the continuum are the highly functional "optimal" families (Level 1). (See Appendix I for the Diagram of Family Assessment Schema.)

The midrange family is just above the borderline or polarized family, of which the Maguires, whom we met in Part Two, were a sterling example. In this latter kind of emotional system, as we saw, *control* was the paramount issue with which everyone in the system was struggling. In the Maguires' polarized emotional world, a sense of orderliness had indeed been established—but because it was based upon tyranny rather than consensus, it had a desperately fragile, provisional feeling.

In borderline families, the system feels perpetually threatened by mutiny from within. This is why a family member's thinking the "wrong" kind of thoughts or having the "wrong" kinds of preferences (such as the Maguires' son wanting eggs instead of pancakes) can be perceived as a dangerous challenge, and send the family despot into a frenzy. It is almost as though the tyrant must shake those ideas right out of the offending person's head. That was why, in that instance, Matt Maguire had slammed into his car and driven off without a word—a shocking act of symbolic abandonment.

An important point to be noted is that in these control-focused, Level 4 families, a very common method of gaining control is to go "out of control"—develop intractable symptoms. A family member may become anorexic and starve herself, or bulimic, like Katie Maguire, or miserably depressed and suicidal—and thus rivet the entire family's attention upon her or his problems. The afflicted person is then "powerless" to change, but since achieving a sense of control is the dominant concern in these systems, *powerlessness is often the most powerful stance available.* Thus, even though she or he may be developing very real and dangerous (perhaps even lethal) symptoms, attaining a sense of self-determination seems to make all the attendant suffering worth it. In polarized systems, *gaining control is felt to be far more important than are such things as attaining emotional gratification or having good feelings about the self.*

Heading Off Potential Anarchy

In the oppressive world of the polarized, Level 4 family, a severe and highly unpleasant form of governance has been imposed upon everyone within the group. Nevertheless, potential anarchy and chaos have been headed off, and it is true that borderline systems are much less disorienting and disturbing than are the severely dysfunctional, Level 5 systems a rung below them on the Beavers Scale—for there is nothing more upsetting than incoherence, a sense that reality itself is in flux. The truth of this statement is made very evident when one encounters a family in acute pain, as were the Andersons at the time of Dave's hospitalization at Elmcrest (see Part One).

What is most pronounced about the Level 5 family in pain is its pervasive atmosphere of hopelessness and despair. The feeling tone, in these distressed emotional systems, is one of utter lostness—of being astray in a murky, confusing place in which there are no distinguishable guideposts and the landscape is continually shifting. From time to time, someone in the family seems to discern the outline of some other member of the family, but even as he does so, that person's shape changes—for nothing in the Level 5 system remains consistent and clear for very long, and no one in the system is prepared to take a coherent personal stand and maintain it.

Indeed, the idea of taking a firm, clear personal stand is considered unthinkable, for it would involve the recognition that separateness and differentness exist—the dangerous knowledge that I am I, and you are you, and that because we are separate individuals, you can leave me or I can leave you (or change, get older, become ill, die). In Level 5 families, the basic biological and social truths of growth, development, aging, and death are being desperately avoided and frantically denied. The members of the emotional system, and the system itself, are psychologically stuck—suspended in time, in a world in which nothing is resolved, nothing changes, and the same old patterns keep repeating.

It is as if, in these impaired, Level 5 families, there is an active conspiracy to blur distinctions between persons, to blur individuality, a basic respect for the unique experience of different members of the group. The system may ride roughshod over its members' subjectivity in an enmeshed style ("We are all alike, in perfect harmony; and we always think and feel the same things") or they may do so in a distancing, emotionally disengaged, or outright hostile fashion, denying that the relationships matter anyway ("You're just a hopeless mess, and always were; I don't give a damn about you, or anyone else in this crazy family, either"). Both these methods of dealing with important attachments can be understood as efforts to avoid confronting past or potential experiences of separation and loss, including those old griefs and losses that may have been traumatic.

It is in any case, *loss*—loss of all kinds, including those inevitable losses that are simply on the human books—that the members of the severely dysfunctional system cannot manage, because loss is felt to be completely intolerable. As Robert Beavers observed in *No Single Thread*, an early report on his family research project, "The ability of a family system to tolerate the pain of loss due to growth and development, aging and death, opens up a panorama of possibilities for human encounter with awareness, acknowledgment and acceptance. Change is inevitable with the passage of time, and a true human encounter produces change in all the participants. Browning's question: 'Can we love but on the condition that the thing we love must die?' suggests this intimate and poignant relationship between closeness and the awareness of finiteness and death."

The severely disturbed family's desperate endeavor is, however, to alleviate or avoid its unmetabolized, unresolved grief and pain completely—and in the ongoing attempt, the family members make copious use of confusion, denial, and mystification, which lead to greater and greater dysfunction. For although the central struggle of the Level 5 system is that of achieving a sense of clarity and coherence, clarity is in fact what everyone in the family perceives as dangerous, if not to say downright terrifying.

The Midrange System's Great Achievement: Control Is Internalized

What it is vital to bear in mind is that as the family moves upward from the least competent position on the Beavers Scale—where all is formlessness and bewilderment—order and control *are* being established. And while it is obvious that the borderline, Level 4 family goes about solving the problem of coherence at great emotional cost, by establishing a dicta-torial, oppressive system, its members are still far better off than are the people in the chaotic systems below them on the Beavers health and func-tioning continuum.

The family at the midrange level represents still another—and this time very substantial—progression upward on the Beavers Scale, for at Level 3, both the issues of coherence and of control have already been dealt with and resolved. Midrange emotional systems are well organized, and the basic rules that the members of the family are expected to live by are very clearly articulated. No wild control battles are needed in order to enforce them (which is why the family dictator is no longer needed) because midrange families have made a momentous discovery: *They have figured out how to maintain control and stability by making use of the power and influence inherent in close emotional relationships.*

At this level of family development, control need no longer be imposed upon the group by a tyrannical leader/oppressor. Control and order are not maintained by pressures exerted from outside the individual members of the group; control has migrated and is located inside the people in the family; it has become self-control at this point. Now, the emotional system's extensive and elaborate "regulations for experiencing, being, and behaving" are regulations that everybody in the family has loyally inter-nalized. Nobody is in the dark about what the basic rules are, and what things are expected of them.

According to Dr. Leonora Stephens, the midrange system's central, most important achievement is its discovery that the power inherent in close emotional attachments can be harnessed and made use of to control the everyday functioning of everyone within the group. "What these fami-lies have realized is that if a relationship is truly important to you, you can be influenced by your own feelings to think along certain lines, and to behave in particular ways." The theme song of the rule-bound family is always, adds Stephens, "If you loved me, you would do . . . whatever. Be home by six o'clock. Never say anything critical. Walk the dog in the evenings. Make friends with my boss's wife. Be more (or less) religious. *Abide by the rules*, in other words."

The members of the Level 3, midrange system dwell in the land of "shoulds," "oughts," and "You know very well you are supposed to . . ." In this kind of rule-bound emotional system it is, for example, always more important for a woman to behave in the ways that a good, loving wife and mother is supposed to behave than it is to actually *feel* loving at the time that she is doing it. The rules of the system (rules for being and behaving) reign supreme; and the rules take clear precedence over—and often serve to stifle and extinguish—that small, vitally important inward-facing beam we use when we are trying to focus upon our own subjective reality.

A husband may, for instance, subscribe to the rule that a really caring woman always wants to stay home with her family in the evenings. He himself often comes in from work feeling worn down and depleted, and while he doesn't actually want to talk much, he lets her know that it's important to him that she hang around.

She, on the other hand, might actually prefer going out to a movie, or going shopping or having dinner with a friend on an occasional evening. But if the partners inhabit a midrange emotional system—and the spoken or unspoken rule is "A good wife always wants to spend the evening hours with her husband and family"—all traces of the traitorous *thought* that she might want to do something quite different with her time are very likely to disappear from her own awareness (though not without leaving residues of obscure guilt or resentment).

Suppose, however, that on a particular afternoon this woman is asked to join a group of her office colleagues for an impromptu happy hour to celebrate a particular success, or simply to get together before the oncoming weekend. Given that she inhabits an emotional system in which there exists an important rule to the effect that a loving wife always wants to go straight home at the end of the day, she is faced with two possible options. In a midrange, Level 3 world, she can either conform to the rule and feel obscurely frustrated and deprived, or she can challenge the family tenet, go out with her colleagues—and probably feel tense and guilty throughout.

Whichever course she chooses, the regulation itself remains inflexibly in place, because at this developmental level, the system's rules do not come into question. Quite the opposite: The rules governing the emotional system are viewed as vitally necessary and of far greater importance than the real wishes and feelings of anyone living inside it. The rules serve to safeguard the system, and to ensure that the people in it will do the right, good, and loving things.

The Midrange System's Great Failing: Closeness Has Been Traded in for Predictability

At the midrange level of family functioning, the list of possible rules is almost endless, and the members of the system are made to feel that failing to abide by the rules shows that you are a bad, wrongheaded, uncaring (or unfeminine or unmasculine) person. For instance, rules such as "A good woman always lets her husband make the big choices, and she acts as if she supports those choices whether she happens to agree with him or not" and "A couple in a good relationship will always want to go to sleep at the same time" may be among the emotional system's important precepts. And if these rules are on the family books there are, once again, only two possible alternatives: One can choose either the way of compliance, or the way of rebelliousness and guilt.

The internalized rules of the Level 3 system do, most assuredly, regulate everyone's behavior effectively and serve to establish order, predictability, and control. But the basic dilemma inherent in these rule-driven families is that when obedience to the "shoulds," "oughts," and "you-are-expecteds" becomes predominant, it becomes difficult to make contact with one's own inner world—with what one really does think and need and want. "You should call your parents once a week" is, for example, a rule that an adult daughter may obey, but it feels vastly different to call the folks because it's expected, and to do so because one is really eager to talk to them.

In these rule-bound emotional systems, a tough and exacting deal has in fact been struck: Closeness has been traded in for predictability. What has been sacrificed, in the service of the rules and regulations, is intimate relating itself.

"In this kind of world," as family expert Leonora Stephens explains, "the other person *can't know me.* Suppose I am someone who wants to stay up late and read—because I really need some quiet time alone, and can get along happily with less sleep—but I feel forced to retire at ten P.M., because that time is written into our family by-laws. Or suppose I want to go off for an evening, or even have a weekend visit with an old friend, and in our family the rule is that it's simply out of the question—as woman of the house, I'm expected to be there, and to function as home base. If that's so, I may follow the rules and stay at home when I'd rather not (feeling put-upon and resentful) or I may not follow the rules, and end up feeling like a guilty, bad person. But what I won't have, in this midrange world, is the inner flexibility to even *think* about whether or not the rule itself makes any sense to me."

In an emotional system in which thinking, feeling, and behaving in compliance with the rule system is of consummate importance, it becomes extremely difficult for a person to figure out who she really is and what she actually does want, and then to share that knowledge with an intimate other. She herself would find it hard to know what she wants, for in this kind of emotional world the distinction between actually wanting to go to sleep at the same time as one's spouse, and feeling obligated to do so, is the important distinction that gets lost. In the midrange family, however, what one does is, by and large, what one is supposed to do and what is expected.

Under the Watchful Eye of the "Invisible Referee"

The members of the rule-bound system behave as if they are being constantly watched, appraised, and scored by an unseen authority on high, or what Robert Beavers has termed "the invisible referee." This referee may, as Beavers observes in *Psychotherapy and Growth*, "be abstract or personified. In many families it is a 'they,' the faceless order of 'good' people. . . . The referee, abstract or concrete, subjugates all family members with standards of thought, behavior and feelings that are pathetically insensitive to people's needs."

In such a family atmosphere, feelings are rarely experienced and expressed spontaneously. The rules themselves take precedence over the needs, wishes, and well-being of any member of the group. And even though the pressure to be one's real self continues to exert itself, the system's regulations for being a worthy person exert counterpressures of even greater strength.

Inevitably, under the powerful sway of the referee system, the people in the family become genuinely uncertain about whether they are thinking certain thoughts and behaving in certain ways because they want to, or because it is wanted of them. For in order to even entertain a particular feeling one must have the sense that having that feeling is justified (and not against the rules).

Obviously, abiding by such stringent regulations calls for monumental sacrifices of important aspects of one's own inner world, which is always bubbling with rich complexities, abundant ambivalences, conflicting motives, wishes, and desires—all of which are wonderful to air (and share), if at all possible, within the haven of a close and trusting relationship. But in midrange emotional systems, the basic, never-ending struggle is to be the "good, right-thinking" kind of person that "they" or "everyone" (the spectral referee or company of watchers) will find acceptable.

Intimacy

The difficulty inherent in the midrange system is the insurmountable fact that *when it comes to getting intimate, no surrogate for the real self will do.* The blanket of emotional constraint and thought constriction that descends upon everyone in the Level 3 family—affecting both their inner worlds and their lives together—makes it almost impossible for people to think their own authentic thoughts, feel their real feelings, and give expression to them freely and readily.

And, in reality, the way of intimacy is not without its own inherent threats and dangers. As psychologist Stephen Mitchell has observed, "Intimacy is not a primrose path, but a process which includes risks, choices, and anxieties. Intimacy necessarily entails accommodation which no matter how freely undertaken, inevitably generates a pull toward a reclaiming of the self." In other words, becoming genuinely close to another person brings one into closer contact with one's *own* genuine thoughts and actual feelings—which can generate problems if those thoughts and feelings happen to fly in the face of the all-important rule system.

The rule-bound family system is plagued by a conundrum, which is that the inner pressure to be one's own real self and to meet one's own quite reasonable autonomous wants and needs is ever present in human life and continues to exert itself. At the same time, in a midrange emotional world, the rules and regulations for right living are more important than any individual in the group, and the members of the family are struggling bravely to think, feel, and behave in the ways they know they "should"—which makes the achievement of true intimacy difficult (if not impossible).

The fundamental dilemma, in a midrange emotional system, is that not only outward behavior but subjective reality itself has to be brought into line with the rules. This is the reason why, at this middle level of family health and functioning, intimacy is the critical developmental issue, the focal problem that everyone within the system is struggling to resolve.

A Basic Mistrust of Human Nature

Why is it that the rules and regulations for thinking, feeling, and behaving are experienced as utterly indispensable in these families—as so much more important than the real thoughts, wishes, and needs of the individuals in the group?

The answer is that *Level 3 families are pervaded by the belief that human nature is essentially unworthy and bad, and that nobody could ever be relied upon to behave in a good, loving fashion in the absence of strong rules to steer his or her behavior.*

It is for this somewhat melancholy reason that the rule-bound family's endless list of precepts and directives is felt to be essential to the system's cohesion, its maintenance, and its survival as an ongoing, functioning entity. There is no optimistic expectation that a family member might do loving, caring things simply because he or she feels loving and actually wants to behave lovingly; the rules are needed to ensure that people behave in the properly caring and affectionate manner no matter what their actual feelings may be.

The rules have been brought into play, and have proven very useful, in the establishment of a smoothly functioning form of family government; but they do become an active hindrance when it comes to spontaneous, close relating. For in these Level 3 systems, it is simply not really safe to come out and say, "This is *me*, and here is what *I* really think and how *I* truly feel." What one thinks and feels may not be in the family rule books—and in any case, certain thoughts, feelings, and behaviors have been declared out of bounds at the outset.

If, for instance, a female has internalized the family rule "An angry woman is an *ugly*, bad woman," she will never know what to do and where to go with the normal anger that she does occasionally experience. And, if she does catch herself feeling rageful, or worse yet, expressing her rage, she is very likely to feel guilty and to experience herself as a bad, worthless human being.

The members of the midrange family find it almost impossible to get past the internal barrier of rules, edicts, and regulations and to make contact with their own genuine thoughts and feelings—which is, of course, what makes intimacy so hard to achieve. For true intimacy always has to do with people attempting to come to grips with who they really are, and what they do think and feel (as distinct from simply knowing who they should be, and what they ought to think and feel). One can never really come to know another if one hasn't gotten reasonably well acquainted with one's own self beforehand.

Becoming truly close to someone else involves, moreover, the willingness to come to the intimate other with the most honest (if not always commendable and admirable) information about oneself that one has at hand. Genuine *relationship* involves having a place to go with the bad news as well as the good news—with the fullest inner report possible, not one that has been censored and deleted.

Genuine relationship involves being able to bring one's messily ambivalent or downright negative feelings out into the open, and to do so with a sense of safety—which in turn must derive from the knowledge that one will be accurately heard and attended. For example, a husband may say to his wife, "You know, hon, I often dread coming home from work because it seems as if all of you start jumping on me at once—you, with a list of complaints, and the kids, who start fighting if they don't get my total and complete attention. And the truth is, at that point in the day, *I'm* feeling strung out, anyhow."

In a midrange system, such a statement is likely to be heard as hateful, horrible, and rejecting. The rules decree that a good husband and father would never have such negative thoughts and feelings as these; he would be gladdened by the prospect of coming home and being with his family in the evenings. The wife's response, in this rule-bound system, may be "You can't possibly mean what you're saying" or "Can't you be like other fathers? What's the matter with you, anyway?" In translation, this means that a good, loving man would do, feel, and think completely otherwise.

The wife in this family is telling her husband that his subjective experience is bad, and unacceptable to her. But in a healthier and more competent emotional system (the adequate or optimal family), the partner would be highly unlikely to respond to her husband's complaints with a rule about how he "should" rightfully feel. She would be able to hear and react to him as *who he is* at that point in time, and her own response might be along the lines of "I know you're too tired and rattled when you get home to do much giving out to us, so let's set things up so that you'll have a little quiet time alone when you first come in. But then, as we both know, I *am* doing the lion's share of the parenting these days, so we'll also have to work out some time in which I can do some venting (and get your help and your advice, as well). Maybe it's just a matter of doing some schedule shifting; and we can make your homecomings more pleasant."

With this kind of feedback, which makes him feel that he has been heard, understood, and not unduly condemned, the husband can then begin to get his real frustrations (and perhaps a number of his other personal issues too) into focus, and stop feeling as if his family is overwhelming him. But telling it like it really is (which is to say, becoming intimate) always does involve taking chances. It involves taking the *big* chance of making oneself vulnerable to the other person by saying forthrightly, "This is really who I am, and this is how I truly feel."

This can only be hazarded if one believes that the response is likely to be reasonably benevolent and supportive—that being honestly oneself is within the pale of the humanly permissible. For being heard and understood helps one not only to clarify one's "bad," "traitorous," unwelcome feelings but also to get to work on resolving them—and, as noted earlier, this is the loving service that true intimates offer to one another routinely.

CHAPTER 15

Her Side of the Genogram— an Enmeshed Family System and a Quasi-Incestuous "Family Affair": Toni Gifford

The Giffords' ranch-style house, situated in a countrified suburb along the Connecticut coastline, was set back among evergreens and shrubberies. The living room, which was long and comfortable-looking, was furnished with a pair of love seats and several large upholstered chairs that looked as if they would be easy to curl up and read in. Most of the furniture was covered in patterned variations of blue, blue-green and pale green, and the soft tan rug contained flecks of these same soothing, underwater colors.

We were five in number and sat in a rough semicircle. A large drawing pad was on my lap, a pad upon which I was beginning to construct a genogram—a schematic outline of the Gifford family's history, including the history of their important emotional relationships. (See Chapter 5, "The Genogram: The Family's Existential Blueprint for Being.")

Present were Toni, thirty-six, a master's-level nurse and teacher of nursing; her husband, Henry, thirty-nine, a lieutenant commander in the Navy; and Toni's mother, Antonia (after whom Toni was named), age fifty-seven, who was living with the family. Seven-year-old Emily was sprawled out on the rug, working on a drawing of the family, using her Magic Markers and a sheet torn from my sketchbook.

There would soon be another member of this nuclear group, for Toni was pregnant and a few weeks from her delivery date. Given that she was thirty-six years old, she had chosen to have amniocentesis, so the Giffords knew the new baby would be a daughter. Toni informed me cheerfully that her maternity leave had just begun; she patted her great belly as she spoke. She looked pleased with herself, and extremely pretty in an artless, healthy-looking way. Her auburn hair, cut to shoulder length, bounced around the base of her neck and caught flickers of the afternoon sunlight.

Toni's mother, Antonia, gray-haired, with stern, classic Italian features, sat on a straight, plastic-backed chair that she had brought in from the kitchen (although, as I'd noted, there was plenty of more comfortable seating available). I wondered if she was trying to indicate that she was just taking time out from her housework and cooking tasks, and might have to opt out from this discussion at any moment. Her expression was tense and wary.

Henry Gifford, who'd sat down at one end of the love seat on the opposite side of the fireplace, looked alert, erect, at attention. He was very much the military man, trim, well-muscled, neither tall nor short (about five feet ten or eleven inches in height) and neither homely nor memorably handsome. With his light-brown hair and gray, assessing eyes, he looked like both a regular American guy and a man who is used to taking charge of situations. His arms were crossed over his chest.

Was it that particular body position, the posture of self-defense, or was it his military bearing that made me think that Henry would probably participate very little in a set of family interviews that could become intense and emotionally demanding? I cannot say, but this first impression did prove accurate in certain respects. Henry came from a family system that was distant and disengaged in the extreme, and his own habitual stance was that of the loner and outsider—but my expectation that he would hold himself aloof from these discussions, and remain uninvolved, proved to be dramatically mistaken.

The Boundary Between the Self and the Other: A Red Flag

"You, of course, are quite familiar with genograms," I had said at the outset to Toni Gifford, as I held my pencil poised over the sketch pad on my lap. Many family therapists use the genogram clinically, and Toni was not only a nurse with advanced training; she had also been trained in family treatment, was on the faculty of the University of Connecticut School of Nursing at Storrs, and held a master's degree in community mental health as well. (It was at Yale's School of Nursing that Toni had heard me lecture and had signed on to the list of volunteers for the family study in which I was engaged.)

She nodded as if to say of course; then she laughed and said apologetically, "I'm afraid you'll find us very ordinary; nothing that much *happens* around here; we're pretty quiet." She laughed again and said, "It's my sister Diane's family you should be talking to." I hesitated, pencil poised, intrigued by this comment.

Our interviews had not even quite begun, and yet Toni seemed to be telling me that I could not possibly be as interested in her as I would have been in her more compelling and dramatic sibling. The remark seemed to reverberate with the echoes of long-ago rivalries, and I wondered whether Diane had had a more favored role in the family ("the charming one," or even "the princess") while Toni herself had felt herself to be "the also-ran." That comment was, in any case, the first intimation I had of what was to emerge as a family leitmotif—an omnipresent theme which had to do with the passionate feelings (both loving and competitive) between the women in this emotional system, and the relative lack of connection between the women and their men.

Toni turned to her mother, who seemed abstracted, as if her thoughts were turned elsewhere. "She ought to interview Diane's family, don't you think?" Toni asked brightly. Her voice had risen slightly, and Antonia's face, frowning in repose, broke into an unaccustomed smile.

"Oh, yes, lots of drama *there;* that daughter's husband's family is— they're all totally cuckoo. But," Toni's mother added, with a lift of her shoulders, "most of them are down in Florida now." She folded her hands in her lap.

I glanced at Henry, who was smiling agreeably but who did not seem to be joining in. He did meet my eyes, but his arms remained crossed and his attitude was watchful; it would, I thought again, be very difficult to connect with him, for he had an air of calm reserve that I feared would prove impenetrable.

I turned to Toni, ready to continue with my sketching of some rudimentary family information. "Is Diane an older sister or a younger one?"

But although I had directed the question to Toni, it was her mother who responded. "Toni is the oldest; she's Antonia, too, after me. Diane is my second. Then there are Thomas Junior, Barbara, and Charlie," Antonia said, with pride in her voice. I glanced at Toni swiftly, for when one member of the group answers for another, it is viewed as a therapeutic red flag. It is frequently a signal that individual boundaries—the distinction between the self and the other—are not being sufficiently respected.

As a family clinician, Toni Gifford was surely well aware of this. But she merely grinned at me, and raised an eyebrow as if to say that theory was one thing; applying it in one's own family was another matter entirely. I paused. In this particular instance, it could be also be the case that not only questions of self/other differentiation, but issues of competition were at play. Antonia had put herself forward as the progenitor of the family and the natural spokesperson for the group, as if it were she, not her daughter, who should be basking in the conversational limelight. Toni seemed comfortable about ceding center stage to her mother, and I answered Antonia by saying, "Five children: You have quite a good-sized family."

She nodded, looking worried but gratified. "I do, and we're all close. We've always *been* close, at least on my side of the family—not my husband's; they were never that way. They kept their distance, but with us, it was always every Sunday, every holiday; you got together, aunts, uncles, cousins. That was the way you did it, you didn't question. It's the Italian way, you stay close to your family."

Her side of the family, she was saying, was the good one.

The genogram I was in the process of constructing was still fairly sketchy, but it already contained the horizontal line that represented the marriage of the parental couple (Toni and Henry) in this present household. At one end I had drawn the round circle that designates a female and inserted "Toni, age thirty-six" within it; at the other end I had drawn the square that symbolizes a male and written "Henry, age thirty-nine" inside. Above the marital line connecting them, I had written "twelve years," and below it had drawn a descending line. At the bottom of this was the round circle designating a female, inside which "Emily, age seven" had been noted.

Now, having learned that Toni was the oldest of five siblings, I swiftly jotted in the new information, adding a number of new circles and squares. Inside these were the names of her sisters and brothers, as well as the names of their spouses and children. The diagram I was creating contained the most obvious family facts, and yet a primitive outline of the group—basically, who was in it—was emerging. I hesitated, for I had several conflicting agendas.

The most important one was to keep everyone involved. If we focused too intently upon Toni's family of origin (the natural direction in which this discussion was tending) it would permit Henry to remain in what might be his ordinary stance, that of the onlooker, the outsider. This, I believed, could happen very easily, and I realized that I was feeling pulled in several directions.

If I kept my attention upon Toni's family of origin, Henry might tune out. I felt some tension rising within me, and wondered: Was this my own early-interview-stage jitteriness or a reflection of some divisive tension within the group itself? Were the members of this family having trouble getting together and staying affectively involved? I had the strong sense of being forced to make hard choices—the sense that if I paid attention to one person, another (or others) would feel disregarded, uncared for, ignored. This was certainly true in regard to Henry, whose silence was very powerful, and who could be lost to the process completely.

What was happening here? I was feeling under some pressure, feeling as if there were a protocol, a set of rules I was supposed to abide by, but I didn't know what they were. If I continued down the path I was on—went on talking with the grandmother and focusing upon Toni's family of origin—it seemed doubtful that everyone in the group could be relied upon to remain engaged and connected.

The Giffords in terms of family atmosphere (civilized and pleasant) and mode of interrelating (neither intensely control-oriented, as in the borderline family, nor fundamentally incoherent, as in the severely dysfunctional family) seemed to me to be emerging as a midrange system on the Beavers health and functioning scale. For in rule-bound, Level 3 systems, there is often not sufficient interest and concern about where people in the family actually *are*, emotionally speaking—what the various individuals are truly thinking and feeling—to keep others in the family group attentive and involved. In a midrange family world, the major focus is upon keeping the rule system itself operating smoothly, and everyone within it behaving in the "right," acceptable ways.

Not to be forgotten, moreover, was seven-year-old Emily, who, with her pensive eyes, seemed to have the face of an adult placed upon a child's body. At the moment, she was intent upon her drawing, but she was listening and had to be kept as actively involved in the discussion as possible. I hesitated, unsure about how to proceed, for my own strong sense was that the Giffords had a set of rules and expectations relating to this encounter, and I couldn't possibly know what they were. All I did know was, first, that those rules and expectations *were* there, because I felt myself bumping up against them—and, second, that the next step I took could be a very wrong one.

"I will surely want to talk much more about this side of the family," I said at last to Toni and her mother, pointing to the line of siblings I had drawn upon the sheet, which looked suspended in the empty whiteness of the paper. I hadn't yet sketched in the marital line of the last generation, the one joining Antonia and her own spouse, Toni's father.

I decided that I had to do so before continuing. Above Antonia's five married children, and those children's own families, I drew the circle that would represent Antonia, the square that would represent her husband, and then a line depicting the connection between them. Toni had told me, on the telephone, that her parents had separated several months earlier; that was why her mother was living with her now.

I decided to reserve any questions about that for later, and said to Toni, "All that I want to ask you, at this moment, is whether or not you are much closer to one of your brothers or sisters than you are to any of the others. Is that the case? Or do you share pretty much the same degree of closeness with all of them?" To my surprise Toni, who'd seemed so eager and so ready to respond that she could hardly wait for the ending of a question, hesitated for a very long time. She looked at her mother uncertainly, and then turned back to me.

"That's hard to answer, I don't know if I am or if I'm not." She turned back to Antonia again. "What do you think, am I closest to Diane, maybe?"

"Definitely," her mother replied. "You and she are closest." Toni turned, nodded, and said to me, "That's right." I drew the double line that signifies "close emotional connection" between the two sisters.

Diane was one year younger, as I saw from the chart. I looked up from the genogram and met Toni Gifford's eyes once again.

I suppose that the fact that she had solicited her mother to answer for her had registered on my face; Toni blushed and giggled. I smiled in response, and shook my head wryly. This was a minuscule little textbook example of what we both knew to occur in families that operated in an emotionally enmeshed, overconnected style. In such enmeshed families, one person can readily answer for another person because individual separateness and differences are not being fully recognized.

Of course there is, it must be emphasized, nothing inherently better or worse about a family's customary way of connecting and being with one another. A family's interactional style is, it bears repeating, just what it is— *a mode of human relating*—and not necessarily linked to either competent functioning or psychological disturbance. But when one family member is able to tell another family member what she's really thinking and actually feeling ("You and Diane are closest"), some blurring of the boundary between self and other can be inferred.

Toni Gifford, at age thirty-six, had turned to her mother to be told whether she herself was closer to one of her sisters or brothers than the others—and, if so, which one of those siblings it might be. There was, it seemed to me, at least one systemic rule at play here: a rule about interpersonal boundaries, to the effect that "a good daughter doesn't separate and differentiate herself from her mother too completely."

And perhaps another equally important family rule was the one that Antonia had signaled at the very outset of the interview: "A good family is one in which everyone is and remains close." Had I been stepping into an off-limits area by asking Toni whether she was closer to any particular one of her siblings than she was to the others? It could be the case that, within this tightly connected emotional system, acknowledging such differences in one's feelings about the various members of the family was not within the realm of the permissible.

For Toni had turned, almost automatically, to her mother, as if to run a rule check—"What do you think, am I closest to Diane?" Had she been asking her mother whether owning up to especially warm feelings about one of her siblings was allowable, or had she literally been asking her mother to tell her what her feelings actually were? In either case, Toni had, on being told that she and Diane were closest, turned back to me at once, looking gratified: "That's right."

Apparently, feeling closest to this particular sister was in sync with the system, in the family rule books, and Toni was feeling the "correct" feelings—the feelings she was expected to feel.

"When One of Us Has a Headache, We All Take an Aspirin"

Toni's mother hadn't hesitated for a moment when asked; she did have a firm idea in her own mind that Toni felt a certain way—that is, closer to her sister Diane than to any other sibling. Antonia was quite sure that Toni felt closest to Diane, and had she paid little heed to Toni's own initial uncertainty. Rather than permit Toni to take a little time, puzzle the matter out for herself, and come to her own conclusions, Antonia had her daughter's answers ready and waiting. "You are closest to Diane," she had told Toni firmly, thus expropriating the independent thinking of her adult offspring.

In thus asserting that she knew exactly what Toni's real thoughts and feelings were, this mother was failing to pay any attention to what Toni's own report on her inner reality might have been. According to psychoanalyst John Zinner, M.D., highly enmeshed family systems can be thought of as systems in which projective identifications—which always involve perceiving charged aspects of one's own inner world as existing in another person—are occurring on a grand scale.

In these relational systems, as he observes, "people prejudge or form ideas about one another which are not actually based on who the person is, but on what has been *put into* the mental picture of the other person." What is involved here is one person's asserting her remarkable capacity to know what is inside another person (as Antonia *knew* which sibling Toni felt closest to) better than that individual knows these things herself.

Attributing Aspects of One's Own Inner Experience to Another Person: Projective Identification

When members of a family confuse aspects of their own inner worlds with the inner experience of those around them, they cease to have hunches, hypotheses, or opinions about what another individual in the group may be thinking and feeling; they simply *know* what the person's thoughts and feelings are, without ever being told—and they know them with perfect certainty. They know the other person's thoughts and feelings because, in such instances, they themselves have put them there (by means of projective identification) in the first place.

Projective identification is, it will be recalled, a psychological mechanism that involves ridding the self of certain denigrated (or, in some cases, cherished) aspects of one's internal world and then seeing these aspects as existing outside, in another person. In this case, as I came to understand later on in the interviews, what Antonia was actually doing was imposing a highly charged aspect of her own inner world on her eldest female child. For Antonia herself had had a sister to whom she'd felt intensely close and whom she viewed as a much more "interesting" and exciting person than she was.

Toni had, to be sure, solicited her mother's answer to my question, as if she had not yet worked out her own answers for herself. It was as if she were waiting, childlike, for her mother to tell her who she was and how she felt; between the two circles representing Toni and Antonia, I sketched in the triple lines denoting an overinvolved, somewhat unseparated relationship. Then I added a question mark next to the triple lines, to remind myself that this was no more than conjecture on my part.

The family in which Toni Gifford had been reared was, one might hypothesize, the kind of group that is indeed extremely close and caring, but which operates like a single-headed organism—somewhat like an octopus, whose individual tentacles (the people in the system) are not really separate, distinct individuals, clearly distinguishable from one another.

This was merely initial guesswork. But later on in my conversations with the Giffords, Toni began to complain about the ways in which the closeness of her family tended became too intense, demanding, downright oppressive. She sometimes felt, she admitted, as if she were gasping for air and for some personal space of her own. "We all—my brothers and sisters and their families, and my grandmother and my aunts and uncles—live within a twenty-mile radius of each other," she'd told me, "and it's as if, when one of us has a headache, all the rest of us have to take an aspirin."

Everything that happened to anybody in Toni's highly resonant family of origin was experienced as if it were happening to all of them, and among the numerous things that were happening at the time, the ending of her parents' marriage loomed very large. Toni and Henry were, themselves, about to have a baby daughter, and at the same time, Toni's mother and father were talking about divorce. Just as a new person was about to enter the emotional system, an important part of that system's foundation was cracking and splitting apart, and there seemed to me to be some real uncertainty about whether people should be celebrating or mourning.

The Key to the Giffords' Front Door

We had fallen silent, and after a few moments Emily looked up from her drawing questioningly as if to ask, "Why has everyone stopped talking?" From where I sat I could see that there were three figures on her paper—

a tall daddy, a smaller mommy, and a little girl standing next to Mommy; all of them were smiling, all holding hands. "That looks good, Emily," I said, with a smile, and she told me that it was almost finished. I noted that her live-in grandma, who cared for her during the day when her mother was at work, was not included in the seven-year-old's drawing of her family.

It was time to put the constructing of the genogram on hold, and to ask this only child (soon to be an elder sibling) a few questions about how she perceived herself as an individual. I began talking to Emily about the ways in which she thought she was just like other seven-year-old girls, and the ways in which she thought she might be a little different.

The youngster cocked her head and looked at me assessingly, as if there might be some trick or joke involved. She was, she told me, *like* other seven-year-olds because she was in second grade, and most seven-year-olds were in second grade. She was different from other seven-year-olds because she was a different person. She might perhaps talk a bit differently, she said reflectively, then added gravely, "And I probably *look* different too."

"In what ways do you look different?" I glanced around and realized with a sense of relief that everyone present—mother, father, even Antonia—seemed to be highly engaged in this conversation.

Emily said that her hair and her eyes might be different from those of other seven-year-old girls; her parents and grandmother looked at her in surprise. Her hair, Emily explained, was short (in point of fact, her shiny, dark hair was cut to shoulder length, like her mother's), and most of the other second-graders had hair down to the middle of their backs. Her eyes might be a different color, also.

"What color are other seven-year-olds' eyes?" I asked interestedly, and Emily said that they were mostly brown and blue. "And what color are *your* eyes?"

"I don't know for sure," she replied guardedly, and everyone started laughing and talking at once. Henry Gifford was, I noticed, leaning slightly forward in his seat, his interest piqued by the things his daughter was saying. "Do you think your mommy knows, perhaps?" I asked Emily, with a smile.

She turned to look at Toni, "Mommy, *do* you?" Jumping up, she went and stood directly in front of her mother. "What color *are* my eyes, Mommy?" she asked insistently, standing up and drawing her face close to Toni's.

Mother and daughter gazed at each other for a long moment, while the little girl's father and grandmother looked on with expressions of vicarious but intense pleasure. In this brief, sweet interval, I felt myself relaxing, felt as if my stopping to focus everyone's attention upon the child had been the key to the family's front door, and that at this moment, the Giffords' door was being opened wide to me.

"Home": The Need to Live Within Toni's Family's Magic Twenty-Mile Radius

My self-congratulations were short-lived, for as I went on talking with the child, I realized that Antonia's attention was slipping once again. I had asked Emily to tell me a few things about her daddy—what was he like as a person? The question made Emily start giggling and rolling her eyes, as if to say that now she was going to let all of her father's secrets out. But apparently, the subject of her son-in-law was one that wasn't able to hold Antonia's attention. The grandmother's thoughts were clearly elsewhere, and she looked pained, as if preoccupied by a kind of mental toothache.

Despite the giggles and all-knowing looks, everything that Emily was saying about her father was positive and flattering. Her daddy took her to her horseback-riding lessons, she told me, and did a lot of nice *unexpected* things with her as well. He had, for instance, taken her out for a submarine sandwich after her lesson yesterday afternoon.

Of course in these public circumstances—that is, a family interview—the daughter could be depended upon to present her parents in the most positive of lights. Children of this age are adept in the politics of the family, and it was unlikely that Emily would say anything that could possibly get her into trouble after my departure. Still, Henry Gifford's cheeks turned a rosy color, and he looked unabashedly delighted.

Antonia was seeming ever more distracted; her retreat into the kitchen was, it seemed to me, imminent. I made some hurried notations on the genogram, feeling torn once again. I would have liked to linger on this discussion, especially when Henry told me that he considered it important to schedule such special father-daughter events with Emily because they had so little time to spend together.

He was, as he explained, currently stationed at the Governors Island base off the coast of Manhattan, and commuted to his job, which was over three hours of traveling time (one way) from his home in Connecticut. He had been doing this for two years, and had eventually found the six-hour commute so exhausting that he'd begun returning home only on an every-other-weekend basis.

Had it not been imperative to draw Antonia back into the conversation, I would have explored the subject of how this demanding arrangement had come into being. For the wooded coastal town in which the Giffords lived was not only 140 miles from Henry's workplace in New York City, it was almost an hour from Toni's teaching job at Storrs. Their pretty house (owned by them) was, however, within the magic twenty-mile radius of everyone in Toni's original emotional system. In purely geographical terms, she was currently living nearer to the family of her childhood than she was to her own husband or her job.

What Had Transformed a Problematical but Long Relationship into a Relationship That Was Suddenly No Longer Bearable?

In what was nothing other than a bald-faced bid to regain the grandmother's attention, I turned to Toni at that point, and asked her if she could give me a few adjectives that might best capture her *mother's* important qualities as a person. Toni laughed and looked at Antonia in the same mischievous "I will tell all" way that Emily had looked at her dad a few moments earlier. To my relief, Antonia smiled slightly, then shifted in her seat, as if her return to this discussion were not a mental but a physical phenomenon.

"She's very maternal. High energy. A worrier. *Very* emotional, a purebred Italian . . . the big disciplinarian, when we were younger." Toni laughed again, as if to soften the severity that might possibly be heard in her words.

Her father, Thomas, had been the opposite. Thomas Baxter (called Tom) was, in his daughter's view, a man who was "controlled" and "sensitive" but "always under a lot of internal pressure" because he kept everything to himself and never talked to anyone about his feelings. He had, however, been the family softie—the one to whom the children would run with complaints about their demanding disciplinarian of a mother. "My dad would always listen and be empathic to what we were saying, but he was never capable of setting limits," Toni said. "He left that to her, I suppose," she added with a swift, somewhat apologetic glance at Antonia.

It was the first hint of any negativity between mother and daughter—an underlying current of resentment that never did resurface until the closing phase of the interviews, when I was meeting with Toni Gifford alone. During this conversation, I put to her the question of what the first sentence of her own autobiography might sound like. "I was born adult," she'd responded promptly, in a somewhat irate tone of voice.

Toni believed she'd simply been a little adult from day one. From the very beginning of her life, she'd felt burdened by responsibilities; as the eldest of five siblings, she'd been expected to be her mother's chief assistant and help out with the practical work of the household. But the really massive burden, the struggle she'd been engaged in as long as she could remember, was the effort to resolve the family's ongoing problems, most specifically her parents' marital difficulties.

She had, she said, always felt tremendously responsible, always felt that it was necessary to take care of her parents—and she believed now that she actually parented them more than they had ever parented her. "Somehow it was *my* duty—*I* had to keep them together. So I was always very vigilant, always checking things out, always eternally *wary*," Toni told me.

Toni Gifford's father, now fifty-eight, was not Italian but of mixed Polish and English parentage. Tom Baxter was retired; his last job had been as the director of housing on a submarine base, and he was living on a disability pension. Although she did not say so at our first, joint interview, Toni had once idolized the father of her childhood, and had felt closer to him than to almost anyone else. She was sorely disappointed by the man he had eventually become, and by the shoddy ways in which his life had turned out.

Her parents had been married for thirty-seven and a half years, Toni Gifford told me. I jotted the number above the line joining Tom and Antonia and waited. . . . The ensuing silence was a short one. It was Toni's mother who continued, in a raised and clear but curiously flat tone of voice. "My husband and I are separated. He walked out on me, just like that, after all that time and all those years together. He's had another woman living with him—or did have." Antonia shrugged as if to say anything was possible. "Someone told me, about a week ago, that this person had moved out. I don't know where his head is at right now."

I drew a single slash across the marital line; this symbolizes separation (while a double slash stands for divorce). "Do you want to talk about what's been happening in your life, just recently—or would you rather leave it for another time?" I asked Antonia directly. She shrugged again, this time to indicate that she was perfectly willing to go on.

"The girlfriend, I guess, moved into his new apartment two weeks after he'd moved out of the house. So he was living with her there, for a couple of months; that's ended now, I understand. But he's always had his affairs, throughout our whole marriage; I mean, this is nothing new to me." As her mother spoke, I glanced at Toni, wondering what it would be like for a daughter to hear this. The expression on her face was clouded and doubtful.

Antonia went on to say that she herself was far from understanding just why her marriage should be breaking up now, after all these years together. "It's something that came on so fast—something that I never expected, although my husband's always had a lot of psychological problems." Then she added, as if in explanation, "He did have a serious drinking problem, one that went on for, oh, almost ten years. He still goes to AA every day of his life, even though it's been—how long?"

She appealed to Toni, who shook her head and said that she wasn't sure. Antonia supplied her own answer immediately. "It's over twenty-five years, but he still goes every day," she told me. Tom Baxter had spent a considerable part of his lifetime—a quarter of a century—in the role of a recovering alcoholic. His behavior, in terms of track record alone, signaled an intense struggle to handle those feelings that he'd "always kept to himself"—both by attempting to medicate himself with liquor and by going outside the marriage to find what had not been found inside it. The long relationship between Toni's parents had obviously been a somewhat painful and problematic one; but what had happened in the recent past that had transformed it into a relationship that was unbearable?

An Incest-Tinged "Family Affair"

"There were, you know, other women, almost from the beginning," Antonia said, giving me an odd look, as if making a quick calculation before deciding to continue. "Including my own sister," she said.

I was silent, unsure for a moment that she'd said what I thought I had heard.

"He even got involved with *her,*" Antonia went on, in the same flat tone of voice. "And my sister and I had been very, very *close.* My sister was my best friend, before that happened." With these words, and for the first time, I heard outright agitation in Antonia's voice.

"Your husband had an affair with your sister?" I repeated, very quietly, and the grandmother nodded. She had folded her hands on her lap and was pressing them together. "So these were the things I had to live with, to keep hushed up at the same time. Everything was kept under wraps; I mean, he and I, we didn't discuss things; the kids didn't even know what was going on." She fixed her gaze upon her daughter, who didn't meet it.

"That's the kind of a person I am, I kept everything inside," the mother added, sounding anxious and uncertain. It was her rage about her husband's recent abandonment, I thought, that was unleashing these public revelations.

Antonia glanced at Henry briefly, as if to gauge her son-in-law's reactions, then turned her gaze rapidly away. Henry shifted his position on the love seat, crossed one leg on top of the other; it felt to me (rightly or wrongly) like a gesture of impatience or even disapproval.

We Just Stopped Talking

Antonia sat there looking blank for a moment, then continued speaking. "Over the years Tom—my husband—got very much inside himself and the two of us never communicated. It wasn't that we were fighting all the time, or anything like that; it was just that we never *talked.* And in the end, we really didn't have anything to say to each other. We were just two people, going our own ways, and we had nothing in common."

Antonia shrugged, as if to say "So, that was that," and at the moment, the strangest notion popped into my own mind. What I was thinking about was this woman's former close and very trusting relationship with her own sister—a relationship that had clearly soured over time, and become laced with envy, outright sexual rivalry, and anger. I was thinking, too, about the strong and forceful certitude with which Antonia had stated that Toni was closer to her sister Diane than to any of her other siblings. Was it Antonia's fantasy that the *good* parts of that once valued but now spoiled sibling relationship were not irreversibly lost, but lived on in the close bond between her own two eldest daughters?

Had she, in other words, split off a prized part of her own inner world (that warm, fuzzy, sisterly fusion) and projected it into Toni and Diane's relationship so that she could perceive it as reposing there safely, far from further destruction and harm?

Projective identification can, as noted earlier, involve ridding oneself of highly cherished (as well as devalued and repudiated) aspects of the inner self as a means of protecting "what is good" from internal attack—that is, from assaults generated by one's own rage, resentment, and hatred. If Antonia could no longer share the same loving, intimate relationship with her own sister, Rita, she could at least take comfort in perceiving this intense connection as being both alive and out of harm's way—stored for safekeeping, so to speak, in the close relationship between Toni and Diane.

Family Names

The quasi-incestuous affair between Toni's father and her aunt had occurred over three decades earlier, around 1961 or 1962, as Antonia remembered it. She and Rita had both been married at the time, and both were mothers of young families. Antonia's own five children had all been born by then, as had the first of her sister's two children. She herself would have been around twenty-eight, Antonia believed, and her older sibling twenty-nine.

Aunt Rita was, I learned, the elder of the two daughters of that generation (a third daughter had died in babyhood). As Toni's mother spoke, I was sketching the new information into the Gifford family's increasingly crowded and complex genogram. Antonia's own father, a chicken farmer, had died twenty years ago, but her eighty-three-year-old mother—also named Rita—was still very much alive.

Gazing down at the genogram, I took note of the fact that Aunt Rita had been named after her own mother just as Toni had been named after *her* mother, Antonia. There seemed to be an intriguing tradition, on this maternal side of the family, of naming one's firstborn female child after oneself. And in a way, in this first act of affirmation of the newly arrived infant, the mother's message seemed to be "You and I, who bear the same gender and the same name, are in some deep way one and the same female human being."

The act of naming is a powerful one, freighted with intimations about who the newborn is supposed to be—and often, with notions about what parental missions she or he may have been put upon the earth to fulfill. The females on the maternal side of Toni's family were perhaps not expected to become differentiated, autonomous adults who grow up, separate from home base, and go off to create lives of their own; rather, they were expected to remain bonded to the mother and the original family in a state of everlasting self-and-other fusion.

In biology, when a cell divides, the two resulting entities are called a mother cell and a daughter cell; they are, however, identical in form and substance. In a way, these joint Ritas and Antonias brought to mind a similar kind of female undifferentiation; certainly, if Aunt Rita's behavior indicated anything, it indicated serious problems in maintaining appropriately firm interpersonal boundaries. She had crossed a forbidden sexual divide and invaded her own younger (and close and trusting) sister's marital relationship.

Aunt Rita's violation of a strong sexual taboo—one does not get involved with a sibling's mate—displayed a fundamental lack of awareness of where her own intimate turf ended and where her younger sister's began. It was as though the women in this family were so intertwined and entangled that to go outside the emotional system—even to find a romantic partner—had somehow seemed less problematic than simply getting hooked up with someone inside it.

Aunt Rita had, in a wonderful way, found a means of flagrantly rebelling against the family, while at the same time abiding by what was probably one of its most fundamental rules: "The women do not ever leave the family; they remain tightly bonded and emotionally close, *no matter what else they may do.*" The affair with her brother-in-law had been, I suspected, Rita's way of remaining inside this demanding, somewhat confining emotional system and at the same time, striking a mutinous blow for autonomy and freedom.

A Husband and Two Sisters: The Myth of Philomela

Rita had not only deceived and betrayed the younger sister who was also her close intimate; she had also changed forever the lives of the five nieces and nephews who were Antonia and Tom's small emotional dependents. For as parents, Antonia and Tom were not only the creators and builders of a family structure; they were also responsible for its ongoing physical and psychological maintenance. The illicit affair between Aunt Rita and her brother-in-law, Tom, had been an assault on this structure's very foundation—an assault, in my view, with an almost mythological resonance.

And in fact as this tale of intrafamily passion emerged, I found myself remembering the Greek myth of Philomela (which is the story of how the nightingale got its song). In that myth the king of Thrace, Tereus, falls passionately in love with his wife's sister, Philomela, and, while escorting her on a voyage to his palace, he rapes his hapless young relative. Then he cuts out Philomela's tongue, so that she cannot tell anyone what has happened, and leaves her stranded and imprisoned on a far-off, isolated island.

But the mute, violated girl manages to weave the story of what has occurred into a lovely tapestry and succeeds in having it delivered to her sister Procne, King Tereus's wife. Procne "reads" the tapestry and understands.

Enraged but self-controlled, the queen obtains young Philomela's release and secretly imports her into the palace. Then Queen Procne executes a terrible revenge upon her husband by slaying their own young son, Itys, and serving him up to his father, King Tereus, for his dinner. After supping well, the horrified king is apprised of the ghastly truth: He has just eaten his own offspring. Thus has this husband and parent's savage rape of his sister-in-law served to exact a real and terrible sacrifice from the young and innocent new generation.

In the aftermath the king, appalled and infuriated by the realization of what he has been tricked into doing, pursues the fleeing women in order to revenge himself and destroy them. But at the moment when he overtakes and is about to kill the sisters, the watching gods intervene and transform all three of them into birds of the air. Tereus becomes an ugly bird with a huge beak, Philomela becomes a swallow (who can only twitter because her tongue has been cut out), and Procne becomes a nightingale.

This is, according to myth, why the nightingale's song is the sweetest, saddest plaint of all—Procne can never forget the baby son she has slain in order to achieve her vengeance. But the myth of Philomela is, in its essence, the story of the breaching of a sexual taboo—a breach involving two sisters and a husband—and the way in which the life of their luckless offspring is served up as a form of existential recompense.

In the myth itself, of course, the women assert their bond of blood and act in concert against the offending male outsider. But the story now being told to me was a different one, for in her own older sister, Antonia had found no such friend and ally. For her, even crueler than Tom's unfaithfulness must have been the fact that Rita had come from within the sanctuary of the family (supposedly a place of safety from sexual marauders) and not from the much less trusted world outside it.

But perhaps worst of all had been the shocking loss of the sense of close-ness and oneness with her older sister—"She was my *best friend*," Antonia had said—and of the intimate relationship that they had once shared. Antonia had sounded, or so it seemed to me, far more upset and aggrieved when describing *that* betrayal than she had when talking about the ending of the marriage itself.

Affairs and Alcohol

The affair with Rita had been Tom's first betrayal of her and of their family, according to Antonia. But, after that affair had ended, her husband's infidelities had continued. Beforehand, Tom Baxter had been at his life's peak performance level: He owned several farms, was involved in a successful real estate business, and was a visible member of the town council of Putnam, Connecticut.

But afterward, although slowly at first, a downward spiral had begun. There had been what Antonia called "drinking problems," and then seri-ous business and financial problems had developed. There had also been a mysterious but crushingly large debt, whose derivation no one was able to explain, even now, many years later, but which had sent both the business and the family (they'd had to sell their home) into temporary bankruptcy at one point.

Somehow, the affair with Rita sounded as if it had been a watershed event in the life of this family—the transitional moment when things had started changing for the worse. I asked Antonia if she knew how long that relationship had lasted, but she wasn't sure.

"I *do* remember not speaking to my sister for a very long time *after* that—almost three years—and this was very upsetting to my parents, when they learned about it. My mother was *very* upset by this whole thing." Her voice was rising indignantly, as if the affair's impact upon her mother had been as distressing to her as had been her sister's and her husband's perfidy and her own misery and woe. How had she herself learned of the affair's existence? I inquired.

Antonia snorted, then answered that it had become so obvious it would have been impossible to overlook. "The four of us always used to go out together, as couples—we're a very close family. And I noticed that every time we went anywhere, Tom would hold the door for her, walk with her, and I'd end up walking with my brother-in-law. They always went off by themselves, and when it came to dancing, Phil and I would sit and watch them. . . . At the end of the evening, I'd always say, 'Gee, you'd think *Phil* was my husband.' "

She sighed, then said, as if in explanation of Rita's position: "My sister wasn't happy with her husband. It was a bad marriage from the start; they had nothing in common." These were, I recognized, the very words Antonia had used to describe her relationship with her own husband.

Tom and she had been living parallel lives without *sharing* their lives, Antonia had stated, and had had "nothing in common" eventually. Was this a family which shared a tradition to the effect that the women stayed closely connected to one another, but as wives didn't connect to their men? And if this was the case, had the marriage of Toni and Henry Gifford been affected by this aspect of her extended system's relational agenda?

"My husband would always flatter my sister, as her husband Phil never did," Antonia continued explaining, as if anxious to keep her own peace with this long-ago matter. "Tom would, you know, tell her how much he liked her dress, and how pretty she looked in it, and he'd run to light her cigarette. After a while, you couldn't ignore it; Rita and I had words, eventually." She shrugged, as if to say "What other option had I?"

"I even told my mother, but my mother couldn't, or *wouldn't*, believe it. I stopped going to my parents' on Sundays, which we'd *always* done. But I couldn't go—Rita and her family would be there. For three whole years this went on, but after a while my mother came to me and said, 'You know, this is tearing the family apart, and it has got to stop.' So in time, for that reason, I forgave her." Antonia lifted her shoulders briefly in that shrug which proclaimed her helplessness. Her wifely injury, unlike that of Queen Procne in the myth, had never been avenged, righted, or resolved. The matter had simply been packed away and put up in the family's attic, so that the extended group's former closeness could be restored.

"You yourself are absolutely sure they did have an affair?" I asked her, searchingly. For there was, of course, the possibility that this "affair" had been nothing other than the jealous fantasy that Antonia's mother had wanted to believe it was. But Antonia shook her head ruefully, as if to warn me not to waste my time with such fanciful ideas. "Yes, my husband admitted it to me. He told me, later on, that they did; but of course I knew it anyhow." I glanced down at the genogram to ascertain what Toni's age had been at that time; she'd been somewhere around eight or nine.

Antonia had said that she had tried to shield her kids and had "kept everything that was happening inside." But I wondered how much Toni, as the eldest sibling in the family, had actually known about what was going on. To what extent had she, like the child Itys in the myth, been "consumed" by the traumatic events occurring in the adult generation?

It is usually the case that the children in a family know far more about what is happening in the adult generation than the grown-ups can possibly imagine. The youngsters are alert and aware, at a subjective, feeling level—as they *must* be, for getting on the caretakers' emotional wavelength is adaptive. If one thinks in terms of physical and emotional survival, the bottom line is that it is the parents' loving care and protection upon which the children are utterly dependent. Staying attuned to the nurturers makes the best of biological sense, which is why the young people in a family will often unconsciously perceive everything that is happening—know the whole story without necessarily knowing any of the particular facts.

The Life of the Family Party

I wondered how cognizant of her parents' difficulties Toni Gifford, as a child, had actually been. When I asked her what she remembered knowing, Toni's eyes widened, and she moved her torso back, as if my words were a strong breeze to which her body was responding automatically.

She had, she answered vaguely, "perhaps heard" about her father's affairs, but on the whole, he had kept them pretty secret. There had been lots of family secrets—things she hadn't known about, growing up—financial problems, among other things. But she certainly hadn't known anything about the affair with her aunt, she assured me.

At that moment, Emily looked up, said with an exaggerated, false-sounding enthusiasm, "Mommy, look at my drawing; it's almost finished!" She had, it seemed to me, picked up her mother's anxiety, and was attempting, in an almost automatic fashion, to divert her mom's attention away from these problematic topics.

"Emily, have you heard your mother and your grandma talk about some of these things before?" I asked her.

"I dunno, maybe." She shrugged. "I think so." She didn't look at me while answering.

Toni laughed, sounding embarrassed, then patted her daughter's head and resumed replying to my question in a thoughtful, almost meditative tone of voice. "Maybe, though . . . in a way . . . I did. There are, you know, certain experiences that you tend to block out and not recall very easily—maybe because they're too painful to deal with. But I do have one very distinct memory, my father lighting my aunt's cigarette in this really sexy, Humphrey Bogart way—" She turned to her mother suddenly, "Remember that?"

Toni turned back to me, said that all she could remember was that one incident, and her parents fighting about it afterward, yelling and screaming. "Other than that, I don't recall much of anything." She looked like a frightened little girl at this moment. The sunshine in the room faded abruptly, as if a celestial dimmer had just been turned down a notch. The light would not be with us much longer on this short winter afternoon.

"But still, I always had a lot of respect for my aunt," Toni added suddenly. "Because she always was very generous to us and very loving."

I was startled, almost bowled over by this statement, and Toni, alert to my reactions, hurried to explain it. "My aunt is just a giving kind of a person, and she has a lot on the ball, *whatever* she did. . . ." Instead of allying with her injured mother, Toni Gifford seemed to be allying with her exciting, self-absorbed aunt. But Antonia herself did not look offended, and when I glanced at Henry, he said, with a wryly amused smile, "I was just thinking that if Rita were here, she'd be dominating this conversation completely."

This elicited a laugh from Toni. "Right, right." She looked at her mother, who began laughing too.

"How would she manage to make that happen?" I directed the question to no one in particular.

"*Whatever* way—but she'd be controlling everything, that's for sure," Henry replied, and they all laughed again, in a tender, indulgent fashion. Her sister had been a schoolteacher before she retired, Antonia told me, as if in justification of Rita's tendency to take charge, and always dominated whatever conversation she happened to be in. Antonia looked proud of her sibling at that moment, and not particularly annoyed with her.

I felt perplexed. Had Toni's mother reserved all her rancor for her husband, and simply forgiven her sister completely? And did Toni have no daughterly identification with her mother's betrayal and her pain, no feeling of grievance about the family-wide distress her aunt's behavior had let loose? No matter what Rita had done, once upon a time, nobody in this family seemed to harbor any serious negative feelings toward her.

"She dominates whatever she's *doing*." Henry was enjoying and prolonging this talk of Rita, in an animated tone of voice. "Right, she does," his mother-in-law seconded him, nodding her head and smiling. "My sister's very outgoing," she said to me, almost smugly. Despite the central, seemingly injurious role that Rita had played in these close relatives' lives, she seemed to be eliciting more affection and admiration than anything else. Clearly, they adored her; she was, in some curious way, the life of the family party.

Female Archetypes: The Sexual Woman and the Moral, Dutiful Woman

It was as if the family group shared a powerful fantasy about Rita—and, for that matter, a fantasy about Antonia, too. The two sisters seemed to have been cast as female archetypes, alternative images of what a woman can possibly be and become.

Rita, in the family pantheon, was the erotic goddess; she spoke for generosity and pleasure, surrender to passion, self-indulgence, and lack of personal responsibility. She knew how to take for herself what she wanted;

she was, moreover, lots of fun to be around. Antonia, on the other hand, was the vision of the mother goddess—self-abnegating, moral, thoroughly conscientious, and probably somewhat sex-phobic and gratification-phobic as well.

Antonia knew how to give and nurture, but, I suspected, felt thoroughly unwanted and irrelevant when there was no one to care for (which was why baby-sitting for her working daughter had been a role around which her life could so readily be organized). While Rita was overentitled, Antonia lacked a sense of personal entitlement and of responsibility toward her own needs as a separate person. She was, perhaps, the winner in the realm of ethics, but the clear loser in the great arena of love.

Both of the sisters had, very clearly, grown up within a family environment in which it was assumed that a woman cannot be sexual *and* responsible simultaneously. The warring needs within a woman—to realize herself as an erotic being and to maintain her moral values and meet her obligations—were, in their own original family, considered to be totally irreconcilable.

It was as if, within the family culture, these images of femininity had been severed. The split between female sexuality and responsibility could never be resolved and reconciled in order to achieve a harmonious balance between them. Instead, these aspects of womanhood had been parceled out between different members of the family. Rita was, it appeared, the one to whom sexuality had been delegated, and Antonia was the one to whom duty and morality had been assigned. In this emotional system, the very idea that one could be a mother *and* a sexual person was neither conceivable nor sanctioned. So clearly, Rita's role in the family was to provide the excitement and stimulation, while Antonia's was to provide the accountability and dutiful control.

A Daughter's Divided Allegiance

I wondered what Toni, as a prepubescent girl, had made of the striking differences between these larger-than-life adult female figures. A scene sprang to my mind: eight-year-old Toni watching her father light her aunt's cigarette and excitedly aware of the flame springing up between them. She had never forgotten the moment.

In identifying with her rejected mother's role in the events of that time, Toni would be identifying with a devalued, denigrated woman, who had, moreover, been abandoned emotionally. In identifying with her boisterous aunt, she would be identifying with a victorious female, but one who had wounded her own parent. Given two such starkly differing models, a daughter could be eaten alive simply trying to choose between them.

I looked directly at her and said, "Your aunt sounds like a powerful kind of person. I have a feeling that there's a lot of respect and esteem for her, even though she has played a funny role here—having an affair with your father, I mean." I felt almost embarrassed at the strangeness of my having to remind her of this quasi-incestuous betrayal.

Toni must have realized it; she looked disconcerted. "Well, she's—" She was unable to complete the sentence.

"She's just *nice*," put in Henry affectionately, explaining that Aunt Rita had lived with them for a brief while. Rita's own long marriage had broken up earlier this year; Henry had enjoyed having her in the household for that short period of time. I felt fairly certain, on hearing this, that the recent breakup of Rita's marriage had led, in a billiard-ball-like fashion, to the sudden breakup of Antonia's own.

"My aunt is *kind*," explained Toni, "and she's always had a mind of her own and believed in what she did; I have no problems with that. She has a positive attitude. She knows what she wants, and she gets it and doesn't la-di-da around. She just *lives life*. There are a lot of people who are put off by her, but hey—she knows what she wants; she does her thing, and that's it." While Antonia was, as Toni had said, a "worrier," Rita could readily gratify herself, without being overly troubled by concerns of conscience.

Judging from her eloquent remarks on her aunt's behalf, Toni's allegiance to her own mother seemed to be a divided one. For in praising Aunt Rita, Toni was also not-so-subtly criticizing her mother's very different, overly responsible, self-sacrificial style of relating—and yet, for a daughter, it is her mother who is the primary model of a female human being. Toni could not win for losing, because the more she might try to be like Rita, the victorious, in-charge female, the more she betrayed her mother—and those parts of her mother with which she was herself deeply identified and which lived on inside her.

Intimate Sharing: Who Knows the Family Secrets and Who Doesn't

"I'm really amazed to hear that the two of them ever *had* such an affair," Henry observed, shifting position so that he was sitting farther back on his seat, arms folded over his chest once again. "Because I didn't think that Toni's father and her aunt got along *at all*. I never knew anything about this *at all*," he repeated, staring at his wife and his mother-in-law.

I was taken aback, too—taken aback by the fact that he seemed not to have ever heard anything about these highly charged family matters. Had Toni never even talked about this affair, never gone over the details as she remembered them, never speculated about it all with the person who was presumably her closest adult intimate?

Perhaps she was, in fact, showing the ultimate loyalty to her mother (and abiding by one of her family's most powerful covert rules) by never sharing her inmost thoughts and her feelings with a man. For to the extent that she and Henry didn't really talk to each other and had "nothing in common," mother and daughter would stay solidly bonded, emotionally entangled, united—as the women in this family were supposed and expected to remain.

CHAPTER 16

His Side of the Genogram— a Chilly, Distanced Family: Henry Gifford

When it comes to styles of relating and being with one another, the family in which Toni's husband had grown up could not have been more different from her own.

For the members of Henry Gifford's family of origin had all been socialized to take care of their own needs in a highly independent, autonomous fashion; people rarely came too close for personal comfort. The major problem seemed, in fact, to have been the opposite one: It sounded as though there had been precious little emotional contact. Henry's family emerged, in his description of them, as a group of fairly distant individuals who happened to be living together under one roof.

This disengaged style of family relating was described earlier (in Chapter 4, "Styles of Relating"), as were some of the technical terms— "emotionally isolated"; "centrifugal"—commonly used to describe it. The Beavers researchers prefer the term "centrifugal," because in this kind of system, the emotional forces are vectored primarily in an outward direction. As Robert Beavers writes in *Psychotherapy and Growth*, "Sources of gratification are viewed by this group as existing essentially outside, not inside, the family." Family members tend to distance themselves from one another and to seek solace elsewhere, often in intense, compensatory relationships with peers.

As one can readily imagine, the experience of living in this kind of system is always one of a woeful dearth of emotional supplies. In Henry's early family world, as he described it, there seemed to have been a profound lack of mutual connectedness and very little sense of warmth, reciprocal concern, and belonging. At this point in his life, he retained minimal contact with the world of his childhood; and he told me, without a tremor of sadness or self-pity, that he felt close to no one at all in the family he'd grown up in.

On one occasion—this was relatively early in my interviews with the Giffords—I asked Henry to tell me his thoughts about the very different, excitingly emotional family system he had married into. At that meeting, which was several weeks after the birth of the Giffords' second daughter, Henry's wife, daughter, and mother-in-law were all present (as was the new baby, Laura, who slept peacefully in her bassinet through most of the conversation).

The idea of making a public pronouncement about Toni's family seemed to strike Henry as funny or daring; he laughed. "They're a *large* family," he replied, selecting his words carefully. "And they *will* get into each other's personal business a whole lot more than my family ever does."

Antonia was, I noticed, regarding her son-in-law with a somewhat wary, skeptical expression. "But most of them are pretty nice," maintained Henry. "They treat me nice. In fact all of them treat me *real* nice. . ." I strained forward to try to catch the rest of the sentence, for his voice was dropping.

"Do you like the emotionality?" I asked him.

"No," he replied. I waited, but he added nothing.

"You don't like it," I said, after a silence.

"No."

"You never missed it in your own family, where it sounds as if people were somewhat disconnected?" I persisted.

"Nope," he said unequivocally, and Toni said, "That's true, he doesn't like the emotionality of my family at all."

A Football Hero's Son

Henry Gifford had been the eldest son, though not the eldest sibling, in a family that viewed qualities associated with maleness (autonomy, independence) and male achievement as the most valued attributes. Indeed, his mother's girlhood ambition, as printed in the caption beneath her high school graduation picture, had been to marry a football star and become the mother of three boys who would all grow up to be football stars themselves.

His father, William Earl Gifford, had been a sergeant major in the U.S. Army. At the time of his parents' marriage, Henry's dad had, in fact, been the local football hero; years later, Henry himself had become the star of the high school team in the small Georgia mill town, Thomaston, in which both his mother and father had grown up.

Henry's dad, now deceased (he had died twelve years earlier, at the relatively young age of fifty-six), had been the youngest son in a large southern family that had once been prosperous, but had suffered huge financial losses and an enormous comedown. At one time, the Giffords had owned and operated three different farms, but during the Great Depression of the 1930s all of their properties were lost. "The family lost it *all*, lost everything they had, and had to move into town so that my grandfather could get a job in the mills. But my dad *did* grow up to be a big athlete—that was when he was in high school. Then, when World War Two rolled around, he joined the Army and went off to war."

It sounded, in a way, as if Henry's father had been in some sense the Gifford family's Joseph—its youngest son and the restorer (at least to some degree) of its sense of hope, honor, and standing. For by becoming a renowned football hero (of statewide as well as local fame, according to Henry), Bill Gifford had recouped some portion of the family's self-esteem at a time when they'd been devastated by the loss of their farms and sorely humbled by their total and terrible poverty.

Henry's father, as the son told me with some pride, had been the only member of the Gifford family who'd ever managed to shake the dust of Thomaston, Georgia, from his shoes and go somewhere else; Henry's uncles had all stayed there, spent their lives working for the mills. His dad's ticket out of town had been a football scholarship; but Bill Gifford had attended college for only a year, or perhaps two, for when World War II erupted he'd left his studies and enlisted in the armed services.

"My father went off to World War Two and then came back to Thomaston an Army guy," recounted Henry, beginning to sound somewhat guarded and wary.

I wondered why, or whether I was misperceiving him somehow.

But in fact, as I later realized, I wasn't—not at all. What I was tuning in to at that moment was Henry's sense that we were moving into an area that might be full of family land mines—certain matters which, although they hadn't been thought about for years, could, if disturbed in any way, prove still "live" and explosive.

A Man Who Couldn't Share His Inner Life

Henry Gifford had been eleven years old when his father—a man's man and a hearty social drinker—left the United States for Korea. It was the early 1960s and this stint in Southeast Asia was to be Sergeant Major Bill Gifford's last tour of military duty before his retirement from the armed services.

But when his father came home from Korea (Henry was just over thirteen, at the time) he'd seemed transformed. Bill Gifford had come back a sour, remote loner, and was now, according to his son, a man who had "a bad problem" with alcohol. "That caused a lot of fighting in the family—verbal fights, not physical. I didn't like that; it was very painful; I didn't like it at all," the now thirty-nine-year-old Henry recounted.

He was using the word "painful," as I couldn't fail to remark, without any resonance of grief in his own voice. It was as if Henry were, at an intellectual level, well aware of how hard things had been at home, but was, at a feeling level, unplugged and disconnected from the real hurting that had been going on.

As if in reaction to this disconnection between words and affect, I could feel a sense of discomfort rising within me. But I simply asked Henry, in a calm tone of voice, to tell me a little more about his father, give me some idea of what kind of fellow he had been.

His father would not be an easy person to describe, Henry Gifford countered. He inhaled deeply, and his chest expanded. I waited, looking at the dark blue wool sweater and neatly ironed khakis he had put on for today's meeting. Last time we'd met, I recalled, he had been wearing a plain maroon sweater and spotless work trousers of the same kind. It was as though his around-the-house clothes were as impeccably clean and de-individualized as a uniform.

"Well, can you give me a few adjectives that might describe his major qualities?" I prompted.

Henry told me that his father had been a tall man, large and good-looking.

I smiled. "What was he like as a person?"

Henry's expression didn't change. "Strict. Selfish. A man who couldn't share his inner life at all." I took the time to write these comments on the genogram slowly, then looked up at Toni and Antonia. Both his wife and his mother-in-law seemed taken aback.

Had he just told me something that his wife and mother hadn't actually ever heard before? Or had he violated a fundamental, unspoken rule of this family, a rule to the effect that "the males in this system never open up and make themselves vulnerable by sharing their inner thoughts and feelings with anyone"?

The Son of an Emotionally Absent Father

Turning back to Henry, I reflected that the son of such a father (a man described as completely unavailable, and in any case, as drinking heavily) is twice impaired when it comes to dealing with the negative feelings that inevitably, like toxic sludge, come to permeate his inner reality. The son is impaired, first of all, by the restrictive societal expectations laid upon men in general—the notion that being a real male involves behaving in ways that are relatively stoic and unemotional, and neither talking much nor thinking much about one's feelings or inner states of being.

The son of such a father is, in the second place, impaired by the parent's impairment, for the youngster's internal working model of an adult male is the model provided by the male parent. And for Henry Gifford, achieving manhood would involve identifying with a man who'd become ever more withdrawn, psychologically handicapped in some mysterious way, and debilitated by his increasing, quite severe problems with alcohol. How could the son of such an affectively absent, incapacitated masculine figure possibly take in a caring, loving, proud, accepting sense of self? How could his "selfish," damaged dad provide the growing boy with a good internal representation of adult manhood and of the man that he himself might someday become?

One way of dealing with this kind of dilemma is to place a self-imposed ban upon inner experiences in general. If the son is longing for connectedness with a parent who is both flawed and unavailable, then he may experience it as far better to have *no* such painful longings than to experience the feelings of shame and rejection that arise in tandem with them. But the difficulty inherent in this sweeping kind of solution—"Back off, don't feel things at all"—is that suppressing one's emotionality means getting rid of good feelings as well as bad ones. The analogy would be to the use of anesthetics while undergoing surgery: If one feels nothing, pain may be suppressed, but so is the ability to experience pleasure.

Henry Gifford had been on the cusp of the great changes of adolescence when his father returned from Korea; it was close to the time of his father's retirement from the armed forces, and Bill Gifford had come home to Thomaston, and to his family, a confirmed alcoholic.

Alcohol, and a Son's Pain

Many, many months later, Henry Gifford was to tell me how wrenching and difficult this first discussion of his early life had been for him.

"I hadn't looked back on my family, hadn't thought about them much at all. As far as I was concerned, it wasn't great—okay?—but it was long, long behind me. So much so that when I talked to you about all of that stuff, a lot of it was news to Toni and Antonia. Because I don't dwell on that kind of stuff, it's not on my mind ordinarily."

"It may dwell inside *you*, anyway," I risked saying; I felt pretty comfortable with him by then.

"It very well may," he answered evenly. The two of us were meeting by ourselves on that occasion, for what was to be one of our last interviews before the Giffords departed for Henry's new posting in Europe. "It probably *does* guide my life a great deal, but I block it out a great deal too; it's *painful*," he acknowledged suddenly.

He hesitated briefly, then added, "I don't want to *deal* with feelings, because I don't want to get hurt. I find that when I open myself up, I'm not quite sure what's going to happen."

I had, at that moment, been making a minor adjustment to my tape recorder, but I looked up to see that there were tears standing in his eyes; I jumped slightly. "Are you crying, Henry?" I asked him quietly, and he nodded. "A little bit. It's just that, when I open myself up about certain things, I could start to cry. It brings back certain things—it's kind of automatic. It's almost as if I'm a little boy again, and I don't *like* that feeling. You lose a little control, see, and it's that kind of response that I don't want to get out of hand." I nodded, acknowledging that I heard and understood what he was saying.

He was clearly moved, but also disconcerted and embarrassed. While confessing to these feelings was in some ways, as he then said, "a relief," it was in other ways uncomfortable and even "shameful."

But, when I asked him what was so *wrong* with a man's crying once in a while, he looked at me as if I'd asked him something bizarre. "It's just not something a man *does*," he stated flatly, looking at me as if I'd just arrived from the moon and he was trying to explain human life to me.

It was the way of the world, as far as he was concerned, a veritable rule of being: Truly masculine males didn't pay a great deal of attention to their inner worlds and very rarely, if ever, shared their private thoughts and feelings with anyone (although manly males might turn to drinking to relieve them). This was, it seemed to me, a powerful but covert rule of male behavior in both his and Toni's original families, and Henry was, as I could see, struggling valiantly to obey it.

Never mind what his own real thoughts and actual feelings might be: What a man was expected to think and feel was of far greater importance than what that man *did* think and feel at the moment! A short while earlier, when I'd talked to this macho naval officer about the brimming tears in his eyes, Henry had said in a subdued tone of voice, "There's a *lot* of them, there inside me." But that admission had been in clear violation of the extended family's rules, which decreed that men were not supposed to open up, share their inner thoughts and feelings, cry, make themselves vulnerable in any way whatsoever.

Such a sex-stereotypic vision of what the *right kind of male* should do, think, feel, and experience is omnipresent in the midrange family system, where, as Robert Beavers has observed, "there is great concern for rules and authority . . . [and] strong, silent males abound." At this level of family development (Level 3 on the Beavers Scale), abiding by the rules for thinking, feeling, and behaving is always viewed as far more important than is knowing what one's thoughts and feelings about a given issue actually *are* at any given point in time.

While there is, in these rule-bound, Level 3 families, neither incoherence nor chaos (as is seen in Level 5) nor a need for dictatorial control (as is seen in Level 4), the rules of the emotional system are so firmly in place that they seem to have taken over the system entirely. *The rules rule the system and everybody living within it.* Thus, these unwonted tears of Henry Gifford's were (as I think both of us knew) an aberration, completely out of bounds; and once his tears dried he would, I believed, put them out of his mind as quickly as he possibly could.

Walling Off the Pain

I'd certainly had no indication, when the topic of his father's drinking problem first arose, that Henry's recounting of his family's history was having so profound and unnerving an effect upon him. At that early stage of the interviews, he gave no hint that such was the case; most of our discussion was carried on in what seemed to be a relatively unemotional question-and-answer sequence. Henry Gifford was very much the naval officer, in complete self-command, and he answered each query briefly and straightforwardly, in an unruffled, neutral tone of voice.

He himself had, as he'd told me, become a high school football hero in his own time. Not only had he been a star football player, but he'd been the all-around leading athlete at the very same high school his dad had once attended. Of the three children in the Gifford family (he had a sister three years his senior and a brother eighteen months younger) only Henry had become the heroic male of his mother's dreams and aspirations; but there had been little or no closeness between them.

Why had that been so? He wasn't sure, Henry allowed, but he believed it had had a lot to do with the huge amount of turmoil in the household—most especially after his dad's return from his Korean tour of duty in the early 1960s.

"What is your fantasy about what got your dad's drinking problem going?" I asked Henry. "Do you have any hypothesis about it—any thoughts or ideas about what might have happened to him during that period of time when he was away?"

He looked at me, puzzled, as if such a consideration were none of his concern and indeed a completely foreign idea. "I never really thought about *why* he drank. I just have a great deal of resentment that he *did* drink, because by drinking he—he wasn't my friend."

"I'm still wondering if there was some incident in Korea," I said musingly, talking to him but also reflecting aloud. "Did you ever talk to your mother about that—ask her what her own theory about what had happened to your dad over there might be?"

He hadn't. Henry's voice remained even and expressionless, but his features seemed to have hardened. "I never discussed things like that with my mother—or with my father either, for that matter. An example of how much I *don't* discuss things, which is kind of revealing, is that after my dad died I was going through the family papers and discovered that my mother had been married before. My brother, it turns out, knew that, but it's not something I ever discussed with my mother. Those are the kinds of things—I don't get too personal—I don't touch on those kinds of things—"

He spoke in sentence fragments, but his message was a very clear and intelligible one. What I heard him saying was that he had managed to erect inner walls against "knowing," against thinking certain thoughts and having certain feelings—thoughts and feelings that, if he did permit them access to awareness, would be a source of intolerable pain and unresolvable inner conflict. Those internal partitions had once served a vital protective function; the only problem with such defenses is that they often remain in place long beyond their time of usefulness and prevent *new* information from coming in—for example, the news that things have changed, and it really is safe to come out now.

An Emotionally Detached, Prematurely Self-sufficient Little Boy

Henry was the middle of three siblings, and the older of the family's two sons. His sister, Marcy, three years his senior, had been married for almost twenty-five years, was in a "solid" marriage, and had children who were almost grown. She was, in her younger brother's view, a "very strong, together sort of person"; I asked him if he felt close to her.

"Marcy is a very admirable person," he answered evenly, "but no, we were never close." Glancing at his family's side of the genogram, I noted that there was only an eighteen-month age difference between Henry and his kid brother, Curtis (now thirty-eight). But when I inquired about his relationship to Curtis, Henry said that he felt no real connection to him either.

"It's so *interesting*," burst out Toni, at that point, "because the two sons have just that little age difference, a year and a half, between them. And Henry's mother will talk to Curtis about everything, but will talk to Henry about nothing at all. I mean," she added hastily, as if worried about offending her husband, "It's not exactly *nothing*—"

"I don't ask *her* about anything, either," Henry cut in to say, with an edge in his voice. I drew in a double line between Curtis and the mother,

Rosemary, to signify that this was a close relationship—indeed, it was the only close relationship that had appeared on Henry's side of the genogram thus far. Later on in the course of the interviews, this double line was to become the triple line that signifies "overclose relationship." Henry's mother and his brother shared a bond that was inappropriately intense— and, in this macho, military family, this younger brother was gay.

Henry did not know whether others in the family were aware of Curtis's homosexuality. His brother had confided the information to Toni's younger sister Diane, who had told Toni, who had told Henry; but the two brothers had never openly discussed it. The two of them never, reiterated Henry, discussed matters of a "personal" nature at all.

"Yes," continued Toni, "but it's so *interesting* how the pair of them are treated so differently—maybe because they respond differently, too. They're just total opposites." She had seemed uninvolved, but came alive suddenly around the emotionally significant issue of siblings who are utterly different kinds of people. I thought of her and her "more interesting" sister Diane, and of those other paired siblings, her dutiful, responsible mother, Antonia, and her dashing, high-stepping aunt Rita. It was as if both families of origin had located certain particular charged qualities in these sets of siblings in order that they might play out their different parts in the family's ongoing drama.

In the current instance, Henry's younger brother, Curtis, was the warm, sensitive brother (and his mother's confidant) while Henry was the stand-offish emotional distancer. With so absent a male figure in his own life, had Henry, as a young boy, feared that his own masculinity could be swallowed up if he let himself get too connected with a woman? Unlike Curtis, who had stayed close to the mother, Henry had established solid, if not almost impassable, interpersonal boundaries between himself and his female parent.

I tapped my pencil on his mother's name on the genogram. Then I looked at Henry and said, "If you were to give me a thumbnail description of Rosemary, how would you describe her?"

"She's a martyr," he answered coldly, without hesitating.

"Not at *all* a strong woman, like your older sister, Marcy?"

"No, she's always made the sacrifices for everyone else." His voice was disapproving. His mother had, he allowed, willingly supplied the "monetary goods" whenever asked, and had looked after him by washing his clothes, taking care of him, cooking his meals. "I didn't have to *do* anything," he explained, "and it was highly unusual for me to even participate in cleaning the house." Why did this sound like a list of complaints rather than a grateful account of the myriad ways in which his mother had been a nurturant, caring person and looked after him?

"So, even though you were growing up in a family in which your father was a—a not very approachable guy—it sounds as if you didn't much appreciate all of the sacrificing that your mother was doing anyhow. Is that right?"

"I *did* appreciate it," Henry contradicted me, with the same frosty reserve in his voice. At that moment, Antonia got up and looked into Laura's bassinet anxiously. "Should we wake her for her bottle?" she asked Toni. "She'll get up when she's hungry, never mind," her daughter replied.

"So, you appreciated the things your mom was doing—and yet I don't get a feeling that you felt close to her." No, Henry agreed, he didn't, not at all.

"How do you explain that? Here's somebody doing all these nice things for you . . . ?" He shook his head as if baffled and said, "Christ, *I* don't know how to explain it, do you?"

I didn't, but once again had the odd notion that he had found the thought of getting close to his mother a highly dangerous one, for reasons that weren't at all clear to me. And, at the same time, I found myself wondering whether *somewhere* in this chilly family galaxy there had been some star, however faint, that had cast its small glow upon the detached, prematurely self-sufficient little boy.

Disconnecting from the Hurting

I turned to his wife. "How do you explain all of this, Toni?"

"How do I explain him not being close to her?" She parroted my words, but merely looked at me blankly. Then she said apologetically, "I was just kind of spacing out here." I stared at her, dumbfounded; her attention had drifted elsewhere. It was as if she were responding to her husband's atypical openness and emotionality by turning an internal hearing aid all the way down to the Off position.

I turned back to Henry and asked him if his mother had ever tried to reach out to him, to engage with him in an emotional way.

"No, she didn't," he said, curtly, "but that's because *I* didn't want it, okay?" A southern inflection, at least in certain words, was becoming ever more pronounced as he spoke. "See, what you've got to understand is the way in which *I* disconnected from the family—and I *did*. I intentionally stayed out of the house as much as I could, because I didn't like being there—there was too much hurt going on."

He stopped, looked at me as if waiting for a response. "Tell me about that," I said, at last.

"The hurt was my father drinking, and my mother getting on his case about it. If I didn't have to be there, I didn't have to participate in that hurt, understand? So I was gone as much as I could be. From about fourteen years old on, I was *out* of there." He spoke firmly and decisively, but as before, the hurting that he talked about was not discernible in the tone of his voice. How had he managed to be out of there? I inquired.

"How was I doing that?" He repeated my question as if its answer ought to have been obvious to anyone. "I played *sports*. I played sports year 'round and didn't come into the house until seven o'clock at night. Then I got me a job and worked until nine o'clock, and on weekends I didn't have to be at home either, because now I had a job. Okay?" His southern accent was becoming ever broader as he talked on. "When I went out to college, I *went* out to college—I didn't come home. No, I did come home one summer, and I said, 'That's it, I ain't coming home no more; this is *not* good.'"

Henry Gifford had, it occurred to me, been the loyal son who becomes the football hero that his mother and father had certainly wanted. Indeed, his dad, stationed in Paris in the mid-1960s, had sent the rest of the family back to the States a year before his own return so that his boy could become the star athlete at the same high school that he himself had once attended. And yet, throughout his adolescence, the affirming echo of his parents' approval had been denied him; Henry's father had never even attended the games.

I asked him how his dad had tended to behave when he was drinking—how the fights about his drinking ordinarily began. "Would he go around being surly, or would your mother start the quarreling by trying to hide the liquor, or by lashing out and scolding him, trying to get him to stop?"

"She'd yell at him, mostly, but it wasn't that he was being mean or being abusive. When he'd get drunk, my dad would just fall asleep in a chair. I resented that, because it meant he wasn't *there* for me. When I played sports and stuff, he never came. . . . He wasn't there for me. I didn't *want* him there," he admitted immediately, "because I was afraid he might be a little—tipsy. So I didn't appreciate that."

"You never had the sense that your dad was a trusted ally, a buddy," I said.

"No, I'd just as soon he *not* be there," Henry replied stoutly, "because I was afraid he might embarrass me. He didn't ever truly do that, except maybe once. But . . ."

"But," I echoed him, and he continued.

"But there was always the potential."

His father had become the town football hero as the son of a bankrupt, impoverished farmer, and Henry had become the town football hero as the son of a drunk. As a tale of a boy's growing up and leaving home, the story that Henry Gifford was relating was a sad one.

A Loner and an Outsider

"It sounds as if you must have had your bags packed, emotionally speaking, for a very long time," I remarked quietly. "It sounds as if, coming from the place you came from, your way of dealing with things was to say, 'Don't bug me, I want out.' "

He didn't reply for several moments, but the expression on his face had softened, become thoughtful. "That's true, and also I had very few friends at the time. The two things are probably interconnected—one, that I disengaged from my family, two, that that carried over into my personal life, with other people. I had very few friends, too, because if you *have* friends, you leave them or if you don't, they leave you. Remember, being a military brat, I'd moved every two or three years, okay? And that's *hard.*"

I nodded. I found myself struck, at that moment, by his availability and by the degree of his self-awareness. "You felt like a perpetual outsider," I then said, and he nodded.

It had gotten even harder, he added, when the family stopped moving from one Army post to another Army post and settled down in his parents' hometown of Thomaston, Georgia. At that point, when Henry himself was about to enter high school, the Giffords had bought a house, the first they'd ever owned. But his mother had gone out and gotten a job; she was no longer at home when he came in after school. His father's posting was at a base in Atlanta, Georgia—more than an hour's travel from Thomaston—and when he *was* in the house, he was drinking and unavailable anyway.

As I sketched in this information, I could not fail to remark upon the odd fact that in this present generation there was also a dad working some distance from his family: Henry himself.

"*Now* I was in a small-town high school," he continued, "and I did make friends. But this was real different from a military environment, where it was *expected* that you'd move on every two or three years. Here, the kids would always be reminiscing about things that went on in elementary school—reliving things—and I felt out of place."

In a small town, I observed, you are either in or you're out; you are either one of the gang or— But Henry interrupted me before I could get to the end of my sentence. "I actually was 'in'; I was a very popular person; I played sports and I did well," he insisted. I didn't reply. But then he exhaled a sigh, said, "Okay, but I *did* feel very much an outsider."

"Lonely," I wrote on the genogram.

CHAPTER 17

Opposites Attract—or Are They Opposites? The Merging of Two Family Styles

Gazing down upon the details of the Giffords' emerging genogram, one couldn't fail to be struck by the vast differences between the emotional systems each member of this pair had come from. Henry Gifford's was a Southern Baptist, military background, and he had grown up in a family setting in which isolation and personal distance were the norm. Toni Baxter had been reared in a mixed Polish-English and Italian family (it was the Italian connection that counted) in which "privacy" and "separateness" were not only dirty words, but viewed as forms of betrayal. What could have attracted these two people, from such diametrically opposite kinds of family worlds, to each other in the first place?

Actually, such an "attraction of opposites" is a not infrequent romantic occurrence, and for the most obvious of reasons: Each member of the couple seems to be bringing into the relationship a wonderful dowry—which is to say, a piece of something that the other is missing. Toni must, for example, have seen in Henry the firm self boundaries in which she felt herself to be so lacking. *He* would never take an aspirin for a headache that was not his own; more likely, he would not even be aware of having any headache whatsoever.

Henry, for his own part, must have seen in Toni a person who had easy access to the inner world of feeling that he usually did his best to avoid and deny (because that had been his own family's way of dealing with such matters). He could warm his chilly toes and fingers at the fires of his partner's ready sociability and her emotionality. Such a couple ought, one would imagine, to live happily ever after; the edges of their inner puzzle pieces appear to fit together so perfectly.

At a very practical level, moreover, Henry could—as an officer in the Navy, whose career constraints would be sure to keep him on the move—help his wife in the difficult work of making the separation from a home base that was hard for anyone in her emotionally entangled system to leave. For clear, external reasons (no fault or act of treason on her own part) he would take her away from the magnetic twenty-mile radius in which her family existed; this understanding, in an armed services family, was an obvious part of the marital contract.

The Giffords had, in fact, lived in other parts of the country—and in Canada, too—for much of their married life. Their return to her family's orbit had occurred with Henry's final posting at the naval base on Governors Island, slightly less than two years before the time of our interviews. As I stared down at their family map, I wondered once again what had prompted them to opt for the difficult commuting arrangement in which they were currently involved. Was there emotional distance between the members of this pair (so that living near Toni's family had been more important to her than living with her husband), and had this been their way of dealing with it? It was certainly the case that the more Henry had opened up during this interview, the more Toni had seemed to tune him out.

The Lure of the Familiar

The His and Hers sides of the Giffords' genogram served not only to highlight the differences in the partners' family backgrounds, but to underscore the many things the members of the pair had in common. Both Toni and Henry had observed the unraveling of a marriage in remarkably similar circumstances, and both had been roughly eight years old when their fathers began trying to medicate and control their feelings by using alcohol. Both members of the couple had watched their disappointed, emotionally abandoned mothers berate their increasingly incompetent and disabled fathers in a maladaptive, doomed attempt to maintain some form of communication (even an angry one) with them. Toni and Henry had both been witnesses to the ending of a relationship in which two partners ultimately have nothing more to say to each other.

There were still other, subtler early life experiences that the Giffords, as a couple, shared. In a family of origin like Toni's, whose members are permitted to say anything and everything, it is often true that all can talk (or scream or yell) but that no one is actually listening. In a family of origin such as Henry's, nobody ever does much talking, and so nobody in this emotional system gets heard either. Thus, while their family backgrounds would appear to have been profoundly different—so much so that they would share no assumptions about familial life whatsoever—what *both* have learned, in their original systems, is that making oneself heard, and being understood as the person who one is, is an aspiration not to be dreamed of.

One of them has come from a setting in which the interaction never stops, and the other has come from a setting in which it never quite gets started; but at an emotional level, the basic relational precept that each internalized is a similar one: *You cannot make yourself heard, and therefore cannot get your needs met* is the fundamental belief they share, and the law that has been written into both partners' internalized family statutes. This is something that neither of these "opposites" realizes when they first meet and fall in love—a not uncommon kind of romantic pairing.

An important reason why these two find each other so attractive (at least initially) is that they do seem so wonderfully different. And they *are* different, in terms of their usual ways of being and relating—that is, what they know how to do well, and how they customarily behave. She has the ability to be emotionally expressive, for she has grown up in a family environment in which anyone can say anything at any decibel level whatsoever. He, who comes from the kind of family in which nobody can say anything meaningful or real, is enchanted.

She holds out the promise that he will be tutored in the language of feelings, get himself heard, and have his emotional needs legitimized and dealt with . . . at last. To her, he, too, holds out a wonderful kind of promise, for he isn't emoting at high pitch; he can be quiet and listen. He can hear her through to the end of what she has to say—something that never happened in her family of origin, where everybody was always highly vocal but no one was really being heard or responded to.

One can readily understand why each mate finds the other's ways of being and behaving such a source of hope and relief. These two fully expect to get together, create a system that will repair and make up for what was so fundamentally amiss in each of their original families, and then live harmoniously ever after. But, while the members of the couple do behave very differently from each other—and, indeed, each one does have a skill in which the other is deficient—the seeming differences between them exist at the level of behavior only. For, even though she is well able to talk expressively, and he is awfully competent at being quiet, at an emotional level they have a great deal in common.

Both of them subscribe to the family-wide belief that getting one's affective needs heard and gratified cannot possibly happen. In the emotional world with which each of them is so familiar, this kind of option for being in a close relationship simply did not exist. Intimacy—that is, *being able to say who one truly is, and what one really needs, and being heard by the intimate partner*—is simply out of the question. There was no option of this kind in either Henry or Toni's inner rulebook, and indeed the very prospect of getting close to someone else was something that *both* of them found terrifying.

Given that this is so, what tends to happen over time is that a person like Toni Gifford talks and talks until she comes to feel that her spouse is being silent but not really hearing her. She experiences this as a deep betrayal, for it is freighted with the emotional meanings of the betrayals that came earlier.

A person like Henry Gifford, on the other hand, truly more and more dismayed by so much unfamiliar emoting, often begins to speak less and less as his partner's impassioned demands on him seem to be increasing. He experiences her as engulfing; her powerful needs, he fears, will over-whelm him, swallow him up alive. The people in his own family of origin didn't share their feelings with one another because they experienced emotional closeness as too sticky, too dependent, and potentially painful.

The circumstances are ripe for the reemergence of the basic family tenet that each member of the pair brought to the relationship in the first place: *You cannot make yourself heard, and therefore cannot get your needs met.* This bedrock rule for relating will surely become the law of the marital realm and a model for the next generation—unless the partners come to recognize that there *are* other ways of connecting, other options for being in an intimate relationship.

But in the Level 3, midrange emotional world in which the Giffords seemed to belong, simply being who one actually is—and being heard, understood, and accepted by the intimate partner—seems like an impos-sible dream. This is why, at a very practical level, operational rules for thinking, feeling, and behaving are experienced as utterly necessary; it is the rules and regulations that will keep the emotional system well organized and running smoothly and efficiently—no matter how little those rules may actually have to do with what the people in the family really are thinking and feeling.

Disciplining Emily

It was toward the close of our discussion of Henry's early life in his family of origin that he mentioned that his grandmother (on the maternal side) had once told him how worried she'd always been by the bad whippings that his father had doled out. "She used to say that he spanked us quite severely; I don't remember it that well. I do remember his hitting me with a belt—not that I ever got real hurt," he said, shrugging the matter off. "But my grandmother *has* talked to me about how afraid this made her."

The whippings had ceased completely at the time that his father left for

Korea. "I stopped getting hit when I was about eleven years old—when he went off; that was it. He came back, and it didn't happen anymore." After Korea, I reflected, Henry's father seemed to have abdicated his familial role, including this form of negative connection to his child. Henry's dad had, in a real sense, *never* come home, because on his return to Thomaston he'd already begun drinking so heavily.

"Your brother, Curtis, once made the comment," said Toni to Henry, "that he remembers getting beaten so hard that he thinks he began to hallucinate." Henry shook his head, shrugged again, observed that he himself had never had such an experience.

I asked him if he himself had memories of his brother's being severely spanked, and the question seemed to strike Henry as an amusing one. "Dad gave whippings to *everybody;* you always got your turn. You know, if you screwed up, the belt came out." His mother had also "been known to give whippings with a belt," he added, in the same lighthearted, amused tone of voice. "That was part of discipline, and it's not uncommon down south. That's the way it is; you screw up, you pay the price. They're very strict; it's 'Yes, ma'am' and 'No, ma'am.' I don't think I had an unusual situation as far as punishment goes."

It was time to wind down and end today's interview, and I was about to do so when I noticed the disturbed expression on Toni's face. She was holding the baby, who had been fed and changed and was now fast asleep against her shoulder. "Any thoughts about this, Toni?" I asked her.

"Well—we *did* get hit as kids, in my family, but never by my father. He never hit us once. My mother was probably the one—I don't remember ever getting hit with a belt—she may have come after us with a wooden spoon, once or twice, but even that seems pretty severe, when I think of it." The thought of corporal punishment was clearly one that she found agitating.

"Henry says it wasn't only his family; it was part of the culture around them." I inclined my head in his direction, and he quickly nodded agreement. "That *is* the military culture," he said, "and that's the down-south culture and that's not unusual. I mean I don't have any scars or anything, not physical scars."

"None that we can see," I said, with a smile.

"Yes, those other scars may be there." He surprised me by replying in a serious tone of voice.

I took a deep breath and looked from Henry to Toni to Antonia, letting my gaze linger on each face for several moments (Emily was at a birthday party that afternoon). "Here we are and here we've *been* for a couple of hours," I said, "sitting and talking together very peaceably. But what, in this family, might be a hot topic—something that could have the people in this room running around and tearing their hair out in no time?"

The Giffords, including Toni's mother, jumped slightly and looked at one another quickly; then they all started laughing. "If you were looking for something that could occur—" began Toni. But Henry joined in at that moment, and I couldn't hear anything but the fragment at the end of her sentence, which was "—disciplining Emily."

"That's right, I was going to say that myself," Antonia said to her daughter eagerly. The introduction of this topic seemed to activate Toni's mother, bring her into a conversation that hadn't seemed to involve her overly much, thus far. Antonia was wearing gray today—a gray skirt and sweater—which harmonized well with her soft gray hair, but had the effect of muting her presence into the background. She leaned forward in her seat, and I waited for some further explanation, but the company had fallen momentarily silent.

"We have different views on that, at times," Toni said primly, at last. And what would her own views be? I asked her.

She had proposed the topic with relish, but now seemed hesitant to continue. "Probably, it's— I don't know." She looked at her husband nervously, then looked back at me. "Emily and I have a close relationship, and I don't believe in hitting. I believe in talking things out, and having a rationale for doing what you're doing. And Henry will come home on the weekends—" She halted for a moment, as if to get her bearings. "What happens then is typical," she concluded vaguely.

"Typical?" I shrugged, as if to say I didn't understand.

"Yes, I have control over her all week, and he doesn't. And then he comes home on the weekends, and wants to *be* in control, and there's no negotiation around that. My perception is that he gets agitated with her more easily, and is more likely to get real critical, and to hit her or use methods like that if he's not getting her to respond." Henry didn't do a whole lot of this, she hastened to add, but then went on to say: "If you want to know the hottest thing that would get me fired up, it's that." This statement suggested the existence of an emotional triangle.

Emotional Triangles: A Tense Twosome and a Third Party

Emotional triangles are, it will be recalled, relational patterns that basically involve a tense twosome (in this case, Toni and Henry) who bring a third party (seven-year-old Emily) into a disagreement going on between them. Triangles develop when a problem or issue that two people are having cannot be confronted, dealt with openly, and ultimately resolved—and children are often wonderful candidates for this third-party job.

As family theorist Murray Bowen has written, "the triangle is the smallest stable relationship system. A two-person system may be stable as long as it is calm, but when anxiety increases, it immediately involves the most vulnerable other person to become a triangle." In other words, when a problem that *two* people are having cannot be negotiated and settled, there is a natural tendency to draw an available third party into the field of play.

Triangling in the third person offers a means of deflecting or detouring, but in any case *lowering the intensity* of, the original conflict. If Toni and Henry Gifford were experiencing some real discomfort and disappointment in their own relationship, then arguing about how a child should be disciplined could help them to avoid facing the problem between them too directly or squarely.

It was not hard to imagine Henry, returning home after a week or two away from his family, feeling needy and famished for a kind of warmth and nurturance that he had never really had and still didn't know how to ask for (or receive). If Toni didn't meet his suppressed dependent needs, but went about her usual business of mothering Emily, one could readily comprehend the ways in which his own resentment and frustration would mount. He would find fault with his daughter and discipline her harshly, as a way of expressing the anger he felt toward the wife whom he experienced as ungiving and withholding (failing to meet those needs that he was experiencing, but certainly hadn't asked her to meet in any way that she could possibly understand and comply with).

By this means—getting into a harsh interchange with Emily—he could not only punish Toni but secure her total attention (however negative that attention happened to be). Triangling Emily into their relationship may have made life somewhat unpleasant, but it also made it far less likely that the emotional pressures in the couple's relationship would ever reach their boiling point; Henry was not attacking his wife directly.

It is in this way that family triangles serve both positive and negative functions. On the plus side, they keep the intimate pair's charged issues under reasonable control; on the minus side, they prevent the buildup of so much emotional energy and pressure that the couple feels forced to confront and deal with the basic conflict between them. Emotional triangles don't help to resolve problematic relational matters in a twosome, but they do help to stabilize them and to keep them relatively bearable.

In this particular instance, the husband-wife-daughter triangle in which the Giffords appeared to be embedded did commit Toni and Henry to a series of endlessly repeated skirmishes about how a child should be controlled and corrected. But their inability to collaborate about disciplining Emily focused their disharmony upon that subject and was, perhaps, helping them stave off other, more problematic battles—the *real* battles about what was happening in their relationship—which both of them unconsciously (or very consciously) feared. Were there (as I'd begun to suspect) some very real difficulties that the Giffords, as a couple, were experiencing at this time?

Another Common Family Triangle: Wife, Husband, Mother-in-Law

If she had seemed curiously abstracted during parts of the conversation about her husband's early life in his own family, Toni was vitally absorbed in the discussion we were having now. Her hazel eyes were wide, her cheeks flushed with the rosy color of annoyance, and when she spoke her voice was louder than it was ordinarily. "Another thing that happens is that my mother will hear me protesting and telling Henry, 'I don't like that,' and then she'll get all upset herself."

Another emotional triangle, this one involving the prior generation, was now becoming manifest. I turned to Antonia. "So then when *you* get upset, what do you tend to do—just talk to Toni about what's happening?"

Antonia drew back slightly, as if the question had struck her as an accusation. "I don't do anything; I try not to get involved," she responded at once.

But then, almost immediately, she amended that statement. "Come to think of it, one morning—it wasn't too long ago—I *did* get involved." She smiled one of her rare, unexpected smiles, and the three of them began laughing; everybody knew the incident to which she was referring. It had occurred within the past couple of weeks, when Emily was given a pair of new roller skates. Her father had set a rule to the effect that she was not permitted in the living or the dining room when she had those roller skates on.

"Emily was wearing her skates and she was looking for her daddy, and by mistake had put two feet inside that door." The grandmother gestured in the direction of the dining room. "So I said, 'Emily, you're not supposed to be in here.' Just then Henry saw her and he thought that she was skating in there, which of course she wasn't supposed to do. Then he tried to discipline her." Antonia shot a disapproving glance at her son-in-law, pursed her lips, and said nothing further.

I thought of the fiercely judgmental parents of Henry's childhood—not only his father but also his mother had hit him with a strap—whom he had internalized and who lived on inside him. The boy who had been whipped when he "screwed up" carried within him a picture of a relationship between a misbehaving child and a morally entitled, rigidly authority-enforcing parent. In the present situation, it was he who was the stern figure in command.

Thus it is that in certain familiar, demanding situations, our old parental scenarios are activated. Henry would require of Emily the same flawless, exemplary behavior ("Yes, ma'am" and "No, ma'am") that had been required of him. "So did he discipline her by spanking her?" I inquired of Antonia.

She shook her head; he had not, on this occasion. "I just took off her new skates," Henry explained, "and told her they were being put away— and of course she went ballistic, started hollering and screaming."

"You'd have thought he was *murdering* her," said the grandmother, "and I just couldn't take the screaming, so I started screaming at *him*. I said, 'Henry, leave her alone!' And he said to me, 'I'll take care of this; don't you get involved.' But I felt so *bad* for her, because it really wasn't her fault. She was just looking for him, and he happened to walk through at that time; she wasn't disobeying, not really." Antonia's voice had risen indignantly. What had been a humorous memory of a moment earlier was no longer anything funny; she was rearguing Emily's case quite seriously.

"This kind of thing can be hard on Antonia," Henry said to me, in an equable, reasonable tone of voice. "She'll hear Toni and me trying to discipline Emily, and of course she hears all the crying and the yelling and resentment. It's a ticklish situation, because of course she—having raised a family—wants to give us advice. But at the moment that something is happening, we're not necessarily being receptive."

"Not at the moment, no," Antonia murmured coldly.

As Henry described the typical sequence of events, it was he and his wife who were allies in disciplining their child. The pair of them were correcting Emily together; the outsider and disapprover was his mother-in-law. But Toni herself had characterized the situation somewhat differently earlier, when she'd suggested that it was she and Henry who were on opposite sides of the net when it came to the subject of discipline.

I turned to her; she had been silent throughout this interchange. "Do you have something to add to the discussion?" I asked.

"Not really," she replied. There was a sense of something edgy and unresolved in the air.

A Family Rule About Women and About Men

I asked Toni whether, in the aftermath of a family blowup, the lid was just put right back on the problematic matter immediately. Or did differences tend to be negotiated and resolved in such a way that people understood what had happened and felt fairly satisfied about how that issue would be handled in the future? "No, I don't really think much gets negotiated," she answered uneasily.

"It may get negotiated, but it doesn't get resolved," said Henry. I was about to ask him to elaborate upon that statement when Antonia said flatly, "The lid gets put back on."

"I don't think it *is*," Henry put in swiftly, a statement whose actual meaning was unclear to me. There was a brief silence. "Well, I do tend to pull back after one of these things," he admitted, as if this last remark had been challenged. "Antonia tends to pull back a bit herself—and I appreciate that. Sometimes even Toni will pull back, so usually we don't process things at all; it just sort of goes away after a while."

I smiled. "And then it pops out again?"

Henry shrugged lightly. "It pops out again, because it's bound to. It's part of my quirky makeup, I imagine. Toni would like to change me in a number of ways; she'd like me to process things with her a little bit better." He looked hurt yet sulky, like a little boy who would like to please the grown-ups but at the same time cannot endure the humiliation of giving ground. "And sometimes I try to process things with her, but it doesn't work out too well. So I pull back pretty fast."

Henry was used to being the family outsider, and he knew well how to disengage. I glanced at his wife, and was struck by the sad expression on her face. "What do you think, Toni?" I asked her, and she sighed, shook her head.

"I think he said it pretty much like it is. I myself think we should do more—and *could* do more—and I would *like* to do more communicating around that issue, and have the same expectations. I mean, what to expect of a child and how to raise a child—we should *talk* about that. And I would like to, but it just doesn't happen." She raised both her arms, palms outward, in the universal gesture of prayer and supplication.

I had closed the sketch pad on my lap, but now I opened it again. "I have a notion," I said, my gaze cast down on the Gifford family's genogram, "that during the week, when Henry's away, there's a kind of silent understanding between Toni and Antonia. I have the idea that they're in pretty much full agreement about the ways in which Emily should be disciplined. And then, when Henry comes home on the weekend, there's suddenly this big, exciting daddy around, and Emily gets pretty steamed up and starts testing the limits." As they watched, I traced out the shape of a Toni-Antonia-Henry triangle with the tip of my forefinger, but said nothing about it aloud. I was trying to indicate, without words, that there was something happening among the three of them; Toni stared at me, eyes widening and then nodded.

"That's right, Emily *does* get pretty testy," she said, her voice brightening as if I'd said or done something that had made her feel understood or recognized. Then, after a moment's thought, she added, "I liked that comment you made, too, about a 'silent understanding' between myself and my mother—because this is something I've thought about a lot. Wishing, I mean, that I could have that with Henry—and not only relating to discipline. It's just a sense of being on the same wavelength."

If, she explained, she saw a mess in the kitchen, she would clean it up; if her mother saw it, then her mother would take care of it. Very little discussion was necessary: "It's a feeling of being in sync about what's happening," said Toni. "But with Henry—" She stopped, then restarted her sentence at the beginning. "With Henry, it sometimes seems as if we're on totally different wavelengths about almost everything."

Taken aback, I glanced at him swiftly, but he seemed curiously unshaken by what he had heard. I looked down at the Giffords' genogram again.

Toni, like the other women in her family, was having trouble making an intimate connection with a man. Also, as far as Aunt Rita was concerned, it was clear that no matter how much overt admiration Toni might express for her aunt's self-absorbed, self-gratifying approach to life, it was Antonia to whom she was most deeply, if covertly, loyal. *As a mother*, Toni wanted to be just the same as her own mother, and experienced herself as being so—as on the same wavelength pretty much all of the time.

In this domestic triangle involving a wife, a husband, and a maternal grandmother, it would expectably have been the marital pair who were the closest allies and most committed life partners. But clearly it was the two women who were the real intimates—the ones "in sync"—and it was Henry who seemed to be the odd man out.

Such a highly independent, emotionally isolated position was, of course, the one he had assumed very early in his life in order to avoid getting involved in his parents' hurting and their troubles. It was a position with which he was highly familiar, and yet I wondered how he really felt about it.

In any case, it seemed fairly evident that a powerful rule was at play within the Giffords' wider emotional system, a rule about the ways in which females could relate to males, which was making itself felt very strongly all the way down through the decades. It was a rule to the effect that women should be extremely leery about ever getting involved with men, because a man would surely let a woman down and bring her grief if she ever allowed herself to become vulnerable, open to him, trusting, and truly connected. This was what made a disengaged, somewhat isolated male such an attractive proposition to the females in this familial world: Such a man would never challenge a woman to become truly intimate with him (he'd prefer alcohol or some other form of escape) because he wouldn't want to be intimate himself.

An Idyll in the Azores

It was not until my next meeting with the Giffords (I was interviewing the couple alone, this time) that I talked with Henry Gifford about that period of his young adulthood when he'd first met and fallen in love with his wife. "What things about her first attracted you to Toni? I mean, what were the particular qualities that drew you to her?"

Henry hesitated, looking disconcerted, and Toni laughed her nervous little social laugh.

After a few moments, he said, "I felt comfortable with Toni. She was a person I felt I could be close to. She was just *fun* to be around." If the words themselves were not conspicuously romantic, the expression on his face had become dreamy, as if he'd been transported to a world of remembered happiness.

I smiled and asked him to name a couple of the things he'd liked about her in addition to the fact that he felt comfortable with her. "Tell me a little more about the Toni that you met, and the qualities she had that made her feel like someone special to you." Toni laughed again, sounding embarrassed. She had been intent on watching the baby drain her bottle, but now gazed across at her husband intently.

"Her qualities," Henry repeated my words thoughtfully. "It was her openness. It was the strong physical attraction we had to each other. And we didn't seem to play games—emotionally, I mean—so that it was just different from the way it was with other girls. Still," he added, "when I left the base in Maine—which was where we'd met; Toni worked in a nearby hospital—I thought that was pretty much it. I went to Spain, and I didn't think I'd ever see Toni again."

I was surprised by the ease and finality with which he had disconnected, at that point, and the colorless tone of voice in which he now described it. "So there was no lightning flash, no sense of 'Aha, this is the person'?" I asked.

He shook his head, "I wasn't in love with her," he said flatly. At that moment Toni shifted Laura to her shoulder in the traditional burping position, but kept her gaze fixed upon her husband. I thought she looked hurt, but perhaps only because I myself would have been.

"So, then—what changed?" I asked him.

"What changed?" He repeated my words, as he had before, then paused, looking thoughtful. "After I left, Toni got in touch with me again, and we corresponded for a while," he resumed. "I came back to the States over the Fourth of July, and I went to see her. I was approaching a point in the Navy where I could get out if I wanted to, but I'd been asked to stay in. Toni wasn't working at that time, and I was going to an island in the Azores, so I invited her to come along with me. She accepted, and it was only after living closely with her during that time frame that I fell in love with her. Because she was such a nice person," he added, his voice growing husky.

I glanced at his wife, expecting her to join him in the evocation of a special time of their courtship, but she didn't. The two of them had lived together in just two tiny rooms, Henry was recounting, with "the same little bed, and we were with each other constantly. She was just real nice to be around," he said, looking moved once again.

"And that's when you decided to get married?" I prompted, but he shook his head. "It wasn't then, it was after she left. She'd gone back to the States just a couple of weeks before I did, and in that time without her I felt terribly lonely. I didn't like that at all, so when I got back I asked her to marry me. And she did," he concluded on a note of self-satisfaction. He was, nevertheless, sounding choked. There were tears in his voice, and his eyes were glistening.

"How does it make you feel to talk about it now?" I asked him quietly.

"Somewhat emotional," he acknowledged, as if admitting to a fault.

"Yes," I said, "I thought that I might've seen tears in your eyes. . . . Which part of the story are the tears about?"

Henry shrugged. "Just all of the emotions associated with that time. There's nothing about the story itself that makes me weep—it's just that it's an emotional story."

What I'd actually been asking, I explained, was which particular emotion he was feeling, and which part of the story it was connected to. "Are you feeling sad or happy or nostalgic for that idyllic time—wishing it were still the same way between you and Toni now?"

"Oh, no," said Henry quickly; he was feeling happy more than anything else. I glanced at Toni, whose face wore a somewhat irritated expression. "What are you thinking about?" I asked her.

"I'm perplexed about the emotional piece of it," she replied. I wasn't sure what she meant. "You're perplexed?" I shook my head as if to say I didn't quite understand. "By which you mean to say 'surprised'?"

"No, not surprised, but perplexed—that he could say that it's a happy feeling that he's so upset about. That piece doesn't fit for me," she objected.

"In what ways doesn't that particular piece fit for you?" I asked her, stealing a quick glance at Henry, who seemed to have snapped to parade attention and whose expression had become impassive.

Toni shifted the baby from her shoulder to her lap, then wiped milk from Laura's lips with a clean white diaper. "Oh, that one would get upset about a happy feeling. I don't see Henry getting upset—I mean, he hardly ever *gets* upset—so to me it would seem more associated with a painful feeling than anything happy." She was disturbed, it seemed to me, by his unaccustomed display of open emotionality. It was as if he were disobeying a fundamental rule of their relationship, which was that she was the member of the couple with the feelings and he was the member of the couple committed to maintaining personal space and creating distance between them.

"But then again," Toni continued, "maybe he just can't connect with the painful feelings, because his ability to deny and block is tremendous."

"To deny and block," I echoed her cool, devaluing words back to her slowly.

"I mean, this could just be my own view," she backtracked guiltily, "and I of course don't really know for sure. But for me, getting teary-eyed and upset over a happy memory—that just doesn't fit." Instead of eagerly joining Henry in the joyful recollection of their island sojourn, Toni Gifford had become annoyed and critical. Did she feel that her husband was encroaching upon what was customarily her turf in the relationship they shared?

I turned to him and said, "Let me ask you something, Henry. If you *did* have any sad feelings connected with this very poignant memory of that time, what would they be?"

He answered, without hesitation, "Oh, the deep bonding that went on there," and I felt not only his sadness, but the sudden haze of wistful longing and of sorrow that had descended upon both members of the pair. Toni was, at one and the same time, pursuing her partner for intimacy, and warding off each and every move toward intimacy that he made—for in her own inner world, what she *knew* was that getting close to a man could only cause pain, and was in any case, a thoroughly terrifying, untenable idea.

The Competent Nurturer of a Needy Male

Looking down at Henry's side of the genogram, where disconnection and estrangement seemed to be the norm, it occurred to me that the intense intimacy that he and Toni had shared during their stay in the Azores must have been a thoroughly novel experience for him.

"I am thinking, Henry," I said musingly, without looking up, "that this whole time when the pair of you lived so closely in those two little rooms, and were together all the time, sounds like nothing that you'd ever had before in your lifetime."

"I never really thought about it, but yes, that's partly true," he answered guardedly.

Picking up on the word "partly" I said, "Or perhaps you *did* experience this kind of closeness much earlier in your life, long ago—maybe in a time that's lost to memory now. But it sounds as if these feelings of—of real human connection were something you'd been struggling along without for a very long time."

"Yes, but it wasn't anything that bothered me or that I missed," Henry objected, "because it wasn't anything I was thinking about most of the time." This time however, his voice did sound pained, even if it was a pain he was unwilling to admit to in words.

I turned to Toni, asked her how it made her feel to see Henry so moved by the memory of their idyllic stay on that island base. She shrugged her slender shoulders and hesitated before replying. "It makes me feel kind of sad," she said slowly, "that he didn't have that experience—that closeness—when he was growing up. That's pretty hard to have to reflect back onto and acknowledge. And I feel sorry for him, too—that it was that way for him."

Her voice was low and, at that moment, empathetic. But then she went on to say, "I suppose, if I were to look at my own role in this, I'm in a helping profession. And maybe part of the attraction was to fill in for him that piece that he didn't have, because it was just *easier* for me. It's *always* been easy for me to be in a position of providing—of taking care."

What she was saying was that her spouse had come into this relationship with a basic lack within himself, and that their unconscious contract had involved her trying to supply what he needed, in terms of warmth, emotionality, and closeness.

I reflected upon the fact that Toni's mother had, in her own time, been the competent nurturer of a disadvantaged male. Antonia had raised the children and overseen the family's business interests, saving what could be saved during the crucial decade when her husband, Tom, had been drinking and becoming increasingly ineffectual. Toni's sense of Henry as needful and incomplete had, perhaps, made him seem a safer and more reliable potential partner. She knew how to provide for this kind of male, and he was someone with whom she was deeply familiar.

"What other things about Henry attracted you, when you were first getting to know each other?" I asked her, then smiled and added lightly that she had been the one who was the pursuer, and it was she who had gotten into contact with him after he'd left his station in Maine. Toni laughed, but then answered seriously, "He was a very, very responsible person. He seemed like a trustworthy person, he was established, he was moving on with it, and he was a gentleman. We seemed to communicate well—a lot of things seemed to click. He was very much a gentleman," she said approvingly, "and that was something I really admired."

Henry looked pleased. "Toni had only been out of college a short time, and I'm three years older—I wasn't going to treat her like a college girl," he said.

"He was very polite, very socially poised; he treated me like a woman," Toni continued. I asked her to elaborate upon what "treating her like a woman" had actually been like, in terms of his behavior. "He opened the door for me" was all that came to her mind. I had a sudden vision of her father gallantly opening the door for sexy Aunt Rita while the rejected Antonia, and Phil, Rita's husband, trailed reluctantly behind them. A real woman, in Toni's view, received such gentlemanly homages and attentions.

"I was twenty-seven years old," continued Henry, "and the fact of the matter is that there's a great deal of difference between what you do in college and how you behave in later life. I didn't date college girls after leaving college, and professional women expect to be treated in a certain way. So I didn't even think about that—I treated her as a professional woman," he said proudly.

"Yes, right," Toni seconded him, then shifted the baby on her lap. Laura had started whimpering, but not urgently. "What is it that you want, miss?" the mother asked her, leaning over to nuzzle her neck. "You can't be hungry again." Henry, watching them, leaned so far forward on the love seat that he had to hold on to the edges of the long cushion beneath him in order to maintain his balance. He looked as if he were about to spring across the small space that separated him from his wife and baby daughter, or as if he were already joined with them in his imagination.

A Way of Dealing with the Threat of Abandonment

Gazing down upon my ever more elaborate map of this pair's extended emotional system, I found myself lingering, with a sense of fascination, upon the correspondences on the Hers and the His sides of the family genogram. Both members of the couple had grown up as witnesses to a male-female relationship in which the adult mates had eventually had nothing good (or nothing at all) to say to each other. Toni had been the oldest offspring, and Henry the older male offspring, of a mother who'd been perceived as a self-sacrificing martyr—a style of child-rearing that places a heavy burden of guilt upon the youngster, who comes to feel deeply complicit in and responsible for the parent's sufferings.

Both partners were also the children of alcoholic dads, and their fathers' alcoholism had emerged at roughly the same point in their childhoods. I remarked upon all of these things aloud, adding that it was no wonder that the pair of them had, as Toni had said, "seemed to communicate well" at the outset; they'd had so much in common.

"Yes," put in Toni eagerly, "and the drinking problem was, I think, something we had—it was one of the things we connected around, in the beginning." She had seated Laura on her lap, facing outward, and was now holding her arms outward and jiggling her as she spoke; the baby looked mollified and contented for the moment.

At the time when their relationship was forming, I continued, it sounded as though both had been well able to communicate, and to share their common experiences. But now, I added somewhat tentatively, I had the impression that they seemed to be complaining of a certain inability to do their emotional laundry by talking things over and processing the issues between them. Was this impression accurate, I asked, and if it was, what had happened to change things? I had directed the question at no one in particular; it was Toni who answered.

"That's interesting; it seemed to happen over time. I think it was partly the result of my going on to do what I wanted to do in terms of my own career; that seemed to create a big difference. He didn't want me to go to work." I thought immediately of what Henry had said a short while earlier—that he'd experienced the good years of his early family life as having ended around the time when his mother got a job. Toni's going out to work had perhaps been experienced as a second, and similar, abandonment.

I turned to him and said, "It sounds as if your becoming a latchkey child felt to you like a big turning point in your life. And I wonder if perhaps Toni's starting work felt to you like a huge potential loss—that you could lose your beloved partner, your special woman, in the same way that you'd lost her before."

"I never *thought* such a thing," Henry objected.

I shrugged, said somewhat apologetically that it had merely been a sudden notion that I'd had, something that had flashed through my mind at that moment.

"But I suppose," he amended slowly, in a tone of bemusement, "that it could very well have led me to make the same kind of response I'd made in the past. Which was the response of disengagement."

Henry Gifford was, it seemed to me, a man who would have kept his emotional bags packed at all times; detaching himself from a threatening situation was a strategy with which he was highly experienced. Faced with the internal threat of desertion, it was not at all unlikely that he would do what he'd always done before: tune out; disengage affectively.

One way (a very commonplace way) of dealing with the fear of being stranded emotionally is to be the one who does the emotional withdrawing first. If, at one time in his life, he himself had felt abandoned, he was henceforth always poised and on high alert to initiate any necessary action himself. Such a life attitude may have left him feeling somewhat lonely, completely on his own, but at least it *did* leave him feeling in control.

The Demands of Intimacy

Laura, getting tired of being bounced on her mother's lap, had begun voicing objections again. "She's almost ready for her nap," said Toni, turning the baby, holding her in her arms cradle style, and humming for a few moments.

But she didn't excuse herself to go and put Laura upstairs in her crib. Toni seemed intrigued by this conversation about Henry's "response of disengagement" and the link between the present and his past. "This is really interesting, because I remember our first year of marriage," she began eagerly, then turned to her husband as if asking his permission to continue; he shrugged, as if to say she could.

There had been a time, about six months after they were married, when Henry had felt uninterested sexually, and totally turned off. "He just wasn't sexually attracted to me anymore," said Toni, "and I remember trying to find out—you know—what's going *on* here." The words were accompanied by a wounded, embarrassed little laugh. "And I kept prying . . . I kept prying, and finally he blurted out the strangest comment. He said, 'You're here all the time. You're sort of like a mother, in a way.' Which I took to mean that the infatuation was gone. This was a real hurt to my ego, but I *do* remember him saying that."

For her this must have been the worst of histories repeating itself. Being rejected as a sexual partner must, I thought, have touched off a series of associative explosions deep within her: How cruelly similar it was to the abandonment she had already seen her mother experience. To the extent that Toni was highly identified with her mother, making herself vulnerable to a man would not have been easy in the first place. If she had succeeded in doing so, early in the relationship, then Henry's powerful sexual recoil must have been experienced as the awful (yet somehow expected) punishment for ever having expected anything to be different.

But what was his own explanation for the fact that he'd abruptly lost all sexual interest in the middle of their first year of marriage? "Do you have some idea, now, of what that was about?" I asked him. He shook his head; he didn't. There was a long silence, which I broke by murmuring that curious comment—"You're sort of like a mother"—aloud, but in a muted, reflective tone of voice. It occurred to me that if having sex with your wife becomes unconsciously linked to feelings about your mother, then intercourse could be experienced as something much akin to incest.

"I didn't think of her as a mother," Henry said now. "I just had no minimal desire. I don't know what it was; I was just not *moved.* That was really strange for me," he hastened to add, "because that's not the case with me, most of the time." He glanced at his wife swiftly, as if appealing to her for confirmation of the normality of his sexual appetites. She blinked rapidly several times, but didn't respond otherwise.

When I asked him what had made that period of sexual disinterest end, Henry said he couldn't remember. It hadn't taken very long, he assured me, and Toni began to laugh. "What are you laughing about?" I asked her. "That comment that it didn't take too long," she said ironically, rolling her eyes heavenward.

"Hey, I was back to chasing you around the house before we left the base at Newport," Henry objected with a laugh. She didn't answer.

"All of this must have been pretty bruising for you," I said to Toni quietly, and she nodded. But when I asked her for her own theory about what had been happening at that time, she had no clear idea. She did blurt out a few fragmentary suggestions: They, like other couples, had gone through a series of stages in their relationship; there had been an infatuation, and they'd married; then there had been a certain recoil. Her voice sounded hesitant and unsure.

"Did you feel that sense of recoil yourself?" I asked her.

Toni shook her head. "I didn't really, not then, but as time went on there *were* things that made me pull back. We couldn't really communicate—that became obvious. For the first few months I'd stayed at home, and I thought, 'Well, I'm going to cook him these good meals.' But then he'd come home from work, and we would sit at the table and there wouldn't be that much to say. I guess I wanted some positive reinforcement, such as 'This is a good meal, honey.' But I remember sitting there watching him eat the meal, and then he'd go and sit in front of the TV. That's all there was, and my feeling was 'Oh, my God.' " Toni's voice had taken on a complaining, sing-song quality. The baby, in her arms, was now sleeping peacefully.

"After a while I began working, and I'd come in and want to talk about my day, but it was clear he really didn't want to hear about it. Then, too, I wanted to go out with my friends from work, but he didn't want me going out with my friends from work," she said resentfully.

Henry had insisted upon her presence while he, at the same time, maintained the huge amount of interpersonal space to which he was accustomed. I wondered if he had shorted out sexually as a way of making his intimate partner back off. Six months into the marriage, he might have been finding this much intimacy somewhat hard to bear.

I said, "It sounds to me, Henry, as if one of the things your earlier experiences had taught you was how *not* to stay too close to anybody for any length of time. So it must have felt a bit strange, early in the marriage, having another person around you so much—a person who was 'like a mother, there all the time,' and also liable to ask for intimacy at any given moment."

"That's probably true," he responded, meeting my gaze with soldierlike directness. "Even today, the demands of intimacy are hard to take."

CHAPTER 18

Alcohol and the Family

Henry Gifford's rank in the Navy—that of lieutenant commander—must, I reflected, have been superior to the highest Army rank (sergeant major) that his father had ever attained. And in the wake of our extensive discussion of Henry's boyhood, I'd been thinking about the competitive feelings that can spring up between a son and his father. During today's interview, with just the couple, their two-month-old baby, and myself in attendance, I asked Henry if, before his father's death, this obvious difference in status had ever been an issue between them.

"Sergeant major . . . for a lifetime career, that's not great, is it?" I observed somewhat dubiously, and Henry reared back in his seat, as if unpleasantly startled.

"No, it's *tremendous*," he retorted quickly. "It's *very* prestigious, and not many guys get that far. In the service, see, you can do it one of two ways. You can either be an officer or you can be an enlisted man. The qualifications for being an officer are that you must have a college degree—if you *don't* have a college degree, you're not an officer."

"And your dad didn't have one, I suppose," I said.

"My dad didn't have a college degree." He nodded. "But it was a very prestigious rank," he stated again, almost chidingly. At the same time Henry seemed to be evading my eye, and was looking oddly stiff and uncomfortable. I didn't understand.

"So you'd say that your dad was pretty much *pleased* with where he got to be, in his career—that he felt proud?"

"Yes, he did," replied Henry, sitting bolt upright, shoulders high, stomach sucked in, as if at attention. Still, wasn't it true, I asked, that his own current prospects, as a lieutenant commander in the Navy, were vastly different from what his father's had been? "In terms of moving upward, you're in a whole other ball game, aren't you?"

Henry shook his head. "I *am* an officer, a senior officer, but I'm not going anywhere else in the Navy. I get out, in less than three years, as a lieutenant commander." The note of reproof in his voice was becoming ever more distinct. He seemed to be resisting the idea that he'd outstripped his parent in any way whatsoever, as if the very suggestion made him highly uncomfortable.

As male contenders in the game of life, adult sons frequently do find it difficult to remain at ease with the disparities of success and failure that may exist between themselves and their fathers. When a son clearly outperforms or outranks (as in Henry's instance) his own father, he will often become vulnerable to the unconscious fantasy of not only provoking rivalrous rage in the male parent but of losing the "internal father's " love, to whatever extent it may live on inside him.

Obviously, once in the grips of such an unconscious assumption, the more the son succeeds in the world, the more his internal relationship with the father (the good, loving dad within) feels threatened, under siege. And in truth, unless the older man has been secure and self-confident himself—personally invested in, and well able to identify with, his son's achievements—both of them may experience the growing son's advances (especially those that surpass the older man's) as akin to a destructive attack upon the parent.

But in the opposite kind of situation—when a son is strikingly *less* successful in his career than his father has been—things aren't really demonstrably easier either. For even though the son in question may love his father deeply, he will still experience himself as being in a somewhat discomfiting, or perhaps even unbearable, one-down position. In some instances he may even feel that he has been completely defeated by his overpowerful parent, and is thus not fully competent to assert himself as a male. In short, when it comes to the impact of success and failure on their mutual relationships, adult sons and their fathers always exist (or so it seems to me) in an unavoidably intricate and somewhat precarious balance.

A Somewhat Ominous Life Transition

I was taken aback, if not mildly alarmed, on learning that Henry Gifford, a healthy man still under the age of forty, would soon become a retiree. "What do you think you'll do after leaving the Navy?" I asked him.

Henry shrugged. "Get a job. Doing what, I don't know. I have applied to graduate school for information management systems, because I happen to like playing around with computers." He sounded vague.

I turned to his wife and said, "So you're going to be married to a graduate student, Toni?"

She jumped slightly; once again, her thoughts had been elsewhere. "Oh, I don't know, is that what you said?" she asked her husband absently.

"I've got to get a job doing something," Henry continued, "and the fact of the matter is that most of the officers do different things when they get out—such as become a contractor who works for another contractor who sublets for the Navy for various projects. Some guys sell houses, a lot of guys sell insurance. . . ." He sounded more and more dubious as he spoke. "It's whatever you happen to fall into," he told me.

The life transition that loomed ahead of him would, it seemed to me, affect him and his family in ways that none of them had yet fully recognized or realized. For as the child of a military man who had then spent his own young adulthood in the armed forces, Lieutenant Commander Henry Gifford was totally used to the predictability that life in the services provides.

This predictability is, in a certain real sense, a form of parenting in disguise. For in the military setting, a person is told what time to get up, exactly what to wear, when to take each meal, what tasks must be accomplished during the day, what time to go to sleep, and who are the people in authority. Everything one needs to do is made explicit, as is the relationship of each individual in the hierarchy to each other individual in the hierarchy. One could not reproduce the situation of childhood in a more precise and accurate fashion. As Dr. Kent Ravenscroft, a psychoanalyst who has worked extensively with a military clientele, has observed, "Instead of parents, there are clear-cut *rules* of the organization—rules which tell you exactly what to do, and when and how it must be done."

Thus, despite its overt emphasis upon masculinity and independence, life within the military world is structured in such a way as to meet many covert needs of a highly dependent nature. And the loss of that institutionally mothering embrace was, it seemed to me, going to force Lieutenant Commander Gifford to pose many life questions to himself very suddenly. "Do you ever give any thought to reenlisting?" I asked him.

Henry shook his head decisively. "In the *Navy*—no. I will get out in twenty years, and for regular commissioned officers, there isn't any such thing as reenlisting." He could not, he explained, remain in the service if he wanted to, and in any case, he didn't.

I looked at Toni, who still seemed abstracted, and said, "He couldn't stay in if he wanted to, and yet he's been in the military for almost his entire lifetime. Won't it be strange for him?" I asked her.

She jumped slightly, said vaguely, "Oh . . . what do *I* think?" I stared at her, taken aback once again by her curious way of spacing out. Her life partner was discussing matters that were vital not only to herself but to all of them, and yet her mind had gone meandering elsewhere. She just didn't seem to be emotionally present.

"What were you just thinking about?" I asked her. Toni shrugged lightly, laughed her ready laugh, then said casually, "Oh, that it probably *will* be weird, getting out. Because there's been so much structure in the Navy, and the office environment is kind of similar wherever in the world you happen to be—in terms of what you wear to work and what you do there, and of how you socialize in the office, and so forth."

Henry regarded her thoughtfully, then conceded that social relationships in a military setting probably were vastly different from those in "regular" offices. "The military does provide structure," he said. "It does provide somewhat of a cocoon; big organizations do that." However, it was his belief that—aside from the strictly social aspects of office life—most things would not be that different once they had left the Navy and entered the world outside. Toni looked at him skeptically, but didn't actually respond.

A Study of Adopted Boys: The Intergenerational Transmission of Alcoholism

How serious was the risk that Henry Gifford, the biological son of an alcoholic father, would himself develop problems with alcohol at some stressful point in his lifetime? Actually, Henry's chances of developing a drinking-related disorder were some three to five times higher than those of the son of a nonalcoholic parent. Although the genetic mechanisms involved are far from well understood, there is stronger evidence for the intergenerational transmission of alcoholism than there is for any other form of psychiatric disturbance.

The fact that alcoholism often runs in families has been recognized for centuries; Aristotle, Plato, and Plutarch were among the ancient Greek writers who noted the existence of a strong tendency for the drinking behavior of children to resemble that of their parents. But until the recent past the influence of genetics and the role played by environment (the alcoholic parent's behavior obviously sets a powerful example) proved difficult to tease apart. It is only within the last two decades that solid data supporting the existence of a link between heredity and vulnerability to alcoholism have appeared in the scientific literature.

The most compelling evidence for such a linkage comes from a series of adoption studies carried out in Scandinavia, the first of which was published in 1973. This landmark investigation, led by alcohol researcher

Donald W. Goodwin, M.D., created an elegant new model for sorting out the differential effects of heredity and environment in the eventual development of pathological drinking.

The Goodwin team selected as their study subjects a group of male Danish adoptees who had been separated from their biological parents before the age of six weeks. The boys had been adopted in the Copenhagen area sometime between 1924 and 1947, and most members of the sample—some 60 percent of them—were around thirty years of age when the research project got under way.

The Goodwin project was, it should be mentioned, a joint American and Danish effort. The U.S. researchers were Dr. Goodwin, Samuel B. Guze, M.D., and George Winokur, M.D.; the Danes were Fini Schulsinger, M.D., and Leif Hermanson, M.D., both of Copenhagen. The advantages of using a Danish sample of adoptees stemmed from the fact that the Scandinavian countries keep centralized national registries. The Scandinavians record and retain extensive information about their citizens, including information about parents of babies who have been put up for adoption.

If, for example, an adoptee's natural parent was once hospitalized for alcoholism, this information will appear on the offspring's family record. American adoption agencies, on the contrary, have little information about the drinking habits of the baby's biological parents, and adoption records are in general far more difficult to gain access to, even for legitimate scientific purposes. Furthermore, U.S. citizens are far more mobile than the Danes; American adoptees, once grown, would undoubtedly have been far more difficult to locate.

These factors made the Danish sample an ideal group for study, and the results obtained from the Goodwin team's research did prove remarkably compelling. For it was found that among male adoptees with a biological parent who had received a hospital diagnosis of alcoholism, the *incidence of drinking-related problems was four times greater* than among a matched control group of adoptees with no alcoholic parent. Even though these sons of alcoholics had been adopted before the age of six weeks and had therefore almost never been exposed to the drinking parent, they were clearly differentially vulnerable to developing problems with alcohol themselves. This was a telling argument in favor of some mysterious underlying difference in the hard-wiring of the children (at least, the male children) of alcoholic parents.

The Goodwin findings were, moreover, consistent with the results of a study of alcoholics and their half-brothers and half-sisters, which had been published just one year earlier (1972) by psychiatric researcher Marc A. Schuckit, M.D., in collaboration with George Winokur, M.D., and Dr. Goodwin himself. In this study, alcoholism was defined as "drinking in a manner that interferes with one's life," and the diagnosis of alcoholism was consequent upon serious social repercussions, such as a divorce, a job loss, two or more traffic arrests, or a hospitalization directly resulting from excessive drinking.

What the Schuckit data revealed was that children reared apart from their natural parents were significantly more likely to have a drinking problem if a biological parent was alcoholic than if a "surrogate" (that is, a foster or adoptive) parent suffered from alcoholism. In other words, if the child was *not* genetically linked to the parent with the drinking problem, then simply growing up in the presence of an alcoholic parent figure did not seem to enhance the youngster's risk of someday becoming an alcoholic himself. This supported the idea that heredity might be of greater significance than the more obvious miseries of being reared in an alcoholic, and therefore often disruptive and depriving, family environment.

Replicating Familiar Family Patterns

Any interviewer worth her salt must carefully inquire about alcohol throughout the family once she realizes that the system is a "wet" one. I had asked Toni and Henry directly, in the course of our initial meeting, whether the drinking problems of the last generation had ever become manifest in this one. Both members of the pair had assured me easily and confidently that neither one of them had ever experienced any difficulties around alcohol, and watchful Antonia had nodded her agreement.

Nevertheless, according to Dr. David Treadway, author of *Families Under the Influence*, anyone who grows up in a family in which one parent displays a strong behavioral pattern is at risk for repeating that pattern— whether it involves an overclose relationship between a parent and child, or problems with separation, or infidelity, or pathological drinking. This tendency to repeat family patterns doesn't have to do with alcoholism per se, as Treadway observed in the course of a conversation, but the additional risk relating to alcohol abuse is that a strong genetic predisposition is also being passed along.

In point of fact, however, the experimental research has indicated that the risks related to nurture (growing up in an alcoholic household) are far less potent than those related to nature (being the child or grandchild of an alcoholic). In family therapist Treadway's view, nevertheless, those risks are still patently present. And in any case, as he notes, individuals who have grown up in alcoholic families will—no matter how much or how little they actually drink—experience a sense of tension and anxiety around drinking that is not dissimilar to that of the outright alcoholic.

These people are, suggests Treadway, "mental alcoholics," for it is a person's relationship to alcohol—not how much he or she may be drinking at a given time—that is important. "If you have grown up in this kind of a family, you don't ever drink casually, the way that a normal person would," as this psychotherapist (who grew up in an alcoholic family himself) told me.

The Transforming, Terrifying Substance

In the eyes of the immature offspring, alcohol takes on the guise of a magical, immensely frightening potion, which seems to have the power to transform the behavior of everyone around him. What the child has seen, in his or her formative years, is that bad things can happen when the adults in the family are drinking. Life can, in fact, become terrifying and out of control—but just when something will actually happen is completely unpredictable.

What makes things so unpredictable is that, even in alcoholic families, people are by no means getting completely drunk all the time. There is usually a certain amount of social drinking that is appropriate and doesn't necessarily lead to a negative outcome. But then, for reasons that are totally unclear to a child, the behavior of the grown-ups is transformed. Someone who was being nice a moment before may suddenly become abusive and start screaming, or someone who has been properly parental may become frighteningly seductive—and what is happening seems to be mysteriously related to the substance that the person is drinking. It is the feared, powerful, strangely exciting fluid in the glass that can turn the protective and parental, civilized Dr. Jekyll into the terrifying Mr. Hyde.

The Sons and Daughters of Alcoholic Parents: Specific Risks

Although both Toni and Henry were the biological children of alcoholic fathers, and although both had had the experience of being raised in a household in which a parent's drinking was out of control, it was Henry about whom I felt a degree of uneasiness. For he, as the son of an alcoholic father, was genetically primed for developing problems around the drug, while Toni had no similarly enhanced vulnerability.

A recent overview of all family studies involving the transmission of alcoholism from parent to offspring has indicated that the daughters of alcoholic fathers are at no greater risk for becoming excessive drinkers than are ordinary civilians. (The daughters of alcoholic mothers *are* at greater risk, however.)

Males, on the other hand, show enhanced vulnerability if either the biological mother *or* the biological father has suffered from alcoholism;

but then, alcoholism is predominantly a male disorder. Statistics gathered in the most recent, large-scale survey of alcoholism in the United States (called the Epidemiological Catchment Area Studies) clearly serve to underscore this statement. These figures indicate that almost one quarter of all males (23.8 percent) show symptoms of pathological drinking at some time during the course of their lives, while the rate for females is dramatically lower (4.6 percent). The male-to-female ratio of problem drinkers is thus a striking five to one.

In Henry Gifford's case, the fact that he was almost forty years old had to be viewed as a most positive factor, for alcoholism tends to have a youthful onset; Henry had already traversed the critical years between the late teens and the early forties when male vulnerability to alcoholism is at its zenith. Nevertheless, the news of his imminent retirement from the Navy did mean that he would soon be facing some demanding new threats and challenges.

Retirement could, in and of itself, be a significant anniversary event in his mind, for his father had begun the descent from hearty social drinker to isolated, sour drunk during the period just before his own retirement from the armed forces. Henry had to be carrying within himself a negative internal model for how this phase of life might be handled. How would he deal with the inevitable pressures and tensions of the coming transition?

In the most realistic and practical terms, this man in the middle years of his life would soon be faced with the loss of a work environment to which he was well acclimated, in which he knew how to operate effectively and competently. The move into the unfamiliar arena of private industry was likely to prove somewhat disorienting, because the military's style cannot be easily transposed into the far less rigidly structured work life that exists outside it.

For example if, in a military setting, an officer commands a subordinate to have his men paint a room that is eight feet by ten feet, and to have the task completed by three o'clock, the task *will* be completed when the officer returns. But in a civilian environment, the subordinate may refuse by saying that he is too busy and cannot handle the job at this particular time. Or, the subordinate may agree to do the task in principle, but ignore the three o'clock deadline.

Then, when the person who has given the instructions returns, he may find that only a third of the room has been painted and that most of the job remains unfinished. Called upon to explain why this is so, the subordinate may merely shrug and say that he couldn't get the men to work fast enough, or that there wasn't more than one painter available, or that there weren't enough paintbrushes to go around. In manifold ways, the military man's expectations—that the orders that are given *will* be followed promptly and to the letter—are likely to be violated routinely in a private-industry setting.

As far as Henry Gifford was concerned, simply having to learn how to function effectively outside the structured environment to which he was so accustomed might well make him feel that he had lost his basic anchorage and his sense of his life's direction. According to Yale alcohol expert Jerome Schnitt, M.D., who has worked extensively with veterans, the somewhat rocky transition from the military to the civilian world often leaves the retiree feeling disappointed, confused, angry, and hurt. "The individual may start thinking dismal thoughts such as 'I'm past my peak,' 'I'll never be appreciated,' 'I'll never go anywhere,' and 'I'm finished,' and it is at this point that the terrible sense that life is no longer good—or that it's all over—frequently sets in."

Such thoughts and feelings are commonly encountered in people who become problem drinkers around the time of their retirement, as psychiatrist Schnitt observes. "Typically, it has to do with a loss of role," he explained, "and with a terrible sense of loneliness and alienation."

If Lieutenant Commander Henry Gifford did feel lonely and alienated at the time of his departure from the Navy, to whom could he turn for support, understanding, and feelings of solidarity? As a couple, the Giffords seemed to be having trouble making contact, collaborating, and helping each other with their individual and mutual issues and concerns. While Toni and her mother were in harmony and "in sync," Henry was the family outsider. As he ventured beyond the familiar cocoon of the Navy—an environment in which he felt recognized and valued as a male, and yet could get his dependent needs met—he was going to need a committed, loving partner, someone upon whom he could depend. But would he permit himself to be vulnerable and lean on her when necessary, and if he attempted to do so, would she permit that to happen?

Gone, Period

There had been a long, almost four-week, interval between my last interview with the Giffords (when the focus had been on Henry's family of origin) and today's meeting. Given Henry Gifford's complicated commuting schedule, and my own interviewing schedule at that time, this was the earliest time we'd been able to manage.

By then, spring was on its way; on the drive northward up the Connecticut coastline, I'd noticed that the sap was running in the willow trees, which looked vibrant, and that the sunlight shone down upon the hills and meadows from a different, higher angle in the sky.

As I'd pulled into their driveway, a compactly built man with white, softly waving hair was just coming out of the Giffords' garage. He acknowledged my presence with a brusque salutation, and then walked across the front of the grass, around the side of the house, and out of my view. I rang the bell, which I heard chiming in the interior.

Toni, when she answered the door, asked me at once if I'd met her father on my way in. I turned and looked in the direction in which the gruff-seeming stranger had disappeared. "Oh. I didn't realize that was your dad. Do you think he might like to join us?" Blushing, she said in a flustered manner, "Oh, no, he'd never—it wouldn't go well—he can be peculiar, and he'd refuse anyway." Her father had just come over to help out with some of the household chores, she explained, and would be leaving as soon as he'd gotten the family lawnmower repaired.

This afternoon the Giffords' house seemed almost eerily quiet, for only the couple, little Laura (an unusually pretty baby, who was growing more so from one visit to the next), and I were present. Antonia had gone to visit her own mother, eighty-three-year-old Rita; and Emily, who'd just turned eight two weeks ago, had gone to a sleepover at the home of a schoolmate. I had the distinct impression that Toni and Henry were pleased, or even relieved, to see me.

On this occasion we sat in the living room, with the baby on her mother's lap through much of the long conversation—which commenced, as every interview subsequent to the first one does, with some of my own thoughts, reflections, and questions concerning what we talked about the last time.

"I want to ask you something, Henry," I said, my voice tentative. "It seems to me, thinking about your childhood, that it sounded somewhat . . . lonesome. It sounded, too, as if there was a scarcity of supplies, in terms of the emotional support that it offered a growing human being?" What had begun as a statement had ended as a question. "Sure," he answered succinctly, as if mine had been a yes-or-no question.

"It sounded as if you really had to withdraw and say to yourself, 'Okay, I'm going to have to take care of *me*, and live on my own resources.' Is that fair to say?"

"Sure it's fair to say," he answered briskly. I asked him if there had been a time when it had been otherwise, a time when living in his family had seemed somewhat different to him.

Henry shifted in his seat, gave me a somewhat nonplussed look, rubbed his smooth-shaven chin for several moments. "Oh, Christ, maybe at eight and younger," he responded at last. "We functioned more as a family back then. My mother didn't work. My father was more of a social person back in those days."

I noted with a glance at the Giffords' genogram that he had turned eight years old in 1958. Then I asked him if he remembered anything about just why things had changed. "Is there any incident that comes to your mind, or something that dramatizes the fact that things got so different in the family at that time?" Henry shook his head. There had been no sudden event, no dramatic happening that he recalled; but his home life had altered signficantly in the years between eight and fourteen.

When he was eight the whole family had returned to the United States from a two-year posting at an army base in France. It was then, he explained, that his parents had bought the house in Thomaston, Georgia, the small town in which both of them had been raised. "My mother ended up going to work there, so we became latchkey kids. Maybe that's when I started feeling so left alone—because now there wasn't anyone there for me. My mother and father didn't come home until about five or six, so we three kids were pretty much on our own, just hanging out in the neighborhood. My sister wasn't going to be there for me—she's three years older—so the two of us lived in a different time frame; we were in different worlds entirely." He cleared his throat.

"Marcy didn't want to be your little mommy?" I asked him with a smile.

"No, she didn't; she had no desire to do that." I heard the flash of a momentary anger in his voice. "There's quite a gap between an eight-year-old boy and an eleven-year-old girl," he added, reverting to his more customary reasonable stance, "and my brother, Curtis, and I didn't have anything in common at all." He cleared his throat again. "A couple of years after that, in the early sixties, my father took off and went to Korea for eighteen months. Gone, period," he stated, with bleak finality. "When he came back he was a changed man."

"I Don't Think My Father Was a Philanderer"

Henry had, he continued to maintain, no particular theory about what had happened to his father during that crucial eighteen-month period when he was away from home. "It was probably the isolation; it's a pretty bleak landscape. It's *cold*, and the Korean people are quite different from you and me. Even today they're very different. When you go over there, you find yourself in this closed-off environment in which there's just a lot of guys around, with nothing to do with their time. And I think maybe it just drove—" The ending of his sentence was provided by a brief shrug of his muscular shoulders.

Henry's working hypothesis seemed to be that it was the barrenness of the Korean terrain, and the sense of social isolation, that had turned his dad from a convivial drinker into the detached and distant drunkard that he had become. But certain other hypotheses presented themselves to my own mind. One was the possibility that his father had been happier, during that eighteen-month absence, than he'd ever been before in his lifetime. Had Sergeant Major William Earl Gifford begun drinking in order to bring back with him from Korea some sense of celebration, some remnant of a great happiness that he had known there?

I wondered if something very meaningful and important had happened to him in Korea—some experience that was utterly outside the realm of his ordinary existence. I wondered, too, if on his return to the dailiness of family life, Henry's father had begun pickling and preserving this special experience inside himself. "Has it ever occurred to you that your dad might have fallen in love with someone else while he was out there?" I asked Henry, in a musing, speculative tone of voice.

Henry dismissed the entire notion summarily. "I don't think so. I don't think my father was a philanderer. I don't think he was a woman-chaser, and if he was I never knew about it. I *never* got that impression. My mother never accused him of that." He sounded highly anxious, as if the idea itself were completely untenable.

When someone is so totally convinced as this, so sure that all further discussion is out of the question, the suspicion arises that the idea being proposed is one against which he is in fact highly defended. But there was, in any case, no point in pursuing a matter that this middle-aged son of a deceased father clearly found disturbing. Henry Gifford seemed to want no part of any speculations (or for that matter, to think at all) about what had caused his ebullient, outgoing father to cross the fateful line that separates an occasionally hard-drinking man's man from a withdrawn, isolated alcoholic.

Necessary Caveats

Family Levels and Genetic Loading

At this point, a couple of necessary caveats are in order. First, it ought not to be supposed that because alcoholism has been addressed within the context of a family at the midrange developmental level, these families are more prone to serious drinking problems than are other families on the Beavers Scale. Alcoholism can and does occur in family groups across the entire spectrum, for the drug is a commonplace of our culture, very widely used for a myriad of purposes and reasons.

Such reasons can of course range anywhere from the celebratory and ceremonial (toasting in the New Year; drinking to the bride and groom), to the easing of mild social apprehension (the cocktail hour before a dinner party), to the disinhibition of certain proscribed feelings and impulses (mainly relating to sexuality and aggression), to blatant self-medication for states of anxiety or depression. Any individual's motivations for drinking—and the reasons why some people may become afflicted with alcohol problems of life-shaping seriousness and severity—are notoriously complex. Thus, while genetic loading is certainly an important part of this picture, it cannot be mistaken for the picture in its entirety.

The underlying purposes that alcohol serves in differing family systems are also an important factor, and one that cannot be ignored. And, as family expert Leonora Stephens has noted, the drug is used in very different ways by families at differing positions on the Beavers health and competence continuum. For example, in a Level 5, severely dysfunctional system, alcohol may serve as an excellent obfuscating device; getting drunk is certainly helpful when it comes to inducing confusion, memory loss, and the like. "Alcohol helps people to forget," as psychiatrist Stephens points out, "and to expel from awareness those things that might cause pain, or perhaps just make them acutely uncomfortable."

According to Stephens, alcohol is put to somewhat different kinds of use in the borderline, Level 4 family. Here, problems centering around alcohol tend to become manifest in one or more of the intense power struggles with which these control-oriented systems are riven. As mentioned earlier, one very commanding way of gaining control is to "go out of control"—developing the uncontrollably addictive symptoms associated with such conditions as obesity or alcoholism. Then, no matter how much the family tyrant may rant and rave, the afflicted family member remains "helpless" when it comes to stopping his or her overeating or excessive drinking. The superior power of addiction has trumped the tyrant's power, and in the face of the afflicted person's compulsion, it is the tyrant who is rendered helpless.

At the next rung upward on the Beavers Scale—midrange, Level 3—one finds, once again, that alcohol is being used in different ways and for different purposes. For in a rule-bound emotional world, the drug often serves as a pressure releaser—a means of keeping the pervasive, system-wide feelings of anxiety, guilt, and resentment within tolerable bounds. Everyone within the family is experiencing a sense of emotional constriction—the members of the system are being asked to live in an emotional framework that allows almost no space for personal growth—and alcohol can be most helpful in assuring that the tensions within the group remain under control. In these families, liquor is used to preserve the system's stability, and ensure that the all-important family rules go unchallenged.

Moving upward to those families at the high end of the Beavers Scale—adequate, Level 2; optimal, Level 1 (see Part Six)—what one sees are alcoholic beverages being used for primarily pleasant, life-enhancing reasons, rather than for purposes of stifling tension, grabbing control, or obfuscating the sources of suffering. Nevertheless there are, as Leonora Stephens notes, situations in which families that are functioning at an adequate or optimal level have a potent alcoholic heritage. What then? In such cases, does genetic loading or family health tend to prevail?

In any specific instance, suggests Stephens, this is a question that only a fortune-teller can attempt to answer. Generally speaking, though, the younger generation of such a family will have enough ego strength to take the bad genetic news into account, and be careful to do nothing to harm themselves. For example, a maturing adolescent male, loaded for bear in terms of alcoholism in the extended system, may decide to jog a few miles a day rather than take a drink in order to relax himself. Or, having realized that taking one drink makes it impossible to not take two drinks, and then three or four, he may quickly decide that taking no alcohol is the safest course.

In any event, children reared in competent, well-functioning family systems have learned to value and care for themselves—and they behave accordingly. If there is alcoholism in the family, they remain aware of the fact that they have a potent biological problem—an inherited defect, like a propensity to develop asthma—and they are mindful not to do the equivalent of the asthmatic person who moves in next door to a factory belching smoke. Healthy families produce offspring with enough sense of self-worth and self-esteem to look out for themselves.

A Risk Is Not an Inevitability

A second and equally important caveat has to do with genetics itself. The threat of an "alcohol gene" has put many concerned parents into a state of permanent alarm, and it is therefore vital that it be understood that every biological son of an alcoholic parent or grandparent is not carrying a ticking time bomb—his genetic doom—within him. As alcohol and family systems theorist Stephen Wolin has pointed out, the biological orientation now fashionable in scientific circles is "damage-oriented," and focuses far too intently upon all that can possibly go wrong. What is deemphasized, in the process, is what can—and, with much greater frequency, actually *does*—end up going right.

According to psychologist Wolin, the statistics indicating that genetic loading for alcoholism exists are scientifically sound, and do represent a very real phenomenon. Still, the very *same* statistics indicate that the majority of biological offspring of alcoholics, whether raised in an alcoholic home or not, actually do very well. "These children neither develop substance abuse nor do they develop other forms of psychopathology," as Wolin told me in the course of an interview. "In fact, as far as we can tell, these kids are simply indistinguishable from normals."

Thus, while genetically oriented thinkers have paid great attention to the existence of an enhanced risk of alcoholism in the children of alcoholics—a risk raised between threefold and fivefold, depending upon the sex of the child and that of the alcoholic parent—there has been much less emphasis upon the important fact that *while one third of these children do go on to develop drinking problems, some two thirds of them (70 percent) do not.* The important lesson here is, in other words, that a higher risk is not—and should not be confused with—an inevitability.

CHAPTER 19

Intimacy, Self-knowledge, and Self-esteem

Intimacy was the central issue with which the Giffords, as partners and as leaders of a family, appeared to be struggling. And over time, as our interviews proceeded, I came to realize that a certain visual image of the pair was continually intruding itself upon my own imagination. It was the image of two people who are always struggling to get nearer to each other and yet are always being bounced off and backward by an invisible barrier of heavy glass that stands between them.

This wall was constructed of deeply ingrained family rules—most especially rules about how a female should relate to a male ("Women should be warm and forgiving toward other women, but deeply suspicious and reluctant about ever becoming emotionally connected to a man"); and how a male should relate to females ("A man should keep his inner world sacrosanct and never permit his spouse to know about his real thoughts, feelings, worries, weaknesses, and vulnerabilities"). It was these and similarly powerful, well-learned rules about women and men—rules that seemed almost designed to foster a state of mutual distrust between the sexes—that were, I believed, preventing the real human encounter for which both Toni and Henry were yearning.

Intimacy is invariably the foremost concern in the midrange family. For in these emotional systems, a myriad of rigid, stringently observed internalized regulations and precepts exert very effective control over every member of the group—a situation that does support the emergence of smoother, more organized functioning of the family group as a whole, but serves to block the emergence of true relationship between its individual members.

Toni Gifford was, in my view, an amiable, appealing woman; Henry was her sturdy, reliable mate. The pair of them ran a pleasant, orderly household and were deeply engaged and involved in the process of their parenting. I felt that there was love between them, but also a lack of closeness that was frustrating to them both. It was as if they were stymied by the entire concept of what it meant to be intimate: How on earth did one go about making it happen? Neither member of the pair seemed to have any kind of interior road map or diagram when it came to achieving closeness in a bonded male-female attachment.

Furthermore, as mentioned earlier, becoming genuinely intimate with another person inevitably generates a tug in the direction of greater contact with one's own genuine thoughts and actual feelings. In a midrange system, this can be experienced as hazardous, not only to the system but to the self. For, as theorist Stephen Mitchell has observed, a person who has never quite established meaningful connections and "whose essential attachments are to constricted and painful experiences" *hope itself can feel very dangerous.*

Why, precisely, is hope experienced as dangerous? In my view, it is because the very notion that true emotional gratification could be achieved—that one could be accepted, cared for, heard, and responded to as the particular person one actually is—might lure the real, authentic self out from behind its wall of protective defenses, and into the strange and unaccustomed open. One could permit oneself to become unthinkably exposed and vulnerable in the (perhaps illusory) belief that there could be a relationship really different from the relationships one has known, and with which one is so thoroughly familiar.

To move out into the emotional open would, moreover, necessitate a revamping of the world within. It would mean letting go of deep, unrequited longings for the parents' unconditional love—which is to say, for a love that was simply always there, not contingent upon one's compliance with the rules and regulations for thinking, feeling, and behaving. It would entail, moreover (and this can feel dangerous), coming into conscious contact with one's own pain and suppressed anger about early needs that having once gone unmet, now never will be. What is involved here is, in other words, an extensive emotional overhaul—a reordering of one's basic internal blueprint for being in an interaction between intimates.

Plainly, for both of the Giffords, the model of a marriage was of a woman screaming for intimacy and a man who was not responding. Henry's principal strategy, as a growing male, had been to not feel the "hurting" in the household. Toni's adaptation, as a growing female, had been to assume the role of the "competent little adult"—the impossible (for a child) burden of taking care of her parents and resolving all the problems in the household. Both of them had succeeded, nevertheless, in getting on with their lives in an orderly, goal-directed fashion. They'd managed to establish good careers and to court, marry, and rear their young family—in brief, to move well and reasonably effectively through the successive tasks of early and middle adulthood and of the family life cycle.

But if the emotional barrier that separated them continued to stand firmly in place, that was (or so it seemed to me) in the service of preserving the illusion that by never getting dangerously close to someone else one could avoid the threat of pain ("too much hurting"). The thick glass wall that kept the Giffords securely apart had been erected for reasons of safety and security; but what I did come to realize, with great force and poignancy, was the degree of loneliness and isolation that each of them was experiencing behind it.

A Problematic, Distance-Creating Rule: You Don't Confront, You Withdraw

As the handling of the fracas about Emily and the roller skates had indicated, an important rule in the Gifford family was "Instead of resolving conflict, you back off." This particular episode was just one among many examples of how the parental couple tended to retreat from problematic differences—in that particular instance, differences about how a child should be disciplined. Thus it happened that issues emerged and re-emerged without any real effort to confront, understand, and resolve them.

So important was this rule that it was the first statement that sprang to Toni's mind when I asked the Giffords (I was meeting with the couple alone on this occasion) if they could identify a few of the rules that everyone in this family could agree were pretty important.

"You don't deal with conflictual issues openly," Toni blurted out immediately.

Then she added, after a moment's uneasy silence, "There's a real idea here that you don't *deal* with conflict, that conflict's not good."

"Yes," Henry agreed, "we don't like to have confrontations among ourselves, and if there's a way to avoid it, that's what will happen." The topic seemed to make both of them uncomfortable.

"Come to think of it, that might have been a rule in my own family, growing up," Toni said, adding that aside from the time when her father had been actively drinking, there hadn't been a lot of open quarreling in the household. There had been withdrawal instead.

Henry, shifting his position, folded his arms over his chest and observed that in a way his own family had not been awfully dissimilar. "When my father was drinking, my mother wouldn't have anything to do with him. Oh, she might yell at him, and stuff like that, but he'd just sit back and take it." I recalled his saying earlier that he'd stayed out of the house in order to avoid the quarreling and "hurting" going on there; now it sounded as though his mother had been doing all the berating and his father not responding—as if her fireworks had been met by his silence.

"It seems as if, in both your families, there was a real standoff in the older generation," I remarked.

"I definitely *worry* about that," Toni shot back swiftly, "because I think you need to deal with—confront—issues. But I don't—if he won't . . ." She looked at her husband somewhat resentfully, but said nothing further.

"You have a hard time getting me to confront issues," Henry said blandly, as if agreeing to take responsibility as the rule's originator. "Because I don't *do* that. Problems make me uncomfortable, to the point where I sometimes think it's better not to deal with them." He grinned suddenly and said facetiously: "Besides, if you ignore them, they may go away."

There was another brief silence. I could see, by her expression, that Toni was disturbed by this remark. "I guess that I—in order to deal with that approach—have gone in the same direction myself. Which may or may not have to do with an old script of my own. You know, it's 'You don't confront—' " She stopped and shrugged helplessly.

Such a rule, I reflected, seemed almost crafted to prevent the emergence of intimacy between the pair. For what it meant, in translation, was "Don't talk openly to your partner. Saying what you really think and feel about a charged issue would be dangerous to the emotional system and is, in any case, not permissible." It was as if, throughout the Giffords' extended family, the lack of intimacy between a woman and a man were being actively legislated.

A Guaranteed Recipe for Rage

This particular rule about not confronting conflictual issues was, most certainly, a guaranteed recipe for producing abundant quantities of silent rage. For close relationships always do involve some differences in point of view, and sometimes quite strong disagreements that simply have to be dealt with. As Robert Beavers has written, "Conflict in family systems is comparable to ambivalence in the individual. Both are ubiquitous and inescapable, and health consists in *resolving* [my italics] the conflict at the individual or family level, not in avoiding or denying it."

To the degree that they were not dealing with their conflicts, those unprocessed conflicts were being quietly stockpiled. But the Giffords' rule—"Instead of resolving conflict, you back off"—continued to hold sway in their family realm, unquestioned.

A Marital Deal

As our interviews continued, it became ever clearer that Toni Gifford had real complaints about her marriage, and that these had to do with her husband's lack of emotional availability. What she wanted, most of all, was more intimate disclosure in the relationship, and to confront their conflictual issues far more forthrightly—if Henry would only do his share in terms of helping to make that happen. Her belief was that she stood ready to throw open the gates of her inner world, if only he were the kind of partner who could accept the invitation, move closer, and do some opening up on his own part.

The sense of lonely stalemate that both were experiencing was something for which she blamed him, and for which Henry accepted full responsibility. "I know I don't meet all of Toni's intimacy needs, her conversational needs, and those kinds of things," he admitted regretfully. He seemed to share the belief that any lack of intimacy in the relationship had to be his own fault because he was constitutionally incapable of getting close to anyone.

Toni's mother certainly held that view as well. During one of the early interviews, Antonia had observed (in her son-in-law's presence) that Henry could sometimes pass a whole day without saying much more than a sentence or two. The family myth (which everyone clearly subscribed to) was that if only this too self-contained and silent male were able to get in touch with his feelings, then the couple could immediately achieve the intimacy for which both of them pined. But what seemed nearer to the truth was that if Toni Gifford had married a man who didn't want to talk about his inner experience it was because she didn't really want to talk about *hers*— that she was as afraid of being intimate as he was.

The Giffords were, it seemed to me, in an unconscious collusion, and the deal they had made was the following one: "Let's never open up to each other, because that would involve truly looking inside ourselves and perhaps coming into contact with certain feelings that could be too painful for bearing." As long as she focused her conscious energies on chasing after her husband for intimacy, Toni need not focus her attention on certain carefully sealed-off and suppressed aspects of her own inner world—most especially, raw, conflict-ridden feelings associated with having been "born adult" and pressed into her family's service at the very outset of her existence.

Being Valued, and Valuing the Self

What Toni was avoiding, I believed, was the realization that she felt an inner emptiness, a lack of good emotional supplies stored up within. For if one thinks in childhood-developmental terms, it is in the course of being nurtured, having our needs met, and experiencing our parents' pleasure in our unfolding accomplishments that *we learn how to nurture ourselves, meet our own needs, and take pleasure in being the particular individuals we are.* In the most basic sense, *parental cherishing is incorporated as cherishing of the self—that is, self-esteem.*

The early family is the medium in which the growing child's sense of who she or he is as a person is being structured, and it is within the context of the first relationships that the individual's sense of worth and importance is slowly being internalized. But Toni had had, since time immemorial, the feeling that the responsibility for saving her parents' marriage was hers to bear.

As the eldest of five children, moreover, and as the family's self-described psychological caretaker, she'd had to do far more of the giving out than she'd ever been entitled to take in. Also, at a very practical level, she had been drafted into domestic service very early, as her duty-driven mother's chief assistant. But it was not until my last interview with the Giffords, on the eve of the nuclear family's departure for Italy, that the full extent of Toni's hitherto underground feelings about this became fully manifest.

"My mother was never available, emotionally; she was always obsessed with 'I've got to clean' or 'I've got to cook,' and—I would say—very narcissistic and self-absorbed," recounted Toni disapprovingly. "She was very much into her *own* needs and whatever it was that *she* had to get done next. I mean—I remember ironing my father's undershirts, because they all *had* to get ironed. And I remember being seven years old, and having to come in to peel the potatoes, because the potatoes *had* to be peeled—and I didn't *want* to; I wanted to be outside playing." She sounded like an offended, sulky child at this very moment.

"But my mother was always *obsessed* by what she had to do," she repeated. "The house had to be clean, and everybody had to take a bath on Sunday night, and everybody's hair had to be curled on Saturday night, and you had to dress for church on Sunday. There was never, ever any five minutes for sitting down and *talking* to you."

"Are you saying that you couldn't really talk to your mother? You couldn't tell her who you were and what was happening in your life?" I asked. This was after all, a very different view of the relationship from the one in which the two women were totally and wordlessly "in sync."

Toni nodded, "Right, and I think that she was never available to me as a parent—that we kids had to parent *them*. We all had to do that, but *I* was the one who had to be the expert—to read the right books and try to figure out what was going on. *I* was the one who had to explain to my mother that alcoholism was a problem—an addiction, a disease, whatever—and what you had to do about it. . . . My aunt Rita is exactly the opposite," she added, a comparison that seemed to come out of nowhere.

"But I don't know what *that* has to do with it," she admitted immediately, looking flustered. I didn't know either, and waited for some clarification; none followed. But it did occur to me that the indefatigable Aunt Rita, who'd recently married for the second time and moved to Florida, was the only female in this glued-together family who had managed to bend the rigid bars of the rule system and ultimately walk right through them, away into a different kind of life.

In a way, Aunt Rita's high junks were an expression of the covert rebellion and tension that are always being experienced throughout the rule-bound system. She broke the rules on behalf of *everyone*, which was, perhaps, part of the reason why people found it possible to be so tolerant and forgiving of her behavior. She had, come to think of it, staged a riveting demonstration of the fact that *not* living by the rules was among life's possible options.

The Parental Imperative: An Existential Pact

Toni Gifford, in the course of growing up, had always struggled to meet the needs of others and to keep the family from flying apart; she had, however, never really made much contact with certain vital aspects of her own inner experience. What had been disregarded, in her family of origin, was the so-called "parental imperative." This is, according to psychotherapist Judith Grunebaum, the irreversible responsibility that the adult generation bears toward the child it has created and brought into the world.

"Children are inherently entitled to unearned care from their parents," writes Grunebaum, explaining that "this entitlement is due to the universal biological and social conditions of an infant's vulnerability." Our human birthright is the unconditional love and caring of our parents. *But some parents turn that existential pact on its head: They require unconditional love and caring from their children.*

"If excessive support and concern are expected from the child for the parent, the child becomes 'parentified,' " as Grunebaum observes. Toni Gifford was, in reality, less a person who had been "born adult" than she was a child who'd never quite gotten a chance to do her growing up—because along the way, her own legitimate developmental needs had been squashed. She knew how to meet the needs of and take care of others but was, it seemed to me, having trouble knowing who *she* was and how to take care of herself.

This was because, during the years of her early growth—a time during which, it bears repeating, we learn to value, care for, and reassure ourselves as a function of having been valued, cared for, and reassured by our caretakers—she had been co-opted into pseudo-adulthood by her distracted and tension-ridden parents. Instead of being attended to and cared for like the immature youngster she was, she herself had had to do the lion's share of attending and caring. And if now, in the high noon of her own adult life, she was struggling against a sense of inner impoverishment and insufficiency, it had to do, I believed, with her having been parentified—become adult without really having been a child.

For a very fundamental question that Toni had not asked herself, in a lifetime of taking care of others, was *"Who am I when I'm not taking care of other people—and if I am not caring for other people, do I exist at all?"*

A Subterranean Contract: The Pursuer-Distancer Relationship

Given the collusive fashion in which the Giffords' present-day relationship was structured, Toni's own impaired ability to connect with her feelings was something that she need never acknowledge or consciously realize. For both she and Henry never doubted for a moment that it was *he* who had the problems when it came to relating intimately. He was, in a very real way, helping to protect her from the pain of ever having to look inside, for by not opening up and sharing his inner world with her, he maintained the emotional distance that she required.

She, in turn, as part of their unconscious arrangement, protected him from his denied needs for nurturance and dependency. For as long as he focused his energies upon the escape from intimacy, he could maintain his vision of himself as a self-sufficient human being, a person who needed nothing in the way of support or sustenance from anyone. This was the posture he had adopted as the son of a physically and then emotionally absent father, and of a partnerless mother who had been perceived as somehow dangerous and to be avoided as much as possible.

Perhaps, given her "unattached" status, Henry's mother's requests for intimacy had been experienced by her developing son as scary, quasi-incestuous requests to step into his father's place and be her companion. Or perhaps the growing boy had felt that coming too close to a woman could be overwhelming, that a woman's needs could engulf him and swallow him up alive—that a female could berate a male into becoming a drunk. Was there, moreover, a question in his own mind about whether his kid brother, Curtis, who was extremely close to their mother, had dealt with a lurking incestuous possibility by turning his sexuality in another direction—that is, by directing his erotic attentions toward other males?

In a telephone conversation I had with Henry just a few days before the Giffords left (I'd called to say good-bye), he detonated one of those postinterview bombshells that can catch a person completely unawares. It was in the course of a discussion about his younger brother (who, in his own opinion, "had been mothered too much") that Henry happened to mention that during their father's absence in Korea his mother had often slept in the same bedroom with her two young sons. "I think Curtis *needed* that," he explained, carefully, "because he was always very sensitive, highstrung, very intelligent. . . . He's much *more* intelligent than I am."

He himself had been eleven and his brother nine and a half years old at that time—that is, in the pubescent period when strange new sexual saps are rising and flowing throughout the body. What Henry was describing sounded like a highly problematic situation that must have been, at some level, downright scary for a young, developing male.

And, after we'd said our last good-byes and hung up the telephone, I couldn't help but wonder: Had this very sense of the scariness inherent in getting too close to a woman so abruptly turned Henry off when, six months after his marriage, he'd found himself in bed with a sexual female beside him? A wife who seems, in fantasy, "too much like a mother" becomes taboo as an object of desire—and loss of desire could be seen as a solution to the problem, a salutary form of self-castration that would prevent the unconsciously forbidden act from ever taking place.

According to the Giffords, that situation had resolved itself eventually (they disagreed on how long it had taken to do so) and Henry's sexual interest had revived within the year. But at present, well over a decade after the mysterious difficulty of that time had evaporated, he was still on the run from open exchange, dependency, and closeness. As he had once fled a subtly threatening intimacy with his mother, he was now fleeing intimacy with his wife.

Toni and Henry were involved in a subterranean pact, which involved each mate's taking charge of certain unacceptable thoughts and feelings for the other one. It was she who carried the emotionality both for herself and for her husband. But it had not escaped my notice that whenever Henry showed himself as full of feeling and vulnerable in our discussions (for example, when the story of his father's drinking and his own childhood alienation was emerging) she had appeared to "space out" and allow her thoughts to go wandering elsewhere. Even more striking was the way in which, just after tears had sprung to his eyes while describing their blissful time together in the Azores, Toni had spoken of his "tremendous ability to deny and block his feelings." Not surprisingly, Henry's tears had dried up immediately.

In that exchange, it seemed to me, he had violated a basic rule of their relational bargain: *She* was to be in charge of (and therefore in control of) all the expressivity in the system. Her instant and negative reaction to his rare display of intense emotion had been that those particular feelings were basically wrong ones; her husband's explanation of why he'd been so moved didn't "fit" or make sense to her. Toni had not responded to his evocation of their island idyll soothingly or with loving memories of her own, nor had she even urged him to continue.

I wondered if, for her, emotionality in a man would be experienced as something deeply disturbing and frightening. Given the family havoc that her own father's temperamental antics had created (his extramarital affairs, drinking, and wild business dealings made me speculate about the possibility that he had actually been experiencing bouts of mania), I could see why Toni might perceive a male with feelings as a male who was potentially out of control. What was clear was that her husband's stepping out of his customary role as the detached, inaccessible man had somehow scared her and evoked an angry reaction also. It seemed quite evident that she wanted more intimacy in the relation *unless and until* the opportunity to have it actually presented itself.

In the Giffords' emotional system, which is a commonly encountered kind of projective-identification system known as the "pursuer-distancer relationship," the partner who (like Toni) always appears to be seeking greater connectedness depends upon the partner who (like Henry) always appears to be eluding connectedness to make sure that too much intimacy never does threaten. As part of their unconscious collaboration, it was her job to ceaselessly pursue him for more closeness, and his duty to run fast enough so that the space and personal distance *both of them required* could be maintained. And while this made real intimacy between them impossible, it did help them both avoid the acute pain of coming into contact with early conflicts that had never been confronted or resolved.

In his very being Toni's husband embodied, for her, her own disowned needs for personal space, her suppressed wishes to be self-absorbed and to take care of her own needs instead of taking care of other people (for example, by taking aspirin for someone else's headache). In her very being Henry's wife embodied, for him, those disavowed needs for nurturance, dependence, and emotionality that had been forsaken early in his life, as he assumed his defensively detached, super-independent "I don't need anyone" stance.

Early in our talks, Henry Gifford had said that he disliked his wife's family's emotionality (and by implication, Toni's as well). But just as she had married a man who talked little and was walled off from his feelings, he had married a woman whose easy sociability and capacity to take care—she was a nurse by profession!—knew no bounds. Although, at a conscious level, Henry was unaware of wanting to be needy, vulnerable, close, and nurtured, he depended upon his wife to pursue him with her never-ending pleas for more closeness, more intimacy, more warmth. Thus it is that we evacuate aspects of our inner experience that we find it impossible to tolerate, and then locate these qualities in those with whom we are most closely intertwined.

In Shusako Endo's novel *Scandal*, there is a journalist who becomes obsessed by his need to expose a much honored, pious author as a sanctimonious hypocrite who is in fact involved in a horde of secret depravities. But as a woman character remarks astutely to the scandal-mongering reporter, "You've sniffed out an image of yourself in Mr. Sugaro, and you hate him for it." Sniffing out an image of oneself in the other happens most frequently between people who are in close relationships—in couple and family relationships, and even among friends. Another name for it is projective identification: that is, projecting out and then perceiving *in the other* thoughts and feelings that are too painful or conflictual to contain within the boundaries of one's own being.

Follow-up

It was in the course of a routine follow-up call to the Giffords that I heard their latest news, and it certainly caught me by surprise. My series of interviews with the family had been completed six months earlier, and I had not talked to them in quite a while. Today's call had been prompted not only by a wish to touch base with them, but also to ask about whether Henry had been summoned for duty in the Persian Gulf (the Mideast war was just winding down to its completion at that time). Toni told me that he had not been involved in the action there, but had in fact been reassigned. He would be stationed at the naval base at Naples, Italy, for the next two years, and she and the children would be going to Italy with him.

What surprised me—and led me to assume that this was good marital news—was that Toni was clearly choosing to put herself far out of the reach of the circle of people upon whom she regularly depended for intimacy and support. She would be leaving behind not only her mother but her younger sister Diane, with whom she shared a confiding relationship. And she would be leaving behind, as well, the visits from her father, who enjoyed helping out with the household repairs and who stopped by frequently to see her and the children.

Toni had "disappointments" about what her father had done with his life, as she'd certainly acknowledged, but even if her present-day feelings about him were laced with regret and disenchantment, she still did care about him deeply. She worried about the state of his health, which was not good in general, and about the fact that he continued to smoke more than a pack of cigarettes daily. (I had noted, by the way, that both she and Henry had seen an initially ebullient and admired father deteriorate, in his latter years, into a diminished and somewhat unsavory character. This was another growing-up experience that these partners had in common.) But then there were also Toni's two younger brothers and two younger sisters, and their husbands, wives, and children, as well as the other relatives in her extended family (Great-grandmother Rita, for instance), who were all integral parts of the tapestry of Toni's current life. In Italy there would be no one to meet her intimate and social needs other than Henry and their own small children.

It seemed to me that things must be going well between the pair if she had weighed not only these considerations but her own teaching and nursing career, and then decided that being with her husband was more important than all these factors combined. In the important language of behavior, Toni was declaring that their being together was her most important priority.

"Congratulations, it sounds like a decision for the marriage," I blurted out impulsively.

"Oh, do you think so?" Toni responded, in a dubious-sounding tone of voice. They were to leave the United States in mid-June, and we agreed that I would come out to see them before their departure.

A Certain Kind of Child-Adult Dialogue

It was a Saturday in late April when I drove out to see the Giffords, but it was turning out to be an unusually hot, sun-drenched afternoon. I found them as lighthearted as I'd ever seen them. Henry, in an open-collared white oxford-cloth shirt, with sleeves rolled up over his muscular arms, exuded a certain vitality and sexiness. Toni looked different in a way I couldn't quite decipher until I realized that she was wearing bright lipstick, which she'd never worn during our previous meetings. She was dressed in a silky print blouse, dark walking shorts, and new-looking loafers.

In the time between my last visit and this one, Laura had metamorphosed from a lap baby into a toddler. As we talked she lurched from toy to toy, the most bewitching little drunkard imaginable. Every once in a while she would squat on her chubby little haunches, babbling happily at an object upon which her attention had become focused. Emily was, I noticed, looking a bit plump, and the expression on her face seemed somewhat graver in repose.

I asked Toni, first of all, if her decision to accompany Henry had been difficult to make. It had sounded to me, I added, like a really big decision for the marriage. "Or am I misinterpreting?" I met her gaze directly.

It *had* been a big decision, she began to reply.

"It was complicated," Henry cut in swiftly. "We bought *this* house because, basically, we didn't want to have to move again after I left the Navy. But when you come right down to it, that's meant that we've had to live apart for three years—and I'm about to take off again. So we looked at it realistically, and now we're talking two more years, okay? And how often could she really visit me over there?" He hadn't quite responded to the question I'd asked—Was Toni's deciding to go with him to Italy a big decision in favor of the marriage?—but had instead grabbed hold of the conversational ball and gone dribbling down the court in another direction entirely.

I looked at Toni, my gaze focused and unswerving, as if inviting her to continue where he had left off. Henry, however, seemed unwilling to permit that to happen. "Also, she's always wanted to go to Europe," he continued, "and this may be the last opportunity ever. Another thing was that she was getting burned out at her job—overextending herself—and then, with me away, she'd have no relief with the kids over the weekends. So it was a whole combination of things." His voice sounded firm and sensible, but carried an overtone of anxiety. Once again, the whole question of the marriage was being sidestepped adroitly.

I shifted position, turning my entire torso in Toni's direction. "Do you remember some of the things we talked about earlier, Toni?" I asked her directly. "I mean—about the problems that you guys were having communicating and making contact? And about the ways in which you were feeling more in sync with your mother than with Henry . . . ? Has something changed?" I realized wryly that the sound of my voice was eagerly hopeful, and reflected that I have caretaker issues of my own to deal with.

For in a very real way, I, too, had been born adult; throughout my childhood, I'd been the worshipful little confidante of my own unhappily married mother, and I spent a lot of those years wanting nothing more passionately than a future in which *she* would find the joy and happiness of which my stern, much older father had deprived her. I'd been invested in listening to and sympathizing with my mother, and filled with fantasies about a great by-and-by in which her life would be totally changed and immeasurably better, when she would be in another marriage and living with a man who valued her true worth and adored her (as I did). It was almost as though I'd been *her* loving parent, and dreaming of a glorious time when she would be fully grown up, married, and living happily ever after.

I, like Toni Gifford, had been a parentified child, and internalized a sense of responsibility for fixing all the family problems around me (my mother's problems, most especially). Now, with hypnotic ease, I had gotten ensnared in an old script of my own, one in which I was cast in the role of the rescuer—the one who will, magically, solve everyone else's difficulties and make their lives happier and better. But in truth (a truth I certainly never recognized until many years later) when a child grows up within the context of this kind of parent-offspring dialogue, that child learns a great deal about how to listen to and nurture other people, but is far less skilled when it comes to knowing how to *be listened to* and how to receive the nurturance that she herself (or he himself) requires.

A Great Life Gamble

It was Toni whom I'd asked about whether there had been positive changes in the relationship, but once again, it was Henry who hurried to reply. "No, there's still that problem," he said stoutly and forthrightly. "I *don't* meet all her intimacy needs—her need to talk about the things that are happening until she's sort of worked them out. And we've discussed what it might turn out to be like over there; we're still discussing that *a lot*, right now. Because she's not going to have her sister Diane right nearby, and she won't be able to get on the phone and talk stuff over, and that'll make a difference *of course.*

"But then," he added after the briefest of pauses, "there's the kids to consider. Emily definitely doesn't want me to go away without her, and then little Laura seems like she'd miss me a great deal too. So it's not really any one factor; it's multiple factors that went into making this decision." Henry seemed to be involved in running interference, trying to block and prevent his wife from getting control of the ball and perhaps saying things he might not want to hear.

"So you don't see this as a decision that Toni is making in order to be with you, or a decision to move closer, or a decision *about* the relationship at all?" I asked him explicitly. Then, to my own surprise, I heard myself adding wistfully, "I guess I thought, when I heard the news, that it had to do with a nice thing that was happening between the pair of you."

Clearly, I had become invested in a happily-ever-after ending, with the Giffords sailing off together to Italy. They were, once again, connecting to that hope-filled child within me, or at least to that part of my own inner world which had been dedicated to making the lives of the parental generation (even in fantasy) better and different. There still lived, somewhere inside me, a child who had wanted to relieve the suffering of a beloved caretaker so that she could be happier, more contented, better able to take care of me. But Henry's response, delivered in a neutral tone of voice, was that while considerations about the relationship might have been part of the picture, they had not, he thought, been "the overriding factor" in the decision to go to Europe as a family.

I was taken aback. "Not the overriding factor for Toni, you mean?"

He nodded. I leaned forward in my seat. "So you don't see this, Henry, as a decision that Toni is making to try to move closer to you in any way?" I asked him.

He shrugged lightly, unrolled and then rerolled one of his shirtsleeves more neatly. "There's some of that, but I don't think it's the overriding thing," he repeated.

If his wife had, by any chance, meant to tell me that she *was* going to Europe with him because she cared about their being together, she had effectively been precluded from doing so. Henry had prevented not only a possibly negative comment but also any positive statement from ever being uttered.

I wondered if, for him, the very notion that Toni's decision was based upon powerful attachment feelings and her investment in their relationship would have been experienced as downright alarming. For feelings are notoriously subject to change and variability; if Toni's feelings *did* change, she could back off from the current decision and unmake her choice at a moment's notice. All the other "multiple factors" that had gone into the making of Toni's decision—most important, the need of the children to not be separated from their father—would be far less subject to intermittent fluctuations in the couple's relationship. Toni's choice to accompany Henry would then *not* depend upon whether she really loved him or not.

It is, I reflected, just this lack of belief that loving, satisfying things could happen *in the absence of an enforcing rule* that brings the rule-driven system into being. For once the Giffords could agree upon the appropriate behavioral rule (such as "A good mother wouldn't keep her children from being with their father for two whole years") the rule itself assumes the quality of an eternal verity. The choice is then taken out of everyone's hands, for it is no longer based upon whether or not the relationship happens to be a warm and gratifying one.

I felt a stab of concern. Toni was leaving behind her those close family members upon whom she now depended. She was also relinquishing a developing career as a nurse/therapist that I believed she very much valued. In Europe, she would be in a position similar to her mother's: that of the dependent female. What would happen when she was feeling hungry for emotional feedback, and there was no one to go to with these needs but her spouse?

I smiled at her and said lightly, "Well, then, is that how the decision was made? Is what he's saying correct, or is it wrong in your opinion?"

Toni returned my smile, but her facial expression was blank. "I think there *is* a little bit of that here," she replied. I shook my head to tell her that I didn't quite understand what she meant, but she said nothing further for the next few moments.

"I guess I've wondered if, perhaps, we were together more, then things might not be so stressful," she began again slowly, as if gathering her thoughts along the way. "These past three years have been—oh, the most stressful ever. And even though I'm totally aware that Henry and I are different from each other, in terms of communicating, I've thought that maybe without all the added stress of our jobs and the commuting, things might not be so tough. There *are* these moments when I think that without all the added stuff we've been dealing with, things could be easier. . ." Her voice trailed off, and she looked at Henry uncertainly.

Of course, her mother's help had alleviated some of the stress, Toni went on to say, but she'd come to the realization that neither she nor her mom—nor for that matter, anyone else in her family—handled stress very easily. "People get uptight if there are too many demands; we all get too uptight. If I look at my father, for instance, I think he could have been a much more successful person, and done a lot more with his life, if he could have managed the stresses better." She sighed. What she had recently come to recognize, with a fresh clarity, was how much the strains and tensions of each individual member reverberated throughout the entire system.

"If someone gets a migraine headache, the wires buzz and everyone's on the telephone immediately. But maybe I don't *care* about that migraine; maybe I don't even want to *know* about it," she complained. While she did enjoy the constant interchanges with her relatives—the warmth and closeness that came with being one tentacle of the family octopus—suffering through every tremor the whole organism experienced was something she was finding ever more burdensome and wearying.

"Still, I didn't want this—my decision to go—to be anything related to my wanting to get away from the family," Toni hastened to add. "I don't know if the family even had anything to *do* with it; that's not the top of my priorities, you know."

"What *is* your top priority?" I asked her.

She paused, then laughed. "You're real good at asking questions," she responded evasively. I laughed, too. Emily, who was snuggling next to Toni, moved upward on the large chair they shared and threw an arm up and around her mother's shoulder. Henry uncrossed his legs, then crossed the bottom leg over the one that had been on top. He leaned forward slightly and said, lightly and teasingly, "It's not often you get put in a position where you have to answer all the questions, Tone."

"What's a priority?" she repeated, looking at me as if to make certain about the exact nature of the question to be answered.

"*Top* priority," I replied, and she laughed again. But when the laugh faded, her expression grew thoughtful and serious. "What's top priority? I'd say probably it's the kids. Emily wanted to be with Henry, and then Laura wouldn't see him for another couple of years."

"Were you worried about missing him yourself?" I ventured.

"Yes. Probably," she answered vaguely, almost as if motivated by politeness. "There was probably some of that there, but I don't know if I really got in touch with that as much." I glanced at Henry, whose facial expression betrayed no reaction to what she had just said.

"Why is it so hard to get in touch with that?" I asked quietly. Then I smiled and added, "It's as if it's the last thing on earth you would ever admit to." I turned to Henry: "If she ever *does* admit it, you'd better be sure to get a signed confession." We all laughed, and Laura looked up from her pile of toys and started laughing along with us. Then she picked up a stuffed toy rabbit and toddled over to show it to her dad.

Toni's expression grew serious once again. "I don't know," she said haltingly. "Maybe it's because these past few years I've had to live without him. I'm not good at getting in touch with these things; I don't even know if I thought about it consciously. That I'd ultimately miss Henry, I mean, and that things would get too tough if he weren't around at all. There's some of that thinking in there, but I don't know if it was *the* thing that made me make the final decision."

I felt, at that moment, that the Giffords were involved in a complicated dance, in which each partner's movements were circumscribed by the fear that if he or she dared to take a step the other would not follow along. This was why they needed the very rules that were limiting and constraining them in terms of the ways they could relate to each other.

On impulse, I turned to Henry and said, "Are *you* as afraid of feeling dependent on somebody else as Toni is?" He looked up swiftly from the stuffed toy he had been admiring with Laura, a startled expression upon his normally impassive features. "Oh, yes," he said fervently, "I am."

His feelings, I thought, were like a vein of precious ore that has been exposed; they glinted there, very close to the surface, and could be mined if only Toni could permit him to have them. But if she were able to accept him as someone who was in fact hurting and uncertain at times, would he be capable of listening to her without feeling invaded and overwhelmed by her emotionality?

They were moving from a situation that seemed almost designed to circumvent intimacy—he commuted to the naval base in New York; she commuted to her own job and had established a comfortable domestic rhythm with her mother—and into a situation in which the demands for intimacy would inevitably escalate. Would the immense journey and relocation ahead of them—which would surely force their turning inward for mutual support in a strange environment—change things between them? This was, it seemed to me, the great gamble that the Giffords were taking.

A Sink-or-Swim Solution to the Problem of Intimacy: Moving Upward from Midrange, Level 3

Some people, it is true, learn how to swim by means of slow, careful instruction, while others learn to swim by simply leaping into the water and swiftly teaching themselves the moves they need to master in order to keep afloat. It was this latter course—a sink-or-swim solution to the problem of intimacy—that Toni and Henry Gifford were now in the process of attempting.

They were, most certainly, moving into a situation highly likely to induce high emotional demand and create the conditions that would either shift the system upward in a Level 2, adequate direction or precipitate a downward slide toward the borderline, Level 4 position on the Beavers Scale. For once they were abroad, Toni would be bereft of her usual intimate resources, and Henry would be without his customary capacity to be alone—off by himself on the base at Governors Island for days and weeks at a time. In a foreign country, with no housing currently available on the naval base itself, the Giffords would find themselves living in far more intimate circumstances, and seeing much more of one another and their children than they saw of the people around them.

In so radically changed an external situation, would these two partners be able to take the first tentative steps out from behind the barrier of ingrained rules and regulations that separated them, and that both of them had erected? Doing so would feel extremely threatening, for in a midrange emotional system, which is pervaded by pessimism about what can be hoped for from other human beings, the rules serve to give the system its basic structure, its sense of safety and security. The rules ensure that things will, by and large, move along in their predictable—*not intimate, but predictable*—familiar patterns.

Thus, while the rule-bound emotional system may not feel individually fulfilling or gratifying, it is reliably orderly and stable. One can depend upon the people inside the system to behave in expected, "appropriate" ways—for example, "*Men don't cry* (though they can, at times, drink too much in an effort to handle painful feelings)." In the case of the Giffords, each partner/parent had brought into the marriage certain well-learned family precepts, habits, styles of being, ways of defending against pain. Both partners were still entrenched, to some significant degree, in old childhood loyalties. And yet both were longing for some alternative—some better, different way of being together than either of them had ever known or could even imagine.

As Robert Beavers has noted, many couples are, like the Giffords, initially attracted to each other because both are searching for something that is missing within the self. That is, a person like Toni, who is lusting for a sense of separateness, is drawn to a person like Henry, who is lusting for a sense of connection. She is drawn to him because he clearly *knows* about separateness, while he is drawn to her because she is well versed in an emotional language whose very alphabet he has great difficulty understanding.

But alas, what often follows is that the partners, instead of respecting the potential teachings of the other—*the important things that could be learned from that very different other person's approach to life*—begin losing sight of what each of them was hungering for, and what was so attractive about the other in the first place. The clinical truism that couples usually divorce for the very same reasons that they initially selected each other is, in Beavers's view, based on the fact that so many people see in their chosen mates a way of finessing the difficult process of growing up into full, separate personhood.

The underlying idea here is, as Beavers explains, " 'If I can marry this person, I'll have solved the problem of separateness.' Or, 'If I can marry that person, I'll have solved the problem of connection.' " But, observes Beavers, "it doesn't actually work that way." This developmental shortcut—using a surrogate to fill in a missing piece of one's own internal world—is really a detour that leads absolutely nowhere; and, over the course of time, the very qualities that were once attractive about the partner become unbearable.

For, before very long, each partner is putting forward a different agenda in terms of what is the correct and proper, *right* kind of behavior. *She* feels that people should express warmth, and *he* feels that people should have self-discipline.

It is, however, impossible to use another person to achieve a sense of separateness—or connectedness—in one's stead and on one's behalf. Becoming a whole person requires that one learn to take responsibility for, and to integrate into one's own internal world, *both* needs—the dual needs for growth and differentiation, *and* for loving and connecting—that are part of our human birthright, and that exist (however denied or repudiated) within every one of us.

In Order to Be Intimate, One Must Make Oneself Vulnerable

Would the Giffords discover, in the crisis-inducing situation in which they were placing themselves, a way of being together as whole, yet separate persons? Toni and Henry were, it seemed to me, deeply scared of each other—frightened about the hurting that could follow if they ever dared to open up and make themselves vulnerable. Yet, at the same time, both were feeling isolated and lonely, and they were looking—however inchoately and incoherently—for some way out of their mutual dilemma.

Could these partners in life and in parenting ever, I wondered, reach a point at which each of them viewed the other as benign? Was it possible for each to see the other as a real ally, on the same side—as *trustworthy, even if very different* in strengths, weaknesses, needs? Could Toni and Henry Gifford ever regain that sense of camaraderie, of having "lots of things in common," and of sexual passion that they'd experienced earlier in their relationship?

In order to do so, each would have to give up the hopeless effort to legislate the other's behavior ("Be more intimate!" "Give me more space!") and both would have to work together to negotiate a new relational bargain, in which basic goodwill and acceptance were assumed to be present. This would involve deep risks, most especially the risk of moving away from the midrange system's predictable, familiar rules. It would involve the members of the couple making themselves truly vulnerable to each other, for *in the absence of vulnerability, intimacy cannot and never does exist.*

A Vision of the Giffords

Would the Giffords ever move beyond the carapace of suspicion and pessimism about what could happen between a woman and a man that permeated both their families of origin? It was anybody's guess. Still, driving homeward that afternoon, I glanced into the rearview mirror and noticed that there was a small smile playing around my lips. I had, as I realized immediately, caught myself in flagrante, in the midst of an elaborate fantasy about them.

I was imagining the entire family, now in Italy, strolling along a Mediterranean beach, somewhere around the beginning of twilight. In my fantasy, Emily and Laura were lagging behind their parents, filling their pails with seashells, while Toni and Henry ambled along, watching the soaring gulls swooping down over the surf in search of their evening meal. Then Henry, dropping his arm across his wife's shoulder, asked Toni what things she was thinking about, and what was on her mind—and she told him, and he listened to her, with empathy.

Such a happening would, as I knew in the cool light of reality, involve Toni's not only confronting her *own* deeply ambivalent issues about intimacy, but also challenging one of her family's most fundamental strictures: the unstated but well-heeded rule to the effect that a woman and a man could only live together as affectively distant antagonists. Then I sighed, thinking that for both the Giffords, making a true *friend* of one's partner would involve moving onto strange ground. It would mean moving upward on the scale, and into another kind of emotional world entirely.

PART FIVE

FAMILY BOUNDARIES
AND
THERAPEUTIC TASKS

CHAPTER 20

Self Boundaries and
Family Boundaries

When it comes to loving and being loved, we tend to do it in patterns reflective of the past—patterns absorbed in our families of origin, which have become woven into our ways of thinking and being as an internal diagram for being in close relationships. We bring into our present-day relationships powerful expectations of *what is likely to happen (based on what has happened) between emotionally involved intimates.* These expectations affect not only what we see in the important people in our lives, but also how we interpret what we see—and this interpretation, inevitably and in turn, affects the ways in which they then see and respond to us.

Put simply, what we perceive in the here and now has been shaped and patterned by the residues of many earlier experiences; we behave accordingly, and are perceived in the anticipated ways, often eliciting the very feedback that was expected.

A woman who has, for example, grown up in an overintense, enmeshed father-daughter relationship may make the unconscious assumption that this pattern will recur in an overinvolved relationship between her daughter and her husband. Indeed, she may later find that she is involved in the same kind of emotional triangle, this time involving herself, her husband, and their own developing daughter; the daughter may, in turn and on cue, have actually begun behaving toward the mother in a competitive, challenging fashion.

Or perhaps the mother—in the hope of preventing this feared but expected triangular pattern from ever emerging—takes a completely opposite but equally extreme tack. She may use her parental power to block any signs of normal affection between what seems to her a potentially dangerous pair: the father and the female child.

This mother might find it difficult to imagine the many other sorts of relationships that could exist between a daughter and her dad. For the mother's inner model of an adult woman and man and their developing daughter stars the younger female as the threatening usurper and rival. Or, to phrase that another way, the mother's own experiences would make it difficult for her to conceive of a secure boundary around the parental marriage, a boundary *not* being invaded by her female offspring.

And, to the extent that she insists upon seeing her daughter in that particular role, the mother is superimposing a transparency of the past upon current reality; she is seeing a piece of her own self and her own history in the "contending younger female" of the present. Therefore, if a problematical mother-daughter situation does (as is probable) emerge, it is very likely that the parent herself is violating the vitally important boundary between her separate self and that of her sexually maturing child. It is the mother who cannot recognize who her daughter actually is, as a unique individual, for she has projected aspects of her own old inner conflict into the person of the younger female and is now busily identifying vicariously with the daddy-vamping siren whom *she herself used to be.* The mother is seeing in her daughter an image of the young temptress that she herself has placed there—and she is responding to that image as if it were real (as it may come to be).

In such a situation, the vitally important boundary between self and other is being breached by this unresolved dilemma; the marital and the parental boundaries are being invaded, as well. For the daughter is being brought into the realm of the marriage, where no member of the younger generation ever belongs; and the mother cannot effectively guide and nurture a child to whom she is relating as if the child were a seductive, menacing challenger and peer.

At least three important intrafamily boundaries are being violated: the boundary demarcating self from other; the boundary demarcating the marital couple from the offspring; and the generational boundary demarcating those who nurture and those who are nurtured by them.

What Is a Boundary, Anyhow?

A boundary is what separates a part from a larger whole. In family-theory terms, it is the imaginary line that marks off a particular subunit (such as the individual, or the parental couple, or all the children in the family) from all that is outside its border. Problematic, distress-producing family boundaries readily fall into three major areas: the self-other boundary, the generational boundary, and the boundary between the family and the world outside it.

Boundaries and Rules

A vital function of boundaries is that of producing predictabilities about the ways in which the members of the various subgroups within the family will behave.

To some considerable extent, boundaries are based upon *rules* about how people in the family are to relate—rules about who may do what and on which occasions. Take, for instance, a fairly ordinary rule: "The children may not start eating dinner until the grown-ups are seated." This is not only a statement about the way in which members of the group are to behave at mealtime; it is also a declaration about where the boundaries are drawn—the children are in one group, different and separate from the parents, who are clearly the rule-makers, the people in charge. The rule about when one can eat is itself boundary-setting, because it creates a clear distinction between the leaders of the family (the parental subsystem) and their young dependents (the child subsystem).

There are, of course, occasions when a simple family rule such as the above does not have to be observed—for example, if the parents happen to be eating out that night with friends. But even in this case, the generational boundary is being enforced. The adults who have created the rule can change the rule to suit the circumstances, but clear-cut lines of authority between parent and child are being maintained.

Family rules, both explicit and implicit, prescribe the behaviors that are permissible between and within different subgroups of the organization. For example, only those within the marital boundary will be expected to relate to each other sexually; they will surely be expected to exclude other family members from this private domain. If, however, the father in a family should make a romanticized quasi-girlfriend of a favorite daughter (as Matt Maguire had seemed to be doing when he sent young Katie that gift of chocolate roses, while neglecting to give a Valentine's Day gift to his wife), he would be violating two boundaries—the marital boundary, and the boundary of the parental subsystem. His behavior would constitute emotional exploitation of his child, whether father and daughter became involved in an overtly sexual relationship or not. In short, family boundaries may be thought of as *the rules that determine who is within which subgroup within the overall system; that is, who can do what, and with whom, and on which particular occasions.*

Boundary Number 1: The Self Boundary

Suppose a casual acquaintance were to say to me, "I'll bet you love to travel," and I were to reply that no, I don't really enjoy traveling that much. I would, in the course of this exchange, have told that person something about who I actually am—about the preferences of the individual who actually dwells inside the private space I inhabit.

But if, on the other hand, my parent or spouse were to step in and answer for me by saying enthusiastically, "Yes, she's a *dedicated* traveler, and she always comes along whenever I go anywhere," I might feel that my ability to respond authentically had been swiftly and automatically trumped.

Depending on some crucial variables—my relationship with the person who has answered in my voice, and the context in which this exchange has taken place—I may experience myself as being thoroughly infantilized (unable to speak for myself) or invaded (prevented from saying what another person seems anxious not to hear). In such a circumstance, a *boundary infraction* has occurred. Someone has trespassed upon my individual territory and is transmitting information as if from within me. That individual is speaking as if he or she knows who I am better than I do.

If this kind of thing should happen frequently, my sense of privacy, safety, independence, and control over my inner world would in time be seriously compromised and eroded. For each of us needs a sense of our own individuality and separateness—a separateness that is permissible and respected—as much as we all need a sense of being part of a greater whole, which confers upon us feelings of comfort and of belonging.

Boundary Number 2: The Couple Boundary

Just as an intact boundary around the self differentiates what is "me, myself" from everyone and everything in the world of the "not-me," an intact boundary around myself and my partner guards the special marital turf, which belongs to us and is ours alone. In family-theory terms, our "spouse subsystem" is a subunit within the larger unit of our nuclear family group (which is itself a subunit of our extended family) and occupies a space that must never be trespassed upon by those who belong outside its vitally important perimeter.

According to the well-known theorist Salvador Minuchin, M.D., the boundary around the couple is crucial to the healthy functioning of the family enterprise as a whole. As he and co-author H. Charles Fishman point out in *Family Therapy Techniques*, the vital task of the adult partners is "the development of boundaries that protect . . . [the relationship,] giving them an area for the satisfaction of their own psychological needs without the intrusion of children, in-laws and others. The adequacy of these boundaries is one of the most important aspects of the viability of the family structure."

Woe, in a word, to those who inhabit an emotional system in which the all-important boundary around the marital couple is not being respected. When someone who belongs solely *outside* the pair becomes involved in matters that belong within the couple subsystem, everyone within the family will be profoundly affected. If, for instance, a mate's parent or a particular child is considered a far better confidant and companion than the intimate partner, a great emotional toll will be taken. For when the marital boundary is being violated in some fashion, systemwide problems inevitably develop.

Suppose, to cite another example, a mother complains to her growing son about his father's inadequacies and failures. In this situation, she is crossing a boundary and bringing her child into the marital sphere, where the youngster has no place and does not belong. She is overstepping the marital boundaries by doing so; and she is contravening the parental boundaries as well. For she is nurturing her child in a smothering, demanding manner, and at the same time asking her child for the kind of solace, understanding, and redress that only a spouse (not an immature youngster) can be asked to offer to a grown-up.

This is not only a serious infringement of a lawful generational boundary, but a form of emotional exploitation as well. If, moreover, the son's designated mission is to "save" his mother, he is bound to fail, for whatever he does will be wrong in her eyes (and therefore to some degree in his own). If the son should turn out to be a failure, like his father, he will clearly disappoint her hopes and wishes for a better future. But if, on the other hand, he should manage to go off and create an independent, successful life of his own—a life in which he and his new family thrive—he will carry within himself the awful sense that by leaving his mother behind he has abandoned his true responsibility and become the male disappointer he was pledged never to become. This is a no-win situation in one of its most striking, purest forms.

How does the son, on reaching his maturity, handle this "To win is to lose" dilemma? He may do so in a variety of ways, all of which involve making sure that if he does succeed, that success is compromised in some fashion. For even though, at a conscious level, he does want to prosper in his life, at an unconscious level he knows there is a price to pay for doing so—that to really grow up and leave his mother (not simply in the physical, but in the psychological sense) will be to destroy her.

Very frequently, the son's way out of such a quandary will be to shoot himself in the foot, symbolically speaking—turn a career success into a career failure (in actuality or in fantasy), or go through one or more completely unrewarding relationships, or become addicted to drink, drugs, or food. What the once-parentified son is quite likely to do in later life is, in other words, *be a disappointment* in some way or another.

The Family Organism

If one conceives of the family as a biological system with a high degree of organization, it is clear that no single element of the "family organism" can be thought of as functioning independently of the other component systems or subgroups that are all parts of a larger whole. In the instance cited above, for example, the woman's relationship with her son will affect not only the marital and parental subgroups but the boy's position within the sibling subgroup as well.

As his mother's "special child" and intimate companion, he will be raised above the junior generation—and yet not be accepted as a full-fledged member of the adult generation, either. He is neither completely in the marriage nor completely out of it—nor is he quite within the younger generation, since he is nurturing his parent instead of being nurtured by her.

The boundaries of at least two important subgroups of the family organization (that around the couple, and that between generations) are being subverted. This will affect the functioning of the entire emotional system, for each of its subunits is interconnected with its other subunits, and all exist in a complex, dynamic balance with one another.

An analogy to the human body might readily be made here, for it is obvious that any organ can affect the human body very dramatically. A person's heart cannot stop beating nor his liver stop functioning without destroying the organism itself. The part can affect the whole, just as the whole is always more than the mere sum of its component parts. A human body is something other—*greater*—than a mere collection of biological systems. Similarly, a family is a structured entity that is always something far greater than the sum of the individual members it comprises.

That *the part can impact upon the whole* is, however, the fundamental idea upon which modern systemic theory is based. All family-systems' theories and therapies take as their starting point the assertion that every subunit of the emotional system is deeply interconnected with every other subsystem, so that if change occurs in one area—in the couple's relationship, for example, or even in the behavior of one single individual within the group—systemwide changes inevitably follow.

Thus, if the overclose self-other boundary between the too tightly bonded mother and son were to be shifted and loosened, while the distant, disengaged relational boundary between the son and his father were being simultaneously reconnected and strengthened, then many other aspects of the family organization and hierarchy would shift in a more appropriate and functional direction. Not only would the marital and parental boundaries be redrawn, but the sibling subgroup would have to change as the son lost his special place in his mother's heart and he was moved back into the children's generation in which he belonged.

According to authors Minuchin and Fishman, it is the parental couple who provide the offspring's most important and indeed mesmerizing "model for intimate relationships, as expressed in daily interactions. In the spouse subsystem the child sees ways of expressing affection, of relating to a partner who is stressed, and of dealing with conflict as equals." What the child witnesses will eventually become part of his or her own values and expectations as the youngster comes into ever-increasing contact with the world outside the family cocoon.

The family's customary mode of transacting emotional business and constructing boundaries will later become the *natural* ways of relating and drawing boundaries, having been incorporated as an internal diagram or blueprint for living. Hence, a son whose mother was rejecting of his father and fiercely overconnected to him as her future savior is highly likely to struggle with the inner expectation that his own wife and his own male child are fated to fall into the same kind of "couplehood" eventually. So powerful may this expectation be that he withdraws in indignation—and then feels himself to be excluded, just as he always expected he would become.

We humans are the most wonderful of alchemists when it comes to transforming the boundaries that exist within our heads into the very real and present boundaries that are part of our everyday, current reality.

Boundary Number 3: The Family Boundary

Let me pause to take the analogy between the human body and the family as a complexly interrelated, biological entity one necessary step further. It is certainly obvious that however intact and well functioning an individual's internal organs may be, he or she cannot long prevail in a milieu in which adequate sustenance or shelter is not available.

As living organisms we depend upon a lively give-and-take with the external environment—we must import the supplies that we need (such as digestible food and uncontaminated water) and keep out what may possibly be harmful (spoiled food, polluted water, potentially dangerous strangers). Or, to take an even simpler example, we must breathe in air and exhale carbon dioxide. We are engaged in a variety of such continuous transactions between "inside" and "outside," and so what we require is a delimiting membrane, which is porous and yet capable of shielding us and protecting us from harm.

Families require such invisible but emotionally real borders around themselves as well. They must be capable of differentiating clearly between who and what belongs "inside" and who and what belongs "outside" the boundary of the nuclear group. The demarcating lines they draw around themselves must be penetrable enough to permit new things to happen and new members to enter the system (to welcome a new baby or a new daughter-in-law, for instance) and flexible enough to allow the maturing and individuating members of the group to depart on schedule into their own separate, adult lives without feeling guilty and traitorous.

At the same time, the family's boundaries must be sufficiently firm and secure to keep those within the intimate system feeling held, cared for, and protected. There must be a sense of a psychologically enclosing outline drawn around a special kind of place: a safe haven containing all kinds of potentially necessary resources, of both an emotional and a very down-to-earth and practical nature. A healthy, functional boundary around the total family offers everyone inside a concurrent sense of union and of closure.

Distress at the Boundaries

In severely troubled families, such as those located at the lower end of the Beavers Scale (Levels 4 and 5), problems at one or more of the important boundary lines—the self-other boundary, the generational boundary, and the boundary between the family and the world outside it—have predictably developed. The diagram on the facing page illustrates the usual nature of these problems in the most simple and graphic of terms.

In the perturbed and *enmeshed* family, as can be seen, the boundary separating each individual from any other individual in the group tends to be fuzzy and blurred. The group's insistence on perfect harmony and consensus creates an environment in which the capacity to be a separate self that is not confused with someone else's self is often nonexistent.

In the perturbed and *disengaged* family, on the opposite hand, the boundaries between the self and the other are not mushy, but far too rigid and impenetrable. In this emotionally distant system, each individual is like an isolated astral body adrift in a wide, empty, dark sky. Aside from the jagged, brief illumination offered by lightning flashes of hostility, the people inside the family are totally unable to make real affective contact. Clearly, the self-other boundaries within the enmeshed and disengaged groups are mirror-images of each other.

In both emotional systems, however, the generational boundary looks pretty much the same. It is always overly dilute, and it ranges from weak to seriously compromised to downright absent.

In an enmeshed system, for example, a lonely member of the senior generation (say, a father) may turn to one of his daughters and make of her

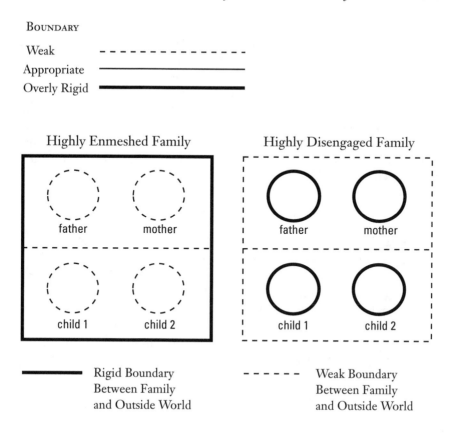

BOUNDARY

Weak - - - - - - - - - - - - - -

Appropriate ————————————

Overly Rigid ████████████████

Highly Enmeshed Family   Highly Disengaged Family

father   mother

child 1   child 2

father   mother

child 1   child 2

████████ Rigid Boundary Between Family and Outside World

- - - - - - Weak Boundary Between Family and Outside World

a loving equal and a companion. By effectively saying to his child, "I need you to meet certain needs that are not being met in my marriage with your mother," he is not only abdicating his parental role but asking his dependent offspring to be his intimate caretaker. He is thus violating the boundaries of both the parental and couple subgroups, for he is requiring that his daughter fill emotional needs that more properly belong within the marital sphere.

In distressed and enmeshed systems, as the distinguished marital and family therapist Stuart Johnson has pointed out, "the parents are usually trying to *look* like parents. In disengaged systems, though, the parents are often behaving more like angry, competitive peers." This was certainly true in the Andersons' Level 5 household (see Part One: "Level 5: The Family in Pain—Ghost-Ridden, Leaderless, Confused"). The parents of "defiant, oppositional" Dave Anderson were without real authority and often sounded like angry, demanding adolescents themselves.

At the third important family boundary—the boundary around the total family as an entity—the mirror-image effect reappears. In enmeshed families, this psychological fence tends to be inflexible and difficult to cross; the system's emotional grip is fiercely tenacious. In this kind of family, an adult daughter's bedroom may be left untouched, ready and waiting for her imminent return, twenty years after she has grown up and left the household. In a disengaged family system, on the other hand, the total group's boundary line can range from too dilute to completely absent. There is often no sense whatsoever of a special, sheltering psychic space; these affectively distant systems feel depriving, unprotected, and unbounded.

Therapeutic Tasks

Understanding what is meant by a boundary is a necessary prelude to the full appreciation of tasks, or therapeutic homework assignments. These clinical devices (a sampling of which will be described in the following chapter) are basically aimed at either weakening overly rigid boundaries or firming up boundaries that are perilously fuzzy, weak, or even totally lacking. The cardinal purpose of a task is, as shall be seen, to bring about a shift in the customary functioning of the family organization—an apparently minor change, which can often, in a seemingly miraculous, inexplicable fashion, bring about sweeping changes in everyone's behavior.

CHAPTER 21

Family Tasks

The very interesting assumption underlying all therapeutic tasks is the novel idea that new ways of behaving can often lead to new kinds of learning—that *enhanced insight and self-understanding may follow upon rather than precede new kinds of behavior.*

We are, of course, all quite used to the opposite idea, which is that new kinds of insight can produce changes in one's view of oneself, and thus changes in behavior; this is, indeed, the bedrock assumption upon which psychoanalytically oriented therapies are based. But the wonderful contribution of clinical homework assignments has been the demonstration that things can happen the other way around. By merely shifting the rules and doing things a bit differently—even in apparently trivial ways—it is possible to initiate completely different ways of thinking about the self and about others in one's intimate environment. And in this fashion, what has begun as a series of minute alterations in the usual script can on occasion produce huge differences in the story's eventual outcome.

Recipes for Change

Therapeutic tasks or "homework assignments" are nothing other than simple (but often devilishly ingenious) behavioral exercises designed to give the members of a distressed couple or family group a taste of what being in a better-functioning, more clearly well-bounded emotional system would be like. For by shifting the operational rules of the system, even in a very minimal fashion, a dissonance between the group's internal script and outer reality can be created. The tasks (a sampling of which is offered in the pages that follow) foster an *emotional awareness* of the ways in which important family boundaries are being routinely and habitually violated.

Consider, for example, an instance in which there is a dispute between a mother and a father about the "correct" way to go about putting their three grade-school-aged children down at bedtime. The mother's role, in this ongoing conflict, is to be perennially soft and gentle; she can spend all the time in the world being with the youngsters, talking to them, reading to them, singing lullabies, and the like. She can, in other words, meet their needs for nurturance as they slowly settle down into their individual night worlds. But, because she is completely unable to set reasonable limits about what time the lights should go out, the bedtime ritual is getting more and more extended.

This is a source of intense annoyance to her husband, whose antithetical role is to set the rules ("Pick up your toys!"), enforce them, and maintain authority. He can be frankly harsh at times, for it is he who embodies all the discipline of the marital pair. The couple's running quarrel about how to handle bedtime is, moreover, eroding both the quality and the quantity of evening time that they are able to spend together. It might even be suspected that the wife's intimate needs are being met far more in the relationships with her children than in the relationship with her husband, and that she wants to keep intimate time with him down to a minimum.

In any event, the problems at bedtime are either creating escalating tensions in the marriage or have developed as a way of dealing with marital tensions that preexisted. In truth, it is often easier for partners to fight about such things as how to put the children to bed than it is to fight about the really scary matters, such as disappointment or even despair about the relationship itself. This, of course, is how and why emotional triangles develop.

But it is clearly the case, as clinician Stuart Johnson observes, that an emotional system in which she only nurtures and he only limit-sets involves the mates in a fundamentally competitive, adversarial kind of process. "They are *fighting*," observes the clinician, who was for many years the director of family therapy at the Yale Psychiatric Institute, "and I am assuming that what is hidden behind that fight about bedtime is a marital fight, something going on between them."

The adult partners are, in other words, violating not only the self-other boundary but the generational boundary as well. They are playing out some marital problem around a parenting issue, thus bringing the children into an intimate arena in which they do not belong.

At an overt level, the members of the couple are clearly involved in a power struggle. They are in a polarized "If I win, you lose" interpersonal battle, competing about whose style of caretaking is the indisputably "right" one. But it may be conjectured that at a more covert level they are in collusion. For each of them has moved into a highly exaggerated, polarized position—almost a caricatured role—a phenomenon that usually indicates the partners are engaging in an exchange of projections and involved in an unspoken deal.

The main rules of their system (which is a projective-identification system) decree that *he* will carry and express all the aggression in the relationship and *she* will carry and express all the vulnerability for the pair. The wife and mother is then free to experience herself as devoid of any anger or need to discipline the children; she leaves it to her husband to feel the need to assert control and do all of the limit-setting on her behalf.

He, on the other hand, experiences himself as free of uncomfortably tender feelings and sticky emotionality; he depends on her to express the softer, more nurturant needs and wishes that have been banished from his own inner world. Each has projected onto the other, and sees in him or her, aspects of the self that cannot, for some reason, be consciously owned and tolerated—and each is now blaming the partner for containing such unacceptable qualities.

When members of an intimate pair "split the conflict" in this fashion (in this case, an internal conflict about softness/nurturance versus hardness/discipline with which *both* are struggling) their personal boundaries become blurred and uncertain. For in this kind of situation, each member of the pair is usually carrying certain denied and repressed thoughts, feelings, and ideas for the other one. The aggressive parts of the mother's being are lodged in her mate; the open, needy, vulnerable aspects of the father's inner world are being expressed in his partner's behavior. A major first step in resolving this dilemma would be to establish firmer individual boundaries around each of them.

In this kind of circumstance, a simple clinical device such as the odd day/even day parenting task may help the partners establish the vital self-other boundaries that projective identifications tend not only to blur but to demolish. If the couple can agree to abide by the elementary rules of this task for a period of time, they may be able to shift the relationship from a state of perpetual combat to a win-win resolution. For what this task's ordinances dictate is a way of interacting in which both members of the pair can be winners—a way of collaborating instead of competing endlessly about whose is the most appropriate, acceptable parenting style.

Be warned, however: Easy as these rules may sound, they are not always easy to put into action. What happens next is highly dependent upon the intensity of the power struggle in which the partners are engaged.

Odd Day/Even Day Parenting Task (Task 1)

The basic recipe for this therapeutic assignment involves putting *both mother and father in complete control of parenting*—not simultaneously, but on alternating days. In the situation given above, for instance, the wife might be placed in sole command of getting the children to bed on Monday, Wednesday, and Friday, while the husband did it his way on Tuesday, Thursday, and Saturday. On Sundays, the parents would be permitted a day off from the task. According to family therapist Johnson, the pair can use this time to "practice their pathology" by returning to the battle about whose style of parenting is the superior one.

The couple would, it must be noted, have to make an initial agreement about what they both considered to be an appropriate bedtime—nine to nine-fifteen P.M., for example. Then their rotation of command would serve to demonstrate to them (by means of their own experience) their own ability to collaborate around goal-setting—a negotiated lights-out time—and yet to attain that goal in their two very different and unique kinds of fashion.

The parent who is the more easily manipulable "softie" might initiate the going-to-bed process a half-hour earlier, since she will surely feel more comfortable with ample space in which to do her emotional connecting. But limit-setting is *up to her* at that point; she must meet the agreed-upon time goal. The parent who is the disciplinarian would probably be able to begin getting the children to bed somewhat later (he doesn't need as much time) but would have to allow enough space in which to do the amount of nurturing with which he is able to feel comfortable.

This alternation of authority creates a collaborative, collegial situation: By shifting the leadership position on a daily basis, both members of the couple get to be in control of parenting (sequentially) and are at the same time released from the acrimonious struggle for total authority, which neither could ever win decisively.

The odd day/even day task, which now exists in many clinical forms and variations, was first used by the famed Italian analyst Mara Selvini Palazzoli as a way of breaking up control struggles around the parenting of a child. Taking turns gives *both* partners what each could never achieve separately: undisputed sway over the domestic scene, at least during certain designated time periods. Gaining control means sharing control, and sharing it with one's separate and very different, but not thereby misguided and wrongheaded (or downright ill-motivated), mate.

Odd Day/Even Day Variation (Task 1A)

A variation on the basic recipe given above might be for one parent (say, the nurturer) to be in sole command on her day, but able to enlist her partner's assistance. According to these rules, on her designated days *he must do whatever she asks him to do.* On his alternate days, the disciplinarian is in charge of the entire process, but his partner has previously agreed to assist him in whatever ways he may require.

By following this behavioral agenda, the members of the couple will be committed to an agreement about who is captain and who is first mate in a steadily fluctuating routine, instead of engaging in an ongoing (and destructive to their children) quarrel about who is the true caretaker in authority.

Role Reversal (Task 1B)

Another clinical strategy that might be useful in this situation would be to divide the nighttime ritual into its two major components—nurturing the children, and setting limits—and giving half the overall task to each parent. Using this format, the mother would be (as usual) the nurturer and the father (as usual) the limit-setter on Monday, Wednesday, and Friday, but on Tuesday, Thursday, and Saturday they would reverse roles and each would take on what was customarily the other parent's part of the job.

On the odd days of the week, then, the father would involve himself in talking with the children, reading them stories, and getting them settled down and ready to retire. The mother's main efforts would be centered around bedtime itself, for her job would be to get the kids into bed and to be responsible for making sure that they remain there. On the even days the parents would switch back, and each would return to the role with which he or she has been overly identified and is so pathologically comfortable.

This task is useful in interrupting the ongoing exchange of projections—which, as therapist Johnson observes, have a self-reinforcing quality. For, typically, the more the wife behaves like a softie, the more the husband sees her as weak and manipulable—so spineless that she would permit the children to stay up until midnight if he didn't move in and interfere. And, the harsher and more authoritarian is the father's stance, the more the mother sees him as cold, unloving, and dictatorial. Jumping into each other's behavioral shoes tends to break up the circularity of the couple's projective-identification system.

By means of this sweeping alteration of their standard roles, each person gets to experience *what it feels like* to do the nurturing or limit-setting with which he or she is so unversed. In the best of circumstances the mates can then begin to recognize the critical nature of both parenting functions (for the children do have to be nurtured at bedtime, *and* also put into bed and kept in bed) and to recognize the differing strengths and weaknesses each of them brings to these equally important activities.

Breaking out of their predictable script helps to shift the partners out of an adversarial process and into a cooperative one—and, not incidentally, helps them disentangle their marital dilemmas from an unresolvable power struggle about how children should be parented. Role reversals, which can be used in a wide variety of situations, also enhance self-other boundaries by inducing in each person an empathetic awareness of what it feels like to be in the other person's position. It is a step in the direction of reclaiming the disowned side (hers, about limit-setting and self-assertion; his, about being tender and vulnerable) of the inner ambivalence.

Note: An alternative way of carrying out this particular task would be to alternate on a weekly instead of a daily basis. In this format, the mother is in charge of limit-setting for six consecutive days. She has nothing to do with nurturing, but is responsible for getting the children to bed and making sure they stay there. The father is in charge of bedtime nurturance, which involves stories, conversation, reading, and so forth; but once the children *do* go to bed, he is out of the picture.

The following week, the couple's polarized roles flip back into their more customary positions. Obviously, the rationale for this therapeutic assignment is identical with the rationale for the odd day/even day role reversal given directly above.

Odd Month/Even Month Parenting Task (Task 1C)

In this version of the basic assignment, the time frame is broadened and the rules are altered to deal with a parental power struggle in a slightly different fashion. Before describing these rules, however, let me sketch in the kind of circumstance in which an odd month/even month rotation of command could prove extremely helpful and effective.

Imagine a situation in which the mother of two preschoolers tells the children that it's time to pick up their toys, which are at the moment strewn all over the living room. It is getting close to bedtime, and the overtired youngsters raise objections and don't want to obey her instructions. As the mother becomes more and more annoyed and insistent, the father moves into the dispute and says to her: "What's the big deal? Leave the kids alone; we can pick up the toys ourselves after we put them down to sleep."

What has actually occurred in the course of this small interaction? And if similar incidents recur repeatedly, what is really going on between the members of the couple, and between them and their small offspring? For one thing, the mother's leadership capacities are being compromised, for her spouse is taking a stance that is superior to hers (he can veto her decision unless she is ready to quarrel openly with *him*) and allying with the younger generation in a manner that will surely undermine her rightfully managerial role in the family organization.

The father is taking the role of children's defender, of buddy, and of good guy, while forcing his wife into the opposing, far more negative position of demanding yet disempowered disciplinarian. He is at one and the same time assuming a subordinate role (orienting toward his mate as if he were a member of the defiant child generation) and a superordinate role (by interfering with her capacity to enforce commands). Obviously, the ongoing functioning of the family organization is going to be vitally and negatively affected, *as it always is when parents are not united in their position.* A way of dealing with this kind of triangular issue (children and dad against mom) is to have the parents share decision-making by alternating the top-dog status.

In this version of the command-rotation task, the couple may take any two troublesome family issues, and then agree that they will abide by the following behavioral contract: For the next month *she* will be in charge of one of these problem areas (such as making sure that the children pick up their toys) while *he* assumes control of the other area (such as settling disputes that arise between the youngsters when the entire family is at home). She is then to be the sole arbiter of the toy-picking-up situation, and he is to support her authority—just as she supports his own efforts to make sure the children resolve their differences and squabbles, which he will do *in his own way and in his own style.*

After a month, the parents switch: The mother takes control of settling the quarrels, while the father assumes charge of the daily toy cleanup. In the meantime, *both* partners are building important new skills, for they are operating within an emotional system in which "You do it your way for a month, and I'll support you" and "I'll do it my way for a month, and you'll support me" are the important behavioral directives being followed.

The ultimate effects of this routine would be to move Dad out of his partial membership in the child subsystem (where he was behaving as a peer to his own offspring and joining with them in a rebellious stance toward his wife) and back up into the adult subsystem in which he properly belongs. Not only will the generational boundary be profoundly affected; the integrity of the marital boundary will be affected as well. For now, instead of feeling undermined and angered by her partner's behavior, the wife will feel respected and supported in her mothering efforts.

Note: The odd month/even month task assignment can be carried out as an odd week/even week task if that is the time frame preferred. Whether one alternates any of the above tasks by months, weeks, or days will clearly depend on how well the children respond to these alternations in parental behavior. Some children may find the daily changes prescribed in an odd day/even day task confusing and difficult to tolerate, while others will fall into this fluctuating routine with huge pleasure and enjoyment—"It's Daddy's night to tell us stories!"

Task 2: Town Meeting

This remarkable therapeutic homework assignment was first described to me by Betsy S. Stone, Ph.D., a clinical psychologist in private practice in Stamford, Connecticut. The simple instructions are as follows: Everyone in the family has to come to a town meeting, ready to state an important want or a need. That want or need can be anything within reason. After everyone has heard everyone else's need, the parents are to go off to a separate place and talk about what the children have said they need, while the children go off by themselves and talk about needs that the parents have communicated. Then, after a twenty-minute interval, the larger group reconvenes. The members of the two family subgroups (the sibling subsystem and the adult subsystem) now converse together about the results of each smaller group's private discussion.

That is all; but what might the carrying out of this behavioral task look like in action?

Dr. Stone describes one instance in which she herself called such a town meeting in her office, because she felt that the family she was treating might not do their therapeutic homework assignment otherwise. In this case, the presenting problem had to do with an adolescent daughter whose parents had grown alarmed because the girl seemed to be growing secretive and they suspected that she might be getting involved in certain experiences of an unknown but vaguely sexual nature.

Stone asked the parents, who had initially come to consult with her by themselves, to bring the whole family (which consisted of the couple and their two daughters, ages fourteen and ten) in to see her. It was in the course of therapeutic work with the entire group—work which at that juncture was feeling stuck and resistant to change—that the psychologist initiated the task described above. Handing each member of the family a small slip of paper, she said, "Write down something that it would be important for you to have." ("State a need," in translation.)

Each of the daughters was readily able to enunciate a very specific, concrete request. "The ten-year-old wanted to have her ears pierced, as many of her friends had done, and the fourteen-year-old wanted her own telephone; both requests were reasonable and appropriate. The father said that what he wanted was to have everyone in the family be at home when he came in from work; what Mom wanted most was for her two girls to get along. That was *her* need," reiterated the psychologist, with a fleeting smile.

The parents then went to the office anteroom to sit and talk together about the children's needs and what might be done to facilitate meeting them, while the children used the clinician's office to engage in a similar discussion. "I flitted back and forth between them," relates Stone, "and found that they were really able to carry out the task very well."

The mother and father talked about whether or not the younger daughter could have her ears pierced, and what the consequences might be, and who was going to pay for it if they agreed that it could happen. Should the procedure be paid for out of the child's own savings? And come to think of it, if they agreed that the older daughter could have a telephone, who would be responsible for the installation and the monthly bills?

"The adults really focused on money, while the children tended to focus on evaluating their parents' needs rather than on trying to *address* those needs. And the girls decided that it was reasonable for Dad to want them to be at home when he came in, but it wasn't reasonable for Mom to insist that they get along with each other."

When the town meeting reconvened, the children said, "Dad, we can be home when you get home most of the time; but some days we can't. We'll let you know in the morning if we think we may *not* be at home, but we may not know ourselves, in advance. In the ordinary course of things, though, we will always try to warn you." To their mother, on the other hand, the daughters said: "Listen, Mom, we don't get along all the time— and we *can't*, because there are things that we don't really like about each other. But when we argue, we'll do it in our own rooms and work out our problems by ourselves."

What these two daughters were telling their mother was that they needed to *have* their differences and not attempt to remain glued to each other in the undifferentiated sisterly harmony of their earlier childhood. They were also saying that they required space in which to argue their differences out between themselves—without having their mother leap into the fray and become overinvolved in their own separate relationship.

The parents, in the course of their own private discussion, had agreed that their younger daughter could have her ears pierced. They had also concluded that the older girl could have a telephone if she was willing to pay for half the installation from her own savings. What had happened seemed relatively minor, and yet carrying out the task served to strengthen the boundary around the child subsystem (the mother was being requested to stay out of the center of her daughters' relationship). As matters developed, the task also enabled the youngsters to resist being invaded by certain issues that belonged in the marital domain alone.

"Two weeks later, when the family returned," reports Stone, "the daughters came in and talked (with a bit of therapeutic assistance) about the fact that they thought their parents needed to do some work on their own relationship. They said they thought that Mom was feeling really lonely for Dad, and perhaps the pair of them needed a bit of marital help— not much, just a small amount."

The rules of the task, which clearly separated the marital subsystem and the child subsystem into two distinct discussion groups—which were then instructed to hold private talks and come to their own collective conclusions—brought the real distinction between these two important subsystems into high relief. This served not only to strengthen the generational boundary, but to prevent emotional leakage from one subgroup into the other.

In fact, the town meeting task affects boundaries at *all* levels of the family organization. At the individual level, articulating an important subjective need is a way of locating a self boundary—of saying "This is who I am, and this is what's important to me." Also, the rules of this therapeutic task serve to promote intimacy, for in the process of disclosing an important need one is not only telling others in the group a good deal about what one's private concerns actually are but also having attention and respect accorded to one's own individuality.

Task 3: Sharing Negative Feelings

This clinical device can be extremely helpful in emotionally overconnected, relentlessly positive, and harmonious family atmospheres, where the emphasis is on consensus and presenting a happy face (whether or not it happens to coincide with one's inner experience). The simple instructions for the task are that each family member must talk for a brief period of time—five to ten minutes, depending upon the size of the group—about whatever happened during the day that was distressing, angering, hurtful, or frightening.

While the speaker holds forth, everyone else in the group must pay respectful attention and not respond until the entire communication has been completed. At the conclusion of each such personal broadcast, others in the family are free to offer sympathy and to ask if there is some concrete way in which help might be offered. Would some joint problem-solving be useful? And might a big hug be welcome? But what usually proves most beneficial is *simply being heard.*

It should be said that this is not an easy task for certain families to tolerate. For when the individual members' interpersonal boundaries are blurred, they often find each other's pain difficult or impossible to tolerate. Instead of being able to let a family member voice his or her distress, the others feel as if they've got to take it away immediately—fix it on the spot—or alternatively, to run away, because one's own pain about the other person's pain is too agonizing to experience.

In a projective-identification situation—that is, a situation in which self-other boundaries are blurred—the listener or listeners are reacting to their own pain about the other person's pain, and they usually find that pain completely unbearable. They simply have to get the person to stop emoting. Indeed, the hardest thing for many people to understand is that when a beloved other is suffering one cannot reach in and try to wrest their pain away. Nor must one make space between oneself and the other. For the human truth is that simply *hearing about* the loved person's pain and distress can be both a loving and healing experience for everyone concerned.

Note: Some families find it so difficult to discuss any kind of negative events openly that they may find it useful to begin this task by reporting only experiences that, though unpleasant, are relatively inconsequential.

Task 3A: Sharing Positive Feelings

In families at the opposite end of the affect spectrum—families in which an atmosphere of remorseless misery prevails—the primary thoughts and feelings being communicated are depressive, angry, or complaining ones. In this kind of negatively toned emotional system, the basic Task 3 rule would be reversed; the instruction would be for each member of the family to discourse for five or ten minutes about some *pleasureful* experience that has taken place during the course of the day.

In this case the positive parts of life are being routinely banished from the shared family terrain. Indeed, there may be a competition for the role of the individual with the worst problems, because the negatives tend to receive more parental attention than do life's pluses. This clinical assignment is designed to actively counter such an orientation and to help each member of the group *make contact with and pay attention to those gratifying aspects of existence* that they all seem so committed to ignoring.

In essence, what both these feeling-sharing tasks support is the understanding that it is possible to be a separate, whole person—someone who is happy at times and downcast at other times—and yet remain in good emotional contact with other members of the intimate circle simultaneously.

Task 4: Resolving Conflict

The instructions for this remarkably effective strategy can be used by any feuding pair within the family group, whether they be husband and wife, siblings, or a parent and a particularly targeted "impossible" child. The easy instructions for this quarrel-settling task are as follows: As soon as a fight begins to develop, the person who is getting angry should be given ten to fifteen minutes in order to tell the partner exactly (1) why she or he is angry; (2) what she or he thinks the basic issues are; and (3) what feelings (such as hurt or fear) lie just beneath the surface of the anger being communicated.

To illustrate how this therapeutic device might influence an emerging argument, let me return to a situation described earlier: the one involving a father who had stepped in and neutralized his wife's efforts to get the children to pick up their toys. Now, let us suppose that in this husband's somewhat childlike orientation to his wife, he himself is behaving a bit rebelliously; he often leaves the bathroom strewn with wet towels, no matter how often or how nicely she asks him to hang them up after his shower. And one enchanted morning, she becomes utterly and volubly furious.

The angry scene that develops is, in the husband's view, like a sudden tornado that has struck the entire household (and his innocent self) out of nowhere. He doesn't see it as something generated out of his own behavior, but rather as emanating from his wife's incomprehensibly shrewish need to attack him—and he counterattacks immediately.

The problem, for the wife, is that she considers his having dropped the wet towels on the floor as an act meant to deliver a message, which is that her needs and wishes are of no significance whatsoever. *She experiences his behavior as a direct assault upon her self-esteem*, and she feels that by dropping the towels he has consciously set out to denigrate and hurt her. In so doing, however, she is confusing the *effect* of his action with its *intent*, which was certainly lazy and thoughtless but very possibly not meant to be harmful or attacking.

The husband, in turn, feels unjustly reviled and thoroughly misunderstood. As he sees it, his wife is not attacking his thoughtless behavior; she is attacking him as a person. Why else would she be making such an emotional extravaganza out of something so trivial as his having failed to hang up the towels? While she has indeed mixed up the deed itself with its motivation, *he hears her as denouncing not his behavior but himself as a bad human being*. And, very naturally, he in turn defends himself.

In the view of family therapist Stuart Johnson, who devised this particular version of the conflict-resolution task, angry intimates are often quarreling about two very different things, while neither of them realizes this to be the case. One subject is the behavior itself (the husband's having left the bathroom strewn with towels); the other is the underlying motivation for the act. "In this case, because the wife feels so hurt, she is assuming that he *meant* to hurt her and that he's therefore a low-down evil human being. He, on the other hand, is defending his motives, which he insists were not evil. . . . Basically, they are in a fight in which she's saying 'My apples are better than your oranges' and he's saying 'No, my oranges are better than your apples'—they're not even arguing about the same thing."

The pair are then very likely to be caught up in an escalating vicious circle of intensifying attack and counterattack that is far too confused and confusing to ever be concluded amicably. The fight about this event becomes a fight about many other events, and they segue swiftly into a situation in which they are trading insults, blame, and memories of past injuries and grievances of all kinds.

Had they, however, declared a cease-fire in place and moved into Task 4 in an early phase of this conflict (as soon as she began communicating her rage about the state of the bathroom) the ensuing scene might have been played out completely otherwise. Instead of getting into a battle in which each lost sight of the other person, and of what he or she might be thinking and feeling, the wife's communiqué to her husband might have proceeded along the following lines:

1. *Why am I angry?*

I'm angry because I'm being made to feel like a nag; I ask you *constantly* to hang up the towels after using them. Sometimes you get irritable about my asking you, and sometimes you agree to my request very nicely—but in either case you seem to forget pretty soon anyhow. And the fact is that after you leave for the office (even though I have to be out of here shortly afterward, myself) *I'm* going to have to go into the bathroom and pick up every one of those towels! And when I do that, it's going to make me even *angrier*, because I'll feel that you're behaving like one of the children and that I have to be the only adult in the entire household.

It really makes me feel as if we aren't quite sharing this parenting job, but that you're just one more child that I've got to care for. I just can't seem to get through to you, and no matter how many times I ask you, you always seem to, quote, forget, unquote, this minor matter, which I've told you matters to *me* enormously. It's clearly something unimportant, but if it's important to your partner how *can* it be unimportant for you? If you really care about another person, doesn't what matters to that person (however trifling) merit your attention?

To me, that's what loving is about. To me, showing love and concern has to do with trying to meet the other person's needs just as well as trying to meet your own; but that's just not *happening* here. What's happening is that I'm getting the message that the last thing on your mind is *my* needs, and that what I want is something you can't be bothered to take very seriously. Every third day or so, you forget all about my request and leave the bathroom in a mess, even though I've told you how much it bothers me. And at this point—whether I say it aloud or whether I don't even mention it—the fact that you *do* keep forgetting infuriates me.

2. *What are the issues?*

To me, the basic issue is that what I want just doesn't seem to figure in your thinking. You just seem so self-absorbed and into yourself that you can't be bothered to pay any heed to something that I've *told* you irritates me on an almost daily (or at least twice-a-week) basis. What this tells me is you find me awfully easy to ignore. And it makes me feel, too, as if I'm a big, finger-wagging mom relating to a little, naughty boy—which is making me really *uncomfortable*. I'd like to think of us as being equals, who are *sharing* responsibilities, but instead I'm feeling more like an angry mama with her bad little son—and I get the feeling that you're somehow *pushing* me into that role.

3. *What are the feelings underneath the anger?*

My main feeling is one of being totally disregarded, and it's all too familiar a feeling for me. As you well know, I was a bit of a waif and a raga-muffin—my parents never took care of me, even so far as dressing me for school was concerned. My mother was in many ways a loving person, but she never paid a reasonable amount of attention to the grooming needs of a child. I didn't have clean clothes to wear, and I often left for school without even having had my hair combed: I wasn't being *watched out for*, even on that very basic level. And it's not news to you that where my father was concerned, it was much worse; he hardly ever even *spoke* to me, and he made it impossible for any of us kids to connect with him at all. It was, as I look back on it—and as I think about the things a young child needs from her parents—annihilating. So now, when you ignore me as you sometimes do, I don't just feel ignored, I feel *violated*. It's as if what you're really saying to me is "I don't need to listen to you, because actually you don't exist at all."

Often, by the time the distressed person has gotten to the feelings underneath the anger, much of the anger has in fact dissipated. And the other person, having heard her out, can more readily understand the impact of his behavior upon her. He will also be more capable of understanding and empathizing with her—something that would be unlikely to happen in the heat of an ongoing battle.

The rules of the task serve not only to block the fight's escalation but to keep the quarreling twosome focused on the issue that has arisen at the moment (in this case, the state of the bathroom) rather than on all of the problems and indignities of the past. To complete the assignment, however, two final edicts must be observed. The first is that *after the angry person has had her say, the partner is not supposed to respond.* His job is simply to hear her out from the beginning to the end of her communication.

Secondly, in exchange for receiving this opportunity to vent her feelings without interruption or fear of counterattack, *she must promise not to bring up the issue at any moment outside the designated task time.* This gives both people a sense that the situation is under control—the wife in the above example cannot mount a new blaming attack about the wet towels at any time that she feels the impulse to do so. And at this juncture—after her initial rage has died down and he has begun to comprehend its sources—

the partners can start negotiating, and can work out a way to manage the relatively mundane matter of the towel-strewn bathroom.

Comment: This therapeutic task's greatest impact is clearly at the self-and-other boundary. Instead of getting into a confusing exchange of negative projections in which (metaphorically speaking) the wife kicks the husband and he kicks her back, so she kicks him harder and then he kicks her harder, the gong sounds almost immediately and the fight is halted before Round 1 is even under way. The rules then enjoin the person who is angry to say clearly, "It is *I* who feel this way, and while the way I feel doesn't necessarily correspond to the way *you* would feel in a similar situation, there are in fact personal, historical reasons for my resonating to this particular experience—and it is of the greatest importance, to both of us, that you come to understand and respect them." The quid pro quo that the other person receives is that, having heard her out, he is assured that she will not re-attack him on the subject, and the quarrel can be halted with a realistic, goal-oriented negotiation.

Task 5: Family Contracting

The purpose of this assignment is to create a clear-cut set of family regulations, but what must be said at the outset is that the more healthy and competent a family already is, the easier they will find this task to perform. This is a case in which, alas, the well functioning are able to become more well functioning, while families at the lower end of the Beavers Scale have difficulties even arriving at an agreement, much less abiding by the rules they have devised. At the time of Dave Anderson's discharge from Elmcrest hospital, for example, the family's attempt to work out a home contract led immediately to an all-out battle.

The creation of a set of family by-laws occurs in the following fashion. First, the parents, as the leaders of the family, sit down together and create a rough draft of a set of rules. These may involve spelling out who does what and under which circumstances, and may include everything from Mom's agreeing not to throw temper tantrums when she is under stress to teenage Jim's getting home on time to meet his ten o'clock weeknight curfew. It can involve enunciating clearly each individual's fair share of the household chores (walking the dog; taking out trash; washing dishes) and the privileges and consequences attached to carrying them out or failing to do so.

Once the parents have created a working paper of this kind, they invite the children to a family-wide discussion that will edit the rough draft into a final jointly created document. At this juncture, it is important that the youngsters be made to realize that these initial "rules of the game" are not going to be imposed upon them by the adults, and that their own feedback will be welcome. The children are to let the adults know where the regulations are too strict or too lenient—or where they may be dead wrong, for that matter.

The children are also expected to make suggestions about *other* ideas that they believe the parents should put into consideration (perhaps lunch out with Dad in exchange for helping him wash the car) but that have not been included in the rough draft.

At this point, the grown-ups retire with the additional data, and whatever parts of it seem reasonable and plausible *to both parents* can be incorporated into the contract. Where the youngsters' suggestions and changes are considered inappropriate or unworkable, the reasons why this is so are to be fully explained to them, with the assurance that all of their input is being taken very seriously.

The final results of this joint effort will be the family's behavioral guidebook—a set of clearly articulated rules that everybody understands that they've agreed to try their best to live by. And because each member of the group (from the youngest to the oldest) has been busily negotiating for his or her own rights and responsibilities, the boundaries between the self and the other members of the group will be enhanced.

As Stuart Johnson notes, the boundary between the generations will also have been clarified and strengthened in the course of these negotiations, because the parents have created the initial version of the contract together, then opened it to discussion by the wider group, and finally retired together to work the document into its final form. This requires that they collaborate and reach agreement between themselves and then present a united front in their negotiations with their offspring—a joint leadership position which, as mentioned earlier, is crucial to the overall vitality and well-being of the family organization as a whole.

Tailor-made Tasks

In practice, the family in distress is usually given very specific therapeutic homework assignments that are tailor-made to fit its own particular circumstances. A task-oriented therapist may at times prescribe therapeutic homework for the entire family, and at other times give differing tasks to different members of the group. These tasks are always designed to give the individual or the family a taste of the honey of what life could be like if one did things just a little bit differently.

At times, a therapeutic assignment will sound somewhat quixotic and perhaps incomprehensible (or even nutty) to the person or family receiving it. This is particularly true of homework tasks that are more indirect and paradoxical in nature, such as those that were used with the Andersons. (See Chapter 6, "Closely Connected People: The Family Script, Projective

Identification, and Paradoxical Tasks.") A number of paradoxical strategies are now commonly in use, and they often sound as if they make no logical sense whatsoever. But these devices are, as mentioned earlier, very potent clinical curveballs.

The Ultimate Therapeutic Assignment

The ultimate therapeutic task of any of our lives is undoubtedly that of forgiving the wrongs that have been done to us, for unless and until we are ready to give and receive such forgiveness, we can never really put those wrongs behind us. The dilemma here is, however, that the ability to forgive is itself rooted in an emotional system in which people are able to *hear* criticisms and to take personal responsibility for their words and actions (which, given that most of us cannot lay claim to being utterly faultless, *will* be flawed, foolish, and hurtful to others from time to time).

This, in turn, presupposes *a family script in which the words "I'm sorry," and forgiveness for one's very human errors, exist. It presupposes an emotional system in which all understand that, being human, we cannot expect to achieve a perfection that involves never receiving or giving out (however inadvertently) any slights, insults, or injuries. The best we can hope to achieve is an atmosphere in which differences that lead to conflicts can be faced directly, ventilated fully, fought about if necessary, understood empathically, worked through, resolved, and ulti-mately forgiven.*

In many families, though, nothing of the sort ever happens. Instead of being able to forgive one another's inevitable wrongs and failings, each member of the group seems to treasure, hoard, and count over and over again the many early griefs and indignities that have been visited upon her or him. Everyone scrambles for the moral high ground, from which a torrent of blaming is hurled down: It is the parents, sister, brother, grand-mother, or stepparent—or the entire family—who is basically at fault for all the bad things that have ever happened in one's life, or that may be happening in it right now.

According to Stuart Johnson, however, this strategy for dealing with the past does no more than identify a perpetrator and a victim—and it tends to leave the victim (the "inner child") lying there bleeding from an emotional wound that he or she believes cannot ever be stanched. Inevitably, the unfinished business of the past—which is the pain that has never been confronted, experienced, resolved, *and forgiven*—becomes the business of the present. For until we find it possible to forgive and let go, that pain and conflict repose within us, stored and awaiting eventual recy-cling in a new generation, whether we can acknowledge this to ourselves or we cannot.

Task 6: The Task of Forgiving

How, one might well ask, could a person possibly go about pardoning and putting to rest the injustices of the past if he or she happens to dwell in the kind of emotional system in which forgiveness is not even conceived of as a viable option? The following task, outlined to me by Stuart Johnson (who has made use of it in many forms), is truly a wonderful feat of emotional engineering. It is like a great prefabricated construction that can be lowered right into the center of the family and assembled rapidly, so that a structure for forgiving is in place where no such structure ever existed earlier.

The easy instructions for this therapeutic assignment can best be given in the context of a clinical example. One very commonplace instance might be that of a young married daughter, with small children of her own, who is beaming anger and enmity at her parents—letting them know that she is enraged with them because of the many ways in which they always have failed her and now continue to do so. The reasons for the daughter's anger are never quite specified (the parents believe it may have to do with problems in her own marriage, for the dissension did emerge at that time), but whenever anyone initiates an effort to break the gridlock and confront the issues, a nonproductive, irrational discussion ensues, and a new emotional standoff emerges.

In this particular case, the guidelines for the forgiving task might be as follows. The parents (or one of them) would launch the action by going to the daughter and saying, "Something is terribly wrong between us, and we have scratched our heads trying to figure out what it is, but we can't come up with any answers other than the obvious one, which is that there seem to be a whole lot of issues from the past—issues that have do with *us*—which remain unresolved. And while this is difficult and bothersome for us, we're far more concerned about what it may be doing to *you*, because we know, from our own experience, that when someone is dragging along a lot of unresolved stuff from the past it sorely limits that person's capacity to enjoy both the present and the future. So, while we're feeling bad for ourselves about all this tension, we're feeling even *worse* on your behalf—for no matter what you may be thinking, we really do care about you, and we're worried about your being stuck in a place that's in fact very limiting and unpleasant."

The phrasing of this opening statement is, suggests Johnson, of critical importance; it must be thought about and composed very carefully in advance. For in order to undercut the daughter's possible resistance to the subsequent phases of the task, what must be stressed is *not* the feud's effects on the parents, but its effects on the daughter herself.

The second step of the forgiving task is to work out a plan for the married daughter to meet with one or both parents (as she chooses) on her own. The ground rules for this meeting, and its stated purpose, are as follows: The daughter will be given the opportunity to sit down with her parents for a set period of time—minimally, a half hour; maximally, an hour—and expound upon and ventilate her charges and her complaints about them, in their entirety. The parents' promise, made at the outset, is that they will *not* attempt to defend themselves, nor will they try to parry or refute her accusations (no matter how outrageous those accusations may sound) with any proofs of their utter inaccuracy.

Their goal, to which they must steadfastly adhere, is to sit with her, meet her gaze, feel her pain, and *just listen.* The content—what the daughter says—should be seen, in Johnson's view, as "mostly rubbish and debris"; *it is the process of hearing her out that is of crucial importance.* And last—this is the definitive goal of the entire endeavor—the parents must take clear responsibility for anything they have done, however inadvertently, which might have hurt her in the past.

They must take ownership of—and tell their child that they truly apologize for—those things that she needed and didn't get, and those things that she didn't need and did get; the things that she wanted that they failed to give her, and the things that she didn't want (perhaps knowledge of their own marital difficulties) that were visited upon her. They must meet her eye, tell her straightforwardly that they are truly sorry for whatever impact their own human failings may have had upon her, and ask her forgiveness for them.

The effects of this encounter can be nothing short of dramatic. And if not immediately, then somewhere down the line (after whatever number of such sessions turn out to be needed) the daughter will run out of complaints, forgive her parents (because she loves them), and put an end to the era of bad feeling, which appeared to be without termination. That she do so is, as Johnson explains, not only important to the parents but *vital* to the daughter herself, for *no one among us can ever get free of anything that she or he hasn't forgiven.* To the extent that we go on lugging the angers of the past along with us, throughout our life's journey, the past has in fact defeated us.

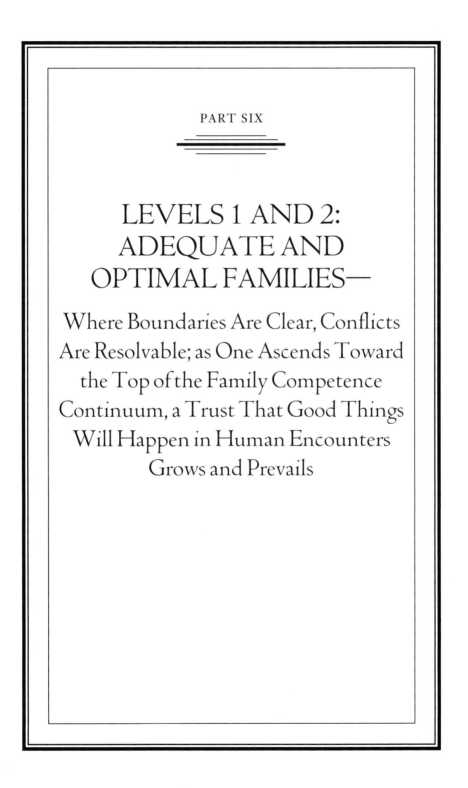

PART SIX

LEVELS 1 AND 2: ADEQUATE AND OPTIMAL FAMILIES—

Where Boundaries Are Clear, Conflicts Are Resolvable; as One Ascends Toward the Top of the Family Competence Continuum, a Trust That Good Things Will Happen in Human Encounters Grows and Prevails

CHAPTER 22

An Important Part of Loving:
Acknowledging Human Separateness

We were sitting in the Walkers' small, thickly carpeted family room. At the far end of the wood-paneled room was a small bookcase that held an impressive display of family trophies. "Quite an awards cabinet," I'd commented, noting that the family had automatically seated themselves in what structural theorists such as Salvador Minuchin would view as a visibly "healthy" arrangement.

The parental couple, side by side on the piano bench, sat so near to each other that their upper arms touched. Frances and James Walker thus constituted a discrete and separate subsystem (the "executive subgroup"), and no member of the younger generation had hurried to sit himself or herself down between them.

Their three children (that is, the "sibling subgroup"), who ranged in age from seven years to almost fifteen, had placed themselves close together on the small love seat. The resulting clear differentiation between these two important subsystems within the family was like a tableau of good government in action. It was as if the Walkers, in the very act of sitting down together, had recognized a certain inherent orderliness in their relatedness.

With my open sketch pad upon my lap, I was in the process of constructing the Walkers' family genogram. There was Frances, age forty-two, director of the marketing and advertising department at a major life insurance company in Hartford, and her husband, James, forty-four, who was an accountant and the proprietor of his own small but prosperous accounting firm. The children, who had ranged themselves in order of ascending age, were James Michael (Jamie), age seven; Debra, age thirteen, and Lyla, who would be fifteen at the end of December.

The Walkers had been married for sixteen years. I looked around at each member of this African-American family in turn. Frances Walker's complexion is the golden color of honey. The couple's daughters and their son are neither as light as their mother, nor do they have their father's milky-chocolate hue. It is as if a most precise genetic alchemist, working with the pair's hereditary palette, has mixed their pigments together and produced their children's soft, matte-brown skin tones.

"Is this a first marriage for both of you?" I inquired, turning to gaze directly at the parents. This is a question I ask routinely, but the pair of them looked startled. It was as if I'd asked them if they'd committed a bank robbery recently, and if so, whether or not the robbery had been successful. "Oh . . ." It was the father who responded, after a pause. "The first marriage, yes." One of the teenage girls began pushing against the other's shoulder, and the pair of them started to giggle.

The rest of us began laughing too. "Don't mind us, we get silly," Frances Walker apologized, trying to look appropriately serious. I hadn't been with the family for more than a very brief time, but I was enjoying their sense of playfulness and already feeling relaxed. This in itself told me a great deal about the Walkers, because one cannot feel at ease and relaxed in an emotional minefield.

A Matter of Mood Tone

My interviews with the Walkers began in late November 1992, and over the next several months, I met with the family as a whole unit and in varying types of subgroups (for example, "parental," "sibling," "sisters") and talked to each of them individually as well.

It was well past St. Valentine's Day when our regular conversations began to taper off; and although, in the course of our sessions together, I had come to know each member of the family separately (and all of them together) extremely well, my initial gut assessment of the Walkers never did change much. This family would, as I realized fairly quickly, fall into either a "high adequate," Level 2, or outright "optimal," Level 1, placement on the Beavers family health and functioning continuum. (The ways in which the adequate family and optimal family differ from each other will be explained further along. But for now, suffice it to say that these two groupings are far more similar than they are different, which is why the Walkers can ably represent both family categories here.)

What specific factors most distinguish healthy, high-functioning families from those below them on the Beavers Scale? One very reliable indicator is the family's emotional climate, its mood tone—in the simplest terms, *what it feels like to be with them.* According to family expert Leonora Stephens, M.D., "The affect in the optimal family is one of affirmation, even joyousness. These people take a real *delight* in one another—not only in their samenesses but in their differences as well."

For instance, most of the individuals in a particular family may be athletes and sports lovers, while one son is the bookworm and "our family philosopher"; in a competent, well-functioning emotional system, this child's differentness is, as Stephens explains, "not only accepted, but actively enjoyed." It is as if, within that small culture, the members of the social group are infused with the belief that *one can be who one is,* and that good things will happen in human encounters. One does not have to be just like everyone else to achieve a sense of belonging.

This kind of acceptance seems to be part of the very air that the members of the healthy family breathe in and out. It is evidenced not only by the things that people in the system *say* to one another, but in a multiplicity of nonverbal cues and gestures as well. It was, most certainly, readily observable in the Walker family's facial expressions, in their body postures, and in their way of meeting one another's gaze in a very clear, focused, and directed manner. These are wordless ways of communicating, of saying "I see you, I care about you, you matter, I *appreciate* the ways in which you are different, and enjoy the fact that you are the person you are."

Explaining Healthy Functioning

It was at the end of our first interview, as I was putting away my taping equipment, that I found myself alone with James Walker for a brief time. Frances and fifteen-year-old Lyla had rushed off to get their coats; they were running late for Lyla's piano lesson. Seven-year-old Jamie was getting his coat too—he was going down the street to play—and the thirteen-year-old, Debra, was upstairs returning a phone call.

"You asked if this was a first marriage, and it is," the father said reflectively, as if he'd not yet stopped thinking about this particular question among the many that I'd posed to them. "But this isn't just the *first* marriage, it's really the *only* marriage—the only marriage that either of us is planning to have."

"That's quite an endorsement," I responded with a smile, zipping up my quilted parka. He smiled, too. "It is," he agreed, as he saw me courteously to the door.

I went down the frozen, slightly slippery front pathway in front of the Walkers' yellow frame house in the gathering dusk. I was reflecting that although I still knew relatively little about these parents' families of origin, making some educated guesses would be easy. James Charles Walker and Frances Townsend Walker had come from fairly loving and stable backgrounds—of that I could be fairly certain; in fact, I would bet my hat on it.

But in the course of our subsequent discussions, I was to discover how very wrong I was. James Walker's early life narrative could, in fact, have been the prologue to a disaster—and yet it had proven to be anything but one. This caused me, in turn, to reflect upon how much trickier it is to explain health and competent functioning, in the face of early adversity, than it is to explain the existence of difficulties, symptoms, and pathology. (See Chapter 23, "Why Some Children Thrive Despite Early Family Trauma.")

The Model of a Dad

It was not until the Walker family interviews were well under way that the father's own history began, somewhat haltingly, to emerge. I recall how, at the outset of that meeting, I'd flipped through my thick drawing pad until I came to the Walkers' genogram, and noticed that (given the amount of time we'd already spent together) there was surprisingly little information there.

Our conversations had, thus far, been very oriented toward the family's present-day life. As for the parents' own families of origin, all that I'd jotted down on the page were the names of James's father and grandfather, and the fact that both members of the marital pair had come from a family in which he or she was one of six siblings. This evening, I was meeting with the parents alone, and it was high time to find out more about the families that each of them had come from.

I decided to start out with James's side of the family diagram, for though I'd always found him quite forthcoming, I find it best to make sure that any males in the company are drawn into an active role in the conversation as soon as possible. "I want to find out more about all of these siblings—six on your side, six on Frances's," I said, with a smile, my pencil aloft over the sketch pad.

I laughed, "Of course I *do* know that your father's name is the same as your name—" The Walkers laughed too, for during our first interview I'd gotten momentarily fuddled by the fact that James himself was named after his father—he was James Charles Junior—but his own son James was not the Third. "Right, he's James Michael," put in Frances, in her lively, accommodating manner.

"And your mother's name?" I met James's eye and waited.

"Elinor," he said softly, and then spelled it.

I drew a circle, wrote "Elinor" beside it, at the opposite end of the long line designating her marriage to James Senior, leaving plenty of room to include the five younger siblings that I knew were to appear. "Right now, I'd like to know about these other guys," I said, tapping the page lightly with my pencil. "Your age is forty-four, so who's next?"

"Of the siblings?"

I nodded, and James responded clearly, almost in the stentorian voice of an expert giving testimony, "I have a sister, Eliza, and a brother, Stephen. He's the one who's now deceased."

"Oh. Yes," I said quietly. Toward the closing moments of our last interview, in response to a question about "worst times" that the family had experienced, James had talked about his younger brother's untimely death of a heart ailment three years earlier. Stephen had been awaiting a heart transplant at the time and had died before a donor organ became available.

"Did you know this brother-in-law pretty well?" I asked Frances now, and she nodded quickly. "Yes. Oh, yes," she replied fervently; she had, she added, felt extremely close to him. During our last discussion it had seemed to me that the children knew this uncle somewhat less well, I remarked, for they'd appeared somewhat taken aback and shaken by their dad's obvious pain when the subject of his brother's death had arisen.

"Our kids had only spent short periods of time with their uncle Steve, because he had moved to Georgia with his family. Atlanta, Georgia," James explained. "So it wasn't that often that we got together as families, and it was mostly at large gatherings in various people's homes."

Also, put in Frances, the children hadn't been very much aware of what was happening at the time of their uncle's sudden death. "It all happened so *quickly*, more or less in a very rapid series of phone calls in the night. Then the two of us went up by ourselves for the funeral, and the children stayed with friends while we were there." Frances stopped speaking, turned to look at her husband solicitously.

Then she turned back to me. "They didn't *feel* all of what was happening," she murmured, then sighed. I turned to James, asked him gently, "How old was your brother at the time of his death?"

He answered swiftly, "He was thirty-six." There was an elongated silence, and after a while I realized that the Walkers were expecting me to be the one to break it.

I looked down at the open sketch pad on my lap, then asked James awkwardly, "And your sister, Eliza—how old is she?"

The question sounded inane in my own ears, and I regretted the words as soon as they were spoken. But the husband, seeming relieved and almost grateful, said, "Eliza's two years younger than I am, so she would be forty-two."

I jotted in the information and asked immediately, "And who's next in line?"

"That's it, for my mother's first marriage. Then I have two stepbrothers and a stepsister," James replied. I looked up quickly. "Oh, I see," I said, although I felt myself stiffen in surprise.

This piece of news did not, I realized, fit in with my own preformed notions. It was as though I'd run smack into an inner wall, solidly constructed of my own theoretical beliefs and convictions. I felt rattled momentarily by the impact, for this was not turning out to be the solid, secure home base that I'd been so confidently expecting James Walker to have come from.

"So then. . . . Who was your mother's first husband?" I asked him, trying not to look as taken aback as I felt. The answer to this question was, of course, one that was already written down on my sketch pad; his father had been James Charles Walker Senior, as James told me patiently.

"I see," I said. "So your parents were divorced," I murmured.

"Yes, they divorced," he responded. His folks had, as he went on to explain, been married for some nine years; the marriage had ended when he himself was about six or seven years old.

I hesitated, finding it difficult to integrate this news of early and profound disruption with the unusually capable, energetic, emotionally connected husband and father whom I saw before me. "Did you see much of your dad after that?" I inquired.

"No, I did not. There was a long period of time—" James halted, seemed to ponder what he would or would not reveal to me next. But then he did go on. "As a matter of fact, after my parents divorced I probably didn't see my father between the ages of six and"—he sighed—"oh, about twenty-six years old."

"Twenty-five or twenty-six." Frances Walker, nodding, echoed her husband's words.

They were both staring at me, waiting for me to say something, but I found myself feeling confused and at sea. Given this history of stark abandonment, how could James Walker have possibly become the kind of a parent he'd become? Without even quite realizing that I meant to ask this question aloud, I exhaled deeply and heard myself say, "Wow, so how in the world did *you* ever learn how to be a dad yourself?"

He laughed lightly; the question seemed to please him. "Well, I had a stepfather," he reminded me. "And I had plenty of other men around who were examples of how to be a good dad. I think, too, some part of it comes naturally," he added, as if gratified to think of the real hurdles which he'd been capable of overcoming. Frances was nodding her head rhythmically as he spoke.

Mysteries of the Last Generation

When I asked him how long his mother had been alone before remarrying, James Walker was not completely certain. He believed that it had been about a year and a half. The first child born to Elinor's subsequent marriage was his brother Mark, now thirty-five years old; then came Donald, two years younger. Last and youngest in the family was Margaretta, two years younger than Donald. I realized, at that moment, that their surname must be different from his own. "And what is your stepfather's name?" I asked, my pencil poised above the sheet of paper.

James answered, "Bailey—Dwight Bailey was his name," just as the gong of the half-hour sounded in the background. Perhaps it was the confluence of the chime and his use of the past tense that made me ask whether or not James's stepfather was still alive.

"Yes, he is," James replied, but added nothing further. Another silence followed, and I felt as if I'd been traveling along a road that had come to an abrupt and unexpected ending.

"So then, you didn't see your own father for this remarkably *long,* twenty-year period." I returned directly to the topic that had paralyzed us, for no other topic of conversation seemed possible at this moment.

"My father's whereabouts were unknown," James said evenly.

"Did he just vanish, disappear—or how, exactly, did things happen?"

He paused momentarily, then chose to sidestep the question. "My mother *did* establish a new relationship, a whole new life, with someone else. We were living in Tuskegee then—Tuskegee, Alabama. We lived there at the time of their divorce and her remarriage, and we lived there a short time afterward."

Did he think that this new relationship of his mother's might have had anything to do with the breakup of his parents' marriage? I inquired. But the very notion seemed to strike James as ludicrous, and he dismissed it with a smile and a shake of his head. "My stepfather came along later on. As to *why* my parents divorced, though, I don't really know. . . . I think they just grew apart." He shrugged briefly as if to say that this was sufficient explanation, and all the explanation that he himself required.

The mysteries of the last generation, and most particularly of that long-ago divorce, were matters about which he seemed content not to know and was perhaps even unwilling to speculate. "Anyway, to round out this story," he continued, "we all moved north in the 1950s, and we had no *idea* where my father was as we were growing up."

The family's decision to migrate to upstate New York had been prompted by the fact that Dwight Bailey, who was working at a gas station and earning thirty-eight dollars a week, had learned from a relative that an auto mechanic could earn as much as eighty dollars a week for the same kind of labor in the North. "For my parents, the difference between thirty-eight dollars and eighty dollars a week was a very, very *tempting* one," recounted James, with a smile, crossing one leg over the other, and folding his arms across his chest easily. "So we loaded up the car and came north. Of course my father went first, and found a job—my *step*father, I mean."

"You said 'my father,' " I interrupted to observe, "and so he really did *feel* like a father to you, I think?"

James nodded his agreement, said appreciatively, "I spent all of my young life with him knowing him as my father, and he *treated* us like a father. There was no distinction made between my stepbrothers and sisters and any of *us* as being only half-brothers and half-sisters. Even now, we don't even consider that—"

"—and that's a term I haven't even *heard*." Frances leaned forward to underscore his comments eagerly. "We just don't make those distinctions *at all*. Between stepfather or stepsister—"

"—or half-brother." Her husband nodded.

"Yes, half-brother or half-sister." She nodded back at him, but went on explaining matters to me. "Which is why even *hearing* the terms now, as we're speaking, is somehow striking. . . . It's strange." What she was saying, I believed, was that there was nobody in this family who was only halfway inside; if you were in the system, you were naturally considered a fully accredited part of it.

Still, glancing downward at the brief note I'd jotted on her husband's side of the family genogram—"Moved north in 1956, with stepfather"—I couldn't help but reflect that when he'd left the South as an eight-year-old boy, James Walker had been leaving his deepest, earliest memories of a completely different father somewhere behind him. And while it seemed evident that he had been fortunate enough to have a reparative experience with a truly nurturing, caring stepfather, being raised *as if* he were the son of his mother's new husband was not exactly the same as being the man's own son in reality.

And as they grew older, James told me, he, Eliza, and Stephen (that is, the three children of his mother's first marriage) had begun writing to various relatives on the paternal side of the family. They were attempting to make contact and perhaps reconnect with their real father, or at least discover his whereabouts. But no one in the entire family had heard from him, and nobody seemed to have any idea where he might be.

The Idealized Parent Imago

James Walker's son, Jamie, was now around the same age as he himself had been when his own father (at least, from the seven-year-old child's point of view) had vanished from the face of the planet. Gazing, now, at the adult man I wondered how, as a young boy, he had construed what was happening in his world and how he had explained his father's disappearance to himself.

In his groundbreaking book *The Analysis of the Self*, theorist Heinz Kohut describes the natural evolution of infantile narcissism and grandiosity ("I am at the center of the universe, and all that happens within it revolves around me and is under my command") to the more modulated and mature, healthy narcissism of adult life.

"Healthy narcissism" is, of course, a synonym for "self-esteem," which is to say that relatively stable sense of one's own self-worth and essential lovability. The self-esteem of maturity is neither grandiose nor omnipotent, but accompanied by an awareness of one's own realistic human shortcomings and limitations.

Early in our lives, Kohut says, we learn to esteem ourselves by basking in the luminous aura of our enchanted parents' admiration. That is, the rudimentary seeds of our good feelings about ourselves germinate and slowly grow within the rich soil of these first, crucially important love relationships. It is the caretakers' spontaneous delight in our unfolding skills and capacities that provides us with a mighty sense of our own wondrousness and excellence. We feel tremendously important in the human world as a function of our importance to them.

The naturally exhibitionistic young baby's self-delight and self-aggrandizing tendencies are thus nourished (or as Kohut would say, "mirrored") by the admiring parent's empathic responding to his or her small personage and slowly accruing accomplishments. The parents' evident joy in the feats and successes of their offspring provides the child with the needed narcissistic supplies. For the child needs to feel, first, that he or she is perfect, and second, that this perfection is recognized by those who matter most in his or her own circumscribed universe.

According to psychoanalyst Kohut, the nascent self of the developing baby is at best poorly differentiated from the self of the nurturing caregiver. In other words, the very small human being does not initially have a distinct, well-bounded sense of "me, myself" but instead experiences the self as amorphously merged and fused with the self of the beloved parent. The parent's praise and affirmation are, therefore, perceived as emanating not only from the outside environment but from *within* the self as well.

Although in actuality the young child is exceedingly weak, vulnerable, and needful, the normal grandiosity of early life (what Kohut called the "grandiose self"), supported by the confirming, validating responses of the nurturer, makes the baby feel crucially important to the ongoing function of a cosmos whose very center he or she occupies. But over time, and most inevitably, the narcissistic supplies flowing in from the admiring, comforting attachment figure will be interrupted, not reliably there when required. Things happen, such as Mom being unavailable when desperately needed—perhaps simply out for a social evening, when baby awakens feeling anxious and frightened to find only a baby-sitter (the *wrong person*) there to console and care for him or her.

These small existential jolts, which Kohut termed "tolerable failures" in empathic responding, serve to provide the offspring with a succession of small opportunities to learn how to care for and empathize with his or her own self. For in the (temporary) absence of the vitally necessary narcissistic feedback, the reassurance and affirmation that came from the parent must now be provided from within the psyche itself.

Such brief, manageable lessons in self-soothing eventually teach us, suggests Kohut, how to give to ourselves the loving support and calming that had initially come in to us from the outer environment (in human terms, always the social environment). And if all has gone well during the course of development—which is to say, if the parents have been able to "respond to and confirm the child's innate sense of vigour, greatness and perfection"—then what was initially our caretakers' high estimation of our goodness and innate worth undergoes transformation and is internalized. Thus it is that parental mirroring, which Kohut equated with the "gleam in the mother's eye," ultimately becomes the steady gleam of confidence and self-regard that emanate from within the individual human being.

The Child's Need to Exalt and Venerate the Parent

Parental mirroring is not, in Kohut's schema, the sole form of narcissistic relatedness that the growing child requires. Equally essential to psychological development is the child's *need to exalt and venerate the parent* in what is called the idealizing relationship. Here, instead of being a perfect person who is being admired by a loving other, the offspring *admires* the beloved other extravagantly. This "idealized parent imago" is, write Kohut and co-author Ernest S. Wolf, an attachment figure "to whom the child can look up and with whom he can merge as an image of calmness, infallibility and omnipotence."

The youngster's own fantasies about the caretaker's amazing qualities ("My dad is the strongest person in the world") are, in fact, being projected into the wildly admired other and are perceived as existing there. In this form of narcissistic relatedness, the developing child's self-image is enhanced by his wonderful illusions about the parent's magnificent powers. The child experiences himself as partaking of the strength and mightiness of the father with whom he feels so deeply linked and identified. Such fantasies about the caretaker as invulnerable and flawless flood the child with feelings of safety, pride, and well-being.

Because the establishment of an idealizing relationship will ultimately have a profound impact upon the offspring's own capacity to set goals and form inner ideals, *the child's need to admire the parent in this endearingly extreme, often highly unrealistic fashion is a developmental imperative.* That is why the attachment figure will usually be idealized, even in what appear to be highly inappropriate circumstances—for example, when Dad is in fact a petty tyrant, an alcohol addict, or even serving a sentence in jail.

What is in fact being attributed to the parent is the dependent child's own internal vision of imagined flawlessness and superiority. Over time, however, just as the youngster's early grandiosity and omnipotence will be cut down to size by life's unavoidable disappointments and blows, so his or her sense of the adult caretaker's exalted worthiness and perfection will slowly but inexorably deflate down to an understanding more consistent with reality.

Still, as Kohut and Wolf write, "however great our disappointment as we discover the weaknesses and limitations of the idealized . . . [parent imagos] of our early life, their self-confidence as they carried us when we were babies, their security when they allowed us to merge our anxious selves with their tranquillity—via their calm voices or via our closeness with their relaxed bodies as they held us—will be retained by us as the nucleus of the strength of our leading ideals and of the calmness we experience as we live our lives under the guidance of our inner goals."

What were once overblown good feelings about the other are, in short, eventually internalized in the form of good feelings about the self—that is, self-esteem. Thus, over the slow course of development, the idealized relationship with the caretaker leaves the offspring with a wonderful residue, a kind of magic dust.

For when the initial glorification of the parent eventually gives way (as it inevitably does) the maturing child is left with a deep feeling of inner worth that has derived from the original identification with the adored and passionately adulated caretaker. As psychoanalyst John Zinner has observed, however, success in this normal developmental process *does* require that the parents be "emotionally available, and willing to tolerate both the child's idealization and de-idealization of them. Parental loss or behavior that betrays the trust their child has placed in them may lead to an abrupt and massive de-idealization."

The parent must slide from his or her high pedestal slowly, not tumble from it so abruptly that the youngster's capacity to reinternalize the idealized image of the parent is overwhelmed. For should the "Emperor" parent lose all his new clothes too shockingly and suddenly, the child's own sense of inner worth and his ability to form ideals and goals will usually be profoundly affected.

While disillusionment with the exalted caretaker is surely in the human cards, it must occur bit by bit, in a series of tolerable, manageable small frustrations and setbacks. I could not therefore fail to regard very seriously the fact that in James Walker's early life this normal developmental process had been sharply and radically interrupted.

Given that a natural object of any seven-year-old boy's wish to relate in an idealizing fashion is certainly going to be his own father, how had this man managed to survive his parent's loss in so seemingly intact and capable a fashion? I was curious, even awed. We have such a *multiplicity* of explanations and theories about pathology and the development of "problems in living," but so little understanding of what underlies healthy adaptation and human resilience.

Had the stepfather who had stepped into James's daddy's shoes very soon afterward parented the little boy so well and so caringly that this early trauma had been rendered somehow manageable? A famous comment of Nietzsche's—"That which does not destroy me strengthens me"—came into my mind at that moment.

"How did you find your dad again?" I asked James. "Or did he find *you*? Or what eventually happened?" To my surprise, an expression of pleasure crossed his face, and he smiled.

The Prodigal Parent

James Walker didn't reply for several moments; his thoughts seemed to have drifted elsewhere. I waited, absently reading the logo on his aqua-and-navy sweatshirt ("Denver, Colorado") over and over again, wondering idly if he'd actually been there. He cupped his hand under his face, stroked his jawline with his fingers several times, then leaned forward and said in a lively voice, "Well, it was a long, *long* time. We'd made many, many efforts to try and find him by writing to relatives on his side of the family, but that never got us anywhere. And we'd tried at various times to go through the Veterans Administration, because he did serve in the military—"

I interrupted to ask whether the word "we" referred to himself and his siblings, or to himself and his mother. Who, exactly, had been involved in these efforts? "Principally me, my brother Stephen and my sister Eliza," he responded easily, then continued as if relishing the telling of the story.

The three siblings had written to the V.A. and to the Army in an effort to track their father down, hoping that one or another of these huge organizations would have some knowledge of his whereabouts. By that time, recounted James, the three of them were all moving into their late teens; it was not until he himself had reached college that they'd finally received a favorable response from the Veterans Administration.

Here James paused and laughed a deep bass laugh, the sound of pure satisfaction and enjoyment. "One day, then, I received a letter from my brother Stephen, saying that he'd heard from the V.A. They wouldn't tell my brother where my father was, but they *would* tell my father how to get in touch with *him*. So they did. Then my father contacted Stephen, and we *all* found out where he was." He was gazing at me with so triumphant an expression that I almost expected him to say, "And then we lived happily ever after."

But he merely inhaled, let a deep breath out very slowly. "I was living in

New York State at the time; Albany, New York. And it turned out that he was right in New York City. *Right in New York City,*" he repeated with emphasis, "and he'd lived there for a number of years. *So* nearby, and *we* didn't know it!" He shook his head back and forth slowly several times, as if to underscore the oddness of this circumstance.

Then James resumed, "I was out of school by then, working for the New York State Department of Social Services, and I traveled a *lot.* So on one trip I had to go to New York City, and while there I made a call to St. Luke's Hospital, which was where he was working at the time. And it was really strange, because I had no idea what my father would even *look* like! Nor did he have any idea of what *I* would look like." His eyes had grown wide, perhaps with remembered apprehension, but he laughed again in the same pleased, gratified fashion. "It was a very, very emotionally *wrenching* moment when we met," he said, meeting my eyes fully and directly as he spoke.

"I can imagine that it was," I responded, not averting my gaze although I was finding the intensity of the moment almost painful. This story of a son's meeting with his father after a twenty-year separation seemed to have a mythic resonance, an echo of the story of the Greek hero Ulysses— who, on meeting his grown son, Telemachus, after a twenty-year absence, suddenly throws off his beggarly disguise and reveals his true identity as the missing parent, saying, "I am that father whom your boyhood lacked and suffered pain for lack of. I am he." James grew quiet, and the three of us sat there stiffly for a while, not saying a word.

Then he went on, his voice sounding more composed, under control. "It was also kind of *awkward*, because I didn't know how to respond to him; he didn't know how to respond to *me*, either. But I just saw this big smile. And he looked at me, and it grew across his whole face, and then he looked down at my feet and said, "Yeah, you're *my* son, all right."

James slapped the side of his knee, laughing. Frances and I began laughing too, although I wasn't completely sure what the joke was. "Big feet, is that it?" I asked him, and he beamed his approval at me.

"That's right, that's *right.*" I felt commended, like a student who has just made an intelligent comment in the midst of an intricate, somewhat convoluted lecture. "We—my dad and I—had only a short period of time in which to talk," he continued, "because I was there on business and there were other people traveling with me; they were sitting outside, waiting for me in the state's car. So we spoke only briefly, exchanged addresses, and said good-bye, and I left." James shrugged briefly as if to say "End of story," but a moment later his face was alive with excitement again.

"But *then*—I'd already gotten into the backseat, and the car was pulling away, when I turned around," he recounted. "And there, *running* behind the car and down the street and *chasing* the car was *my father*! And he signaled me to roll the window down, then pressed a fifty-dollar bill into my hand," he concluded jubilantly.

"So that was it," he added, by way of epilogue. "After that first meeting, we wrote to each other often and we saw each other, too, from time to time. Later on, *much* later, when I graduated from business school, he did attend and there he met my mother again. . . . After all those years." His voice had dropped, grown soft and thoughtful, and the look on his face was dreamy.

I myself was lost in thought, wondering what his long-absent father's chasing him down the street and pressing a fifty-dollar bill into his hand had actually *meant* to James Walker, as a newly adult young African-American professional. It was a question that I was aching to ask him, but I felt hesitant to do so at this particular moment; and I decided that I would ask it later on.

A Boy and His Dad

One year after this "wrenching" reunion with his long-absent father, James told me, he'd decided to leave his job at the New York State Department of Social Services and go back to graduate school to study accounting. He was accepted at the Tuck School of Business at Dartmouth, and began his studies there the subsequent fall.

A year later, in 1976, he and Frances had gotten married. Their older children, Lyla, now fifteen, and Debra, now thirteen, were born two and four years later, respectively. But there was a six-year age difference between Debra and the couple's youngest child, Jamie. The Walkers' son wasn't born until 1985 and was therefore the only one of the children who never got to meet James Charles Walker, Sr. For in 1982 James's dad suffered a stroke and a heart attack, and he died of heart complications within the following year.

"If you were to give me a couple of adjectives that might best describe your father," I asked James now, "what do you think they would they be?" He gave me a slightly perplexed look. "I mean, of course, your biological father, not your stepfather," I clarified my question, but he shook his head as if he had nothing whatsoever to say.

"I realize that you didn't have a big experience of him, growing up," I murmured, as if to soften the question as the silence continued to stretch itself out. Then I added diffidently, "Would you say, for example, that he was 'calm,' a 'cool' and very 'collected' sort of person?"

As far as I was concerned these particular adjectives were no more than randomly chosen examples, but they seemed to hit a bull's-eye of immediate response. "Oh, *yes* . . . ." He let out a long sigh of air with the words, as though his agreement came from somewhere very deep inside him. "I would say that he was very, *very* controlled, yes. He was very calm, very intelligent, very well organized."

"Me-tic-u-lous," put in Frances, with a comfortable laugh, putting stress on each and every syllable of the word.

"Meticulous, yes." James exchanged a friendly look with his wife and placed his arm across the sofa behind her. Then he turned back to me expectantly, and the two of us exchanged a smile. "Are those adjectives that you would use to describe *yourself* as well?" I inquired lightly.

It was no more than a fishing trip on my part, but he jumped slightly, said, *"Yes,"* emphatically, and then chuckled at his own response.

"Absolutely, he is so much *like* his father! It's *amazing*," Frances, with a laugh, put in warmly, her voice a rich tremolo with a captivating little break in the middle of a word here and there. "An amazingly striking resemblance, if you think—" She didn't finish what she was saying, but turned to her husband instead.

I turned to James also. "What was your dad doing for a living, by then? Not working as a shoemaker at St. Luke's Hospital, I suppose," I added lightly, for I knew James Senior had been a shoemaker back in Alabama. Was it my imagination, or did this innocuous-seeming question make James Walker tense up ever so slightly? His father had been working as an orderly at St. Luke's at the time that they'd gotten together again, he said shortly.

I had the odd suspicion that James might be defending his dad from *me*. Was his concern that I might think less of this "meticulous, controlled, calm," and self-contained parent because his father had not been an educated man with a job of recognizably good (white-collar) status? I felt like saying to him outright that I myself had come from an immigrant, blue-collar background, and that there had been father-problems in my own early life as well. But although it might have eased this moment of social disquietude, it would have been highly inappropriate in the context of these interviews.

I fell silent, a silence that I was afraid both he and Frances might be misinterpreting. The telephone began ringing in the kitchen; after several rings, I heard Debra answer it and launch into a high-pitched, laughing conversation. A frown crossed her mother's face briefly, and I recalled that Frances had expressed some concern about how much homework time this adolescent daughter was squandering on lengthy phone conversations with her friends.

James's gaze was, however, locked upon mine. He didn't seem to be at all distracted by what was occurring slightly offstage, in the wings of this intense conversation. His expression at this moment was, it seemed to me, somewhat downcast, as if a momentary cloud were passing over his usually animated, expressive face. I found myself thinking about this adult son's ardent protectiveness and loyalty toward a father who had by no means been a loyal, caring protector during the years of dependence when it had mattered most vitally.

I asked, my voice sounding hesitant in my own ears, "When you did see your dad again, after all that time, you must have had some feelings about this guy who'd just—just dropped out of sight for all those years. Or were you just so happy to see him that you didn't have any bad feelings at all?"

James shook his head. "I didn't have any bad feelings, because I didn't have any *reason* to have bad feelings—to the best of my knowledge, he hadn't done anything terribly wrong. True, he wasn't in my life for a large *part* of my life—"

I was staring at him in amazement. "But doesn't that in itself seem kind of wrong, for a kid?" I heard myself saying—or should I say blurting out? His lack of resentment seemed almost unfathomable to me; had he no empathy for the little boy he had been, the seven-year-old child whose father had vanished from his world so totally and so completely?

"It was something that I missed. . . . It was a *void*," he acknowledged quietly. I could hear the note of sadness in James's voice, but there was no spirit of blame or anger whatsoever. "Yes, that's what I mean," I said, retreating gently; I wondered if he was in denial about his painful feelings or if, on the contrary, he had been able to come to terms with some very distressing early experiences in ways that I didn't completely understand.

Tumbling Tumbleweed

I glanced at Frances, noticed that she was leaning backward in her seat like a passenger in a car that is accelerating at an alarming rate and is already well over the speed limit. I decided to take my cue from her and back away from this hazardous topic, or at least to do so for the meanwhile. Dropping my gaze, I sat staring down at the genogram on my lap—most particularly at the small square representing their son, under which I'd written "Jamie, age seven." I said nothing for the next several moments, but James was unwilling to allow the discussion of his father to rest in the place where we'd left it.

"There was no dislike for him, because there wasn't—because I *did* have a father," he stated, in an even, strong, reasonable tone of voice. "And I had a very *good* father. Very supportive, a hard worker and a good provider. For a long time, my father worked three jobs—two full-time jobs and a part-time job also." Dwight Bailey had not only driven a maintenance truck for the city of Niagara Falls, but he'd also been a bus driver and worked as a contractor at the same time. "He poured concrete, installed patios, driveways, and sidewalks. He'd tear them up and put in new ones. My father—my *step*father, that is—was a very *strong*, powerful man, and people used to admire his physique."

A look of boyish admiration came into James's eyes at this moment, and I glimpsed the young child in the mature adult man. "He was not a tall person, but he was a very forceful, strong sort of guy. In fact, he would just scratch his head and his biceps would simply *swell up*, and people were amazed. He never lifted weights or anything; it just came from hard work."

But then James added, "He and my mother *did* have their problems, but he was always very, very good to us."

The problems in his mother's second marriage had, he believed, resulted from the fact that she was a deeply religious woman—"not a fanatic, but a very religious person"—and had become ever more so over the years. "My father, on the other hand, always loved the good life." Here James made a rueful, ironic face, but laughed aloud at the same time. "He loved to party, drink, have fun, and he had an excellent sense of humor; he made *everybody* laugh." He himself laughed again, as if visualizing some remembered scene, but then added, in a sharper, more critical tone of voice, "It did seem to me that he could be somewhat—well, irrational at times."

How so, I asked, but James looked stumped, as if this weren't the easiest question to answer. After a long pause, during which he seemed to be scanning backward through his recollections, he said slowly, "I just can't bring to mind right now a particular subject that we argued about. But if we *were* arguing, he would make his point by saying something like 'Grass is green, isn't it?' And of course you'd have to agree. So then my father would say, '*All right*, then . . .' " James grinned, and Frances laughed.

"That's my *point!*" she mimicked her father-in-law jokingly.

"In other words, 'I rest my case,' " I added, and the three of us giggled together, releasing tension.

"My father was just not the kind of person you could argue with in a rational, logical way." James sounded highly entertained and yet really annoyed with the man simultaneously. Still, I hadn't failed to take note, throughout this conversation, of how comfortably his two different fathers seemed to coexist in his own mind and in his thinking. James Walker never did refer to Dwight Bailey as anything but his father in ordinary conversation; I heard him use the word "stepfather" only when he was distinguishing between the two men for my benefit.

"If I were to ask you, What was the most important thing you ever learned from your father?, what do you think your answer would be?" My voice was reflective and musing and I cocked my head to one side, smiled, met his steady gaze directly.

"Is this Dwight Bailey or James—Dwight?" asked Frances immediately.

My eyes still fixed upon her husband's, I shrugged lightly as if to say to him, "Your choice." "She's talking about my father—about James," he turned to tell Frances decisively, then turned back to me.

"I don't know *what* I learned from him. I think I *inherited* some things from him . . . some traits."

I shook my head, smiling slightly, as if to say he wasn't quite responding to the question that I'd posed. "Can you think of something that you actually *learned* from him? It doesn't have to be something positive; it can be positive, negative, whatever."

He nodded, said in halting phrases, "Well—I think—I may have learned—that it's important to keep in touch with your family."

I nodded and said: "By his not doing it." I was amplifying upon his answer, but my own voice, as I heard it, was far less convinced than it was questioning.

"By his not doing it," James repeated, nodding in agreement simultaneously. "Not only with us but with his own brothers and sisters, because he didn't keep in touch with *them*, either. They had no idea where he was, and they'd been close when they were younger. Very, very close. My brother Stephen was named after *his* brother, and my sister Eliza was named after *his* sister. But when he disappeared, he just disappeared; no one had any idea for years and years where he was. Whether he was dead or alive, sick or well . . ." His voice trailed off on this mystified and somewhat plaintive note.

"Did your aunt and your uncle have any idea why he disappeared from sight in that way?" I asked. James shook his head, said, "No, none."

"And you still don't know?"

He shook his head again. "We still do not know; that's right; he just did it. We did discover, later on, that he was ill—he had the heart ailment that he eventually died from—but it wasn't the kind of illness that would have prevented him from keeping in touch." He was speaking in a neutral tone of voice now, and I asked him in a similarly even, level tone whether he thought that the ending of his parents' marriage had caused his father to vanish from an entire former lifetime in that manner.

"I can't say that because I don't know," James replied, almost formally. But after a moment he added slowly, "I think he probably spent time in the South, and like most people eventually just migrated north looking for opportunity and excitement, a different way of being . . ."

"But it does sound as if he was very disconnected," I said, my eyes staring straight into his sympathetically. "It sounds as if he'd gotten into what you might call a 'tumbling tumbleweed' kind of life—" I stopped in mid-sentence, for his startled expression told me that he had heard this last remark in a spirit in which it hadn't been meant. His wife shifted in her seat uncomfortably, cleared her throat.

"No, I don't think so; that's not the impression I got," James stated tersely and almost coldly.

I was in no doubt about the fact that I'd made a misstep, but it was one that I couldn't quite fathom at that moment. It wasn't until much later, in the course of interviews with other black families (both single-parent and intact), that I came to understand the sensitivity that exists in the African-American community in regard to the widespread stereotype of the absent, disconnected, nonproductive black male. When I had said "tumbling tumbleweed," they had heard me saying (or so I later came to believe) "shiftless, good-for-nothing drifter."

But at that juncture, although I didn't understand exactly what it was that was being heard amiss, I did have the presence of mind to turn to his wife and ask, "Frances, what are your own thoughts about this long disappearance? I mean, what's your own understanding of what might have happened, or how do you describe or explain this in your own mind?"

"I'm not sure, I'm not sure, but I did know—I could *see*—the loving and caring that were there," she said fervently and supportively. Then her expression became somewhat doubtful. "I'm not sure," she repeated, her voice low, "and I think one of the reasons why I insisted that James reconnect with his father was that there were so *many* unanswered questions. . . . It's just unfortunate that we ran out of time, because we didn't realize his dad was as ill as he was.

"They were just getting together, and I think beginning to catch up, when his father went into the hospital. Then we'd go back and forth to visit, but not really to stir him up. Not to get him upset; just really to spend time with him. We did think he was going to get better, and that later on we'd really get a chance to delve into where he'd been, what had happened to him during—" Frances halted in mid-speech, looked swiftly at her husband, then looked back at me.

She met my gaze fully and directly. "To me, his dad was *not* the kind of person you would think of as having been adrift or just blowing around in the wind during those years. He was very neat, very organized; he *looked* great; he looked *wonderful.* We just had no idea he was as sick as he was; I was shocked when I got the phone call, and in fact we brought his body here for the funeral. He's buried here in West Hartford, in the graveyard of our own church, which is just a few miles away. But it did take us by surprise, because at that time everything was just sort of opening up. We were about to really get to *know* him, after all those years."

She had been speaking swiftly, in a voice charged with affection and regret. In the brief silence that ensued I turned to look at James, saw that his momentary ire had vanished completely. An expression of satisfaction and good nature had now returned to his features, and I wondered if he were merely feeling gratified by this almost automatic outpouring of his wife's support. Or was the sense of contentment and emotional closure that I could see reflected in his features due to his not only having found and reconnected with his father, but with his having been able to bring him home again permanently? James's dad was buried in his adult son's churchyard, not more than a few miles from where we sat.

A Lot of Love, a Lot of Sharing, a Lot of Caring

The next time I met with the Walkers, the entire family was present. "So, tell me," I began by saying, "what is it *like*, living in this family?" This broad question, not surprisingly, met with total silence.

The Walkers looked at me, then at one another, then back at me with smiles of bewilderment and embarrassment. "Anyone at all can answer," I added, and then waited expectantly for something to happen. Nothing did.

I looked from one member of the assemblage to the other. "What is it like, living here?" I repeated. "Anybody who feels like answering, please speak up."

James Walker laughed, surveyed the other people in his family teasingly. "No one wants to go first, huh?" the father inquired. They laughed too, but nobody spoke. I dropped my gaze, stared at the six-sibling lineup on each parent's side of the genogram. Then I looked up to find that Frances's open-eyed gazed had locked, radarlike, upon mine.

She gave me the impression that she wanted to speak, but that so many potential answers were coming into her mind that she couldn't settle upon any one of them in particular. "Somebody ought to go *second*, then"—I smiled at the mother—"and then the next person can be the first one."

Frances returned my smile, but still made no reply. When it came right down to it, I realized, she was having trouble admitting me across the family threshold.

I reflected that she, as a high-powered executive with a considerable staff under her charge, might well have conflicted feelings about surrendering control and making herself vulnerable. I said nothing, and it was the father who spoke up at that moment.

"I think it's pretty *easy* to live in this family," James commenced slowly. "There's a lot of humor . . ."

"Yes, I can see that," I agreed quickly, and everyone smiled. I glanced quickly at Frances, who seemed relieved that her husband had begun speaking.

"There's a lot of cooperation," James added then. "A lot of love, a lot of sharing, a lot of caring," he went on, and his wife nodded.

The father looked at his children, said reflectively, "There isn't a need for strong discipline, because the values are laid down and everybody seems to understand them, and abide by them. So there isn't a need to impose discipline"—he sat up suddenly, ramrod straight on the piano bench, as if taking command militarily—"or at least, not *very often*," he amended jokingly. "So—" The rest of his remark was lost in a babble of the girls' high-pitched laughter and comments. Then everyone was talking at once, making it impossible for me to hear what any one person was saying. When the hubbub quieted down, however, Frances began to chime in. "I think that there are areas of—of *intensity* as well," she said, in that gentle yet authoritative tone of voice. "Because we are all involved in a lot of things, and we all stay on the move."

"We all have our own separate lives," she explained, "and we're all doing lots of different things. We bring it together in this family, and so there's a *lot* going on." What she was saying was that in this family, people invested themselves in their own interests as distinct and different individuals and yet remained profoundly connected.

It was almost as though she had read a book on healthy family functioning and were giving me all of the correct answers before I got to ask the questions. For it is in fact this very expectation—that each person within the group will naturally pursue his or her own separate interests and then bring back into the home some of that outside energy and intensity—that perpetually reinvigorates the healthy family and gives it its special sense of aliveness and vitality.

Frances drew in a long breath, then exhaled deeply. "This all adds to the general intensity, and I think from time to time we've just got to stay *still* . . ."

I was aware of the way in which the mother, as she spoke about everyone's separate activities adding to the "general intensity," was leaning forward in the direction of her children as if to bridge any potential distance that might suddenly loom between them. "You mean you've got to slow down, cool your jets," I murmured, and she nodded in agreement.

"I think from time to time we've just got to stay *still*," she repeated, "to—oh—reflect on ourselves and what we're doing. We miss some things, and we have to play catch-up from time to time." Her gaze swept the circle of faces that were turned toward her, then turned back to meet mine.

"What do you think you miss?" I inquired quietly.

She looked uncertain, and made no reply.

"Are you saying that in the rush you just don't hear each other from time to time?" I proposed, after a few moments had passed.

Frances nodded immediately. "I think that's *it*. I think that—well, James and I work full-time, and they're in school, plus they have their extracurricular activities." She was telling me that in her view the search for some balance between each person's individual world and the intimate world they all shared as a family had to be continually active—that equilibrium wasn't something that one could count on to just happen naturally.

While everyone had, by all means, to be encouraged to follow his or her own individual pathway, they all had to remain aware of one another and in good affective contact. Otherwise, there was the ever-present danger of someone straying too far from the family pack and suffering the pain and potential hazards of isolation.

I turned next to her seven-year-old son, and asked him, "What about it, Jamie? Can you add anything to what your mom and dad are saying?"

The boy's attention had wandered, and he jumped when I addressed him directly; everyone laughed. Debra put her arm around her little brother's shoulder. "Are you in shock?" His mother leaned toward Jamie, asked coaxingly, "What's it like, being in this family? Do you like being in this family?"

The youngster shook his head up and down enthusiastically. "*Yeahhh*," he said.

"Why?" Frances prompted him.

"I don't know, I just do," Jamie replied, and the family's easy laughter sounded again. Then the father, eyes fixed upon his son, added, "I think everybody has to be somewhat self-reliant, and somewhat independent, too. Because they all have to do for themselves at various points in time. They have to be able to prepare their own meals from time to time."

"Even Jamie?" I smiled at the boy. "Do you have to do that from time to time?" He nodded his head up and down proudly.

"He'll have to fix himself a sandwich, grab himself a snack," said the father.

"Some cereal in the morning," added Frances, and her husband continued.

"We *encourage* that; we want our kids to be self-reliant, to be able to do things for themselves and not be completely dependent on someone else. For instance, everybody needs to know how to wash dishes, iron clothes, do their own washing, too. I think those things are important—"

He was stopped in mid-sentence by a burst of laughter from the sofa. The girls were engaged in an exchange that I couldn't quite grasp, and I asked Lyla to explain to us what was happening. "Oh, I was just telling Debra that she needs a little more *experience*, on that front," stated the older of the two sisters dryly.

I asked this eldest sibling if she would like to add to what others had already said about living in this family. "How do *you* find it?" I asked her. Fifteen-year-old Lyla answered, without hesitation, that it was "secure" and that she knew always that she'd be taken good care of. "You know you can depend on rides, and money if you need it," she explained. "It's just like—*security*," she reiterated.

"So it's a pretty safe place to be?" I asked, and she nodded. Then I turned to the middle sibling, Debra, and asked her what she would have to say about living here.

"Nothing," she replied.

"Nothing? Just—nothing?" I repeated, with a smile. Her parents looked at their middle child in amazement.

"Nothing," Debra repeated firmly, clearly reveling in the drama of this moment. She straightened her wide-rimmed glasses over the bridge of her nose, then stole a glance at her mother, who merely rolled her eyes. This pubescent girl was letting all present know that the perfect family was not a family that she wanted to be any part of, but nobody seemed overly concerned. Evidently, it was safe here to feel differently and to be contrary.

Family Roles

It was in the course of that same, all-family interview that I asked the Walkers a playful question, one that I knew they would enjoy. This was the question of whether there were certain roles or character parts that people in this family tended to fit into.

"In lots of families," I explained, "there is someone who is the clown and someone who's always in trouble; somebody may be the angel here, and somebody may be the one who . . ." I paused and looked around at the amused faces of the parents, the slightly perplexed Jamie, the giggling teenage daughters. "I'm hearing a little *laughter* around here," I said.

When I asked Debra if *she* had such a role, and if so, what it might be, she was ready with her reply. "I'm the one who's always in trouble," she said drolly, and without a moment's hesitation. This brought forth a rush of laughter and comment from the other people in the family.

I smiled and asked her what sorts of trouble she was most likely to get into. She paused, her expression growing serious and thoughtful, then murmured that it usually had to do with talking on the phone too long, and sometimes it had to do with getting a bad grade. As she spoke, her voice pitch was dropping. I had the impression that this middle child liked to seek the family spotlight but then felt shy and diffident when it actually landed upon her.

I asked her then what *other* things she might do that would reliably land her in the family doghouse, but Debra could think of nothing else. So I let the matter rest there, and turned to the eldest sibling, Lyla.

Lyla couldn't think of a role that she had, and asked me to suggest more of the possible categories. I smiled, "Oh, the complainer, the devil, the one who's always sane and logical, the one who's always emotional—" I began reciting.

But at this point she held up her hand, halted me right there: "I'm *emotional*," she said, definitively. "I'm probably the one who likes to argue the most, also," added the teenager, looking around at the other people in the family as if for confirmation. Everyone except her little brother laughed and nodded; he appeared to be lost in his own thoughts, at the moment.

I interrupted this conversation to lean toward Jamie and ask if he was perhaps thinking about which of the roles was *his* role. He nodded in a weighty, significant manner, which brought forth universal smiles and some suppressed laughter. Thirteen-year-old Debra put her arm around her little brother's shoulders again, giving him a hug and a squeeze.

I told Jamie to go on thinking, and that I would get back to him in a very short while. Then, turning back to Lyla, I asked her which topics in particular she tended to get into arguments about.

"Anything, really," she admitted. "If I disagree, then I'll start arguing about it." The most recent such incident that she could describe had occurred just yesterday, in her Sunday school Bible class, when someone had made what she considered to be a sexist comment; she had chewed him out.

How, I asked, had her fellow student responded? "He didn't say *anything*." Lyla grinned; her dad, laughing, put in, "That fella said to himself, 'Whoa, better leave this woman alone!' "

Now it was young Jamie's turn. I asked him what role he thought *he* had in the family, but he remained uncertain. When I asked him if he was, perhaps, "the angel," he shook his head dubiously. He said he couldn't say for sure; he didn't think so.

But when I asked him if he might be "the complainer," he nodded his head in agreement and said solemnly, "Yes." This evoked hoots of laughter from his sisters and much negative head-shaking on everyone's part. Clearly, no one in the family agreed with him, and I found myself laughing with them.

At the same time I was reflecting upon the fact that there was something basically life-affirming about the quality of this family's humor. The Walkers could surely share a joke, and did so readily, but the jokes they made were not attacking ones and were not being made at any family member's expense.

In distressed, dysfunctional emotional systems, this is very rarely the case. In troubled families, nothing tends to be funny at all—or if humor is present, it is of the assaultive, denigrating variety. The pathological family script is a deadly *serious* melodrama, one in which there is neither character development nor resolution of any difficulty, and in which the selfsame plot repeats itself ad infinitum. Everyone is stuck inside the system, in set roles and complementary relationships that are rigidly fixed and unchanging. What is lacking is the healthier family's capacity to step outside the drama—and even the stage frame—and to regard itself with amusement. In order to do so, *a sense of humor is a basic necessity.*

And what was significant about the Walkers' interchange was not only its humorous quality, but the fact that the discussion did not seem to be generating any hostility whatsoever. This meant that the individuals inside the system were capable of stepping outside the system and reflecting playfully about the role that each of them was enacting within it.

The Sheriff

I noticed that thirteen-year-old Debra's expression was pensive, and asked what *she* believed her brother's role in the family to be. She said, without a trace of sarcasm, that he was the angel. But older sister Lyla wasn't sure that she agreed. "Probably, he *is* the angel, but he's not completely perfect," she said forthrightly. "Still, he's probably the best out of all of us," she added, a somewhat enigmatic afterthought.

I would have asked her what she meant had I not noticed the boy's gaze fixed attentively upon his dad. I asked James Walker what *he* thought his son's role in the family to be; he turned and looked at his child pensively for several moments. Then he said softly, "Oh, I think he's a sweet little kid. He likes to joke and clown around, to jump me when I'm not paying attention to him. And he likes to be very affectionate—receive and give affection."

This father was not so much responding to me as he was reflecting aloud, in a voice that was vibrant with tenderness and emotionality. The sense of loving connection in this family was extraordinary; in fact, it was downright enviable.

James Walker's own role in his family was, as he saw it, "that of an enforcer." His wife, on hearing this, reared back in her seat, then turned to stare at her husband, her expression a parody of horror and incredulity. She giggled.

"You think of yourself as a kind of sheriff, then?" I inquired, and he nodded.

"Yes, the one who maintains stability, discipline, that kind of thing," James said calmly. Frances's expression was becoming ever more extreme, a caricature of perfect disbelief and amazement. "You're the *sheriff*?" she demanded. "How so?" She giggled again, and the children began giggling along with her.

"I think that when things need to be attended to, and they haven't been attended to, it's my job to see that they finally get done," he maintained seriously; but his wife, with an incredulous smile on her face, said, "This is sounding like *Gunsmoke* to me."

My own thought was that if this dad was indeed the family sheriff, he seemed to wear his badge very lightly. I was thinking, too, that the members of this family were having to do some serious searching in order to sort out what their own individual roles might actually be. In distressed, dysfunctional families, these "parts" are usually far easier to discern, for very often the people in the system have had certain preformed, predesignated roles imposed upon them. In many instances there is a pathological script, which seems to demand that someone be an "angel" or a "devil" or a "slut" or a "savior"; the appointed individual's role is set and waiting to be played out. In healthier family organizations, on the other hand, people are freer to create their own roles, and the emotional system is flexible enough to accommodate them.

Frances was now humming the theme music from *Gunsmoke*, and I said to her, with a nod in her husband's direction, "What do you think of that self-characterization?"

"I don't view him that way at all," she said decisively. In her opinion, James's role in the family was more accurately that of "the serious one."

"That's just what *I* was thinking," burst out fifteen-year-old Lyla, as soon as her mother had spoken. "He's *definitely* the most serious person in the family!" I turned at once and looked at Debra questioningly; she nodded and said only, "Yes." But young Jamie, when he was asked in turn, said he thought that his dad was very serious—the most serious person in the family—but that he was a little bit like a sheriff also.

Interpersonal Curiosity

In a way, the youngster was making an important point, for in healthy emotional systems an individual is always far *more* than his designated role in the collective script. Thus, while James Walker might be the most "serious" person in his family, he could clearly be playful (when Jamie jumped on him unexpectedly, for example) and while the father was perhaps exaggerating his position as "law enforcer," he was obviously playing that role to some degree as well. In well-functioning systems, a person may be "the most serious one," but that is not all he or she is seen to be.

In distressed families, on the other hand, the members of the cast tend to occupy roles that have been preformed rigidly and seem to be set in cement. Dave Anderson's family role as "bad, betraying male" in relation to his "rightfully angry" mother had this air of having been created *for* him in advance. And he was, as is usual in this kind of emotional system, viewed as *being* his role; it was as if there were no other parts or aspects of his self than those that the Andersons' pathological script appeared to require.

As psychoanalyst Edward R. Shapiro and episcopal clergyman A. Wesley Carr observe in their joint work, *Lost in Familiar Places*, "In many families where individuals manifest severe personal problems, the members have a striking lack of curiosity about one another. Instead, they are often remarkably certain that they *know* [my italics], understand, and can speak for other family members without further discussion. If individual members attempt to challenge assertions about who they are, they encounter bland denial, unshakable conviction, or platitudinous reassurance. Even though such assertions are usually incorrect and frequently lead to escalating disagreements within the family, this cycle is difficult to interrupt."

In less competent, poorly functioning families, the emotional system shapes the individual's role, and the individual *is* that role and can be nothing otherwise. In better-functioning, healthier families, on the other hand, people tend to create their own roles, which are not unidimensional and *which can change over time* as both individual and family development proceed and continue.

Loving the Distance

When I asked the Walkers if they could tell me what some of the family's most memorable happy times had been, they merely looked at one another, nonplussed. Frances shook her head as if to say that no such event was coming into her mind at this moment. I was surprised, and had to fight the urge to propose suggestions—a large family reunion? A vacation they'd taken? What I was looking for, I explained, was an occasion that they could remember as having been a wonderful experience for all of them.

But they seemed to be unable to focus upon a particular occurrence, and Frances shook her head again. "I think the answer's probably different for each of us," she said, in a doubtful, musing tone of voice. "We've certainly shared good times, when there are weddings and other kinds of special occasions—and that's *great*," she appended enthusiastically. "But then we share in other kinds of things"—she sounded graver and more serious again—"when one of us is being honored or highlighted: Debra making state and then going on to regional in the cheerleading competition; James being named man of the year by the local chapter of the National Council of Negro Women, as he was last week; Lyla being accepted for a trip to Australia . . ." The mother's gaze lingered on each member of her family as she or he was being singled out.

I looked at Lyla, who had sat bolt upright at the mention of her forthcoming journey to Australia. "Wow, you're going to Australia," I said. "When?"

"This summer," she responded, in a voice charged with excitement.

Frances was now looking fondly at her son. "Jamie was just selected as student of the week, two weeks ago," she added gently.

There was a brief silence. "Debra got pretty *far* in that cheerleading competition," put in the father, thoughtfully.

"And *she* was just named mother of the year," burst out Lyla, gesturing in Frances's direction. Then she pointed out the trophy that her mother had just received, which stood between one that Jamie had gotten for field hockey and one that Debra had won at softball. There was such a sense of mutual pride, affection, and belonging here that I said impulsively, "Hey, can I *join* this family? You sound like a great bunch of people," and we laughed at the oddity of the comment.

So many factors (not the least of which were age and race) made this the silliest of notions, and yet I was thinking, not without a sense of wistfulness, what growing up in a family such as this one would have been like.

Frances Walker, her expression becoming pensive again, said, "The way I see it, we all *rejoice* in those good things, and we don't feel threatened. But it's a big deal for any one of us to get involved in something, and to win. Or to lose, for that matter, because losses—those are important also. And we've *lost*, too." Her voice had that crack of emotionality. "There are things that we haven't really gotten."

She was looking at her daughter Debra, and said quietly, "We lost at the regional cheerleading competition, and we all *felt* that, I believe. But we all wanted to be there, and to be part of it . . ." Frances turned to look at her husband and said feelingly, "And to me, it was interesting that in losing, Debra handed something to you? I'm not sure what it was, but I saw *something*. And she gave *me* the flower . . ."

Her voice trailed off softly, and I said to Debra, touched, "What did you hand your dad? Do you remember?"

"No," said the thirteen-year-old flatly and dismissively, a reply that was met with peals of laughter. "It was a ribbon," her father said at once.

Each of the contestants in the cheerleading competition had been given a ribbon and then a flower at the outset, he explained.

"And afterward, her dad asked her if she was upset," Frances interrupted to tell me, "because the other girls were crying, and *she* wasn't crying. To me, it was just interesting," she repeated, "because even though she didn't articulate it, in giving *him* the ribbon and *me* the flower, Debra seemed to be saying 'I'm glad you're here.' "

I turned to the adolescent girl and said, "When your father asked if you were upset, what did you say?"

"No," she answered shortly, but she had a sardonic twinkle in her eye. At that moment, the half-hour gong of a clock sounded. I looked at my watch, and so did Frances. It was three-thirty in the afternoon, and I was aware of the fact that Lyla had to be driven to a schoolmate's house at four o'clock.

"You *weren't* upset?" I turned back to Debra dubiously. "Even after having made it through the state competition, and gotten that far?" She shrugged, shook her head assuredly. "Why *not*?" I asked, tempering my air of wry disbelief with a friendly smile. But Debra, unfazed, only shrugged lightly and said, "I don't know for sure. . . . I guess I was happy to get *that* far, to get where I was." In reaching the regional level of the cheerleading contest, she explained, she had gotten further than she'd ever expected to go.

I realized that she meant what she said. For while Debra Walker had not emerged as a finalist in the last stage of the competition, she had come away from the experience bearing clearly in her mind the positive aspects of the situation, which represented the full half of the cup rather than the empty one.

A long pause followed, during which I looked at each family member in turn. "What I hear you all saying," I said at last, my voice tentative, "is that in terms of good times in this family, every one of you has had certain special things happen which everyone *else* has been able to enjoy . . . Is that what you're saying?"

The question was directed to Frances, who nodded and said, "Sure, sure. But we've *lost* as well," she reminded me immediately, as if she feared I might perceive the situation in an unrealistically rosy fashion.

"We've also had some good times on trips," observed the father at that moment. "We went to Disneyland, and we had a fantastic time, though we were all doing different things in different groups."

There was something really delightful about the Walkers, I thought, and I said aloud, "I get the impression that there's a certain respect, in this family, for the fact that people will probably want to do their own and perhaps very different things. And I have the idea, too, that there's a real acceptance of differences—and yet you're all pretty close."

I turned to the second daughter, Debra, confident that she would puncture any balloon of unjustified idealization. "Am I getting a correct impression? Would you agree or disagree?" I asked her.

The teenager nodded, and said briefly, "Yes," as if at some level she hated to admit it. "You have your space here," put in her mother levelly, at that moment. "And you're allowed to *have* that space."

This was, in my own opinion, an important part of what made *this* family as well functioning and competent as they obviously were; an important part of loving is acknowledging human separateness. As the poet Rainer Maria Rilke has so beautifully phrased it, "Once the realization is accepted that even between the *closest* human beings infinite distances continue to exist, a wonderful living side by side can grow up, if they succeed in loving the distance between them which makes it possible for each to see the other whole against the sky."

CHAPTER 23

Why Some Children Thrive
Despite Early Family Trauma

Is there a link, objectively speaking, between a disruption in early attachment bonds and the development of emotional disorder in adulthood? Are there solid data demonstrating that injurious life experiences (such as the abrupt disappearance of James Walker's father from the seven-year-old boy's life) inevitably lead to psychological aftereffects, either in the immediate wake of the event or as a delayed reaction in later life?

Most of us would assume that some negative sequelae *will* ensue, in the guise of troubled relationships, mental or physical symptoms, or a variety of problems in living. But in fact, there appear to be many instances in which *no* such adverse aftermath ever appears.

While it is obviously true that severe early stressors (family losses due to parental death, divorce, desertion) enhance the risk of later emotional difficulties, a large and growing scientific literature has demonstrated that there is in fact *no* predictable one-to-one, cause-and-effect relationship between early trauma and later psychological disturbance.

Even in the face of early loss and calamity (adversities far more extreme than anything ever encountered by Mr. Walker), a significant number of children do remarkably well. In some mysterious fashion, these youngsters (more than half the sample, in most scientific studies of at-risk populations) are able to make their way through emotionally inflamed family situations without getting seriously burned.

Instead of becoming overly sensitized to the possibility of further loss and disappointment, or totally overwhelmed by their sufferings, these sturdy at-risk children grow up to experience themselves as effective adults, well tempered by the environmental challenges that they have proven themselves capable of managing. "Sweet are the uses of adversity," wrote Shakespeare in *As You Like It;* he likened adversity to "a precious jewel" when one is enriched by it instead of succumbing to it—for in the process, the hardy individual develops an inner sense of fortitude, mastery, and competence.

But how might one account for the consistent finding that *some* severely stressed children are able to fare surprisingly well, while others, embroiled in similarly demanding circumstances, fare very badly? In the course of the past several decades, a growing band of researchers has been studying so-called resilient youngsters in an effort to ascertain what specific protective factors are helpful when it comes to shielding at-risk children from sustaining long-term psychological harm. This field of scientific inquiry is intriguing for a number of reasons, the foremost being its focus upon explaining health rather than explaining pathology.

Born "Invulnerable"?

It has now been well documented, in several excellent longitudinal studies, that severe stress in childhood augments the risk of emotional disorder and also of delinquency in young adult life. This seems in line with one's good common sense; but how to explain the so-called invulnerable children—present in every at-risk population studied—who have grown up in situations that are just as potentially harmful, and who yet have been capable of going on to construct stable, productive, reasonably untroubled lives?

How and why does this happen? Are the crucially relevant factors at play simply inborn, intrinsic to the "invulnerable" child's temperament? To be sure, the earliest studies of resilience were dominated by the pervasive belief that the major differences between at-risk children who became symptomatic, and those who survived relatively intact, were genetic in origin. The fundamental theoretical assumption in the field was that some babies simply come into the world with sturdier constitutions; they have a higher natural immunity to the anxieties and fears to which their distressing early experiences have exposed them. And for a while, this "born sturdy" explanation appeared to be the best—or indeed, the *only*—reasonable explanation of invulnerability.

But with the passage of time, and the accumulation of a good deal of additional research, the concept of a genetically based indestructibility has slowly but inexorably passed out of scientific fashion. At present, few scientists talk about resilience in terms of innate, constitutional factors alone. While inborn makeup is still considered an important part of the overall picture, it is also considered but *one* aspect of a highly complex interaction between the child, his or her nuclear family, and the wider environmental reality. The modern-day approach to the understanding of psychological resilience under stress is far more detailed and multifaceted: Resilience is, one might say, seen in terms of an existential balance sheet—a life ledger that takes into account not only the risks to the growing child but the range of encouraging, supportive resources available.

Consider, for example, a quality or capacity that is to some degree innate: high intelligence. There is now good scientific evidence demonstrating that higher intelligence and academic achievement serve a protective, buffering function for children undergoing adverse life experiences. Still, it is obviously true that high intelligence and good scholastic performance do not always go hand in hand. When it comes to academic achievement, a number of other considerations—such as the child's level of self-esteem, work strategies, sense of efficacy, and belief that life events are generally under his or her own control—are also of critical significance. And while high intelligence can indeed have a protective effect in the presence of severe stressors, it is far likelier to do so if the child's native capacities have brought him or her affirmative strokes from the environment—support, praise, and positive feedback from those people who matter most to him (parents, valued teachers, important peers).

What the ever-expanding resilience literature has in fact made clear is that there are no easy, single ("born invulnerable") answers here. Any comprehensive assessment of psychological risk and resources must involve not only inborn personality factors—some babies come into the world with "easy" and some with far more "difficult" temperaments—but the pivotally important temperamental fit between the baby and the caretaking figures to which he or she must adapt.

One mother may, for instance, feel perfectly capable of managing a difficult infant, while another feels assaulted and overwhelmed by the baby's continual discomfort and incessant demands. Or a bookish, intellectual little boy may be just the son one father desires, while another father would like to toss him back into the sea and fish out a strong and strapping athlete instead. Genetically endowed qualities, capacities, and vulnerabilities take on added power and value—or lose something of their force and significance—as a function of important other people's responses to those particular characteristics.

Furthermore, when evaluating the total picture of risks and resources in the life of any child undergoing stress, a great variety of additional variables must also be taken into account. These include the intensity of the trauma (psychologist E. Mavis Hetherington has provided solid evidence that marital tensions and quarreling inflict more emotional damage upon the children of divorce than does the divorce itself), the duration of the event, and the number of life changes and consequent adaptive demands that ensue. For instance, in the wake of a divorce, does the family have to move from one neighborhood to a different, perhaps much worse and unfamiliar one? And is a formerly nonworking mother forced to seek outside employment, so that she suddenly becomes dramatically less available to her offspring?

According to resilience researcher Dr. Michael Rutter, there is, despite all these variables, a common central theme that emerges from all the recent studies of resilient children. Rutter suggests that *what really matters most for children undergoing stress are two major protective features: "stable affectional relationships," and "experiences of success and achievement."*

The first of these key factors is significant because the presence of an emotionally available caregiver serves to buffer and dampen the anxious, burdened youngster's fears and feelings of disorientation. As Dr. Rutter observes, "The simplest paradigm is children's immediate emotional response to an anxiety-provoking situation; perhaps the most striking feature is the extent to which children's distress is reduced by the presence of a parent or some other person with whom they have a close relationship." In the case of very young children, as he remarks, it is even true that the mere presence of a comfort blanket can provide great reassurance; the blanket is a symbolic and reassuring reminder of the essential mothering figure's involvement and her concern.

It is of course the case that there are many situations in which an at-risk youngster has either a precarious, unstable relationship with a parent, or perhaps has no relationship with that parent whatsoever (this was so for James Walker, who'd had no contact with his father between his sixth and twenty-sixth years). But even in such far from ideal circumstances, maintains psychologist Rutter, a reliable, secure relationship with the other parent can "substantially mitigate" any potentially damaging effects. *"What seems important for protection,"* writes Rutter, *"is a secure relationship with someone"* (my italics).

The second key feature cited by the researcher, "experiences of success and achievement," is important because setting and attaining goals—even minor ones—aids the stressed child in staving off the sense of utter helplessness that crisis and trauma engender. The capacity to accomplish something (perhaps nothing more complicated than giving the mother needed assistance in caring for the younger children) can imbue the youngster with a sense of personal agency, of having a role and making a difference when so much of life feels as if it is spinning out of control. Experiences of success and achievement serve, in short, to counter feelings of powerlessness, hopelessness, passivity.

Furthermore, as researcher Rutter points out, "coping successfully with stress situations can be strengthening; throughout life, it is normal to have to meet challenges and overcome difficulties. The promotion of resilience does not lie in an avoidance of stress, but rather in encountering stress at a time and in a way that allows self-confidence and social competence to increase through mastery and appropriate responsibility."

Sweet indeed can be the uses of adversity, at least in circumstances in which the dependent child is challenged but not overwhelmed by them.

A Stable Affectional Relationship: James Walker

It was in the course of my long meeting with the couple alone (our third interview) that I asked James Walker to give me a few adjectives that would describe his mother, Elinor. He smiled, but said nothing for what seemed like a long time.

I waited, then glanced down at the genogram. "The words you gave me for your dad were 'controlled,' 'meticulous,' 'cool,' " I said reflectively, staring at the family chart on my lap.

I looked up again to find that he had a slightly amused but tender expression on his face. "My mother is a very loving and caring person," he said. "Passionate. Not well educated, but articulate, and"—he smiled—"definitely someone who likes to involve herself in everybody else's business."

At this Frances sputtered audibly, as if trying to prevent herself from giggling aloud. "Well intentioned, *but* . . ." James didn't finish the sentence, for he had met his wife's eyes and the two of them laughed together. I looked down at the genogram, put the tip of my pencil on the round circle under which I'd written "Elinor," then looked up again and said to him in a musing tone of voice, "If I were to ask you to complete the following sentence: 'I learned from my mother that . . .' what do you think your answer might be?"

He looked at me in surprise, but nevertheless responded without hesitating. "What my mother provided for me was *a base*. From which I haven't strayed very far. She gave me a sense of values, a sense of right and wrong; I think that's what I got from her." His voice was deepening into a masculine bass as he spoke, yet simultaneously growing fuller and more vibrant with feeling.

Then Frances added, her tone also serious, that her mother-in-law had a *strong* sense of family, and that she adored the grandkids, who adored her right back.

"I also have to say that she's very kind and modest," James put in.

"Mmm, and *warm*," agreed Frances, nodding.

His mother was, James went on to explain, a religious person. She'd always insisted that the whole family go to church even though he and his brothers and sisters often hadn't wanted to. And although for a long time after leaving home, James himself hadn't wanted any part of the church, it was something he'd come back to, eventually.

"Probably, it's because of her," he said, sounding more and more moved—almost elated—as he spoke. If his mother hadn't provided that kind of foundation, he added feelingly, then he probably wouldn't be connected with the church in the way that he was now. James had told me that his mother was a "passionate" person, and he was sounding passionate himself.

What I seemed to hear him saying was that the sense of this parent's caring and her purposefulness—once experienced by him as loving nurturance coming *to* him *from* her—had become transmuted, over time, into a capacity to nourish his own self as well as a sense of being firmly oriented in the same moral universe that she had always inhabited. His internal mother, an ongoing source of security and guidance, appeared to be active, vital, and very much alive inside him.

Experiences of Success and Achievement; James Walker

Toward the close of my previous interview with the Walkers, James had mentioned that from his earliest boyhood onward there had always been "an expectation" that he would go to college someday. Now I asked him where he thought this expectation had actually come from. Had the source been his mother, Elinor? His mother and his stepdad, perhaps? I paused, looked at him questioningly, but he shook his head as if to say that I was chugging along on a completely wrong track.

Nobody had ever really told him that he *had* to go to college, he replied; it was an expectation of his own—one that was simply there, inside him. "I never thought that I wouldn't go, never even thought about *not going*," he stated, with certainty in his voice. But when I went on to ask him if he believed, in retrospect, that this ambition to go on with his studies had been kindled in the high school he'd attended, it was as though I'd pressed a magic switch. James's expression abruptly tightened and hardened.

"I certainly don't think it came from the school," he said curtly, in a tone of voice that was uncharacteristically grim. Then he explained that although he'd performed fairly well in high school, and had asked his counselor for letters of recommendation to the school of his first choice—which was the State University of New York at Albany—he'd been turned down. The alternative route he'd taken had been via a community college, which he'd attended for two years, graduating cum laude. At this time, he'd applied to the state university at Albany again, and been admitted immediately.

"While I was there, I worked in the admissions office," the father recounted, "and there, I was in a position to read recommendations that came in for other students." James hesitated briefly, then explained that he'd also gotten to read the recommendations that his own high school counselor had sent in for him two years earlier. That letter had contained only three lines: "James is a Negro. I believe he comes from a poor family. I don't think he would do well in college."

That was it, James Walker reiterated, staring at me, just those three lines; he added that they explained why he hadn't been accepted by Albany in the first place. He seemed, I thought, gratified by the obviously startled look on my face, but he didn't continue. There was a silence.

Both he and Frances were regarding me with carefulness, and I had the feeling that there was something they were needing to hear me say; they both looked so wary and so vulnerable. "My God, what a hell of a story that is," I murmured at last, sinking downward in my chair, expiring deeply as though the breath had been knocked out of me. But then I looked up to meet James's gaze fully and directly, said, "That must have sent you through the ceiling. You must have been totally enraged."

His expression, which was cool and slightly distant, didn't alter. "I was—disappointed," he replied, with a wry smile.

I wondered then, as I was to wonder throughout the course of these interviews, what this man had done with his rightful anger—anger at the father who had disappeared from his life for some twenty years, anger at the real harm that had been done to him by a high school counselor's blatant prejudice, anger about the other deprivations and slights that a boy growing up black and poor in this country must surely have suffered.

But if James Walker did have some deeply unacknowledged rage within him, with which he was unable to make any conscious connection, it was certainly hard to discern any outward sign of it. He was, by and large, an engaging, friendly, easy man—someone who focused on the full side of the cup rather than the empty one.

"Anyway, for *whatever* reasons, I always had the expectation of going on to college, but my parents didn't have the money, and couldn't afford to send me," he went on. "So when I was in high school, I was playing sports like all the kids, and I wanted to play football. And I *did* play football— right through high school, and the first two years of college." We seemed to have passed beyond the moment of maximum disquiet, at least for the time being, and he was looking and sounding comfortable with me again.

More than that, James looked as if he were actively enjoying this telling of his tale. "At that time, which was while I was still in high school, I had a cousin who was working at a big place called the Long Lane Country Club. Through him, my cousin Calvin, I got an opportunity to work there, washing dishes, and I did—for a dollar and twenty-five cents an hour." He smiled ironically, shook his head in mock disbelief, as if the memory of those minuscule wages was almost comical now.

The way he'd gotten to college, James explained, was by washing dishes every night until midnight and saving up the money he earned. "That's how I went to college; I *paid* for it," he said, with evident pride. He was letting me know that the successes that he'd achieved in his life had not come easily, but had been earned by his own determined efforts and striving.

There had never been any tuition grants or scholarships, he added. "I paid for it all," James repeated, his voice sounding almost jubilant. "Basically, I put myself through all my schooling, because when I got to college, I continued working throughout." He was leaning forward, radiating such satisfaction that if he'd had suddenly jumped up, thrown his hands in the air, and shouted, "I did it all by myself!" I wouldn't have been overly astonished.

I smiled. "So it sounds as if you'd picked up a few pointers from that hardworking stepfather of yours, Dwight Bailey. *He* was, after all, holding down three jobs at once. . . ." It was less an observation than a question, but for some reason it made us all laugh.

"I would have to say so, yes," conceded James, looking intrigued by that particular thought. For a few moments the three of us sat there without exchanging another word, but with what seemed to me a feeling of being linked and connected.

Three Levels of Early Love Bonding

John Bowlby's theory of human attachment has, over the course of the past three and a half decades, lent itself to careful experimental observation in a fashion never previously available to psychoanalytic thinkers—for no one has actually ever observed an id, an ego, or a superego in action, and thus Freud's ingenious and compelling mapping of the mind can never be either disproved or definitively verified. What *has* proven possible, though, is the study of early infant-parent relatedness, by means of the ethological methods that Bowlby originally championed.

This approach to animal behavior (the animal, in this instance, being human) involves the precise and painstaking scrutiny of particular behaviors along with the attendant effort to understand those behaviors in terms of the adaptive functions they serve. And one very well tried and productive experimental method widely used in this flourishing area of research, the "strange situation" procedure, was first introduced into the field by Bowlby's famous disciple and colleague, psychologist Mary Salter Ainsworth. The technique involves a simple but elegant observational strategy, which has provided a window into the basic nature of early infant-parent attachment and enabled psychological researchers to look at this potent first relationship in wonderful and unexpected detail.

The strange situation is an event consisting of several brief component episodes (many variations on the unadorned form given here exist). As described by John Bowlby in *A Secure Base*, the first of these episodes involves a period during which the mothering person and her young child are observed from behind a one-way mirror in a room (actually, a laboratory fitted out to look like a playroom) with which the baby is completely unfamiliar. Not only are there unaccustomed toys in this new setting, there is also a "stranger"—another person present whom the small youngster has never seen before.

In the second stage of this experiment, the mother leaves the room for a brief period; during her short absence, the small youngster's response to being left in a strange room with a stranger is meticulously noted. And finally, when the mother returns and the pair are reunited, the manner in which the baby greets her—whether joyously, or with anxious clinging behavior, or perhaps with apparent indifference—is carefully recorded.

An impressive quantity of observational data has now emerged from such strange situation research, much of which involves variations on the basic scenario described—the mothering person departs briefly, leaving the young baby (Salter's original study was done with one-year-olds) in an unfamiliar room with a stranger; then the mother returns. This work has led to the recognition of at least three stable types of caregiver-infant relationship. These are known as "secure," "anxious-avoidant," and "anxious-resistant" patterns of attachment.

As described by Bowlby in *A Secure Base*, "The pattern of attachment consistent with healthy development is that of *secure attachment* [my italics], in which the individual is confident that his parent (or parent-figure) will be available, responsive, and helpful should he encounter adverse or frightening situations. With this assurance, he feels bold in his explorations of the world and also competent in dealing with it." This fortuitous state of affairs is, as Bowlby notes, promoted by an attachment figure who is sensitive to her child's signals, affectively available, and lovingly there for him when he needs her protection, solace, or assistance.

The second form of relational configuration, *anxious-resistant attachment*, is one in which the child "is uncertain whether his parent will be responsive or helpful when called upon. Because of this uncertainty he is always prone to separation anxiety, tends to be clinging, and is anxious about exploring the world." This kind of emotional bond is prone to develop when a caregiver is sometimes available and receptive, but at other times inaccessible, unhelpful, or disconfirming of the child's actual experiences. The selfsame pattern may also develop when actual and very real parent-offspring separations have taken place, or in situations involving an attachment figure who continually threatens to abandon if the child's behavior doesn't show improvement.

The third type of parent-child bond, *anxious-avoidant attachment*, is one in which the youngster has "no confidence that, when he seeks care, he will be responded to helpfully; on the contrary, he expects to be rebuffed. Such an individual attempts to live his life without the love and support of others. This pattern is the result of the individual's mother constantly rebuffing him when he approaches her for comfort or protection," as author Bowlby describes it. There is now, as Bowlby notes in *A Secure Base*, a considerable body of clinical evidence suggesting that this type of early attachment pattern leads to a variety of personality problems in adulthood, a very common one being compulsive self-sufficiency—that is, an incapacity to either receive or to give out emotional nourishment, even within the context of one's most intimate relationships.

Much work on early attachment bonding has now been carried out in both retrospective and prospective (and therefore, predictive) studies of mothers and their young babies and toddlers. And according to researchers working in this area of child development, there now exists an impressive scientific literature on the subject—one that supports the view that our characteristic patterns of relating intimately become established very early in our lives, and that such patterns tend to have a certain perdurance and stability.

What this experimental work with young babies and their mothers has also demonstrated with great clarity is that securely attached children will generally respond to life's challenges with hope, confidence, and a belief that they can deal successfully with whatever obstacles they encounter, while anxious, insecurely attached children begin to show signs of helplessness and defeatism almost from the very outset. *A secure relationship with someone seems to inspire a kind of inner optimism and trust, the deep belief that something good will happen if only one perseveres long and hard enough.*

Earning One's Keep: Frances Walker

Frances Townsend Walker, like her husband, had been the child of an enormously hardworking, hard-driving man. This certainly came as no surprise to me; in the course of interviews with many other African-American families who'd recently ascended into the middle class, I'd come to recognize that a shared and strong belief in the work ethic was of paramount importance.

As experts Alice F. Coner-Edwards and Henry E. Edwards, M.D., observe in their brief but illuminating essay "The Black Middle Class: Definition and Demographics," the people who do manage to make it from the lower to the middle or upper middle classes are those who have gotten up there by means of their own bootstraps. They have worked hard for whatever they've achieved.

An important prerequisite for any black person's attaining higher status is, as Coner-Edwards and Edwards observe, that individual's own belief that a person of color *can* achieve the same benefits and privileges enjoyed by others in the society. But these newly middle-class African Americans also, they write, "believe that they must work hard to achieve this status. . . . These families shun getting by, or laziness." My own impression, picked up during interviews with a number of these hardworking families, was that the threat of being perceived as an "idle, slothful black person" was a negative social stereotype that was always nipping at the middle-class African American's heels.

When I asked Frances for an adjective or two that would best describe her father, her immediate response was "strong-willed."

"A *hard* man," added her husband, albeit softening the phrase with a low, good-natured guffaw. I turned to Frances, asked her how, exactly, this hardness had made itself manifest.

Her father had, she explained, simply believed that you had to earn your keep. He'd let his children know, very early in their lives, that he would support his children for eighteen years; after that, it was up to them; they were on their own. "My dad simply believed that you had to earn your keep," she repeated unequivocally, "and he was just *driving*. He was strong on values about honesty and trust, and working hard, and not getting anything for nothing. *Those* kinds of things. . . He was tough on us," she admitted, meeting my eye.

James grinned, shot her an impish look, and said, "Tell her about how he farmed you all out." Their eyes met, and the two of them burst out laughing.

Frances, turning back to me, explained that her father had felt that there were too many females in the house—which was small—and that there wasn't enough work to keep them all busy. For that reason, he'd sent Frances's older sister Letty to their grandmother's house, which was directly across the way. "To *stay*," James put in equably but decisively, as if reasserting his original point.

On the genogram, I had already sketched in some information about the birth order and present circumstances of the children in Frances's family. Letty was, I noted, two years older than Frances herself, and was the fourth in this row of mainly female siblings. All the daughters in the family had completed college, while the one male—Clifton, second in line and now forty-six years old—had gone off in his late teens and joined the Marines.

Letty had, I learned, been ten years old when she was sent across the way to live with their grandma. Frances herself had been sent to another relative—"someone who lived not far away, within walking distance," she added quickly, as though offering explanations on her dad's behalf. She had been in sixth grade when that happened, she believed, and therefore must have been around twelve years of age.

Looking down at the maternal side of the genogram, I reflected that Frances, a middle daughter herself (fifth in a row of six siblings), had been farmed out to another family when she'd been roughly the same age as her own middle child, Debra, was right now. And I wondered whether Frances Walker might be experiencing any "anniversary tensions" in regard to this particular child's having reached the age of her own family banishment.

"There were just the two of them, Constance Wright and her mother; they were distant relatives of my father . . . cousins of some kind," Frances now told me, looking uncertain about what the blood relationship had actually been. I wasn't sure whether or not she was saying she had been sent off to *live* with these relatives, and this was the next question I asked her.

"I didn't sleep there, no," she replied. She'd simply gone over to her other family's house every day after school, and helped out with whatever chores needed doing. "Every day in the summer, too, I would get up in the morning and go over there and stay until about five in the evening, do whatever work needing doing. . . . And my sister did the same thing at my grandmother's house," added Frances, her manner calm but her voice sounding oddly hollow, devoid of its usual warm and vibrant tonal changes, as if she were speaking to me from a long distance away.

I paused, then said, "That, I suppose, felt pretty *hard* to you guys?" Even as I spoke, she was nodding in agreement. "At the time it *did*, at the time it certainly did," she answered fervently, with her more customary presence and immediacy.

Her eldest sisters Anne and Sue had, as she explained, been put in charge of keeping their own family's house, "helping to clean, doing whatever. . . But *all* of us had to learn to cook and clean and do all of the chores, which my dad felt we would not do otherwise—Letty and me, I mean, because the older siblings, the sisters particularly, were there and would probably do the brunt of the work. He wanted to make sure that we did it *firsthand*, so we learned it from . . ." Frances's voice trailed off, and there was a silence.

I did nothing to interfere with that silence, for my own thoughts had gone rambling in another direction entirely. I was wondering whether Constance Wright and her mother had actually been distant cousins of Frances's father, or whether they'd merely been the kind of "kinfolk" who, though in reality biologically unrelated, are accepted as belonging within the family's boundaries anyhow. Such augmented families flourish within the black community, and will often care for each other as lovingly and tenderly as the best of blood relatives would.

As sociologist Andrew Billingsley, Ph.D., describes it in *Climbing Jacob's Ladder:* "There is an element in African-American family life which [the sociologist] Carol Stack calls 'fictive kin' and others call 'play mother, brother or sister, aunt, uncle, or cousin.' This can still be a strong basis for family unity in the African-American community. Indeed, our own children have so many 'aunts,' 'uncles,' and 'cousins' unrelated to them by blood that they can hardly keep track of them. Whenever they are in need, however, or reach a particular transition in their lives, they can count on assistance from these 'appropriated' family members."

This extended network of actual and "adoptive" kinfolk creates an effective mutual support system, which, in the survival culture that the African-American community has historically been, and to a great extent still is, often has real consequences not only in terms of the emotional sustenance offered but in very tangible economic terms as well. But as a number of experts on ethnicity and family therapy have observed, this broadened sense of family belonging has resulted in a situation in which the line the family draws around itself is normatively somewhat different. In black families, the family boundary is not necessarily synonymous with the boundary around the *nuclear* family, as is usually true of other ethnic groups. Indeed, as researcher Robert B. Hill observes in *The Strengths of Black Families*, one of the great unrecognized sources of vigor and resilience within the African-American community (whose failings and pathologies are, as he notes, far more scrupulously documented) may well be the way in which all kinds of real and fictive kinfolk join together to form networks of familial belonging and cooperative assistance.

This characteristically black family pattern of reciprocal involvement and caring may, as Howard University social scientist Harriet Pipes McAdoo has suggested, even be the wave of the not-so-distant future in the culture at large. For as McAdoo points out, the social forces buffeting *most* families at the present time—increasing divorce, economic hardship, and the fact that in many households with young children there are two working parents—are creating vast reservoirs of need for communal, extra-nuclear-family backing and support. "Black families have managed to sustain their families under pressures that are now being shared by a growing number of non-black families. Many other American families are adopting and developing life-styles and parenting approaches that have been present for a long time within the extended kin-help patterns of the black community," McAdoo writes.

A Second Surrogate Parent

"Did your dad ever get any income from your work for the Wrights?" I asked Frances, then said lightly, "Or was he just getting you out from underfoot?" She didn't smile, but shook her head in the negative very vigorously, as if to dislodge the notion of wages from my own thoughts at once.

"No, what actually happened was that Constance Wright and her mom sort of took me under their wing. They did all of my school shopping, would purchase my school clothes, and they would just—" She stopped, seemed to speculate for a few moments. "My dad certainly did *not* want me to accept any money; he said to them, you know, 'This is not for money.' He told them up front that this is what he wanted me to do, and Letty to do, and that no one was expected to pay us. So buying me my school things was *their* way, this was what Constance and her mother would do."

Frances was, I realized, looking at me as if fully anticipating that I would misperceive in some fundamental way what this entire arrangement had been about. I went on to ask her what her mother's feelings about this arrangement with the Wright family had been. Had her mother been in favor of it, by and large?

"She didn't object to it; she thought it was fine," Frances replied quickly. "Keep in mind that we were all living in the same neighborhood, and very, very close. *I* became pretty close to the Wrights, and actually we all still *are*. The kids call Constance 'Grandma' now, because I became that close to them, and we're still close now."

James turned in her direction, leaned toward her, and touched her forearm lightly. "Even your mother calls Constance your second mother," he remarked, with a half-smile. "Yes," she answered. "Oh, yes," then turned back to me. In the background, I heard the telephone in the kitchen start ringing.

"I think I became closer to the Wrights than my parents ever expected, particularly than my *mother* ever expected," resumed Frances, in a gentle, grateful tone of voice, "and this was even more so after my father died, when we became *really* close and that family really did look out for me." Frances Walker's goodwill and affirmative orientation toward the world were, it seemed to me, like a boomerang that always returned to her with many of the positive, gratifying things that she was giving out.

Still, how odd I found it that she and her husband should have had these remarkably similar pieces of early history in common. James Walker had been a young boy who'd forged a relationship with an encouraging, supportive "second father," and he'd found himself an intimate partner whose own attachment to a sympathetic and supportive "second mother" had been among her most profound and formative experiences.

Clearly, both members of the pair had the inherent capacity to engage in positive ways with these "supplemental parents" and to elicit their genuine involvement and concern. And this capacity—to engage warmly and affirmatively with the available caregivers in their lives—had to be recognized as a powerful and influential personal resource available to each of them during the years of his or her childhood dependency.

CHAPTER 24

Love: Unconditional, or Conditional/Earned

What is it that brings the gratifying kind of parent-offspring bond termed secure attachment into being? The answer is, the unconditional love of the caregiving parent—a free-flowing, spontaneous, and genuine commitment to the child that is proffered with no inappropriate strings attached.

The child who is loved unconditionally is not ever being asked to *earn love* by becoming the nurturer's comforter, confidant, or caretaker. Nor is the child being asked to live out the lost dreams and unmet expectations that the parent was never able to realize—to be a better version of the parent, the person the parent wishes he or she could have become. Unconditional loving is never given or withheld depending upon whether the child is willing to become the particular sort of individual that the parent has in mind (an "I'll love you *if . . .*" type of relational framework).

The love of the attachment figure is, in a word, noncontingent. *The youngster need not struggle to obtain her love* by means of his heroic and continuous (but never completely successful) efforts to meet her needs for solace, sustenance, narcissistic enhancement, or the like. Quite the opposite: The unconditionally loved child is meeting the parent's needs by virtue of his very existence; she loves him for just plain being there. The nurturer's love is not, in brief, fluctuating up and down like the needle of a barometer, becoming less or more available depending upon the acceptability of the child's behavior.

There will be, most certainly, a host of situations in which a parent will be heartily annoyed, disapproving, or even frankly disturbed by her child's actions. But, as marital and family therapist Stuart Johnson observes, "the mother won't *stop loving the youngster* when she's feeling critical or distressed by the things he happens to be doing."

A child may, for example, be failing to do his homework, or be raiding the refrigerator and overeating alarmingly in the parent's absence. But still, the parent's basic love for the child will not be withdrawn because an overweight child or a child who's doing badly in school is viewed as unworthy of her further concern and involvement. Where love is granted unconditionally, one may disapprove of behavior, but the basic continuity, reliability, and predictability of the attachment are never seriously brought into question. The child is, very simply, loved "for his own sake, as a person in his own right," to quote the great theorist Ronald W. D. Fairbairn.

Earned Love

Love that must be earned from the parent has a different tone and feeling entirely. This kind of loving always has the word "unless" attached to it, like the proverbial can tied to the dog's tail. The message being transmitted repeatedly, and across a variety of interpersonal channels (words, attitude, gestures, facial expression, voice pitch, inflection), is one that may start out in any of a host of ways—"*Unless* you're obedient . . ."; "*Unless* you show me great respect . . ."; "*Unless* you accept the way I need to see myself . . ."; "*Unless* you bring a sense of pride to this family . . ."—but the message invariably concludes in the selfsame fashion.

What is being communicated is that the parent's love is conditional upon the child's behaving in the approved and acceptable ways. Thus, the full and unabridged communication always reads, "*Unless* you do X, Y, or Z, I will withhold my love from you or may withdraw from the relationship entirely." Or, at a somewhat more subterranean level, the completed message may even be the following: "*Unless* you accept my projections of those dissociated thoughts and feelings that I cannot consciously 'own' as aspects of my own inner being—and respond by enacting your assigned role and living out these denied parts of myself in your *own* life—I will find it impossible to respond to and acknowledge you. I may not even find it possible to interact with you at all."

This powerful, demanding, and extremely confusing kind of communication was, it will be recalled, the customary mode of message transmission within the Anderson family's household. Dave's mother's most passionate interactions with her teenage son invariably took place when the boy was standing in the symbolic shoes of her wild, impulsive, "impossible" father. The adolescent boy was personifying and portraying for Susan Anderson the charged role of a person from her past—that irresponsible, abandoning first male in her life, whose loving commitment to her had always felt so insecure and ultimately proved so tenuous.

In acutely troubled families one often finds, as theorists John Zinner and Roger Shapiro have observed, that "the relationship between parents and split-off aspects of themselves projected onto their children replicates the family relations of the parent when he was a child." It was, in any event, true that—in a striking and peculiar, but basically disastrous manner— Dave Anderson was "earning his mother's love" by enacting the role of the impossible man with whom she (at a level outside her own awareness) still craved a sense of continuing contact.

Seeking Love Strategically

In a relational system pervaded by the belief that love has to be earned— one in which love is never freely given but instead is doled out in exchange for certain "good" behaviors—a sense of the attachment figure's dependability and steadiness cannot develop in a natural, organic manner. When love must be endlessly struggled for, it is difficult for a fundamental belief in the caretaker's ongoing caring to develop.

In this kind of emotional system, moreover, there is a sense that the parental nurturer can never be fully satisfied. She is always likely to want more of whatever is required—obedience, for example—or she may want to see the child's submission manifested differently, or may reward obedience (or not reward it) in a random manner that makes no coherent sense to the child whatsoever. And, as Yale psychologist Dr. Jesse Geller notes, love that is contingent upon behavior tends to be granted only in a strategic fashion.

The mothering figure will be loving only as *a reward for certain behaviors*—and, not surprisingly, the child also learns to seek love in a similarly strategic and tactical manner. The child takes for granted what seems perfectly obvious, based upon his or her own experiences: That love can never be attained in straightforward and uncalculating ways.

The youngster's all-pervasive sense that the nurturer's love must forever be acquired (and is therefore always on the verge of being lost) makes him feel as if he is living at the edge of a precipice, and could tumble into it at any moment. He is filled with the dread of some nameless but terrible happening—something that could go irretrievably awry at any given moment. He could do something utterly intolerable, make the fatal misstep that brings about the loss of the nurturing person's affection, caring, and protection. The dependent child lives in apprehension, for his fear is that the nurturer may withdraw her love at any moment, and that if she does withdraw from the attachment, the fault will be no one's but his own.

The true horror of this relational dilemma actually lies in the youngster's own (mistaken) belief that whatever happens will be under his control. His firm belief is that if he relaxes his vigilance even briefly it may well be his own foolish mistakes or stupidity that bring the feared event to pass—the loss of the parent's affection and whatever sense of safety and orientation the attachment confers. His feeling is that *one false move on his part, and he may be abandoned,* either temporarily or on a permanent basis.

For the young, dependent child this kind of threat is experienced as threatening to existence itself. Certainly, the recent explosion of research with very young infants (see Part Three, "The First Loves of Our Lives") has produced considerable scientific evidence supporting John Bowlby's original hypothesis that we humans come into the world biologically prewired to establish a love bond with an adoring, nurturing, and protecting caretaker.

It follows that in situations in which this vitally important attachment seems imperiled, the child feels as if his very existence is on sufferance and on probation; he experiences himself as being in enormous danger. He must be wary and shrewd; forthrightness and spontaneity are completely out of the question. The dependent child cannot simply be who he is (a less-than-perfect human being) but must instead evaluate each and every one of his deeds and actions in advance. He must remain in a state of constant alert about what is wanted by the parent—what will "sell" in the relationship, in terms of eliciting the desired responses or even just the beam of the caregiver's undivided attention.

Says clinical psychologist Geller, "The child who is secure in the knowledge that he's loved unconditionally will come into the house and feel as if he's being *embraced,* even though the parent may do no more than glance at him, ask a question or two, make a few offhand remarks. But the child who feels unsure about the attachment will enter the house vigilantly, look around carefully, try to gauge the state of the atmosphere and figure out what the parent's mood may be."

Even as the child makes this appraisal, adds Geller, he will be figuring out what might be the best tactic of approach; that is, what can be said that the parent will be willing to hear and will respond to. The child may, for example, talk about an A that he received on a math test, when in fact it is *also* true that he was the last kid to be picked to play on either side of the baseball team and he is struggling with painful feelings of hurt and rejection.

The contingently loved child is not at liberty to be who he really is—a boy with an A on his test, who is also in need of some nurturance and comforting. It is his never-ending task to shape himself into someone who will be found acceptable and worthy of love by the caretaking parent. In this kind of emotional framework, it is clearly the case that *the dependent youngster is always tirelessly performing.*

In the process of doing so, it must be added, he is also learning to ignore, deny, and repress from awareness those aspects of his internal and external experience that might threaten the existence of this vitally necessary relationship. *The maintenance of the attachment with the mothering figure (which, no matter how flawed, provides the human child with a basic sense of safety and protection) is of paramount importance.*

Love and Exploration

The very phrase "unconditional love" seems to convey the notion that unlimited supplies are available. The phrase "earned love," on the other hand, seems to suggest the notion that love exists as a finite resource, one that can be depleted or even used up entirely. This is why the child who is loved unconditionally feels little anxiety about the possibility of the caretaker's love supplies drying up, while the child who is loved only "on condition" of certain behaviors lives with the constant fear that the nurturer's love may lessen or perhaps dissipate completely.

Thus, while the unconditionally loved child is infused with a sense of optimism, self-confidence, and personal entitlement, the child who is endlessly engaged in the task of obtaining the parent's love is assailed by feelings of self-doubt, mistrust, and uncertainty. His inchoate but very potent fear is that she may withdraw emotionally or even leave him—and he will then be cast off into a terrifying and limitless abyss, in which he must inevitably perish.

It is thus of mortal importance that he meet the nurturer's demands, comply with her requirements, be the person she needs and wants him to be. He is, however, never completely certain about just how to go about carrying out this confusing assignment, and it is for this reason that the world in which the insecurely attached child lives feels like an extraordinarily unpredictable, hazardous place. And inevitably, the impossibility of placing any real trust in the reliability of the attachment has an inhibiting effect upon the small child's ability to explore the world around him.

This is no mere speculation, for more than two decades of research on attachment bonding (much of it carried out using strange situation techniques) have clearly documented something that many of us already knew in our bones anyhow: There is an inverse relationship between the insecurity of a child's primary attachment and his ability not only to explore the world around him but to rebound from stressful experiences. The less safe and protected the youngster's home base in the world happens to feel, the harder it feels to leave it behind him. For when one's base camp feels unsteady and undependable, small forays into the surrounding environment come to seem like highly dangerous enterprises.

Learning "Not to Know"

Not only is it more difficult for the insecurely attached child to make forays into the world around him, it is far harder to explore the world within the self as well. For when the caregiver's love is extended on a contingent basis only, the child must not merely do the right things— behave correctly and make himself acceptable in the parent's eyes—but also think the right kinds of good, loving thoughts. If one is loved only conditionally, it feels profoundly unsafe to have (or at least be aware of) "bad," hostile, or just plain ambivalent feelings toward the very person upon whom one depends so absolutely and profoundly. Because of the child's essential doubts about the steadiness of a relationship that feels somewhat imperiled already, the mere idea of closely examining his own real (and therefore complex) feelings about the attachment figure *feels* alarming.

It seems downright menacing to be too curious about the parent's failings and shortcomings, or to linger upon the ways in which one actually does experience her as bad, punishing, and depriving. Given the dubious state of the attachment itself, the rageful feelings engendered by such thoughts are almost intolerably threatening.

The child's fear is that the mothering person (who is always scrutinizing his behavior so critically and carefully anyway) may be able to see right through his head and know exactly what kinds of "bad" thoughts he is thinking. And, given that her love and nurturance are being offered to him only "on condition," his automatic reaction is to swiftly banish all the "bad," angry thoughts from conscious awareness. For the omnipresent danger is that if his own thoughts and feelings are hateful and unloving, she will know about it somehow, and respond in kind to him.

The young child's way of experiencing the world is, furthermore, suffused with magical thinking. The youngster may know, at one level, that good witches and bad witches don't really exist, but another part of him believes in witches very deeply. There is, moreover, a far hazier internal boundary between what is occurring in imagination and what is occurring in reality. Children are frequently unable to make a very clear distinction between the thoughts they have and the actions that they are actually taking.

Thus, if a child happens to be harboring hostile, destructive feelings toward a mothering person who has frustrated him, these angry feelings may be equated in his own primitive thought processes with the sense that he is actually attacking or destroying her. This puts the utterly dependent and needful offspring into a state of mounting tension and anxiety. His inner experience is one of somehow harming the very person upon whom his life depends.

In order to deal with this situation, which feels lethally alarming, the psychological mechanism known as "splitting" is brought into play. The vulnerable child cleans up his inner act by systemically sweeping the "bad," unwelcome thoughts and feelings from his own conscious awareness. They are removed not only from the caregiver's knowledge but from his own; he is rendered as ignorant of their existence as she is.

It is in the service of preserving the vitally important bond with the nurturer, at any emotional cost whatsoever, that he perceives not only her but his own inner world through glasses that are, if not exactly rose-tinted, certainly defensively distorted. But as part of this ongoing effort to isolate his idealized image of the "all-good" parent—and to split it off from suppressed negative internal images of the "all-bad," unloving parent— the youngster must deny and block out segments of emotionally incompatible and therefore unwelcome information.

There are things that the child who is loved only "on condition" cannot know about (perhaps the extent of the parent's rejecting feelings) lest they prove too damaging or threatening to the continuing existence of the vitally important relationship. The problem is that in this very process of "not knowing" (splitting), the youngster's ability to learn is impaired. For, as Professor Geller points out, "curiosity, interest and exploration are the basis of *all* learning."

The very capacity to wonder—"I wonder where the stars come out from at night?"; "I wonder what happens to the leaves in winter?"; "I wonder what makes an airplane go up in the sky?" "I wonder if my cat knows who I am?"; "I wonder how high the highest fireman's ladder can go?"; "I wonder where people really go when they die?"—is inevitably affected, for the child who is forced to shut down important aspects of his thought process in regard to the parent becomes inhibited in many other aspects of the learning experience as well.

He has found it safer to avoid thinking too much—especially about areas that have emotional valency—and so cannot retain an open, expansive approach to new experience or even bring into play the full range of his intelligence, thoughtfulness, and awareness. Knowledge itself feels dangerous, for there is always the sense that lurking just around the next corner there may be things it's better not to know.

Using Aspects of the Past That Are Felt to Be Positive

The most important thing that he'd learned from his biological father, James Walker had told me, was that "staying connected to the people in your family" is essential. In other words, he'd learned to behave in a way that was the total opposite of the original model.

When I asked James what had been the most important thing he'd learned from his *other* father—his stepdad, Dwight Bailey—he surprised me by framing his response in the negative once again. "I think what I learned from him were some things *not* to do. In terms of being a father," he explained, softening the comment with a wry, regretful smile.

"My father didn't spend a lot of time with us, and when he talked about things, they were adult things. He didn't take a lot of interest in us *as* children, and in the 'children' kinds of things we did. But," added the middle-aged man reflectively, "he did try to teach us how to work, and the *meaning* of work." He paused, looked at me, and I nodded, urging him to continue.

"For instance, he would often take me out with him on Saturday mornings when he had to go and shovel stone—to prepare a driveway or a swimming pool, something of that sort. He'd waken me early, get me out of bed, take me with him, because, as he'd tell me over and over, 'This is what *you'll* have to do if you don't get an education.'" An amused expression crossed James's face, and he laughed. "Now I don't think I really *needed* to be told that, in the first place!"

"But he was, in any case, pushing you along to continue your education?" I inquired, thinking, at the same time, about the ways in which this husband and father had managed to improve upon his two early male parent models—to do certain things very differently in his own adult life, while retaining a sense of emotional connection to them both.

"Right, and he *was* supportive," he replied thoughtfully. "He was encouraging. He *never* did anything to hinder me in that regard, although he wasn't a well-educated person himself." James Walker was capable of feeling warmth and gratitude, as well as disapproval, of the varying aspects of his stepfather's behavior. He was, in other words, capable of containing his ambivalence, his mixed positive and negative feelings about the other.

This capacity is always linked to the ability to consciously "own" and take responsibility for mixed feelings about the goodness and the badness within one's own self—an ability in turn predicated upon not sweeping major aspects of one's internal experience out of sight and out of conscious awareness. In the wake of James's reply, I sat there quietly for several moments, tapping the point of my pencil on the Walker side of the genogram.

I was reflecting upon the fact that some people find it feasible and natural to alter what they perceive as problematic aspects of their early family experiences, while others behave as if they're on automatic pilot—compelled to re-create those problematic experiences and to repeat them. What made the difference? What made changing the early models possible? My own working hypothesis was that this important capacity—*to do things differently in one's own adult life*—was made possible or not possible depending upon how secure and solid the first, most primary relationship was felt to be.

If one has grown up feeling safe in the caregiver's love, one can "own" and take responsibility for the bad, angry, vengeful thoughts and emotions that arise from time to time without feeling that the attachment itself is being frighteningly endangered. One can have full access to one's knowledge of her goodness and badness—and of one's own loving *and* hating— without the terrifying threat of losing her nurturance and protection completely.

This sense of security in the resilience of the relationship (the "secure base" of which James Walker had spoken) engenders a certain confidence about exploring life's possible options, allowing novel information into the system, altering and improving the original familial models. James had, for instance, found it possible to make changes in the family script by incorporating his stepfather's industry and work habits into his own life, while rejecting the older man's sense of remoteness from the children and his lack of engagement with the younger people's activities.

It felt safe to be different, and he could be flexible, because being different from the paternal model didn't raise the internal threat of losing contact with the "internal parent" completely. When one has learned how to operate from the secure kind of base with which James Walker's mother had provided him, one can remain affectively connected to the past without having to resurrect and relive it, without needing to have things happen in the same old familiar, predictable (if often painful) ways over and over again. One can *use* aspects of the past that are felt to be positive and helpful, and lay the other parts to rest.

The Family Boundary

The adjectives that I'd jotted on Frances's side of the genogram, just above and to the right of the square designating her father, William, were "strong-willed," "hard man," "important that you earn your own keep," "worked in construction," "strong on values, such as honesty, trust, not getting anything for nothing."

When I was at work on the Townsend side of the family chart, I'd asked Frances for some terms that might most readily describe her own mother's qualities, and the relevant answers sprang to her lips without a moment's hesitation. Mary, her maternal parent, was "kind," "giving," "a generous sort of person." She was also someone who liked to please, explained her daughter.

"Someone who *lives* to please," amended James, with an amused but affectionate expression.

"How old is Mary right now?" I asked Frances, who told me that her mother had just turned sixty-two. I wrote that number down on the genogram, then asked, "And William?" She jumped as if startled, then replied in a voice that had fallen abruptly to little more than a hushed whisper, "He's deceased."

Frances sounded almost frightened, as if she thought her father or his spirit might be here in this room right now, disapproving of the fact that he was being discussed.

Drawing a slantwise line through the square box representing William (the customary way of depicting death on a family genogram), I said quietly, "When did he die?" She responded in the same low voice, "When I was sixteen."

"When you were sixteen," I echoed her words sympathetically, and our gazes locked. I asked her what had caused her father's death, and she answered, looking shaken, "He had a heart attack." Judging by the expression on his daughter's face, William Townsend might have died last week, and yet a quick glance at the family diagram told me that he had actually died some twenty-six years earlier.

"Was it a sudden heart attack?" I asked her.

She nodded. "He walked out of one room into the other. Literally, in a matter of three minutes . . ." She didn't go on. After a few moments, I asked her whether the people in her family had been aware of his having a heart condition, and Frances nodded. Her father had suffered a serious heart attack eleven years earlier, and been sent home from the hospital with the information that his days were numbered; but he had outlived that diagnosis by over a decade, with no trouble whatsoever in between.

"And then one evening he just . . . walked out of the living room," recounted Frances. "My younger sister Mae was there, and I was there, and my mother was there. . . . My folks were just getting ready to turn in. She, my mother, was picking up a few things; she liked everything neat and clean. And he said to her, 'You should come on to bed.' And she said, 'Oh, I just want to neaten things up here,' and then she went in there after him. . . . I can still remember her scream."

She shivered. She was looking directly at my face, but her eyes were so blank and unseeing that she seemed almost like a sleepwalker. I was slightly startled when she continued speaking. "That was it, and that was, I'm sure, three minutes at most." Her voice was low, but there was a note of complaint in it, as though an event so tragic should have been allotted more than this cruelly short space of time in which to occur.

There was an uneasy silence, which I broke by asking her how long her parents had been married at the time of her father's death. She was uncertain. "I myself was sixteen at the time—" Frances was just starting to do the calculation aloud, when James interrupted her by saying, "Your sister Anne is the oldest, and she's now forty-seven, so they'd have to have been married at least as long as—" He halted suddenly, for she was shaking her head decisively.

"Anne is my *mother's* daughter," she explained. All conversation ceased abruptly, and James stared at his wife in amazement. This news had plainly taken him entirely by surprise, and an astonished smile slowly spread itself across his face. "From a prior relationship, no doubt," he commented drily.

He was, as we all knew, alluding to our earlier conversation about "real" siblings and half-siblings in his own family of origin, and there was something so weirdly comic about the way in which this bit of information had emerged that the three of us burst out laughing.

"Had you never *heard* about Anne's being a half-sister? Or is it possible that you *did* know about this at one time, but then just forgot about it later?" I asked James, who shook his head in slow wonderment, as if to indicate that he himself couldn't be sure.

He looked intrigued, and I was intrigued, too. I am always surprised when unexpected, revelatory bits of family information pop up in the course of these interviews—even though such revelations happen with peculiar frequency. It is hard to understand why these strangely similar episodes or fragments of experience tend to emerge on both sides of a genogram—often, as in this instance, to the great surprise of the participants themselves. But the regularity with which this happens does make me think that we humans must have some wonderfully unknown sources of knowledge about one another: Otherwise, how could we be so thoroughly ingenious in our ability to gravitate toward those who are, for thoroughly unarticulated reasons, deeply known and profoundly familiar?

James said, his expression perplexed, that, come to think of it, he did seem to remember having known at some earlier time that Anne was a half-sister; but it was not something he'd ever thought about.

"But that's because the rest of us don't ever think about it," Frances burst in eagerly, speaking with energy and warmth. "Anne's never been *different* from the rest of us, and we were all so close. My dad was so very close to her, too; he never ever treated her as if she weren't his own, and she called him Dad, just like the rest of us." Her voice, no longer muffled but clear and rising, was resonant with feeling.

"And my sister was really *young*, no more than a baby, when they got married, I believe," she added, then said, almost as an afterthought. "My father had been married before, and his first wife died." She herself, Frances went on to explain, had been named in her father's first wife's honor. "My middle name is Ruth," she told me.

"And that's where your middle name comes from?" I asked. I wasn't sure how she herself had construed this act of naming, but I found it somewhat surprising. "Yes, from his first wife," she replied levelly, meeting my eye.

I couldn't tell whether this was pleasing to her or not. But it seemed to me as though her family had opted, through the medium of a new birth, to include their father's lost partner in the emotional system—to value and preserve that aspect of his earlier history by keeping something of this first wife's memory alive. The boundary that Frances's family of origin had drawn around itself was, in my opinion, clear and stable, yet at the same time flexible, generous, and inclusive.

What I Learned from My Mother

The most important thing that she had learned from her mother, Frances Walker told me, was "a sense of independence." I was looking at the genogram, but looked up quickly when she said this. Frances had told me just a short while earlier (with a faintly disapproving air) that Mary had never learned how to drive a car or keep a checking account or pay the household bills throughout her entire marriage.

Her mother had not "come of age" until after her husband's death, according to Frances, for only then had she learned how to care for herself—and she'd been taught by her almost adult offspring. So if one of these women had learned "a sense of independence" from the other, it seemed to me as if it had been the parent who'd learned it from the daughter. Frances nodded her agreement when I said so.

Her mother's vivid example had, she explained, taught her that she herself wanted to conduct her own adult life very differently in this important respect. "I just wanted to make sure that *I* never got into a position where I needed to have someone else taking care of me," she said resolutely, "and that's not the kind of relationship that *we* have," she added, glancing at James quickly, then turning back to meet my eye directly once again.

I looked at each member of the couple in turn, then smiled and said that I could see this was indeed the case. But how had she, as the child of a dependent woman, known how to go about behaving in such antithetical ways? "*Wanting* to do the opposite thing, and knowing *how* to do the opposite thing are very, very different," I said, with a question in my voice, adding that she, as the daughter of a dependent female, was probably far more well versed in knowing how to be a dependent female herself.

My own thought was that she, like her husband, had known how to stay connected with certain aspects of her same-sex parent's behavior that she admired and approved of heartily—in this case, her mother's great kindness and generosity. But she (again like James vis-à-vis his father and stepfather) had also been capable of doing certain things differently. She'd made changes in the basic diagram for female adulthood that she'd observed while growing up, improved the design in ways that were more consonant with the kind of person she was interested in becoming.

She had known from her teen years onward, Frances told me, that she wanted to carve out for herself a mentality that was different from her mother's. "I wanted to feel that I didn't ever have to depend on someone else for my existence, for my sense of being. That I would always be able to take care of myself."

Frances Walker seemed and sounded so clear-headed, firm, and strong that when I asked her my next question—"What, in your own mind, is the most important lesson you learned from your father?"—I wasn't at all prepared to see her eyes start filling up with tears.

Father Love

Her voice dropped to a whispery hush once again. What she had learned from her father was the real importance of every single day, the middle-aged daughter told me shakily, and of living life to its very fullest. "I think that my dad had understood clearly, and remembered well, what the doctors had said to him—that he was *not* going to live. But he didn't ever let that stop him in any way at all, and I think he *enjoyed* his life; he had lots of friends, and he enjoyed the family—oh, *enormously*. And you know, as tough as he was on us, I believe he was bringing us up that way because he knew he wouldn't always be around—to take care of us—he was just not sure *how long* he . . ." Here she halted, unable to go on speaking, and began wiping around the bottoms of her eyelashes with her fingertip.

Her husband reached over and touched her on the shoulder lightly; I dropped my gaze to the sketch pad on my lap in order to give the pair of them a moment's privacy. For a short while no one said anything further, and then Frances and I both started talking at the same time.

She began, "And he—" and I said, not without a painful twinge of jealousy, "It sounds as if you had a *strong* sense of your father's love for you." My thought was that she was fortunate to be longing for a relationship that had been deeply gratifying and was no more, while I, the daughter of a remote, silent, tyrannical father, longed for one that had never gotten off the ground at all.

"Oh, *yes*," she murmured.

"But I interrupted you," I apologized.

"I just wanted to say that I think he—" She stopped again, inhaled. There was a reverberating quake in her voice that made it hard to speak, and she was struggling to keep it under her control.

"I think he wanted to make sure that we *made* those connections . . . with his mother . . . with the Wrights—" Again she halted abruptly, as if we were in the midst of an emotional terrain in which (these many years after her father's death) a rich loam of loss and sorrow still lay very close to the surface.

"You mean, connections with everyone who could help care for you after he was gone?" I asked, in a voice as subdued and low-pitched as her own.

"Uh-huh," she said softly, and I saw the shimmer of refracted light from a tear that was sliding silently down across her cinnamon-colored cheek. The wonderful aura of strength and self-confidence with which this woman seemed imbued was, I thought, the patrimony of a strong and forceful father who'd been an emotionally trustworthy individual and who had loved his girl child since her birth.

Her dad, as Frances Walker described him, had been a rough-hewn, hard-driving man who could drink too much and become "bossy and irrational" on certain, fortunately rare, occasions. But William Townsend had also taken an impassioned pride in his children's accomplishments, and he'd accorded them an affection that could always, always be depended upon.

As she talked on about her father, Frances ceased all efforts to hide the fact that she was weeping, although she clearly found it somewhat disconcerting to weep in my presence. At one point, I ventured to ask her, my voice tentative, if she could tell me what she thought her tears were mostly about. "Are those tears for your father's having loved you so, and his being gone? Or are they about your wanting him to take care of you and wishing he were still here to do so?" But even as I asked these questions, Frances was shaking her head as if to say with no uncertainty that she was crying about none of the above. "Probably, it's because he can't be here to see the end result. The grandkids," she murmured in a muffled voice.

What she was crying about, I realized, was the fact that her father hadn't lived long enough to see what kind of a grown woman his girl had become. He couldn't know about the educational level she'd achieved, the fine career she'd established; he couldn't ever meet the man she had married or come to know the three young descendants he would have liked and enjoyed so heartily.

She was crying because her dad could not see for himself how successful a father he *himself* had been, what a fine job of raising a daughter he had done.

CHAPTER 25

Resolving Conflict, Managing Power

It is not to be supposed that any emotional system, however functional and well operating, will exist without some degree of conflict. Conflict is—it bears repeating—an inevitable and inescapable part of every family's life. This is true both at the individual level and the group level, for we each contain conflicting feelings (ambivalences), and there are always bound to be differences and varying points of view among the different members of a multi-person group.

Conflict is ubiquitous, and no family will move through its developmental cycle marvelously free of life's controversies, hardships, difficulties, and crises. What *does* characterize families at the upper (adequate and optimal) end of the Beavers Scale is not an absence of dissension and dilemmas, but rather the group's capacity to traverse its crises and to resolve its internal conflicts in a satisfactory fashion along the way.

The manner in which the members of the Walker family dealt with conflict was clearly demonstrated to me later on in the interviews, when the subject of family vacations came up again. In addition to that trip to Disneyland, which they'd cited as a family high point, the father told me, they'd gone to San Francisco together a year earlier.

"Oh, yes, that was *wonderful*," the eldest girl, Lyla, said immediately, a dreamy, faraway expression on her face.

"That was a *good* time." James glanced at his daughter briefly, his mobile features alight with satisfaction. Then he turned to focus his gaze upon me in his open, friendly manner. I realized, with a slight start of surprise, that he wore a trim pencil-thin mustache, which I had somehow never noticed earlier.

"Actually, Frances had a convention out there," he explained, "and we all decided that we were going to tag along and have some fun. *Every* year she has a conference somewhere, and we went with her once and had such a good time that now she plans the trip so that all of us can come too."

He paused, turned to smile broadly at his wife while continuing to address me. "And while we're there, we would *like* for her to do her own thing, because not only does she have business, she wants to go to *every* seminar and *every* exhibit possible." Frances had begun giggling under her breath, and I heard the children laughing softly also. "At the same time, she likes to plan out very carefully all of the things that *we're* supposed to do. But we four sort of have *our own ideas*, and we just want to have *fun*." The entire family was now laughing out loud, and I found myself joining in.

I turned, said to Frances with a smile, "So Mom wants to make it educational, hmmm?" She nodded, shrugged. "Yes, all of the cultural things . . ." There was another small ripple of communal laughter, and I looked around at the rest of the group.

"So what do you guys do *then*?"

James answered, his voice jocular: "We spend a *lot* of time at the health spa and at the pool and just walking around town, seeing various things."

"The sightseeing in San Francisco was—" Lyla drew in a deep, awed breath, but didn't arrive at the end of her sentence.

"The rest of us like to have it real loose and not very structured, and Frances likes to have things *very* structured, well organized," the father continued mischievously. "You know, it's 'We're going to this science exhibit for twenty minutes,' and 'We're going to be at this plaza for a half-hour,' and 'We'll be at this art gallery between ten-thirty and noon,' " he mimicked his wife, and they all began laughing again.

The year before last, Debra and Lyla began telling me in almost the same breath, they had all gone to Atlanta together. "And before that, Chicago," said Frances, "but I think the Atlanta trip was the turning point for me." An irritated expression crossed her features momentarily, and she added, "Because after that Chicago trip, I think I told you all that you weren't coming with me again!"

I looked at her in surprise. "I said to them, 'That's *it*.' I said, 'No more family trips, I'm going alone, you guys will not spoil it for me.' She was smiling now, but there was still some real ire in her voice. "You won't do this, you'd rather not do that—"

"No, it was Rosa, Rosa Parks that really *did* it," Lyla interrupted her mother to say excitedly.

I looked at the daughter, and then at Frances, and then back at Lyla again. I certainly knew *who* they were talking about—Rosa Parks, the black seamstress and civil rights activist who'd sparked the Montgomery, Alabama, bus boycott of the mid-1950s by refusing to surrender her seat to a white passenger. But what could Rosa Parks have to do with the Walkers and their vacation? I smiled and shook my head at all of them uncomprehendingly.

Lyla grinned, suppressed the grin swiftly, looked at her mother slyly, then laughed outright. "What happened was that when we were in Chicago, Rosa Parks turned up unexpectedly at some mixer my mom was attending—some people had brought her along with them, I guess. So she, my mother, called up to the room and said, 'Everybody come on down, come on down *quick!*'—and it was late to begin with. So then we all had to take a shower, get dressed and everything, and by the time we got down there, we had missed it. We'd missed Rosa Parks, and my mom was so— she was *so furious.* She said to us, like, 'Don't ever come on these trips *again!*' "

I heard the mother's infectious giggle above the laughter that resounded immediately. "After Chicago, I told them, 'This is *it*, the *last* time you're coming with me,' " Frances took up the tale. "I told them, 'You people don't know how to *enjoy* yourselves!' And yet I think that at the same time, without even realizing it, I was beginning to do a little backing off myself. Because when they started talking about wanting to come along again on the Atlanta trip, I said to myself, 'I am not planning *a thing* for anyone to do.' "

The rest of the family laughed, but she added earnestly, "It was inter-esting, though; it seemed as if they came a little closer to *my* way of doing things just as I was backing off—and we had a wonderful time." Frances paused, looked around at her children and her husband affectionately. "We've had great times *since* then—in Atlanta, in San Francisco, this past year. Because I think something happened at that point that we didn't real-ize, or that perhaps *I* wasn't realizing myself.

"I mean, there it was, *my* agenda," she explained ardently. "And I wanted so badly for them to do the things that *I* wanted them to do that it was really putting limits on the kinds of things that *they* wanted to do. But what was interesting was what then happened in Atlanta—which was that without my making any plans or even *saying* anything, they began to make remarks, things like, 'Well, aren't we going to go to Martin Luther King's birthplace?' and 'Aren't we going to see Spelman College?' " She drew in a deep breath, held it, exhaled, and added, "Somehow, without my ever saying 'Okay, guys, if you're coming on this trip, here are the things you're going to do,' I backed off, and they in turn moved closer."

She looked around at the other members of her family, but no one said anything. Then she laughed, added good-naturedly, "I knew I *needed* to back off after that blowup, because you were all looking at me as if I had two heads!"

"Yes, we've had our arguments, but *Rosa Parks*—" Lyla turned to me, her expression condescending. "I can't really think of *anything* that set my mom off as badly as that one."

Managing Power

Power and its management are always a major concern (overtly or covertly) in *all* human groupings, among which the family group can most certainly be counted. And, as one ascends the Beavers Scale from the least capable and functional to the most capable and functional families, clear differences in the ways in which power-related issues are managed become strikingly apparent.

In families at the bottom of the continuum (Level 5, severely disturbed) there is no executive level of the family, no leader or pair of leaders who are in charge. These basically structureless, ungoverned families have no clear, discernible hierarchy; the only rule is that there are no reliably consistent rules; "Anything goes" is the household's fundamental credo. As a result, writes Robert Beavers, "family functioning appears chaotic, since control is carried on by a variety of covert and indirect means."

In Level 4 (polarized or borderline) families, the situation has improved to some degree, because at least someone—the tyrant—has taken charge. But the control the dictator has assumed is so all-encompassing that it is humanly unendurable, and these families tend to get embroiled in bruising power struggles "alternating with ineffective but persistent efforts to establish dominance-submission patterns," as Beavers observes.

At the next higher level (Level 3, rule-bound or midrange), matters have certainly improved dramatically, but are still far from ideal. For in midrange families, as Beavers notes, power struggles and discipline without negotiation are typical." In the Gifford household (see Part Four, "Level 3: The Rule-Bound Family"), it will be recalled, the disciplining of eight-year-old Emily was a very real sore point and source of ongoing tension between Henry, his wife, and his mother-in-law. But the three of them seemed locked in a stalemate when it came to negotiating this "hot" issue to a mutually acceptable resolution; instead of discussing (let alone dealing with) this ongoing source of distress and bad feeling, the Giffords tended to back off, so that their attempts at resolution never even seemed to get off the ground.

Level 2, adequate families can best be understood as occupying a position between the midrange and optimal groupings on the Beavers clinical scale. These families are still somewhat prone to use the coercive, guilt-inducing tactics of the rule-bound families below them; and yet their mutual understanding of how the emotional system operates (who is in charge, and under which circumstances) has come into strikingly sharper focus. The family's rules, leadership, and hierarchy are now well defined and evident to all concerned; in this important respect, the adequate family resembles the optimal family at the scale's summit.

How are power issues handled by Level 1, optimal families? According to Beavers, one sees in these families a comfortable balance between structure and flexibility. "The hierarchic structure of the family is well defined. . . . There is a concomitant flexibility that permits frequent changes in function and approaches to problems," as he explains.

Within the optimal system, the rules of the family game are not only distinct and well articulated; they can also be readily modified or changed as changing life circumstances may warrant. In these highly competent, successful families, notes Beavers, "intimacy is sought and generally found, a function of frequent, equal-powered transactions combined with respect for each others' viewpoints."

Differentiating Between Adequate and Optimal Families

At this point, it might be useful to pause briefly and address a still-unanswered question: How does one go about making the distinction between those families seen as adequate and those families considered to be optimal on the Beavers competence continuum? Actually, these two groupings do not differ very sharply; the adequate family and the optimal family are far more alike than dissimilar.

Families at this healthier end of the continuum share certain fundamental characteristics "in terms of the importance of family life, caring for members, and relatively low incidence of psychiatric disturbances," as Beavers and colleague Robert B. Hampson write in their book *Successful Families*. These co-authors observe that both the adequate and the optimal family seem equally capable of raising competent, sound, well-functioning offspring.

Families deemed adequate do all of the right, appropriate things in terms of meeting the developmental needs of their individual members. Still, the pulleys of the family's organization tend to strain and creak at times, and its wheels don't always move around easily. In adequate families, according to Beavers and Hampson, one simply doesn't find the same relatively constant sense of closeness and joy—that real *delight* in one another's company—that is so evident in the optimal families a notch above them on the Beavers Scale.

In distinguishing between these two kinds of families, both of them so admirably well functioning, it is always useful to bear in mind the adequate family's location on the Beavers Scale, *in between* the midrange and the optimal levels. Thus, while adequate families clearly have much in common with the optimal families above them on the clinical ladder, they also bear some resemblance to the somewhat less competent, rule-bound families a rung below.

The adequate family is, for example, like the midrange family in its tendency to be control-oriented and to "attempt to resolve conflict by intimidation and direct force," as Beavers and Hampson note. This is the reason why "family members seek greater overt power, and the parental coalition is less emotionally rewarding, though effective. The interaction in these families, though still adequate, produces less intimacy and trust, less joy, and less spontaneity" than one sees in the optimal families just above them on the family functioning graph.

In short, while adequate families carry out the tasks of family living very ably and well indeed, they don't manage to do so without some real pain and individual loneliness, some uncomfortable grinding of the emotional system's gears. One might say that the adequate family achieves, by means of its steadfastness, caring, and conscious efforts, what the optimal family achieves smoothly and naturally due to its inherent flexibility, sense of goodwill, and deep-seated belief that positive things will happen in human encounters.

Pulling Rank

Families located toward the high end of the Beavers continuum are by no means without their developmental dramas and occasional issues of serious contention. Thus it came as no startling news to me that within a family such as the Walkers—whose composition included two developing young females—tensions relating to the budding of adult sexuality, the lingering dependence of childhood, and the equally powerful surge toward individuation and separateness would come bubbling upward periodically.

Debra and Lyla Walker were now in the midst of the adolescent metamorphosis, a period during which enormous, relatively discontinuous changes in the young person's physical and mental capacities are inevitably creating a demand for psychological reordering, a profound, far-reaching internal rearrangement.

During this dizzying period of their existence, as psychoanalyst Theodor Lidz observes in *The Person*, youngsters are thrust toward adulthood by the very changes in their size and contours. They must also, writes Lidz, "cope with a new inner pressure that creates strange feelings and longings, and adds an impulsivity and irrational force with which they have had little experience." But because these strange new stirrings and sensations are profoundly connected to their feelings about their parents, most youngsters find it hard or impossible to come to their parents for help—which is why the maturing adolescent frequently feels angrily bereft of what have hitherto been her or his most trusted, reliable supports.

Certainly, when I met with the Walker girls alone, it didn't take very long for these adolescents' ambivalent feelings toward their parents (especially their father) to make themselves known. Thirteen-year-old Debra said, very plaintively, that there was actually nobody in the family whom she could really *talk* to, not in the ways that she could talk about her problems with her friends. This confession met with visible incredulity on Lyla's part.

"Weren't you at all aware of Debra's feeling that way?" I asked her, and the older sister shook her head. "Not really. I've never even thought—it never even seems like she *has* any problems, at least I've never heard her talk about them with anybody." Then she gazed at Debra with a doubting frown, as if to say "I'm not sure I believe this."

Without lingering on the issue of Debra's problems (existent or nonexistent), I embarked on a series of sentence-completion questions that I sometimes use to direct a conversation and keep it lively and focused. "In my family, my father is always the one who . . . ?"

I stopped, awaiting Debra's input, but no conclusion was forthcoming. After a long silence, the teenager simply shrugged as if to say she was stuck and couldn't think of a thing. I said nothing further for the next several moments, and neither did either of the girls. But then: ". . . gets on your *nerves*," Debra finished suddenly, with a giggle. "*Right*, I agree with that one!" Lyla put in promptly, giggling too.

I smiled, raised an eyebrow, said reflectively, "Gets on your nerves . . . in what way?"

Neither daughter answered immediately; they merely exchanged an all-knowing look. Then Lyla said, with an offended air, "He just . . . I don't know . . . It *bothers* me that he doesn't say please and thank you. And if you put up some objection, all he says is, 'I don't really think I have to *beg* you to do this.' " She was imitating her father's deep bass voice and his solemn, superior expression. She burst out laughing, and Debra laughed, too. But then Lyla added indignantly, "It's not really *begging*, it's just common courtesy. And let's see, what else?" She glanced at her younger sister questioningly.

"He tells *you* what to do, but he doesn't want to do stuff himself," Debra joined in animatedly. "Like, he tells *us* to clean up the house while he sits there watching television. And he acts like the *girls* have to do everything." She paused, looked at me eagerly, as if hoping this remark would elicit an angry feminist response on my part.

I said, "It sounds as if you're both feeling that there's a girl-guy thing that goes on in this household." Then I looked questioningly from one sister to the other and back again. Debra merely nodded, but Lyla said testily, "The other day my father came home, and we had to clean up the whole house because we were going to have *company*, or something like that. He made us clean up the entire kitchen, and Jamie stayed downstairs and watched his cartoons. Even though it's *his* job to take out the trash, *I* had to do it. It's that kind of thing: My father *does* make us do more of the work." She pursed her lips and added, "My mother divides it up more evenly."

"With Jamie doing more of the chores?" I asked. Both girls chimed in at once—"Right, right"—nodding their vehement agreement. I made no comment, but I did have the thought that *most* parents, when faced with the need to get the house straightened up quickly for company, would *want* to press their older, more capable and experienced teenagers into service and keep a still unskilled and probably clumsy seven-year-old as much out of the way as possible. My own suspicion was that it might not have been gender so much as it was age that had been at issue on this particular occasion.

"Also, my dad *pulls rank* all the time." Lyla was still warming to her indictment. "Even if he's totally *wrong*, and everybody's sitting here disagreeing with him. . . . No," she amended with a sudden giggle, "*I'm* usually the one disagreeing with him! And he'll just act like 'I don't want to discuss this matter anymore.' " She sniffed contemptuously, once again mimicking her father's condescending distaste for a discussion that he clearly viewed as far beneath him.

"Oh, he won't *say* that in so many words," she conceded straightaway, "but he's *implying* it. It's like he's saying, '*I'm* the adult here, and *you* don't understand things.' " Then she looked at me searchingly. "*You* know what I mean," she said.w "He pulls rank." A parent *has* rank, I thought, amused and charmed.

"Doesn't your mom ever do that, pull rank?" I asked her.

"No, not really," Lyla responded earnestly. "She just—well, my mom usually just gives up and starts laughing." She herself laughed, and Debra, grinning, nodded slowly and significantly as if to underscore the veracity of her older sister's statement.

It was true, Lyla admitted immediately, that whenever she herself got going, everybody groaned and begged her not to get anything started. The sisters exchanged a knowing look and started giggling again; I found myself laughing with them.

"So *you're* the one who likes to get the heavy discussions going here?" I asked the older sister jokingly.

"Right," she said emphatically, but added that she really *did* know when to stop, while (in her opinion, at least) her sister didn't seem to know that at all. "*She* crosses the line; she crosses the line *a lot*," said the adolescent primly, adding that in her view, there was a point where a person needed to know how to stop, but that Debra crossed it, and just kept going and going.

Turning to her younger sister, Lyla said forthrightly, "I mean, I don't want to insult you or anything—" The sentence hung in the air. But far from seeming the least bit offended, Debra looked more thrilled by this statement of her effrontery than she was anything else.

"When *I* argue, I'm probably more respectful," Lyla added. "*She* shows no respect when she argues." Debra burst out laughing, and her laughter was so infectious that we couldn't help laughing, too. "So it sounds as if you go in for mud wrestling," I said to her ironically.

"She does, she *does*," put in Lyla, who, though she was laughing, sounded annoyed. But Debra wasn't backing down; their father, she said, told them to do all the things that he didn't want to do himself, and that made her mad. "That gets me really *mad*," she reiterated scornfully. "He thinks that the girls should do stuff, and he shouldn't—because he's the *man*, and he wears the *pants* in the family."

Very clearly, these daughters and their dad were very busily engaged in creating some emotional distance between themselves—an important, even vital task at this phase of family development.

Oedipal Fears and Necessary Distance

As Theodor Lidz points out in *The Person*, young adolescents' relationships to their families, though changing, are still very much family-centered. "Along with the upsurge of sexual feelings there is some reawakening of oedipal attachments," he writes. "The sensuous and affectional attachments to the parent of the opposite sex, even though under the ban of repression, are the obvious channels into which the sexual feelings can flow. The oedipal attachments have to be resolved once again but at a different level, and this time the sexual feelings will not be repressed so much as *redirected away from the parent*" (my italics).

The cute, flirtatious little girl of age four or five, who once charmed her dad by climbing up on his lap and telling him she wanted to marry him, now finds herself the inhabitant of an adult woman's body with all of its appealing curves and softened outlines. Obviously, crawling up on Daddy's lap and being hugged and caressed by him is out of the question; and that is why developing complaints and harboring resentments is often the daughter's way of reassuring herself that she wouldn't want to do so anyhow.

At this pivotal point of her development, it is necessary that she make some comfortable distance from him. Her trajectory is outward from the family as she begins moving forward in her own life and starts focusing her affections on males who are her peers. And Father, in the presence of this erstwhile girl-child—now, with startling suddenness, a sexually maturing, attractive young woman—feels impelled to draw back and create some distance himself.

The pretty young female in his household is in some sense a stranger, one who may cause him to ruminate subliminally about what it would be like to be young (and the suitor of a young woman) once again. This is why, according to Lidz, "either just prior to the onset of puberty or early in adolescence . . . [the daughter] turns from her father and her father turns away from her." This can, adds the clinician, "leave the girl feeling deserted, lonely, and even empty."

But at this important developmental transition, when anxiety about the merest suggestion of incestuous attraction is a very real and powerful subterranean family theme, a comfortable distance between fathers and their flowering female adolescents is something that feels absolutely necessary. And how better to create such a distance than by amassing mutual grievances and getting into all kinds of disputes, differences, and arguments?

In a way, by asserting his paternal authority and ordering his daughters around (to the degree that he was doing so), James Walker was reminding both them and himself that while they might look like desirable young females, they were still his children. And he himself was not their peer or equal (nor by any means their suitor); he was the person in charge here. What was being reinforced, by all the parties concerned, was the clear boundary separating the two generations.

"As the real upsurge of sexual feelings gets under way, adolescents begin to turn away from their attachments to a parent, unconsciously and even sometimes consciously concerned by the sexual aspects of the attraction," as analyst Lidz writes. "They begin to find fault with the parent, criticizing him or her, convincing themselves that the parent is not attractive and not [a love] object worth seeking."

This ongoing criticism and fault-finding soon spread, as Lidz notes, to include the parent of the same sex. For an adolescent daughter, this is of course the mother and rival, upon whom she is nevertheless still very dependent and with whom she feels highly identified. This is all part of the young female's predictable (if predictably painful) struggle to work herself free of the sheltering and yet increasingly confining, restrictive family chrysalis—to liberate her own unique, adult self from the powerful, predominating influences of *both* parents, and their external and internal dictates.

"Tell me," I asked Debra, thoughtfully. "Do you get that same feeling vis-à-vis your mother and your father—that your dad pulls too much rank on your mom?"

She looked at me blankly. "What do you mean, rank?" I wondered if she were getting tired, tuning out, or merely going on a temporary side trip to Mars, as adolescents so frequently will do.

"I mean what Lyla was talking about earlier—your father pulling rank on the girls," I explained. "Your mom being, of course, a girl," I added, with a smile. The teenager didn't return my smile; she merely shook her head, looking bemused and thoughtful. "No, there's a *difference*, because my dad pulls rank with the girls, but not with the women," she answered. "You know?"

I nodded. My own thought was that at this developmental transition, when both these young females were grappling with a number of perplexing questions relating to their oncoming adulthood (such as "What are the possibilities for me, as a woman, actually going to *be*?" "What are the roles of men and women?" "When, someday, I have a partner of my own, how can I expect him to treat me?"), the internal road maps for the future that each of them was engaged in constructing were highly likely to be remarkably benign ones.

For when a father admires, appreciates, and respects his wife, as was so evidently the case in this family, a daughter can welcome the signs of her own approaching maturity and, as family expert Lidz observes, "feel secure that she will be loved and find satisfaction in life as a woman."

Sheriff or Partner

It was somewhere around the midpoint of our interviews that I asked Frances Walker just why she'd found so ridiculous the whole notion of her husband's role in the family being that of "the sheriff." And what, in her mind, would be the right word to describe his role? I asked her.

James was, Frances replied, more of a partner in the household than he was anything else. In her view, moreover, as the kids got older and older, the balance of power in the family was continually shifting. The girls, especially, were now playing an ever more important part in the family decisions being made. "This isn't a dictatorial kind of a household," stated Frances, then paused, turned to look at her husband probingly. "Anyhow, that's how *I* see it."

The word "sheriff," I realized, sounded coercive in her ears. So I asked her if the term "coach"—or "executive"—might capture her husband's family role more precisely. Frances shook her head, a slight furrow appearing between her eyebrows; she didn't like the term "co-executive" either, when I then suggested it.

What we were really talking about here, I explained, was setting family rules and enforcing them when necessary. "How about 'co-president'?" James put in, his tone of voice droll and whimsical. Frances smiled, but nevertheless shook her head again. "No, not really. He isn't . . . No, I think those titles are just so *strong*."

She was, I realized, beginning to look genuinely uncomfortable; what we were talking about really mattered to her. So I quickly asked her once again what *she* thought the right word or term might be.

"I can't move away from 'partner' . . . 'liaison,' perhaps," she said slowly. "Because to me, we're all like linkages in—in—" She stopped short, as if having abruptly run out of explanatory fuel.

This didn't encompass the leadership capacity that James was trying to include here, I observed, aware that I might be pushing things a bit, but still not grasping exactly what aspects of the other terms she found disturbing.

That question was, apparently, a good one to ask. For Frances, her face alight with something like relief, shifted forward on the sofa and clasped her hands together on her knees, looking attentive and even excited— almost like a schoolgirl who knows she may be called upon next in class and *knows* she has the perfect answer in mind. "Oh, I *see* that part," she said animatedly, "but it's not as if—" She paused and looked as if she'd lost her train of thought for the moment.

Then she turned to stare into her husband's eyes intently. "I think he has a *strong* presence in this household." She was addressing me even though her gaze was fixed upon his. "And I think that presence is respected—looked to—*counted* on—but it's not an overbearing one." Then she added that it wasn't the case that he was "it," the sole person in charge here. Her voice, though not at all loud, was commanding in its ardor and intensity.

What Frances was telling me (and James) was that in her view there was no sense of a top dog in this household. "Do *you* see what I'm trying to say?" Frances appealed to her husband, her voice cracking slightly as it always seemed to do in moments of high emotion. James had placed the tips of his fingers together in a bridge, as if in thought or prayer, and bowed his face down over them briefly. Now he looked up at her and said with quiet fervor, "I don't see me as dominating in this household, not *at all*."

I smiled, asked him what other word or term he would use to describe his family role. He smiled back, but at the same time said with some seriousness that he wasn't sure that he even knew a right word to describe it. To some extent, he saw the entire family as a kind of corporation, and all its members as a board of directors. And there really wasn't any *permanent* chairman of the board, he added at once, flashing a roguish grin at his wife. The couple paused, exchanged a long, wryly affectionate look, but at the same time Frances nodded her head in agreement, and said, "That's right, that's *right*."

"Of course from time to time, somebody *will* chair it," James elaborated upon his corporate metaphor. "And then at other times there will be a *co-chair*." All of the children had input as directors of the corporation, from time to time, he went on to say, but he halted when Frances suddenly said, "Oh!" as if struck by an important thought.

Both James and I looked at her expectantly, but she simply sat there for a long, silent, speculative moment. Then she looked at her husband, a question in her eyes and in her tone of voice as well. "*You* mentioned the board of directors," she said to him, "and what came to *my* mind was a team. This really *is* a team," she added fervently, "and one where all of us have really got to be functioning and operating."

"But of course a team has somebody calling the plays," I said to her quickly, with a comical expression on my face.

"So then can *I* be the quarterback?" James turned to ask his wife imploringly, and the three of us burst out laughing.

High-Functioning Families: Power; Flexibility; the Welcoming of Difference

The above conversation can serve as a remarkably apt illustration of the way in which power issues are typically handled in capable, high-functioning families. First of all, it was plain that these two people were really operating as equals in the family's governance. Frances Walker's struggle with the word "sheriff" had centered upon the implication that it meant her husband was the boss—and therefore the only person in the household wearing the shiny star of authority on his lapel.

Clearly this was not the case here, for one couldn't fail to notice the way in which James continually checked back with his wife for her reactions to his remarks, as she in turn kept checking in with him for his feedback. Each member of the pair was obviously quite sensitive to, and very open to, the other's input and responses. This was, I thought, why Frances kept on returning to the notion that they were "partners" in the family's governance—that while her husband had a real presence in the family, and one that everyone counted upon, he was really not the sole person in charge here.

Not only were these partners equal-powered and respectful of each other's viewpoints, but as parents they were also open to their children's input and contributions. This is characteristic of healthy, competent systems such as this one. In these families, *the children are expected to exercise their choice-making powers while they are still very young* (for example, getting to decide on which movie the family will go to) because it is readily understood that making a responsible decision is a way of saying "Hey, everybody, this is who *I* am!" In healthy families, this defining of self is actively encouraged, for in these relational systems, individual differences are not seen as threatening, but are both welcomed and celebrated.

Still another important attribute of high-functioning families—their natural *flexibility in the face of changing situations and circumstances*—had been evidenced in these parents' conversation as well. For Frances's comment to the effect that as the children got older, they were taking on more and more decision-making powers, was developmentally quite appropriate. And James's remarks about how different members of the family sat in the board chairman's seat at different times and on different occasions reflected the same intuitive ease of response. The Walkers clearly had a whole range of possible responses at their fingertips (depending on the issue, the circumstances, and so forth) and were not locked into the one or two rigid options for reacting that one sees in families lower down on the Beavers Scale.

In this family, being one's own individual self, with one's own wishes, needs, and preferences, was not seen as badness or betrayal. In this family, differences were not merely tolerated, they were seen as enriching. People could and did disagree; but it was easy to figure out how Mom felt about a certain situation, as compared with how Dad saw that situation, as compared with how each of the children saw it. Individual differences were not only being respected; they were being encouraged to flourish.

Here, in short, *there was space allotted*—a plot of personal territory in which each member of the family was being permitted to grow without sacrificing his or her own sense of place and belonging within the larger relational system. It is this sense, that one can get close to others without being swallowed up alive in the family's emotional program, that makes intimacy feel safe and even imaginable.

CHAPTER 26

Journeying Home

What had James Walker done with his anger? As my conversations with the family stretched from late winter to the middle of spring, I found myself perplexed by this middle-aged dad's apparent lack of negativity toward a father who had disappeared from his life so totally between his sixth and twenty-sixth years. James seemed to harbor no real rancor, chagrin, or pain about what had occurred—and frankly, I couldn't understand it. Where had that little six-year-old boy's feelings about his absentee parent *gone* to?

If only James Walker, as an adult, had once expressed some real affect about what had happened to James Walker as a child! If only he had made some emotive comment, even in passing ("That was a hard and confusing time for me, but I managed to get through it"), I would have found it easier to think that he had truly been able somehow to put the narcissistic wound of this early abandonment behind him. But what James Walker had said to me was "My father never harmed me."

This would have been quite true if a father were under no existential obligation to the child he had brought into the world, if a father did his son no harm by simply walking off and seeming to forget his very existence! What had me baffled was this man's inability to express (perhaps even to experience) any feeling about what seemed so patently obvious— that it had been hard for a six-year-old boy when his father left the family, hard for that boy to waken to the reality that his dad had gone away and was not returning.

A parent's disappearance is no small happening in a person's life, and this eldest son had to have been deeply shaken at the time—to have wondered why his dad wasn't there, where he'd gone, when he was coming home again. Also, at this stage of psychological growth, children are still magnificently egocentric; they tend to feel guilty and responsible for much that is happening around them, including matters over which they have no control whatsoever. A little boy of six might readily have become preoccupied by a litany of awful possibilities—"My daddy left us because he didn't love me"; "My dad left because I was a bad boy"; and similar sorts of self-inflated, overresponsible notions.

At the very least his father's disappearance from James's life, when he himself was still a very young child, must have caused pain. And yet what seemed evident (this middle-aged man had the track record to show it) was that the pain had not been overwhelming.

Still, this strange absence of any anger about what had happened to him in the past posed a perennial question mark in my own mind. It was, moreover, a factor that didn't fit in with the optimal family picture, for in families at the high-functioning end of the Beavers continuum one doesn't tend to encounter those prohibited emotions or forbidden states of feeling (such as anger) that are so ubiquitous in families lower down on the scale. In adequate and optimal systems, "bad" feelings are viewed as part of the human package rather than as dark, dangerous, or potentially destructive forces.

In these very capable families, a full range of emotions can be expressed, because all feelings—not just those that are in line with the family's mythology and its agenda—are taken to be the "facts" of someone's existence at a particular moment in time (not, it should be said, until the end of eternity). In these families, angry feelings and sad feelings aren't only tolerated, they're *embraced*, just as are warmth, happiness, and joy." There are no subliminal demands that one bottle up—or perhaps completely deny—one's feelings about aspects of life that are, or have been, hurtful or enraging.

In healthy emotional systems, the members of the family can experience their sorrows openly, be soothed in their grief, talk about sad times with sadness—as Frances Walker had done when remembering her father's sudden death twenty-six years earlier. But it is, by and large, in *less* functional systems, where human grief and complexity are being disavowed in a multiplicity of ways, that one sees heroic efforts to push the bad, sad, or angering things (of the past or in the present) out of sight and engage in the mutual pretense that these injuries have never happened—or that if they did, it doesn't really matter.

This is why, when it comes to the overall assessment of family health and functioning, a good diagnostic rule of thumb is that the better functioning the emotional system happens to be, the less will such avoidance tactics exist within it. As Robert Beavers writes, members of healthy families "are quick to pick up emotional pain or unusual behavior in each other, and approach problems with directness and an expectation that something can be done. In other words, myth is not used to cloud and distort reality perceptions."

In adequate and optimal families, joyful and affiliative subjects as well as disturbing, upsetting, and potentially divisive matters are equally admissible within the intimate group's ongoing discourse. This *readiness to acknowledge and to embrace the hard and distressing parts*—the sorrows, vulnerabilities, losses, griefs, and feelings of anger intrinsic to the human condition—*makes it possible for the people in the family to experience all of their affects* and to feel quite naturally entitled to do so. This is why I found James Walker's lack of anger so puzzling.

A Psychic "Keep off the Grass" Sign

Once, during the course of an interview at which all family members were present, I asked the father what he himself considered his best qualities—his greatest assets and personal strengths—to be. (Everyone present, it should be said, was being asked this question in turn.) James didn't hesitate a moment before replying. "I think I'm a fairly well-rounded person—a balanced individual, mentally and physically. I think I operate well under pressure, and I *like* being under pressure. I manage people and situations well; I think I have good administrative abilities."

He paused briefly, as if to mentally review what he had said, and then added thoughtfully, "What I like *best* about myself, I suppose, is that I *care* about people—about how they relate to me and react to me. I get along pretty well with most people, and it matters to me whether they like me or they don't. And when they don't, I try to find out why, what's the issue—what's going on?—and if it's within reason, work it out.

"I'm willing to make accommodations," James appended, and I nodded my agreement. He was certainly describing the attractively outgoing, courteous, affirming person I had always found him to be . . . and yet that question mark persisted in my mind. There was something here that eluded me, something I found myself unable to fully comprehend.

Why was this individual, who was so readily expressive and so affectively available throughout our many interviews, so inexpressive and so relatively unavailable when it came to one particular subject? And why, each time the conversation circled back to the topic of his father's desertion of the family, did an invisible but very real psychic "Keep off the Grass" sign seem to make its presence felt almost immediately? This kind of semiautomatic reaction can be a therapeutic signal that one is moving into a charged area of discussion—one that may well contain a buried, but still live emotional land mine.

Why, in the course of our conversations, had James never given vent to any emotionality—never acknowledged that it might have been tough, or that he'd felt lost for a while? Once again, I wondered: Why did this lively, intelligent, curious individual seem to know almost nothing about why his parents' marriage had ended, or about what had motivated his father's twenty-year absence? Was James Walker out of contact with his issues, unaware of his own psychological insides?

If so, then at some period of stressful family transition—perhaps around the departure of a grown child, when a parent is being left behind and may be feeling abandoned—this father's own past in his original family did threaten to repeat itself in some freshly updated and modernized scenario. Unless he had managed somehow (perhaps within a religious context, by bringing his sorrows to church) to truly feel his hurt and anger—to mourn what had been suffered, to *forgive his own father* and let go of all the pain inevitably connected to an early loss of this magnitude—there remained the real possibility that aspects of his own internal world were being disavowed, split off from his own conscious awareness.

In this kind of situation, the internally generated pressure to resurrect one's raw, unprocessed feelings—the sorrow and the rage that have never really been dealt with—and to work on them anew remains ever present. An emotional time bomb could, in other words, be ticking away just below the delightful, optimally functioning surface of this household.

Explaining Health

I was somewhat amused to learn in my interviews with the Walkers that it was the male in this family who did the weekly grocery shopping, and the lion's share of the laundry as well. But if James's adolescent daughters were busily (predictably) chipping away at the paternal idol—viewing their dad as sexist and overbearing—his seven-year-old son, Jamie, still had stars in his eyes where both his parents, but especially his father, were concerned.

Once, when this youngest sibling and I were talking together about a drawing he had made (a picture of the entire family), I asked Jamie who, among all the people on the page, was the person he himself felt closest to. "My mom and *my daddy*," the little boy replied glowingly, a slow, beamish smile spreading itself across his face.

I tried not to laugh; the two of us were involved in a serious one-on-one interview. "Your mom and your daddy," I repeated, then stared down at the drawing intently for the next few moments. At seven, Jamie was such a delightful, sturdy, handsome, good-natured youngster that it was easy to understand why he was in fact the "angel of the household," why everyone in the family adored him.

After a brief silence, I asked him in a reflective tone, "Who then, do you think, is the person in the family that you're least, *least* close to?"

"My sisters," Jamie answered without hesitating.

"*Both* of them?" I asked him.

"Yes," he replied, nodding slowly, with a solemn, portentous air. This time I couldn't suppress a smile, for not only was I charmed by his gravity and seriousness; I was also thinking of the way in which his older sisters had answered this same question. Both Debra and Lyla, when asked, "Who, in this family, would you say you feel the very closest to?" had answered with alacrity, "Jamie."

On this particular afternoon, after talking with Jamie for a long while, I stayed on to visit with his parents briefly. The three of us had no formal interview planned for today, a warm Sunday in late May, but it didn't take me long to become aware that they were both looking at me expectantly and attentively. They were waiting for something, and it was, I quickly realized, feedback of some sort from my side. I had spent so much time, and talked so intensively with the various members of the family and with the family as a whole; not surprisingly, Frances and James were becoming curious about my own reactions to what I'd heard during the course of these long, probing conversations.

I saw no reason for not responding to them openly and honestly, and I started out by admitting, with a somewhat rueful smile, that the story of the husband's early boyhood had me feeling baffled. "It's *easy* to see the many ways in which you're a pretty self-assured, confident parent," I said to James forthrightly, "and so when you started telling me about what had happened with your dad—about his not being there, between ages six and twenty-six—my own thought was that gee, if you were having all kinds of problems with your own fathering right now, explaining why that was so would have been simple, *elementary*." I laughed, and the couple did too.

I looked down at the Walkers' genogram, which was sitting open on my lap. "I could have just pointed to this, and said, 'Yes, here's the reason,' " I added, staring at the paternal side of the family chart; I touched my finger to it lightly, traced an enclosing circle around the two square symbols depicting James and his biological father. Then I said, "What I'm finding harder to explain is why you're *not* having problems—why you're the very competent, able parent that you are." We all laughed again at the odd nature of this dilemma, and I murmured something about theory and real life sometimes being very different matters indeed.

Then the three of us lapsed into a long, but relaxed and easy silence. I realized, after a while, that the partners were waiting patiently for me to continue, so I said almost apologetically, "In a way, it's harder to explain *health*, harder to explain how you survived this"—I ran my fingers over James's side of the genogram again—"as well as you obviously did . . . ?" What had begun as a statement ended as a question. But the father, his facial expression composed, merely shrugged his shoulders briefly as if to say that he really had no special insight or explanation to offer.

"Just looking at the way you did manage makes me wonder . . ." I went on, in a muted, hesitant tone. "Can you imagine your *own* son, whom you're so close to, and who is now seven years old . . . What would it have been like for *him*, if you'd disappeared from his life one year ago?" I met the father's gaze, saw anxiety in his expression. "It would've been pretty terrible for him, don't you think?" I asked.

"Yes, I *do*," James answered feelingly, as if he found it easier to empathize with his son's imaginary pain than with his own pain—a pain that had once been very real and palpable. I hesitated at this point, unsure about whether or not to move onward in the same candid spirit in which this conversation with the couple had begun. But both Frances and James were staring at me fixedly, eyes enlarged, as if they were hearing an engrossing story or watching an extremely absorbing (but slightly frightening) film. Both had shifted forward in their seats, and were sitting on the edge of the sofa, their bodies leaning toward me.

I looked from one member of the pair to the other, wondering where each of them wanted to go from here. At that moment, Frances met my gaze and nodded, as if she somehow knew what I was thinking and was giving me the signal to continue. Still I hesitated, alert to the fact that the area we were now moving into might prove perturbing. I would have to proceed judiciously at every step along the way.

Mental Anniversaries

While it often goes completely unnoticed and unremarked (unless an individual or the family happens to be in therapy), many people seem to observe what may be thought of as mental anniversaries—sudden upsurges of anxiety or malaise relating to an old bereavement, which is being commemorated internally. Such anniversary reactions may be linked to a specific date or to a season—the day of one's mother's death, or the memory of the way the dogwood trees were then erupting into bloom—and induce great suffering despite the fact that conscious thoughts of that long-ago loss are very far from anyone's awareness.

Anniversary reactions may at other times be elicited by certain circumstances in one's current life that feel painfully familiar. These are situations that bear a symbolic similarity to (and are thus distressing reminders of) griefs that one experienced earlier—reaching the age of one's mother at the time of her death, for example. Or it may happen that when one's child reaches the age at which a significant loss was experienced (Jamie was now around the age that James had been when his own father departed), seemingly forgotten but in reality raw and unresolved conflicts associated with that loss are sometimes reactivated.

The intensity of such anniversary reactions may range anywhere from complete emotional upheaval to a vague but persistent sense of discomfort—often without any link to that past grief ever being consciously established. It seemed quite clear to me, however, that nothing of the sort was happening in the present-day life in this particular household. The relationship between James and his son was obviously a tender and loving one, and there was no suggestion whatsoever that a family scenario related to abandonment was in the process of being replayed.

Still, in the course of today's conversation with the Walkers, I talked about the phenomenon of anniversary reactions anyhow. What one often saw, I explained, was that when a child got to be somewhere around the age at which the parent once experienced a painful loss, the feelings associated with that loss start mounting in the parent again.

"That parent may not then be at his best with his child; he may not even feel able to know *how* to be a father to a child that age," I added, reflectively. What followed was a silence, during which James sat staring at me unseeingly. He seemed lost in thought, almost in a trance, as if mesmerized by the things I had been saying.

At last, growing concerned, I said, "What seems very *clear* to me, though, is that this kind of thing isn't happening here . . . ?" What had started out as a statement had again become a question along the way. And the question being posed, as I myself realized, was "Why isn't it?"

I was asking James Walker to explain to me just how a little boy who'd been abandoned by his dad at the age of six had grown up to parent a family of his own so competently, lovingly, and well. And he, responding to this question almost as if it had been asked aloud, said fervently and with gratitude, "I give a *lot* of credit to my mother and my stepfather."

The Strengths of Black Families

As researcher Robert B. Hill observes in *The Strengths of Black Families*, very little academic or public attention has been given to those adaptive patterns of black family life that have made stability, survival, and advancement possible in an unfriendly and uncaring wider environment. "Most discussions of black families tend to focus on indicators of instability and weakness," notes Hill. "With few exceptions, most social scientists continue to portray black families as disorganized, pathological and disintegrating."

In an early (1971) study carried out under the auspices of the Urban

League, sociologist Hill and his colleagues examined the opposite side of the coin in a careful, rigorous fashion. Looking at patterns of black family life that had made it possible for certain families to prevail in the face of what were indisputably awesome social realities, these investigators isolated and identified the five major strengths of African-American families: strong kinship bonds; strong work orientation; strong religious orientation; strong achievement orientation; and flexibility of family roles.

This quintet of adaptive characteristics is to be found, according to Hill, in the large numbers of black families (usually ignored by scholars and the media) who are neither weak, nor disintegrating, nor unstable, as the "typical" African-American family is popularly imagined to be. These important ethnically based strengths may well have been critical when it came to cushioning the blow of a six-year-old boy's father seeming to vanish from the face of the earth, never to return.

In the year and a half during which James's mother had been the sole breadwinner for herself and her three children, she and her family had not been socially isolated or stigmatized (as can happen in an affluent white suburb); on the contrary, this single parent and her youngsters seemed to have been firmly ensconced within a powerful social and religious network. In order to make ends meet, she had found it necessary to hold down two jobs simultaneously—one as a domestic, and another as a waitress in the Greyhound bus terminal.

Nevertheless, as James recounted, when his mother was out at work "there were the neighbors next door who kept an eye on us, and with whom we spent *lots* of time. . . . We never felt as if we were *alone*. We played with kids in the neighborhood, and it felt safe. . . . We weren't scared or isolated; we just felt like we were part of this larger community." As he spoke, his deep but resonant voice seemed to be taking on the chanting, almost sing-song cadences of someone who has drifted off in time and is in another place entirely.

"During the whole period we were growing up, I *did* help take care of the other children in the family, and in some respects, I helped play the role of a father . . . even a mother, to some extent"—James's expression was becoming ever more faraway and dreamier—"because I *knew* how to diaper my younger brothers and sisters, and I *knew* how to feed them and to bathe them; I could do everything a parent could do.

"*So*"—the word emerged with an unexpected force and passion, as if he'd suddenly catapulted back from the past and into the present—"in answer to your question, I think I learned a *lot* about parenting, just in the course of helping out." There was real pride in his face and in his voice; in fact, this was as close to bragging as I'd ever seen James Walker come. What I heard him telling me was that he had received his basic training in parenting in the process of acting as his mother's assistant parent—and she had, I imagined, been telling him what a helpful, remarkable, wonderful little boy he was at every step along the way.

What did seem apparent was that this resourceful woman had not, when necessity forced her into the role of family breadwinner, been over-whelmed. She had been able to get on with her own life (she'd remarried after a brief, year-and-a-half interval), and there was no sense of her having screamed and raged or fallen into a state of helpless despair at any time before that. She had certainly never conveyed to her children the feeling that they were, as a group, bereft, deprived, in the midst of a family disaster. Her eldest son, in his middle years, had been able to say that he'd always felt secure and cared for, that "her love for me was never in doubt."

James's mother, left by her ex-husband to raise their three young youngsters on her own, did not seem to have looked into her young male child's face and seen there the despised features of a spouse who had betrayed her and left the family economically stranded. Quite the oppo-site; according to her son, she had always tended to talk to the children about their absent father in a positive, almost mythologizing fashion.

James himself had only a few episodic memories of his father, dating from before the age of six. Among them were a couple of luminous, extremely vivid visual images—a time when his father had doled out candy to the kids from a magical footlocker full of sweets; another time when his father had taken him to the store to buy a gun-and-holster set for Christmas. Aside from that, most of what the children knew about their truant dad they knew because their mother had told them. And according to James, she had always described him to them as "a well-dressed person, very meticulous . . . a classy kind of guy, for whom she had a lot of respect and a high regard." The image that she had kept alive for them was of a man they could be proud to call their father.

Whatever bitternesses may have existed between herself and her ex-husband—they *had* divorced, after all!—James's mother had been able to keep them quite separate from anything that was happening between herself and her offspring. She seemed to understand intuitively that her children's fantasies and visions of their absent father would inevitably have some real impact upon the kinds of images they developed about them-selves. And, wisely, she had never talked him down.

"I Knew Where Everything Was"

Over time, the Walkers and I had developed certain rituals about where each of us would sit during the interviews, and we'd also worked out ritu-als about what would happen at each meeting's close. Frances always hurried off at once to attend to some bit of waiting business; the children, if present, scattered; and James lingered for a while, chatting with me as I put my gear together. Often, he reflected on what had transpired during the discussion; I'd come to look forward enormously to these moments of thoughtful epilogue.

Once, as I was packing up my tapes, microphone, and recorder, he told me that he'd suddenly realized, in the course of the interview, why he had married Frances in the first place. "It came to me while I was listening to her talk," he said quietly, "that besides her being an attractive person, what was important to me was that she was from the South, and from a very *common* kind of family—I felt comfortable with that."

"By 'common' you mean 'ordinary'?" I'd asked him, and he'd nodded. "Plain folks, yes; folks who would be able to relate to my family well. I didn't have to worry about them being of different educational levels, or one of us coming from a more moneyed background than the other—and that was one of the things that helped to cement my liking for Frances. Also," he added almost as an afterthought, "I *liked* the fact that she was an independent person, someone who could function on her own without depending on me. Because I'm the same way myself."

At the close of today's conversation, however, James's wife surprised me by not rushing away to return a phone call or to ferry someone to a friend's house or to religious school or a piano lesson. At first I thought she was lingering in order to say good-bye: I was about to leave on an annual working vacation, and this was to be our last meeting before the summer. But I soon realized that there was more on her mind than just that.

I was in the process of rolling up the extra-long extension cord of my tape recorder, which tended to get tangled; but I stopped to look at Frances searchingly and questioningly. She seemed distracted and wore a speculative frown, as if there were something on her mind that she was struggling hard to come to grips with. "You look very thoughtful," I remarked with a smile.

She shrugged lightly and said vaguely, "Oh, I've just been trying to think about what you've been saying . . ." I wasn't sure exactly what she was referring to, but asked with equal vagueness, "And you have some thoughts about that?"

She shrugged again and answered hesitantly: "Oh . . . I was just making a connection here. . . . It was really what *you* said . . . about people kind of marking anniversaries in their head, you know?" I nodded, but Frances didn't see me do so. She had turned to look at her husband, and now she touched her hand to his shoulder lightly.

"I was thinking about what *she* said," she murmured to him in a low and intimate voice. By "she," she meant me; it was almost as if she'd forgotten that I was still present. "About people maybe not remembering something that happened, or even thinking about it at all, and yet still *observing* it in some way. . . . And what I was thinking about was Tuskegee . . ." The couple's gaze had locked in an intense, radarlike stare that made me feel like an intruder.

"Tuskegee. Oh," James said doubtfully, taken aback. But that was all he said. There was a silence, a moment of such utter stillness that it was almost like a lapse in time; even the clock seemed to have stopped ticking in the background. "Yes, well, it could be . . ." he said at last, and then both Walkers seemed to recollect my presence.

Frances turned back to me to explain. This past summer the entire family had visited Tuskegee, Alabama, which James had never seen again after having left there some thirty-five years earlier, at the age of seven and a half. "That trip was *amazing*," she told me eagerly, her voice breaking slightly on the word "amazing" in that particular manner that never failed to charm me. "Because we drove there straight from Atlanta, and we all *joked* about it from the time we left until the time we arrived. The kids, when they heard where we were going—and that James hadn't ever been back there since age eight—were just going on and on about how we were all going to get *lost*, just hopelessly lost." She smiled. "They just kept going on and on—'Dad, you'll never *find* anything. Are you serious? You really think you're going to *find* those places, after all this time?' And they kept saying, 'Daddy, *turn around.*'"

The Walkers had both started laughing; Frances had to pause a moment before continuing. "But you know, we were just *amazed* when we came to each place and he'd say, 'Well now, up here is where such-and-such should be'—and it *was* there, just the way he'd said," she told me excitedly. "Then, after a time, we got to this house—it used to be their neighbors' house—and it had this big 'Beware of the Dog' sign on it. So there we all were, and we were saying to him, 'Don't go in! These people don't *live* here anymore! Is this a ghost you're chasing? *Don't*, don't get out of the car!'" She rolled her eyes, was interrupted by her own laughter again. I waited, captivated by this tale.

"So of course he does get out," continued Frances, after a moment, "and he knocks on the door, and the next thing we all remember is just all this *screaming*. We hear his voice saying 'I'm so-and-so,' and seconds later there's this elderly lady *embracing* him. I'm hearing '*James!*' and I'm hearing 'That's my baby!' and then her daughter comes out and says to him, 'Oh, yes, we used to play together.' And he remembers her, too, of course. Then they all wanted us to come out of the car, and we did. . . . We visited with them, and they all reminisced about both their families, and about what it was like when they were all kids. It was just . . . just *amazing*," Frances repeated delightedly.

I turned to James and saw that his face was now suffused with pleasure, an almost beatific joy. He now took up the telling of the tale. "My family had left Tuskegee when I was about seven and a half or eight, and this was the first time I had been back. Since *that* age. And still, I remembered the city well enough so that I could find my way around. The *whole* city," he reported almost ecstatically.

"First, I went to the Catholic school, where I started at the kindergarten, and to the house where we used to live, on Church Street. Then I found the house of the lady who took care of us when my mother wasn't home. I went right to where I used to get my hair cut. . . . To the Greyhound bus station where my mother worked . . . the service station where my father worked until our family moved north. The *second* place that we lived, just before we left, which was on the other side of town. And then the elementary school I last attended." He looked and sounded jubilant, even overjoyed.

"You know, we'd just stopped off and didn't stay in Tuskegee for more than a brief period of time, but it was probably the *best* feeling that I had in a long, long time," said James happily. He looked transported, as if what had been reawakened in him there were intense feelings of what it had been like to be a little child—the vividness, the palpability, the clarity, the magical quality of the young child's experience.

"I was astonished that I seemed to know my way around the city so *well*," he added. He had come back to the place where, as a boy of six, he had lost his father, but it was as if he were reliving an experience of mastery. He knew his way around, and could manage what needed to be managed very ably.

"It was all very, very *intense*—the biggest high I've been on in a long time," said James, then gave his wife a sheepish look. "I don't think anybody else in the family enjoyed it, or felt it, nearly as much as I did— but I sure *did enjoy it*." He laughed, and Frances joined in.

Then she turned to me and said warmly, "It was just remarkable to see him react this way, because he is, you know, usually pretty low-key. I've never seen him quite *like* that." She laughed again. "And the next thing I know, he stops the car, jumps out of the car, because now he sees a pay phone. And of course he has to call his mother—and to go through all of this with *her*, tell her what's just happened."

Smiling, I turned to James, whose face was alight. "So it sounds to me as if you were—were flooded by some very joyous feelings, as if you had an almost euphoric experience," I said.

But his only response was to murmur, almost as though speaking to himself, "I think the reason that I was able to remember it all so *well* was because I'd gone through the layout of the city, in my own thoughts, so often. And I probably remember less now about how to get around than I did before I visited—before *we* visited," he amended, with a quick glance at his wife. "I'd kept going over it and over it, in my mind, from the time that I left there until—oh, until the time that I returned.

"Because I think it was always there, a longing to go back. . . ." He sighed deeply, a sigh not of sorrow but of satisfaction. "I reconnected," he said quietly; he paused, then added: "I knew where everything was."

APPENDIXES

Directions for Mapping One's Own Family on the Beavers Systems Model

1. Fill in answers to questions on Self-report Family Inventory.
2. Add up columns *as directed.*
3. Use your scores to locate your family's position on the Beavers Systems Model.

SELF-REPORT FAMILY INVENTORY

For each question, mark the answer that best fits how you see your family now. If you feel that your answer is between two of the labeled numbers (the odd numbers), then choose the even number that is between them.

	YES: Fits our family very well		SOME: Fits our family some		NO: Does not fit our family
1. Family members pay attention to each other's feelings.	1	2	3	4	5
2. Our family would rather do things together than with other people.	1	2	3	4	5
3. We all have a say in family plans.	1	2	3	4	5
4. The grown-ups in this family understand and agree on family decisions.	1	2	3	4	5
5. Grown-ups in the family compete and fight with each other.	1	2	3	4	5
6. There is closeness in my family but each person is allowed to be special and different.	1	2	3	4	5
7. We accept each other's friends.	1	2	3	4	5
8. There is confusion in our family because there is no leader.	1	2	3	4	5
9. Our family members touch and hug each other.	1	2	3	4	5
10. Family members put each other down.	1	2	3	4	5
11. We speak our minds, no matter what.	1	2	3	4	5
12. In our home, we feel loved.	1	2	3	4	5
13. Even when we feel close, our family is embarrassed to admit it.	1	2	3	4	5

Southwest
Family
Institute

		YES: Fits our family very well		SOME: Fits our family some		NO: Does not fit our family
14.	We argue a lot and never solve problems.	1	2	3	4	5
15.	Our happiest times are at home.	1	2	3	4	5
16.	The grown-ups in this family are strong leaders.	1	2	3	4	5
17.	The future looks good to our family.	1	2	3	4	5
18.	We usually blame one person in our family when things aren't going right.	1	2	3	4	5
19.	Family members go their own way most of the time.	1	2	3	4	5
20.	Our family is proud of being close.	1	2	3	4	5
21.	Our family is good at solving problems together.	1	2	3	4	5
22.	Family members easily express warmth and caring toward each other.	1	2	3	4	5
23.	It's okay to fight and yell in our family.	1	2	3	4	5
24.	One of the adults in this family has a favorite child.	1	2	3	4	5
25.	When things go wrong we blame each other.	1	2	3	4	5
26.	We say what we think and feel.	1	2	3	4	5
27.	Our family members would rather do things with other people than together.	1	2	3	4	5
28.	Family members pay attention to each other and listen to what is said.	1	2	3	4	5

		YES: Fits our family very well		SOME: Fits our family some		NO: Does not fit our family
29.	We worry about hurting each other's feelings.	1	2	3	4	5
30.	The mood in my family is usually sad and blue.	1	2	3	4	5
31.	We argue a lot.	1	2	3	4	5
32.	One person controls and leads our family.	1	2	3	4	5
33.	My family is happy most of the time.	1	2	3	4	5
34.	Each person takes responsibility for his/her behavior.	1	2	3	4	5

35.   On a scale of 1 to 5, I would rate my family as:

1	2	3	4	5
(My family functions very well together.)			(My family does not function well together at all. We really need help.)	

36.   On a scale of 1 to 5, I would rate the independence in my family as:

1	2	3	4	5
(No one is independent. There are no open arguments. Family members rely on each other for satisfaction rather than on outsiders.)		(Sometimes independent. There are some disagreements. Family members find satisfaction both within and outside of the family.)	(Family members usually go their own way. Disagreements are open. Family members look outside of the family for satisfaction.)	

*Self-report Family Inventory: Mapping One's Own Position
on the Model*

1. SCORING AND PROFILE GUIDE

For each numbered item, enter the score from the family questionnaire. For those special items that are marked with an (R), do not enter the score itself; enter 6 minus the score. Thus, if the score on item #18 is 5, enter 1 (6–5=1); if the score is 4, enter 2 (6–4=2), and so forth.

Once the entries are completed, add up the two columns.

Health/Competence	Cohesion/Style
2 _____	2 _____
3 _____	15 _____
4 _____	19 (R) _____
6 _____	27 (R) _____
12 _____	36 _____
15 _____	
16 _____	*Sum:_____*
17 _____	
18 (R) _____	
19 (R) _____	
20 _____	
21 _____	
24 (R) _____	
25 (R) _____	
27 (R) _____	
28 _____	
33 _____	
35 _____	
36 _____	

Sum:_____

Now, turn to Diagram of Family Assessment Schema, next page.

DIAGRAM OF FAMILY ASSESSMENT SCHEMA

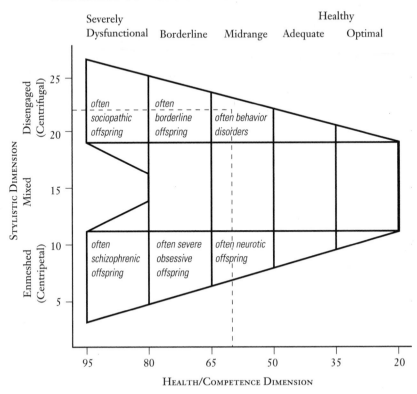

In order to find your family's position on the chart, simply do the following:

- Locate your Health/Competence score on the horizontal axis; draw a line upward.
- Locate your Stylistic Dimension score on the vertical axis; draw a line inward.
- The intersection of these two lines represents your family's position on the Family Assessment Model.

In the example above, the Health/Competence Score is 60 and the Stylistic Dimension score is 22. The family is therefore functioning at a Midrange level, with a somewhat emotionally distant style.

(The Self-report Family Inventory and Diagram of Family Assessment Schema were adapted by the author from *Successful Families: Assessment and Intervention*, by W. Robert Beavers and Robert B. Hampson.)

Interview Outline: A Sampling of the Topics Raised, Questions Asked, Self-reflective Exercises Frequently Used in the Course of Interviewing Families

Section A: Questions Always Addressed, Although Not Invariably in This Particular Order

1. Construction of family genogram
2. What have been the memorable ups and downs in this family?
3. Early memories
4. Please list three important family rules
5. What are the things that people in this family enjoy doing together?
6. What are the things you often talk about?
7. Who does which kinds of things with whom (activities/contact)?
8. What are the things about the family that members (or a particular member) would like to see changed?
9. How have the people in the family managed difficult times?
10. Who has the power in this family?
11. How are people punished? Is this fair?
12. Do you feel as if you all speak the same language—the same feeling language, the same thinking language? Or do people often misunderstand the thoughts and feelings that others in the family are trying to convey?
13. How is the topic of sex dealt with in this family? Is it a subject that is ever talked about? Which people in the family have conversations about sex?

14. What is each person's job or role in this family? For example, who is the complainer? Who is the angel? Who is the devil? Who is crazy? Who is always sane and logical?
15. What do you all do for fun, and how often do you do it?
16. What is your religion, and how do you practice or not practice it? How do you celebrate the holidays?
17. If the parents are an interfaith couple, which religious rituals are observed?
18. How is money managed and how are decisions about money made? Does money tend to be a source of tension in this family?
19. How is anger displayed when people in the family are feeling angry? For example, is there yelling and screaming? Is one particular member of the family always angry? Is there someone who is never angry at all?
20. How do the members of this family show one another love and affection?
21. Does the issue of divorce come up when there are troubles in the family?
22. What is mealtime like? (Note: Some experts consider this a metaphor for the family's life together.)
22. What are family vacations like? Who usually makes the decisions about them?
23. Every family has secrets. In some families the secrets are bigger, and in others the secrets are smaller. What are the secrets in this family?
24. If you can cast yourselves forward and imagine a photograph of this family being taken five years from now, who would be in the picture? What's happening in the family? What is the relationship with the extended family like—especially the relationships with parents, siblings, grandparents?
25. What values does this family tend to emphasize? (Covers topics such as the family's beliefs about achievement and success; its attitudes about religious observance; its involvement in the community; the roles of men and women in the family's structure are raised—see Section C of this Appendix.)
26. What are the patterns in this family that you children don't want to see repeated in your own families when you are grown up? What are the parts of this family that you'd like to see preserved? (Obviously, this is asked only of members of the family who are old enough to answer; but, it must be said, some young children were able to come up with remarkably thoughtful replies.)
27. If you were going to tell or write the story of your life—which would of course begin when you were an infant in your *own* family—what would the first sentence of this autobiography be? (This question was

posed to everyone in the family who was old enough and willing to try to answer it.)

Section B: Questions Sometimes Asked

1. Is there a topic that you want to be sure to get to during the course of our talk today—something that you may consider crucial to my understanding of how this family works?
2. I'm going to ask you (wife and mother) to begin the discussion by telling me what you think your husband would like to see covered in the interview today. Is there a topic that you believe he'd really like to see brought up? (Same question is directed to the husband and father before either parent gets to answer.)
3. Speaking metaphorically, if you think of family life as a house—with a living room, kitchen, bedrooms, bathrooms, and so forth—which room would each of you be happiest and most comfortable in?
4. Here we are, sitting peacefully together and having a very relaxed conversation. But what I am wondering is whether there's a surefire issue—a topic that, if raised, would in no time have everyone arguing, or at least feeling terribly upset.
5. It sounds as if we're now exploring something that happens often. Tell me, or, better yet, show me, how it typically happens.
6. What is your fantasy about how this argument could end differently—have a different denouement or conclusion?
7. Everybody here seems to agree that X (for example, a particular in-law) is a wretched, wicked, trouble-making person. But are there certain ways in which he or she is not wicked, or on occasion even helpful and supportive? If so, tell me about them.

Section C: Questions Related to Changing Marital and Parental Roles*

1. There has been a considerable shift in societal expectations about male and female rights and responsibilities within the family structure. In your own opinion, who should be expected to do the following: 1) care for the home, cook, and shop; 2) make major family decisions; 3) have a career; 4) be sexually faithful to spouse; 5) have responsibility for care of children; 6) be sexually aggressive; 7) have interests and activities that do not include spouse; 8) determine how money is spent?

**Sections C and D are by Janine Roberts, as quoted in *Family Therapy Sourcebook*, by Fred P. Piercy, Douglas H. Sprenkle, and Associates.*

The possible responses to each of the above questions may be one of the following: the wife; the husband; both; neither.

2. How closely do your answers to this set of questions correspond to the way things actually happen in your household?
3. Do you feel you have been influenced by society's changing attitudes on marriage and divorce? If your answer is yes, then can you talk more specifically about that?

Section D: Questions Relating to Parental-Family-of-Origin Themes, as These Pertain to the Present-Day Family's Script, Its Myths, and Its Beliefs

1. Tell me if you (mother or father) can recall any interactional scenarios, any events that kept occurring over and over again in the family in which you grew up?
2. In your own family of origin (again, addressing a parent), were there legends that had been passed down from generation to generation? Do you believe that these legends (good or bad) are being subscribed to and passed along in this family as well?
3. What was a story commonly told to outsiders about your family?
4. What subjects could be discussed within your family of origin?
5. What subjects could not be discussed directly?
6. Are there similar themes in this family—subjects that cannot be openly discussed and challenged? If so, what are the family beliefs about which everyone must share the same "party line"; that is, the themes or family myths that cannot ever be confronted or talked about openly?

Section E: Sentence-Completion Questions

1. The family I come from could best be described as . . .
2. In my family, my mother was always the one who . . .
3. If there was a topic that couldn't be discussed in my family, it was . . .
4. In my family, my father was always the one who . . .
5. In my family, I was always the one who . . .
6. The greatest strength about my family was . . .
7. Disagreement in my family was handled by . . .
8. I learned from my mother that . . .
9. I learned from my father that . . .
10. To me, family "events" (birthdays, holidays, etc.) were . . .
11. An emotion rarely expressed in my family was . . .
12. In my family, I usually felt closest to . . .

13. In my family, I usually felt most distant from . . .
14. When I was out in public with my family, I usually felt . . .
15. A myth my family perpetuated was . . .
16. If I were to give a title to a book about living with my family, it would be . . .
17. What I like best about my family is . . .
18. If I could change anything about my family, it would be . . .

Author's note: I would not like to give the impression that my interviews with families were organized so as to ensure that all of the above questions and thematic issues were addressed in a systematic way. Quite the contrary—my tendency was to use these background materials to organize and direct my own thinking as the conversation progressed. Generally speaking, I liked to let the families themselves set the direction of these semistructured interviews as much as possible. The members of each family did, after all, know the intricacies of their emotional system far better than I did; and to the degree that they were willing to take the lead in ushering me into their world, I let it happen that way.

Selected Bibliography

Ackerman, Nathan W. *The Psychodynamics of Family Life: Diagnosis and Treatment of Family Relationships*. New York: Basic Books, 1958.
———. *Treating the Troubled Family*. New York: Basic Books, 1966.
Ainsworth, M.D.S. "Object relations, dependency and attachment: A theoretical review of the infant-mother relationship." *Child Development*, 40:969–1025, 1977.
Ainsworth, M.D.S.; Bell, S. M.; and Stayton, D. J. "Individual Differences in Strange Situation Behavior of One-Year-Olds," in H. R. Schaffer, ed., *The Origins of Human Social Relations*. London: Academic Press, 1971.
Alford, C. Fred. *The Psychoanalytic Theory of Greek Tragedy*. New Haven: Yale University Press, 1987.
American Psychiatric Association. *Diagnostic and Statistical Manual of Mental Disorders*. 4th ed. (DMS-IV). Prepared by the Task Force on Nomenclature and Statistics. Washington, D.C.: American Psychiatric Association, 1994.
Aponte, Harry J. "Underorganization in the Poor Family," in Philip J. Guerin, Jr., *Family Therapy: Theory & Practice*. New York: Gardner Press, 1976.
Bacal, Howard A., and Newman, Kenneth M. *Theories of Object Relations: Bridges to Self Psychology*. New York: Columbia University Press, 1990.
Bagarozzi, Dennis A., and Anderson, Stephen A. *Personal, Marital, and Family Myths: Theoretical Formulations and Clinical Strategies*. New York: W. W. Norton & Co., 1989.
Balint, Michael, M.D. *The Basic Fault*. Evanston, Ill. Northwestern University Press, 1979.
———. *Primary Love and Psychoanalytic Technique*. New York: Liverright, 1965.
———. *Thrills and Regressions*. London: Hogarth Press, 1959.

Bassoff, Evelyn, Ph.D. *Mothers and Daughters: Loving and Letting Go.* New York: Plume Books, 1989.

Beattie, Hilary J. "Eating disorders and the mother-daughter relationship." *International Journal of Eating Disorders*, 7:453–460, 1988.

Beavers, W. Robert. *Psychotherapy and Growth: A Family Systems Perspective.* New York: Brunner/Mazel, 1977.

———. *Successful Marriage: A Family Systems Approach to Couples Therapy.* New York: W. W. Norton & Co., 1985.

———. "Beavers Systems Model," in C. N. Ramsey, ed., *Family Systems in Medicine.* New York: Guilford Press, 1989.

———. "A Clinically Useful Model of Family Assessment," in C. N. Ramsey, ed., *Family Systems in Medicine.* New York: Guilford Press, 1989.

Beavers, W. Robert, and Hampson, Robert B. *Successful Families. Assessment and Intervention.* New York: W. W. Norton & Co., 1990.

Beavers, W. Robert, et al. "The Beavers systems approach to family assessment." *Family Process*, 24:398–405, 1985.

Beavers, W. Robert. Personal communication.

Beebe, Beatrice; Feldstein, Stanley; Jaffe, Joseph; Mays, Kathleen; and Alson, Diane. "Interpersonal Timing: The Application of an Adult Dialogue Model to Mother-Infant Vocal and Kinesic Interactions," in Tiffany M. Field and Nathan A. Fox, eds., *Social Perception in Infants.* Norwood, N.J.: Ablex, 1985.

Beebe, Beatrice; Alson, Diane; Jaffe, Joseph; Feldstein, Stanley; and Crown, Cynthia. "Vocal congruence in mother-infant play." *Journal of Psycholinguistic Research*, 17:245–259, 1988.

Beebe, Beatrice. Personal communication.

Bennett, Simon, M.D. *Tragic Drama and the Family.* New Haven and London: Yale University Press, 1988.

Benjamin, Jessica. *The Bonds of Love.* New York: Pantheon, 1988.

Bettelheim, Bruno. *The Uses of Enchantment: The Meaning and Importance of Fairy Tales.* New York: Vintage Books, 1989.

Bilich, Marion. *Weight Loss from the Inside Out: Help for the Compulsive Eater.* San Francisco: Harper & Row, 1983.

Billingsley, Andrew. *Climbing Jacob's Ladder: The Enduring Legacy of African-American Families.* New York: Simon & Schuster, 1992.

Bion, W. R. *Experiences in Groups.* New York: Basic Books, 1961.

Black, Claudia. *It Will Never Happen to Me.* New York: Ballantine Books, 1981.

Black, C.; Bucky, S. F.; and Wilder, Padilla S. "The interpersonal and emotional consequences of being an adult child of an alcoholic." *International Journal of the Addictions*, 21:213–231, 1986.

Blanck, Rubin, and Blanck, Gertrude. *Marriage and Personal Development.* New York: Columbia University Press, 1968.

Blankenhorn, David; Bayme, Steven; and Elshtain, Jean Bethke. *Rebuilding the Nest: A New Commitment to the American Family.* Milwaukee, Wisconsin: Family Service America, 1990.

Blos, Peter. *The Adolescent Passage: Developmental Issues.* New York: International Universities Press, 1979.

Bollas, Christopher. *The Shadow of the Object: Psychoanalysis of the Unthought Known*. New York: Columbia University Press, 1987.

Boscolo, Luigi; Cecchin, Gianfranco; Hoffman, Lynn; and Penn, Peggy. *Milan Systemic Family Therapy: Conversations in Theory and Practice*. New York: Basic Books, 1987.

Boszormenyi-Nagy, Ivan, and Spark, Geraldine M. *Invisible Loyalties*. New York: Brunner/Mazel, 1984.

Boszormenyi-Nagy, Ivan, and Krasner, Barbara R. *Between Give and Take: A Clinical Guide to Contextual Therapy*. New York: Brunner/Mazel, 1986.

Bowen, Murray, M.D. *Family Therapy in Clinical Practice*. New York: Jason Aronson, 1978.

Bowlby, John. *Attachment and Loss*, Vol. 1: *Attachment*. London: Hogarth Press, 1969.

———. *Attachment and Loss*, Vol. 2: *Separation: Anxiety and Anger*. New York: Basic Books, 1973.

———. *Attachment and Loss*, Vol. 3: *Loss: Sadness and Depression*. New York: Basic Books, 1986.

———. "The nature of the child's tie to his mother." *International Journal of Psychoanalysis*, 39:1–23, Part 5, 1958.

Box, Sally, ed. *Crisis at Adolescence: Object Relations Therapy with the Family*. Northvale, N.J.: Jason Aronson, Inc., 1994.

Box, Sally; Copley, Beta; Magagna, Jeanne; and Smilansky, Ericca Moustaki. *Psychotherapy with Families: An Analytic Approach*. London: Routledge and Kegan Paul, 1981.

Boyd-Franklin, Nancy. *Black Families in Therapy: A Multisystems Approach*. New York: Guilford Press, 1989.

Bretherton, I., and Waters, E. *Growing Points of Attachment Theory and Research*. Monograph of the Society for Research in Child Development, 1985.

Bruner, Jerome; Cole, Michael; and Hoyd, Barbara, eds. *Mothering: The Developing Child*. Cambridge, Mass.: Harvard University Press, 1977.

Buber, Martin. *I and Thou*. New York: Charles Scribner's Sons, 1970.

———. *The Knowledge of Man: Selected Essays*. Atlantic Highlands, N.J.: Humanities Press International, 1988.

Cadoret, R. J., et al. "Development of alcoholism in adoptees raised apart from alcoholic biologic relatives." *Archives of General Psychiatry*, 37:561–563, 1980.

Carter, Betty, and McGoldrick, Monica, eds. *The Changing Family Life Cycle*. 2d ed. Boston: Allyn & Bacon, 1989.

Cashdan, Sheldon. *Object Relations Therapy: Using the Relationships*. New York: W. W. Norton, 1988.

Cath, Stanley S.; Gurwitt, Alan R.; and Gunsberg, Linda, eds. *Fathers and Their Families*. Hillsdale, N.J.: Analytic Press, 1989. Distributed solely by Lawrence Erlbaum Assoc.

Cath, Stanley S.; Gurwitt, Alan R.; and Munder, John Ross, eds. *Father and Child: Developmental and Clinical Perspectives*. Boston: Little, Brown and Co., 1982.

Cazenave, Noel A. "Black Men in America," in Harriet Pipes McAddoo, ed., *Black Families*. Beverly Hills and London: Sage Publications, 1981.

Cazenave, Noel A., and Smith, Rita. "Gender Differences in the Perception of Black Male-Female Relationships and Stereotypes," in Harold E. Cheatham and James B. Stewart, eds., *Black Families: Interdisciplinary Perspectives.* New Brunswick, N.J., and London: Transaction Publishers, 1991.

Chance, Michael, and Jolly, Clifford. *Social Groups of Monkeys, Apes and Men.* New York: E. P. Dutton & Co., 1970.

Cheatham, Harold E., and Stewart, James B., eds. *Black Families: Interdisciplinary Perspectives.* New Brunswick, N.J., and London: Transaction Publishers, 1991.

Chethik, Morton. *Techniques of Child Therapy.* New York: Guilford Press, 1989.

Cloninger, C. R. "Inheritance of alcohol abuse." *Archives of General Psychiatry,* 38:861–868, 1961.

Collins, R.; Lorraine, Leonard; Kenneth, E.; and Searles, John S., eds. *Alcohol and the Family.* New York: Guilford Press, 1990.

Comer, James, M.D. *Maggie's American Dream: The Life and Times of a Black Family.* New York: Penguin Books, 1988.

Coner-Edwards, Alice F., and Spurlock, Jeanne, M.D., eds. *Black Families in Crisis: The Middle Class.* New York: Brunner/Mazel, 1988.

Cotton, N. "The familial incidence of alcoholism: A Review." *Journal of Studies on Alcohol,* 40:89–116, 1979.

Cramer, Bert. "Assessment of Parent-Infant Relationships," in T. Berry Brazelton and M. W. Yogman, eds., *Affective Development in Infancy.* Norwood, N.J.: Ablex, 1986, 27–38.

Darwin, C. *On the Origin of Species by Means of Natural Selection.* London: John Murray, 1859.

Davis, Katherine E. B. Personal communication.

DeCasper, Anthony J., and Fifer, W. P. "Of human bonding: Newborns prefer their mothers' voices." *Science,* 208:1174–1176, 1980.

DeCasper, Anthony J., and Spence, Melanie J. "Prenatal maternal speech influences: Newborns' perceptions of speech sounds." *Infant Behavior and Development,* 9:133–150, 1986.

DiLeon, Joseph H., M.D. *Children's Drawings as Diagnostic Aids.* New York: Brunner/Mazel, 1973.

Dlugokinski, Robin J.; Dlugokinski, Eric L.; Caputo, Lisa M.; and Griffin, Richard B. "Children at risk for emotional disorders." *Clinical Psychology Review,* 8:417–440, 1988.

Edwards, Audrey, and Polite, Craig K., Ph.D. *Children of the Dream: The Psychology of Black Success.* New York: Doubleday, 1992.

El-Guebaly, Nady, M.D., and Offord, David R., M.D. "The offspring of alcoholics: A critical review." *American Journal of Psychiatry,* 134:357–365, April 1977.

Elkin, Michael. *Families Under the Influence: Changing Alcoholic Patterns.* New York: W. W. Norton & Co., 1984.

Emde, R. N. "Changing models of infancy and the nature of early development." *Journal of the American Psychoanalytic Association,* 29:179–219, 1981.

Endo, Shusaku. *Scandal: A Novel.* New York: Dodd, Mead, 1988.

Erlich, Gloria C. *Family Themes and Hawthorne's Fiction: The Tenacious Web.* New Brunswick, N.J.: Rutgers University Press, 1984.

Fairbairn, W. Ronald D. *Psychoanalytic Studies of the Personality: An Object-Relations Theory of the Personality.* London: Routledge & Kegan Paul, Ltd., 1952.

———. "Observations of the nature of hysterical states." *British Journal of Medical Psychology,* 27:105–125, 1954.

———. "On the nature and aims of psycho-analytical treatment." *International Journal of Psycho-Analysis,* 39:374–385, 1958.

Fantz. R. L. "Pattern vision in newborn infants." *Science,* 140:296–297, 1963.

Ferreira, Antonio, J., M.D. "Family myth and homeostasis." *Archives of General Psychiatry,* 9:457–463, 1963.

Feldman, Larry B. *Integrating Individual and Family Therapy.* New York: Brunner/Mazel, 1992.

Field, Tiffany M. "Infant gaze aversion and heart rate during face-to-face interactions." *Infant Behavior and Development,* 4:307–315, 1981.

Field, Tiffany M., et al. "Discrimination and imitation of facial expressions by neonates." *Science,* 218:179–181, 1982.

Fogel, Gerald I., M.D. ed., *The Work of Hans Loewald: An Introduction and Commentary.* Northvale, N.J., and London: Jason Aronson, 1991.

Fox, Hannah. Personal communication.

Fraiberg, Selma; Adelson, Edna; and Shapiro, Vivian. "Ghosts in the nursery: A psychoanalytic approach to the problem of impaired infant-mother relationships." *Journal of the American Academy of Child Psychiatry,* 14:387–422.

Framo, James L. *Explorations in Marital and Family Therapy.* New York: Springer Publishing Co., 1982.

Freud, Anna. *The Ego and the Mechanisms of Defense.* New York: International Universities Press, 1946.

Freud, Sigmund A. *Beyond the Pleasure Principle,* in *The Standard Edition of the Complete Psychological Works of Sigmund Freud.* Vol. 12. London: Hogarth Press, 1961.

———. *Civilization and its Discontents,* in *The Standard Edition of the Complete Psychological Works of Sigmund Freud.* Vol. 18. London: Hogarth Press, 1961.

———. "Remembering, Repeating, and Working Through," in *The Standard Edition of the Complete Psychological Works of Sigmund Freud.* Vol. 12. London: Hogarth Press, 1961.

Gabbard, Glen O., M.D. *Psychodynamic Psychiatry in Clinical Practice: The DSM-IV Edition.* Washington, D.C., and London: American Psychiatric Press, Inc., 1994.

Galanter, Marc., ed. *Recent Developments in Alcoholism.* Vol. 5. New York: Plenum Press, 1987.

Gallant, Donald M. *Alcoholism: A Guide to Diagnosis, Intervention, and Treatment.* New York: W. W. Norton & Co., 1987.

Gary, Lawrence E. *Black Men.* Beverly Hills, California: Sage Publications, 1981.

Garner, D. M.; Garfinkel, P. E.; Schwartz, D.; and Thompson, M. "Cultural expectation of thinness in women." *Psychological Reports,* 47:483–491, 1980.

Geller, Jesse D. Personal communication.

Genovese, Eugene, D. *Roll, Jordan, Roll: The World the Slaves Made.* New York: Vintage Books, 1976.

Glick, Ira D.; Clarkin, John F.; and Kessler, David R. *Marital and Family Therapy.* 3d ed. New York: Grune & Stratton, 1987.

Goldberg, Arnold, ed. *The Future of Psychoanalysis: Essays in Honor of Heinz Kohut.* New York: International Universities Press, 1988.

Goodwin, Donald W. "Alcoholism and heredity." *Archives of General Psychiatry,* 36:57–61, 1979.

Goodwin, Donald W., Schulsinger, Fini, Hermanson, Lief, Copenhagen; Guze, Samuel B., St Louis; and Winokur, George, Iowa City. "Alcohol Problems in Adoptees Raised Apart From Alcoholic Biological Parents." *Archives of General Psychiatry,* 28:238–243, 1973.

Greenberg, Jay R., and Mitchell, Stephen A. *Object Relationships in Psychoanalytic Theory.* Cambridge, Mass., and London: Harvard University Press, 1983.

Grinberg, Leon; Sor, Dario; and Tabak de Banchedi, Elizabeth. *Introduction to the Works of Bion.* New York: Jason Aronson, 1977.

Grizenko, Natalie, M.D., and Fisher, Christina. "Review of studies of risk and protective factors for psychopathology in children." *Canadian Journal of Psychology,* 37:711–721, 1992.

Grotstein, James S., M.D. *Splitting and Projective Identification.* Northvale, N.J., and London: Jason Aronson, 1985.

Grunebaum, Judith. Personal communication.

———. "From Discourse to Dialogue: The Power of Fairness in Therapy with Couples," in *One Couple, Four Realities: Multiple Perspectives on Couple Therapy,* Richard Chasin, Henry Grunebaum, and Margaret Herzig, eds. New York and London: Guilford Press, 1990.

Guntrip, Harry. *Psychoanalytic Theory, Therapy, and the Self.* New York: Basic Books, 1973.

Gurman, Alan S., and Kniskern, David P., eds. *Handbook of Family Therapy.* New York: Brunner/Mazel, 1981.

Haley, Jay. *The Power Tactics of Jesus Christ and Other Essays.* Rockville, Md.: Triangle Press, 1986.

———. *Problem Solving Therapy: New Strategies for Effective Family Therapy.* San Francisco: Jossey-Bass, 1978.

———. *Uncommon Therapy: The Psychiatric Techniques of Milton H. Erickson, M.D.* New York: W. W. Norton & Co., 1973.

Haley, Jay, ed. *Changing Families: A Family Therapy Reader.* New York: Grune & Stratton, 1971.

Hamilton, Edith. *Mythology.* Boston: Little, Brown and Co., 1942.

Hamilton, N. Gregory, M.D. *Self and Others: Object Relations Theory in Practice.* Northvale, N.J.: Jason Aronson, Inc., 1990.

Hammer, Signe. *Passionate Attachments: Fathers and Daughters in America Today.* New York: Rawson Associates, 1982.

Hansen, Connie. "Living in With Normal Families." *Family Process,* Vol. 20, March 1981.

Hardy, Janet B., and Zabin, Laurie Schwab. *Adolescent Pregnancy in an Urban*

Environment: Issues, Programs, and Evaluation. Washington, D.C.: Urban Institute Press, 1991.

Helzer, John E.; Burnam, Audrey; and McEvoy, Lawrence T. "Alcohol Abuse and Dependence," in N. L. Robins and D. A. Regler, eds., *Psychiatric Disorders in America.* New York: The Free Press, 1991.

Hetherington, E. M. "Divorce: A child's perspective." *American Psychologist,* 34:851–858, 1979.

Hetherington, E. M., et al. "Coping with marital transitions." Monograph of the Society for Research in Child Development, 57: serial no. 227, 1992.

Hill, Robert B. *The Strengths of Black Families.* New York: W. W. Norton & Co., 1989.

Hinshelwood, R. D. *A Dictionary of Kleinian Thought.* London: Free Association Books, 1991.

Hoffman, Lynn. *Foundations of Family Therapy: A Conceptual Framework for Systems Change.* New York: Basic Books, 1981.

Hofling, Charles K., and Lewis, Jerry M., eds. *The Family. Evaluation and Treatment.* New York: Brunner/Mazel, 1980.

Horwitz, Robert A. Personal communication.

Hotchner, Tracy. *Childbirth and Marriage.* New York: Avon Books, 1988.

Huggins, Nathan Irvin. *Black Odyssey: The African-American Ordeal in Slavery.* New York: Vintage Books, 1990.

Hughes, Judith M. *Reshaping the Psycho-analytic Domain: The Works of Melanie Klein, W. R. Fairbairn, and D. W. Winnicott.* Berkleley, California: University of California Press, 1989.

Humphrey, Laura Lynn, and Stern, Steven. "Object relations and the family system in bulimia: a theoretical integration." *Journal of Marital and Family Therapy,* 14:337–350, 1988.

Imber-Black, Evan; Roberts, Janine; and Whiting, Richard, eds. *Rituals in Families and Family Therapy.* New York: W. W. Norton & Co., 1988.

Johnson, Craig, and Connors, Mary E. *The Etiology and Treatment of Bulimia Nervosa: A Biopsychosocial Perspective.* New York: Basic Books, 1987.

Johnson, Stephen M. *Humanizing the Narcissistic Style.* New York: W. W. Norton & Co., 1987.

Johnson, Stuart. Personal communication.

Kagan, Richard, and Schlosberg, Shirley. *Families in Perpetual Crisis.* New York: W. W. Norton & Co., 1989.

Kantor, David, and Lehr, William. *Inside the Family: Toward a Theory of Family Process.* New York: Harper & Row, 1976.

Kantor, David, and Okun, Barbara, eds. *Intimate Environments. Sex, Intimacy, and Gender in Families.* New York: Guilford Press, 1989.

Kaplan, Louise J. *Oneness and Separateness: From Infant to Individual.* New York: Simon & Schuster, 1978.

Karen, Robert. *Becoming Attached: The Unfolding Mystery of the Infant-Mother Bond and Its Impact on Later Life.* New York: Warner Books, 1994.

Karpel, Mark A., ed. *Family Resources: The Hidden Partner in Family Therapy.* New York: Guilford Press, 1986.

Keesey, Richard E. "A Set-Point Theory of Obesity," in Kelly D. Brownell and John P. Foreyt, eds., *Handbook of Eating Disorders: Physiology, Psychology, and Treatment of Obesity, Anorexia, and Bulimia.* New York: Basic Books, 1986.

Klein, Melanie. *Envy and Gratitude and Other Works, 1946–1963.* London: Hogarth Press, 1975.

Klinnert, M. D. *Facial Expression and Social Referencing.* Unpublished doctoral dissertation prospectus. University of Denver, Psychology Department, 1978.

Klinnert, M. D.; Campos, J. J.; Sorce, J. F.; Emde, R. N.; and Svejda, M. "Emotions as behavioral regulators: Social Referencing in Infancy," in R. Plutchik and H. Kellerman, eds., *Emotion:Theory, research and experience,* Vol. 2. New York: Academic Press, 1983.

Kohut, Heinz, M.D. *The Analysis of the Self: A Systemic Approach to the Psychoanalytic Treatment of Narcissistic Personality Disorders.* Madison, Connecticut: International Universities Press, 1971.

Kohut, Heinz, and Wolf, E. S. "The disorders of the self and their treatment." *International Journal of Psycho-Analysis,* 59:413–425, 1978.

Lachkar, Joan, Ph.D. *The Narcissistic/Borderline Couple: A Psychoanalytic Perspective on Marital Treatment.* New York: Brunner/Mazel, 1992.

Landry, Bart. *The New Black Middle Class.* Berkeley: University of California Press, 1987.

Lax, R. F. "Some comments on the narcissistic aspects of self-righteousness." *International Journal of Psycho-Analysis,* 56:283–292, 1976.

Lerner, Harriet Goldhor. *The Dance of Intimacy: A Woman's Guide to Courageous Acts of Change in Key Relationships.* New York: Harper & Row, 1989.

Lemann, Nicholas. *The Promised Land: The Great Black Migration and How It Changed America.* New York: Alfred A. Knopf, 1991.

Lewin, Roger A., M.D., and Schulz, Clarence, M.D. *Losing and Fusing: Borderline Transitional Object and Self Relations.* Northvale, N.J., and London: Jason Aronson, Inc., 1992.

Lewis, Jerry M., M.D.; Beavers, W. Robert, M.D.; Gossett, John T., Ph.D.; and Phillips, Virginia Austin. *No Single Thread: Psychological Health in Family Systems.* New York: Brunner/Mazel, 1976.

Lewis, Oscar. *Five Families.* New York: John Wiley & Sons, Inc., 1962.

Lewis, Robin J.; Dlugokinski, Eric L.; Caputo, Lisa M.; and Griffin, Richard B. "Children at risk for emotional disorders: Risk and resource dimensions." *Clinical Psychology Review,* 8:417–440, 1988.

Lidz, Theodore. *The Person: His and Her Development Throughout the Life Cycle.* New York: Basic Books, 1976.

Loewald, Hans, W., M.D. *Sublimation: Inquiries into Theoretical Psychoanalysis.* New Haven: Yale University Press, 1988.

Luepnitz, Deborah Anna. *The Family Interpreted: Feminist Theory in Clinical Practice.* New York: Basic Books, 1988.

Luthar, Suniya S., and Zigler, Edward. "Vulnerability and competence: A review of research on resilience in childhood. *American Journal of Orthopsychiatry,* 61:6–22, 1991.

MacFarlane, Aidan. "Olfaction in the development of social preferences in the human neonate in parent-infant interaction." Ciba Foundation Symposium 33 (new series). Amsterdam: Associated Scientific Publishers, 1975.

McAdams, Dan P. *Stories We Live By: Personal Myths and the Making of the Self.* New York: William Morrow & Co., 1993.

McAdoo, Harriette Pipes, ed. *Black Families.* Beverly Hills: Sage Publications, 1981.

McAdoo, Harriette Pipes. "Factors related to stability in upwardly mobile Black families." *Journal of Marriage and the Family,* 40:761–776, 1978.

McGoldrick, Monica, and Gerson, Randy. *Genograms in Family Assessment.* New York: W. W. Norton & Co., 1985.

McGoldrick, Monica; Pearce, John K.; and Giordano, Joseph, eds. *Ethnicity & Family Therapy.* New York: Guilford Press, 1982.

Madhubuti, Haki R. *Black Men: Obsolete, Single, Dangerous? The Afrikan American Family in Transition.* Chicago: Third World Press, 1990.

Mahler, Margaret S.; Pine, Fred; and Bergman, Anni. *The Psychological Birth of the Human Infant: Symbiosis and Individuation.* New York: Basic Books, 1975.

Manfield, Philip. *Split Self/Split Object: Understanding and Treating Borderline, Narcissistic, and Schizoid Disorders.* Northvale, N.J., and London: Jason Aronson, 1992.

Mathew, R., et al. "Craving for alcohol in sober alcoholics." *American Journal of Psychiatry,* 136:603–606, 1979.

Meltzoff, Andrew N. "The Roots of Social and Cognitive Development: Models of Man's Original Nature," in Tiffany M. Field and Nathan A. Fox, eds., *Social Perception in Infants.* Norwood, N.J.: Ablex, 1985.

Meltzoff, Andrew N., and Moore, M. K. "Imitation of facial and manual gestures by human neonates." *Science,* 198:75–78, 1977.

Middleton-Moz, Jane, and Dwinell, Lorie. *After the Tears: Reclaiming the Personal Losses of Childhood.* Pompano Beach, Fla.: Health Communications, 1986.

Miller, Alice. *Prisoners of Childhood: How Narcissistic Parents Form and Deform the Emotional Lives of their Gifted Children.* New York: Basic Books, 1981.

Miller, E. J., and Rice, A. K. *Systems of Organizations.* London: Tavistock Press, 1967.

Mills, Theodore, M., with Rosenberg, Stan. *Readings on the Sociology of Small Groups.* Englewood Cliffs, N.J.: Prentice-Hall, 1970.

Minuchin, Salvador. *Families & Family Therapy.* Cambridge, Mass.: Harvard University Press, 1974.

Minuchin, Salvador, and Fishman, H. Charles. *Family Therapy Techniques.* Cambridge, Mass.: Harvard University Press, 1981.

Minuchin, Salvador, and Nichols, Michael P. *Family Healing: Tales of Hope and Renewal from Family Therapy.* New York: The Free Press, 1993.

Mitchell, Stephen A. *Hope and Dread in Psychoanalysis.* New York: Basic Books, 1993.

———. *Relational Concepts in Psychoanalysis: An Integration.* Cambridge, Mass., and London: Harvard University Press, 1988.

Muir, Elisabeth E., and Thorlaksdottir, Eyglo. "Psychotherapeutic intervention with mothers and children in day care." *American Journal of Orthopsychiatry,* 6:60–67, 1994.

Nadelson, Carol C., and Polonsky, Derek, C., eds. *Marriage and Divorce: A Contemporary Perspective.* New York: Guilford Press, 1984.

Napier, Augustus Y., Ph.D., with Whitaker, Carl, M.D. *The Family Crucible: One Family's Therapy—An Experience That Illuminates All Our Lives.* New York: Bantam Books, 1980.

Nichols, Michael. *Family Therapy: Concepts and Methods.* New York: Gardner Press, 1984.

Ogden, Thomas H., M.D. *Projective Identification and Psychotherapeutic Technique.* Northvale, N.J., and London: Jason Aronson, 1991.

———. "On projective identification." *International Journal of Psycho-Analysis,* 60:357–373, 1979.

Ortmeyer, Inge. Personal communication.

Piercy, Fred P.; Sprenkle, Douglas H.; and Associates. *Family Therapy Sourcebook.* New York: Guilford Press, 1986.

Pincus, Lily. *Death and the Family: The Importance of Mourning.* New York: Pantheon Books, 1974.

Pincus, Lily, and Dare, Christopher. *Secrets in the Family.* New York: Pantheon Books, 1978.

Pinderhughes, Elaine B. "Treatment with Black Middle-Class Families: A Systemic Perspective," in Alice F. Coner-Edwards and Jeanne Spurlock, M.D., eds., *Black Families in Crisis: The Middle Class.* New York: Brunner/Mazel, 1988.

———. "Black genealogy: Self liberator and therapeutic tool." *Smith College Studies in Social Work,* March 1982.

Pittman, Frank S., III. *Turning Points: Treating Families in Transitional Crisis.* New York and London: W. W. Norton & Co., 1987.

Pollock, V. E.; Schneider, L. S.; Gabrielli, W. F.; and Goodwin, D. W. "Sex of parent and offspring in the transmission of alcoholism: A meta-analysis." *Journal of Nervous and Mental Disease,* 173:668–673, 1987.

Ravenscroft, Kent, M.D. "Psychoanalytic Family Therapy: Approaches to the Adolescent Bulimic," in Harvey J. Schwartz, M.D., ed., *Bulimia: Psychoanalytic Treatment and Theory.* New York: International Universities Press, 1988.

Ravenscroft, Kent, M.D. Personal communication.

Regier, D. A.; Myers, J. K.; Kramer, M.; Robins, L. N.; Blazer, D. G.; Hough, R. L.; Eaton, W. W.; and Locke, B. Z. "The NIMH epidemiological catchment area program." *Archives of General Psychiatry,* 41:934–941, 1984.

Reich, T.; Cloninger, C. R.; et al. "Secular trends in the family transmission of alcoholism." *Alcoholism: Clinical and Experimental Research,* 12:458–464, 1988.

Reiser, Lynn Whisnant, M.D. "Love, Work and Bulimia," in Harvey J. Schwartz, M.D., ed., *Psychoanalystic Treatment and Theory.* New York: International Universities Press, 1987.

Reiss, David. *The Family's Construction of Reality.* Cambridge, Mass.: Harvard University Press, 1981.

Rhodes, Lorna A. *Emptying Beds: The Work of an Emergency Psychiatric Unit.* Berkeley: University of California Press, 1991.

Rilke, Rainer Maria. *Briefe Aus Den Jahren.* 1892 bis 1904. Im Insel-Verlag Zu Leipzig, 1939.

Root, Maria; Fallon, Patricia; and Friedrich, William N. *Bulimia: A Systems Approach to Treatment.* New York: W. W. Norton & Co., 1986.

Rosenwald, George C., and Ochberg, Richard L. *Storied Lives: The Cultural Politics of Self-Understanding.* New Haven and London: Yale University Press, 1992.

Rutter, Michael. "Protective Factors in Children's Responses to Stress and Disadvantage," in M. W. Kent and J. E. Rolf, eds., *Primary Prevention of Psychopathology,* Vol 3: *Social Competence in Children.* Hanover, N.H.: University Press of New England, 1979.

———. "Resilience in the face of adversity." *British Journal of Psychiatry,* 147:598–611, 1985.

Sartre, J. P. *Being and Nothingness: An Essay on Phenomenological Ontology.* Translated and with an Introduction by Hazel E. Barnes. New York: Philosophical Library, 1959.

Satir, Virginia. *Conjoint Family Therapy.* 3d ed. Palo Alto, Calif.: Science and Behavior Books, Inc., 1983.

———. *Peoplemaking.* Palo Alto, Calif.: Science and Behavior Books, Inc., 1972.

Scharff, David, E., M. D. *Refinding the Object and Reclaiming the Self.* Northvale, N.J., and London: Jason Aronson, 1992.

Scharff, David E., M.D., and Scharff, Jill Savege, M.D. *Object Relations Family Therapy.* Northvale, N.J., and London: Jason Aronson, 1987.

Scharff, Jill Savege, M.D. *Foundations of Object Relations Family Therapy.* Northvale, N.J., and London: Jason Aronson, 1989.

Schuckit, M. A.; Goodwin, D. W.; and Winokur, G. "A study of alcoholism in half-sibs." *American Journal of Psychiatry,* 128:1132–1136, 1972.

Scott, Derek, ed. *Anorexia and Bulimia Nervosa: Practical Approaches.* New York: New York University Press, 1988.

Segal, Hanna. *Introduction to the Work of Melanie Klein.* New York: Basic Books, 1974.

Segel, Nathan P. "Repetition Compulsion, Acting Out, and Identification with the Doer." *Journal of the American Psychoanalytic Association,* 17:474–488, 1969.

Shapiro, Edward R., and Carr, A. Wesley. *Lost in Familiar Places: Creating New Connections Between the Individual and Society.* New Haven and London: Yale University Press, 1991.

Shengold, Leonard, M.D. *Soul Murder: The Effects of Childhood Abuse and Deprivation.* New Haven: Yale University Press, 1989.

Sher, Kenneth J. *Children of Alcoholics: A Critical Appraisal of Theory and Research.* Chicago: University of Chicago Press, 1991.

Siegal, Michele, Ph.D.; Brisman, Judith, Ph.D.; and Weinshel, Margot, M.S.W. *Surviving an Eating Disorder: Strategies for Family and Friends.* New York: Harper & Row, 1988.

Silberstein, Lisa R.; Striegel-Moore, Ruth, H.; and Rodin, Judith. "Feeling Fat: A Woman's Shame," in H. B. Lewis, ed., *The Role of Shame in Symptom Formation.* Hillsdale, N.J.: Erlbaum Press, 1987.

Silverman, Doris. "Some Proposed Modifications of Psychoanalytic Theories of Early Childhood Development," in J. Masling, ed., *Empirical Studies of Psychoanalytic Theories.* Vol. 11. Hillsdale, N.J.: Erlbaum Press, 1966.

Simon, Bennett, M.D. *Tragic Drama and the Family: Psychoanalytic Studies from Aeschylus to Beckett.* New Haven and London: Yale University Press, 1988.

Skolnick, Arlene S., and Skolnick, Jerome H. *Family in Transition.* Boston: Little, Brown and Co., 1977.

Skynner, Robin. *Explorations with Families: Group Analysis and Family Therapy.* London: Tavistock/Routledge, 1990.

Slipp, Samuel, M.D. *Object Relations: A Dynamic Bridge Between Individual and Family Therapy.* Northvale, N.J., and London: Jason Aronson, 1984.

Slomowitz, Marcia, ed. *Adolescent Psychotherapy.* Washington, D.C.: American Psychiatric Press, Inc., 1991.

Smith, Peter. Personal communication.

Solomon, Marion F. *Narcissism and Intimacy: Love and Marriage in an Age of Confusion.* New York: W. W. Norton & Co., 1989.

Sorce, James F., and Emde, Robert N. "Maternal emotional signaling: its effect on the visual cliff behavior of 1-year-olds." *Developmental Psychology,* 21:195–200, 1985.

Spitz, René A. "The smiling response: a contribution to the ontogenesis of social relations." *Genetic Psychology Monographs,* 39:57–125, 1946.

Stack, Carol B. *All Our Kin: Strategies for Survival in a Black Community.* New York: Harper Colophon, 1974.

Staples, Robert. *The Black Family: Essays and Studies.* Belmont, Calif.: Wadsworth Publishing Co., 1991.

Steele, Shelby. *The Content of our Character: A New Vision of Race in America.* New York: Harper Perennial, 1991.

Steinglass, Peter, M.D. "The alcoholic family at home." *Archives of General Psychiatry,* 38:478–584, 1981.

Stephens, Leonora, M.D. "Borderline Families," unpublished.

Stephens, Leonora, M.D. Personal communication.

Stern, Daniel N., M.D. *Diary of a Baby: What Your Child Sees, Feels, and Experiences.* New York: Basic Books, 1990.

———. *The First Relationship: Infant and Mother.* Cambridge, Mass.: Harvard University Press, 1977.

———. *The Interpersonal World of the Infant: A View From Psychoanalysis and Developmental Psychology.* New York: Basic Books, 1985.

———. "Mother and Infant at Play," in M. Lewis and L. A. Rosenblum, eds., *The Effect of the Infant on its Caregiver.* New York: Wiley & Sons, 1974.

———. "The goal and structure of mother-infant play." *Journal of the American Academy of Child Psychiatry,* 13:402–421, 1974.

———. "A micro-analysis of mother-infant interaction: Behaviors regulating social contact between a mother and her three-and-a-half-month-old twins." *Journal of the American Academy of Child Psychiatry,* 10:501–517, 1971.

Stierlin, Helm, M.D. *Psychoanalysis and Family Therapy.* New York: Jason Aronson, 1977.

———. *Separating Parents and Adolescents: A Perspective on Running Away,*

Schizophrenia, and Waywardness. New York: Quadrangle/The New York Times Book Co., 1974.

Stone, Betsy. Personal communication.

Storr, Anthony. *The Art of Psychotherapy.* New York: Methuen Press, 1980.

Striegel-Moore, Ruth H.; Silberstein, Lisa R.; and Rodin, Judith. "Toward an understanding of risk factors for bulimia." *American Psychologist,* 41:246–263, 1986.

Sugar, Max, M.D., ed. *Female Adolescent Development.* New York: Brunner/Mazel, 1979.

Sullivan, Harry Stack. *Clinical Studies in Psychiatry.* New York: Basic Books, 1956.

———. *Conceptions of Modern Psychiatry.* New York: W. W. Norton & Co., 1953.

Sze, William, Ph.D. *Human Life Cycle.* New York: Jason Aronson, 1975.

Taylor, Graeme J. "Alexithymia." *Harvard Mental Health Letter,* vol. 5, no. 12:8, June 1989.

Terkel, Studs. *Race: How Blacks and Whites Think and Feel About the American Obsession.* New York: Anchor Books, 1992.

Thompson-Fullilove, M., ed. *The Black Family: Mental Health Perspectives.* San Francisco: University of California Press, 1985.

Tinbergen, N. *The Study of Instinct.* London: Oxford University Press, 1951.

Tolpin, M. "On the Beginnings of a Cohesive Self," in R. Eissler et al., eds., *The Psychoanalytic Study of the Child.* Vol. 26. New York: International Universities Press, 1971.

Treadway, David C. *Before It's Too Late: Working with Substance Abuse in the Family.* New York: W. W. Norton & Co., 1989.

———. "Codependency: Disease, metaphor or fad?" *The Family Therapy Networker,* 14:38–42, 1990.

———. "The ties that bind." *The Family Therapy Networker,* 11:16–23, 1987.

Tronick, E. Z. "Emotions and emotional communication in infants." *American Psychologist,* 44:112–119, 1989.

Van Heusden, Ammy, and Van Den Eerenbeemt, Elsemarie. *Balance in Motion: Ivan Boszormenyi-Nagy and His Vision of Individual and Family Therapy.* New York: Brunner/Mazel, 1986.

Wachtel, Ellen F., and Wachtel, Paul L. *Family Dynamics in Individual Psychotherapy: A Guide to Clinical Strategies.* New York: Guilford Press, 1986.

Walsh, Froma, ed. *Normal Family Processes.* New York: Guilford Press, 1982.

Wesner, David; Dowling, Jerry; and Johnson, Frank. "What is maternal-infant intervention?: The role of infant psychotherapy." *Psychiatry,* 45:307–315, 1982.

White, John. *Black Leadership in America: From Booker T. Washington to Jesse Jackson.* New York: Longman Press, 1990.

White, Michael, and Epston, David. *Literate Means to Therapeutic Ends.* Adelaide, Australia: Dulwich Center Publications, 1989.

Windle, M. "Temperament and Personal Attributes Among Children of Alcoholics," in M. Windle and J. S. Searles, eds., *Children of Alcoholics: Critical Perspectives.* New York: Guilford Press, 1990.

Winer, Robert. *Close Encounters: A Relational View of the Therapeutic Process.* Northvale, N.J.: Jason Aronson, 1994.

Winnicott, D. W. *The Family and Individual Development.* London: Routledge, 1989.

———. *The Maturational Processes and the Facilitating Environment: Studies in the Theory of Emotional Development.* New York: International Universities Press, 1965.

———. *Playing and Reality.* London: Routledge, 1989.

———. *Through Paediatrics to Psycho-Analysis.* New York: Basic Books, 1975.

Winokur, George; Reich, T.; Rimmer, J.; and Pitts, F. N. "Alcoholism: III. Diagnosis and familial psychiatric illness in 259 alcoholic probands." *Archives of General Psychiatry*, 23:104–111, 1970.

Wolin, Steven J., M.D., and Wolin, Sybil, M., Ph.D. *The Resilient Self: How Survivors of Troubled Families Rise Above Adversity.* New York: Villard, 1993.

Wolin, Steven J., M.D.; Bennett, Linda A.; and Noonan, Denise L. "Family rituals and the recurrence of alcoholism over generations." *American Journal of Psychiatry*, 136:589–593, 1979.

Woititz, J. G. *Adult Children of Alcoholics.* Pompano Beach, Fla.: Health Communications, 1983.

———. "Adult children of alcoholics." *Alcoholism Treatment Quarterly*, 1:71–99, 1984.

Zigler, Edward F., and Lang, Mary E. *Child Care Choices: Balancing the Needs of Children, Families and Society.* New York: The Free Press, 1991.

Zilbach, Joan J., M.D. *Young Children in Family Therapy.* New York: Brunner/Mazel, 1986.

Zinner, John, M.D. "The Influence of Shared Unconscious Fantasy on Family Communication," in Jill Savege Scharff, M.D., ed., *Foundations of Object Relations Family Therapy.* Northvale, N. J., and London: Jason Aronson, 1989.

Zinner, John, M.D., and Shapiro, Roger L., M.D. "The Family Group and a Single Psychic Entity: Implications for Acting Out in Adolescence," in Jill Savege Scharff, M.D., ed., *Foundations of Object Relations Family Therapy.* Northvale, N.J., and London: Jason Aronson, 1989.

Zinner, John, M.D. and Shapiro, Roger, M.D. "Projective Identification as a Mode of Perception and Behavior in Families of Adolescents," in Jill Savege Scharff, M.D., ed., *Foundations of Object Relations Family Therapy.* Northvale, N.J., and London: Jason Aronson, 1989.

Zinner, John, M.D., and Shapiro, Edward R., M.D. "Splitting in Families of Borderline Adolescents," in J. Mack, ed., *Borderline States in Psychiatry.* New York: Grune and Stratton, 1975.

Zinner, John, M.D. "A Developmental Spectrum of Projective Identification." Forthcoming.

———. "How Heinz Kohut's ideas enrich object relations family therapy." Forthcoming.

Zinner, John, M.D. Personal communication.

Zuk, Gerald H. *Family Therapy: A Triadic-based Approach.* New York: Human Sciences Press, 1981.

Index

abandonment, parental, 43–46, 86, 87, 93
  in Level 3 case family, 269–70
  in Level 4 case family, 100–102, 105, 107,
    112, 122, 209
achievement orientation, 419
acting out:
  of adolescent delegate, 21–22
  in Level 5 case family, 3–22
  protective function of, 4, 18, 21–22
  self-responsibility vs., 9, 10–11
adaptive responses, of infants, 169–71
adequate families, *see* Level 2 (adequate)
    families
adolescence, adolescents:
  disengaged families and, 57–58
  eating disorders and, 55–56; *see also*
    anorexia nervosa; bulimia
  enmeshed families and, 55
  impact on family of, 139
  of Levels 1 and 2 case family's daughters,
    403–6
  projective identification and, 78–79
  separation from family in, 55, 57–58
  as symptom bearer, 3–20
  see also puberty
adolescent delegates, 21–22, 77
adversity, 371, 374
affairs, extramarital, 19, 68

affection and warmth:
  expression of, 50, 51
  lack of, 51
agoraphobia, 56
Ainsworth, Mary Salter, 377, 378
alcoholism, 264, 273–86
  definition of, 277–78
  family levels and, 284–86
  intergenerational transmission of,
    276–78
  in Level 3 case family, 235–37, 244–48,
    251, 252, 269, 276, 279, 283–84,
    289–90, 293
  risk factors and, 279–81, 286
alexithymia, 132–33
ambivalence, 52, 215
  in Level 4 families, 97–98, 99
  in Level 5 families, 61, 93–94, 97
Analysis of the Self, The (Kohut), 348–50
Anderson family, *see* Level 5 case family
    (Anderson family)
*And to Think That I Saw It on Mulberry
    Street* (Dr. Seuss), 176
anger, 12, 16, 39–40, 49, 60
  conflict resolution and, 331–32
  in disengaged families, 57
  disengagement and, 51–52, 56–60
  in Level 3 case family, 231, 232, 290–91

anger *(cont'd)*
    in Level 4 case family, 98–99, 107–8,
        111–13, 119, 120, 122
    in Level 5 case family, 6, 7, 9, 11, 12, 13,
        15–21, 37–41, 45–46, 49, 58–59
    in projective-identification relationship, 80
animal behavior studies, 164–68, 170–73
Anna Karenina (Tolstoy), 23
anniversaries, mental, 417–18
anniversary tensions, 381
anorexia nervosa, 129, 131
    incidence of, 127
    physical effects of, 55–56, 131
    psychological motivations and, 55–56
antidepressants, 7–8
anxious-avoidant relationships, 182–84, 378,
        379
anxious-resistant relationships, 378
Aponte, Harry J., 125–26
approach-avoidance relationships, 183
archetypes, 238–39
Aristotle, 276
As You Like It (Shakespeare), 371
attachment, 163–91
    Bowlby's studies of, 164–73
    eye-to-eye contact and, 179–84
    to family members, 194, 195
    imitative behavior and, 178–79
    infant-caretaker bond and, 165–71
    principle figure for, 194–95
    protection and, 166–67, 171, 194
    sound recognition and, 176–77
    substructure of, 191
    survival and, 164–67, 172
    visual preferences and, 177–78
    see also first loves
Attachment and Loss (Bowlby), 166–67
autobiographies, first sentences of, 192–93,
        200–205
    examples of, 200–202, 204–5
    musical motifs compared with, 203–4
autonomy, *see* individuality

babbling, of infants, 169
Beattie, Hilary J., 144
beauty contests, weight and, 128
beauty ideals, female, 127–28
Beavers, W. Robert, xxviii, 24, 30, 48, 56,
        59, 61, 211, 215, 242, 247, 290, 304,
        401, 402, 414
Beavers Systems Model (originally Beavers-
        Timberlawn Family Evaluation Scales),
        xxvi–xxix, xxxviii, 23–36

alcoholism and, 284–86
    as developmental schema, xxix
    development of, xxviii
    families' mobility on, 92–93
    family contracting and, 333
    family style and, 50
    five major family systems in, xxviii, 24,
        209
    mapping your own family on, 427–32
    uses of, xxviii–xxix
    see also Level 1 (optimal) families; Level
        2 (adequate) families; Level 3
        (midrange) families; Level 4 (polarized
        or borderline) families; Level 5
        (severely disturbed) families; *specific case
        families*
Beebe, Beatrice, 188–89, 191
being absent while present, 72
Being and Nothingness (Sartre), 195
betrayal:
    in Level 4 case family, 105, 140
    in Level 5 case family, 7, 9, 49, 69, 93
Between Give and Take (Boszormenyi-Nagy
        and Krasner), 117–18
Billingsley, Andrew, 381–82
biofeedback, xxxii–xxxiii
black families:
    middle-class, 379–80
    nonproductive male stereotype and, 359
    strengths of, 418–20
    unity of, 381–82
"Black Middle Class, The" (Coner-Edwards
        and Edwards), 379–80
Blos, Peter, 53, 140
body weight:
    ideal, 128
    lovableness and, 136–37, 156
    set-point for, 134
    see also anorexia nervosa; bulimia
borderline families, *see* Level 4 (polarized or
        borderline) families
Boszormenyi-Nagy, Ivan, 117–18
boundaries, 59, 307–18
    definition of, 310–11
    distress at, 316–18
    of enmeshed vs. disengaged family, 74
    family organism and, 314–15
    family–outside world, 311, 315–16,
        317–18
    generational, 310, 311, 312–14, 316–17,
        320, 325, 334
    of infant, 174
    rules and, 311

self-other, 80–81, 88, 221, 224, 226, 310, 312, 320, 328–29, 333
sexual-generational, 125–26, 141, 148–49
three types of, 310
violations of, 59, 125, 141, 148–49, 221, 224, 226, 231–35, 295, 310, 311
Bowen, Linda, 3, 8, 9, 10, 11, 13, 15, 16, 19, 20, 37–38, 39, 40, 41, 46, 48, 59–60
Bowen, Murray, 51, 66, 259–60
Bowlby, John, 164–73, 199, 377, 378, 379
on critical periods, 164–65
on instinctual adaptive responses, 169–71
social releasers and, 167–69
brain, early structuring of, xxxiv
Bretherton, Inge, 194, 195
British-American family style, 52
Browning, Robert, 211
bulimia, 125–37, 141–49
alexithymia and, 132–33
body viewed as enemy in, 133–35
causes of, 127–29
clinical definition of, 130–31
early life history and, 147–49
incidence of, 127
mother-daughter relationships and, 135, 136–37, 143–44, 147, 155
normal-weight, 129–30, 148
in Level 4 case family, 98, 100, 104, 109, 125–29, 135–37, 141, 142, 143–44, 148–49, 155, 159, 210
onset of, 131–32
physical consequences of, 135–36
psychological motivations and, 126–27

caregiver-infant relationships, *see* infant-mother relationships
Carr, A. Wesley, 366–67
Carson, Richard D., xxiii–xxiv
Carter, Elizabeth A., 44, 138
Cashdan, Sheldon, 174
"catching of fears," 199
cell division, 233
centrifugal families, 50, 54, 59, 242; *see also* disengagement
centripetal families, 50, 53–54, 56, 59; *see also* enmeshment
Changing Family Life Cycle, The (Carter and McGoldrick), 138
Chapman Unit, 3–20, 64, 65, 67
status ladder of, 10–11
Child Care Choices (Zigler and Lang), 195
children:
of alcoholics, 276–86

arrival of, parents and, 44–45
awareness of, 236–37
choice-making powers of, 410–11
disciplining of, 257–59, 261–62
early family trauma overcome by, 370–83
in emotional triangles, 259–60, 320, 324–25
family contracting and, 333–34
family style and development of, 52–58
generational boundary violations and, 125, 141, 148–49, 310, 311, 312–14, 316–17, 320, 325, 334
illegitimate, 19–20, 41–42, 49, 73–74
only, 101, 110
parents exalted by, 350–52
parents' unconditional love of, 293, 384–97
as sibling subgroup of family, 341, 342
as symptom bearer and delegate, 3–22
unconscious perceptions of, 237
see also adolescence, adolescents; infants; parentified children
chronic low-grade depression, 7–8
Civilization and Its Discontents (Freud), 174
cliff, visual, 197–98, 199, 200
Climbing Jacob's Ladder (Billingsley), 381
clinging, by infants, 169, 170–71
closeness, need for, *see* attachment; intimacy
coalitions, xxvi–xxvii, 18
Colorado, University of, Health Sciences Center, 197
Columbia School of Social Work, xxix
communication:
crying as, 170
eye love and, 180–82
of feelings vs. actions, 13
Level 3 family's lack of, 231–32, 255–57, 291
Level 4 family's lack of, 111–12
listening and, 11–13, 48, 89
nonverbal love and, 175–76, 178–79, 188–89, 191
social releasers and, 167–69, 170
visual cliff and, 197–200
community, family unity and, 381–82
competition:
in father-son relationship, 273–74
in Level 3 case family, 221, 273–74
in mother-daughter relationship, 144, 147, 148, 155
conditional (earned) love, 121, 385–86
Coner-Edwards, Alice F., 379–80
conflict, xxii, xxvii
inevitability of, 398

conflict *(cont'd)*
  resolution of, 329–33
  suppression of, 51, 54, 57
Connecticut School of Nursing, University
    of, 220
contending younger females, 310
control, 28
  anorexia nervosa and, 55–56
  bulimia and, 126–27, 135, 141–42, 148
  as core emotional issue, 33–34
  eye love and, 181–82
  fear of loss of, 98, 99, 105–6, 140, 247
  in infant-mother relationship, 181–82, 188
  through intimacy, 212
  in Level 4 case family, 98, 99, 104–6,
    126–27, 140, 141–42, 209–10
  see also rules; tyrants
cooing, of infants, 169
corporal punishment, 257–58, 261
Cramer, Bert, 193
critical periods, in development, 164–65
Crown, Cynthia, 189
crying, of infants, 169–70, 171, 304
  function of, 173
crying, of men, 247, 295–96, 304
curiosity, interpersonal, 366–67

Darwin, Charles, 171–72
death instinct, 151, 152
DeCasper, Anthony J., 176
defense mechanism, *see* projective
    identification
delegates, adolescent, 21–22, 77
dental erosion, 136
depression, 4, 56
  chronic low-grade, 7–8
depressive signals, 199
destructive entitlement, 117
detouring-attacking triangles, 18
development, 163–74
  animal behavior studies and, 164–68,
    170–73
  critical periods in, 164–65
  social releasers and, 167–70
developmental imperatives, 350
*Diagnostic and Statistical Manual of Mental
    Disorders III*, 130
*Diagnostic and Statistical Manual of Mental
    Disorders IV*, 6, 130
dieting, bulimia and, 128
disagreements, suppression of, 51, 54
disciplining, of children, 257–62
  in Level 5 families, 48

disengagement, 50–54, 242–43, 270
  boundaries and, 74, 316–18
  defined, 51
  ethnic considerations and, 52
  leaving home and, 57–58
  in Level 3 case family, 242–43, 267, 270
  in Level 5 case family, 8–9, 56–61, 74
disjointed thinking, 4, 60
distancer-pursuer relationships, 294–97
distrust, xxxi
  in Level 5 case family, 7, 9, 12, 13
divorce, 70, 305
  of author's parents, xxxi
  Level 3 case family and, 226, 230, 240
  Level 4 case family and, 110
  Level 5 case family and, 43
drug use, 4
dutiful woman vs. sexual goddess, 238–39
dysthymia, 7–8

earned (conditional) love, 385–86
eating, causation vs. function of, 167
eating disorders, xxvi, 4
  see also anorexia nervosa; bulimia
"Eating Disorders and the Mother-
    Daughter Relationship" (Beattie),
    144
Edwards, Henry E., 379–80
either/or worldview, 27, 97–98, 104
Elmcrest Hospital, xxxvi, 62
  Chapman Unit of, 3–20, 65, 67
emotional illiteracy, 132–33
emotional incest, 149
emotional legacies, 44–49
emotional triangles, xxii, 309–10
  definition of, 17–18, 259–60
  detouring-attacking, 18
  development of, 320
  in Level 3 case family, 259–62
  therapeutic tasks and, 324–25
emotions, infants' imitation of, 178–79
Endo, Shusako, 297
enmeshment, 50–59
  anorexia nervosa and, 55–56
  boundaries and, 74, 316–18
  defined, 51
  ethnic considerations and, 52
  in Level 3 families, 51, 224, 267
  in Level 4 families, 51
  in Level 5 families, 51, 54–56
ethnicity, and family style, 52
Ethnicity and Family Therapy (McGoldrick,
    Pearce, and Giordano), 52

ethology, 164–68, 170–73
  defined, 164
  function of a behavior and, 173
executive subgroups, 341, 342
expectable losses, 25–26
extramarital affairs, 19, 68
eye-to-eye contact, 179–84
  in anxious-avoidant relationship, 182–84
  eye love and, 180–82

facial expressions:
  social referencing and, 199
  visual cliff experiment and, 197–200
  see also eye-to-eye contact
failure to thrive, 172–73
Fairbairn, Ronald W.D., 385
families:
  core emotional issues faced by, xxii,
    33–34
  emotional power of, xxix–xxx
  as first social organization, xxxiv–xxxv
  formative effects of, xxii, 44
  forms of, xxxvii
  function vs. structure in, xxxvii–xxxviii
  interpersonal curiosity in, 366–67
  maladaptive strategies found in, xxii; *see
    also* emotional triangles; scapegoating
  mates as architects of, xxx–xxxii
  outline of author's interviews with,
    433–37
  relational styles in, *see* family style
  subgroups of, 341, 342
  see also Beavers Systems Model; children;
    fathers; Level 1 (optimal) families;
    Level 2 (adequate) families; Level 3
    (midrange) families; Level 4 (polarized
    or borderline) families; Level 5
    (severely disturbed) families; mothers;
    parents
Families in Perpetual Crisis (Kagan and
    Schlosberg), 44–45
Families Under the Influence (Treadway),
    278–79
family contracting, 333–34
Family Life Cycle, The (Carter and
    McGoldrick), 44, 156
family meetings, 326–28
family myth, 84–85, 291
"Family Myth and Homeostasis" (Ferreira),
    84–85
family organism, 314–15
family–outside world boundaries, 311,
    315–16, 317–18

family roles, 363–65, 415–17, 419
  in Level 4 family, 98
  projective identification and, 78
family script, 76
  see also projective identification
family style, 26, 50–61
  Beavers Systems Model levels and, 50
  centrifugal, 50, 54, 59, 242
  centripetal, 50, 53–54, 56, 59
  change of, over time, 52–54
  enmeshment and disengagement in,
    51–52, 54–58, 224, 225, 242–43, 267,
    270, 316–18
  ethnicity and, 52
  merging of opposites in, 254–72
family tasks, *see* therapeutic tasks
family theory and treatment, major schools
    of, xxiii
Family Therapy Techniques (Fishman),
    312–13
Fantz, Robert L., 177, 178
fat, body:
  cultural views of, 127–28
  set-point and, 134
father-daughter relationships:
  divorce and, 43
  in Level 4 case family, 145, 148–49
fathers:
  absent, 245–46
  of author, xxiv, xxx–xxxii
  inconsistent, immature and erratic, 43,
    45–46, 139
father-son relationships:
  competitive feelings in, 273–74
  in Level 3 case family, 244–49, 257–58,
    273–74
  in Level 5 case family, 12–15
  projective identification and, 78–79
  repetition compulsion and, 154
fear, 86–87
  "catching of," 199
  of change, 158
  of intimacy, 288–89, 291
  of loss of control, 98, 99, 105–6, 140, 247
  Oedipal, 406–8
  visual cliff and, 197–200
feelings, sharing of, 328–29
Feldstein, Stanley, 189
female archetypes, 238–39
Ferreira, Antonio J., 84–85
fictive kin, 381–82
Field, Tiffany M., 178, 181
Fifer, William P., 176

first loves, 139, 161–205
    attachment patterns and, 175–91
    infant survival functions and, 163–74
    nonverbal mode of, 175–76, 178–79,
        188–89, 191
    nurturance and, 166
    protection and, 166–67, 171
    repetition compulsion and, 45–46,
        154–55
    survival and, 164–67, 172
    see also attachment
Fishman, H. Charles, 312–13, 315
flexibility, 34–35, 53, 105, 410–11, 419
"Focus," 10–11
following, by infants, 169, 171
forgiveness, 335–37
Forster, E. M., 175–76
Freud, Anna, 173
Freud, Sigmund, 152, 277
    on alexithymia, 132
    on infant attachments, 173–74, 175
    on repetition compulsion, 45–46, 149–51

Geller, Jesse, 386, 387, 390
generational boundaries, 125, 141, 148–49,
        310, 311, 312–14, 316–17, 320, 325,
        334
genograms:
    definition of, 62
    effectiveness of, 66–67
    of Levels 1 and 2 case family, 341–42,
        344–46, 380–81, 392–95
    of Level 3 case family, 219–24, 226, 232,
        242–53, 267, 282
    of Level 5 case family, 67–75
Gifford family, *see* Level 3 case family
        (Gifford family)
Giordano, Joseph, 52
"good-enough mother," xxxiii–xxxiv
Goodwin, Donald W., 277
grandiose self, 349
groupthink, in Level 5 enmeshed families,
        34
*Growing Points of Attachment Theory and
        Research* (Bretherton), 194
Grunebaum, Judith, 293
Guze, Samuel B., 277

Haley, Jay, 138
Hampson, Robert B., 402
Handbook of Eating Disorders (Brownell and
        Foreyt, eds.), 132, 134
Hansen, Connie, xxix–xxx

Harvard Medical School Mental Health Letter,
        133
Hermanson, Leif, 277
Hetherington, E. Mavis, 372
Hill, Robert B., 382, 418–19
home contracts, 62–63, 333
homosexuality, 250, 294–95
honesty, intimacy and, 217–18
Horwitz, Robert, 100, 102, 108, 109, 110,
        111, 112, 116–17, 118, 123–24, 140,
        141, 143, 144, 145, 159
human contact, need for, 163–64, 172–74
human nature:
    Level 3 view of, 31, 216–18
    origin of personal views of, xxxv, 163
    prior to cultural influences, 176
humor, importance of, 364
hunger, 166, 167
    love vs. food, 173–74
husband-wife relationship:
    detouring-attacking triangle and, 18
    focus on symptom bearer vs., 4–5
    in Level 3 case family, 224, 226, 230–37
    in Level 4 case family, 114–15, 148
    in Level 5 case family, 18–20, 38–39, 49,
        59–60, 75, 86, 93–94
    projective identification and, 79–81
hyperindividualism, 52

identity formation, 78
imagery exercise, xxiii–xxv
imitative behavior, of infants, 178–79
imprinting, 165
incest:
    emotional, 148
    in Level 3 case family, 295
    therapeutic task and, 88
individuality, xxii, xxxvii
    discouragement of, 50, 51, 99–100,
        104–6, 122, 149, 184
    encouragement of, 36, 50, 88, 140,
        361–62, 410–11
    intimacy vs., xxvii, 52–53, 175, 184
infantile narcissism, 348–49
infant-mother relationships, 165–71,
        179–91, 193–202
    eye-to-eye contact and, 179–84
    mother overwhelmed by, 195–98, 200
    mother's facial expressions and, 198–99
    mutual-regulation model for, 185,
        188–89
    secure vs. anxious-avoidant, 182–84,
        378–79

social releasers and, 168–70
space and closeness in, 189–91
visual cliff experiment and, 197–200
Watch, Wait, and Wonder therapy for, 185–88
infants, 163–205
attachment patterns of, 164–65, 175–91, 194
contact created and broken by, 179–81
early parental relationships with, 377–79
failure to thrive in, 172–73
Freud's view of, 173–74, 175
human contact as primary need of, 163–64, 172–74
imitative behavior by, 178–79
instinctual responses of, 169–71
Latin derivation of term, 175
love play by, 179
primary attachment figures for, 194–95
relationships formed by, 193–94
resilience of, 371–74
responses to visual stimuli by, 177–78
smiling by, 168–71
sound preferences of, 169, 179
sound recognition by, 176–77
temperamental inclinations and biases of, 185, 186, 187–88
visual preferences of, 177–78
"inner child," 335
instinct:
attachment and, 164–66
causation vs. function of, 167
social releasers and, 167–69
internal parents, 158
internal tormentor:
in Level 4 case family, 122
in Level 5 case family, 59–60
interpersonal curiosity, 366–67
Interpersonal World of the Infant, The (Stern), 198, 199
intimacy, xxii, xxvii, xxxvii, 287–306
barriers to, 256–57
control through, 212
defined, 179, 256–57
eye-to-eye contact and, 179–84
fear of, 288–89, 291
honesty and, 217–18
individuality vs., xxvii, 52–53, 175, 184
infants' attachment patterns and, 175–91
in Level 3 case family, 240–41, 267, 270–72, 287–306
in Level 3 families, 31–32, 34, 215–16, 287–306

nonverbal love and, 175–76, 178–79, 188–89, 191
pursuer-distancer relationships and, 294–97
self-esteem and, 292–93
space and closeness in, 189–91
vulnerability and, 218, 305–6
Watch, Wait, and Wonder therapy and, 185–88
withdrawal and, 289–90
Intimate Partners (Scarf), xxi, xxii, 155
invisible referees, 29–31, 214–15
"islands of consistency," 192
Italian family style, 52, 222

Jackson, Don D., 102–3
Jaffe, Joseph, 189
Jasnow, Michael, 189
Jewish family style, 52
Johnson, Stuart, 317, 320, 322, 323, 330, 334, 335, 336, 337, 385

Kagan, Richard, 44–45
Kearney-Cooke, Ann, 131, 132
Keesey, Richard E., 134, 135
kinship bonds, 419
"kitchen cupboard theory of loving," 166
Kohut, Heinz, 348–50, 351
Krasner, Barbara, 117–18

Lang, Mary E., 195
language:
early learning not based on, 192
misuse of, 81–84
preceded by love, 175–76, 178–79, 191
Levels 1 and 2 case family (Walker family), 341–424
author's sessions with, 341–48, 354–69, 374–77, 379–83, 390–401, 403–24
Beavers Systems Model level, 342
children's relationships, 362, 416
daughters' adolescence, 403–6
family roles, 363–65, 415–17
family style, 360–63
father as sheriff, 365–66, 408–10
father's childhood abandonment, 344, 346, 351, 356, 358, 370, 373, 412–13, 417
father's description of his father, 354–56, 357–60, 390–91
father's end-of-interview talks with author, 343, 420–24
father's psychic "keep off the grass" sign, 414–15

Levels 1 and 2 case family (Walker family)
    (cont'd)
  father's relationship with his mother,
      374–75
  father's relationship with his stepfather,
      346–48, 356–57
  father's reunion with his father, 352–54
  father's route to college, 375–77
  genogram, 341–42, 344–46, 380–81,
      392–95
  mother's background, 379–83, 392–97
  power issues, 403–12
  sense of humor, 342, 360, 364–65, 399
  vacation-time conflicts, 398–401
  visit to father's childhood home,
      422–24
  younger daughter's cheerleading
      competition, 367–69
Level 1 (optimal) families, xxviii, xxxviii, 24,
      217–18, 339–424
  alcoholism and, 285
  comparisons between level 2 families and,
      32–33, 35, 342, 402–3
  conflict in, 398
  description of, 32–33, 342–43
  power issues in, 402
Level 2 (adequate) families, xxviii, 24,
      339–424
  alcoholism and, 285
  comparisons between Level 1 families
      and, 32–33, 35, 342, 402–3
  conflict in, 398
  description of, 32–33, 34–35, 401–2
Level 3 case family (Gifford family),
      219–306
  affair between mother's father and aunt,
      231–37, 236
  alcoholism of parents' fathers, 233–35,
      244–48, 251, 252, 269, 279, 283–84,
      289–90, 293
  attraction of opposites, 254–55, 256
  author's sessions with, 219–73, 281–84,
      297–306
  disciplining of eldest daughter, 257–59,
      401
  eldest daughter as author's key, 226–28
  emotional triangle, 259–62
  family atmosphere and mode of
      interrelating, 223
  family rules, 223, 224–25, 245, 262–64,
      266, 289–91, 296, 301, 303
  father's brother's homosexuality, 250,
      294–95

father's competitive feelings with his
      father, 273–74
father's Navy career, 219, 274–75, 281
father's side of genogram, 242–53, 267,
      282
female archetypes, 238–39
individual boundary violations, 221, 224,
      226, 231–37
intimacy, 240–41, 267, 270–72, 287–306
lack of male-female connection, 221, 236,
      241, 245, 262–64, 287, 288–89, 290
merging of opposite family styles, 254–72
mother as parentified child, 204–5,
      229–30, 291, 293–94, 299–300
mother's family treatment training, 220
mother's need to live close to her family,
      228–29, 297
mother's parents' separation, 230–31
mother's side of genogram, 219–24, 226,
      232
mother's split identification between her
      mother and aunt, 237–40, 293
newborn daughter, 219, 243, 298
parental imperative, 293–94
parents' early relationship, 264–69
parents' pursuer-distancer relationship,
      294–97
parents' sexual turn-off period, 270–72,
      295
pattern of given names, 232–33
Persian Gulf relocation, 297–303
potential shift to levels 2 or 4, 304–5
sharing/not sharing secrets, 240–41
Level 3 (midrange) families, xxviii, 24,
      207–306
  alcoholism and, 285
  description of, 29–32, 211–13, 401
  enmeshed style in, 51, 224, 267
  human nature as viewed by, 31, 216–18
  intimacy in, 31–32, 34, 215–16, 287–306
  invisible referees in, 29–31, 214–15
  predictability in, 213–14, 275
  rules in, 29–32, 34, 212–14, 216, 217,
      223, 247–48, 257
Level 4 case family (Maguire family),
      98–159
  author's sessions with, 98–102, 107–20,
      123–25, 140–47, 157–59
  breakfast rule, 100–102, 104–5
  comparison of twin sons, 109
  daughter's bulimia, 98, 100, 104, 109,
      125–29, 135–37, 141–49, 155, 159, 210
  daughter's dream, 146–47

daughter's individuation, 140
daughter's overhearing of parents'
  lovemaking, 123–24, 126
family's fear of confronting father,
  111–12
father as family bad guy, 113, 118–20
father as parentified child, 117–20
father's abandonment scenario, 100–102,
  105, 107, 122, 209
father's family background, 107, 115–16,
  120
father's projective identification, 120,
  121–22
fear of change, 157–59
good vs. moody son, 109
mother's family background, 115–16,
  136–37
mother's fear of confrontation, 108, 110,
  112–15
mother's peacemaking role, 114–15
parents' drinking, 124, 125
parents' either/or splitting of anger,
  98–100
re-creation of past events, 120–22, 149,
  151–52
relational model, 115–17
repetition compulsion, 149, 155, 156
sexual-generational boundary violations,
  125–26, 141, 148–49
Valentine's Day gifts to daughter,
  143–46, 155, 311
Level 4 (polarized or borderline) families,
  xxvii, xxviii, 24, 95–159
  alcoholism and, 285
  ambivalence and, 97–98, 99
  description of, 26–27, 97–98
  enmeshed style in, 51
  individuality discouraged in, 99–100,
    104–6, 122, 149
  loss of control feared in, 98, 99, 105–6,
    140
  power struggles in, 33–34
  tyrants and rules in, 27–29, 33–34,
    98–106, 111–12, 113, 154–55, 156,
    210, 401
Level 5 case family (Anderson family), 3–22,
  37–49, 58–76, 81–94
  author's sessions with, 3–4, 7–17, 19–20,
    37–43, 46–49, 59–61, 62–75, 81–86
  family myth, 85
  family script, 76
  father as mystery man, 85–88
  father's family background, 69–73

father-son relationship, 12–15, 65, 70
father's parental relationships, 71–73
father's secret other family, 15–17, 19–20,
  37–43, 46–49, 65–66, 73–75, 82–83, 86
genogram, 67–75
gun threat incident, 3–4
home contract, 62–63
hospitalization of son, 3–4, 6–7, 9, 10, 11,
  62, 64, 65, 67
identity of internal tormentor, 59–60
listening problem, 11–13, 48
lying, 7, 8, 47–48, 49
Mischief Night meeting, 68–69
mother's family background, 42, 43,
  45–46, 68, 69, 139
mother's half-brother, 42, 43
mother's naked shift, 61
mother-son relationship, 9, 15–19, 37–40,
  59–61, 65, 139, 385–86
mother's pain, 42–43, 45–46
mother's rage, 9, 15–20, 37–41, 45–46, 49
projective identification, 76
re-creation of past events, 42–46, 69–71,
  73, 76
repetition compulsion, 45–46
son's dysthymia, 7–8
son's oppositional defiant disorder, 5–7,
  18
son's return to home, 62–65, 333
son's role, 58, 81–84, 85, 366
therapeutic tasks, 86–92, 334
use of language, 81–84
Level 5 (severely disturbed) families, xxviii,
  xxix, xxxviii, 1–94
  adolescent delegates in, 21–22
  alcoholism and, 285
  ambivalence and, 93–94
  anger in, 12
  chaotic power structure in, 33, 401
  description of, 25–26, 210–11
  difficulty of change for, 92–93
  disengaged style in, 8–9, 56–61, 74
  displays of vulnerability punished in, 8
  emotional legacy in, 44–49
  emotional triangles in, 17–18
  enmeshed style in, 54–56
  extremity of family style in, 54
  family style of, 26, 50–61
  fear and, 86–87
  language and, 83
  mystification and disjointed thinking as
    norm in, 4, 26, 47–48, 60, 66
  past as present influence in, 42–43

Level 5 (severely disturbed) families *(cont'd)*
  projective identification in, 76, 77–81
  symptom bearers in, 3–20
libido, 151
Lidz, Theodor, xxxv, 403, 406, 407
listening, 11–13, 48, 89
Looft, William R., xxxv, 163
Lorenz, Konrad, 165
Lost in Familiar Places (Shapiro and Carr), 366–67
love:
  biological function of, 171–72
  conditional, 121, 385–86
  early, memories of, xxxii–xxxiii
  exploration and, 388
  eye, 180–82
  family boundaries and, 392–95
  language preceded by, 175–76, 178–79, 188–89, 191
  learning "not to know" and, 389–90
  managing power and, 401–2
  strategic seeking of, 386–88
  unconditional, 293, 384–97
  weight and, 136–37, 156
  see also intimacy
love objects, xxxvii
  see also first loves
lying, in Level 5 case family, 7, 8, 47–48, 49

McAdoo, Harriet Pipes, 382
MacFarlane, Aidan, 177
McGoldrick, Monica, 44, 52, 138
Maguire family, *see* Level 4 case family (Maguire family)
Mahler, Margaret, 173
maturation process, 53
Meltzoff, Andrew N., 178
menstruation, 55–56, 131
mental alcoholics, 278–79
mental anniversaries, 417–18
mental models, 195
Meyer, Patricia, 156
microanalytic method, 182, 188–89, 191
micro-rejections, 182
middle class, black families in, 379–80
midrange families, *see* Level 3 (midrange) families
military life:
  as form of parenting, 275
  transition from, 280–81
mind, human interactions as basis of, 174
Minuchin, Salvador, 17, 51, 312, 315, 341
mirroring, parental, 349, 350

Miss America contestants, 128
Mitchell, Stephen, 215, 288
Moore, M. Keith, 178
mother-daughter relationships, 310
  bulimia and, 135, 136–37, 143–44, 147, 155
  competition in, 144, 147, 148, 155
  early love in, xxxiii
  "good-enough" mother and, xxxiii–xxxiv
  influence of past and, 110, 144
  in Level 3 case family, 221, 224, 229, 292–93
  parentification and, xxxi–xxxii
  projective identification and, 78
  repetition compulsion and, 155
mothers:
  of author, xxiv, xxx–xxxiv, 299–300
  "good-enough," xxxiii–xxxiv
  as infants' first love, 165–67, 169, 174
  infants' "microrejections" perceived by, 181–82
  instinctual responses of, 170
  negative attention and intrusive caring from, 71–73
  primacy of child's relationship with, 388
  see also infant-mother relationships
mothers-in-law, 70
  in emotional triangles, 261–62
mother-son relationships, 195–97
  in Level 5 case family, 9, 15–19, 37–40, 46, 59–61, 65, 70–73, 92, 139, 385–86
  secure vs. anxious-avoidant, 182–84
  social referencing and, 199
  visual cliff and, 200
movies, X-rated, 125
Muir, Elisabeth, 187
multi-model depressive signals, 199
musical motifs, autobiographical beginnings compared with, 203–4
mystification, 4, 25, 47–48

naked shift, 61
names, significance of, 232–33
narcissism, infantile vs. healthy, 348–49
"Nature of the Child's Tie to the Mother, The" (Bowlby), 169–70
neediness, suppression of, 51–52, 57
negative feelings, sharing of, 328–29
negative maternal attention, 71–73
negativity, feelings of:
  intimacy and, 217
  suppression of, 51, 54
neonates, *see* infants

New Introductory Lectures on Psychoanalysis
  (Freud), 151
New York Times Magazine, xxxii
Nietzsche, Friedrich, 352
No Single Thread (Beavers), 211
nurturance, 53
  good-enough mother and, xxxiv
  of Level 3 needy male, 267–69, 294
  love and, 166
  parentification and, xxxii, 117
  self-, 53, 88, 91, 116–17, 148

object, definition of, xxxvii
object relations family therapy, xxxvi–xxxvii
Object Relations Therapy (Cashdan), 174
odd day/even day tasks, 321, 322–25
Oedipal fears, 406–8
Ogden, Thomas, 79
"only connect," 176
"On Projective Identification" (Ogden), 79
opposing viewpoints, suppression of, 51, 54
oppositional defiant disorder (ODD), 5–7,
  18
optimal families, *see* Level 1 (optimal)
  families
Origin of Species, The (Darwin), 171–72
Ortmeyer, Inge, 132
overprotective mothers, 70–73

Palazzoli, Mara Selvini, 322
paradoxical strategies, 89–90
parental abandonment, *see* abandonment,
  parental
parental attention, need for, 88–89, 91
parental imperative, 293–94
parental mirroring, 349, 350
parentified children:
  definition of, xxxi–xxxii, 117–18, 293–94
  in Level 3 case family, 204–5, 229–30,
    291, 293–94, 299–300
  in Level 4 case family, 117–20
parenting, normal vs. anxious, 44
parents:
  children loved unconditionally by, 293,
    384–97
  children's exalting of, 350–52
  children's puberty and, 139
  in emotional triangles with children,
    259–60
  in emotional triangles with mothers-in-
    law, 261–62
  as executive subgroup of family, 341, 342
  generational boundaries and, 125, 141,

  148–49, 310, 311, 312–14, 316–17,
    320, 325, 334
  infants' early relationships with, 377–79;
    see also infant-mother relationships
  internal, 158
  newborn children's effects on, 44–45
  odd day/even day tasks and, 321, 322–25
  power-sharing by, 36
  power struggles between, 321
  projective identification and, 76, 77–81,
    323
  single, xxxvii
  supplemental, 383
  see also families; mothers
Parks, Rosa, 399–400, 401
past, influence of, xxii, xxv, 37–49, 309–10
  alcoholism and, 276–81
  in construction of genograms, 66–67
  emotional legacies and, 44–45
  on Level 4 case family, 110, 114, 120–22,
    149, 151–52
  on Level 5 case family, 42–43, 69–71, 76
  on Level 5 families, 42–43
  see also repetition compulsion
Pearce, John K., 52
Person, The (Lidz), xxxv, 403, 406
Philomela, myth of, 233–35
phobias, transient, 184
Plato, 276
play relatives, 381–82
pleasure principle, 151
Plutarch, 276
polarized families, *see* Level 4 (polarized or
  borderline) families
pornography, 125
positive feelings, sharing of, 329
power, xxii, xxvi–xxvii
  as core emotional issue, 33–34
  flexibility and, 410–11
  Levels 1 and 2 case family and, 403–12
  managing of, 401–2
  parental sharing of, 36
  parental struggles over, 321
predictability, 311
  in Level 3 families, 213–14, 275
pregnancy, out-of-wedlock, 58, 68, 73–74
prescribing the symptom, 89–90
press conferences, family, 87–88, 91
primary attachment figures, 194–95
primates, adaptive responses in, 170–71
projective identification:
  breaking up circularity of, 323
  definition of, 76–81, 225–26, 297

projective identification (*cont'd*)
    displacement of what is inside the self to
        what is outside the self in, 78–79
    in Level 3 case family, 225–26
    in Level 4 case family, 120, 121–22
    sharing negative feelings and, 328–29
    ventriloquist-dummy model of, 79–80
promiscuity, 4, 21–22
protection, 237
    attachment and, 166–67, 171, 194
Psychoanalytical Psychology, 179
psychoanalytic theory:
    infancy as viewed by, 173–74, 175
    repetition compulsion and, 45–46,
        149–51
Psychotherapy and Growth (Beavers), 48, 215,
    242
puberty:
    eating disorders and, 128
    emotions affected by, 53, 139
    growth spurts in, 138
    hormonal changes in, 138–39
punishment:
    corporal, 257–58, 261
    in Level 3 case family, 257–62
    vulnerability and, 8, 12
pursuer-distancer relationships, 294–97

rage, silent, 290–91
rape, in Philomela myth, 234
Ravenscroft, Kent, 147–48, 275
referees, invisible, 29–31, 214–15
religious orientation, 419
remarried families, xxxi, xxxvii, xxxviii
    Level 5 case family and, 42, 43
repetition compulsion, 149–56
    alternative explanations of, 152–56
    definition of, 45, 150
    familiar patterns and, 155–56
    on family vs. individual level, 151–52
    first loves and, 45–46, 154–55
    in Level 4 case family, 149, 155, 156
    in Level 5 case family, 42, 43, 45–46
    mastering the past and, 152–53
    reconnecting with first loves and, 154–55
"Repetition Compulsion, Acting Out, and
        Identification with the Doer" (Segel),
    153
responsibility:
    home contract and, 62–63
    of parents, 47, 48
    sexuality vs., 238–39
    see also self-responsibility

rigid triads, 17
Rilke, Rainer Maria, 369
role reversal, parental, 323–24
rules:
    boundaries and, 311
    in conflict resolution, 332
    conscious vs. unconscious, 102–4, 125
    definition of, 103
    fear of change of, 158
    in Level 3 case family, 223, 224–25, 245,
        262–64, 266, 289–91, 296, 301, 303
    Level 3 families controlled by, 29–32,
        34, 212–14, 216, 217, 223, 247–48,
        257
    Level 4 families controlled by, 27–29,
        33–34, 99, 101–6, 210
    Level 5 families' lack of, 48
    as relationship agreements, 103
Rutter, Michael, 373

salivary glands, enlargement of, 136
Salter, Mary, 377, 378
Sartre, Jean-Paul, 195
Satir, Virginia, xxx
Scandal (Endo), 297
Scandinavia, alcoholism study in, 276–77
scapegoating, 77
    definition of, xxii
Scharff, Jill Savege, 42
schizophrenia, 56
Schlosberg, Shirley, 44–45
Schnitt, Jerome, 281
school problems, 6, 58, 89
    in Level 4 case family, 100
Schuckit, Marc A., 277–78
Schulsinger, Fini, 277
Science, 177, 178
seating arrangements, 341
secrecy:
    in Level 3 case family, 240–41
    in Level 5 case family, 5–6, 17, 19, 37–43,
        46–49, 65–66, 73–75, 82–83, 86
    symptom bearer and, 5–6
Secure Base, A (Bowlby), 378, 379
secure relationships, 378
Segel, Nathan P., 153
self-esteem, 349
    intimacy and, 292–93
self-other boundary violations, 221, 224,
    226, 310, 312, 328–29, 333
self-responsibility:
    acting out vs., 9, 10–11
    therapeutic task, 88

Separating Parents and Adolescents (Stierlin), 21–22
separation anxiety, 378
severely disturbed families, *see* Level 5 (severely disturbed) families
sexual abuse, female, 11, 44
sexual attraction, 270–72, 295
sexual behavior, sex:
  alcoholism and, 279–80
  in Level 3 case family, 231–39, 271–72, 295
  in Level 4 case family, 123–26
  promiscuity, 4, 21–22
  responsibility vs., 238–39
sexual boundaries, violation of, xxvi, 125, 141, 148–49, 231–35, 295, 310, 311
sexual-generational boundary violations, 125, 141, 148–49, 295, 310, 311
sexual goddess vs. dutiful woman, 238–39
Shakespeare, William, 371
Shapiro, Edward R., 366–67, 386
Shapiro, Roger, 77–78
sibling subgroups, 341, 342
signs, 167–69
Silverman, Doris K., 179
single-parent families, xxxvii, xxxviii
Skynner, A. C. Robin, xxxiv
smell, infants' sense of, 177
smiling, by infants, 168–71, 188–89
  as social releaser, 168–69
Smith, Peter, 4, 5
Social Perception in Infants (Meltzoff), 178
social referencing, 199
social releasers, 167–70
soft feelings, suppression of, 51–52, 57
sound:
  infant-caregiver vocal behaviors and, 189–91
  infant preferences and, 169, 179
  infant's recognition of, 175–76
Southwest Family Institute, xxviii, 24
Spitz, René, 172
spouse subsystem, 312
Stack, Carol, 381
State University of New York, at Albany, 375–76
stepfamilies, *see* remarried families
Stephens, Leonora, xxvii, 57, 86, 99, 211, 214, 285, 343
Stern, Daniel, 180, 182, 183–84, 192, 195, 198
Stierlin, Helm, 21–22
stimulation, optimal level of, 180

Stone, Betsy, 103–4, 326, 327
Strengths of Black Families, The (Hill), 382, 418
Successful Families (Beavers and Hampson), 402
sucking, by infants, 169–70, 171
supplemental parents, 383
survival, 237
  attachment and, 164–67, 172
symptom bearers (identified patients):
  definition of, 4–5
  in Level 4 case family, 98, 100, 109
  in Level 5 case family, 3–20

"Taming Your Gremlin, or, Your Ego May Not Be Your Amigo" (workshop), xxiii–xxv
Taylor, Graeme T., 133
teeth, vomiting and, 135–36
thanatos, 151
therapeutic tasks, 318–37
  conflict resolution, 329–33
  family contracting and, 333–34
  forgiveness and, 335–37
  function and description of, 319–21
  for Level 5 case family, 86–92, 334
  odd day/even day, 321, 322–25
  paradoxical strategies and, 89–90
  sharing negative feelings, 328–29
  sharing positive feelings, 329
  town meetings, 326–28
time-series analysis, of vocal patterns, 190
"tolerable failures," 349–50
Tolstoy, Leo, 23
town meetings, 326–28
transient phobias, 184
Treadway, David, 278–79
triads, rigid, 17
triangling, *see* emotional triangles
"true self," xxxiv
tyrants:
  as familiar partner, 158
  Level 4 families controlled by, 27–28, 33–34, 98–102, 104–6, 111–12, 154–55, 156, 210, 401
  repetition compulsion and, 154–55, 156
  victims' collusion with, 113

Uncommon Therapy (Haley), 138
unconditional love, 293, 384–97
unconscious:
  adolescent delegate and, 21, 22

unconscious *(cont'd)*
    object relations family therapy and,
        xxxvi–xxxvii
    projective identification and, 76, 78, 79, 81
undifferentiated family ego mass, 51
Unfinished Business (Scarf), xxi
unthought thoughts, 192
Urban League, 418–19

ventriloquist-dummy model of projective
    identification, 79–80
violence, child's threat of, 3–4, 6
visual cliff, 197–98, 199, 200
visual stimuli, infant preferences and,
    177–78
vocal behavior, infant-caretaker relationship
    and, 189–91
volunteer families, sources of, xxviii,
    xxxv–xxxvi
vulnerability, 8, 245, 305–6
    honesty and, 218
    intimacy and, 218, 305–6
    in Level 5 case family, 8–10, 12, 43

projective identification and, 78–79
suppression of, 51–52, 56, 57

Walker family, *see* Levels 1 and 2 case
    family (Walker family)
WASP family style, 52
Watch, Wait, and Wonder therapy, 185–88
Winnicott, D. W., xxxiv, 185–86
Winokur, George, 277
withdrawal, instead of confrontation,
    289–90
Wolf, Ernest S., 350, 351
Wolin, Stephen, 286
Wooley, Susan C., 131, 132
work orientation, 419

X-rated movies, 125

Yale Psychiatric Institute, 320
Yale School of Nursing, 220

Zigler, Edward E., 195
Zinner, John, 77–78, 83, 105, 154, 225

MAGGIE SCARF, the author of *Body, Mind, Behavior; Unfinished Business;* and *Intimate Partners,* is currently a senior fellow at the Bush Center in Child Development and Social Policy at Yale University. She is a contributing editor to *The New Republic* and *Self* magazine, and a member of the advisory board of the American Psychiatric Press. She has been a Ford Foundation fellow, a Nieman fellow in journalism at Harvard University, an Alicia Patterson Foundation fellow, has twice been a fellow of the Center for Advanced Study in the Behavioral Sciences at Stanford University, and is a recent grantee of the Smith Richardson Foundation, Inc. She has also received several National Media awards from the American Psychological Foundation. She lives in Connecticut with her family.

ABOUT THE TYPE

The text of this book was set in Janson, a misnamed type-
face designed in about 1690 by Nicholas Kis, a Hungarian
in Amsterdam. In 1919 the matrices became the property
of the Stempel Foundry in Frankfurt. It is an old-style
book face of excellent clarity and sharpness. Janson serifs
are concave and splayed; the contrast between thick and
thin strokes is marked.